EXPLORING OUR
NATIONAL HISTORIC
PARKS AND SITES

EXPLORING OUR NATIONAL HISTORIC PARKS AND SITES

RUSSELL D. BUTCHER

ROBERTS RINEHART PUBLISHERS
IN COOPERATION WITH
NATIONAL PARKS AND CONSERVATION ASSOCIATION

Copyright © 1997 Russell D. Butcher

International Standard Book Number 1-57098-125-6

Library of Congress Number 97-66388

Published by Roberts Rinehart Publishers
6309 Monarch Park Place, Niwot, Colorado 80503

Published in the UK and Ireland by
Roberts Rinehart Publishers
Trinity House, Charleston Road
Dublin 6, Ireland

Distributed to the trade in the U.S. and Canada by Publishers Group West

10 9 8 7 6 5 4 3 2 1

Book design: Paulette Livers Lambert

Cover photograph: © 1997 David Muench,
Gettysburg National Cemetery

Photograph on title page: © 1997 David Muench, USS *Constitution,*
Boston National Historical Park

Printed in the United States of America

To
NERMANA
and to all those who, like her,
find magic in the National Parks
and
To
ELIZABETH
who sees beauty in the world,
as she projects her own rays of sunshine
to everyone around her

CONTENTS

Listing of Parks by State, xii
PRELUDE, xiv
ACKNOWLEDGMENTS, xvii
INTRODUCTION — Paul C. Pritchard, xix

PART I, 1

PARKS CELEBRATING AMERICA'S DISCOVERY, SETTLEMENT, EXPANSION, AND GROWTH AS A NATION

Allegheny Portage Railroad N H Site, 1
Arkansas Post N Memorial, 2
Bent's Old Fort N H Site, 6
Boston N H Park, 8
Cabrillo N Monument, 11
Castillo de San Marcos N Monument, 14
Chamizal N Memorial, 16
Charles Pinckney N H Site, 17
Chesapeake & Ohio Canal N H Park, 17
Christiansted N H Site, 21
City of Rocks N Reserve, 23
Colonial N H Park, 24
Coronado N Memorial, 32
Cumberland Gap N H Park, 34
De Soto N Memorial, 37
Ebey's Landing N H Reserve, 40
El Morro N Monument, 41
Federal Hall N Memorial, 42
Fort Caroline N Memorial, 43
Fort Clatsop N Memorial, 44
Fort Frederica N Monument, 48
Fort Matanzas N Monument, 49
Fort Necessity N Battlefield, 50
Fort Raleigh N H Site, 51
Fort Union Trading Post N H Site, 54
Fort Vancouver N H Site, 56
Friendship Hill N H Site, 58
Golden Spike N H Site, 59
Grand Portage N Monument, 62
Grant-Kohrs Ranch N H Site, 64
Hamilton Grange N Memorial, 66
Harpers Ferry N H Park, 66
Homestead N Monument of America, 69

Hubbell Trading Post N H Site, 71
Independence N H Park, 72
Jean Lafitte N H Park & Preserve, 78
Jefferson N Expansion Memorial, 83
Johnstown Flood N Memorial, 85
Kalaupapa N H Park, 85
Kaloko-Honokohau N H Park, 86
Klondike Gold Rush N H Park, 89
Knife River Indian Villages N H Site, 91
Natchez N H Park, 94
Nez Perce N H Park, 96
Pecos N H Park, 99
Pipe Spring N Monument, 103
Piscataway Park, 105
Pu'uhonua o Honaunau N H Park, 106
Pu'ukohola Heiau N H Site, 109
Roger Williams N Memorial, 111
Saint Croix Island International H Site, 112
Salem Maritime N H Site, 114
Salinas Pueblo Missions N Monument, 116
Salt River Bay N H Park & Ecological Preserve, 118
San Antonio Missions N H Park, 121
San Francisco Maritime N H Park, 124
San Juan Island N H Park, 125
San Juan N H Site, 126
Scotts Bluff N Monument, 128
Sitka N H Park, 132
Statue of Liberty N Monument, 134
Thomas Stone N H Site, 140
Timucuan Ecological & Historic Preserve, 141
Tumacácori N H Park, 142
Whitman Mission N H Site, 145

PART 2, 149
WAR FOR INDEPENDENCE (REVOLUTIONARY WAR)
Historical Sequence of War for Independence Battles and Other Events

Cowpens N Battlefield, 149
Fort Stanwix N Monument, 151
George Rogers Clark N H Park, 152
Guilford Courthouse N Military Park, 155
Kings Mountain N Military Park, 158
Minute Man N H Park, 160
Moores Creek N Battlefield, 163

Morristown N H Park, 165
Ninety Six N H Site, 167
Saratoga N H Park, 169
Springfield Armory N H Site, 172
Thaddeus Kosciuszko N Memorial, 173
Valley Forge N H Park, 174

PART 3, 177
WAR OF 1812, MEXICAN-AMERICAN WAR, etc.

Castle Clinton N Monument, 177
Fort McHenry N Monument & H Shrine, 177
Fort Washington Park, 180

Palo Alto Battlefield N H Site, 181
Perry's Victory & Internat'l Peace Mem., 182

PART 4, 185
U.S. MILITARY VERSUS NATIVE AMERICANS (INDIANS)
(Nineteenth-Century Forts and Battlefields)

Big Hole N Battlefield, 185
Fort Bowie N H Site, 187
Fort Davis N H Site, 190
Fort Laramie N H Site, 192
Fort Larned N H Site, 194

Fort Scott N H Site, 197
Fort Smith N H Site, 198
Fort Union N Monument, 201
Horseshoe Bend N Military Park, 203
Little Bighorn Battlefield N Monument, 205

PART 5, 209
CIVIL WAR PARKS
Historical Sequence of Civil War Battles

African-American Civil War Memorial, 210
Andersonville N H Site, 210
Antietam N Battlefield, 212
Appomattox Court House N H Park, 216
Arlington House, Robert E. Lee Memorial, 219
Brice's Cross Roads N Battlefield Site, 221
Chickamauga & Chattanooga N M Park, 223
Fort Circle Parks, 227
Fort Donelson N Battlefield, 229
Fort Point N H Site, 231
Fort Pulaski N Monument, 233
Fort Sumter N Monument, 235
Fredericksburg & Spotsylvania County Battlefields
    Memorial N M Park, 237

Gettysburg N Military Park, 245
Kennesaw Mountain N Battlefield Park, 251
Manassas N Battlefield Park, 254
Monocacy N Battlefield, 261
Pea Ridge N Military Park, 263
Petersburg N Battlefield, 264
Richmond N Battlefield Park, 268
Shiloh N Military Park, 276
Stones River N Battlefield, 279
Tupelo N Battlefield, 282
Vicksburg N Military Park, 283
Wilson's Creek N Battlefield, 287

PART 6, 291
TWENTIETH-CENTURY MILITARY PARKS

Korean War Veterans Memorial, 291
Manzanar N H Site, 292
USS *Arizona* Memorial, 293

Vietnam Veterans Memorial, 294
War in the Pacific N H Park, 296

PART 7, 297
PARKS CELEBRATING U.S. PRESIDENTS

Abraham Lincoln Birthplace N H Site, 297
Adams N H Site, 298
Andrew Johnson N H Site, 299
Eisenhower N H Site, 301
Ford's Theatre N H Site, 302
Franklin Delano Roosevelt Memorial, 303
General Grant N Memorial, 304
George Washington Birthplace N Mon., 304
George Washington Memorial Parkway, 305
Harry S Truman N H Site, 306
Herbert Hoover N H Site, 308
Home of Franklin D. Roosevelt N H Site, 309
James A. Garfield N H Site, 311
Jimmy Carter N H Site, 312
John Fitzgerald Kennedy N H Site, 313
Lincoln Boyhood N Memorial, 314

Lincoln Home N H Site, 316
Lincoln Memorial, 317
Lyndon Baines Johnson Mem. Grove, 319
Lyndon B. Johnson N H Park, 320
Martin Van Buren N H Site, 321
Mount Rushmore N Memorial, 322
Sagamore Hill N H Site, 323
Theodore Roosevelt Birthplace N H Site, 325
Theodore Roosevelt Inaugural N H Site, 325
Theodore Roosevelt Island, 326
Thomas Jefferson Memorial, 327
Ulysses S. Grant N H Site, 329
Washington Monument, 329
White House, The, 330
William Howard Taft N H Site, 333

PART 8, 335
PARKS CELEBRATING WOMEN IN U.S. HISTORY

Clara Barton N H Site, 335
Eleanor Roosevelt N H Site, 336
Maggie L. Walker N H Site
    (see African Americans section)

Mary McLeod Bethune Council House NHS
    (see African Americans section)
Women's Rights N H Park, 337

PART 9, 341
PARKS CELEBRATING AFRICAN AMERICANS IN U.S. HISTORY

Booker T. Washington N Monument, 341
Boston African American N H Site, 342
Brown v. Board of Education N H Site, 345
Frederick Douglass N H Site, 346
George Washington Carver N Monument, 348

Maggie L. Walker N H Site, 350
Martin Luther King, Jr., N H Site, 352
Mary McLeod Bethune Council House N H Site, 354
Tuskegee Institute N H Site, 356

PART 10, 359
PARKS CELEBRATING WRITERS, ARTISTS, MUSICIANS, etc.

Carl Sandburg Home N H Site, 359
Edgar Allen Poe N H Site, 362
Eugene O'Neill N H Site, 363
Frederick Law Olmsted N H Site, 364
Glen Echo Park, 365
Hampton N H Site, 367
John Muir N H Site, 368

Longfellow N H Site, 370
New Orleans Jazz N H Park, 372
Saint-Gaudens N H Site, 373
Saint Paul's Church N H Site, 374
Vanderbilt Mansion N H Site, 376
Weir Farm N H Site, 377
Wolf Trap Farm Park for the Perf. Arts, 379

PART 11, 381
PARKS CELEBRATING TECHNOLOGY AND INDUSTRIAL AMERICA

Dayton Aviation Heritage N H Park, 381
Edison N H Site, 382
Hopewell Furnace N H Site, 383
Keweenaw N H Park, 384

Lowell N H Park, 386
Saugus Iron Works N H Site, 387
Steamtown N H Site, 389
Wright Brothers N Memorial, 390

PART 12, 393
NATIONAL CAPITAL PARKS
(not listed elsewhere)

Constitution Gardens, 393
Kenilworth Aquatic Gardens, 394
National Mall, 395

Pennsylvania Avenue N H Site, 396
Rock Creek Park, 396

PART 13, 401
NATIONAL RECREATION AREAS AND URBAN PARKS

Amistad N Recreation Area, 401
Bighorn Canyon N Recreation Area, 402
Catoctin Mountain Park, 403
Chattahoochee River N Recreation Area, 405
Chickasaw N Recreation Area, 406
Coulee Dam N Recreation Area, 408
Curecanti N Recreation Area, 409
Cuyahoga Valley N Recreation Area, 410
Delaware Water Gap N Recreation Area, 412
Gateway N Recreation Area, 413
Glen Canyon N Recreation Area, 415

Golden Gate N Recreation Area, 417
Great Falls Park, 420
Greenbelt Park, 421
Lake Chelan N Recreation Area, 422
Lake Mead N Recreation Area, 423
Lake Meredith N Recreation Area, 426
Oxon Hill Farm/Oxon Cove Park, 427
Prince William Forest Park, 428
Ross Lake N Recreation Area, 429
Santa Monica Mountains N Rec. Area, 433
Whiskeytown-Shasta-Trinity N Rec. Area, 435

PART 14, 437
AFFILIATED PARKS

American Memorial Park, 437
Benjamin Franklin N Memorial, 437
Blackstone R. Valley N Heritage Corridor, 437
Chicago Portage N H Site, 438
Chimney Rock N H Site, 438
David Berger N Memorial, 438
Delaware & Lehigh Nav. Canal N Heritage
    Corridor, 438
Father Marquette N Memorial and Museum, 439
Gloria Dei (Old Swedes') Church N H Site, 439
Green Springs H District, 439
Historic Camden, 439
Ice Age National Scientific Reserve, 440

Illinois & Michigan Canal N Heritage Corridor, 440
International Peace Garden, 440
Jamestown N H Site, 440
McLoughlin House N H Site, 441
Pinelands N Reserve, 441
Port Chicago Naval Magazine N Mem., 441
Quinebaug & Shetucket R Valley N Heritage
    Corridor, 443
Red Hill Patrick Henry N Memorial, 443
Roosevelt Campobello Internat'l Park, 444
Sewall-Belmont House N H Site, 444
Touro Synagogue N H Site, 444

PART 15, 445
NATIONAL TRAILS

Appalachian N Scenic Trail, 445
California N Historic Trail, 445
Ice Age N Scenic Trail, 445
Juan Bautista de Anza N Historic Trail, 446
Lewis and Clark N Historic Trail, 446
Mormon Pioneer N Historic Trail, 447
Natchez Trace N Scenic Trail, 447
Nez Perce (Nee-Me-Poo) N Historic Trail, 448

North Country N Scenic Trail, 448
Oregon N Historic Trail, 448
Overmountain Victory N Historic Trail, 449
Pony Express N Historic Trail, 450
Potomac Heritage N Scenic Trail, 450
Santa Fe N Historic Trail, 450
Selma-to-Montgomery N Historic Trail, 451
Trail of Tears N Historic Trail, 452

PART 16 OTHER NATIONAL PARK SYSTEM AREAS, 455

PART 17 POSSIBLE NEW PARKS, 465

PART 18 THREAT AFTER THREAT, 473

NATIONAL PARKS AND CONSERVATION ASSOCIATION; A BRIEF HISTORY, 501

NATIONAL PARK STANDARDS FOR ESTABLISHMENT AND PROTECTION OF NATIONAL PARKS AND MONUMENTS, 508

EPILOGUE, 513

FURTHER READING, 514

INDEX, 516

List of Parks by State

Alabama
Horseshoe Bend
Tuskegee Institute

Alaska
Klondike Gold Rush
Sitka

Arizona
Coronado
Ft. Bowie
Hubbell Trading Post
Pipe Spring
Tumacacori

Arkansas
Arkansas Post
Fort Smith
Pea Ridge

California
Cabrillo
Eugene O'Neill
John Muir
Manzanar
Whiskeytown
   San Francisco area
    Fort Point
    Golden Gate
    San Francisco Maritime
Santa Monica Mountains

Colorado
Bent's Old Fort
Curecanti

Connecticut
Weir Farm

Florida
Castillo de San Marcos
De Soto
Fort Caroline
Fort Matanzas
Timucuan

Georgia
Andersonville
Chattahoochee River
Chickamauga & Chattanooga
Fort Frederica
Fort Pulaski
Jimmy Carter
Kennesaw Mountain
Martin Luther King, Jr.

Hawaii
  Hawai'i
   Kaloko-Honokohau
   Pu'uhonua o Honaunau
   Pu'ukohola Heiau
  Molokai
   Kalaupapa
  Oahu
   USS *Arizona* Memorial

Idaho
City of Rocks
Nez Perce

Illinois
Lincoln Home

Indiana
George Rogers Clark
Lincoln Boyhood

Iowa
Herbert Hoover

Kansas
Brown v. Board of Education
Fort Larned
Fort Scott

Kentucky
Abraham Lincoln Birthplace

Louisiana
Jean Lafitte
New Orleans Jazz

Maine
St. Croix Island

Maryland
Antietam
Catoctin Mountain
Chesapeake & Ohio Canal [from
  Washington,DC to Cumberland,
  MD]
Monocacy
Thomas Stone
  Baltimore area
   Fort McHenry
   Hampton
  Washington, DC, area
   Clara Barton
   Fort Circle Parks
   Fort Washington
   Glen Echo
   Greenbelt
   Oxon Hill Farm
   Piscataway

Massachusetts
Springfield Armory
  Boston area
   Adams
   Boston
   Boston African American
   F.L. Olmsted
   J.F.K.
   Longfellow
   Lowell
   Minute Man
   Salem Maritime
   Saugus Iron Works

Michigan
Keweenaw

Minnesota
Grand Portage

Mississippi
Brices Cross Roads
Natchez
Tupelo
Vicksburg

Missouri
George Washington Carver
Harry S Truman
Jefferson National Expansion
Ulysses S. Grant
Wilson's Creek

Montana
Big Hole
Bighorn Canyon
Grant-Kohrs Ranch
Little Bighorn Battlefield

Nebraska
Homestead
Scotts Bluff

Nevada-Arizona
Lake Mead

New Hampshire
Saint-Gaudens

New Jersey
Edison
Morristown

New Jersey-Pennsylvania
Delaware Water Gap

New Mexico
El Morro
Fort Union
Pecos
Salinas Pueblo Missions

New York
Eleanor Roosevelt
Fort Stanwix
Home of F.D.R.
Martin Van Buren
Saratoga
Theo. Roosevelt Inaugural
Vanderbilt Mansion
Women's Rights
  New York City area
  Castle Clinton
  Federal Hall
  Gateway
  General Grant
  Hamilton Grange
  Sagamore Hill
  St. Paul's Church
  Statue of Liberty
  Theo. Roosevelt Birthplace

North Carolina
Carl Sandburg Home
Fort Raleigh
Guilford Courthouse
Moores Creek
Wright Brothers

North Dakota
Fort Union Trading Post
Knife River Indian Villages

Ohio
Cuyahoga Valley
Dayton Aviation
Hopewell Culture
James A. Garfield
Perry's Victory
William Howard Taft

Oklahoma
Chickasaw

Oregon
Fort Clatsop

Pennsylvania
Allegheny Portage Railroad
Eisenhower
Fort Necessity
Friendship Hill
Gettysburg
Johnstown Flood
  Philadelphia area

E.A. Poe
Hopewell Furnace
Independence
T. Kosciuszko
Valley Forge

Rhode Island
Roger Williams

South Carolina
Charles Pinckney
Cowpens
Fort Sumter
Kings Mountain
Ninety Six

South Dakota
Mount Rushmore

Tennessee
Andrew Johnson
Cumberland Gap
Fort Donelson
Shiloh
Stones River

Texas
Amistad
Chamizal
Fort Davis
Lake Meredith
Lyndon B. Johnson
Palo Alto Battlefield
San Antonio Missions

Utah
Golden Spike

Utah-Arizona
Glen Canyon

Washington
Coulee Dam
Ebey's Landing
Fort Vancouver
Lake Chelan
Ross Lake
San Juan Island
Whitman Mission

Washington, DC
  African-American Civil War
    Memorial
  Constitution Gardens
  Ford's Theatre
  Fort Circle Parks
  Frederick Douglass

Kenilworth Aquatic Gardens
Korean War Veterans Mem.
Lincoln Memorial
LBJ Memorial Grove
M. McL. Bethune Council
  House
National Mall
Pennsylvania Avenue
Rock Creek Park
Theo. Roosevelt Island
Thos. Jefferson Memorial
Vietnam Veterans Memorial
Washington Monument
The White House

West Virginia
Harpers Ferry

Virginia
Appomattox Court House
Booker T. Washington
Colonial
Fredericksburg & Spotsylvania
G. Washington Birthplace
Green Springs
Jamestown
Maggie L. Walker
Manassas
Petersburg
Prince William Forest
Red Hill Patrick Henry
Richmond
  Washington, DC, area
  Arlington House
  George Washington Parkway
  Great Falls
  Wolf Trap

Wyoming
Fort Laramie

Outside the U.S.

Guam
War in the Pacific

Puerto Rico
San Juan

U.S. Virgin Islands
Christiansted
Salt River Bay

PRELUDE

I was one of the fortunate ones. In school I had teachers who made the study of United States history interesting, if not downright fascinating! There were classes on the early European explorations of the New World and the first colonial settlements along the eastern seaboard; the Euro-American expansion westward across this vast continent and the resulting cultural collision between the newcomers and the indigenous Americans; the War for Independence against Britain; the Civil War between the North and South; the history of politics, legislation, and constitutional law; biological explorations of America; and the history of increasing mobility across the country and the impact that that mobility has had upon the use and abuse of the land and its resources.

For me, these and other academic studies were not merely dry, boring subjects from some irrelevant, distant, dust-gathering past. Rather, the events and people were given meaning through the quality of inspired teaching and through insights into the past's relevance to the present and future course of this great nation.

Whether you also were fortunate enough or not to have had your interest in and appreciation of U.S. history sparked in school, I hope you will find this book a helpful and stimulating reference to the national historical parks. Most of all, my hope is that the descriptions on these pages will inspire you to learn more about our history by visiting many of these wonderful and priceless national treasures. Visits to these parks will offer you the opportunity to share in the enriching experience of U.S. history. Whether you are a life-long citizen or an immigrant from another land, savoring some of these places will surely light the flame of fascination and appreciation for the people and events that have led to the America of today—people and events that have influenced the lives of us all.

Each of the approximately two hundred historical units of the National Park System has some fascinating story to tell—many of them are happy stories, while others reveal tragic aspects of American history. I have personally derived enormous pleasure from visiting many of the units of the National Park System that commemorate significant people and events of our past. Among the most meaningful and memorable experiences have been my visits to the following:

• The Statue of Liberty and the immigration museum on nearby Ellis Island, which I visited with a very dear friend who is herself an immigrant. I felt her own deep emotional response to this national monument honoring all immigrants in U.S. history. From her I gained insight into the meaning of the courage and effort it takes to come to America in the hope of achieving, through hard work and commitment, a better life and enhanced opportunities for happiness and success. I sensed, even more than previously, a profoundly deep feeling that the freedoms, privileges, responsibilities, and quality of life that most Americans enjoy must never be taken for granted. The sacrifices and risks that so many immigrants have been and continue to be willing to take are what has helped make this nation great. It is the immigrant's courage that has helped immensely to create the rich and enriching ethnic and cultural diversity of American society. This diversity has helped produce a unique and ever-strengthening national unity and cultural richness unknown anywhere else in the world.

• The site of Jamestown, on scenically beautiful Jamestown Island on Virginia's tidewater James River, is where I visualized something of the awesome sacrifice and bitter hardships faced by those early colonists from England. Had not those and other early settlers been willing to risk all, including their very lives, what would our nation have ever become? This part of Colonial National Historical Park is a place to seriously contemplate the past.

• Valley Forge, where General George Washington and his weary troops wintered over, weighed down with the feeling that they and other American soldiers were inadequately equipped and poorly prepared to defeat the British troops in the Revolutionary War and win independence for the American colonies. What if those feelings, those fears had proved correct? Or fearing defeat, suppose those soldiers had just given up—where would we be today? A place like this makes you stop and think about the courage it took for the soldiers to do their best to fight for the cause they believed in—ultimate victory over the redcoats that would allow the United States of America to be born and grow as an independent nation.

• Independence National Historical Park prominently features Independence Hall, in which the Declaration of Independence was adopted and the stars-and-stripes design of the United States flag was chosen. Here, as well, the U.S. Constitution was hammered out by the members of the Constitutional Convention "to form a more perfect Union." To walk through this steepled, red-brick building and realize what all has occurred within its hallowed walls is an awesome experience!

• The Chesapeake & Ohio Canal, extending over 180 miles from Washington, D.C., to Cumberland, Maryland, is a major example of this country's nineteenth-century canal-building era. For today's visitors, this former commercial transportation corridor offers exceptional recreational opportunities, such as delightful canoeing and mule-towed boat tours on the canal, and hiking and bicycling along the towpath. Of my many hikes in the vicinity of Great Falls, I've most enjoyed springtime, when the rich Potomac River bottomland forest has been filled with a concert of bird songs.

• Civil War battlefields, such as Manassas and Fredericksburg & Spotsylvania, in Virginia; and Gettysburg, in Pennsylvania, where in the peacefulness and beauty of today's pastoral landscapes, it is a challenge to visualize the horrendous fighting, human suffering, and dying that once occurred in these and so many other bitterly contested places. At one forest-bordered meadow, where there had been a terrible slaughtering of both Union and Confederate soldiers, the tranquillity that I was privileged to enjoy was broken, not by the sounds of warfare, but by the clear, sweet notes of a bobwhite quail calling from a hedgerow nearby. Hearing that beautiful bird in this once blood-stained and war-shattered place made me realize even more what a miracle it was that the beauty of this Virginia countryside and other Civil War battlefields has been healed. And what an even greater miracle it was that our bitterly divided nation was reunited after all the hateful killing finally came to an end. Experiences like this can make you think thankfully about our United States of America.

• The majestic Lincoln Memorial, overlooking the Potomac River in Washington, D.C., honors the life and accomplishments of the 16th President of the United States, Abraham Lincoln. This inspiring columned place, with its large statue of Lincoln seated, has long been the site of peaceful civil rights and other demonstrations, including Martin Luther King, Jr.'s, "I Have a Dream" speech in 1963.

• The enormous sculpted heads of George Washington, Thomas Jefferson, Abraham Lincoln, and Theodore Roosevelt at Mount Rushmore, in the pine-covered Black Hills of South Dakota, is a sight that cannot help but inspire the viewer. It is a mystery how the sculptor and his stone carvers figured out the precisely calculated proportions and measurements, so that from any angle and in any lighting, the four sculptures look just right.

• El Morro is a spectacular, ponderosa pine-framed sandstone bluff in western New Mexico, where it is fascinating to see ancient Indian petroglyphs and historic Spanish and American inscriptions that were carved into the rock by early travelers passing by this great landmark.

• Pecos and Salinas Pueblo Missions, in New Mexico, are the sites of Pueblo Indian villages at which seventeenth-century pioneering Spaniards built Franciscan mission churches in an effort to establish Christianity among the indigenous peoples of this frontier region of the New World. An aura of mystery seems to pervade the ruins of these now long-abandoned villages that were once bustling with the activities of their people and filled with the laughter of little children; and church edifices that were once filled with the sounds of organ music, singing, and prayers.

• Fort Davis, in the scenic Davis Mountains of West Texas, and the ruins of Fort Union, in New Mexico, were two of many nineteenth-century U.S. military forts established across the Great Plains and the West. These military outposts were positioned to help protect the rapidly growing numbers of Euro-American travelers and settlers from attack by Indians. These are good places to contemplate how this influx led to fear-fueled uprisings and raids by many of those native peoples, who foresaw the loss of their vast traditional hunting grounds and an end to their ancient way of life.

• Fort Point is an excellent example of nineteenth-century coastal defense fortifications. Built to help protect San Francisco, California, from attack by foreign warships, it is a fabulous place from which to view the mouth of San Francisco Bay and the comings and goings of ships, with the mighty Golden Gate Bridge directly overhead and spanning across to the headlands of Marin.

• Pu'uhonua o Honaunau is one of three parks on the west coast of the Big Island of Hawai'i established to help perpetuate the rich traditional culture of the native Hawaiian people. This tranquil and delightful palm-shaded place by the sea was a refuge for persons who had broken ancient and sacred taboos. Sitting by a pond beneath the tall coconut palms, I found this magical place to be still a tranquil and beautiful refuge for contemplative thought and healing inspiration.

If you really want to *feel* some of the historical heartbeat of the United States of America, I cannot urge you too strongly to go out and savor some of these national historic parks and sites. For me, the research and writing of this tome has been entirely a labor of love that has given me a major shot of patriotic adrenaline.

—*Russ Butcher*

ACKNOWLEDGMENTS

I am deeply grateful to the numerous National Park Service superintendents and their staffs for the invaluable help and advice they provided during the preparation of this book. My thanks to the National Parks and Conservation Association; to its former president, Paul C. Pritchard; its former senior editor, Sue E. Dodge; and others for their desire to produce this companion volume to the long-running *Exploring Our National Parks and Monuments*, recently issued in its ninth edition. I am, of course, grateful to my parents, Mary and Devereux Butcher, for initiating the latter book way back in 1947 and carrying it through eight editions, and I am extremely grateful to them for encouraging my interest in the national parks. My thanks to Rick Rinehart and Roberts Rinehart Publishers for publishing both books; a special thank you to my editor, Toni Knapp, whose thorough editing and thoughtful suggestions, along with very helpful suggestions by the association's editorial staff, have enhanced the text; and my thanks to Belinda MacMaster for her excellent assistance on the word processor. And I am especially grateful to my very dear friend Nermana Ligata for the inspiration as well as the marvelous professional help she has given me that made both volumes of *Exploring . . .* bigger and better than they would otherwise have been.

—*Russ Butcher*

INTRODUCTION

PAUL C. PRITCHARD

Former President, National Parks and Conservation Association

America's "crown jewels"—Yellowstone and Yosemite, for example—all but define the National Park System for many visitors, while the cultural sites included among the system's 374 units are often overlooked or misunderstood.

Longevity is partly responsible. In the earliest days of the system, most parks singled out for inclusion were areas with spectacular landscapes, examples of the primeval New World. It was only later that we came to realize that historic sites—places where events significant to the nation's development occurred—were an equally important part of America's heritage.

While the natural parks and monuments represent nature's superlatives—the tallest, the largest, the deepest—the cultural parks represent a part of who we are. This is a nation whose historical events began long before Christopher Columbus, evolving in waves of human endeavor over many centuries. The cultural parks celebrate America's discovery, settlement, and expansion. They commemorate the Civil War and wars with Mexico and the Indians. They celebrate U.S. presidents and the contributions of women, African Americans, musicians, artists, writers, and inventors, as well as the influence of technology and industry.

Cultural sites are important to our understanding of our nation today and how we've arrived at this point. And by the same token, Russ Butcher's *Exploring Our National Historic Parks and Sites* is an important and original assessment of the cultural resources within the National Park System. There is nothing comparable to this work. There are homogenized documents that try to compress all sorts of facts into totally neutral statements about what the visitor will find at our cultural sites, and there are others that document the temperature or the routes of access or similar logistics about the sites—but there's nothing else with heart.

This tome is a companion to one that was first published fifty years ago and authored by Devereux Butcher, Russ's father. Since that time, *Exploring Our National Parks and Monuments* has been updated and reissued nine times—with the latest edition revised by Russ Butcher himself.

Like his father, who served as executive director of the National Parks Association (today known as the National Parks and Conservation Association) and as its first magazine editor, Russ also has a long and distinguished affiliation with NPCA and the national parks. America is lucky to cultivate individuals who devote their lives to a public purpose and who inspire in their children that same commitment.

We should be grateful, too, for Russ's important contribution to our understanding of our premier cultural sites and the rich national heritage of which we are stewards.

PART 1

PARKS CELEBRATING AMERICA'S DISCOVERY, SETTLEMENT, EXPANSION, AND GROWTH AS A NATION

ALLEGHENY PORTAGE RAILROAD NATIONAL HISTORIC SITE

ALLEGHENY PORTAGE RAILROAD NATIONAL HISTORIC SITE, consisting of 1,500 acres in the Allegheny Mountains of west-central Pennsylvania, was established in 1964 to protect and interpret the remains of an unusual passenger and freight railroad portage that was completed in 1834. This ingenious device connected two major stretches of the Pennsylvania Main Line Canal and slashed travel time between Philadelphia and Pittsburgh from over three weeks to only four days.

A series of five rail incline planes stair-stepped up each side of the Allegheny Mountain Range, climbing over 1,000 feet. Initially, passengers and freight were transferred from canal boats to railroad cars. The system was soon simplified by the creation of sectionalized boats that were floated onto flatbed railroad cars. Passengers and freight no longer had to be transferred, but remained on the packet-boat sections for the entire canal-and-railroad trip.

As the National Park Service says:

> [The boat's sections] were hauled from the water by stationary steam engines, then pulled by locomotives at about 15 mph over the long grade to the first incline. In a small shed at the foot of the incline, workers hitched three cars at a time, each with a load averaging 7,000 pounds, to the continuous cable that moved over rollers between the rails. This cable was pulled at about 4 mph by a stationary steam engine beneath a large shed at the top of the incline.

> During the portage's busiest periods, six trains an hour were pulled up each incline. When possible, the operators used cars descending on the other track to counterbalance those ascending, lessening the strain on the engines.

Five of these inclines carried the cars to the summit. On the near-level grades between inclines, the cars were drawn by horses or locomotives. . . . Upon reaching the Johnstown canal basin [to the west], the boat sections were eased into the water, reassembled, and floated down the canal's Western Division to Pittsburgh. In 6 hours, the boats had traveled 36 miles, ascended 1,398 feet, and descended 1,172.

While the portage was a clever invention, it was plagued with problems. Steam-engine boilers exploded from time to time, and the hemp rope would sometimes break. The latter difficulty was resolved when "wire rope" cable was installed.

Near the crest of the mountain is the Lemon House, built in the early 1830s as a tavern that offered refreshments for railroad passengers. Among other historic structures in the park are Skew Arch Bridge that was built as a wagon road over the railroad; 901-foot-long Staple Bend Tunnel—the first railroad tunnel in the United States; engine house #6 foundation, covered with an exhibit shelter containing a full-scale model of a stationary steam engine; a stone quarry used for railroad construction; railroad bed inclines 6, 8, 9, and 10; and stone sleepers, early railroad ties. The portage was made obsolete by completion of the Pennsylvania Railroad's main line across the state in 1854, and was abandoned in 1857.

The site's visitor center provides interpretive exhibits, a 20-minute introductory movie, a full-scale model of a steam locomotive used on the railroad, and publications. Living-history demonstrations and other interpretive programs are offered during the summer months. Interpretive boardwalks and trails lead from the vicinity of the visitor center and Lemon House. There are no camping facilities in the national historic site, but a picnic area is provided approximately 1.5 miles from the visitor center which can be accessed by hiking or by vehicle. Lodging and meals are available in Hollidaysburg, Duncansville, Ebensburg, Altoona, and elsewhere in the region; and meals are available also in Cresson and Gallitzin.

IF YOU GO: Access to the site is by way of the Gallitzin exit from U.S. Route 22, 12 miles west of Altoona or one mile east of Cresson. Further information: Superintendent, P.O. Box 189, Cresson, PA 16630. Telephone (814) 886-6150.

ARKANSAS POST NATIONAL MEMORIAL

ARKANSAS POST NATIONAL MEMORIAL comprises 389 acres on the banks of the Arkansas River in southeastern Arkansas. It was established in 1964 to commemorate events that occurred in or near the national memorial, spanning nearly three centuries. It also commemorates all those people of many nationalities and cultures who endured enormous hardships and even sacrificed their lives in the settlement and early development of lands that were or subsequently became part of the United States of America.

France had claimed a vast region of North America, and in the 1680s entrusted to Parisian Henri de Tonti the task of establishing frontier trading posts and settlements in a wide area of the lower Mississippi River valley. This colonization and commercial development was intended to give validity to France's grand scheme of controlling the resources-rich empire that stretched westward from the Appalachian Mountains, and from French Canada south to the Gulf of Mexico.

In 1686, de Tonti dispatched six of his men to begin construction of a fur-trading post near the Quapaw Indian village of Osotouy, about 18 river miles upstream from the Arkansas River's junction with the Mississippi. They built a small house of cedar logs and roofed it over with bark. But this tiny frontier outpost was not to become the successful settlement de Tonti had envisioned. The European market for furs had become saturated, causing prices to tumble and leading France to ban fur trading south of Canada. Consequently, by 1700 his dream was dead and his fledgling *Poste de Arkansea* (or *Akansea*) may even have been abandoned.

By the 1720s, however, France's interest in the vast Louisiana empire was rekindled. A Scottish entrepreneur, John Law, was given the charter to colonize the region. For his own personal investment, he chose a site near the former Arkansas Post, which was strategically located about midway between newly founded New Orleans to the south, and a French fort and settlements in the Illinois country to the north.

Law brought nearly 50 French immigrants to his Arkansas colony, and rustic pavilions, cabins, and storehouses were quickly built. A visitor, in 1722, observed that "everything seemed to promise that it would soon become flourishing." Simultaneously, a small military garrison was established about three miles southeast of the colony, near the junction of the rivers. But Law's financial empire suddenly collapsed, leaving his Arkansas colony to struggle on its own. By 1723, only 20 residents remained. The garrison stayed on for several years to help maintain the French alliance with the friendly Quapaw Indians, but it departed when a Roman Catholic Jesuit priest briefly took over the leadership of the remnant community.

As French supply boats plied up and down the Mississippi and as the English and French became increasingly hostile toward each other over claims to the vast interior of North America, the French decided to establish a stronger military presence at Arkansas Post. In 1732, a small fort was built at the site of de Tonti's post, while a number of French fur traders settled nearby. In 1749, the warring Chickasaw Indians, prompted by their English allies, raided and burned down the Arkansas Post village. Shortly after this setback, and further discouraged by a major change in the course of the Arkansas River, the French moved the post in 1751 to a place about 40 river miles upstream from the Arkansas' junction with the Mississippi—a site that is at today's national memorial. The new location was called *Ecores Rouges* (Red Bluffs).

To provide a stronger defense against Indian raids, a larger fort was built, with a garrison of 40 men. A dozen or so houses and other buildings were enclosed by a high picket stockade, within which were the officers' quarters, barracks, storeroom, chaplain's quarters, chapel, hospital, bakery, powder magazine, and jail. The village nearby housed some 30 Frenchmen and a dozen or so slaves. Almost as soon as the fortified settlement was completed, however, it was abandoned. Arkansas Post was again relocated, this time to a site only six miles from the mouth of the Arkansas, with a 60-man garrison to help protect French boat traffic on the Mississippi.

In 1762, after being defeated by the British in the French and Indian War, France surrendered to Britain all the lands east of the Mississippi, while ceding to Spain its Louisiana Territory west of the great river. The Spanish flag was raised over Arkansas Post in 1770 and the fort was renamed Fort Carlos III, in honor of the king of Spain.

The newest location of the post was unfortuitous, as it was annually hit with often disastrous flooding by the river. Consequently, in 1779, the post was once again moved back upriver to the vicinity of the present national memorial. Here the fur-trading enterprise became more successful than it had ever been under the French. The pelts and hides of many species of fur-bearing mammals, such as beaver, otter, mink, marten, raccoon, fox, bear, deer, and buffalo (bison), were exchanged by the Quapaws and other trappers for such items as traps, rifles, powder, flints, knives, scissors, axes, articles of clothing, cloth, wool ribbon, and beads.

The American Revolution reached briefly westward to the Mississippi River valley. In 1783, a 100-man force of British soldiers, American renegades, Chickasaw Indians, and black partisans, retaliating against Spain's support of the American colonists in their push for independence from Britain, crept up on the post under the cover of darkness and attacked the village. Although they were unsuccessful in breaking through the fort's defenses, they succeeded in carrying off a number of village residents. A rescue party of a hundred Quapaw warriors chased after the attackers, encircled them, and forced the release of most of the hostages.

Following this attack, the fort was gradually destroyed by the river's steady erosion of the *Ecores Rouges* site. A new and stronger fortification, renamed Fort San Esteban, with a 50-man garrison, was established in the 1790s to protect the adjacent Arkansas Post village that consisted of more than 100 residents and roughly 30 houses. With the new fort, the residents felt more secure in the face of persistent aggressions by the Osage Indians.

In 1800, following the French Revolution, France succeeded in forcing Spain to return the Louisiana Territory. But then France suddenly found itself strapped for cash. In 1803 it sold the vast Louisiana Territory (extending from the Mississippi to the Rocky Mountains and from the northern edge of Texas to Canada) to the United States for $15 million. The fort on the bluffs overlooking the Arkansas was officially handed over to U.S. officials in 1804 and renamed Fort Madison, honoring the Secretary of State, James Madison. At this time, Arkansas Post consisted of about 120 residents. In 1812, the 16-man U.S. garrison departed and the fort was allowed to fall into ruin. No trace remains of it because of the river's steady erosion of the bluffs.

Arkansas Post next developed into an American frontier fur-trading settlement, complete with a U.S. government fur-processing factory. This facility was so poorly managed that it operated for only five years. But by 1810, Arkansas Post had grown to nearly 900 residents and about 20 houses. In 1819, the Arkansas Territory was established by the U.S. Congress, and Arkansas Post became the territorial capital. The town's population mushroomed. Some large homes and important businesses were built. A newspaper, the *Arkansas Gazette*, was founded. A real estate boom took off, fueled by lots of land speculators.

In just two years, however, the territorial capital was moved from Arkansas Post to the higher elevation and more central location at Little Rock. Following this setback, Arkansas Post next became a major center for cotton production on rich lands formerly occupied by the Quapaw Indians, and a key cotton-shipping port on the Arkansas River with the arrival of the steamboat. Arkansas entered the Union as the 25th state in 1836.

In 1861, at the start of the Civil War, Arkansas followed other southern states by seceding from the United States and joining the Confederacy. A Confederate fortification, Fort Hindman, was built at Arkansas Post, with a 5,000-man garrison to defend it. In January 1863, however, a 30,000-man Union force came upriver, backed by a fleet of three iron-clad gunboats, four boiler-plated "tinclads," and two other gunboats. This flotilla unleashed a tremendous bombardment that overwhelmed the Confederate defenders, hammered the fort, and damaged or destroyed most of the town's buildings. What remained of the fort and much of the town subsequently disappeared beneath the ever-shifting course of the river.

In 1929, Arkansas Post became a 21-acre state park honoring the site of the founding of Arkansas. Today, the national memorial continues to protect and interpret the history and historical remains of this important site.

The memorial also contains a rich variety of Arkansas alluvial habitats, from bottomland deciduous forest to wetlands along Post Bayou. Unfortunately, much of the original wetlands has been sacrificed to efforts at riverbank stabilization and to the Arkansas River Navigation Project.

Among the dominant trees are sweetgum; nine species of oaks—most notably southern red, cherrybark, blackjack, post, willow, and water; eastern red cedar; several kinds of elms; loblolly pine; a species of hackberry called sugarberry; bald cypress; American sycamore; eastern cottonwood; honeylocust; pecan; water, bitternut, and mockernut hickories; and scattered bush palmettos, flowering dogwoods, and redbuds. Other plants include boneset, goldenrods, ironweed, rose mallow, wood sorrel, Mayapple, spring beauty, bluet, violets, cattail, highbush blackberry, muscadine, southern dewberry, trumpet creeper, honeysuckle, cat briar, moonseed, supple jack, Virginia creeper, scuppernong, giant cane and other grasses, and the resurrection fern that grows on oak trees.

Mammals include whitetail deer, bobcats, coyotes, red foxes, armadillos, opossums, raccoons, gray and red squirrels, and an occasional mountain lion and black bear. Alligators also inhabit the area.

Of the many species of birds, there are anhingas; great blue and green-backed herons; wood ducks and many species of wintering waterfowl; ospreys; Mississippi kites; bald eagles; wild turkeys; bobwhite quail; barred and other owls; belted kingfishers; red-headed, red-bellied, pileated, and other woodpeckers; blue jays; Carolina chickadees; tufted titmice; Carolina, marsh, and other wrens; eastern bluebirds; a multitude of warblers including prothonotary, yellowthroat, and hooded; summer and scarlet tanagers; cardinals; indigo and painted buntings; redwings; meadowlarks; and orchard and northern orioles.

The memorial's visitor center features exhibits, an interpretive film, and publications. Interpretive trails and paths wind through some of the natural habitats and lead past the sites and remains of historic points of interest. A nature trail leads around the tip of the peninsula that juts into the river; another path encircles Park Lake; and a primitive nature trail tracks along Post Bayou. The Park Service urges visitors to be alert for snakes and poison ivy, and to use insect repellent to discourage ticks and chiggers.

Two informative publications are *The Arkansas Post Story*, by Roger Coleman (Southwest Cultural Resources Center, Santa Fe, NM) and *Colonial Arkansas 1686-1804: A Social and Cultural History*, by Morris Arnold (University of Arkansas Press).

While camping is not allowed, the memorial does provide a picnic area. Lodging and meals are available in Dumas, Gillett, DeWitt, and other nearby communities.

IF YOU GO: Access to the memorial is 84 miles southeast of Little Rock, by way of U.S. Route 65 to Dumas, then 15 miles north on U.S. Route 165, and 2 miles east on State Route 169; or 6 miles south of Gillett on U.S. Route 165 and 2 miles east on State Route 169. Further information: Superintendent, Route 1, Box 16, Gillett, AR 72055. Telephone (501) 548-2207.

BENT'S OLD FORT NATIONAL HISTORIC SITE

BENT'S OLD FORT NATIONAL HISTORIC SITE, comprising 800 acres on the Great Plains of southeastern Colorado, was established in 1960 to protect the site of an Anglo-American trading center. As the most important trading post on the Mountain Route of the Santa Fe Trail, the center carried on a profitable business from 1833-1849. It did business with Plains Indian tribes such as the Arapaho, Cheyenne, and Kiowa, as well as with Mexicans and American trappers and explorers.

William and Charles Bent and Ceran St. Vrain came west from Missouri. By 1833, they had selected this strategic location in the Arkansas River valley to set up their business under the name of Bent, St. Vrain and Company.

Bent's Old Fort National Historic Site, southeastern Colorado [NPS]

The fort was set amid buffalo (bison) hunting grounds and was built as a fortified community measuring 180 feet long by 135 feet wide. It was surrounded by a thick, 15-foot-high adobe wall that was topped by gun turrets. Within its walls were over 30 rooms, including living quarters; trade rooms; workshops for carpenters and blacksmiths; a council room for meetings with the Indians; warehouses; and a corral and plaza.

Because William Bent proved adept at negotiating trades with the Indians, Mexicans, and American trappers, he became the fort's manager. In 1837, he married a Cheyenne Indian, Owl Woman.

Charles Bent devoted much of his time to buying trips to and from St. Louis, Missouri, where he obtained merchandise for the fort and for company stores in Santa Fe and Taos, New Mexico. St. Vrain helped manage the Santa Fe business and traded for Navajo blankets and Mexican merchandise for trade at the fort. Bent's Fort did a big business in trading merchandise from St. Louis and Santa Fe for buffalo robes brought by the Plains Indians. The Indians, in return, received such items as horses, firearms, kettles and knives, tobacco, and cloth.

But Bent's Fort, for all its success, was more than a commercial trading center. It also served as a cultural meeting place—as neutral ground where problems between the various Indian tribes or between Indians and Anglos could be discussed and solutions negotiated.

In 1846, U.S. General Stephen W. Kearny's Army of the West used Bent's Fort as an advance base from which to launch a successful invasion and takeover of New Mexico during the war with Mexico. Charles Bent was named the first United States governor of New Mexico, while William Bent continued for a short time with the Indian trade at the fort. As a result of a decline in trading due to an epidemic of cholera, William finally gave up in 1849. The fort was partially blown up and he may have deliberately tried to destroy it on his way out. He subsequently constructed a new trading post 40 miles farther down the Arkansas River valley.

In 1975, the National Park Service began the careful reconstruction of the old fort, aided by archaeological research, historical drawings, and diary descriptions. The national historic site offers an interpretive video, publications, and a gift shop, where visitors can purchase authentic trade items. There are regularly scheduled tours and living-history demonstrations throughout the summer. Picnicking is permitted, but camping is not. The site is open daily, except on Thanksgiving, Christmas, and New Year's Day.

IF YOU GO: Lodging and meals are available in La Junta and Las Animas, as well as in Pueblo and Trinidad. Access is by way of various highways crisscrossing southeastern Colorado, including southeast from I-25 at Pueblo on U.S. Route 50 to La Junta, then eight miles east on State Route 194; or northeast from I-25 at Trinidad on U.S. Route 350 to La Junta and eight miles east on Route 194. Further information: Superintendent, 35110 Highway 194, La Junta, CO 81050. Telephone (719) 384-2596.

BOSTON NATIONAL HISTORICAL PARK

BOSTON NATIONAL HISTORICAL PARK consists of 41 acres in 16 sites in Boston and Charlestown, Massachusetts. It was established in 1974 to protect, interpret, and focus national attention on significant places and the events that helped to spur the American colonies toward independence from Britain. Most of the properties are linked by the 2.5-mile Freedom Trail (a national recreation trail), which runs from an information kiosk on Boston Common through downtown Boston, across Charlestown Bridge, and loops through Charlestown.

Among the park sites are the following:

Faneuil Hall (below Government Center, near the intersection of Congress and North streets) is owned by the City of Boston and jointly managed by the city and the National Park Service. It is referred to as the "Cradle of Liberty," because town meetings that were held here included those opposing oppressive British taxation—notably the Sugar Tax of 1764 and the Stamp Act of 1765. These debates were reported throughout the American colonies and helped unify public opinion in favor of American independence.

Built by wealthy merchant Peter Faneuil, the red brick hall was constructed in 1742 to provide space for market stalls, town meetings, and other public functions. After a fire in 1761, the building was rebuilt, and it was this structure in which the debates over Britain's abusive taxation were held. In 1805, the hall was enlarged to accommodate the growing needs of the city. The famous architect of the time, Charles Bulfinch, expanded the height and width of the structure without altering its exterior architectural style.

In subsequent years, other national topics were debated here, including slavery, temperance, and women's suffrage. Since a major renovation in the

USS *Constitution*, Boston National Historical Park [David Muench]

1970s, the second floor has continued as an important public meeting center, while a marketplace occupies the ground floor.

Old South Meeting House (at 310 Washington Street) was built as a Congregational church in 1729. Because it was the largest structure in colonial Boston, it was sometimes used for public meetings that were too large for Faneuil Hall. The most significant of those was the gathering of 5,000 irate Bostonians, on December 16, 1773, to discuss the British tax on imported tea. Following this stormy meeting, a group of colonists dressed as Indians walked down to Boston Harbor, boarded the three British cargo ships, and dumped 400 crates of tea overboard. In retaliation for the "Boston Tea Party," Britain shut down the Port of Boston, and thus brought the American colonies sharply closer to their unified desire for independence.

The Old South Association, a private organization, is protecting the building, sponsoring interpretive exhibits and programs, and holding special events that carry on the American tradition of promoting the freedom of speech.

Old State House (at 206 Washington Street) dates from 1713 and housed the seat of the Massachusetts Bay Colony's government, as well as municipal and county governmental offices. So important was this oldest public building in Boston to colonial politics and philosophy, that it has been called the most important public building in colonial America. It was here, in 1761, that lawyer James Otis, who campaigned against "taxation without representation," spoke out eloquently and forcefully against the British policy of issuing search warrants—just on *suspicion* of hiding smuggled merchandise—

without enumerating specific charges against persons accused. As John Adams described Otis' speech:

> Otis was a flame of fire. Then and there was the first scene of the first act of opposition to the arbitrary claims of Great Britain. Then and there the child Independence was born.

In the Old State House's Representatives Hall, the Massachusetts Assembly started debating colonial rights, that ultimately led to the colonies' rebellion and war for independence from Britain. Following independence, this building continued to serve as the seat of Massachusetts government, until the new, gold-domed state house was erected in 1798. Today, the historic building is maintained by the city in cooperation with the National Park Service, and it houses an informative museum of the history of Boston, sponsored by the Bostonian Society.

Paul Revere House (at 19 North Square, in Boston's North End) is the oldest house in the city, dating from around 1680. While Paul Revere lived here in the late 1700s, he participated in the Boston Tea Party. On April 18, 1775, he made his historic horseback ride, to carry the warning to American patriots in Lexington and Concord that the British troops were rushing from Boston to seize weapons and ammunition hidden in Concord. The early colonial urban-style house was rescued from threatened demolition and restored by the Paul Revere Memorial Association in 1908. It is open to visitors daily.

Old North Church (at 193 State Street) was made famous when Paul Revere instructed the church's sexton to place two lanterns from the 190-foot-tall steeple to warn American patriots in Charlestown that British troops were heading from Boston out to Concord, crossing by boat. Today's steeple is a replica of the original, which was knocked down in a hurricane in 1804, the replacement of which was also toppled in a hurricane in 1954.

Bunker Hill Monument (in Monument Square, bounded by High and Bartlett streets in Charlestown) is a 220-foot-tall granite obelisk rising from the top of Breed's Hill. It celebrates the valor of Americans in their first significant military confrontation with British soldiers in the War for Independence (the American Revolution), on June 17, 1775. The building at the monument's base provides exhibits of the fierce slaughter, in which the redcoats succeeded in capturing the hill and driving off the patriots. However, they suffered nearly 50 percent casualties of their 2,200-man force at the hands of the first American colonial army. Visitors today may climb the 294 steps of the monument to view the surrounding city.

Charlestown Navy Yard, dating from 1800, built and serviced U.S. naval ships for many years, climaxing during World War II. The historic frigate, the USS *Constitution*, is docked here for public viewing. This beautiful sailing ship fought against the Barbary pirates and was engaged in the War of 1812 against the British navy. Nearby, the USS *Constitution* Museum interprets the history of "Old Ironsides" and other naval history. Also berthed close by is the destroyer, the USS *Cassin Young*, built and active during World War II. The 30-acre Navy Yard complex administered by the National Park Service includes other structures, notably the Commandant's House, the beautiful mansion that dates from 1805.

IF YOU GO: Park visitor centers are located at 15 State Street (across from the Old State House), in downtown Boston; and adjacent to Dry Dock #1, near the USS *Constitution*, in Charlestown. Walking the entire Freedom Trail from Boston Common to Bunker Hill Monument may take visitors most of a day or parts of more than one day. A red line on the pavement leads the way through most of the distance in either direction. Visitors driving into the Boston area are advised to avoid bringing their cars into the congested downtown city center. Instead, take public transportation, or follow signs from U.S. Route 93 to the Charlestown Navy Yard and walk or take public transit from there.

Lodging and meals are abundantly available in and around Boston. The Park Service offers interpretive walking tours of the downtown stretch of the Freedom Trail from mid-April through November; and there are daily interpretive talks at Faneuil Hall and Bunker Hill Monument, as well as tours of the World War II destroyer USS *Cassin Young*. The U.S. Navy offers daily tours of the *Constitution*. The park is closed on Thanksgiving, Christmas, and New Year's Day. Further park information: Superintendent, Charlestown Navy Yard, Boston, MA 02129. Telephone (617) 242-5601.

CABRILLO NATIONAL MONUMENT

CABRILLO NATIONAL MONUMENT, comprising 144 acres, was established in 1913 to celebrate the first European landing on the west coast of what became the United States, by Portuguese shipbuilder and navigator Juan Rodriguez Cabrillo, in 1542. (Some historians believe Cabrillo's name was actually Portuguese—João Rodrigues Cabrilho, while others claim he was born in Spain.) The national monument protects part of Point Loma—a 422-foot-high, coastal sage scrub-covered headland at the mouth of San Diego Bay in Southern California.

Exploring under license of the King of Spain, Cabrillo's historic expedition, up the west coast of North America, began in Navidad, Mexico, on June 27, 1542. Sailing in three ships—the flagship 100-foot-long galleon *San Salvador,* the smaller *Victoria,* and a brigantine, the *San Miguel*—the expedition of over 200 men proceeded up the coast of Baja California, first pausing at Cabo San Lucas at the tip of the Baja peninsula, and then sailing 15 to 20 miles each day. Sixty-two days after setting forth, the ships arrived on September 28 at a harbor that Cabrillo called San Miguel (subsequently renamed San Diego Bay) where they remained for six days. While there, the explorers encountered a few Indians, some of whom were wearing wild-animal furs.

From the sheltered bay, the sailing ships continued north, landing at San Miguel Island, which is now within Channel Islands National Park. There, Cabrillo seriously injured himself in a fall. On the expedition's return to the island, after sailing north to near San Francisco Bay, Cabrillo died. The ships were left under the command of Cabrillo's pilot, Bartolomé Ferrer (or Ferrelo), who then sailed northward again as far as Oregon, before returning to Navidad in April 1543.

In 1602, Spanish explorer Sebastián Vizcaino visited San Diego Bay, changing its name from Cabrillo's "San Miguel" to San Diego. Vizcaino urged Spain to use this sheltered harbor as a major port for Spanish galleons crossing the Pacific Ocean from the Philippines, but his suggestion was ignored.

Nearly two centuries after Vizcaino's expedition, the Spaniards finally built a small fortification, Fort Guijarros, on Ballast Point along the eastern shore of Point Loma. The only military engagements occurred with the firing of shots in 1803 against the American ship *Leila Byrd,* following a failed attempt to impound the ship and arrest its crew, and in 1828 with the firing of the fort's guns at another American ship, the *Franklin.*

In the early 1800s, San Diego Bay became an increasingly popular harbor for maritime trade. After California became a state of the United States in 1850, whaling became a major pursuit and a key whaling station for the processing of whale oil was established on Point Loma. The slaughter of the Pacific gray whale, however, decimated its population and came close to wiping out the species. Fortunately, its numbers have increased. Today, thousands of these great mammals, measuring up to 40 feet long and weighing up to 40 tons, pass by Point Loma on their 12,000-mile round-trip migrations between their summer feeding grounds in the Bering and Chukchi seas off Alaska, and their winter calving habitat in Baja California lagoons.

The most prominent historic landmark in the national monument is the restored and refurbished, white-washed brick-and-sandstone Old Point Loma Lighthouse. The structure is a simple Cape Cod-style house, measuring about 30 feet long by 20 feet wide, with 22-inch thick outer stone walls. The light tower rises 15 feet from the center of the two-pitch roof of the house. A narrow spiral staircase leads up to the light. The structure was completed in 1855 as one of eight original lighthouses built along the West Coast. These buildings were erected in response to rapidly increasing numbers of sailing ships from the East Coast and elsewhere drawn by California's Gold Rush, sparked in 1848 by the discovery of gold near Sacramento.

The lighthouse was in use for only 35 years. At its lofty perch atop Point Loma, the light was sometimes obscured by low clouds and coastal fog. Consequently, in 1891 the old lighthouse was abandoned and fell into disrepair, and a light station close to sea level became the new beacon of safety for mariners.

The national monument was initially only a quarter-acre of land immediately around the old lighthouse and was under the jurisdiction of the

War Department. In 1933, it was finally transferred to the National Park Service, and the crumbling lighthouse was carefully rehabilitated over the next two years. From 1941-1946, the monument was closed to public access so that the old lighthouse could serve as a signal tower verifying the identity of military ships during World War II. In late 1995, the lighthouse was refurbished with 1870s and 1880s reproductions to accurately depict this era. In 1959 and 1974, the national monument was expanded to its present acreage.

A 14-foot-tall sandstone statue of Cabrillo, carved by Portuguese sculptor Alvaro DeBree in 1939, stands near the visitor center. It was actually commissioned for the 1939 World's Fair in San Francisco, but was delivered late. A controversy then ensued between the governor of California and San

1855 lighthouse, Cabrillo National Monument, San Diego, California [Russ Butcher]

Diego's State Senator Ed Fletcher over where the statue should be erected—either in Oakland or San Diego. Fletcher's persistence resulted in its being brought to Point Loma in 1949, as an appropriate celebration of Cabrillo's historic voyage.

Another of the attractions at the national monument is the opportunity to view the migrating gray whales, from late December through February, on their way south to the calving lagoons in Mexico. Tidepools on Point Loma's outer rocky shore provide a glimpse of the ecologically rich intertidal life—such things as seastars, crabs, limpets, sculpin, anemones, and nudibranches. Much of the monument supports the native coastal sage-scrub habitat. The Bayside Trail winds through some of the latter, affording great panoramas of San Diego Bay, with sailboats, whale-watching and deep-sea fishing excursions, and U.S. naval ships passing by.

Three especially interesting publications are *Cabrillo National Monument*, by Joseph E. Brown (1981); *The Old Point Loma Lighthouse*, by F. Ross Holland (1978); and *A Harbor Worth Defending*, by Barry A. Joyce (1996).

IF YOU GO: The national monument offers guided and self-guided walks, tours of the old lighthouse, and interpretive exhibits, programs, and publications. During the whale-watching months, special programs are offered on the whales. Lots of lodging and restaurants are available in San Diego.

Access from the I-5/I-8 freeway junction is by way of Rosecrans Street, right onto Cañon Street, and left onto Catalina to the monument entrance. Further information: Superintendent, 1800 Cabrillo Memorial Dr., San Diego, CA 92106. Telephone (619) 557-5450.

CASTILLO DE SAN MARCOS NATIONAL MONUMENT

CASTILLO DE SAN MARCOS NATIONAL MONUMENT, comprising 20 acres at St. Augustine, in northeastern Florida, was initially established in 1924 as Fort Marion National Monument. Then under the War Department, it was transferred to the National Park Service in 1933, and given its present name in 1942. It protects and interprets a major Spanish colonial fort that was begun in 1672.

For many years, Castillo de San Marcos was the northernmost military outpost of the widespread Spanish empire in the western hemisphere. It successfully guarded Spain's hotly contested territory along what is now the coast of Florida, Georgia, and the Carolinas, from its main colonial rival—England. It remains the best example of Spanish colonial fortification architecture in the United States.

In 1564, France had established a small fortified colonial settlement called Fort Caroline (see Fort Caroline National Monument), about 30 miles to the north of Castillo de San Marcos, on the banks of the St. John River. The following year, a Spanish military expedition that had set up a base at St. Augustine was initially unsuccessful in trying to seize the French outpost. But a hurricane wrecked a fleet of French warships that had sailed from Fort Caroline to attack the newly founded Spanish settlement. This setback enabled the Spaniards to successfully attack both Fort Caroline to the north and the survivors of the shipwrecked fleet to the south. Most of the French at both places were killed, and the latter place was named Matanzas for the slaughter of between 200 and 300 Frenchmen (see Fort Matanzas National Monument).

This Spanish triumph ended France's threat to this region of North America. But in 1586, an English force under the command of Sir Francis Drake burned St. Augustine. With the founding of Jamestown in Virginia in 1607 (see Colonial National Historical Park), the attack on St. Augustine by English pirates in 1668, and establishment of Charleston in what is now South Carolina in 1670, Spain finally got serious about building a major defensive installation by constructing Castillo de San Marcos. In contrast to the nine earlier Spanish fortifications at St. Augustine that were built of wood, this massive structure was built of masonry (*coquina stone*).

When the English occupied the town of St. Augustine in 1702, they tried for 50 days to break through the fort's defenses, but were unsuccessful and settled with burning down the town on their way out. The Spaniards rebuilt St. Augustine and erected new defenses along the northern and western

Castillo de San Marcos National Monument [NPS]

sides of the community, creating a medieval-like walled city.

In 1740, the British again attempted to defeat the Spanish military in their fort, but after nearly a month's siege, they gave up. In response to this latest attack, the Spaniards expanded the fortification to provide enhanced defenses for Matanzas Inlet, which the enemy had blockaded during the bombardment. The British finally did take over Castillo de San Marcos and Fort Matanzas when Spain turned Florida over to Britain at the close of the French and Indian War. The *castillo's* defenses were further improved under the British military, who held it for 21 years—through America's War for Independence, and were then required to hand Florida back to Spain under the terms of the Treaty of Paris in 1783.

In 1821, Florida was ceded to the United States and the *castillo* was renamed Fort Marion. Over the following years—during the Seminole Indian War, the Civil War, and the Spanish-American War—it was used to keep prisoners.

The great fort is a square-shaped structure containing guard rooms, storage rooms, a chapel, and a central courtyard—the *plaza de armas*. Just outside this main structure is a small shot furnace, in which cannonballs were heated. The red-hot shot then was used to set the enemy's wooden warships on fire. Diamond-shaped bastions are located at each corner of the fort. A moat that surrounded the fort on all sides is now only on three sides. And there is a never-completed triangular-shaped structure, called the *ravelin*, which was designed to protect the single entrance across the moat on two drawbridges and into the fort.

Today the fort offers interpretive exhibits in the former storage rooms. Visitors are cautioned to be careful when walking through the fort to be aware of uneven stone steps and other surfaces and to keep children from climbing on walls and cannons. The national monument provides interpretive programs and living history demonstrations, as well as a self-guided tour.

IF YOU GO: The park is open daily, except on Christmas. Lodging and meals are available in St. Augustine. Access to the fort from I-95 is by way of State Route 16 exit, and U.S. Route 1 to historically interesting downtown St. Augustine. Further information: Superintendent, 1 Castillo Drive, St. Augustine, FL 32084. Telephone (904) 829-6506.

CHAMIZAL NATIONAL MEMORIAL

CHAMIZAL NATIONAL MEMORIAL consists of 55 acres along the Rio Grande, in El Paso, Texas. It was established in 1974 to commemorate the peaceful resolution of a 99-year international boundary dispute between the United States and Mexico.

Prior to the construction of dams and irrigation projects upriver, the lower Rio Grande would frequently shift its course and thereby also change the international boundary, which was addressed in provisions of the Treaty of Guadalupe Hidalgo of 1848. This treaty mandated that the boundary be situated along the middle of the river, and it also stipulated that if the river suddenly cut a new path—a process called *avulsion*—the boundary would remain at the river's prior location. But if there were a gradual shift through erosion and new land deposition, the boundary would be shifted.

In the late 1800s, a 600-acre parcel of land in Mexico, known as the Chamizal (for a species of plant growing there), was severed by the river's new course. While Mexico still claimed ownership of the tract in 1895, a dispute arose over whether the severing process had been sudden or gradual. For Mexico, this controversy also became highly symbolic of powerful "Yankee imperialism" versus Mexican nationalism and sovereignty.

An arbitration decision in 1911 called for dividing the tract equally. But the United States refused to recognize the arbitration commission's ruling—arguing that the decision should have gone either all one way or the other, rather than slicing up the disputed land.

Finally, in 1962, U.S. President John F. Kennedy and Mexico's President López Mateos agreed on a compromise, which was legally approved by both nations the following year. It fairly divided the controversial parcel and authorized the concrete lining of a channel through the Chamizal, thereby forcing the river to remain there. In 1964, President Lyndon B. Johnson and Mateos officially declared the long-running dispute finally resolved.

Chamizal National Memorial not only commemorates this triumph of international diplomacy, but it celebrates this peacefully negotiated compromise as a model of international dispute resolution for nations throughout the world.

Mexico has established its own park—the 760-acre Chamizal Federal Park across the river channel. It features a highly acclaimed archaeological museum and other facilities.

The U.S. national memorial visitor center provides interpretive historical exhibits, an acclaimed documentary video and an art gallery. There are also indoor and outdoor musicals and other cultural performances, among which are the Siglo de Oro Drama Festival in March, Sunday concerts from June through August, El Paso/Zarzuela Festival in August, and the Border Folk Festival in September.

An informative publication is *Chamizal National Memorial*, by Luis Torres (Southwest Parks and Monuments Association).

IF YOU GO: Picnicking is allowed in the memorial, but camping is not. Lodging and meals are available in El Paso. The memorial is located in south-central El Paso, and may be accessed from I-10 to Paisano Drive or Delta Street to S. San Marcial Street to the park entrance. Further information on the memorial and on exhibits and cultural events: Superintendent, 800 S. San Marcial St., El Paso, TX 79905. Telephone (915) 534-6668.

CHARLES PINCKNEY NATIONAL HISTORIC SITE

CHARLES PINCKNEY NATIONAL HISTORIC SITE, consisting of 28 acres in Mount Pleasant, South Carolina, was authorized in 1988 to com-memorate the life of Charles Pinckney (1757–1824). He was an officer in the War for Independence (Revolutionary War), was one of the primary framers of the U.S. Constitution, served in the state assembly and four terms as governor of South Carolina, served in the U.S. House of Representatives and Senate, and was minister to Spain during President Thomas Jefferson's administration. The site also protects and interprets Pinckney's ancestral home and country estate, Snee Farm, which once encompassed more than 700 acres. In 1990, the property was acquired by the National Park Service, as the result of a success-ful fund-raising campaign that combined private contributions with public funds. Today, historic highlights include the brick foundations of structures dating from the time of Pinckney ownership and a tidewater house dating from the 1820s.

The site has a visitor center in the historic house, in which interpre-tive exhibits and an audiovisual program are presented. Trails lead visitors through the property. While camping is not permitted, there are picnic facili-ties. Lodging and meals are available in Mount Pleasant and elsewhere in the Charleston area.

IF YOU GO: Access from I-526 is by way of the Long Point Road exit east-bound and continuing three miles to the site entrance; or by way of U.S. Route 17 north from Charleston to Long Point Road, then east one-quarter-mile to the site. Further information: Park Ranger, 1214 Middle St., Sullivan's Island, SC 29482. Telephone (803) 881-5516.

CHESAPEAKE AND OHIO CANAL NATIONAL HISTORICAL PARK

CHESAPEAKE AND OHIO CANAL NATIONAL HISTORICAL PARK, encompassing 19,236 acres, was initially placed under the care of the National Park Service in 1938. It then was established as a national monument in 1961, and changed to a national historical park in 1971. It protects and interprets the C & O Canal, which was constructed from 1828 to 1850 and extends 184.5 miles from Potomac River tidewater, in Washington, D.C., to Cumberland, Maryland.

Building a canal along the Potomac River had been a dream of President George Washington. When construction was launched by President John Quincy Adams, this project was an ambitious undertaking that its investors predicted would become a vital commercial link between the nation's capital on the eastern seaboard and the Ohio River region beyond the Appalachian Mountains. As construction proceeded northwestward, the canal's progress was plagued by disputes over acquiring the rights-of-way, and there were shortages of manpower, building materials, and funding. The canal was about 60 feet wide, 30 feet deep, and climbed more than 600 feet through 74 locks.

One of the major features of the canal is the Paw Paw Tunnel near Milepost 155, historically called one of the "Wonders of the World." It took 14 years (12 more than anticipated) to blast this 3,118-foot-long tunnel, from start of construction until it was opened to canal boat traffic. Another part of the canal is the beautiful pink-and-white quartz sandstone Monocacy Aqueduct, at mile 42.

The canal idea originally called for construction continuing much farther west of Cumberland. But by the time the last stretch of the canal was finally completed to Cumberland in 1850, the Baltimore & Ohio Railroad, which had begun construction on the same day as the canal, was already running its trains to Cumberland. In fact, it had been for the previous eight years. The rail route offered faster and often cheaper service than the canal could provide. And then the B & O extended its rails west to the Ohio River and beyond. Consequently, after all the time, effort, and money, the canal was largely obsolete prior to its completion. It was competitive only in transporting such products as coal, flour, and grain in its 90-foot boats.

Twelve years after the C & O Canal began, its operation was disrupted by extensive damage during the Civil War. In 1862, when Confederate troops crossed the Potomac River from the Confederate state of Virginia into Maryland, canal locks were dynamited, boats were destroyed, and mules used to tow the boats were stolen. This havoc ended when the Union troops defeated the Confederates at the nearby, horrendously bloody Battle of Antietam and forced the Southerners to retreat back across the Potomac (see the text on Antietam National Battlefield).

In 1889, major flooding caused further costly damage. Then, in 1924, another severe flood terminated what was left of the waterway's dwindling commercial activity. Some stretches of the canal have never been restored to hold water.

In January 1996, a major flood of the Potomac River again extensively damaged the canal. Congress appropriated $22 million to help fund repairs, while another $1.4 million was obtained through the National Park Foundation's C & O Canal Restoration Fund appeal for private donations. Some of the restorative work was carried out, with the help of volunteers, during the following months. But in September 1996, yet another major flood, from heavy rainfall that fell on the Potomac River watershed before and during Hurricane Fran, caused further damage. Fortunately, this most recent flooding was no-where near as destructive as before; and fortunately as well, most of the major reconstruction work had not yet been accomplished. As a result, the majority of the funding is still available, as work continues.

Hiking the canal's towpath and canoeing or boating on the canal have become increasingly popular pastimes. One person who frequently enjoyed walking the towpath in all seasons was U.S. Supreme Court Justice William O. Douglas. In the early 1950s, a plan resurfaced for paving over the canal to create a parkway. Douglas strongly opposed this highway

Chesapeake & Ohio Canal National Historical Park [William Clark/NPS]

scheme. On January 3, 1954, The *Washington Post* editorialized that "the pro-posed parkway along the old C and O Canal . . . will stir enthusiasm of many Washing-tonians. . . . By utilizing the old canal—no longer either a commer-cial or scenic asset. . . ." On January 19, Douglas wrote to the newspaper: ". . . I wish the man who wrote that editorial . . . would take time off and come with me. We would go with packs on our backs and hike the 185 miles to Cumberland. I feel that if your editor did, he would return a new man and use the power of your great editorial page to help keep this sanctuary untouched."

The *Post* editorialized on Jan. 21, "we are pleased to accept Justice Douglas' invitation to walk the towpath. . . ." Justice Douglas led an eight-day hike with 37 other people, including the *Post's* editorial writer, from one end of the canal to the other. This event received so much news coverage that it caused an outpouring of public support for protecting the canal. In 1977, Congress passed legislation, signed by President Jimmy Carter, dedicating the canal to Justice Douglas, in recognition of his leadership that scuttled the parkway proposal and saved the canal.

Since the National Park Service acquired the canal, its value for hik-ing, bicycling, horseback riding, canoeing, boating, and mule-towed canal tours has increased manyfold. Mule-towed boat rides run from mid-April to mid-October—from Georgetown in Washington, D.C. (Telephone [202] 472-4376); and from Great Falls Tavern in Maryland (Telephone [301] 299-2026).

Canoe, boat, and bicycle rentals are provided at Thompson's Boat Center, located at the junction of the canal, Rock Creek, and the Potomac, in Wash-ington, D.C. (Telephone [202] 333-4861); Fletcher's Boathouse, just off Canal Rd., in Washington, D.C. (Telephone [202] 244-0461); and at Swains Lock (Lock 21), off River Rd. (State Route 190), just over two miles north of Potomac, MD (Telephone [301] 299-9006).

The park includes a rich river-bottomland flora and fauna. Among the forest trees are American sycamore (many of which are of exceptional size), tulip tree, river birch, several hickories, walnut, boxelder, red maple, sassafras, sweet gum, black tupelo, flowering dogwood, eastern redbud, shadbush, Virginia pine, and eastern red cedar. A few of the wildflowers are bloodroot, bluet, Dutchman's-breeches, spring beauty, yellow trout-lily, Mayapple, and downy phlox. Ferns include Christmas, hay-scented, cinnamon, bracken, leathery grape, and spleenwort.

Among the park's mammals are whitetail deer, red and gray foxes, raccoons, opossums, striped skunks, muskrats, cottontails, and gray and fly-ing squirrels. A long list of birds includes great blue herons; wintering tun-dra (whistling) swans; Canada geese; many ducks such as mallards, pintails, blue-winged teal, wood, and ring-necked; bald eagles; red-shouldered, broad-winged, and other hawks; ruffed grouse; bobwhite; wild turkeys; cuckoos; barred owls; belted kingfishers; red-bellied, red-headed, pileated, and other woodpeckers; blue jays; tufted titmice; white-breasted nuthatches; Carolina and house wrens; eastern bluebirds; wood thrushes; numerous warblers including prothonotary, black-and-white, chestnut-sided, prairie, yellow, Kentucky, hooded, ovenbird, Louisiana waterthrush, yellowthroat; yellow-breasted chat, and American redstart; cardinals; indigo buntings; song, white-throated, and other sparrows; redwings; northern orioles; scarlet tan-agers; and American goldfinches. There are also turtles, black snakes, and the poisonous copperhead.

One of the scenic highlights of the park is Great Falls, where the Poto-mac cascades and plunges between the walls of rugged gorges. The falls are espe-cially exciting to watch and hear during periods of high water. They may also be viewed from the Virginia side (see Great Falls Park).

IF YOU GO: The park's main visitor center/museum, located in the historic Great Falls Tavern, 11710 MacArthur Blvd., Potomac, MD 20854 (Telephone [301] 299-3613), provides interpretive exhibits, programs, and publications. Other visitor centers are located at 1057 Thomas Jefferson St., NW, Washing-ton, D.C. (Telephone [202] 653-5844); at 326 E. Main St., Hancock, MD (Telephone [301] 678-5463); and at the Western Maryland Station Center, Canal St., Cumberland, MD (Telephone [301] 722-8226).

Group camping, such as scouts, is allowed with a free permit at Marsden Tract, a few miles south of Great Falls. There are also hiker-cycler campsites for tent camping located at roughly five-mile intervals between

Swains Lock and Evitts Creek (approximately the upper 168 miles of the canal). And there are primitive drive-in camping areas at McCoys Ferry, Fifteen-mile Creek, and Spring Gap. Picnic facilities are located at many places along the canal. There is also a 20-site tent camp at Antietam Creek.

Lodging and meals are available in Washington, D.C.; Harpers Ferry, WV; Hancock and Cumberland, MD; and elsewhere in the vicinity of the park. Snack bars are located at Williamsport, Great Falls, Fletcher's Boathouse, and Swains Lock and are open from April to October. Further information: Superintendent, P.O. Box 4, Sharpsburg, MD 21782. Telephone (301) 739-4200.

CHRISTIANSTED NATIONAL HISTORIC SITE

CHRISTIANSTED NATIONAL HISTORIC SITE consists of 27 acres in the port town of Christiansted, on the West Indian island of St. Croix, U.S. Virgin Islands. It was established in 1952 to protect and interpret the Danish colonial history and architecture of this island.

The French took possession of and named St. Croix (Holy Cross) in 1650, establishing initial plantations, townsites, and fortifications. It was not until 1733, under the flag of Denmark, that the island's economy really began to grow and flourish. It was then that the Danish West India & Guinea Company purchased the island, after acquiring earlier the two nearby islands of St. Thomas and St. John. Within two decades, sugar-cane cultivation became the island's major enterprise, and sugar production created great economic wealth during the eighteenth and early nineteenth centuries. The sugar planters and merchants created an opulent lifestyle for themselves. Many of the buildings and homes in Christiansted, the island's largest town, reflected this period of wealth. Today, some of these buildings are protected within the national historic site.

The end of the island's era of luxury began in 1820, when competition from the cultivation of sugar beets elsewhere in the world caused a sharp drop in the price of sugar. Import barriers against St. Croix sugar were imposed by countries growing sugar beets. Most island planters ended up in debt, with their properties being foreclosed upon. In 1848, slavery, which had helped make sugar-cane plantations exceptionally profitable, finally ended. The once thriving sugar industry was virtually history.

Following the U.S. Civil War, the United States attempted to acquire St. Thomas and St. John islands. Even though Denmark agreed to sell, the U.S. Senate blocked ratification. In 1902, an attempt to purchase all three islands failed. But the United States finally succeeded in buying the islands from Denmark in 1917 for $15 million.

Among the historic highlights of the national historic site:

• Fort Christiansvaern, fronting on Christiansted Harbor, is an outstanding example of seventeenth- and eighteenth-century Danish colonial fortification architecture. It was built mostly of bricks that were previous-

Customs House and Steeple Building, Christiansted National Historic Site
[Larry Ulrich]

ly carried as ballast in Danish commercial sailing ships. Construction of the fort was essentially complete by the mid-1700s. A Danish military garrison was headquartered there until 1878. It subsequently served as a courthouse and police offices.

• Old Danish Customs House is where the colonial government levied taxes on exports and imports. This imposing structure was begun in 1751, but most of it was built in the late 1820s.

• Scalehouse, dating from the mid-1800s, is where the Customs Service inspected and weighed exports and imports.

• Government House was originally two separate eighteenth-century residences that were expanded and joined in the 1830s for use by the colonial government.

• Danish West India & Guinea Company Warehouse was built in the late 1740s. It was used for company offices and storage of supplies and merchandise. In 1833, it became a Danish military depot, and was subsequently a telegraph office.

• Steeple Building was the island's first Danish Lutheran church, the Church of our Lord of Sabaoth, dating from 1753. The attractive steeple was added in 1794. The building has also been used as a military bakery, hospital, and school. It presently houses the national historic site's museum.

The site's headquarters is located in the Old Danish Customs House. Visitors are urged to begin a walking tour at the fort, where there is a small visitor center that provides publications, various interpretive materials, and gifts. Interpretive exhibits are provided in the Steeple Building.

IF YOU GO: Food and lodging are available in Christiansted and elsewhere, including at many resorts on St. Croix. Further information: Superintendent, P.O. Box 160, Christiansted, U.S. Virgin Islands 00820. Telephone (809) 773-1460.

CITY OF ROCKS NATIONAL RESERVE

CITY OF ROCKS NATIONAL RESERVE, comprising 14,407 acres in southern Idaho, was authorized in 1988 and is jointly administered by the National Park Service and the Idaho Department of Parks and Recreation. About one-third of the area is in private ownership. The reserve protects imposing granite spires, columns, and other beautifully weather-sculpted rock formations, some of which rise as much as 60 stories high. Part of the granite dates back more than 2.5 *billion* years ago. Both the older and younger rocks stand side by side in a section of rocks called the "Twin Sisters," the younger dating back a "mere" 25 million years ago.

Both the older and the younger rock formations started as molten matter within the earth's crust. Gradually these substances became hardened rock that was eventually exposed to and shaped by the forces of erosion. Fractures, cracks, and fissures developed that led to the creation of these massive granite forms: spires, columns, and pinnacles, as well as caves, arches, and hollowed out bathtub-like depressions. The processes of erosion are of course continuing.

The spectacular City of Rocks was a prominent landmark for pioneer travelers heading westward along a segment of the historic nineteenth-century California Trail, traces of which are still visible within the reserve. Emigrants traveling along the various routes through this area left behind historic inscriptions and messages written in axle grease. One of those emigrants, James F. Wilkins, described this incredible landscape in 1849:

City of Rocks National Reserve, Idaho [NPS]

We encamped at the city of rocks, a noted place from the granite rocks rising abruptly out of the ground. They are in a romantic valley clustered together, which gives them the appearance of a city.

Activities in the area include hiking and rock climbing. There are about 100 primitive campsites in the reserve. A visitor center is open daily, providing interpretive information, as well as updates on the conditions of gravel roads, weather conditions, rock-climbing regulations, and camping. Lodging and meals are available in Burley, about 50 miles north of the reserve, and supplies are available at nearby Almo. Bed-&-breakfast inns are available in Almo, Albion, and Oakley.

IF YOU GO: Access from Boise and the west is by way of I-84 to Declo, exiting south onto State Route 77, proceeding through Albion, Elba, and Almo, and continuing two miles southwest of Almo to the reserve. From Pocatello and Idaho Falls, access is by way of I-86 and I-84 to the Declo exit and south through Almo. From Salt Lake City, access is either by way of I-84 to north of Snowville and Utah State Routes 39 and 42, or proceeding farther on I-84, taking the Sublette exit, and continuing west through Malta, Elba, and Almo. There is also a seasonal route through Oakley by way of State Route 27. Further information: Superintendent, P.O. Box 169, Almo, ID 83312. Telephone (208) 824-5519.

COLONIAL NATIONAL HISTORICAL PARK

COLONIAL NATIONAL HISTORICAL PARK, in the Tidewater area of eastern Virginia, was established as a national monument in 1930 and then renamed as a national historical park in 1936. Consisting of 9,327 acres, it protects and interprets part of the site of the first permanent English settlement in North America that was founded on Jamestown Island, on the James River, in 1607, and the site of the decisive American-French victory over the British forces in the Battle of Yorktown, at the mouth of the York River. This triumph quickly hastened the end of the War for Independence (Revolu-tionary War). These two units of the park are connected by the 23-mile Colonial Parkway.

Jamestown

In May 1607, three English square-rigged sailing ships, the *Discovery, Godspeed,* and *Susan Constant,* dropped anchor near the mouth of the James River and sent ashore 104 men and boys to establish a colonial settlement for the Virginia Company, of London, England. The colonists chose a site on a low, forested, marshy island about 50 miles upstream, on the north shore of the river. It turned out to be a poor location to settle, but was chosen because it seemed a good strategic position to defend against possible attack by Spanish warships. The men built a fort that contained rustic, thatch-roofed

Surrender Field, Yorktown, Colonial National Historical Park [David Muench]

dwellings, a church, a storehouse, and other structures. The river and settlement were named in honor of England's King James I.

Just over a year after the first colonists arrived, a small glass-making factory was established near Jamestown. The 'tryal of glasse' shipped over to England was the first factory-manufactured product made in North America. Although glass-making seemed to offer great hope for the struggling colony's economic viability, this venture had only limited success, and was followed 12 years later with a second, better-financed enterprise that was nevertheless plagued by problems, resulting in the production of little or no glass.

One of the Englishmen who had been actively promoting and participating in the Virginia venture was veteran world traveler Captain John Smith. He soon emerged as a strong leader and was elected president of the community's council in September 1608. He quickly implemented strict discipline, enhanced the settlement's defenses, and insisted that farming be expanded. He was adamant that "He who does not work will not eat." Smith's leadership came to an abrupt end, however, when he was accidentally wounded by gunpowder burns and was forced to return to England in 1609.

Hardships beset the budding community from the outset. A fever that was likely typhoid claimed the lives of many colonists. The oppressively humid heat of the "sickly season" of summer was unbearable. Perishable provisions spoiled. The island's brackish water was undrinkable. An abundance of mosquitoes and other pesky insects made life miserable. And then came the damp, cold first winter, in which over 60 colonists perished from illnesses and starvation, before urgently needed new supplies and additional settlers were able to reach the colony. Two winters later, the death toll reached 500, leaving only 60 individuals. In 1610, a large group of new settlers arrived from England, just in time to rescue Jamestown from an otherwise virtually certain abandonment. Many of those arriving were indentured servants who were to spend a few years working off their servitude before becoming free.

To snatch the colony from the jaws of defeat required overdue strong leadership, discipline, and incentives for working. This scenario finally began coming together under the direction of Sir Thomas Gates and Sir Thomas Dale. Stiff penalties were handed out for offenses. For instance, those avoiding labor were imprisoned; a second offense was punishable by death. Swearing was met with a death sentence. Attending church was required; anyone failing to do so was deprived of rations, while a second-time offender was whipped and a third-time offender ended up in the gallows. A rebel had his limbs painfully stretched over a circular frame, his tongue pierced through with a bodkin, and was then chained to a tree or post and left to die.

Because the Virginia Company was an investor-owned enterprise, the settlement was expected to begin reaping financial rewards for the company's stockholders. Yet, the early years at Jamestown were anything but profitable. In addition to disillusionment, diseases, high mortality, lack of skilled craftsmen, famine, and crop failures, there was almost constant conflict with the native Indians who were alarmed over the rapid takeover of their traditional tribal lands by these newcomers.

Initial attempts to put the colony on a sound financial footing proved fruitless—until 1612, when John Rolfe received tobacco seeds from the West Indies that flourished and produced tobacco that became highly popular with English smokers. Tobacco then became the cash crop that provided the economic base for the growth of the colony. It was also Rolfe who married the beautiful Indian maiden, Pocahontas, the daughter of Chief Powhatan.

In the beginning, the Virginia Company tried to impose tight political and economic controls over the colony's affairs. Company officials soon yielded to appeals for some degree of limited self-government. In 1619, a representative legislative body was created—the first freely chosen, elective governmental assembly in North America. At the outset, local laws enacted by this body were subject to possible veto from London. Also in the beginning, the legislature served as both a law-making body and a court that handed down sentences upon those violating its laws. There was not yet a separate and independent judiciary to perform this function.

Two other events occurred in 1619: The Virginia Company recruited English maids who arrived the following year to become wives of some of the settlers, and a number of blacks arrived in a Dutch warship, providing a source of labor in the tobacco fields.

In 1622, a major disaster struck the colony. In response to the English settlers' takeover and clearing of lands for tobacco cultivation, the Powhatan Indians retaliated. Nearly 350 colonists were killed—about one-third of the English population in Virginia. While Jamestown was spared this bloody uprising because a friendly Indian boy forewarned the town's people, nearly all outlying settlements—including houses, crops, and livestock—were destroyed. This was a devastating blow to the struggling colony. Of the 5,500 individuals who had come across the Atlantic Ocean to the colony from 1607 to 1623, only 1,200 now remained. More than 4,000 had either died or had been killed, while some 300 had given up and returned to England. The colony's prospects appeared so gloomy by this time that the Virginia Company's royal charter was revoked in 1624 by King James I. Even though Virginia now became a royal colony, under which the British Crown named its governor and council (the latter made up of prominent Virginians), the colonists now actually enjoyed more freedom because the king and his privy council focused so little attention upon the distant colony.

In 1639, the Crown authorized the colonial governor to annually bring together "the burgesses [local representatives] of all and singular plantations there, which together with the governor and council shall have power to make acts and laws for the government." With this significant addition to the colonial law-making process, Virginia now had the beginnings of a bicameral legislature—the council being the upper house, while the freeholders comprised the House of Burgesses (akin to the federal or a state house of representatives). The lower house was not only given authority to pass substantive laws, but also had the exclusive authority to initiate funding appropriations.

In the words of Max Savell, former Stanford University historian, in his textbook, *The Foundations of American Civilization* (1956):

> The establishment of this, the royal form of government in Virginia, was an event of great significance in the history of political institutions in British America, for it meant that the British colonies were to be, in large measure, self-governing. This was in itself a recognition of the fact that the local affairs of these new overseas communities could most wisely be administered by the colonists themselves, rather than by a body of men, themselves unfamiliar with the conditions involved, sitting in London, three thousand miles away.

Over the next few years, the colonists retaliated against the Indians for their earlier devastating uprising, and they came close to wiping out the tribes of the surrounding area. Meanwhile, new colonists were arriving by the shipload. A new land rush led to the creation of Tidewater tobacco plantations, as well as smaller agricultural enterprises farther inland. By mid-century, Jamestown was no longer a commercial or military center. Its only major function was continuing as the seat of the colonial government. Virginia's expanding settlements, consisting of small villages, farms, and plantations, now extended northwestward up the James River nearly 100 miles, to the vicinity of its junction with the Appomattox River, while extending about 35 miles up the York River and about 45 miles up the Rappahannock and south bank of the Potomac rivers.

From the beginning there was periodic conflict within the colony. Perhaps the worst case of rebellion was the havoc caused by rebels under the leadership of Nathaniel Bacon, Jr., who were protesting the Crown's colonial governor, Sir William Berkeley. Bacon had been named to the governor's council, but he became so outraged over the governor's strict policies that he and his cohorts finally took matters into their own hands and burned Jamestown to the ground in 1676. Governmental and other structures were rebuilt, but when the legislative building again burned down in 1698, the colonial capital was moved to Middle Plantation, renamed Williamsburg, just over six miles to the northeast.

Today, the eastern part of the site of the original Jamestown settlement lies within the Jamestown unit of Colonial National Historical Park. Adjacent to the park is the affiliated, 22-acre **Jamestown National Historic Site**, which was established in 1940. It contains the western part of the English settlement, and features the ruins of the seventeenth-century Jamestown church tower and a statue of the Powhatan Indian, Pocahontas. The national historic site is owned and operated by the Association for the Preservation of Virginia Antiquities, a private, nonprofit organization. Also adjacent to the park is Jamestown Settlement, which is run by the Jamestown-Yorktown Foundation, a quasi-governmental agency of the Commonwealth of Virginia. This area features a re-creation of the triangular James Fort and Powhatan Indian village, replicas of the three square-rigged ships like those that brought Jamestown's founding settlers to Virginia, and a museum complex containing galleries on the English settlement and on the Powhatan Indians.

Yorktown

The park's history now fast-forwards about 80 years, to the autumn of 1781. The War for Independence (Revolutionary War) had begun in 1775, with provocative British military actions resulting in the Battle of Lexington and Concord, Massachusetts, wherein Britain had raised its sword against one of her American colonies for the first time (see the text on Minute Man National Historical Park). The Continental Army's General-in-Chief George Washington was then successful in driving British troops out of Boston. In the southern colonies, Americans had wiped out an entire British force at Moores Creek Ridge, North Carolina, in February 1776 (see the text on Moores Creek National Battlefield) and had successfully defended the city of Charles-ton, South Carolina. On July 4, 1776, the colonies had declared their independence from Britain.

While the British occupied New York City and Philadelphia for a time, British General John Burgoyne had been forced to surrender 5,000 troops in a major American victory near Saratoga, New York (see Saratoga National Historical Park), in the autumn of 1777.

This key triumph had finally convinced France to openly join the Americans in their struggle against Britain. With the Franco-American alliance

Moore House, Yorktown, Colonial National Historical Park [David Muench]

formalized in 1778, the French and American forces had begun to take the offensive. Meanwhile, the British had been rampaging through the southern colonies. Georgia and South Carolina had been seized, and British Lord Charles Cornwallis had been placed in command to complete Britain's control of the South.

There had been a number of major battles in the southern colonies. The Battle of Kings Mountain, South Carolina, in October 1780 (see Kings Mountain National Military Park) resulted in Britain's loss of an entire regiment of soldiers. There was the decisive American victory at Cowpens, South Carolina, in January 1781 (see the text on Cowpens National Battlefield). And there was the long, bloody battle at Guilford Courthouse, North Carolina, in March 1781 (see Guilford Courthouse National Military Park). This was an indecisive struggle, in which the British nevertheless sustained such overwhelming losses that Cornwallis had decided to leave the Carolinas and concentrate his forces on seizing Virginia.

Meanwhile, Washington's forces had been facing serious problems of diminishing manpower, military supplies, and funds. A major contingent of French troops had been effectively trapped by a British naval fleet in Rhode Island. And the Americans had been helpless to oust the British forces from their main base in New York City. As Washington wrote in his journal in May 1781:

> Instead of having everything in readiness . . ., we have nothing; and instead of having the prospect of a glorious offensive campaign before us, we have a bewildered and gloomy defensive one.

By August, however, the American general had finally begun to hear some encouraging news: A large fleet of French warships would be arriving in late summer, although not in the New York area, as Washington had anticipated, but in the Chesapeake Bay area, off the Virginia coast. And Cornwallis had established a British naval base at Yorktown, near the mouth of the York River on the Chesapeake Bay, making his army, which accounted for one-third of British forces in America, an attractive target.

General Washington organized a force of some 5,000 French troops, commanded by Comte de Rochambeau, and about 2,000 Americans for a rapid march southward to Williamsburg, Virginia, only 12 miles from Yorktown. Some soldiers were left behind on the Hudson, in New York, successfully deceiving the British into believing Washington was still poised to attack New York City. Arriving in Williamsburg in mid-September, Washington's forces joined General Lafayette's 4,000 Continental soldiers already based in Virginia, plus General Thomas Nelson, Jr.'s, 3,000 Virginia Militia.

At about the same time, the French battle fleet, commanded by Comte de Grasse, arrived at Chesapeake Bay. Five days after the fleet's arrival, a British battle fleet, commanded by Admiral Thomas Graves, was sighted off the Virginia coast. On September 5, the two fleets engaged in the Battle of the Capes, resulting in the British fleet's return to New York to make repairs on its badly damaged ships. The French fleet remained to form a blockade across the mouth of Chesapeake Bay and the York River.

Arriving outside Yorktown on September 28, Washington's allied army opened their siege lines on October 6, 1781. On October 9, the bombardment of British-held Yorktown and Cornwallis' army began. A second and closer siege line was started on October 11 and completed following the seizure of two forward British positions, Redoubts 9 and 10, by hand-to-hand assault on October 14. (*Redoubt* is a French term meaning earthen fort.) With French ships blocking his escape by sea, with allied artillery fire now coming in from destructive point-blank range, having already suffered nine days of continual bombardment, and with supplies dwindling and no hope of rescue by the British navy, Cornwallis requested a cease fire, on October 17, to discuss the terms of surrendering his forces. On October 19, the articles of capitulation were signed by Washington and Cornwallis (though not in a face-to-face meeting), and the defeated British army yielded up its arms, as they marched by the victors.

This historic surrender signaled the last major engagement of the American Revolution. While British troops still occupied key cities, including New York, Charleston, and Savannah, the British people were weary of the war with America. And by the time of the Siege at Yorktown, Britain was waging war with France, Spain, and the Netherlands as well. A major change in British political leadership soon opened the way for final diplomatic negotiations. On September 3, 1783, a treaty of peace was signed, under which the British officially recognized the independence of the United States of America.

So, here, barely 25 miles from where the first permanent English colony began at Jamestown, the American colonial forces at Yorktown effectively ended British colonial rule, 176 years after it began.

Today, the historical park provides two visitor centers: one emphasizes the Yorktown unit; the other focuses on Jamestown. Both centers have excellent interpretive exhibits, programs, and publications, and both are open daily, except on Christmas. They offer self-guided and guided walking tours, as well as driving tours with interpretive pulloffs at points of interest. Among special places to see are the site of Jamestown; the reconstructed Jamestown Glasshouse where glassblowers demonstrate this ancient craft and where blown-glass products are offered for sale; and the scenic drive that loops around Jamestown Island. This beautiful route winds through stands of pines and oaks, crosses open areas of marsh and tidal creeks, and reaches the eastern end of the island where a delightful path leads a short distance to Black Point.

Of the many points of interest in the Yorktown unit are such historic buildings as the Nelson House, Session House, Thomas Pate House, Moore House, and Sommerwell House. Interpretive programs are presented at the Nelson House during the summer. Moore House is open also during the summer months.

Especially informative publications are: *Colonial National Historical Park: The Story Behind the Scenery®,* by James N. Haskett (KC Publications); *Jamestown and the Founding of the Nation,* by Warren M. Billings (Thomas Publications); *The First Seventeen Years: Virginia, 1607-1624,* by Charles E. Hatch (University Press of Virginia); The *Campaign That Won America,* by Burke Davis (Eastern Acorn Press); *The Yorktown Campaign and the Surrender of Cornwallis,* by Henry Johnston (Eastern Acorn Press); and *Colonial Yorktown,* by Clyde Trudell (Thomas Publications).

Two other places of special interest adjacent to the park and parkway are the Yorktown Victory Center (information: [804] 887-1776), located just west of Yorktown on Water Street and run by the Jamestown-Yorktown foundation, and privately owned Colonial Williamsburg, which was magnificently restored by the Colonial Williamsburg Foundation, with generous funding from John D. Rockefeller, Jr. It is situated just off the Colonial Parkway and features not only many beautifully reconstructed buildings, but presents fascinating living-history demonstrations of what eighteenth-century life was like when Williamsburg was the capital of Virginia.

Colonial National Historical Park also protects a wealth of natural values. Of the many species of trees, there are loblolly pines that form beautiful stands on Jamestown Island; a number of oaks including white, post, swamp chestnut, northern and southern red, and black; eastern red cedar; eastern redbud; flowering dogwood; black tupelo; red maple; and a few bald cypresses along such places as Sandy Bay and Back River, adjacent to Jamestown Island.

Mammals include whitetail deer, red foxes, river otters, muskrats, raccoons, woodchucks, and gray squirrels. Of the many birds, there are wintering tundra (whistling) swans and Canada geese; numerous species of ducks, bald eagles, ospreys, bobwhite quail that may be heard calling across open fields in spring and summer; great and snowy egrets; great blue and green-backed herons; American bitterns; Virginia and other rails; mourning doves; yellow-billed cuckoos; barred owls; belted kingfishers; a number of woodpeckers, including red-bellied; blue jays; Carolina chickadees; tufted titmice; white-breasted nuthatches; Carolina and marsh wrens; mocking-birds; catbirds; brown thrashers; wood thrushes; eastern bluebirds; yel-lowthroats and many other warblers; redwings; northern orioles; scarlet tan-agers; cardinals; indigo buntings; American goldfinches; rufous-sided towhees; and song sparrows.

Spring is a wonderful season at Colonial, when flowering dogwoods, redbuds, and many wildflowers are blooming and when a chorus of birds fills the landscape with song. The autumn is also a magical time when many of the deciduous trees turn shades of red, orange, and yellow.

Camping is not permitted within the park, but campground facilities are available nearby. Lodging and meals are available in Williamsburg, York-town, Norfolk, Richmond, and elsewhere in the area.

IF YOU GO: Access to the park is by way of U.S. Route 17 from I-95 near Fredericksburg; by way of I-64 southeast from Richmond or northwest from Norfolk; or by way of State Route 5 from Richmond, a route that passes a number of historic plantations along the north shore of the James River. Further information: Superintendent, P.O. Box 210, Yorktown, VA 23690. Telephone (757) 898-3400.

CORONADO NATIONAL MEMORIAL

CORONADO NATIONAL MEMORIAL consists of 4,750 acres along the Mexican border at the south end of the rugged, forested Huachuca Moun-tains in southeastern Arizona. It was established in 1952 to commemorate the epic Spanish expedition comprising 1,500 men and women, along with hun-dreds of sheep and cattle and more than 500 horses, under the leadership of 28-year-old Francisco Vásquez de Coronado, from 1540 to 1542.

Some historians believe that Coronado and his huge entourage entered what is now the United States in 1540 by way of the broad San Pedro River valley that gradually descends from Mexico into Arizona, just east of Coronado National Memorial. He and his expeditionary colleagues were exploring this region of North America for the Spanish Crown—pri-marily spurred on by fantastic tales of great wealth in gold to be found at the fabled "Seven Cities of Cíbola." While their arduous trek ultimately took them in a golden goose-chase as far as the great buffalo plains of the Texas and Oklahoma panhandles and central Kansas, Coronado and his chroni-clers did explore and describe much of the vast region now known as the American Southwest.

The Spaniards made contact with native Americans throughout their journey—notably a number of the Indian pueblos. At the Zuni Pueblo of Háwikuh, in what is now western New Mexico, the Spanish soldiers attacked the inhabitants and forced them out of their homes so that they could use the great pueblo and its supplies of food for a four-month stay. (Today, the Zunis, a major Pueblo Indian tribe, are widely acclaimed for their artistic talents in creating exquisite stone-and-shell inlaid silver jewelry and intricately carved stone, antler, bone, shell, coral, and fossilized ivory animal and corn maiden fetishes.)

While based at Háwikuh, Coronado dispatched a number of small scouting groups. One such party, led by Pedro de Tovar, encountered the Hopi Indian villages in what is now northeastern Arizona. Another party, led by García López de Cárdenas, reached the Grand Canyon of the Colorado. And Coronado sent yet another small scouting group, led by Hernando de Alvarado, on ahead eastward across New Mexico. This group visited the mesa-top Ácoma Pueblo, the Rio Grande villages north to Taos Pueblo, and, returning southward, proceeded east over Glorieta Pass to one of the largest pueblos of that time—Cicuyé or Pecos, at the gateway between the Rio Grande Valley and the Great Plains to the east (see Pecos National Historical Park).

Coronado's main expeditionary force also proceeded east, spending the winter of 1540-1541 with the Tiguex Pueblo Indians who once thrived along the Rio Grande, near where the city of Bernalillo is today. It was in this vicinity that the Spanish troops engaged in a fierce attack against the Arenal and Moho pueblos, in which many inhabitants were killed.

Coronado's expedition next paused at Cicuyé (Pecos) Pueblo, where a Plains Indian guide told the Spaniards of a land of gold, Quivira, in hopes that the Spanish expedition would get lost and perish out on the vastness of the Great Plains. When Coronado finally awakened to the reality that they had been duped, the Indian guide was put to death, and this bedraggled and demoralized expedition returned empty-handed to Mexico (*Nueva España*). Coronado was subsequently put on trial for his failed mission and barely avoided being convicted. The Spanish Crown viewed the expedition as a monumental failure, though it ultimately proved to have been a major landmark in Spanish exploration leading to colonial development.

Coronado National Memorial is a scenically and ecologically rich park that includes beautiful oak woodlands, amid a setting of mountains, canyons, and the broad panorama of San Pedro Valley and far southward into Mexico. Of the ten species of oaks in the area, there are Arizona white, Emory, silverleaf, Mexican blue, and Gambel. Other trees include pinyon pine, alligator and oneseed junipers, Fremont cottonwood, netleaf hackberry, Arizona sycamore, western soapberry, catclaw acacia, honey mesquite, Arizona madrone, Arizona walnut, and velvet ash. Other plants include Parry's and other agaves (century plants), sotol, nolina, Schott's yucca, ocotillo, and numerous cacti, including Engelmann's prickly pear and cane cholla. Among the numerous wildflowers are paintbrush, penstemon, gilia, and sunflowers.

A long list of grasses includes nine species of the fascinating gramas—sideoats, black, blue, etc.

Mammals include an occasional mountain lion; bobcats; coyotes; gray foxes; whitetail deer; coatis; ringtails; striped, hognosed, spotted, and hooded skunks; and peccaries (*javelinas*). Among the more than 160 recorded species of birds are Gambel and Montezuma quail; roadrunners; great horned owls; 12 kinds of hummingbirds, such as black-chinned, broad-tailed, magnificent, and an occasional white-eared; acorn and other woodpeckers; scrub and gray-breasted (Mexican) jays; painted redstarts and other warblers; black-headed grosbeaks; western tanagers; and hooded and Scott's orioles. Of the reptiles, there are a number of lizards including the beautifully patterned Arizona alligator lizard, and a half-dozen varieties of rattlesnakes.

There are six miles of trails in the memorial, including the one leading from the visitor center up to Montezuma Pass and on up to the 6,864-foot summit of Coronado Peak. The overlook at Montezuma Pass, which is reached both by trail and road, provides an outstanding panorama southward into Mexico. The highest point in the memorial is 7,676-foot-high Montezuma Peak.

Camping is not permitted in the memorial, but it is allowed in the adjacent Coronado National Forest. A picnic area is available in the memorial. The visitor center offers an interpretive video on the Coronado expedition, exhibits, and publications. The memorial's visitor center is open daily, except on Thanksgiving and Christmas. Lodging and meals are available in Sierra Vista, Bisbee, Benson, Tombstone, and Tucson.

IF YOU GO: Access from I-10 (just west of Benson) is south 29 miles on State Route 90 to Sierra Vista, then south about 15 miles on State Route 92, to the Coronado Memorial Road, which soon enters the memorial. Further information: Superintendent, 4101 E. Montezuma Canyon Rd., Hereford, AZ 85615. Telephone (520) 366-5515.

CUMBERLAND GAP NATIONAL HISTORICAL PARK

CUMBERLAND GAP NATIONAL HISTORICAL PARK consists of 20,312 acres in Kentucky, Tennessee, and the western tip of Virginia. It was established in 1955 to protect a scenic stretch of Cumberland Mountain (a ridge of the Appalachian Mountains) and a historically significant natural pass through the mountain.

For many centuries, native Americans traveled back and forth through the narrow gap. Then in 1750, a group led by Thomas Walker became the first white men to discover this passageway, as they searched in vain for a vast land grant to the west of the mountains. For a few years, the frontier wilderness beyond the Appalachians remained closed to eastern colonists, because of hostilities during the French and Indian War. But as these

Cumberland Gap National Historical Park [David Muench]

conflicts began to be resolved, hunters started to explore westward in search of new sources of wildlife. Prominent among these pioneers was marksman Daniel Boone who ventured alone in 1767 on a two-year trek into the uncharted wilderness. In 1775, following the signing of a treaty that officially ended the years of Indian hostilities in this region, Boone set out with 30 companions, including his wife and children, to find a new homeland and mark out a wilderness trail westward from Cumberland Gap into the wilds of Kentucky.

Hundreds, then thousands, of pioneering emigrants from the eastern seaboard moved into the new territory by way of the gap. By the end of the Revolutionary War in 1781, at least 12,000 people had crossed over to Kentucky by way of Boone's Wilderness Road. In another decade, that figure had grown to 100,000. In 1792, Kentucky became the 15th state admitted to the Union, which naturally triggered an even greater flood of settlers. By 1800, more than 300,000 people had poured through Cumberland Gap on their way to a new life in the frontier beyond the mountains.

By the 1820s and 1830s, as canals and railroads were extending westward, the importance of the long-popular gap finally began to wane. During the Civil War, in the 1860s, Cumberland Gap took on a different kind of strategic value, as military forces took advantage of the site. In mid-1861, Confederate troops established seven earthen forts that faced northward from the gap. The following year, Union troops took over the gap and built nine earthen forts that faced southward. Then, in a classic military maneuver, the Confederates severed the Union supply line, thus forcing them to yield up control of the pass. In 1863, however, the Union forces got even by sneaking into Cumberland Gap and destroying the Confederates' supplies, thereby enabling the Union troops once again to claim the stronghold. In spite of these back-and-forth takeovers, no significant battle was ever fought at Cumberland Gap.

An important book on the history of this key transportation corridor is *The Wilderness Road,* by Robert L. Kincaid.

To enjoy this beautiful park today, away from the fast pace of the main highway, visitors may drive Pinnacle Road, which branches from the main highway, just east of the park's western entrance at Middlesboro, Kentucky. This road winds up the mountain to Pinnacle Overlook, from which is a vast panorama across the gap to the mountains extending on south.

The park offers some 50 miles of hiking trails, from short interpretive trails, as near the main campground, to Ridge Trail. The latter begins at Pinnacle Overlook and runs 19 miles northeastward along the spine of richly forested Cumberland Mountain. This trail crosses Gibson Gap, where one of the park's five hike-in campgrounds is located (permits are required), then proceeds on, crossing Butchers Gap at 2,819 feet elevation and Chadwell Gap at 3,385 feet.

Near Chadwell Gap is the site of the historic Hensley Settlement. Founded in 1904, this community of a dozen farmsteads was scattered across a plateau on Brush Mountain. The remote settlement grew to about a hundred residents in the late 1920s and 1930s, before being abandoned by the early 1950s. Three of the Hensley farmsteads have since been restored by the National Park Service.

The park's visitor center, situated near the start of Pinnacle Road, offers interpretive programs, exhibits, trail guides, and other publications. From mid-June to Labor Day, and on spring and autumn weekends, the park offers a variety of family oriented, ranger-guided activities. From Memorial Day to Labor Day, the visitor center is open daily. It is closed on Thanksgiving, Christmas, New Year's Day, Martin Luther King, Jr.'s, birthday, and Presidents Day. The Park Service advises visitors always to use caution when hiking, and to be alert for snakes, poison ivy, poison oak, and poison sumac.

The wide variety of flora and fauna of Cumberland Mountain is typical of the southern Appalachians. Of the trees there are Virginia and pitch pines; eastern hemlock; tulip tree; sassafras; witch hazel; several hickories; beech; a number of oaks, including white, chestnut, northern and southern red, black, scarlet, and blackjack; eastern redbud; flowering dogwood; striped, red, and sugar maples; and royal paulownia. Shrubs include mountain laurel, early azalea, great laurel, and catawba rhododendron. Of the numerous species of wildflowers, there are Mayapple, yellow trout-lily, large-flowered trillium, yellow and pink lady's-slippers, showy orchis, bloodroot, hepatica, partridgeberry, and about 20 kinds of violets, such as bird-foot and sweet white.

Among the mammals are black bears; whitetail deer; gray and red foxes; bobcats; opossums; raccoons; striped skunks; cottontails; chipmunks; and fox, gray, and flying squirrels. Of the many birds, there are numerous kinds of hawks, many of which are seen during the autumn as they ride the rising thermals on their southward migration along Cumberland Mountain; and there are ruffed grouse; wild turkeys; great horned, barred, and other owls; pileated, red-bellied, and other woodpeckers; blue jays; Carolina wrens; wood thrushes; numerous warblers during spring migration, such as chestnut-sided, Kentucky, hooded, ovenbird, and American redstart; rose-breasted grosbeaks; cardinals; indigo buntings; rufous-sided towhees; white-throated and other sparrows; and scarlet and summer tanagers.

The park's main campground is situated just north of U.S. Route 58, near the park's eastern entrance, in Virginia. The five hike-in campgrounds (one is a horse camp, near the Hensley Settlement) are located adjacent to or near Ridge Trail. Picnic areas are provided near the visitor center, at Bartlett Park, partway up Pinnacle Road, and near the main campground. Spur roads lead to trailheads in the eastern part of the park, and a back road leads up to the Hensley Settlement.

Lodging and meals are available in Middlesboro, KY; Cumberland Gap, TN; and other towns in the area.

IF YOU GO: Access is west from U.S. Route 23, 54 miles on U.S. 58 (route of the Wilderness Road), in Virginia; north from I-81, 50 miles on U.S. Route 25E, in Tennessee; or southeast from I-75, 48 miles on U.S. Route 25E (route of the Wilderness Road), in Kentucky. Further information: Superintendent, P.O. Box 1848, Middlesboro, KY 40965. Telephone (606) 248-2817.

DE SOTO NATIONAL MEMORIAL

DE SOTO NATIONAL MEMORIAL consists of 26 acres at the mouth of the Manatee River at Tampa Bay, on the west coast of Florida. It was established in 1949 to commemorate the landing of Spanish explorer Hernando de Soto, somewhere near this site in May 1539. He and his successor, Luís de Moscoso, led a grueling, four-year, nearly 4,000-mile trek that was the first major European exploration of what is now the southeastern United States.

With a license from the Spanish Crown "to conquer, pacify, and populate" the region called La Florida, De Soto led an army of approximately 700 men—cavalry, crossbowmen, lancers, and harquebusiers; a corps of construction engineers, carpenters, and other workers for building boats, bridges, and temporary shelter; a few Roman Catholic friars; and a few women. Included were more than 200 horses and other livestock.

The Spaniards trekked through the seemingly endless, largely forested wilderness of what is now Florida, Georgia, the Carolinas, southeastern Tennessee, Alabama, Mississippi, Arkansas, and eastern Texas. While the expedition anticipated discovering gold and other great riches, as the Spaniards had previously found in Peru and Mexico, it was faced with never-ending hardships without ever discovering the wealth its men were seeking. Again and again they encountered Indians. Some, as in what is now South Carolina,

Reenactment of Spanish explorers at De Soto National Memorial, Florida [NPS]

treated the Spaniards hospitably and presented them with gifts of such things as freshwater pearls. But others attacked the expedition, retaliating against the ruthlessness of these strangers in their midst. Deaths and desertions substantially reduced the size of the expeditionary force as they struggled along.

There were numerous confrontations with the native Indians, as for example in northern Florida, where the Spaniards attacked 400 Indians, killing many and taking others as slaves to serve as carriers for the expedition. Women, too, were taken as prisoners. Those who opposed the harsh treatment were either burned at the stake, shot, or had a hand cut off, as an example to the others. On many occasions, the expedition ousted Indians from their towns so they could establish quarters for themselves.

In Alabama, in the biggest confrontation of the expedition, the explorers suddenly found themselves encircled by several hundred Mabila Indian warriors, who were angered by De Soto's demand that they hand over several hundred Indians to serve as enslaved porters. A fierce fight ensued in which the Indians' town burned down and more than 2,000 Indians were killed. Some of De Soto's most important colleagues were also killed, along with some of the expedition's valued horses.

While De Soto's demoralized men pressed him to return south to their supply ships lying just off the Alabama coast, he stubbornly insisted on pushing farther northwestward across what is now Mississippi. Time and again De Soto proved to be stubborn and inflexible—intolerant of opposition once he had made a decision.

Narrowly escaping a dawn attack by Chickasaw Indians, who resisted supplying the Spaniards with women and porters, the explorers reached the wide Mississippi River in May 1541. Barges were built to ferry them across. In what is now Arkansas, they continued to encounter hostile Indians. They built a fortified stockade around their winter encampment on the Arkansas River, near where Ft. Smith is today. De Soto finally became so discouraged with the continuing failure to find great riches—along with losing his chief interpreter, Juan Ortiz, many of his ablest soldiers, and most of his horses—that he reluctantly ordered the weary expedition back to the Mississippi.

De Soto's next plan had been to build boats and sail down the great river, send for reinforcements from Mexico and Cuba, and establish a coastal base from which to carry on further searches for gold. In May 1542, however, he succumbed to a fever (perhaps malaria) and died. But not before he ordered an attack on a town nearby in which the unarmed native Americans were savagely slaughtered, others were seriously injured, and many women and children were taken captive.

The expedition, now under the leadership of Luís Moscoso, attempted to reach Mexico by way of Texas, but soon retraced their steps once again to the Mississippi, where they commandeered an Indian village for their winter encampment. In 1543, the expedition's 300 remaining bedraggled Spaniards built a fleet of boats and sailed down the river where they were repeatedly attacked by Indians. From the river's mouth they sailed westward across the Gulf of Mexico, finally reaching Pánuco, Mexico, in the autumn of 1543. Not only was the De Soto expedition deemed a total failure because no gold or other riches were found, but also because it failed to open this region to Spanish colonization.

From the Indians' point of view, the Spaniards had been cruel and ruthless toward them and had consequently earned the natives' animosity. Not only were many Indians killed in clashes with the Spaniards, but apparently far greater numbers perished from the ravaging epidemics of European-introduced diseases, such as smallpox, measles, and typhoid, against which their populations had no natural immunities. Ironically, the De Soto expedition's descriptions of the vast region helped to encourage the English colonization of America in the next century.

The national memorial's visitor center provides interpretive exhibits, programs, and publications. A half-mile self-guiding nature trail runs by a mangrove swamp and along the Manatee River shore of De Soto Point. A short spur leads to the ruins of a tabby house from one of south Florida's earliest known American settlements, dating from the early nineteenth century. Tabby was a mixture of oyster shells, lime, sand, and water that produced a cement-like construction material.

Among the flora visitors can identify are black, red, and white mangroves; button mangrove; gumbo-limbo, with its smooth, reddish-brown bark that was historically peeled off in thin sheets and its sticky, oily resin then used to treat gout, yellow fever, and dysentery; southern red cedar and bay cedar; cabbage palm, the official state tree of Florida; the shrubby saw palmetto; the primitive and poisonous palm-like member of the Cyclad Family—Zamia, or coontie; sea grape, with its oval-shaped leathery leaves and grape-like fruit that grows in clusters; strangler fig; live oak; groundsel tree; wax myrtle, the berries of which contain a waxy substance that was once used to make candles; inkberry that grows on dunes; sea oats, a beautiful grass reaching heights of six feet or more and is vitally important in helping to stabilize sand dunes; yellow-flowering prickly pear cactus; seaside goldenrod; sea lavender; saltwort; and several epiphytic airplants—Spanish moss, wildpine, and ballmoss—that grow on trees or other plants and obtain all their nutrients from the air, rain, and sunshine.

Mammals include red foxes, armadillos, opossums, raccoons, and gray squirrels. There are seven varieties of snakes including the colorfully banded Florida scarlet snake, eastern indigo snake, and the diamondback rattlesnake.

Of the many species of birds, there are magnificent frigatebirds; white and brown pelicans; many herons including green-backed and little blue; snowy and great egrets; wood storks; white ibises; roseate spoonbills; several kinds of gulls; five species of terns including sooty and sandwich; black skimmers; bald eagles; ospreys; bobwhite; ground doves; red-bellied and pileated woodpeckers; blue jays; Carolina and house wrens; catbirds; mockingbirds; brown thrashers; a number of warblers including yellow-throated and parula; and cardinals.

The Park Service warns visitors to be alert for poisonous snakes, poison ivy, and sharp-spined cacti. From late December through early April, park staff provide living-history demonstrations at a site near the visitor center.

IF YOU GO: Access to the memorial is made by traveling west from I-75 on State Road 64 for ten miles. Turn north (right) onto 75 Street NW and travel 2.5 miles to the memorial. Lodging and meals are available in Bradenton, Sarasota, St. Petersburg, Tampa, and elsewhere in the area. Further information: Superintendent, P.O. Box 15390, Bradenton, FL 34280. Telephone (941) 792-0458.

EBEY'S LANDING NATIONAL HISTORICAL RESERVE

EBEY'S LANDING NATIONAL HISTORICAL RESERVE comprises 17,000 acres on Whidbey Island, Washington state. It protects a rural area containing an unbroken historical record stretching from nineteenth-century exploration and settlement in the Puget Sound region to the present day.

The reserve includes historic farms, as well as magnificent coastal beaches and bluffs, and views of Puget Sound and distant summits of the Cascade and Olympic ranges.

IF YOU GO: Further information: Trust Board of Ebey's Landing National Historical Reserve, P.O. Box 774, Coupeville, WA 98239. Telephone (360) 678-6084.

Ebey's Landing National Historical Reserve, Washington [NPS]

EL MORRO NATIONAL MONUMENT

EL MORRO NATIONAL MONUMENT, encompassing 1,278 acres was established in 1906 to protect the scenic, 200-foot-high sandstone mesa, known as Inscription Rock, or El Morro (the headland or bluff), in western New Mexico. Hundreds of historic inscriptions were carved into the soft sandstone, as were some prehistoric petroglyph motifs such as bighorn sheep and geometric designs. Atop the huge monolith are the excavated ruins of A'ts'ina (writings on the rock) Pueblo that once housed at least 1,000 people. and a smaller, unexcavated prehistoric Indian village, both occupied from around A.D. 1275 to 1350.

The earliest European inscription was carved into the cliff face by Spaniard Juan de Oñate, who established the initial Hispanic settlement of New Mexico. On April 16, 1605, he wrote: *"Paso por aqi el adelantado don Ju de Oñate del descubrimiento de la mar del sur a 16 de abril de 1605"* (Passed by here the Governor don Juan de Oñate from the discovery of the Sea of the South [Gulf of California], on the 16th of April 1605).

Pasó por aqui . . . . Many other Spaniards inscribed their writings on the great rock, among them the Governor General don Diego de Vargas who successfully reconquered New Mexico for the Spanish Crown in 1692, following the Pueblo Indians' successful revolt against the Spaniards in 1680. Another inscriber was the Bishop of Durango, Martin de Elizacochea, in 1737. Many Americans subsequently passed by El Morro, as well. Among them were artist Richard H. Kern and cartographer Lieutenant James Harvey Simpson in 1849—the first Americans to record many of the inscriptions; a U.S. military party that crossed the Southwest in 1857 with a bunch of camels as experimental pack stock; a wagon train of 26 emigrants in 1858; and a railroad survey crew of 1868.

One of El Morro's important and even life-saving assets for the early travelers was the pool of water at the cliff base. Today, a self-guiding interpretive path passes the cattail-bordered pool and winds around the base of the head-

El Morro National Monument, western New Mexico [Russ Butcher]

land for a quarter mile. Visitors may walk the entire two-mile loop trail, which climbs steeply up and over the great rock. From here they can see A'ts'ina Pueblo ruin and enjoy the surrounding scenic panorama of mesas, sheer cliffs, valleys, and the beautiful pine-filled box canyon at the western end of El Morro.

Inscription Rock is at about 7,200 feet above sea level. This elevation supports an attractive habitat of sagebrush and other shrubs and grasses, pinyon pines and junipers, a few picturesque clumps of Gambel oaks, and scattered, stately ponderosa pines. The rock itself is composed of two sedimentary strata: the soft, porous, pale-yellowish Zuni Sandstone which derives from compacted sand dunes that once covered a vast, Sahara Desert-like expanse of this region around 180 million years ago; and El Morro's harder, less porous caprock of Dakota Sandstone that is from compacted beach and shallow-ocean deposits laid down some 65 million years ago.

An especially excellent publication is *El Morro National Monument*, by Dan Murphy (Southwest Parks and Monuments Association, 1989).

IF YOU GO: The visitor center provides interpretive exhibits, audiovisual programs, and publications. The monument is open daily, except on Christmas and New Year's Day. A small campground is located in the monument. Lodging and meals are available in Gallup and Grants. Access from Gallup is 56 miles south on State Route 602 and east on State Route 53; and from Grants 42 miles west on Route 53. Further information: Superintendent, Route 2, Box 43, Ramah, NM 87321. Telephone (505) 783-4226.

FEDERAL HALL NATIONAL MEMORIAL

FEDERAL HALL NATIONAL MEMORIAL, consisting of a half-acre at 26 Wall Street, in lower Manhattan, New York City, celebrates the site of an earlier structure built in 1703 as City Hall. When the U.S. Congress initially selected New York as the nation's capital city, that building was expanded and became Federal Hall. On the second-floor balcony, George Washington took the oath of office as the first President of the United States, on April 30, 1789.

Congress met in that building from 1785 to 1790, when the national government moved to Philadelphia for ten years (see Independence National Historical Park), before moving permanently to Washington, D.C. The original Federal Hall fell into disrepair after the national government's departure, and it was finally demolished in 1812.

In 1942, the present Greek Revival structure was built, first accommodating a U.S. customs house and then a subtreasury. It boasts a large bronze statue of George Washington, sculpted by John Quincy Adams Ward in 1883. The National Park Service now provides interpretive exhibits and films about George Washington, his first inauguration, artifacts of the late eighteenth century, and information on the original Federal Hall.

Classical music concerts are presented in the hall's rotunda on Wednesdays at 12:30 p.m. and there are Friday afternoon movie programs. The memorial is open Monday through Friday.

IF YOU GO: Lodging and meals are abundantly available throughout Manhattan. Access is best by way of the city's subway or bus system, or by taxi. Further information: Superintendent, Manhattan Sites, National Park Service, 26 Wall St., New York, NY 10005. Telephone (212) 825-6990.

FORT CAROLINE NATIONAL MEMORIAL

FORT CAROLINE NATIONAL MEMORIAL consists of 138 acres in Jacksonville, Florida, and was established in 1953 to protect and interpret the site of the first attempt by France, in the 1560s, to lay claim to this region of North America.

In June 1564, two hundred French Huguenots, led by René de Laudonniére, built a small, triangular-shaped fort and settlement as an initial step in founding an important new colonial empire for France and carving out a new life for themselves.

The heroic effort was plagued by troubles after just a few months. The unity of the colony was torn apart when 80 members of the struggling community, disillusioned by hardships, took matters into their own hands by mutinying. Sailing to the Caribbean, they began to raid Spanish ships and hamlets.

Just as the colonists were about to give up on their settlement, a ship bearing more Frenchmen arrived along the Florida coast in August 1565. But the following month, fearing that these French reinforcements posed a likely threat to their shipping and other interests, a sizeable Spanish force arrived. Coming ashore 40 miles to the south, 500 Spaniards marched north and launched an attack on Fort de la Caroline, killing most of its inhabitants and capturing the colony. Two-and-a-half years later, the French evened the score by carrying out a successful surprise attack, capturing their former fort and killing many of the Spanish defenders.

The national memorial includes an outdoor exhibit, 400 yards from the visitor center. The center offers interpretive exhibits, artifacts, programs, and publications relating to both Fort Caroline and the Timucuan Ecological and Historic Preserve (see Timucuan). Camping is not allowed in the memorial, but picnic facilities are provided. Lodging and meals are available in and around Jacksonville.

IF YOU GO: For access to the memorial—13 miles from downtown Jacksonville—drive east on State Route 10, turn north on either St. Johns Bluff or Monument Road, and continue east on Fort Caroline Road to the national memorial entrance. Further information: Superintendent, 12713 Fort Caroline Road, Jacksonville, FL 32225. Telephone (904) 641-7155.

FORT CLATSOP NATIONAL MEMORIAL

FORT CLATSOP NATIONAL MEMORIAL, comprising 125 acres, was established in 1958 to protect and interpret the 1805–1806 winter encampment site of the Lewis and Clark Expedition, near the Pacific Ocean in northwestern Oregon. The memorial features a replica of the 50-foot-square, fortified cabin compound, set amid a dense coastal rainforest comprised mostly of Sitka spruce and western hemlock.

President Thomas Jefferson dispatched the "Corps of Discovery" under the command of two fellow Virginians, Captain Meriwether Lewis, age 29, who was the president's secretary-aide, and Lewis' good friend, Captain William Clark, age 33. Their mission was to explore the Missouri River to its headwaters, cross the Rocky Mountains, and follow the Columbia River downstream, thereby determining the most direct route to the Pacific Coast. They made accurate maps and charts, contacted native peoples, and kept detailed records in their daily journals of the region's geography, flora and fauna, ethnology, and weather. This was the first significant expedition officially supported and funded by the U.S. government. Its successful results had a profound impact on encouraging the subsequent westward expansion and development of the United States.

After working their way up the Missouri River from St. Louis in a 55-foot keel boat and two smaller, canoe-like pirogues, the 45 men spent their first winter—1804–1805—at Fort Mandan in what is now North Dakota (see Lewis and Clark National Historic Trail). While a few of the men were sent back in the spring with an initial report to President Jefferson, the main group of 33, including a French fur trader and Indian interpreter, Toussaint Charbonneau, his Shoshone wife, Sacagawea, and their infant child, proceeded westward. Sacagawea was both interpreter and diplomat, and her presence assured Indian tribes they encountered that the party had peaceful intentions, since an Indian woman would never accompany a group intent on war. She

Fort Clatsop National Memorial, Oregon [NPS]

was also able to negotiate with her people for a guide and horses, with which to cross the rugged Bitterroot Range in the northern Rocky Mountains.

Upon reaching the Clearwater River, in the Nez Perce country of what is now Idaho (see Nez Perce National Historical Park), the men built five large dugout canoes in which they proceeded down the Columbia River. They arrived at the Pacific Ocean in mid-November 1805, one-and-a-half years after setting forth on their epic trek across the uncharted wilderness.

Nearly continuous gale-force winds and drenching rainfall plagued the party during the first several weeks—a harbinger of miserable winter weather yet to come. While some of the men urged that the expedition should backtrack to drier country to the east of the Cascade Range, Lewis and Clark and a majority of the party were swayed by local Indians who said the elk, to supply their needs for meat and hides for new clothing, were plentiful to the west of the mountains, along the south (now Oregon) shore of the river. The party decided that there were convenient places where they could boil seawater and obtain much needed salt.

The men finally chose the site for their fortified log cabin compound a couple of miles up the Netul (now Lewis and Clark) River from the Columbia. Construction began on December 8 and was all but completed by Christmas. The fort was named for the friendly Clatsop Indians, one of a number of Chinookan tribes in the surrounding region. Along one side of the compound, there were three wall-to-wall rooms for eight or nine men each. Along the opposite side were the quarters for Lewis and Clark; the Charbonneau family; the orderlies' room for the fort's guards; a storeroom for trade goods, elk meat, hides, and other supplies; and a sentry box. These two rows of cabins faced each other across a courtyard, at each end of which was a stockade and gate. It took only two-and-a-half weeks for the men to build the basic structures.

In spite of the virtually continuous torrential rainfall and penetrating, cold dampness that made life miserable, caused much illness, and rotted their buckskin clothing, the hunters among them were more or less successful in providing an abundance of elk meat and hides—the latter being dressed and made into new clothing and moccasins. Through trade and barter, the Clatsop Indians frequently provided them with such other foods as fresh and/or dried salmon and sturgeon; wappato, a root that tasted like potato; eulachon, a small migratory fish that has a high fat content and was a special favorite; a variety of dried roots and berries; and, occasionally, dog meat.

Captain Lewis spent much of his time carefully collecting, studying, and writing in detail about the flora and fauna. He described dozens of local animals and over 30 species of trees and plants of the surrounding area—many of which were new to science. He also recorded how the Indians utilized many plants for food, medicinal properties, clothing, and tools. Lewis wrote of previous epidemics among the various native Americans, who had little or no natural immunity against diseases that were unfortunately introduced by the white man.

Captain Clark also kept busy throughout the long, dreary winter by writing about the geography of the region and preparing a map of their route from the Mississippi to the Pacific. This map was one of the principle contributions of the expedition.

From December 7, 1805, when Lewis and Clark first arrived at the site selected for the winter quarters, until March 23, 1806, when the expedition "bid a final adieu to Fort Clatsop," there had been only a dozen days when it did *not* rain. They had seen the sun only about six times! But as Clark described their departure (his words/spelling),

the rain seased and it became fair about Meridian, at which time we loaded our canoes & at 1 P.M. left Fort Clatsop on our homeward bound journey, at this place we had wintered and remained from the 7th of Decr. 1805 to this day and have lived as well as we had any right to expect, and we can say that we were never one day without 3 meals of some kind a day either pore [poor] Elk meat or roots, not withstanding the repeated fall of rain which has fallen almost constantly. . . .

Six months later, the expedition was greeted in St. Louis with a hero's welcome.

In 1955, on the Lewis and Clark sesquicentennial commemoration, the Clatsop County Historical Society, Astoria Jaycees, and other local groups and businesses contributed to rebuilding Fort Clatsop. Three years later, the site was added to the National Park System. Today, the national memorial not only protects the encampment site and surrounding environment, but provides a variety of interpretive, educational, and summer living-history programs and cultural demonstrations. The visitor center offers audiovisual programs and exhibits, and the Fort Clatsop Historical Association sells publications and other theme-related items. Trails lead from the visitor center to the fort, spring, and down to the canoe landing on the Lewis and Clark River. The Park Service cautions visitors to be careful by the river, as the riverbank is often slippery and unstable.

In lieu of a strictly natural environment, Lewis and Clark entered a significant historic and cultural environment. The members of the expedition met and interacted with many of the local native Americans. As the Park Service points out, the descriptions of these peoples, contained within the expedition's journals, are in many instances the only written information we have of these long-established cultures, which in a matter of only a few years were either permanently altered or disappeared altogether.

The same lack of distinction between natural and cultural resources exists today at Fort Clatsop National Memorial. The entire park is listed on the National Register of Historic Places. This includes not only the fort replica, but also the park's wetlands, sloughs, estuary, and spruce-hemlock forests. The coastal forests, wetlands, elk, and other natural resources surrounding the encampment site are as much a part of the Lewis and Clark story and cultural scene as the fort replica itself.

Trees of the memorial include Sitka spruce, Douglas-fir, western hemlock, grand fir, western red cedar, red alder, cascara buckhorn, western crabapple, willows, and bigleaf and vine maples. Among the shrubs are salal, several huckleberries, bush honeysuckle, Nootka wild rose, thimbleberry, elderberry, salmonberry, and Oregon grape. Beautiful ferns include sword, deer, licorice, maidenhair, wood, and bracken. Of the wildflowers, there are Smith's fairybell, western trillium, wood sorrel, wood violet, yellow flag, touch-me-not, and bittercress.

Among the publications on the fort and expedition are *Fort Clatsop: The Story Behind the Scenery*® by Daniel J. Dattilio (KC Publications); *Lewis and Clark; Voyage of Discovery* by Dan Murphy (KC Publications); and *Journals of the Lewis and Clark Expedition 1804-1806* edited by Gary Molton (University of Nebraska Press).

IF YOU GO: There is a picnic facility near the parking area. Camping is not allowed in the memorial, but three campgrounds are located about seven miles away, including at Fort Stevens State Park. Lodging and meals are available in Astoria, Warrenton, and Seaside. Access from Astoria is five miles south on U.S. Route 101 and Alt. 101. Follow signs to the memorial. The park is closed on Christmas. Further information: Superintendent, Route 3, Box 604FC, Astoria, OR 97103. Telephone (503) 861-2471.

FORT FREDERICA NATIONAL MONUMENT

FORT FREDERICA NATIONAL MONUMENT consists of 216 acres on St. Simons Island, on coastal Georgia. It was established in 1936 to protect and interpret the ruins of a British fort and adjacent community built under the direction of British General James E. Oglethorpe, begun in 1736 and completed in 1748.

This fort and the adjacent village were built in an attempt to help establish Britain's military power in the southeastern part of North America, to challenge Spain's claim to the region, and to give some of Britain's "worthy poor" a chance for an opportunity in the New World. The colony's founder was a politician and military commander who had great compassion for those less fortunate than he.

The city of Savannah was established first, 18 miles up the Savannah River. Then Oglethorpe selected a site on the coast to the south of Savannah for establishment of a fortified settlement—located on the coastal island of St. Simons, which was covered with great, spreading live oaks. He brought 44 men and 72 women and children to a site on a bluff above the Frederica River. The fort was built close to the river, with a battery commanding the river. The fort housed the magazine, storehouses, and officers' quarters, and was surrounded by a rampart with four bastions. Behind the fort was a palisade, within which the village containing the residents' homes and the soldiers' huts and barracks were located. Each family received a house lot measuring 90 by 60 feet, plus 50 acres of farming land. Initially, the dwellings were simple huts. But by the 1740s, some had become substantial Georgian-style red-brick or clapboard houses. The village population totaled about 500 people.

In 1740, Oglethorpe led a military offensive against Spanish Florida, capturing two small forts on the St. Johns River (at today's Jacksonville), but failing to take Castillo de San Marcos and St. Augustine (see Castillo de San Marcos National Monument and Fort Matanzas National Monument). Two years later, a Spanish armada sailed north from Florida to attack and wipe out the British settlements and fortifications in Georgia. In 1743, Oglethorpe sailed back to Britain, and by 1755, Frederica was no longer inhabited and soon fell into ruin.

Today, the monument's visitor center offers interpretive exhibits, programs, and publications. There are also walking tours of the historic points of interest, and summer living-history demonstrations. The monument is open daily, except on Thanksgiving, Christmas, and New Year's Day. Lodging and meals are available on St. Simons Island, nearby Sea Island, and in Brunswick. Camping is not allowed in the national monument, but there are campground facilities located on Jekyll Island and elsewhere in the vicinity.

IF YOU GO: Access to the monument is 12 miles from Brunswick, east by way of the F. J. Torras Causeway (toll) to St. Simons Island and following signs to the entrance. Further information: Superintendent, Route 9, Box 286-C, St. Simons Island, GA 31522. Telephone (912) 638-3639.

FORT MATANZAS NATIONAL MONUMENT

FORT MATANZAS NATIONAL MONUMENT, consisting of 300 acres on the northeastern coast of Florida, was established in 1924 and transferred from the War Department to the National Park Service in 1933. It protects and interprets the place where, in 1565, the Spanish military from St. Augustine (see Castillo de San Marcos National Monument) slaughtered nearly 250 Frenchmen from Fort Caroline (see Fort Caroline National Memorial), whose fleet of warships had been shipwrecked by a hurricane. The French military forces had been intending to attack St. Augustine in an attempt to defeat the Spaniards and take control of this region of North America. The storm's destruction, followed by the *matanzas* (slaughter), put an end to those French ambitions.

With France out of the way, Britain next challenged Spain to its claims in the region by establishing a colony in Georgia in 1733. Seven years later, British forces began to launch an attack upon St. Augustine and its fort by blockading the Matanzas River. The Spaniards were running low on supplies, and had the British blockade been maintained, St. Augustine could have been in serious trouble. But after a brief encounter near the mouth of Matanzas Inlet between two British sloops and several small Spanish boats trying to reach ships carrying provisions for St. Augustine, the British abandoned the blockade long enough for the Spanish supply ships to enter the inlet and sail up the river to the grateful settlement. Lacking adequate naval reinforcements, aware that the Spaniards were now well supplied for a long blockade, and facing the onset of the hurricane season in Florida, the British ended their plan to attack St. Augustine only five weeks after beginning it.

Fort Matanzas National Monument, Florida [NPS]

One result of the British threat was the decision by the Spanish military to construct a small but massive stone fort at Matanzas Inlet, replacing a smaller wooden one. Despite efforts by the British and their local Indian allies to block this project, the fort was completed in two years. In 1743, the British forces attempted one last, futile attack on the Spanish installations. While the British failed to win Florida by military conquest, they finally acquired it under the terms of the Peace of Paris, in 1763. Florida and Fort Matanzas were given back to Spain in 1784, and remained in Spanish hands until 1821, when Florida was purchased by the United States. By the time the United States took over Florida, the fort was already deteriorating after a lengthy period of abandonment.

The visitor center offers a video and interpretive exhibits, and the Park Service offers interpretive programs and walks. Lodging and meals are available in St. Augustine Beach and St. Augustine. Camping is not permitted in the national monument, but campgrounds are available in nearby Anastasia and Flagler state recreation areas and at a number of privately owned camping facilities.

IF YOU GO: The monument is open daily, except on Christmas. Access is 14 miles south of St. Augustine by way of State Route A1A on Anastasia Island. The fort is reached by way of a free ferry across to Rattlesnake Island, which runs daily except when weather does not permit safe passage. Further information: Superintendent, Castillo de San Marcos National Monument, 1 Castillo Dr., St. Augustine, FL 32084. Telephone (904) 471-0116.

FORT NECESSITY NATIONAL BATTLEFIELD

FORT NECESSITY NATIONAL BATTLEFIELD comprises 902 acres in southwestern Pennsylvania. It was established in 1931 as a national battlefield site under the War Department, transferred to the National Park Service in 1933, and given its present designation in 1961. It protects and interprets the site of the fort at which the first major battle occurred, in 1754, in the seven-year French and Indian War between Britain and France.

The battle took place during a heavy summer rainstorm, in a grassy expanse amid the forested wilderness that extended westward from the Allegheny Mountains. This upper Ohio River area was part of the vast region of interior North America, the ownership of which was in dispute between the two nations. French fur trappers and troops were moving southward into the area from Canada, while the English colony of Virginia was claiming the same area.

To urge the French military to withdraw its troops back northward to their fort near Niagara Falls, Virginia's colonial governor dispatched a small force of militiamen under the command of then-Major George Washington. But this attempt to reconcile the problem through negotiations was a failure. The Virginia governor next dispatched soldiers to establish a British fort at the strategic junction of the Allegheny and Monongahela rivers that form the Ohio River (where Pittsburgh is today). But the French military blocked the Virginians and set up their own fortification—Fort Duquesne.

In April 1754, Washington led another military expedition. On May 24, the Virginians established an encampment at the grassy place called Great Meadows. Several days later, helpful Indian scouts notified Washington that a 32-man force of French soldiers was heading their way and was camped at a glen located about seven miles to the northwest of the meadows. In spite of a miserable rainy night, Washington and 40 of his recruits immediately set out with Indian guides. Arriving at just after dawn on May 28, they opened fire on the French, who were caught so off guard that Washington obtained their surrender in a mere 15 minutes. While 10 Frenchman were killed in the brief fight, the Virginians lost only one man. The site was subsequently named Jumonville Glen, in memory of the French commander who was killed there.

Returning to Great Meadows, Washington and his men quickly built a small, circular fortification—a log stockade, storehouse, and protective trenches—which he named Fort Necessity. An expected retaliatory attack by French soldiers from Fort Duquesne was launched on July 3. There were many casualties on both sides during the fierce eight-hour battle. But in the end, Washington's recruits were no match for the more than 600 French soldiers and 100 Indian allies, and he was forced to surrender—the only surrender in George Washington's distinguished military career. After he and his men headed back to Virginia, the French burned down the fort. And so began the French and Indian War, in which the British ultimately won control of a vast part of North America, stretching west from the Appalachian Mountains.

In the national battlefield visitor center, there are interpretive exhibits, a brief slide program, and publications. From there a short path leads to the reconstructed fort. There are living-history re-enactments in the summer. The park also features the Mount Washington Tavern, a historic stagecoach stop dating from the early nineteenth century, that houses interpretive exhibits. And the Jumonville Glen unit of the national battlefield (closed from November to mid-April) offers self-guiding interpretive trails through this scenic area.

IF YOU GO: Lodging and meals are available in Farmington and Uniontown. Access is by way of U.S. Route 40, 11 miles east of Uniontown. The battlefield's visitor center is open daily, except on Christmas. Further information: Superintendent, 1 Washington Parkway, Farmington, PA 15437. Telephone (412) 329-5512.

FORT RALEIGH NATIONAL HISTORIC SITE

FORT RALEIGH NATIONAL HISTORIC SITE comprises 513 acres on Roanoke Island on the northeast coast of North Carolina. It was established in 1941 to protect and interpret the site of England's first tentative efforts at founding a colony in North America, between 1585 and 1590.

Queen Elizabeth I, during her reign from 1558 to 1603, launched England on an unprecedented period of international expansion and territorial colonization. Sir Walter Raleigh, a 31-year-old scholar, poet, soldier, mariner, and the queen's favorite courtier, had envisioned England amassing tremendous riches and power by establishing colonies in such places as the New World. Under a charter he obtained from the English Crown, Raleigh organized a reconnaissance expedition in 1584 that sailed across the Atlantic Ocean to the coastal region soon to be named Virginia (in honor of the Virgin Queen), and that subsequently became North Carolina.

The captains of the sailing ships returned with glowing descriptions of this new land, including its native inhabitants, the Algonquian Indians, who were characterized as "most gentle, loving and faithful, void of all guile and treason." Consequently, in 1585, Raleigh dispatched seven ships and 107 colonists under the command of a skilled navigator, Sir Richard Grenville, to set up a colonial foothold in this wonderful new land. They settled on the northern end of Roanoke Island, hidden behind the Outer Banks barrier islands. The men constructed a small fort to help defend the fledgling settlement against attack by the Spanish and French, and as a base from which to launch attacks on Spanish and French shipping.

When the English sailor, Sir Francis Drake, stopped at Roanoke Island on his way from the West Indies, he found a disillusioned, starving, and homesick population, struggling with meager supplies and facing increasing hostility from the Indians. Drake honored their appeal and took them all back to England. A few weeks later, Grenville, who had sailed to England for new supplies, returned to find the fort abandoned. He left 15 of his men to take care of the settlement and returned to England.

In spite of this initial setback, Raleigh kept his vision alive, and in 1587 sent out a new group consisting of 84 men, 17 women, and nine children, to establish an agrarian colony under a coat of arms and titled Cittie of Ralegh (the City of Raleigh in Virginia). This time, it was to be located at the southern end of Chesapeake Bay, under the governorship of John White. It had been White's plan to pick up Grenville's 15 men at Fort Raleigh and sail north to Chesapeake Bay, but when White's ships arrived, they found that all of the Englishmen had been killed by the Indians.

White sailed back to England to procure more badly needed supplies. Unfortunately, England was being threatened with invasion by the Spanish Armada, thus delaying his return to the colony for three years. When he arrived, the little fort and settlement were abandoned, the houses taken down, and a palisade built. Mysterious clues were all that remained, including the word *Croatoan*, the Indian name for the Outer Banks island of Cape Hatteras, carved into a post. Raleigh made a number of attempts between 1590 and 1602 to locate the colonists and solve the mystery—to no avail. The colonists were never found and no conclusive evidence of what happened to the "Lost Colony" has ever surfaced.

The national historic site features the small earthen fort, reconstructed by the National Park Service in 1950. The reconstructed fort may actually represent a structure used by the group of 15 men in 1586, rather than the original fort built by the first group of colonists. This theory is based on archaeological evidence unearthed in 1992 by Ivor Noel Hume, as reported in *National Parks* magazine ("New Findings at the Lost Colony," by Laura P. McCarty, July-August 1993).

In 1990, the U.S. Congress passed legislation not only enlarging the Fort Raleigh National Historic Site to its current size but expanding the site's scope of interpretation to include events that occurred within or near the site.

In early 1862, Civil War General Ambrose Burnside led a Union military force north from Hatteras Island through Pamlico Sound and captured Roanoke Island from the defending Confederate Army. Although the battle is not well known today, it was crucial to the Union's effort to deny Confederate access to the riverine transportation system into the interior of North Carolina. Two Confederate forts and the Confederate barracks were located on the north end of the present Fort Raleigh National Historic Site. They are not visible today.

Following the island's capture, a Union army chaplain from Massachusetts organized a colony to care for freed slaves and the families of black Union soldiers on Roanoke. This "Freedmen's Colony" was located roughly from the center of the island north to the former Confederate barracks site. Although the colony did not survive the war, it gave hundreds of former slaves an opportunity to begin learning how to take care of themselves in a free society.

At about the time the Wright brothers were experimenting with flight just a few miles across the Albemarle Sound (see Wright Brothers National Memorial), Reginal Fessenden set up a site close to the present day park, where he transmitted the first musical notes over the airways.

The site's visitor center provides interpretive exhibits—including artifacts recovered from the site excavations—programs, and publications. The park also features the Waterside Theater where *The Lost Colony* is performed during the summer months, blending drama, dance, and symphonic music to convey the history of the unsuccessful attempts to colonize this area. Adjacent to the park are the beautiful Elizabethan Gardens, on the shore of Roanoke Sound. This delightful area was created by The Garden Club of North Carolina as a living memorial to those early courageous settlers. Paths lead throughout the gardens, and trails wind through some parts of the park, including a nature trail that loops through a scenic stretch of woods between the shore of the sound and the site of houses adjacent to the fort.

Among the trees at the site are loblolly pine; bald cypress; Atlantic white cedar; sassafras; American sycamore; sweetgum; bitternut hickory; wax myrtle; beech; several oaks including swamp chestnut, southern red, water, laurel, and live oak (the latter near the northern end of its range here); water and black tupelos; American holly; red maple; and Carolina ash.

Camping is not permitted within the national historic site, but a picnic area is provided and campgrounds are located at nearby Cape Hatteras

National Seashore. Lodging and meals are available in Manteo, Wanchese, at several communities on the Outer Banks, and elsewhere in the region.

IF YOU GO: Access to the site is 3 miles north of Manteo on U.S. Route 64; about 67 miles north of Elizabeth City by way of U.S. Routes 158 and 64; or about 90 miles south from Norfolk, VA. Further information: Superintendent, c/o Cape Hatteras National Seashore, Route 1, Box 675, Manteo, NC 27954. Telephone (919) 473-5772.

FORT UNION TRADING POST NATIONAL HISTORIC SITE

FORT UNION TRADING POST NATIONAL HISTORIC SITE, consisting of 442 acres in northwestern North Dakota and adjacent Montana, was established in 1966 to protect and interpret the site of the most important nineteenth-century fur-trading center on the Missouri River. Located on a grassy expanse of shortgrass prairie, it overlooks the river and eroded landscape of bluffs and buttes beyond to the south, and is just upstream from the confluence of the Missouri and Yellowstone rivers.

Fort Union Trading Post was founded in 1828 by a Scottish-born trader, Kenneth McKenzie, who headed the American Fur Company-affiliated Upper Missouri Outfit. The Blackfeet Indian tribe, which had previously traded beaver pelts with the British of the Hudson's Bay Company, initially opposed allowing an American company to set up its business in this area. But with the help of a trapper who had formerly worked for the British and who could speak some of the Blackfeet language, McKenzie was given permission to establish his post.

Fort Union consisted of a palisades-enclosed quadrangle, in which were the Bourgeois (manager's) House; a building providing lodging for company employees; an Indian trading house; quarters for the clerk's office; a company store; storerooms for supplies as well as skins and furs; a fort kitchen; shops for the blacksmith, tinsmith, and carpenters; an icehouse; a gun powder magazine; an enclosure for horses and cattle; and at opposite corners of the palisades, two stone bastions (watchtowers).

For several decades prior to the startup of the post, beaver pelts had been in great demand. But as McKenzie was getting under way, beaver hats went out of fashion. This turn of events could have doomed the fledgling venture, except for the fact that buffalo robes, obtained by Indians from the immense herds of bison roaming the Great Plains, were readily available and of commercial value. Consequently, the Upper Missouri Outfit's business in buffalo robes flourished during much of the 1830s and beyond.

During the peak years of the trading post's operation, about a hundred company employees staffed the site. In addition to Americans, the cosmopolitan enterprise included immigrants from such countries as Britain, France, Germany, Italy, Spain, and Russia.

Coinciding with the founding of Fort Union Trading Post was the coming of the steamboat to this distant stretch of the Missouri in 1832. Not only was it far easier to ship needed trading supplies and other cargo upriver and great loads of robes and furs downstream, but travelers from the east could now more easily come west, stopping at such places as Fort Union. Among the visitors welcomed at the post were scientists, explorers, and painters such as George Catlin, John James Audubon, and Karl Bodmer. The latter produced a beautiful painting of the fort, with Assiniboines encamped near the trading post and on horseback, and the scenic bluffs beyond the river.

During the trading season, the Indians came with abundant quantities of robes and furs, and pitched their tepees on the grassy expanse outside the palisades. As described by the National Park Service:

> The almost ritualistic trading negotiations occurred in the reception room [of the Trade House] as Indian chieftains and fur company clerks made opening speeches, enjoyed a hearty feast, and then shrewdly parlayed furs for weapons, clothing, utensils, beads, and a myriad of other trade goods. In one corner . . . visitors also see furs piled high, the proceeds of a successful trade.

Disaster struck in 1837. An epidemic of the European-borne smallpox ravaged some of the Indian populations. This deadly virus, against which the native Americans had little or no natural immunity, tragically caused widespread loss of life. Among the local Assiniboines, for instance, nearly nine-tenths of their 1,000-member band was wiped out. This, in turn, resulted in a major decline in the trading post's business. Trading recovered from this setback, however, and resumed at a brisk pace over the next few years. But then, in 1857, another smallpox epidemic swept through the tribes, this time decimating the Crow Indians of the Yellowstone River country—a tribe that had mercifully been spared this scourge 20 years earlier. The post's business dropped off again and never really recovered. By the start of the Civil War in 1861, the trading post's profits were only marginal and the fort itself was allowed to run down. By 1864, a U.S. Army general observed that it was "an old dilapidated affair, almost falling to pieces."

For a brief time, the North Fur Company attempted to revive the operation, but soon gave up and sold out to the U.S. Army in 1867. After the fort was dismantled for reuse of materials to help expand the military's Fort Buford, two miles downstream, little remained but the foundations of what had been such a busy enterprise.

When the area became a national historic site, only low mounds and ridges defined where the palisades, bastions, powder magazine, Bourgeois House, and other structures once stood. Since then, the National Park Service has carried out excavations and recovered historic artifacts, such as parts of trapping gear, buttons, bottles, china, and eating utensils. In the 1980s, the Park Service reconstructed some of the fort, including the Bourgeois House, log Indian trade house, fort kitchen, walls, and stone bastions.

The fort is open daily, except on Thanksgiving, Christmas, and New Year's Day. The site's visitor center is located in the Bourgeois House, providing exhibits of many artifacts, publications, and other interpretive material. During the summer months, the site offers guided tours and living-history programs. From Thursday through Sunday of the third weekend in June, an annual reenactment of the fur-trading rendezvous is staged, with "buckskinners" dressed in period clothing and displaying tools and equipment of the trade and handmade items.

A picnic facility is provided near the site's parking area. Camping is not allowed, but a campground is located at the North Unit of Theodore Roosevelt National Park, about 70 miles southeast; and primitive camping is permitted at Fort Buford State Historic Site, two miles east.

IF YOU GO: Overnight lodging and meals are available at Williston, ND, and Sidney, MT. Access to the site is 24 miles southwest from Williston, via U.S. Route 2 and ND Route 1804; 21 miles northeast from Sidney, via MT Route 200 and ND Route 58; or about 70 miles north of the Theodore Roosevelt National Park's North Unit, by way of U.S. Route 85, ND Route 200, and ND Route 58. Further information: Superintendent, RR3, Box 71, Williston, ND 58801. Telephone (701) 572-9083.

FORT VANCOUVER NATIONAL HISTORIC SITE

FORT VANCOUVER NATIONAL HISTORIC SITE, consisting of 208 acres in the city of Vancouver, in southwestern Washington state, was established initially as a national monument in 1948, then changed to a national historic site in 1961. It protects and interprets the site and reconstructed buildings and stockade of what was the most important nineteenth-century commercial outpost in the Pacific Northwest.

In 1825, the powerful British-owned Hudson's Bay Company moved the regional headquarters of its vast Columbia Department from Fort George, near the mouth of the Columbia River, upstream about 100 river miles to Fort Vancouver, on the north bank of the river. This move was intended to secure the British claim to the region known as the Oregon country. Dr. John McLoughlin, a businessman and trained physician from the Canadian province of Quebec, was placed in charge of the company's operation, which encompassed today's Oregon, Washington, Idaho, and British Columbia. His task was not only to create a strong commercial power in the region for Britain, but to keep Americans out of the fur-trading business and maintain peaceful relations with the Indians.

As increasing numbers of American emigrants poured into the Oregon country in the 1840s by way of the Oregon Trail, McLoughlin extended hospitality by selling them needed merchandise and extending credit to help them begin a new life in the frontier. Some emigrants, including missionaries, were provided with temporary lodging at the fortified post until they could get established. While contrary to the Hudson's Bay Company and British objective, McLoughlin's assistance to Americans actually helped bring the Oregon country into United States ownership.

Responding to the popular fashion in beaver hats, Hudson's Bay dispatched brigades of 50 to 200 trappers into the wilderness. These brigade groups consisted of men, women, and children—all of whom helped with the trapping of beavers. Most of this work was carried out in winter, when the pelts were at their thickest. When the brigades of trappers returned to the post with horseback-loads of furs, company clerks then appraised the quality of the pelts, paid the trappers accordingly, and prepared the furs for shipment to London, where they were made into elegant hats.

The post consisted of many buildings, such as the chief factor's (manager's) house, lodging for visitors, quarters for upper-echelon employees, the trade house, storage for furs and general merchandise, carpentry shop, a blacksmith shop, a kitchen and bakehouse, and a chaplain's residence that also served as a school. This entire complex was surrounded by a high palisade. At its peak of commercial activity, as many as 500 people were employed at the fort—a cosmopolitan population that included Indians of various tribes, and people from Britain, France, Germany, Russia, Canada, the Sandwich Islands (Hawai'i), and other countries.

Brigade trapper, Fort Vancouver National Historic Site, Washington [Rick Edwards/NPS]

In 1846, the international boundary between the United States and Canada was established along the 49th parallel in this region. This was far to the north of where the British had envisioned the line would be, thereby placing Fort Vancouver and what became Oregon and Washington within the United States. For another 14 years, the company continued its trading with settlers and Indians. But as the population of beavers dwindled through overtrapping, and as silk hats began to replace the fashion in beaver hats, the post's volume of business steadily declined. Hudson's Bay Company finally left Fort Vancouver in 1860, and by 1866, the decaying fort was burned and torn down.

In 1948, archaeological excavations of the site were undertaken. More than a million artifacts were recovered. Then, beginning in 1966 through

1982, the palisade and five buildings were reconstructed, including the chief factor's house, the Indian trade shop, kitchen, bakehouse, and blacksmith shop. In 1995, the fur warehouse was completed.

The visitor center provides an interpretive video, publications, and exhibits featuring artifacts unearthed during the excavation of the site. Interpretive tours of the reconstructed complex are offered, living-history demonstrations are presented in the blacksmith shop and kitchen, and there are a number of special cultural events during the year, notably the annual reenactment of the brigade encampment in July and a candlelight tour in October. The site is closed on Thanksgiving, the day of Christmas Eve, Christmas, and New Year's Day.

IF YOU GO: Lodging and meals are available in Vancouver. Access to the national historic site is by way of the E. Mill Plain Blvd. exit from I-5 and proceeding east, following park signs to the visitor center on E. Evergreen Blvd.; or by way of the State Route 14 exit from I-205 and proceeding west on Route 14 for about five miles to a right turn onto Grand Blvd., and following park signs to the visitor center. Further information: Superintendent, 612 E. Reserve St., Vancouver, WA 98661. Telephone (360) 696-7655.

FRIENDSHIP HILL NATIONAL HISTORIC SITE

FRIENDSHIP HILL NATIONAL HISTORIC SITE consists of 674 acres in New Geneva, overlooking the Monongahela River, in southwestern Pennsylvania. It was authorized in 1978 to protect and interpret the brick-and-stone Gallatin House. This was the country estate of Swiss-born Albert Gallatin (1761-1849), who was Secretary of the Treasury from 1801 to 1813, in the administrations of U.S. Presidents Thomas Jefferson and James Madison. Gallatin was involved with acquisition of the vast Louisiana Territory from France, and was instrumental in negotiating an end to the War of 1812 with Britain.

Interpretive exhibits and programs on Gallatin's life and accomplishments are presented in the Gallatin House. Ranger-led tours of the house are provided in the summer, while the house is open year-round for self-guided touring. The site offers ten miles of delightful hiking trails that lead along streams and a pond, and through the woods and across meadows that surround the house. The site is open daily except on Christmas.

IF YOU GO: Camping is not permitted, but picnic facilities are available. Lodging and meals are available in Uniontown, PA, and Morgantown, WV; and meals are available in Point Marion, PA. Access from I-68 is by way of U.S. Route 119 northbound to Point Marion; and then three miles north on PA Route 166 to the site entrance. Access from I-76 is by way of U.S. Route 119 southbound to Uniontown and on south to Point Marion, then north three miles to the site entrance. Access from I-79 is by way of PA Route 21 eastbound, and south (right) on PA Route 166 to the site. Further information: Superintendent, RD 1, Box 149-A, Point Marion, PA 15474. Telephone (412) 725-9190.

GOLDEN SPIKE NATIONAL HISTORIC SITE

GOLDEN SPIKE NATIONAL HISTORIC SITE encompasses 2,735 acres at Promontory Summit north of Great Salt Lake, in northern Utah. It was established in 1965 to celebrate the completion of the first transcontinental railroad line across America, on May 10, 1869.

A number of transcontinental railroad alternatives had been urged in the 1840s and 1850s. But the winner in this high-stakes competition was a central route across what became the states of Nebraska, Wyoming, Utah, and Nevada, to Sacramento, California. The idea of this specific rail link received major impetus from surveyor and engineer Theodore Judah. He was a zealous promoter and lobbyist who succeeded in encouraging four prominent California businessmen—Leland Stanford, Charles Crocker, Mark Hopkins, and Collis P. Huntington—to back construction of a rail line eastward from California, to be called the Central Pacific Railroad.

In 1862, soon after the southern states seceded from the Union, a shorter southern rail proposal was ignored, and the U.S. Congress passed and President Abraham Lincoln signed into law the Pacific Railroad Act. It authorized construction of the Central Pacific Railroad from Sacramento, California, and the Union Pacific Railroad westward from Omaha, Nebraska—across the Great Plains and over the Continental Divide. The two would meet somewhere midway.

Each railroad was given incentives—loan subsidies that ranged from $16,000 to $48,000 per mile, plus 10 sections of land for each mile of track constructed, a land subsidy that was doubled two years later. After the groundbreaking ceremony for the Central Pacific in Sacramento, in January 1863, thousands of Chinese and other laborers were put to work, and the race was on. Progress over the rugged Sierra Nevada was slow, backbreaking work, as the men carved out massive cuts and tunneled through solid rock, coped with treacherous landslides, and were harassed by winter snowstorms.

Once over the mountains and onto the awesome, stark vastness of Nevada's Great Basin Desert, construction accelerated rapidly. Thousands more laborers were brought directly from China. The lure of lucrative financial incentives and substantial land grants from the federal government spurred the company onward. At an ever-quickening pace that often reached a mile a day, it covered a remarkable 360 miles in 1868, and peaked at ten miles of construction on April 28, 1869.

Meanwhile, in December 1863, the Union Pacific finally got underway with ground-breaking ceremonies in Omaha. While its crews of survey-

Golden Spike National Historic Site, Promontory, Utah [A. J. Russell]

ors and laborers were spared the challenges of crossing a major mountain range, they were frequently harassed on the Great Plains by Sioux and Cheyenne Indians, who felt hugely threatened by the sudden intrusion of the white man's "iron horse" plowing through the heart of their ancient buffalo domain.

The rails were laid along the Platte and North Platte rivers, passing just to the north of Scotts Bluff, which had for so long been a major landmark for thousands of emigrants on the Oregon and Oregon-California trails (see Scotts Bluff National Monument). In 1868, as they worked across what is now Wyoming, the laborers completed 425 miles, exceeding the Central Pacific's annual record.

Finally, on May 10, 1869, a grand gathering of several hundred people, including the railroads' owners, employees, and well-wishers, celebrated the meeting of the two lines at a place in the Promontory Mountains of northern Utah Territory. With whistles blowing, the Central Pacific's steam locomotive, *Jupiter*, and the Union Pacific's engine No. 119 chugged up to each other, cow-catcher to cow-catcher, amid the wild cheers of jubilant onlookers. Just before the last several iron spikes were hammered into place to hold the rails to the ties, the company presidents tapped four ceremonial spikes into precut holes—two of gold, one of silver, and one of iron, silver, and gold. The ceremony was held at Promontory Summit, which is located about 40 miles north of Promontory Point. At that moment in history, a message was telegraphed across America: "The last spike is driven. The Pacific railroad is finished." The Central Pacific had laid down 690 miles of track, and the Union Pacific's rails extended 1,086 miles.

Sadly, however, the man whom some had called "Crazy Judah" was not there to enjoy the completion of his dream. Just as construction had gotten underway, he succumbed to a fatal attack of yellow fever.

Five days after the hammering of the last spike, regular passenger service was inaugurated. Passengers initially had to change trains, from the one railroad company to the other, at the scruffy excuse for a railroad town that quickly sprang up in the midst of the sagebrush wilderness. But only eight months later, the transfer point was shifted to Ogden, Utah. Promontory then settled down to a more peaceful railroad employees' town that included a depot, restaurant, hotel, roundhouse for locomotive maintenance, water tank, and coal supplies for the smoke-belching engines.

When the Southern Pacific Railroad took over the Central Pacific around the turn of the century, a shortcut was laid across the central part of Great Salt Lake, and the town of Promontory went into steep decline that paralleled the diminishing use of the original route. In 1942, the rails were removed; only a concrete monument remained to mark the historic meeting place. The original steam locomotives unfortunately were scrapped. But by using historic photographs and other data, a company under contract with the National Park Service painstakingly created fully functional replicas.

The new *Jupiter* and No. 119 are now kept at the site's enginehouse, located near the visitor center. A Golden Spike reenactment ceremony is held annually on May 10, and other living-history events occur during the summer. The visitor center provides interpretive exhibits, programs, and publications. One such publication is the excellent *Golden Spike National Historic Site,* by Rose Houk, published by the Southwest Parks and Monuments Association.

The national historic site also protects natural values. Among the area's mammals are mule deer, mountain lions, bobcats, coyotes, red and kit foxes, badgers, porcupines, cottontails, pygmy rabbits, and black-tailed jackrabbits. Birds include red-tailed hawks, prairie falcons and kestrels, black-shouldered kites, short-eared and barn owls, ravens, black-billed magpies, rock wrens, sage thrashers, Brewers and lark sparrows, western meadowlarks, and horned larks. Milk and gopher snakes and Great Basin rattlesnakes inhabit the area, along with a number of lizards.

Among the plantlife, the site supports chokecherry, sagebrush, rabbitbrush, bricklebush, balsamroot, sego lily, common sunflower, globemallow, prickly poppy, primrose, and numerous species of grasses including Great Basin wild rye and several wheatgrasses.

IF YOU GO: Camping is not allowed, but a picnic area is located at the site. Lodging and meals are available in Brigham City, Ogden, Tremonton, and other cities in the area. Access to the site is 30 miles west of I-15 at Brigham City, by way of State Routes 13 and 83, and then following signs on an unnumbered road to the site. Further information: Superintendent, P.O. Box 897, Brigham City, UT 84302. Telephone (801) 471-2209.

GRAND PORTAGE NATIONAL MONUMENT

GRAND PORTAGE NATIONAL MONUMENT, comprising 710 acres in the northeastern tip of Minnesota, was initially designated as a national historic site in 1951. Then, when the Ojibway Indians ceded some of their lands to the federal government, it was established as a national monument in 1958. It protects and interprets both the site of the field headquarters of the Great Lakes region's largest and most profitable late-eighteenth-century fur-trading company, and the 8.5-mile Grand Portage that connected the headquarters on the shore of Lake Superior with the Pigeon River. The Ojibways had previously used this overland portage pathway, which they called *Kitchi Onigaming* ("Great Carrying Place").

The North West Company, which was owned by Simon McTavish, Benjamin and Joseph Frobisher, and other partners in Canada and Britain, controlled a vast expanse of North America's beaver country. The Grand Portage fur-trading headquarters, which was operated from 1784 to 1803, was surrounded by a 15-foot-tall cedar-picket stockade, or palisades. It enclosed a compound containing 16 buildings that included the Great Hall, a business office, kitchen house, partners' house, manager's house, general store, fur store, blacksmith and tinsmith shop, carpentry and cooper shops, and gun powder magazine; while outside the compound was a building for storage of the canoes. The company employed as many as 50 traders, several dozen guides, and over 1,000 canoemen.

Each year in late June or early July, a major rendezvous was held, bringing together more than 1,000 canoemen and voyageurs, many of whom camped outside the stockade. Following this gathering's final festivities that included dance ceremonies by local Indians, the voyageurs and canoemen took off into the far reaches of the north country with their birchbark canoes to bring back a wealth of beaver pelts and other furs.

Grand Portage itself sliced through the forest, bypassing the Pigeon River's impassable lower rapids and waterfalls. In as little as two-and-a-half hours, the hardy men were able to hike this trail rapidly, burdened with some 90 pounds of supplies. The canoes were carried by two men each. Fort Charlotte, at the western end of the portage, provided a temporary storage post for furs and a place to carry out canoe repairs.

The Grand Portage operation processed enormous quantities of furs that were then shipped eastward to Montreal. From there, many were sent on to European markets. The lucrative enterprise at Grand Portage came to an end in 1803, when the company reluctantly decided to move its field headquarters about 40 miles to the north, on Lake Superior's Thunder Bay, Ontario, Canada. When the U.S.-Canadian boundary had recently been determined, Grand Portage ended up in the United States, and the company wanted to avoid paying taxes and duties to the United States.

Today, the national monument features replicas of several of the buildings—the Great Hall and the kitchen house within the stockade, and the canoe-storage building outside. The Great Hall and kitchen exhibit historical furnishings. The canoe house shelters replicas of two birchbark canoes. One is a 36-foot craft like those used to carry up to 8,000 pounds of furs and other cargo on the Great Lakes and the larger rivers, with a crew of eight to ten men. The other is a more maneuverable, 26-foot canoe like those paddled on the Pigeon and other fast-flowing interior rivers.

The Grand Portage is now popular for hiking in the summer months, and also in the autumn when the vibrant colors of foliage set the woods ablaze. It is increasingly popular, as well, for cross-country skiing and snow-shoeing on crisp winter days. Hikers on the Grand Portage may be fortunate to experience the thrill of seeing a gray wolf. Or perhaps a moose, whitetail deer, lynx, bobcat, red or gray fox, wolverine, fisher, marten, mink, river otter, weasel, beaver, raccoon, porcupine, snowshoe hare, or striped skunk.

Among the many species of birds that live in or migrate through the Grand Portage area are common loons; great blue herons; Canada geese, mergansers, and other waterfowl; woodcock and snipe; bald eagles and ospreys; ruffed grouse; great horned, sawwhet, and other owls; pileated, three-toed, and other woodpeckers; blue and gray jays; winter wrens; hermit and Swainson's thrushes and veeries; numerous warblers including the blackburnian, magnolia, black-throated blue and black-throated green, Canada, parula, ovenbird, and American redstart; rose-breasted grosbeaks; white-throated sparrows; crossbills; and purple finches.

Trees of the Grand Portage area include white, red, and jack pines; tamarack (larch); white and black spruces; balsam fir; white cedar; yellow and paper birches; quaking and bigtooth aspens; mountain ash; and red and mountain maples.

A half-mile path leads to the 300-foot summit of Mount Rose, from which visitors look directly down to the stockade and across Grand Portage Bay to Grand Portage Island and the open waters of Lake Superior beyond. During spring and autumn migrations, this summit affords visitors a good opportunity to see many kinds of birds.

Guides, wearing costumes representative of the late eighteenth century, help interpret the area's history, while an annual gathering reenacts the historic fur-traders' rendezvous that were held here for nearly a quarter century. The stockade area is open from mid-May to mid-October. Exhibits and interpretive programs are provided in the Great Hall. There are picnic facilities near the parking area, and a primitive campsite is located at the Fort Charlotte area, for which advance reservations are required.

An informative book on the area's history is *The Grand Portage Story* by Carolyn Gilman, and published by the Minnesota Historical Society.

IF YOU GO: Lodging and meals are available at the Ojibway-owned Grand Portage Lodge (camping facilities also available), just southwest of the monument, as well as in Grand Marais, Minnesota, and Thunder Bay, Ontario, Canada. Access to the monument's stockade area is 36 miles northeast of Grand Marais by way of State Route 61, or 43 miles southwest of Thunder

Bay by way of Ontario Route 61 and State Route 61. Summer ferry service is offered from the boat dock in the monument, out 22 miles to Isle Royale National Park. Further information: Superintendent, P.O. Box 668, Grand Marais, MN 55604. Telephone (218) 387-2788.

GRANT-KOHRS RANCH NATIONAL HISTORIC SITE

GRANT-KOHRS RANCH NATIONAL HISTORIC SITE, containing 1,498 acres in Deer Lodge Valley of western Montana, was established in 1972 to commemorate the nation's frontier cattle era and to protect and interpret the historic Grant-Kohrs Ranch.

By 1860, within a decade of being in the cattle business, Canadian trader John Grant had amassed a sizable herd of cattle largely acquired through his trade with Oregon Trail emigrants. In 1862, he moved his ranching headquarters close to the town of Deer Lodge and constructed a large, two-story home for his Bannock Indian wife, Quarra, and their seven children. One newspaper described the Grant house as "the finest" in Montana.

Four years later, Grant sold the ranch to German-born Conrad Kohrs. Previously a prospector, Kohrs then became a butcher and learned the cattle business by selling beef to mining camps in the region. In 1868, Kohrs courted and married 19-year-old Augusta Kruse, while visiting relatives in Iowa. She took over running the home—everything from cooking and cleaning, to milking the cows and making candles and soap—in addition to raising their three children.

Kohrs' partner was his half-brother, John Bielenberg, who ran the day-to-day ranching activities. This left Kohrs free to handle the business end of the operation. At the peak of their cattle empire, the herds totaled some 90,000 head scattered across ten million acres of open range in Montana, Idaho, Wyoming, Colorado, and Canada. In the 1870s and 1880s, herd quality was improved through the introduction of registered Herefords and Shorthorns.

The expanding ranch headquarters reflected the cattlemen's success. Kohrs added a brick wing to the original Grant house in 1890. A number of structures were added over the years, including barns, a bunkhouse, blacksmith shop, icehouse, and granary.

Kohrs also went into partnership with other ranchers, and diversified by investing his profits in real estate, acquisition of prized water rights, and mining ventures. The crippling winter of 1886–1887 wiped out many northern-plains ranchers. While Kohrs suffered losses, his Deer Valley herds were virtually intact. His recovery was aided by reduced competition for rangeland. The pivotal killing winter also helped transform the cattle industry from its traditional open-range, high-impact nomadic grazing system to a more environmentally disciplined approach. In the meantime, the home ranch grew to 25,000 acres

Sitting room, Grant-Kohrs Ranch National Historic Site, Montana [NPS]

and became a major center for cattle breeding, with up to 10,000 head shipped by rail annually to Chicago's stockyards.

By the second decade of the twentieth century, the once open range of the region was largely fenced by farming homesteaders. By the early 1920s, the ranch had been reduced to about 1,000 acres. In the 1930s, Kohrs' grandson, Conrad Kohrs Warren, began managing the operation, and by the early 1940s was breeding Hereford cattle and Belgian horses.

Conrad Kohrs died in 1920, but his widow, Augusta, lived on to the age of 96. Throughout her long life, she enjoyed being involved with keeping up the ranch. After her death in 1945, Conrad Warren and his wife, Nell, painstakingly preserved the historic ranch buildings, furnishings, and documents.

Today, visitors to Grant-Kohrs Ranch see the evolving cattle industry reflected in its historic landscape and structures: the ranch house and its furnishings; bunkhouse row that once housed the ranch hands and cowboys; the array of barns; buggy shed; blacksmith shop; ice house (subsequently used as the tack room); chicken coop; and feed sheds. Visitors may also see cattle grazing and draft horses working in the tradition of ranchers Grant, Kohrs, Bielenberg, and Warren.

There are ranger-led tours of the ranch house, self-guiding walks around the ranch headquarters complex, and a visitor center with exhibits and a bookstore. Blacksmithing and other living-history demonstrations occur in summer, as staffing permits. The site also offers Cottonwood Creek Trail, a mile-long, self-guiding route where visitors can learn about the natural environment of the ranch, including the riparian habitat.

Of the many books on the cattle industry, especially informative are *The Cowboys* and *The Ranchers*, two volumes in a series on the West by Time-Life Books; *The Trampling Herd*, by Paul Wellman (University of Nebraska Press); *The Range*, by Sherm Ewing (Mountain Press); *The Cattle Kings*, by L.

Atherton (University of Nebraska Press); *We Pointed Them North*, by E. C. Abbott (University of Oklahoma Press); *Free Grass to Fences*, by Robert Fletcher (University Publishers, Inc., for the Historical Society of Montana); and two books relating to the Grant-Kohrs Ranch: *Very Close to Trouble* (lengthy memoirs), by John Francis Grant (Washington State University Press); and *An Autobiography*, by Conrad Kohrs (Platen Press, Deer Lodge).

IF YOU GO: Grant-Kohrs Ranch National Historic Site is a day-use area. While there are no facilities for camping or picnicking on the ranch, both are available nearby, including picnic facilities in the city park. Contact the national historic site for further information on these facilities, as well as on lodging and meals in the surrounding area. The ranch is accessible by either of two Deer Lodge exits off I-90. The ranch is at the north end of town. The site is open daily, except on Thanksgiving, Christmas, and New Year's Day. Further information: Superintendent, P.O. Box 790, Deer Lodge, MT 59722. Telephone (406) 846-3388.

HAMILTON GRANGE NATIONAL MEMORIAL

HAMILTON GRANGE NATIONAL MEMORIAL consists of one-tenth of an acre at 287 Convent Avenue, at 141st Street, in New York City. It was authorized in 1962 to protect and interpret the home of Alexander Hamilton (1755 to 1804), the first Secretary of the Treasury, in the administration of President George Washington.

At this writing (1996), Hamilton Grange is closed while renovations are being carried out. For information on reopening and visitation: Telephone (212) 264-4456.

Regarding access to the national memorial, the National Park Service recommends public transportation—the 8th Avenue IND express subway to the West 145th Street stop, or the A, B, C, or D subway to West 145th Street. Buses also run close to the site: the Convent Avenue bus #3 to 142nd and the Broadway bus #4 to West 145th. Further information: Superintendent, Hamilton Grange National Memorial, 287 Convent Ave., New York, NY 10031. Telephone (212) 283-5154.

HARPERS FERRY NATIONAL HISTORICAL PARK

HARPERS FERRY NATIONAL HISTORICAL PARK, consisting of approximately 2,300 acres in several units around the confluence of the Potomac and Shenandoah rivers, in West Virginia, Virginia, and Maryland, was established as a national monument in 1944 and changed to a national historical park in 1963. Among the themes running through Harpers Ferry's history are transportation, industry, the Civil War, and African-American history. Ever present is the magnificent landscape of rivers and mountains that

Thomas Jefferson once described as "perhaps one of the most stupendous scenes in Nature." When the mantle of forest covering the mountains and river valleys is transformed to the yellow and gold of autumn foliage, it is then an especially magical landscape.

Harpers Ferry was named for Robert Harper, who in 1747 moved from Philadelphia, expanded an existing ferry service, and built a gristmill at what became Harpers Ferry. In 1796, President George Washington helped persuade the U.S. Congress to construct a national armory and arsenal at Harpers Ferry. By 1810, the federal government was producing 10,000 rifles and muskets annually. During the five decades up to the start of the Civil War, the facility manufactured more than 600,000 rifles, muskets, and pistols.

For many centuries, Indians had used this water gap through the mountains, followed by early explorers and settlers heading into the uncharted wilderness to the west. Major east-west transportation facilities were then sliced through the strategic gap. In 1828, construction of both the Chesapeake & Ohio Canal and the Baltimore & Ohio Railroad was begun (see Chesapeake & Ohio Canal National Historical Park). The canal was built along the Maryland shore of the Potomac River, passing opposite Harpers Ferry on its 184.5-mile route between Washington, D.C., and Cumberland, Maryland. The railroad crossed a bridge from Maryland to Harpers Ferry, on its way to the Ohio River region. Another railroad, the Winchester & Potomac, was built along the west bank of the Shenandoah River, through Harpers Ferry, and connecting with the B & O line. The railroads greatly enhanced the

Harpers Ferry National Historical Park [Larry Ulrich]

growth and importance of Harpers Ferry as a prosperous industrial center, but coal smoke from the factories, armory, and homes filled the river valley air.

Far more serious, however, was an event that occurred on the evening of October 16, 1859, when abolitionist John Brown set out on a mission to free the black slaves in the southern states. To obtain 100,000 muskets and rifles, he and 20 supporters, calling themselves the "army of liberation," seized the federal armory. A local militia and a contingent of U.S. Marines, led by Lt. Col. Robert E. Lee, were quickly dispatched. Only 36 hours after the raid began, most of Brown's men were either dead or wounded. The Marines stormed the old armory fire engine station, now called "John Brown's Fort," capturing Brown and several others. Brown was brought to trial, found guilty of treason, and was hanged on December 2, 1859. The national attention that focused on Brown's trial and execution heightened the polarization of public opinion on the moral question of slavery, and helped push the United States toward the Civil War.

Harpers Ferry was in the thick of the Civil War. Its strategic location on key railroad routes and at an important junction between the North and South assured that the town would be coveted by both Union and Confederate forces. Harpers Ferry was in Virginia at the beginning of the Civil War. Just a few hours after Virginia seceded from the Union—in April 1861 to join the Confederacy—U.S. troops set fire to the federal armory, rather than let it fall into the hands of the Confederates. While the arsenal's 15,000 weapons went up in smoke, the Confederates did succeed in putting out the flames at the armory. The equipment for manufacturing weapons was moved to the Confederate capital of Richmond and was used to produce firearms for the Confederacy. When Confederate forces abandoned Harpers Ferry later that year, they destroyed most of the factories and mills, and dynamited the railroad bridge across the Potomac.

During the course of the war, Harpers Ferry changed hands eight times. In 1862, U.S. troops established a military base of operations for penetrating southward into the Shenandoah Valley. In September 1862, when Confederate forces first invaded the North into Maryland, they captured a 12,500-member Union garrison at Harpers Ferry—the largest surrender of Union troops during the Civil War. When Union troops again took over the town, after their victory at the Battle of Antietam (see Antietam National Battlefield), they started constructing fortifications on the surrounding hills to offer protection for the town and railroad. And in 1864 (with West Virginia created as a new northern state on June 20, 1863), Union troops again used Harpers Ferry as a base from which to launch military strikes against the Confederates in the Shenandoah Valley.

During the Civil War, Harpers Ferry became one of a number of Union garrison towns where runaway slaves from the South sought a safe haven. In 1864, a school was started to help educate former slaves. In 1867, just two years after the end of the Civil War, Storer Normal School (later Storer College) was founded at Harpers Ferry to further help these freedmen.

In 1881, former slave and respected journalist and Storer College trustee, Frederick Douglass (see Frederick Douglass National Historic Site), spoke about John Brown at the college. Douglass extolled Brown as a martyr to the cause of liberty. Storer College operated for 88 years. It was closed in 1955, following the landmark U.S. Supreme Court desegregation decision of *Brown v. Board of Education*, a year after legal segregation finally ended. Part of the former college campus is now used as a National Park Service training facility.

Among the park's highlights are the restored buildings of Lower Town, including Harper House, the town's oldest building. A three-to-six-hour ranger-led tour, available during the spring, summer, and fall, includes interpretive programs and exhibits; the ruins of the nineteenth-century industrial center ("Virginius Island") along the banks of the Shenandoah River (a one-to-two-hour tour); the old federal armory buildings restored for use by Storer College (a one to two-hour tour); onto Bolivar Heights, just west of Harpers Ferry (one-to-two hours); a scenic hike on the Appalachian Trail on the Virginia side of the Shenandoah River (three to five hours); and up to Maryland Heights across the Potomac from Harpers Ferry (three to six hours; a rock-climbing permit is required from the Park Service).

IF YOU GO: The park provides a visitor center just off U.S. Route 340 and shuttle buses that take visitors to the Lower Town District. A bookshop, operated by the Harpers Ferry Historical Association, carries titles on all park themes. Lodging and meals are available at Harpers Ferry and other towns in the vicinity. Access is by way of U.S. Route 340, between Frederick, MD, and Charles Town, WV. Further information: Superintendent, P.O. Box 65, Harpers Ferry, WV 25425. Telephone (304) 535-6029.

HOMESTEAD NATIONAL MONUMENT OF AMERICA

HOMESTEAD NATIONAL MONUMENT OF AMERICA comprises 195 acres along meandering Cub Creek, in the farming country of southeastern Nebraska. It was established in 1936 to protect the Daniel and Agnes Freeman land claim—among the first applicants for 160 acres under the 1862 Homestead Act. The monument also commemorates all those people who courageously pioneered in the settlement of the Great Plains and western frontier.

The Homestead Act provided that any citizen or any immigrant intending to become a U.S. citizen could claim 160 acres of government land, with the stipulation that the person claiming the land must make improvements by building a home and planting crops. If, after five years, the original claimant was still occupying the land, it was then his, free and clear. Between 1863 and 1935, more than 275 million acres of public domain lands were deeded over to homesteaders.

Nothing remains of the original Freeman family buildings, where six sons and two daughters were raised. However, the monument does feature the Palmer-Epard log-and-chink cabin, located near the visitor center. It was built

Homestead National Monument of America, Nebraska [NPS]

in 1867, was moved several miles from a nearby homestead, and is typical of frontier dwellings of eastern Nebraska. It contains furnishings, fixtures, and tools representative of the 1880s. The one-room, red-brick Freeman schoolhouse, dating from 1872, is within a nearby separate unit of the monument.

Among informative books are *Sod Walls* by Roger Welsch (J & L Lee Company); *Where the Prairie Began: land of the tallgrass prairie*, by John Madson (Houghton Mifflin); *Pioneer Women* by Joanna L. Stratton (Simon & Schuster); and *Soloman D. Butcher, Photographing the American Dream* by John E. Carter (University of Nebraska Press). And for children, there are *Rough and Ready Homesteaders* by A. S. Gintzler (W. W. Norton); and *Seasons of the Tallgrass Prairie* by Carol Lerner (William Morrow).

From the visitor center, a 2.5-mile self-guiding trail loops by the sites of the Freeman cabin and the brick house that was built by the Freemans in 1876. A longer trail follows a wooded stretch of Cub Creek, then swings through a beautiful, 100-acre expanse of restored tallgrass prairie edged by a hedgerow of osage orange, and passes the Freeman family cemetery. Visitors are urged to be alert for ticks and poison ivy.

IF YOU GO: The visitor center provides interpretive programs, publications, and exhibits of artifacts and historic photographs. Guided walks and living-history demonstrations are offered during the summer months. Camping is not allowed, but the monument provides a small picnic area near the visitor center. Lodging and meals are available in Beatrice and Lincoln. Access to the monument is 40 miles south of Lincoln, by way of U.S. Route 77 to Beatrice, then 4.5 miles west on State Route 4 to the monument entrance. Further information: Superintendent, Route 3, Box 47, Beatrice, NE 68310. Telephone (402) 223-3514.

HUBBELL TRADING POST NATIONAL HISTORIC SITE

HUBBELL TRADING POST NATIONAL HISTORIC SITE, consisting of the 160-acre Hubbell homestead near Ganado, surrounded by the Navajo Reservation in northeastern Arizona, was established in 1967. It protects the historic, long-popular trading post built by John Lorenzo Hubbell in 1883.

Don Lorenzo, as he was respectfully called, not only provided food and other basic merchandise in trade with the Navajos for such things as blankets and jewelry, but he did everything he could to promote their best interests and welfare. As an honest and deeply caring trader, he enthusiastically and successfully encouraged the revival of excellence in Navajo arts and crafts—notably in the weaving of beautiful traditional wool blankets and rugs (such as the Two Grey Hills, Crystal, Ganado, Wide Ruin, and Chinle styles)—and in the making of silver jewelry.

Hubbell Trading Post was also an important cultural meeting place where mutual understandings and trust between the Navajo and the Anglo were nurtured. Hubbell was a healing, reaching-out kind of person who earned the trust of the Navajo people. And this trading post was a healing place that enhanced many lives.

Hubbell married Lina Rubi, and they raised two daughters and two sons. When John Hubbell died in 1930, his youngest son, Ramon, and daughter-in-law, Dorothy, continued to run the post. Today, as a national historic site, the operation continues essentially as in the past, offering for sale or trade many of the same kinds of merchandise—from canned foods to horseback-riding equipment, and offering for sale the high-quality Navajo rugs and Navajo, Zuni, and Hopi jewelry.

Hubbell Trading Post, Arizona [Russ Butcher]

The site protects the stone trading post building; the Hubbell family's New Mexico-style adobe home built in 1901; a small stone hogan built in 1934 in honor of Hubbell; and barns and corrals that recall the days when the post was served by horse-drawn wagons, wagon-drivers, blacksmiths, cooks, and gardeners.

An informative publication is *Hubbell Trading Post National Historic Site* by David M. Brugge (Southwest Parks and Monuments Association).

The site's visitor center provides interpretive exhibits, publications, and weaving and silversmithing demonstrations. There are guided tours of the Hubbell home, as well as a self-guiding tour of the homestead property. Picnicking is permitted, but camping is not. Lodging and meals are available in Chinle, Window Rock, and Chambers, and additional accommodations are available in Holbrook, Arizona, and Gallup, New Mexico.

Site hours are from 8 a.m. to 6 p.m. from June to September, and until 5 p.m. from October to May. Unlike the majority of Arizona, the Navajo Reservation switches to daylight savings time from early April to late October. The site is closed on Thanksgiving, Christmas, and New Year's Day.

IF YOU GO: Access to Hubbell Trading Post is from several directions across the Navajo Reservation. From I-40 the most direct route is from the Chambers exit, 44 miles north on U.S. Route 191 to Ganado and less than one mile west on State Route 264. From I-40 at Gallup, NM, it is 7 miles north on U.S. Route 666, then 48 miles west on New Mexico and Arizona Route 264. From Chinle, near Canyon de Chelly National Monument, it is 36 miles south on U.S. Route 191 and a mile east on Route 264. Further information: Superintendent, P.O. Box 150, Ganado, AZ 86505. Telephone (520) 755-3475.

INDEPENDENCE NATIONAL HISTORICAL PARK

INDEPENDENCE NATIONAL HISTORICAL PARK comprises 44 acres of sites mostly in downtown Philadelphia, Pennsylvania. It was established in 1948 and protects 26 properties associated with the American Revolution and the founding and early development of the United States of America. They include Independence Hall, Congress Hall, Old City Hall, First Bank of the United States, Liberty Bell Pavilion, Carpenters' Hall, Declaration House, City Tavern, Library Hall, Franklin Court, Philosophical Hall, Christ Church, Free Quaker Meeting House, St. George's Church, St. Joseph's Church, Mikveh Israel Cemetery, Second Bank of the United States, New Hall Military Museum, Todd House, Bishop White House, and in Germantown, Pennsylvania, the Deshler Morris House. Independence Hall was designated as a World Heritage Site by the United Nations in 1979.

As the National Park Service says in its interpretive handbook, *Independence*, this park "is perhaps the most significant historical property in the United States—and also one of the most complex." Writing in this same publication, historian Carl Van Doren says:

In the last quarter of the 18th century, Philadelphia was the center of some of the most creative and far-reaching political thought of the modern world. Here, within the space of a few square blocks, in buildings still standing in their original splendor, Americans cast off ancient colonial ties, directed the course of a long and uncertain war to secure their liberties, and instituted a form of government adapted to the new needs of a rising people.

The sense of what John Adams called "this mighty Revolution" is still a presence in the buildings and sites of Independence National Historical Park. The Liberty Bell is a symbol known around the world. Independence Hall, where two great charters of national destiny were adopted, is a shrine to the principles of human rights and self-government.

Independence Hall (on Chestnut Street between 5th & 6th) was planned by a lawyer and speaker of the Pennsylvania Assembly, Andrew Hamilton, and was built under the direction of master carpenter Edmund Woolley, from 1732 to 1748. The original tower was added in the early 1750s, but by 1773, it had rotted so dangerously that it was taken down and replaced by a much shorter and less imposing one. The present tall tower was erected in 1828 and is similar to the original.

This building became the centerpiece of a governmental center. It is valued as an outstanding example of symmetrical, red brick, Georgian-style architecture. The white-steepled structure served initially as the colonial State House of the Province of Pennsylvania. Except for a brief occupancy by the British in 1777-1778, it housed the Second Continental Congress from 1775 to 1783. In 1775, in the building's Assembly Room, George Washington was appointed commander-in-chief of the Continental Army. And here, the Declaration of Independence was adopted on July 4, 1776. In part, this historic document established that:

We hold these truths to be self-evident, that all men are created equal, that they are endowed by their Creator with certain unalienable Rights, that among these are Life, Liberty and the pursuit of Happiness. That to secure these rights, Governments are instituted among Men, deriving their just powers from the consent of the governed, That whenever any Form of Government becomes destructive of these ends, it is the Right of the People to alter or to abolish it, and to institute new Government, laying its foundation on such principles and organizing its powers in such form, as to them shall seem most likely to effect their Safety and Happiness. Prudence, indeed, will dictate that Governments long established should not be changed for light and transient causes; and accordingly all experience hath shown, that mankind are more disposed to suffer, while evils are sufferable, than to right themselves by abolishing the forms to which they are accustomed. But when a long train of abuses and usurpations, pursuing invariably the same Object evinces a design to reduce them under absolute Despotism, it is the right, it is their duty, to throw off such Government, and to provide new Guards for their future security.— Such has been the patient sufferance of these Colonies; and such is now the necessity which constrains them to alter their former Systems of Government. . . .

We, therefore, the Representatives of the united States of America, in General Congress, Assembled, . . . do, in the Name, and by Authority of the good People of these colonies, solemnly publish and declare, That these United Colonies are, and of Right ought to be Free and Independent States, that they are Absolved from all Allegiance to the British Crown, and that all political connection between them and the State of Great Britain, is and ought to be totally dissolved. . . .

In 1777, the stars-and-stripes design of the United States flag was chosen in the same Assembly Room. It was here, as well, that the 55-member Constitutional Convention hammered out the United States Consti-tution in the summer of 1787. As set forth in the document's Preamble, the goal of the convention was "to form a more perfect Union," secure peace among the states, and provide for the nation's defense against foreign enemies by establishing a sufficiently strong central government. The delegates disagreed over just how strong that national government should actually be and how much authority the states should retain. There were lengthy and sometimes bitter debates concerning many complex issues over establishing the framework and guidelines for this new government. But through the exchange of ideas and with compromises that are the hallmark of the democratic pro-cess, the delegates gradually achieved a blending of a strong central government and a confederation of the states that retained to themselves much of their own governmental authority. Fortunately, the language of the Constitution was carefully crafted so as to be flexible and adaptable to changing needs and circumstances through time. The convention's four months of grueling work finally was concluded on September 17, 1787, when "By unanimous consent of the States present," the Constitution was signed. After the required nine states ratified the landmark document, Congress declared the start of the new national government on March 4, 1789.

IF YOU GO: Independence Hall is open only for official National Park Service-led tours, and they are provided on a first-come, first-served basis.

Behind Independence Hall is **Independence Square**, where on July 8, 1776, four days after its official approval, the Declaration of Independence

Independence Hall, Philadelphia [David Muench]

was first read in public. Each year, the Park Service celebrates this great event by presenting a commemoration of the public reading on July 8. The annual event includes participants in colonial dress.]

Flanking Independence Hall are two nearly identical red brick, Georgian-style buildings: **Congress Hall** was completed in 1789 and was built originally to accommodate the Philadelphia County Court House. When Philadelphia became the temporary national capital of the United States, the new Congress convened here from 1790 to 1800. In 1790, the 65-member House of Representatives met on the first floor, while the 26-member Senate met on the floor above, with membership increasing as the country grew.

While Congress was based here, it established the Bank of the United States to hold the government's funds, collect taxes, issue bank notes, and provide for a stable currency and bank credit for the new nation. This bank existed for 20 years (1791–1811) and initially occupied Carpenters' Hall before moving into its own **First Bank of the United States** building, an imposing neoclassical edifice (on 3rd Street between Chestnut and Walnut). It was also during this decade in Philadelphia that Congress admitted three new states to the Union—Vermont, Kentucky, and Tennessee—and established many basic legislative powers and procedures. These included setting a balance of powers between the legislative and executive branches of the federal government and establishing a system of legislative committees. The latter has proven to be vital in drafting legislation and holding public hearings, in which differing public opinions can be heard. To resolve differences between House and Senate versions of bills, conference committees were formed of members from each chamber.

As for the **Old City Hall** that was completed in 1791, the municipal government provided space for the U.S. Supreme Court, from 1791 to 1800. It was here that the court handed down its earliest decisions, some of which helped to define the powers of the new national government as they relate to the states' authority.

Carpenters' Hall is another red-brick, Georgian-style structure near Independence Hall (320 Chestnut Street), dating from 1770. It was built by the Carpenters' Company of Philadelphia not only to house the company operations and provide assistance to up-and-coming carpenters, but to demonstrate the excellent craftsmanship that its guild members were capable of producing. The First Continental Congress met in this building in the autumn of 1774, to air the American colonies' grievances against Britain and to adopt a "Declaration of Rights." This document reviewed a number of oppressive acts by the British Parliament since 1763 that had been constraining American freedoms and rights, and it then listed a number of fundamental rights of the British colonies in America. The Continental Congress also adopted a prohibition against the trade of goods with Britain, acts that ultimately helped set the stage for full independence less than two years later.

On June 7, 1776, the Second Continental Congress, meeting in the Assembly Room of the Pennsylvania State House (now Independence Hall), began to consider several resolutions that called for outright independence of the colonies from Britain. It called for the formation of alliances with other nations to help protect the independence of the American states, and for the creation of a confederation of the united colonies under a governing constitution. Congressional committees were formed to study and debate these resolutions and prepare responses for consideration by the full Congress. Since Thomas Jefferson had already demonstrated great wisdom and a special proficiency in the use of the language, he, at the age of only 33, was chosen to draft a declaration of independence. While preparing this document, he was living on the second floor of a red brick house (at 7th and Market streets), then owned by Jacob Graff, Jr., and now called **Declaration House**.

City Tavern (at Walnut and 2nd streets), originally built in 1773, was a popular gathering place for members of the First and Second Continental Congresses, the Constitutional Convention, and for U.S. governmental officials during the 1790s. The present structure is a reconstruction and provides a tavern that is open daily for lunch and dinner.

Library Hall (at 105 South 5th) was originally built in 1789 and 1790 by the Library Company of Philadelphia, and is the oldest subscription library in America. Members of the First and Second Continental Congresses, the Constitutional Convention, and U.S. Congress used the facility. The present larger library building was completed in 1959 and is open for scholarly research.

Franklin Court (Market Street between 3rd and 4th Streets), near Independence Hall, includes the site of Benjamin Franklin's home that was built in the 1760s. This illustrious gentleman lived here while serving as a member of the Continental Congress and the Constitutional Convention. In addition, he was an internationally known scientist, philosopher, inventor, journalist, printer-publisher, musician, and distinguished statesman. Twenty years after his death in 1790, the Franklin house was demolished. Artistically arranged steel beams now outline where the house once stood.

The Liberty Bell Pavilion (on Market Street between 5th and 6th) contains the cherished emblem of American freedom. A bell that was cast in London, England, in 1751, possibly to celebrate the 50th anniversary of Pennsylvania colony's democratic constitution, known as the "Charter of Privileges," cracked beyond repair upon its first public ringing. A second bell was cast from the first bell and was hung in the tower of the Pennsylvania State House (Independence Hall). It was rung on numerous special occasions for many years, but it, too, developed a crack. In 1846, the crack extended beyond repair. Prior to the Civil War, the abolitionist movement adopted the bell as a symbol for their cause, calling it the Liberty Bell due to its association with the Declaration of Independence and the Biblical verse around its crown. In 1976, at the beginning of the national Bicentennial celebrations marking the independence of the United States, the great bell was moved from Independence Hall to a pavilion nearby. There, visitors may see this powerful symbol and read the Old Testament inscription: "Proclaim LIBERTY throughout all the Land unto all the Inhabitants thereof."

Several sites of the national historical park celebrate the religious diversity, freedom, and tolerance of the "City of Brotherly Love." **Christ Church** (at 2nd and Market streets), completed in 1754 with the addition of its 200-foot white steeple, is viewed as one of the most beautiful eighteenth-century colonial buildings in the country. Among its early members were George Washington and Benjamin Franklin. The red brick **Free Quaker Meeting House** (at Arch and 5th streets) was completed in 1783 and is now the headquarters of the Junior League of Philadelphia. The red brick **St. George's Church** (at 235 North 4th), dating from 1769, is the oldest United Methodist Church building in continuous use in America. Richard Allen, the first black man licensed to preach in a Methodist church, preached here in the late eighteenth century. **St. Joseph's Church** (its site is near 4th and Walnut streets) was founded in 1733 as the first Roman Catholic Church in Philadelphia. And **Mikveh Israel Cemetery** (on Spruce Street between 8th & 9th) was deeded to the only Jewish synagogue that functioned in the colonies during the American Revolution.

Philosophical Hall (at 104 South 5th) is owned by the American Philosophical Society, which was founded by Benjamin Franklin in 1743. The building dates from the late 1780s, and is not open to the public.

Second Bank of the United States (on Chestnut Street between 4th & 5th) was completed in 1824 and is an outstanding example of Greek-Revival architecture. It housed one of the world's major banking institutions of its time. The bank operated under a charter from the federal government, but when President Andrew Jackson vetoed legislation to renew its charter in 1836, it ceased to exist. The majestic building now contains the park's Portrait

Gallery, which includes a large collection of paintings, many by Charles Willson Peale, of colonial and early national governmental leaders.

New Hall Military Museum (in Carpenters' Court, 320 Chestnut Street), a reconstruction of the building where the country's first War Department convened, explores the founding of the Army, Navy, and Marine Corps of the United States.

Among the array of excellent and informative publications on this park and its priceless historical heritage are: *Independence: A Guide to Independence National Historical Park* (National Park Service handbook 115); *Independence National Historical Park: The Story Behind the Scenery®* by Ronald Bruce Thomson (KC Publications); and *Starting America: The Story of Independence Hall,* by Edward M. Riley.

IF YOU GO: The park's visitor center is located at Chestnut and 3rd streets in downtown Philadelphia and is open daily, It provides interpretive exhibits, programs, orientation, and publications. Lodging and meals are available in and around the downtown area. The park's parking garage is located on 2nd Street, between Walnut and Chestnut streets. Further information: Superintendent, 313 Walnut Street, Philadelphia, PA 19106. Telephone (215) 597-8974.

JEAN LAFITTE NATIONAL HISTORICAL PARK & PRESERVE

JEAN LAFITTE NATIONAL HISTORICAL PARK & PRESERVE, consisting of 20,020 acres in four major units in southern Louisiana, protects and interprets significant aspects of human and natural history of Louisiana's Mississippi River Delta region. The units are the New Orleans Unit (the French Quarter), Chalmette Battlefield, Barataria Preserve, and the Acadian Unit, with its three (Cajun) cultural centers.

The park is named for a mysterious Frenchman who came to the French Louisiana colonial territory with his brother, Pierre, around 1802 and was apparently a French privateer and slave trader who preyed upon enemy shipping. With other "Baratarians," he allegedly carried on smuggling of contraband from the Gulf of Mexico, through the Barataria swamplands to New Orleans. He subsequently aided the United States as a guide and advisor during the War of 1812. After the American victory in 1815 prevented the British capture of New Orleans, Lafitte was considered by some an American patriot. Little factual information is actually known about Lafitte, but his legend lives on in the delta.

The **New Orleans Unit** celebrates the rich cultural history of New Orleans. The city was founded in 1718 by Jean Baptiste LeMoyne, the first governor of France's vast colonial territory of Louisiana. This new French commercial and military outpost was named for Philippe II, the *duc d'Orleans*, and an 85-block city grid was platted for future development. The Vieux Carré, measuring approximately one mile by a half-mile, is now a national historic district. It contains buildings dating from the French and Spanish rule. Fronting on the Mississippi River is the four-block-long French Market. At 916 N. Peters Street is the park unit's visitor center where exhibits help interpret the cultural diversity and history of New Orleans and Louisiana's Mississippi Delta region. Musical performances and craft, art, and cooking demonstrations are featured. Ranger-led walking tours of the French Quarter and Garden District are available. Tours provided daily except on Mardi Gras and Christmas are on a first-come, first-served basis, and passes must be picked up in person on the day of the tour.

Although most of the earliest buildings of the French Quarter were destroyed in fires in 1788 and 1794, the city building codes required brick and stucco façades in what became the Creole style of architecture—combining the French inner courtyard with the distinctive Spanish-style iron grill-work balconies, known as galleries.

Jean Lafitte National Historical Park, Louisiana [NPS]

Among the quarter's most important historic structures are the triple-spired Saint Louis Cathedral, dating from 1794, with major changes in 1851; the Cabildo that once housed the Spanish colonial government; and the Presbytère that formerly served as a courthouse. The latter two similar buildings date from 1795 and have Spanish-style arcades and French mansard roofs. The Cabildo was heavily damaged by fire in 1988. The Presbytère contains some of the Louisiana State Museum.

Elsewhere in the quarter are famous Bourbon and St. Peter streets, which have long been a major focus of all-night jazz—a rhythmically soulful musical heritage dating back to the late nineteenth century and typically featuring the trumpet, trombone, saxophone, clarinet, and percussion instruments.

The park's **Chalmette Unit** celebrates the greatest victory on land of the United States over Britain in the War of 1812. The Battle of New Orleans pitted some 9,000 well-trained veteran British soldiers against only 5,000 American militia and volunteers under Major General Andrew Jackson. While the British objectives in the war had been to successfully challenge America's maritime rights and block the westward expansion of the United States, the outcome was British defeat. The Battle of New Orleans was the last battle of the war, and was actually fought after the Treaty of Ghent had already been signed, though not yet ratified. While 2,000 British troops were killed, only 13 Americans lost their lives in the fight that culminated in a last, desperate British attack of less than two hours' duration. The main thrust lasted a mere 30 minutes, on January 8, 1815.

The Chalmette Unit was initially established as Chalmette Monument & Grounds in 1907, under the War Department's administration; was transferred to the National Park Service in 1933; became a national historical park in 1939; and was incorporated into Jean Lafitte National Historical Park & Preserve in 1978. The Chalmette Monument, completed in 1908, is an obelisk honoring the American victory on this battlefield. Another highlight of the park unit is the elegant Beauregard House, the French-Louisiana style, Greek-Revival plantation mansion dating from 1833 and named for the last of a number of private owners, Judge René Beauregard. Adjacent to the park unit is the Chalmette National Cemetery, established in 1864.

IF YOU GO: The Chalmette visitor center provides interpretive exhibits, programs, and publications. There is a 1.5-mile tour drive with interpretive pulloffs along the way. A small picnic area is provided, but camping is not permitted. Further information: Unit Manager, Chalmette Unit, St. Bernard Highway, Chalmette, LA. Telephone (504) 589-4430.

The park's **Barataria Preserve Unit** protects approximately 20,000 acres of ecologically rich Mississippi River Delta wetland and forest habitat, including bald cypress swamp, bayou, freshwater marsh, and natural levee hardwood forest. Among the trees and shrubs are great spreading live oaks (*Quercus virginiana*), water oak, bald cypress, palmetto, red bay, swamp bay, red mulberry, wax myrtle, Florida basswood, eastern cottonwood, leatherwood, sparkleberry, Small's acacia, water tupelo, yaupon, red maple, black mangrove, green ash, and button bush. Among the array of wildflowers are the giant blue iris, spiderwort, showy evening primrose, spider lily, and bur marigold.

Mammals include opossums, nine-banded armadillos, swamp rabbits, beavers, muskrats, raccoons, mink, river otters, bobcats, whitetail deer, and gray and flying squirrels. A wild, coyote-like animal that is believed to be a red wolf-coyote hybrid and the non-native nutria also inhabit the preserve.

Among the extensive variety of birds are great blue and green-backed herons; great and snowy egrets; white, glossy, and white-faced ibises; wood and mottled ducks; barred owls; red-bellied and pileated woodpeckers; Carolina chickadees; tufted titmice; Carolina wrens; parula, yellow-throated, prothonotary, and yellowthroat warblers; cardinals; indigo and painted buntings; redwings; and boat-tailed grackles.

Of the 22 kinds of snakes recorded in the preserve, the most commonly encountered venomous species is the cottonmouth, or water moccasin. Other poisonous snakes are the harder-to-see, less aggressive copperhead and two rarely seen rattlesnakes—the canebrake or timber, and pygmy. Other snakes include the speckled kingsnake, broad-banded water snake, ribbon snake, milksnake, and black-masked racer. Turtles, frogs, lizards, and the American alligator also live in the Barataria.

This part of the Mississippi Delta contains evidence of human occupation spanning at least the past 2,000 years. Pre-Columbian Indian village sites along the bayous have been discovered by archaeologists. By the eighteenth century, the Chitimacha Tribe had settled in this region, with perhaps 4,000 people in roughly 15 villages. This tribe has been known for its beautifully woven, intricately patterned black, red, and yellow baskets made from native cane (*piya*).

With the arrival of French colonists, there was a period of conflict with the Indians that ended with the signing of a peace treaty in 1718. The French Acadians began moving into this traditional homeland of the Chitimachas. As in other regions of America, European-borne diseases such as smallpox decimated the Indian population. Today, there are only just over 700 tribal members and a mere 283 acres of tribal reservation land remaining of what was a far more extensive ancestral homeland.

Beginning in 1779, hundreds of *Isleños* from the Spanish Canary Islands settled along the banks of Bayou des Familles, in what is now the preserve. Subsequently, virgin-growth bald cypress and other trees were cut down for lumber and to clear land for the production of sugar cane. Within the preserve today are house sites, canals, roads, and hunting, trapping, and fishing camps.

Barataria Unit's visitor center is located at 7400 Highway 45 in Marrero, Louisiana, and there are 2.5 miles of boardwalk, another 5.5 miles of trails, 9 miles of canoe routes that are closed to motorized boats, and another 20 miles of waterways open to motorized boats. Ranger-led walks and canoe excursions are provided. Moonlight canoe tours are available on the night prior to and night of the full moon. Picnic areas are provided at several locations, but camping is not allowed. In contrast with the ban on public hunting in national parks, hunting and trapping are allowed in the Barataria Preserve during the designated season. A permit is required. For further information on the preserve: Telephone (504) 589-2330.

The park also contains three Acadian cultural centers within the Acadian Unit.

IF YOU GO: The **Acadian Cultural Center**, headquarters for the **Acadian Unit**, located at 501 Fisher Rd., Lafayette, LA (Telephone [318] 232-0789), provides interpretive exhibits, programs, and publications. The Acadian culture, also called the Cajun, traces its roots from the Vendée area near the west coast of France to *Acadie* (Acadia) in 1604 in what is now the Canadian province of Nova Scotia . Thousands of Acadians perished as they were driven from their homes in 1755. In spite of "*Le Grand Derangement*," several thousand survivors successfully reestablished themselves in Louisiana.

The National Park Service describes their culture as "a rich and exciting culture, nurtured through music, food, the Acadian French language, religion, and extended close-knit families."

The other two Acadian centers are: **Wetlands Acadian Cultural Center**, along Bayou Lafourche and St. Mary St. in Thibodaux, LA (Telephone [504] 448-1375), which presents exhibits portraying the lifestyle of Acadians who lived off the swamps, marshes, bayous, and coastal waters by fishing, hunting, and trapping; and **Prairie Acadian Cultural Center**, located at Park Ave. and 3rd St., Eunice, LA (Telephone [318] 262-6862), which depicts the heritage of the grasslands-based Acadians who grazed livestock and raised crops.

The **Chitimacha Cultural Center**, which is affiliated with the national historical park and preserve, is located on the Indian reservation, just off State Route 326, in Charenton, LA. The center exhibits a brief history of the tribe and some of the basketry. Further information: Telephone (318) 923-4830. **Tunica-Biloxi Museum**, in Marksville, LA, contains one of the most extensive collections of American Indian and European artifacts representing the colonial period of this region. The Park Service assists the tribe's operation of the museum. Further information: Telephone (318) 253-8174.

Another affiliated site is the **Isleño Center** in St. Bernard, LA. It interprets the immigration and settlement of Spanish Canary Islanders *(Isleños)* to Louisiana in 1777. Further information: Telephone (504) 682-0862.

Lodging and meals are available in New Orleans, Thibodaux, Lafayette, and other cities and towns in the region.

Access to the park units is as follows:

New Orleans Unit: From the west, exit I-10 at the Vieux Carré exit onto Basin St., left onto Toulouse to enter the French Quarter, and left onto Decatur to the French Market; from the east, exit I-10 at the Vieux Carré exit, turning left onto Orleans at the bottom of the exit ramp; Orleans becomes Basin St., and directions are as above to the French Market. Telephone (504) 589-2636.

Chalmette Unit: From Canal St. in New Orleans, by way of N. Rampart St. that becomes St. Claude Ave. and then St. Bernard Highway (State Route 46); or take the Chalmette exit from I-10 and follow State Route 47 (Paris Rd.) and turn right onto State Route 46 to the park unit. Telephone (504) 589-4428.

Barataria Preserve Unit: From New Orleans, cross the Mississippi on the Greater New Orleans Bridge to the West Bank Expressway (U.S. Route 90), then left on Barataria Blvd. (State Route 45), proceeding seven miles to the preserve entrance. Telephone (504) 589-2330.

Acadian Cultural Center: From the Lafayette exit at I-10, take U.S. Route 90 and then Surrey St. (State Route 728-8) in Lafayette and proceed to 501 Fisher Rd. Telephone (318) 232-0789.

Wetlands Acadian Cultural Center: U.S. Route 90 from New Orleans to Raceland, then State Route 1 to St. Mary St. in Thibodaux. Telephone (504) 448-1375.

Prairie Acadian Cultural Center: North from I-10 Crowley exit on State Route 13 to 250 W. Park Ave. in Eunice. Telephone (318) 262-6862.

IF YOU GO: A unique aspect of Jean Lafitte National Historical Park & Preserve is the presentation of interpretive programs on board AMTRAK trains—the RAILS (Rangers & Amtrak: Interpreting Landscapes of the States) program—twice each week on the *Sunset Limited* and once each week on the *City of New Orleans*, between Memorial Day and Labor Day. Further information: (504) 589-3882. For fares and reservations call Amtrak at 1(800)-USA-RAIL.

Further information on the park & preserve: Superintendent, 365 Canal St., Suite 3080, New Orleans, LA 70130-1142. Telephone (504) 589-3882.

JEFFERSON NATIONAL EXPANSION MEMORIAL

JEFFERSON NATIONAL EXPANSION MEMORIAL, comprising 91 acres on the west bank of the Mississippi River, in St. Louis, Missouri, was established in 1935. It features the 630-foot-tall stainless steel Gateway Arch, designed by the Finnish-American architect, Eero Saarinen, who in 1948 won a widely contested competition with his bold design. The graceful structure was erected from 1963 to 1965, and celebrates the soaring vision of President Thomas Jefferson and others who promoted the westward expansion of the United States.

From an engineering viewpoint, the Gateway Arch is a dynamic expression of structural forces. As the National Park Service explains:

> The Arch traces the lines of a "catenary" curve, the shape a weighted chain assumes when freely suspended between two points. This is an exceptionally sound shape for a standing arch. All the forces of thrust are kept continuously in the center of the legs and transferred directly to the foundations. The legs of the Arch are equilateral triangles, the most rigid geometrical shape in nature. They taper from 54 feet on a side at ground level to 17 feet at the top. This diminishing taper, aside from its aesthetical merit, greatly reduces wind loading and virtually eliminates stresses caused by oscillations. . . . There is a grand clarity to Saarinen's arch, a harnessing of forces to serve the ends of structure and art. Site, purpose, form, and material are fused into one passionate act of homage, linking westering Americans to our own technological age.

Beneath the arch is the underground Museum of Westward Expansion, which artfully presents a wealth of pioneer and native American artifacts, along with paintings, photographs, maps, and the words of those who participated in this epic time of exploration, settlement, and conflict.

Much of the early nineteenth-century expansion was inspired and actively promoted by President Jefferson. For example, his timely action in purchasing the vast Louisiana Territory from France in 1803 doubled the size

Old Courthouse, Jefferson National Expansion Memorial, St. Louis, Missouri [NPS]

of the United States and the Jefferson-dispatched Lewis and Clark Expedition of 1804 to 1806 set forth from St. Louis and reached the Pacific Northwest coast (see Fort Clatsop National Memorial) on an 8,000-mile round-trip trek through the unmapped wilderness. With events such as these, St. Louis quickly became the leading commercial center serving the vast region of the west.

The memorial is situated on the riverfront of downtown St. Louis, and includes the Old Courthouse that dates from 1839 and is topped by a large dome. This building was the setting for the initial Dred Scott trials of 1847 and 1850 that led to the U.S. Supreme Court ruling in 1857 that slaves were not "persons" or citizens, and consequently did not have standing to sue in federal court. The Dred Scott decision said further that slavery could not be restricted in the territories, a decision that increased national tensions and led to the Civil War.

Three informative books are *Jefferson National Expansion Memorial Administrative History, 1935-1980* by Sharon A. Brown (U.S. Government Printing Office); *The Story of the Gateway Arch* (Jefferson National Expansion Historical Association); and *The Dred Scott Case: Its Significance in American Law and Politics* by Don E. Fehrenbacher (Oxford University Press).

IF YOU GO: The memorial also provides a wide-screen theater; and there is a tram system that whisks visitors to the top of the arch for breathtaking panoramas. The memorial is closed on Thanksgiving, Christmas, and New Year's Day. Lodging and meals are available in St. Louis. Further information: Superintendent, 11 N. Fourth St., St. Louis, MO 63102. Telephone (314) 425-4465.

JOHNSTOWN FLOOD NATIONAL MEMORIAL

JOHNSTOWN FLOOD NATIONAL MEMORIAL comprises 164 acres in Saint Michael, Pennsylvania. It was established in 1964 to memorialize the death and destruction caused in Johnstown by a break in the South Fork Dam on May 31, 1889. Following heavy rains on the night of May 30th, the dam broke, unleashing a disastrous flood of 20 million tons of water that devastated this riverside steel company community and killed 2,209 people. Following this flood, the Red Cross, under the leadership of Clara Barton (see Clara Barton National Historic Site), performed its first major disaster relief program in the United States.

The national memorial, which is located 10 miles northeast of Johnstown, has a visitor center providing interpretive exhibits, an audiovisual program, and publications. The Great Flood is commemorated annually with special programs at the end of May. Other programs are offered during the summer. The site is open daily, except on Christmas. It features the historic Unger House, and several interpretive and nature trails, including the South Fork Dam Abutment trails.

IF YOU GO: Picnic facilities are available, but camping is not permitted, Lodging and meals are available in Johnstown and Ebensburg. Access from Johnstown is about 10 miles to the northeast, by way of U.S. Route 219 to the Saint Michael exit, proceeding east 1.5 miles on State Route 869, turning left onto Lake Road, and continuing 1.5 miles to the visitor center, which is on the right. Further information: Superintendent, P.O. Box 355, Saint Michael, PA 15951. Telephone (814) 495-4643.

KALAUPAPA NATIONAL HISTORICAL PARK

KALAUPAPA NATIONAL HISTORICAL PARK encompasses 10,788 acres on the north coast of the Hawaiian island of Moloka'i. It was established in 1980 to protect and interpret the remote Kalaupapa Peninsula and its history as a leper colony, in which more than 7,000 persons suffering from the dread disease of leprosy have been quarantined and treated since 1866.

The native Hawaiians, as with native Americans in general, lacked a natural immunity to a number of Eurasian-borne diseases. One of these was the chronic infectious disease, leprosy, caused by a bacterium (*Mycobacterium leprae*) that tragically attacks the skin, flesh, nervous system, and other parts of the human body. This scourge was first recorded in the Hawaiian population in 1830, apparently originating from China.

By 1865, the disease had become so widespread that a law was enacted under which leprosy victims were dispatched to isolated Kalaupapa Peninsula. Three years later, a Norwegian medical researcher, Armauer Hansen, discovered the bacterium causing what came to be called Hansen's disease. By the 1870s, over a thousand afflicted persons were quarantined at Moloka'i's hideaway. While research continued, no cure could be found and it was still not known how the disease spread from one person to another.

In 1873, a Roman Catholic priest from Belgium, Fr. Damien Joseph de Veuster, arrived to minister to and help improve the living conditions of the colony. Eight years later, at the age of 45, Fr. Damien himself fell victim to Hansen's disease and died four years later. Although drugs have since been discovered to treat this terrifying disease so that victims no longer have to be isolated, there are less than a hundred elderly individuals still living at Kalaupapa. The park is a tribute to the enormous personal courage of Hansen's disease victims and to those, notably Fr. Damien, who have offered their services to help the victims.

In addition to this human history, the park also protects an area of spectacular mountain, valley, and coastal scenery. The peninsula itself is a flat stretch of land in the midst of a rugged landscape, and thus its name, 'Flat Leaf.' Flanking the peninsula are the highest coastal cliffs anywhere in the world.

One way to view the peninsula is from Kalaupapa Overlook, at the brink of a 1,600-foot cliff. This spectacular viewpoint is reached by way of State Route 460 and then 470 (Kalae Highway) to the Kalaupapa Trailhead. There are interpretive panels at this point that explain the history of the leper colony. To actually visit the national historical park, visitors are required to take a guided tour. Access is by airplane, on foot, or by mule. No one under the age of 16 is permitted, and visitors must have a permit obtained in advance from the Hawai'i State Department of Health.

IF YOU GO: The hike into the park and onto the peninsula, on the Pali Trail, takes approximately 1.5 hours from the trailhead. The park offers no lodging or meals. For information on health permits and park tours, prospective visitors should contact Damien Tours, Box 1, Kalaupapa, HI 96742. Telephone (808) 567-6171; or Ike's Scenic tours, c/o Kalaupapa Settlement, Kalaupapa, HI 96742.

An informative publication on the park is *Kalaupapa National Historical Park and the Legacy of Father Damien* by Anwei V. Skinsnes Law and Richard A. Wisniewski (Pacific Basin Enterprises, Honolulu, 1988).

Further information: Superintendent, Kalaupapa National Historical Park, Kalaupapa, HI 96742. Telephone (808) 567-6102.

KALOKO-HONOKOHAU NATIONAL HISTORICAL PARK

KALOKO-HONOKOHAU NATIONAL HISTORICAL PARK consists of 1,156 acres on the Kona Coast of the Big Island of Hawai'i. It was established in 1978 to protect, interpret, and perpetuate the traditional native Hawaiian culture and activities, archaeological and historical sites and land uses, and to protect scenic and ecological values.

This coastal area is largely comprised of expanses of sharply rugged and barren ʻaʻa lava flows dating from over 1,000 years ago. While much of the area appears inhospitable, the early Hawaiians created a thriving community of hundreds of people that derived *mana* (power) from the land and sea and that continued into the nineteenth century.

The national historical park protects the coastal part of two *ahupuaʻa* (an ancient form of land division)—one called Kaloko and the other Honokohau. According to the National Park Service:

> The ahupuaʻa was an elongated rectangle of land extending mauka (from the mountaintop) makai (to the ocean). Land was divided this way in order to provide the people who lived in the district with all of life's necessities. Terrain ranging from sea level to more than 5,000 feet created a range of vegetation zones supporting a wide variety of plants used in food and medicines, and in making barkcloth, canoes, and houses. Freshwater flowed down from the mountaintop and was easily accessible near the ocean from shallow wells called anchialine ponds. There was a bounty of fish in the ocean, caught with nets woven of plant fiber and fishhooks carved of bone and shell. . . .
>
> There were small local settlements throughout the ahupuaʻa consisting of extended families. People who lived near the ocean provided fish and salt to the inland people in return for crops and materials not found on the coast.

Among the many significant interrelated cultural and natural values of the park are two large, brackish fishponds that were the center of aquaculture, providing a year-round source of food. Kaloko fishpond, near the northern end of the park, is a *loko kuapa*—a bay that was converted to a pond with construction of a massive, 750-foot-long, 18-foot-high seawall of lava boulders. Within this barrier were two sluiceways that were opened during the incoming tide to allow fish of many species to enter the pond, and then closed with a gate so that the majority of the fish could not return to the sea on the outgoing tide. Aimakapa fishpond, toward the southern end of the park, is a *loko puʻuone*—a pond contained by a natural sand beach barrier.

These fishponds were but two of over 100 royal fishponds in the Hawaiian Islands that were an important source of food. Among the many kinds of fish that were raised in ponds such as these were mullet (*ʻamaʻama*), parrotfish (*uhu*), surgeonfish (*kala, palani,* and *pualu*), goatfish (*kumu*), anchovy (*nehu*), milkfish (*awa*), goby (*ʻoʻopu*), and amberjack (*kahala*). Fish populations and the fishponds were carefully managed by the *kahuna* (chiefs) to prevent abuse and overharvesting of the resource and to keep the system in balance.

The park's two ponds also provide vital habitat for native plantlife and for a number of waterbirds, including the endangered Hawaiian coot (*ʻalaeʻkeʻokeʻo*) and the endangered Hawaiian black-necked stilt (*aeʻo*) that visitors may enjoy seeing fly gracefully in small flocks over the ponds, or wade in the shallows in search of food.

The park protects many archaeological and historical sites. They include petroglyphs (*ki'i pohaku*), a recreational stone slide (*holua*) on the east side of Aimakapa fishpond that was used by chiefs, and walled planters on the lava flow that may have been agricultural plots in which were grown such things as sweet potatoes, taro, and gourds and that also may have served as enclosures in which mature hogs were fattened before slaughter. There are village sites with stone platforms that once supported thatched shelters (*hale mau'u*); landings (*paena wa'a*) for fishing and sailing outrigger canoes; temple sites such as the Pu'u'oina *heiau*; a small pool within the lava flow with nearby rock mounds marking its location; assembly areas; fishing shrines (*ku'ula*); and a restored mile-long segment of the historic stone pathway known as the Mamalahoa Trail (the King's Trail) that encircled much of the island in the early to mid-1900s.

As written in the document, *The Spirit of Ka-loko Hono-ko-hau*, published in 1974 by the Honokohau Study Advisory Commission, Hawaiian settlements, such as the one at Kaloko-Honokohau

> . . . thrived, because the ancient Hawaiians touched and understood the spirit, but did not disturb it. . . . Their philosophy was a simple and effective one—"provide for nature and it will provide." . . . To misuse the natural resources at Ka-loko, Hono-ko-hau would bring upon them the wrath of their all-powerful gods Kane, Ku, Lono, and Kanaloa, and devastation to their land.

> Thus the people . . . observed their kapu (taboo) system, a set of regulations and prohibitions governing almost every activity of life, religiously. They believed the kapu were directed by the gods through the kahuna chiefs who imposed them upon the people. Although seemingly rigid and perpetuated by strict enforcement, the kapu system had a purpose. . . . Its edicts contained their respect for nature's mana and the assurances of survival, for many of the kapu were designed to protect the land and conserve its resources which ultimately sustained their needs.

The park is further valued as a place where Hawai'i's most famous *ali'i* (chief), the great *mo'i* (king), Kamehameha I, frequently gathered his armies of men for a place of refreshment on their long marches.

The park also protects a scenic stretch of seashore that combines white sand beaches with contrasting black lava ledges containing tidepools. A grove of coconut palms (*niu*) stands near the shore of Kaloko fishpond. Native Hawaiians have long used the coconut palm for many needs such as food, medicinal properties, building materials, and the teeth of combs.

Other vegetation in the park includes clumps of heliotrope; the rare, orange-flowered *kou* that has long been valued for making durable bowls and platters; *noni* (Indian mulberry), a tree that has been used for medicinal purposes such as treating boils, diabetes, asthma, high blood pressure, and cuts and burns; and small groves of yellow-flowered *milo* (pronounced *mee-lo*)—a tree whose seeds were taken as a laxative, and whose richly colored and beautifully grained wood has been prized for making bowls, bracelets, and other carved and polished objects.

IF YOU GO: Plans eventually will call for construction of a visitor center to help interpret the area's cultural and natural resources. In the meantime, there is a small contact station at Kaloko fishpond. Park headquarters, which is open Mondays through Fridays, is located in Kaloko Industrial Park, just north of the junction of State Route 19 and the Honokohau Boat Harbor road, or about four miles south of Ke-ahole Airport (turn inland off Route 19 onto Hinalani Street, right onto Kanalani Street, and right into the fourth industrial complex driveway). Further information: Superintendent, 73-4786 Kanalani St., #14, Kailua-Kona, HI 96740. Telephone (808) 329-6881.

The National Park Service cautions visitors that they should drive slowly on the very rough unpaved road that leads just under a mile down from State Route 19 to Kaloko fishpond. Visitors hiking in the park are advised to bring plenty of drinking water, sturdy walking shoes, sunscreen, and a hat for shade against the intense, hot sunshine. Visitors are also urged not to swim in the fishponds, both because of their cultural significance and because of fireworms that can inflict a painful sting.

A small picnic area is provided near Kaloko fishpond, but camping is not permitted within the park. Lodging and meals are available in the town of Kailua-Kona and at a number of resort hotels along the west coast of the island.

Among informative publications are *Ruling Chiefs of Hawaii* by S.M. Kamakan (The Kamehameha Schools Press, Honolulu); *Hawaiian Antiques* by David Malo (Bishop Museum, Honolulu); *Shoal of Time: A History of the Hawaiian Islands* by Gavan Davis (University of Hawaii Press); and *Resource Units in Hawaiian Culture* by Donald D. Kilolani Mitchell (The Kamehameha Schools Press, Honolulu).

KLONDIKE GOLD RUSH NATIONAL HISTORICAL PARK,

KLONDIKE GOLD RUSH NATIONAL HISTORICAL PARK, consisting of 13,191 acres in four units in and near Skagway in southeast Alaska, and in the Pioneer Square Historic District in Seattle, Washington, was established in 1980 to commemorate one of the most spectacular gold rushes in North America.

It all got started when George Washington Carmack and two Tagish Indians, Tagish Charlie and Skookum Jim, discovered gold in the summer of 1896 in a Klondike River tributary in the Yukon Territory of northwestern Canada. News of a shipment of gold aboard a boat from Skagway to Seattle in 1897 triggered a frenzied stampede of fortune hunters in 1898. Skagway and

Dyea exploded into bawdy frontier shack and tent cities. Numerous saloons, hotels, and other businesses sprang up to accommodate the thousands who disembarked from ships and attempted the grueling climb over the rugged Coast Mountains on either the White Pass or Chilkoot trails to the Klondike goldfields in Canada. Many hopeful adventurers never made it—some dying along the way and others giving up and heading home, while a lucky few made a fortune.

Today, much of downtown Skagway is protected as part of the national historical park. Many of the buildings are restored, such as the old White Pass and Yukon Railroad Depot, now housing the park's visitor center (at Broadway and 2nd Avenue); Mascot Saloon (at Broadway and 3rd); and Captain Moore's cabin built by Skagway's first settler in 1887 (on 5th).

The park also includes the town site of Dyea and the United States part of the historic Chilkoot Trail. Experienced and well-outfitted hikers may still negotiate this route that climbs through coastal rainforest and follows the Taiya River into its canyon. From there the trail climbs steeply above timberline and crosses over Chilkoot Pass into Canada. (Hikers should ask the National Park Service about customs requirements, before setting out on the Chilkoot Trail.) The Park Service warns that this is a very challenging and potentially dangerous trek. The weather can change dramatically and with little warning, sweeping in with a sudden drop in temperature, accompanied by rain or snow. Hikers are also warned to be on the alert for Alaska brown bears. These large animals can pose a serious danger if encountered suddenly at close range so that they are startled or feel threatened.

The park's visitor center in Skagway provides interpretive programs and information on the park, as well as updates on the accessibility of Chilkoot Trail, weather conditions, and availability of camping places. This facility is open from approximately mid-May to September. The city also provides its own City of Skagway Visitor Center, located in the historic Arctic Brotherhood Building (on Broadway between 2nd & 3rd), offering information on walking and bus tours, charter flights, cruise ship tours, and the Alaska state ferry services.

The National Park Service provides a visitor center in Seattle (at 117 S. Main St.) that provides interpretive exhibits, programs, and publications, as well as information on how to reach Skagway. Lodging and meals are available in Skagway and abundantly available in and around Seattle.

IF YOU GO: Access to Skagway is by car from Whitehorse and Carcross on Highway 2 in Canada, to White Pass, and then down to Skagway in Alaska; by way of scheduled airline flights to Skagway; and by boat, including the Alaska state ferry system. Further information on the park: P.O. Box 517, Skagway, AK 99840, Telephone (907) 983-2921; or Superintendent, 117 S. Main St., Seattle, WA 98104. Telephone (206) 553-7220.

KNIFE RIVER INDIAN VILLAGES NATIONAL HISTORIC SITE

KNIFE RIVER INDIAN VILLAGES NATIONAL HISTORIC SITE consists of 1,758 acres near the confluence of the Knife and Missouri rivers, in west-central North Dakota. It was established in 1974 to protect and interpret the remains of historic villages that were occupied from about A.D. 1000-1100 until 1845 by Hidatsa and Mandan Indians.

By the early eighteenth century, the Hidatsa and Mandan tribes of the Northern Plains Indians were the flourishing culmination of at least seven centuries of established communities along the upper Missouri River. Five summer villages were situated atop terraces above the Knife and Missouri rivers and consisted of earthlodge dwellings. In one of the villages there were as many as 120 of these circular, timber-and-earthen structures, measuring from 30 to 60 feet in diameter and averaging 12 feet in height. Each structure housed from 10 to 30 people. The Indians' winter lodgings were smaller dwellings set under the trees bordering the river, sheltered from fierce winter storms.

The remains of three villages are located within the national historic site: Hidatsa Village (Big Hidatsa Site), just north of a bend in the river; and farther south, along the west bank of the river's meandering course, Awatixa Village (Sakakawea Site) and Awatixa Xi'e Village (Lower Hidatsa Site). Three-foot-deep depressions indicate where the earthlodges once stood.

Preparation for construction of an earthlodge would begin in summer, with the women preparing posts and beams obtained from large cottonwood trees bordering the river. In winter, the men dragged these great logs to the village over ice and snow. Later in the spring, after holes in the ground were dug for the posts, the men used a system of a pole, sling, and rawhide rope to maneuver four massive center posts up and into position. These were joined and secured across the top by horizontal beams. Providing the structure's outer frame were shorter posts, also joined and secured by beams. Over this log framework were then laid thinner rafters, while on top of them was placed a layer of dried prairie cordgrass. Finally, the whole lodge was covered over, adobe-like, with sod or earth. When the dwelling was completed, the Indians would then hold a house-blessing dance ceremony.

In 1833–1834, Maximillian, Prince of Wied (from Germany), visited one of the villages and described the interior of an earthlodge:

> In the center of the hut a circular place is dug for the fire, over which the kettle is suspended. . . . Round the inner circumference lie or hang . . . leather bags, the painted parchment traveling bags, and the harness of the horses. . . . The beds stand against the wall . . . ; they consist of a large square case made of parchment or skins with a square entrance, and are large enough to hold several persons who lie very conveniently and warm on skins and blankets.

The women of the villages cultivated gardens of squash, beans, maize (corn), and other crops, in the rich river-floodplain soil. Berries and roots of certain wild plants were gathered. Fish were caught from the rivers. The men sometimes went off on hunting expeditions to obtain the meat and hides of buffalo. And the warriors also fought to protect the villages from raids by unfriendly nomadic tribes. When the men returned from a successful hunt or battle, the women would offer a festive celebration of dancing, singing, and feasting.

These farming-based villages traded surpluses of their garden produce with friendly nomadic tribes, in exchange for such things as deer skins, buffalo robes, and meat. These communities were also the center of an extensive intertribal trading network that included such things as copper from the upper Great Lakes region, obsidian (volcanic glass) from the Yellowstone region of Wyoming, turquoise from the Southwest, and shells from the Pacific and Gulf coasts. After contact with the white man, trading expanded to include such valued possessions as horses, rifles, and ammunition.

The first documented white man to visit one of these villages was Pierre de la Verendrye, in 1738. A few French, Spanish, British, and American explorers and traders began to travel through the upper Missouri region in the following decades. Two of these villages were visited by the Lewis and Clark Expedition in 1804, as its members spent the first winter of their epic trek to the Pacific Coast at nearby Fort Mandan, a few miles down the Missouri. In the 1830s, two noted painters, George Catlin and Karl Bodmer, recorded scenes of Hidatsa and Mandan village life. Both Bodmer and Catlin produced beautiful paintings of the earthlodges and Indian activities—a cherished historical record.

Tragically, contact with the white man also eventually brought the scourge of disease, against which the Indians had little or no natural immunity. In 1781, a smallpox virus swept through the tribes, decimating their numbers. The village of Awatixa Xi'e was abandoned. Fifteen years later, the survivors returned and built Awatixa Village (Sakakawea Site) nearby.

The reduced population was now easier prey for nomadic tribes such as the Sioux. In 1834, Awatixa was burned to the ground by Indian raiders. Then three years later, another virus epidemic ravaged the population and came close to wiping out the Mandans. The villages were abandoned by 1845, and the remaining Hidatsas and Mandans founded a new village upriver, called Like-a-Fishhook. In 1862, they were joined by neighboring Arikara Indians. In 1885, these three tribes were forced by the white man to leave their village and move onto the Fort Berthold Indian Reservation. Now the descendants, who continue to carry on many of their ancient traditions, are referred to as the Three Affiliated Tribes.

The national historic site provides an impressive visitor center that features an orientation program, interpretive exhibits, and publications. There is also a replica of a full-scale earthlodge. Native crafts are offered for sale.

Earthlodge, Knife River Indian Villages National Historic Site, North Dakota [NPS]

Summer special events and cultural demonstrations may include native American dances, tanning of hides, and gardening. The Northern Plains Indian Culture Fest is scheduled for the fourth weekend in July.

There are ranger-guided interpretive walks during the summer, and self-guiding walks are available, as well. Awatixa Trail leads 1.5 miles from the visitor center to Awatixa Village and back, while Awatixa Xi'e Village (Lower Hidatsa Site) is adjacent to the visitor center. Big Hidatsa Village, containing the greatest number of earthlodge depressions, is a two-mile drive from the visitor center.

Other trails range from about a half-mile to seven miles, leading hikers or cross-country skiers through both prairie grassland and riparian woodland habitats. Visitors are cautioned to be careful along riverbanks, as the land there is often unstable and may slump off without warning.

Picnicking is permitted near the visitor center, but camping is not allowed in the park. Federal and state campgrounds are available near Garrison Dam, 19 miles north of the national historic site. Lodging and meals are available in nearby towns.

IF YOU GO: Access to the site is 41 miles north from I-94 at Bismarck, by way of U.S. Route 83, 23 miles west on State Route 200A, and north several miles through Stanton to the visitor center. From U.S. Route 2 at Minot, it is about 50 miles south on U.S. Route 83, west and south on State Route 200, and then County Route 37 to the park. The national historic site is closed on Thanksgiving, Christmas, and New Year's Day. Further information: Superintendent, P.O. Box 9, Stanton, ND 58571. Telephone (701) 745-3309.

NATCHEZ NATIONAL HISTORICAL PARK

NATCHEZ NATIONAL HISTORICAL PARK, consisting of 108 acres in three sites, was established in 1988 "to preserve and interpret the history of Natchez, Mississippi, as a significant city in the history of the American South." The park includes the architecturally outstanding antebellum estate, Melrose, that dates from 1848, and the early 1840s home of a freed black man, William Johnson. It is expected to include acquisition of the site of the early-eighteenth-century French fortified colonial outpost, Fort Rosalie, that was on the Natchez bluffs overlooking the Mississippi River.

By the mid-sixteenth century, the Natchez area was the flourishing center of at least 30 villages of the Natchez Indians. In 1716, the French, who claimed this region of North America, built Fort Rosalie and maintained relatively peaceful relations with the Indians for 13 years. Then the Indians decided to take back this part of their ancient homeland. They attacked the fort and killed most of the Frenchmen stationed there. In retaliation, a French force struck back at the Natchez people, killing many and chasing the survivors away.

Later in the eighteenth century, this region changed hands several times—from French to British, to Spanish, and finally to United States ownership. In 1798, the U.S. Congress established the Territory of Mississippi, and Natchez was designated the territorial capital. In 1801, the United States signed a treaty with the region's Choctaw and Chickasaw Indians, under which American settlers could travel to Natchez on the Natchez Trace—a centuries-old, 500-mile Indian path through the wilderness between what is now Nashville, Tennessee, and the Natchez area. This important access opened the way for a surge in settlers to Mississippi.

By the early decades of the nineteenth century, leading up to the Civil War in the 1860s, Natchez developed into a significant commercial, social, and architectural hub in the cotton belt of the Deep South. The arrival of the steamboat on the Mississippi in 1811 signaled the start of what came to be called the "Golden Age" of Natchez. The cultivation of extensive cotton and indigo plantations, using black slave labor, brought enormous wealth to plantation owners, planters, and merchants. This wealth enabled many individuals to build large mansions for themselves and their families.

As the city was spared damage during the Civil War, Natchez today contains a rich architectural heritage that includes many of the grand old homes set amid beautifully landscaped, tree-shaded grounds and parks. Many of these lavishly furnished palatial mansions are of imposing Greek Revival architecture, reflecting the great power and wealth of those who built and lived in them.

Natchez National Historical Park's stately mansion, located at 1 Melrose-Montebello Parkway, off Sergeant Prentiss Drive, is a blend of the nineteenth-century Greek Revival and eighteenth-century Georgian styles. Melrose has been characterized as the "Mount Vernon of Natchez"

"Melrose," Natchez National Historical Park [Van O'Guinn]

(George Washington's home, Mount Vernon, overlooking the Potomac River in Virginia).

The Melrose complex, which was built from 1845 to 1848, includes the main house; kitchen house (now housing the visitor center and bookstore); smokehouse; laundry building; living accommodations for the house, stables, and gardening slaves; carriage house; and stables. The columned mansion was built by prominent Natchez planter and attorney, John T. McMurran, and decorated by his wife, Mary. Many of the original furnishings still grace the mansion. Following the Civil War, George Malin Davis, another planter and attorney, purchased Melrose, and it remained in the Davis family for more than 100 years.

The mansion and outbuildings are set amid 84 acres of magnificent trees and other vegetation. Great spreading live oaks, which have come to symbolize these antebellum estates, grow along with beautiful southern magnolias, flowering dogwoods, eastern redbuds, bald cypresses, azaleas, rhododendrons, and a formal flower garden.

The William Johnson House, a brick townhouse, is located in downtown Natchez at 210 State Street. In 1809, Johnson was born a black slave but was freed at age 11. He owned his own barber shop in Natchez, and at age 32, he bought a tract of land, built his townhouse, and even bought some slaves. At 42, he was killed in an argument, and because none of the black witnesses was allowed to present testimony in court, Johnson's murderer was never apprehended and brought to trial.

Among the informative books are *Classic Natchez* by Randolph Delehanty and Van Jones Martin (Martin St. Martin Publishing Co.); *The*

Barber of Natchez, by Edwin Adams Davis and William Ranson Hogan (Louisiana State University Press); and *Antebellum Natchez,* by D. Clayton James (Louisiana State University Press.)

IF YOU GO: The National Park Service provides guided house tours (a fee is charged for the Melrose tour), interpretive programs, walks, and publications. The park is closed on Thanksgiving, Christmas, and New Year's Day. Lodging and meals are available in Natchez. Further information: Superintendent, P.O. Box 1208, Natchez, MS 39121. Telephone (601) 446-5790.

NEZ PERCE NATIONAL HISTORICAL PARK

NEZ PERCE NATIONAL HISTORICAL PARK comprises 2,109 acres in 38 scattered sites in Idaho, Washington, Oregon, and Montana. It was initially established in 1965 to protect and interpret 24 sites on and near the Nez Perce Indian Reservation, in north-central Idaho. In 1992 the park was expanded to add 14 other sites at more distant locations. The park commemorates the history, legends, and culture of the Nez Perce (pronounced like purse), as well as interaction with the white man—explorers, fur traders, Christian missionaries, U.S. military, settlers, and others. Of the sites, four in Idaho are owned by the National Park Service—Heart of the Monster, Canoe Camp, Spalding Mission, and White Bird Battlefield. Bear Paw Battleground, in northern Montana, is operated by the Park Service, under an agreement with the state of Montana. The other sites are a mixture of federal, state, tribal, and private ownerships.

Heart of the Monster, at East Kamiah, is the Nez Perce legendary place of origin. An audio station at the site explains the legend, which says that the Nez Perce people were created from drops of blood squeezed from the monster's heart. This site is located along U.S. Route 12 in Idaho's Clearwater River valley, between Kamiah and Kooskia.

Canoe Camp, located 2.5 miles west of Orofino on U.S. Route 121, is an encampment site by the Clearwater River. There, the Lewis and Clark "Corps of Discovery" rested from their fatiguing travels in the early autumn of 1805, and built five log canoes, before setting forth on the final stretch of their long trek to the Pacific Coast and the grueling winter at Fort Clatsop. (See Fort Clatsop National Memorial and Lewis and Clark National Historic Trail.)

Long Camp, just south of Kamiah on U.S. Route 12, is the site of another Lewis and Clark Expedition encampment. On their return trek in the spring of 1806, they waited for the snow to melt so they could proceed eastward on the Nez Perces' **Lolo,** or **Old Buffalo Trail,** back over **Lolo Pass** in the rugged Bitterroot Range. Regarding the expedition's impre ..ion of the Nez Perce Indians, Captain Meriwether Lewis wrote that they "are the most friendly, honest, and ingenious people that we have seen in the course of our voyage and travels."

The Spalding Mission site is where the Reverend Henry Harmon Spalding founded a Presbyterian Christian mission station in 1836. The Nez

Perce had previously sought information on the white man's religion to add to their own spiritual beliefs. In response to their inquiry, Spalding was sent out from the East Coast by the American Board of Commissioners for Foreign Missions, to minister to the Nez Perce.

Spalding and his wife, Eliza, traveled west with Dr. Marcus and Narcissa Whitman. They reached the Missouri River in April 1836 and then proceeded by covered wagon across the Great Plains, by way of the Platte and South Platte river valleys, and then trekked down the Snake River country of Idaho. They finally reached Hudson's Bay Company's Fort Vancouver fur-trading post, near the mouth of the Columbia River in September 1836 (see Fort Vancouver National Historic Site). Eliza and Narcissa thus became the first women to cross North America by an overland route.

While the Whitmans began a missionary station among the Cayuse Indians, in what is now southeastern Washington (see Whitman Mission National Historic Site), the Spaldings went another 100 miles eastward and founded their mission among the Nez Perce, in north-central Idaho. The initial site was at a spot about two miles up Lapwai Creek from its junction with the Clearwater River. In 1838, they relocated down by the Clearwater, and the main house was built that same year. Over the next several years it was expanded to include a wing housing a school where Eliza taught some of the Nez Perce children. The mission complex also contained a gristmill, sawmill, and system of ponds and ditches to carry water to the mills and to irrigate crops and an orchard. In 1839, the mission obtained a printing press and ran off the first book printed in the Pacific Northwest—New Testament passages from the Bible that were translated into the Nez Perce language.

In 1855, the Nez Perce Reservation was established by the U.S. government, and five years later, when the Bureau of Indian Affairs moved the Nez Perce Indian Agency to the mission site, Spalding and his wife were hired as teachers, from 1862 to 1865, and again from 1871 until Spalding's death in 1874.

None of the original mission structures remain, but the old agency cabin and the later Indian agent's house do remain. The town of Spalding was once a lively community of stores and other businesses, saloons, hotels, and a railroad station. When the Nez Perce Agency was moved to a new location, the town began its decline, with the last store finally closing in 1964.

Also located at Spalding, and surrounding the mission site and the Indian agency cabin, is the historic Spalding Arboretum. It was dedicated as part of the former Spalding Memorial State Park in 1936 and is now part of the national historical park. Landscape engineer, W.S. Thornber, of the Idaho State Bureau of Highways, selected 35 species of trees from all over America and Europe. Today, there are still 22 of those varieties, among them the Scot's, Austrian, ponderosa, and jack pines; white, blue, and Norway spruces; giant sequoia; London plane tree (sycamore); bur, English white, and scarlet oaks; European (weeping) birch; and Norway, silver, and sugar maples.

IF YOU GO: The national historical park's headquarters and visitor center are located at the Spalding site. The center presents orientation programs, ranger-led tours and walks, park site brochures and other publications, interpretive exhibits including displays of outstanding Nez Perce artifacts, and, during the summer, a variety of cultural demonstration programs. Access to the site is by way of U.S. Route 12 and U.S. Route 95, ten miles east of Lewiston, ID. The visitor center is closed on Thanksgiving, Christmas, and New Year's Day.

Other sites in the vicinity of Spalding include the rock formation called the **Ant and Yellowjacket,** just west of the park's visitor center. It explains the legend of Coyote, who tried to settle an argument between Ant and Yellowjacket. Because they ignored Coyote's efforts, he turned them to stone with their jaws fiercely locked in combat. Another legend site is **Coyote's Fishnet,** located about five miles to the west, on the Clearwater, where Coyote hurled his fishnet across one hillside and Black Bear hurled his on another hillside, turning the Ant and Yellowjacket to stone.

A site of a different kind draws attention to **Donald MacKenzie's Pacific Fur Company Trading Post.** It was established in 1812, somewhere along the north bank of the Clearwater, just north of today's city of Lewiston. The post was founded as part of John Jacob Astor's strategy of competing against the powerful British-owned Hudson's Bay and North West fur-trading companies. But this post did not succeed, and it was soon sold to British traders.

South of Spalding is the site of **St. Joseph's Mission,** founded in 1874 by Fr. Joseph Cataldo as the first Roman Catholic mission among the Nez Perce. It is located ten miles south of Spalding, on U.S. Route 95 and then nearly four miles on the spur road to Slickpoo.

A number of Nez Perce War battle sites are also included in the national historical park. This tribe was traditionally at peace with the white settlers. But soon after 5,000 square miles of the original Nez Perce homeland were established as a reservation, under the terms of a treaty in 1855 with the U.S. Government, gold was discovered on the reservation.

A new round of negotiations was begun in 1862, in an attempt to resolve the conflicts between the prospectors and the Nez Perce. While most of the tribal bands attended the negotiations, a major division among them led many tribal chiefs to abstain from signing the treaty of 1863. Those refusing to sign were convinced that the government was demanding too many concessions from the tribe. They became known as the "nontreaty" Nez Perce.

In 1877, under the pressure of an ultimatum, the nontreaty chiefs finally decided to move onto the reservation at Lapwai, instead of risking open conflict with the U.S. Army. On the way to the reservation, however, a number of young warriors attacked and killed several white settlers, to avenge past killings of tribal members. For a tribe that had previously prided itself on being peaceful and never having killed a white man, this was a tragic turn of events.

White Bird Battlefield, located in White Bird Canyon, along U.S. Route 95, about 14 miles south of Grangeville, recognizes the first official battle of the Nez Perce War on June 17, 1877. Several bands of Nez Perce had gathered at White Bird and were attacked by a force of more than 100 U.S. Army cavalry from **Fort Lapwai** and 11 volunteer citizens. Hoping to avoid a confrontation, the Nez Perce sent forth a white flag. But a volunteer fired a shot that triggered the battle. Not one Nez Perce lost his life, while 34 U.S. soldiers were killed. Some 600 troops were then organized to pursue the Nez Perce.

Big Hole National Battlefield (see separate section on this park), in southwestern Montana, is where these Nez Perce, after fleeing from their homeland and crossing Lolo Pass in the Bitterroots, were suddenly attacked by more U.S. troops on August 9, 1877. The army lost 29 soldiers, and somewhere between 60 and 90 Indian men, women, and children were killed.

Camas Meadows Battle Site, a few miles west of the then five-year-old Yellowstone National Park, is where the Nez Perce were successful in slowing the U.S. forces' pursuit, by stealing more than 150 of the military's pack horses and mules. The newspaper in nearby Virginia City, Montana, wrote that "The surprise was sudden and complete." From there, they fled eastward through Yellowstone.

As the Indians attempted to cross over the international border into Canada, the final battle of the war, at **Bear Paw Battleground**, occurred just 40 miles south of the border, near the present town of Havre, Montana. After having traveled some 1,700 miles, they were attacked and forced to surrender to the U.S. troops on October 5, 1877, less than four months after the initial battle. Eventually, the Nez Perce were returned to their reservation in Idaho—a reservation that originally encompassed seven million acres, but was reduced to 757,000 acres, and finally to only 86,000 acres.

In 1986, the U.S. Congress designated the **Nez Perce** (*Nee-Me-Poo*) **National Historic Trail**, to commemorate the Nez Perce's attempt to outrun the pursuing U.S. military troops. Nee-Me-Poo is the traditionally accepted name of the Nez Perce Tribe, meaning "The People."

An excellent scholarly book is *The Nez Perce Indians and the Opening of the Northwest* by Alvin Josephy, Sr. (University of Nebraska Press).

IF YOU GO: Regarding access to many of the park sites, the National Park Service is still working on agreements with property owners of some of the privately owned sites. Visitors are urged to check with park staff to make certain that public access is allowed. Lodging and meals are available in cities and towns throughout the four-state region, including Lewiston, ID; Joseph, OR; Wisdom and Chinook, MT; and Nespelem, WA. Further information: Superintendent, P.O. Box 93, Spalding, ID 83551. Telephone (208) 843-2261.

PECOS NATIONAL HISTORICAL PARK

PECOS NATIONAL HISTORICAL PARK consists of 6,577 acres in three units at the base of the southern end of the rugged Sangre de Cristo Mountains, in north-central New Mexico. It was initially established in 1965 as the single-unit Pecos National Monument to protect the ruins of the once-thriving, extensive Pecos Pueblo that began around A.D. 1300 and the associated ruins of the adobe Hispanic Franciscan mission church complex that was established in the 1600s, was destroyed, and then reestablished in the 1700s.

In 1990, the national monument was renamed Pecos National Historical Park, and expanded to protect the two-section Glorieta unit that commemorates two Civil War sites in the vicinity of Glorieta Pass. (These sites are still privately owned and not open to the public, as of this writing in late 1996.) And in 1991, the 5,500-acre Forked Lightning Ranch was added to the park. It provides vital viewshed protection from the park's ridgetop pueblo and church ruins and protects this historic dude and cattle ranch and its architecturally significant ranch house. The house was designed for rancher "Tex" Austin in the 1920s by the famous Southwest "pueblo revival" architect, John Gaw Meem. The ranch also contains other pueblo ruins, a stretch of the historic Santa Fe Trail, the remains of the Kozlowski Ranch and stage stop and tavern that operated from 1858–1880, and 1.5 miles of the Pecos River and its bordering riparian trees and other lush vegetation.

Pecos Pueblo, at its peak of occupancy between the mid-1400s and the 1600s, had 700 rooms and rose to four and in some places to five stories. In 1540, a Spanish expedition of more than 1,000 people, led by Francisco Vásquez de Coronado, in search of rumored cities of gold, marched north through what are now Mexico and Arizona, and crossed New Mexico—pausing at Pecos Pueblo, then known as Cicuyé. This great pueblo of some 2,000 residents was one of the largest in the Southwest and was a major trading center between the Pueblo Indians of New Mexico and the nomadic tribes of the Great Plains to the east. Pedro de Castañeda, Coronado's chief chronicler, wrote that,

> Cicuyé is a village of nearly five hundred warriors, who are feared throughout that country. It is square, situated on a rock, with a large court or plaza in the middle, estufas [kivas]. The houses are all alike, four stories high. One can walk on the roofs of the whole village, there being no streets to hinder. . . . The houses do not have doors below, but they use ladders, which can be lifted up like a drawbridge. . . . The people of this village boast that no one has been able to conquer them. . . .

While Coronado's expedition was greeted cordially with gifts, it was led off on a goosechase across the Great Plains, and finally abandoned the quest for the elusive golden cities. In 1598, another group of Spaniards, led by don Juan de Oñate, trekked north into New Mexico—to conquer and colonize the region, and to convert the Pueblo Indians to Roman Catholic Christianity. By 1618, Franciscan Missionaries had established churches at many of the pueblos along the Rio Grande Valley. The Christianizing effort next focused on the pueblos to the east, such as Pecos and several south of there in the Salinas Province (see Salinas Pueblo Missions National Monument).

In 1621, Fray Andrés Juárez (Suárez) completed construction of a large adobe church. It was the most massive of all the early mission structures in New Mexico and was dedicated to *Nuestra Señora de los Ángeles de Poriúncula*. With the Indians' labor, it took four years to build. Its adobe walls were eight to ten feet thick—the side walls being reinforced with great buttresses. The structure boasted six bell towers. The nave measured 133 feet long and at its widest was 41 feet across. The flat roof that was supported by large pine logs (*vigas*) was 40 feet high.

Potters, Jemez Pueblo, Pecos National Historical Park [NPS]

The adjoining *convento*, which was gradually expanded over the years, housed the cells (small, sparsely furnished sleeping rooms), a refectory (dining room) and kitchen, and workrooms and classrooms where the Indians were instructed in the Spanish language and in a variety of Spanish woodworking, craft, and horticultural methods. The *convento* also included stables, corral, and garden patio.

During the next 55 years, the Indians became increasingly restive and angry over the repressive and even brutal Spanish rule. In 1680, the pueblos carried out a carefully planned and well-coordinated rebellion, in which many missionaries and other Spaniards were killed, the churches were plundered, and the remaining Spanish population and a few of their Indian allies were forced to leave New Mexico.

Twelve years later, Spanish forces led by Diego de Vargas reconquered the region. The Pecos Pueblo Indians, by now numbering around 1,500 individuals, welcomed the Spaniards and helped them build a first temporary chapel and then, starting in 1705, a new church—the ruins of which rise prominently today. The nave of this structure was 76 feet long, just over half the length of the massive, pre-Revolt church.

By the mid-1690s, Pecos' population had dropped further, to around 700 residents—perhaps the result of a devastating epidemic, or a move by some of its people to other pueblos in reaction to Pecos

Pecos National Historical Park, New Mexico [NPS]

Pueblo's official welcome of the Spaniards. While Pecos maintained a generally cooperative relationship with the new, far-less-repressive Spanish regime in the 1700s, it was nevertheless a pueblo divided against itself. This division was caused by the basic cultural conflict between Spanish Catholic beliefs and practices, and the ancient Indian beliefs and ways of living close to the natural environment. It was a conflict that ultimately helped pull the fabric of this ancient community apart.

Additionally, by the 1760s, the repeated ravages of the nomadic Indian tribes of the Great Plains—notably the Comanches who had for so long been close trading partners—plus the repeated ravages of such European-introduced diseases as smallpox, took their toll on the pueblo population. By the 1770s, only about 200 inhabitants remained. As emigrant and trade caravans began rolling by the pueblo on the Santa Fe Trail in the 1820s and 1830s, only a few survivors occupied a small part of the pueblo. Finally, by 1840, the last 17 or so individuals moved away to Jemez Pueblo, to the west of the Rio Grande. The once great pueblo, which had been a key gateway between the Pueblo and Plains Indians, was left behind to crumble and erode away.

Archaeological excavations of the pueblo, church, and *convento* ruins began in 1915 under the direction of Alfred V. Kidder. He and his associates worked over a span of ten summers, unearthing more than 16,000 Indian and Spanish artifacts, and devising a cultural-development classification system that is still in use by archaeologists today. When Pecos was established as a national monument, the National Park Service started further excavation and stabilization work under the direction of Jean M. Pinkley. Other efforts followed, including research by Alden C. Hayes.

In 1848, by the Treaty of Guadalupe Hidalgo, now-independent Mexico surrendered New Mexico (along with Arizona, California, Nevada, and part of Utah and Colorado) to the United States. This event greatly increased trade on the Santa Fe Trail between Missouri and New Mexico's capital, Santa Fe. The ruts of this historic route can still be detected in some places, including a stretch within the park.

In March 1862, the Civil War briefly touched New Mexico. As part of a broad strategy to ultimately gain control of the gold mines of Colorado and other assets of the West, so as to enhance the economic strength of the Confederacy, the Texas Rangers marched into New Mexico and clashed with Union troops in the vicinity of Glorieta Pass, just west of Pecos Pueblo ruins. An initial skirmish occurred on March 26 in Apache Canyon, in which the Confederates pulled back. Later that day, a second encounter ended in a victory for the Union cavalry.

Two days later the forces again engaged in combat, in the vicinity of the Santa Fe Trail stage stop of Pigeon's Ranch. This seven-hour Battle of Glorieta was a short-lived victory for the Confederates. Union troops had meanwhile climbed across Glorieta Mesa to the south of the pass and wiped out their entire supply train, containing ammunition, food, blankets, wagons, and horses. The Confederates had no choice but to retreat from New Mexico and give up their hope of seizing control of the West's gold.

An especially beautiful book on the park is *Pecos: Gateway to Pueblo & Plains: The Anthology,* edited by John V. Bezy and Joseph P. Sanchez (Southwest Parks and Monuments Association, 1988). Also providing valuable insight into the history of Pecos Pueblo is *The Four Churches of Pecos,* by Alden C. Hayes (The University of New Mexico Press, 1974).

The visitor center, which provides interpretive exhibits, programs, and publications, is an exceptionally attractive, pueblo-style structure that was the generous gift of the former owners of the Forked Lightning Ranch, Mr. and Mrs. E. E. Fogelson. Mrs. Fogelson is best known as the actress, Greer Garson, and it was she who also made possible the protection of the Forked Lightning Ranch by selling it to The Conservation Fund, which in turn donated it to the National Park Service.

The park offers a 1.5-mile self-guiding trail from the visitor center through the pueblo and church ruins. There are no provisions for camping in the park, but Santa Fe National Forest just to the north offers campgrounds. The park has a picnic area. Limited lodging and meals are available in the town of Pecos, two miles north of the park. There are numerous accommodations in Santa Fe, 25 miles to the northwest by way of I-25; and in Las Vegas, NM, 37 miles to the east by way of I-25.

IF YOU GO: Access to the park is on I-25, exiting at Rowe and then north five miles on State Route 63; or at the Pecos-Glorieta exit and then east about seven miles on State Route 50 to the town of Pecos, then south two miles on Route 63. Further information: Superintendent, P.O. Box 418, Pecos, NM 87552. Telephone (505) 757-6414.

PIPE SPRING NATIONAL MONUMENT

PIPE SPRING NATIONAL MONUMENT, comprising 40 acres on the high desert of the "Arizona Strip," north of the Grand Canyon in northern Arizona, was established in 1923 to protect and interpret a historic stone "fort." The monument commemorates pioneer settlement of the West and is representative of Indian-Pioneer interactions on the western frontier.

The water of Pipe Spring has long allowed plant and animal life to thrive in this arid region, and humans have taken advantage of this water source for at least a thousand years. Ancestral Puebloans (Anasazi) cultivated crops near the spring.

Shortly after 1870, when a peace treaty between the Mormon pioneers and Navajos brought an end to the Indians' destructive raids on settlers in this area, the Mormon leader, Brigham Young, directed that the church's tithing herd of livestock for southern Utah be located at Pipe Spring. (A tithing herd was the livestock given to the church that equaled one-tenth of a

The fort at Pipe Spring National Monument, Arizona [NPS]

Mormon family's annual income.) There a fortified ranch-horse complex was built by Anson P. Winsor and his ranchhands with two similar, two-story sandstone houses facing each other, and high connecting stone walls enclosing the courtyard between the houses. One of the homes was built over the spring, providing clear cold water for domestic use and then flowed as a dashing stream through the courtyard and beyond, where it was used for irrigating trees and crops. The ranch was never attacked by Indians. It was known as Winsor Castle (sounding like Windsor Castle in England), and was named for Winsor and his wife, Emeline.

The National Park Service maintains the ranch, including nearby cabins, corrals, recreated gardens and orchards, and period furnishings in the houses that are essentially as they appeared in the 1870s. At its peak of operation, more than 2,000 head of cattle were kept on Pipe Spring Ranch. The property was sold in 1888 to a non-Mormon cattle rancher, B. F. Saunders, and it was sold again in 1906 to Jonathan Heatons, from whom the Park Service acquired Pipe Spring in 1923.

The monument's visitor center provides interpretive exhibits and a short video. A small gift shop and snack bar are located near the center. During the summer, as staffing permits, there are sometimes pioneer crafts and ranching demonstrations. A half-mile history and geology interpretive loop trail switchbacks up the cliffs behind the structures, and provides a broad view of the Arizona Strip country.

Two interesting publications are *Pipe Spring National Monument: Landscape and History on the Arizona Strip* by Lyman Hafen *(St. George* Magazine); and *Kaibab Paiute History, The Early Years* by Richard Stoffle and

Michael Evans (Kaibab Paiute Tribe).

There are no camping or picnicking facilities in the monument. The Kaibab Paiute Indian Reservation that surrounds the monument provides a picnic area and Heart Canyon Campground, a half-mile from the monument. Lodging and meals are available in Fredonia, AZ; and Kanab, St. George, and Hurricane, UT.

IF YOU GO: Access to the monument is 14 miles west of Fredonia on State Route 389; or 85 miles east of St. George by way of I-15 north, Utah Route 9 east to Hurricane, and Utah Route 59 and Arizona Route 389 east to the monument. Further information: Superintendent, Moccasin, AZ 86022. Telephone (520) 643-7105.

PISCATAWAY PARK

PISCATAWAY PARK comprises 4,262 acres along a scenic, six-mile stretch of the Maryland shore of the Potomac River. It was established in 1961 to protect the historic view across the river from George Washington's famous home, Mount Vernon, on the river's Virginia shore.

The park features the **National Colonial Farm**—a re-created eighteenth-century Tidewater farm, where today living-history interpreters in period costumes take visitors on tours (fee) to see such farm animals as Red Devon cattle, sheep, goats, turkeys, and geese; vegetable and herb gardening; and the cultivation of crops. The farm is operated by the Accokeek Foundation, Inc., in cooperation with the National Park Service. The farm practices techniques representative of eighteenth-century farming, when there were no chemical pesticides, fertilizers, or merchandized farm equipment. The farm is open Tuesdays through Sundays, except on Thanksgiving, Christmas, and New Year's Day.

The other features within Piscataway Park are several small parking areas near the shoreline of the river, where one may enjoy the scenic beauty and walk short nature trails. Also within the park boundaries are the remains of Marshall Hall, an early eighteenth-century plantation, with the shell of the manor house, kitchen building, and Marshall family cemetery. A boat ramp and pier are located on the river bank just south of the manor house. The park is open daily, except on Thanksgiving, Christmas, and New Year's Day.

Camping is not permitted in the park, but picnic facilities are provided. Lodging and meals are available in the Washington, D.C., metropolitan area.

IF YOU GO: Access from I-95 (the Capital Beltway) is by way of Exit 3A and proceeding southbound on State Route 210 (Indian Head Highway) for ten miles, then turning in Accokeek onto Bryan Point Road, and continuing to the park entrance and the farm. Further information: Piscataway Park, Superintendent, National Capital Parks—East, 1900 Anacostia Drive, SE, Washington, D.C. 20020. Telephone (301) 763-3600.

PUʻUHONUA O HONAUNAU NATIONAL HISTORICAL PARK

PUʻUHONUA O HONAUNAU NATIONAL HISTORICAL PARK (Place of Refuge at Honaunau Bay), comprising 181 acres on the west coast of the Big Island of Hawaiʻi, was established in 1961 to protect and interpret one of the most important and the largest and most complex of many such refuges in the Hawaiian Islands. The park also helps to perpetuate the traditional native Hawaiian culture. Sacred sanctuaries like this one offered persons who had broken ancient and sacred taboos *(kapu,* a variation of the Polynesian word, *tapu)* a chance to escape from pursuers and safely reach a puʻuhonua and thereby avoid being put to death to appease the gods.

It was long believed that if transgressions of the rules of strictly regulated daily life were not appropriately appeased, the gods would be offended and strike back with punishing disasters such as lava flows, earthquakes, *tsunami,* or famine. The people believed that there was a vital balance between a life-embracing people who lived in harmony with the environment and the vengeful gods who could take life away. If a transgressor were fortunate enough to reach a place of refuge, he or she would be absolved of the offending act by a *kahuna pule* (priest), would thus be given a second chance at life, and could then safely return home, usually within a few hours or several days. Warriors defeated in battle, as well as women, children, the sick, the elderly, and maimed could seek refuge from battles. A strictly enforced *kapu* was the rule against the taking of life within the sacred *puʻuhonua.*

This sanctuary is situated on a low promontory of lava-flow rock by the sea. It is encircled on two sides by a massive ten-foot-high Great Wall. The black lava boulders were fitted together so skillfully, in the mid-sixteenth century, as to need no mortar. The third side of the *puʻuhonua* faces the Pacific Ocean. Within this six-acre enclosure is the thatch-roofed Hale o Keawe (House of Keawe), an authentic reconstruction of a *heiau* (temple) mausoleum, representing the one originally built here around 1650. The latter was the sacred place where the bones were placed of the revered ruling *aliʻi* (chief), Keawe-ʻi-kekahi-aliʻi-o-ka-moku, and subsequently nearly a score of other chiefs of his lineage. This high *aliʻi* ruled over the island of Hawaiʻi during a rare period of peace and prosperity, during the mid-sixteenth century, and he was the great-grandfather of the revered *moʻi* (king), Kamehameha I, who ended the long history of warfare between the islands by uniting all the Hawaiian Islands. Standing guard around the *hale,* now as then, are tall, carved wooden effigies called *kiʻi*—their wild grimaces warning against unwanted intrusions into the sacred *puʻuhonua.*

Also within the enclosure is ʻAlealea Heiau—a platform of boulders measuring 127 by 60 feet and averaging eight feet in height. This was the dominant *heiau* of the refuge, prior to the erection of Hale o Keawe.

Honaunau was also the home of the ruling chief, his queen, and the entourage of lesser chiefs who served him. Where coconut palms rise gracefully above the former palace grounds, just outside the walled *puʻuhonua,* ten or more thatch-roofed palace structures were once located. Fishponds that create an especially pleasant scene beneath the palms are also on the former palace grounds, and were used as holding ponds for fish caught at sea and reserved for the chiefs. (For more on fish farming, see Kaloko-Honokohau National Historical Park.) The beach at beautiful, palm-framed Keoneʻele Cove, next to Hale o Keawe, was once the landing place for the royal canoes. Nearby are Hawaiian outrigger canoes constructed as they used to be, made of *koa* wood with coconut fiber lashings.

When Kamehameha II abolished the ancient religious system and kapu-regulated life of the Hawaiians in 1819, all of the *mana* (spiritual power) that the *heiau* and *puʻuhonua* had for so long represented suddenly ceased to exist. While the Hale o Keawe lost its religious meaning, and was stripped of such things as stick and feather effigies, drums, bowls, spears, and ornaments, it continued for another decade to house the bones of 23 deified god-chiefs, before they were removed and taken to a burial cave.

Kiʻi, carved wooden effigies, Puʻuhonua o Honaunau National Historical Park, Hawaiʻi [Russ Butcher]

In 1902, private funding enabled restorative work to be performed on the Great Wall and the ʻAlealea Heiau platform. And after the park was established, the Hale o Keawe was painstakingly reconstructed. Another historical feature of the park is the 1871 Trail—the path of an ancient trail and part of the King's Trail that encircled much of the island in the mid-1800s. The park's segment passes ancient house and *heiau* sites, cliffs, the shore of Alahaka Bay, the hardened cascades of a lava flow, and a lava tube; climbs Alahaka Ramp; and comes to Kiʻilae, a village that was inhabited until the 1930s.

Among the trees and other vegetation in the park are *noni* (Indian mulberry), a tree that has long been used for its medicinal properties such as treating boils, diabetes, asthma, high blood pressure, and cuts and burns, and that bears foul-smelling, knobby fruit; *kukui* (candlenut tree), the official state tree of Hawai'i, whose nuts were a source of candle fuel and from the trunks of which canoes were carved; *milo,* a rare tree whose seeds were taken as a laxative and whose beautiful wood was carved and polished into bowls and other utensils and carvings; *hala* (pandanus or screw pine), an ancient species that is easily recognized by its stilt-like aerial roots that have been attributed with medicinal properties, fruit that somewhat resembles the pineapple, and narrow, yucca-like fibrous leaves that have long been made into floor mats, fans, sandals, baskets, and other woven objects; *kou,* a rare, orange-flowered tree that has been greatly valued for making durable bowls, utensils, and wooden effigies; and *ti* (pronounced *tee),* the two-foot-long, five-inch-wide leaves of which are used for house thatching and *hula* skirts, as well as cooking and food-storage wrappings. The National Park Service has a handout sheet on these and other plants of the park.

Among the birds are common myna, zebra dove, yellow-billed cardinal (with bright red head), Japanese white-eye, and saffron finch.

Within the Place of Refuge and to the south is a scenic stretch of seashore, combining sandy beaches and black lava ledges that contain tidepools, in which visitors may find such intertidal life as small crabs, sea hares, sea urchins, and small fish and eels.

The park's visitor center provides interpretive displays, programs, and publications. On a self-guiding walk (following numbered points of interest keyed to the park brochure), visitors may see the Hale o Keawe, the grimacing effigies, several thatched huts and shelters, a petroglyph, the palm-shaded fishponds, palm-framed Keone'ele Cove, *heiau* sites, and the massive stone wall.

The park periodically sponsors arts and crafts demonstrations, such as the carving of *ki'i* effigies and outrigger canoes, making colorful featherwork, and weaving and thatching. On the Friday through Sunday nearest July 1, a Hawaiian festival is held at the park, similar to one held at Pu'ukohola Heiau National Historic Site. This event features the colorful Royal Court procession, gift-giving ceremony, and court dancers, followed by extensive arts and crafts demonstrations and workshops.

Two publications that are worthy of mention: *Tracing the Past at Honaunau,* by Dorothy B. Barrere (Hawai'i Natural History Association, Hawai'i Volcanoes National Park, 1994); and *Resource Units in Hawaiian Culture,* by Donald D. Kilolani Mitchell (The Kamehameha Schools Press, Honolulu, 1992).

Camping is not permitted in the park, but there is a picnic area near the shore, south of the Place of Refuge, in the shade of coconut palms and *kiawe* (mesquite) trees. Lodging and meals are available in Kailua-Kona and at a number of resorts along the island's west coast.

IF YOU GO: Access to the park is 22 miles south of the town of Kailua-Kona: 18.5 miles on State Route 11 and 3.6 miles on State Route 160. Further information: Superintendent, P.O. Box 129, Honaunau, HI 96726. Telephone (808) 328-2326.

PUʻUKOHOLA HEIAU NATIONAL HISTORIC SITE

PUʻUKOHOLA HEIAU NATIONAL HISTORIC SITE consists of 85 acres on the northwest coast of the Big Island of Hawaiʻi. It was authorized in 1972 to protect and interpret the site of the last major religious *heiau* (temple) to be built in accordance with the ancient Hawaiian traditions. A prophet (*kahuna*) told warrior chief Kamehameha that he would conquer and rule over all the Hawaiian Islands as a united kingdom, if he would construct a grand temple to the god of war, Kukaʻilimoku, on a summit near the Pacific Ocean known as Puʻukohola (Hill of the Whale), near Kawaihae on the Big Island of Hawaiʻi. The national historic site was also established to help revitalize and perpetuate the traditional native Hawaiian cultural heritage.

With the labor of thousands of workers, the 100- by 224-foot temple platform was built of water-rounded boulders and stones, all meticulously placed so as to require no mortar. Rock walls surrounded this platform on three sides, the fourth being open to the view of the sea. Thatch-roofed structures; carved wooden, grimace-faced effigies; a drum house; altar; and an oracle tower were erected on the platform. When the temple was completed in 1791, Kamehameha invited his cousin, chief Keoua Kuʻahuʻula—a longtime rival for control of the Big Island—to the temple consecration ceremony. But just as the cousin and eleven friends stepped ashore from their war canoes, they were killed. It is not known whether their deaths were premeditated or whether they resulted from a fight that erupted on the beach. The bodies were then presented at the temple altar as a human sacrifice.

Kamehameha subsequently proceeded to fulfill the *kahuna* prediction by becoming King Kamehameha the Great of all the Hawaiian Islands. When he died in 1819, his favorite wife brought about the end of the ancient social and religious taboos and customs. Outward symbols, such as the tall carved effigies and temple structures, were destroyed at Puʻukohola Heiau and elsewhere. Today, only the massive platform remains. In the words of Kalani Meinecke, a Hawaiian scholar:

> Puʻu Kohola is a place of destiny. It is in this hallowed vicinity that Keoua Kuʻahuʻula offered himself to his fate and where Kamehameha realized the clinching of his rise to conquest, dominion and, ultimately, immortality. Today, this National Historic Site stands as the greatest historic edifice to the memory of Kamehameha—he who is regarded as the most celebrated Hawaiian who ever lived.

The park's visitor center provides a few displays, programs, and publications. One goal of this National Park Service area is to continue the reintroduction of native flora and to expand interpretive programs on native plants and their traditional uses and spiritual significance. For instance, the taro or *kalo* has long had a variety of uses. Its root is pounded into *poi* that is rich in vitamins and minerals. The juice helps heal insect bites and other skin wounds,

Arts and crafts, Pu'ukohola Heiau National Historic Site [Russ Butcher]

the pulp when mixed with *noni* fruit and the juice of sugar cane has been taken as a laxative, and the plant itself is symbolic of ancestry and interconnections of the native Hawaiian family. Visitors are not permitted to enter the temple platform area. A trail leads from the visitor center around to a view of the temple, and there is also a shore road that leads to a view of the structure from Spencer Beach Park. Other significant places within the site include the ruins of an earlier temple, Mailekini Heiau, that is down the hill from the great *heiau*; the site of Pelekane, the king's residence at Kawaihae; and the site of the John Young House. Young was a British sailor who became stranded on Hawai'i in 1790 and then became a close friend and trusted business counselor to Kamehameha the Great. He was honored with a Hawaiian name, 'Olohana; was made a full Hawaiian chief; and served as governor of the island from 1802-1812. He also managed lands given to him by Kamehameha. These cherished properties were subsequently inherited by his granddaughter, Queen Emma, wife of King Kamehameha IV.

Lands initially acquired by the National Park Service for the national historic site were generously donated by The Queen's Medical Center, a health care facility begun by the queen and her husband in 1859. The park was expanded in 1990 with another donation of lands from The Queen Emma Foundation, the real estate management subsidiary of The Queen's Health Systems.

As of this writing, Hawaiian cultural demonstrations are presented one day per week, January through September. Other special cultural events are held periodically, climaxed by the spectacular annual Hawaiian Cultural Festival, held on the weekend closest to the 17th of August. Similar to the festival held in July at Pu'uhonua o Honaunau National Historical Park, it features the colorful Royal Court procession, a gift-giving ceremony, and court dancers, followed by a fascinating program of arts and crafts demonstrations and workshops. The latter includes early Hawaiian dances, weaving of coconut-frond bowls, featherwork, pounding of *tapa* (bark cloth), *ki'i* effigy carving, beginning lessons in speaking Hawaiian, games, *lei* making, and net making and fishing.

An especially excellent publication is *Resource Units in Hawaiian Culture,* by Donald D. Kilolani Mitchell (The Kamehameha Schools Press, Honolulu 1992).

Camping and picnicking are not permitted in the national historic site, but facilities are provided at the adjacent county-owned Samuel M. Spencer Beach Park. Lodging and meals are available at communities such as Kailua-Kona and Waimea, and at resorts along the Kohala and Kona coasts.

IF YOU GO: Access to the site entrance is four-tenths of a mile north of the junction of State routes 270 and 19, on State Route 270. Further information on the site: Superintendent, P.O. Box 44340, Kawaihae, HI 96743. Telephone (808) 882-7218.

ROGER WILLIAMS NATIONAL MEMORIAL

ROGER WILLIAMS NATIONAL MEMORIAL consists of a 4.5-acre park on North Main Street in Providence, Rhode Island. This memorial was authorized in 1965 to commemorate the founding of Providence Plantations by Roger Williams (c. 1603 to 1683). Williams promoted the ideal of a democratically governed colony providing religious freedom, tolerance, and the separation of church and state.

Roger Williams was born in London, England, around the year 1603. He came to America in 1631 to separate from the Church of England. In Boston, he suffered under the religious constraints and intolerance of the Puritan founders of the Massachusetts Bay Colony. Williams found that the strong alliance between church and state allowed the passage of civil laws that mandated church attendance and payment of a tax in support of the church. Williams protested against the colony's laws and was banished. He moved south from Massachusetts to the Narragansett Bay area where he started a new settlement named 'Providence Plantations.'

In Massachusetts colony, political activity was under the influence and control of the church, and non-church members were denied the right to vote. The colony of Providence Plantations was founded by Williams on the principles of religious freedom, tolerance, separation of church and state, and governmental democracy. Providence Plantations governed its own affairs in town meetings, except that there were no religious qualifications for voting.

By 1643, four settlements existed: Providence Plantations, Portsmouth, and Newport on Rhode Island, and Warwick. In 1644 and 1663 Williams returned to England to obtain charters for his settlement. These documents became the legal foundation of the new colony of *Rhode Island and Providence Plantations* (the true name of the state today). The Crown of England gave authority to settle on the lands in and around Narragansett Bay, and granted the colony the right to govern itself.

These charters united the four towns into a single government. However, it was the Charter of 1663, signed by King Charles II, that granted the colony full liberty in religious matters. It was called a 'lively experiment' . . . that a . . . civil state may stand and best be maintained with full liberty of religious concernments." This Royal Charter hangs in the Rhode Island capitol building.

A century after Williams' death, the Constitution's Bill of Rights ensured the freedom of religion, and the separation of church and state in the United States of America. Roger Williams' ideas were now part of the laws of a new nation. The Roger Williams National Memorial commemorates the contribution he made to the principles of freedom established in the United States.

The national memorial's visitor center is located at the corner of North Main and Smith streets, and provides exhibits, videos, and relevant publications. The center is open daily, except on Thanksgiving, Christmas, and New Year's Day. Group interpretive programs may be arranged in advance. There are paths with interpretive waysides through the memorial.

IF YOU GO: Lodging and meals are available in Providence. From Interstate 95 north or south, take the downtown exit, take your first left at the light, proceed by taking a right turn at the next three lights. At the last turn, you will find the parking lot for the memorial on the immediate left. Further information: Superintendent, 282 North Main Street, Providence, RI 02903. Telephone (401) 521-7266.

SAINT CROIX ISLAND INTERNATIONAL HISTORIC SITE

SAINT CROIX ISLAND INTERNATIONAL HISTORIC SITE comprises 50 acres, of which 6.5 acres are on St. Croix Island, about eight acres are of intertidal terrain where the range between mean high and low tides is about 20 feet, and about 35 acres are on the mainland, along the tidal estuary of the St. Croix River, in eastern Maine. The area was initially established as a national monument in 1949 and was then redesignated as an international historic site in 1984, in cooperation with Canada's Department for the Environment. It protects the site of the first French settlement, in 1604, in northern North America.

In 1603, the king of France made Pierre Dugua de Mons a *général de corps d'armée* (lieutenant general), granting him complete authority over North America between the 40th and 46th parallels (from just north of today's Montréal, Québec, and Mount Katahdin in Maine, south to today's Philadelphia, Pennsylvania). He was directed to settle, explore, and develop those lands for France. The king also commissioned Samuel de Champlain to serve as the expedition's geographer, since the previous year he had sailed up the St. Lawrence River and had an initial knowledge of the region.

Dugua's five sailing ships experienced a long and stormy crossing of the Atlantic Ocean. Three of his ships sailed up the St. Lawrence River to trade for furs. The other two, carrying 79 men and after initially exploring what is now the coast of New Brunswick, sailed into Passamaquoddy Bay in June, and proceeded up the St. Croix River, where they discovered a small wooded island. Champlain wrote that the island was "*couverte de sapins, de bouleaux, d'érables et de chêne*" (covered with firs [probably white spruces], birches, maples, and oaks). Because of its good anchorage and defensibility, Dugua selected it for their settlement.

During the summer, the men were put to work building a number of structures, including the governor's cabin, dwellings for those of noble birth, barracks for the soldiers, a kitchen house, a storehouse, and blacksmith shop. The settlement seemed to be well underway. But as matters turned out, an unusually early and brutally severe winter began in October, soon cutting off the colonists from the mainland, and coming perilously close to terminating the expedition right there.

In addition to their being isolated and imprisoned on the little island that Champlain had initially described as being "*trés bien située naturellement*" (by nature very well situated), the men lacked fresh water and proper food (they had only salted food), and had inadequate clothing and shelter. Many contracted scurvy from the poor diet, and 34 men died, while others became seriously ill.

To make matters worse, as the long winter finally began to relent, the long-awaited supply ship they had expected in April failed to show up until mid-June. Dugua immediately set forth to find a more suitable place for their settlement. This he located across the Bay of Fundy at what was named Port Royal, near today's town of Annapolis Royal, Nova Scotia. St. Croix Island was obviously abandoned. As increasing numbers of French settlers arrived in North America, other villages were founded, including the one on the St. Lawrence River that grew to become the city of Québec and the capital of the Province of Québec.

As for St. Croix Island, for many years its original name was long forgotten. New England colonists called it Dochet Island. But when the international boundary between the U.S. and Canada was being determined, the original *Île Sainte-Croix* was discovered. The island subsequently served as a neutral meeting spot for American and British representatives during negotiations over the War of 1812. In 1857, a lighthouse was established that continues to be operated by the U.S. Coast Guard as a beacon for boats on the river.

Although no structures remain on the island, excavations have revealed the foundations of buildings and the graves of those who perished during the harsh winter.

IF YOU GO: As of this writing, there is no boat service to the island. Visitors may look across from the top of a hill in the mainland unit of the national historic site, just off U.S. Route 1, eight miles south of Calais, ME. A small interpretive facility tells the history of the island. A picnic area is also provided there. Lodging and meals are available in Calais and other towns along the coast of Maine. Further information: c/o Superintendent, Acadia National Park, P.O. Box 177, Bar Harbor, ME 04609. Telephone (207) 288-3338.

SALEM MARITIME NATIONAL HISTORIC SITE

SALEM MARITIME NATIONAL HISTORIC SITE consists of nine acres along the waterfront of Salem, Massachusetts. It was established in 1938 to protect and interpret nine historic buildings and three historic wharfs that represent the late eighteenth and early nineteenth centuries, when this harbor was among the world's most active international shipping ports.

In the 1630s, Salem became an important New England coastal fishing town. By 1643, commercial sailing ships were carrying cargo such as lumber and dried codfish from New England to the West Indies, and then West Indian rum and molasses to New England or Britain, in trade for manufactured goods. When the British levied heavy duties, taxes, and trading constraints on American shipping, thereby greatly reducing shippers' profits, New England shipping merchants provided major financial support for America's War for Independence (the American Revolution). And when the American colonies declared their independence from Britain, more ship owners from Salem than from any other American port city responded to the Continental Congress' appeal for American ships to attack and disrupt British shipping, and to seize weapons and supplies from their ships for use by the Continental Army. Salem privateers captured over 400 British ships.

Following America's victory in the war, Salem entered its grandest period of maritime trade, with shipowners expanding worldwide. Salem's most prominent shipping merchant was Elias Hasket Derby. Before the War for Independence, Derby ships plied the trade routes between New England, the West Indies, and Europe. During the war, Derby Wharf serviced at least as many privateers engaged in attacking British ships as any other wharf in America. After the war, Derby opened trade with China in 1786. His ships obtained such exotic goods as Chinese silks, china, spices, and tea in exchange for American lumber, dried fish, beef, cotton, and tobacco. Salem's shipping soon expanded further into lucrative trading with India, bringing back cotton fabrics, coffee, tea, pepper, and various spices. Ships sailed out of bustling Salem Harbor "to the farthest port of the rich East," as the city's slogan stated, and plied the seas from port to port on voyages of a year or two, searching for exotic merchandise to trade with other countries or to bring back to America. Ships from the East brought back such art objects as carved ivory figurines, decorative fans and tea caddies, and paintings. Enormous wealth was amassed by Derby, William Gray, Simon Forrester, and many others. And powerful shipping merchants such as these gave their backing to a strong central government for the budding United States of America, helped encourage the ratification of the U.S. Constitution, and consequently benefited from tariffs that discouraged competition from foreign shipping to American ports.

In 1807, however, the decline of the shipping heyday began when the United States slapped an embargo on trade with France and Britain. Most of America's shipping companies were hit hard by this constraint against trade. The War of 1812 cut off further international shipping, and Salem never recovered from the economic impacts of these two events. The last square-rigged ship sailed away from Derby Wharf in the 1890s.

There were once over 50 wharfs extending into Salem Harbor. Three of those remain: Derby Wharf that was started in 1762 and greatly expanded in 1806; Central Wharf, dating from 1791; and Hatch's Wharf. Each of these was lined with a number of warehouses that provided secure places for storing such products as silks; cotton and cotton fabrics; ivory; spices including cinnamon, cloves, and nutmeg; coffee; cocoa; beet sugar; and even gold dust. Two of the warehouses remain: Central Wharf Warehouse, dating from 1805 (now housing the national historic site's orientation center), and the Hawkes House—built in 1780 as a residence—which served as a warehouse from the 1780s to 1799 (now the park's headquarters), as well as the foundation of the Forrester Warehouse, dating from before 1832.

The imposing red brick, two-story Custom House, built in 1819, is where shipping merchants paid customs, import duties, and other taxes, and where the U.S. government issued permits to bring cargo ashore. Behind the Custom House is the Scale House, built in 1829, in which the U.S. Customs Service kept large scales for weighing cargo on board ships.

The Derby House, which dates from 1762, is the oldest brick house in Salem and was built fronting on Derby Wharf. The Narbonne-Hale House, erected in the 1600s, was occupied by various laborers and craftsmen, including a ropemaker and a tanner. And finally, the West India Goods Store, dating from around 1800, served as a popular retail sales outlet for some of the imported foods and other merchandise from around the world.

The site's orientation center, in the Central Wharf Warehouse building, provides interpretive exhibits, an introductory film, and publications on the history of Salem Harbor and vicinity. Historic structures may be visited either on guided tours (reservations may be necessary) or at one's own pace. A Heritage Walking Trail leads from the visitor center, in downtown Salem at 2 Liberty Street, to the orientation center. Group tours of the site are offered seasonally by prior arrangement.

IF YOU GO: Lodging and meals are available in Salem. Access to Salem and the site is by way of a number of routes including I-95 north from Boston, taking the Lowell St. exit (Exit 26) or Route 114 East exit (Exit 25A) to downtown Salem, following signs to the visitor center. The site is closed on Thanksgiving, Christmas, and New Year's Day. Further information: Superintendent, 174 Derby St., Salem, MA 01970. Telephone (508) 740-1660.

SALINAS PUEBLO MISSIONS NATIONAL MONUMENT

SALINAS PUEBLO MISSIONS NATIONAL MONUMENT, consisting of 1,100 acres in three units in central New Mexico, was initially established as the single-unit Gran Quivira National Monument in 1909, then expanded in 1980 with the addition of the Abó and Quarai units. Together they protect the ruins of three Pueblo Indian villages dating back to around A.D. 1300 and the impressive ruins of associated Hispanic Franciscan mission churches of the 1600s. The national monument, located in the Estancia Basin between the Rio Grande Valley to the west and the Great Plains to the east, takes its name from the *salinas* or salines—the nearby playa, or dry lake sediments, where these pueblo people gathered salt used in trade with other villages.

When the Spaniards initially colonized New Mexico in 1598, missionaries of the Franciscan Order set out to convert the Indians to Roman Catholic Christianity. By around 1618, the friars had created missions at many of the pueblos along the Rio Grande. Attention then turned to the Salinas Province pueblos. In 1622, Fray Francisco Fonte began his missionary work at Abó. With the Indians' labor, construction of the Church of *San Gregorio de Abó* began the following year and was completed in four years. Its interior measured roughly 84 feet long by 25 feet wide, and its flat roof, which was supported by large pine logs called *vigas* hauled down from the mountains, was about 25 feet high. This original structure was subsequently expanded to a larger, more massive church that required six years to build and was completed in 1651. As with the ancient pueblo itself, the church at Abó was built of the local red sandstone that naturally outcrops here, near the base of the scenic, pine-covered Manzano Mountains.

The mission complex also included the *convento*, housing the religious brothers and certain devoted followers. There were cells (small, sparsely furnished sleeping rooms), a refectory (dining room) and kitchen, storerooms, and stables. And there were classrooms and workrooms where the Spaniards instructed the Indians in the Spanish language, in Catholic prayers and the sacraments, and in Spanish techniques of woodworking, crafts, music, and horticulture. A patio and corral were also within the *convento*.

In 1626, Fray Juan Gutierrez de la Chica began establishing a similar mission center at the nearby pueblo of Cuarac, or Quarai. With the Indians' labor, an even more massive church than at Abó was erected—the Church of *la Purísima Concepción de Cuarac*. This church-and-*convento* complex was completed in the early 1630s, the church itself taking five years to build. Within its five-foot-thick, red-sandstone walls, this great edifice measured nearly 100 feet long, was 50 feet across at the transept, 27 feet wide at the nave, and its walls rose about 40 feet to the *viga*-supported roof.

The largest of the Salinas pueblos was at what is now the Gran Quivira unit of the national monument. In contrast to the colorful red sandstone of Abó and Quarai, the pueblo and church ruins at *Pueblo de las Humanas*, as the Spaniards called it, were constructed of the local whitish-gray limestone. In

1629, Fray Francisco Letrado began his missionary work at Las Humanas, at first establishing a small church. In 1659, Fray Diego de Santander carried on the work, and started construction of a new church of *San Buenaventura*. This larger structure, measuring 138 feet in length, was never completed.

In the 1660s, the Pueblo Indians of New Mexico became increasingly restive and unhappy over the Spaniards telling them what to do and what to believe. In addition, there were now attacks by the nomadic Great Plains Indians—the Apaches and Comanches—who with horses obtained from the Spaniards had a tremendous logistical advantage over the pueblo people. Las Humanas, Quarai, and Abó were among the most vulnerable pueblos to these sudden raids, in which Pueblo Indians were sometimes taken captive.

Further serious stress was placed on these eastern villages by the prolonged drought of 1667-

Ruins of convent and Mission Church of San Gregorio de Abó, Salinas Pueblo Missions National Monument, New Mexico [Russ Butcher]

1672—the severity of which caused crop failures and widespread famine. As if all these problems were not enough to endure, there were also epidemics of European-introduced diseases, such as smallpox, that swept through the Indian populations, decimating their numbers. In the 1670s, surviving inhabitants of the Salinas Province pueblos gave up, abandoned their ancient homes, and moved into other villages along the central Rio Grande Valley. Las Humanas was abandoned first in 1671, followed by Abó in 1673, and Quarai by 1677.

In 1680, the Pueblo Indians of New Mexico finally took matters into their own hands, organized a plan to throw off the 82-year yoke of Spanish rule, and successfully rebelled. A few days later, 21 missionaries and close to 400 other Spaniards lay dead and all the Franciscan missions were plundered. The remaining Spaniards and their sympathizers were permitted to leave New Mexico, providing a 12-year interval before they returned and reconquered the region in 1692.

The long-silent Salinas pueblos of Abó, Quarai, and Las Humanas at Gran Quivira are now reminders of the attempted dominance by those early Spanish colonists of the ancient pueblo culture. As you stand amid the awesome ruins and the surrounding natural beauty of the landscape, it is possible to imagine the many centuries of pueblo life. It is possible to imagine the arrival of the Spaniards with their religious faith that impelled them to impose their religious and secular views upon these pueblo people. It is possible to stand inside the ruins of these once-great churches and imagine the singing and organ music that once filled these now roofless spaces. And it is possible to imagine the increasing pressures and problems that ultimately conspired to destroy the very fabric of life in these ancient places.

The mission churches of Abó, Quarai, and Las Humanas, along with the great adobe church at Pecos Pueblo (see Pecos National Historical Park) and the church at Jemez State Monument, were certainly great architectural achievements of their time and place. They were once described in glowing terms by the first director of the Museum of New Mexico, Dr. Edgar L. Hewett:

> These five churches . . . constitute a noble group of ruins . . . crude, massive, elemental as compared with the later missions of California, Arizona, and Texas . . . a style not dependent upon ornamentation for its distinction but resting its claim of merit solely upon a . . . formal tradition that perfectly meets the requirements of a unique, elemental environment.

The national monument's visitor center is centrally located between the three units, in the town of Mountainair. The National Park Service offers interpretive programs, exhibits, and publications. An especially excellent book on the national monument is *Salinas Pueblo Missions* by Dan Murphy (Southwest Parks and Monuments Association, 1993). Each monument unit provides a self-guiding trail. There are small picnic areas at each site; and the nearest camping facilities are available at Manzano Mountain State Park, 13 miles north of Mountainair on State Route 55.

IF YOU GO: Lodging and meals are available in Mountainair. Access to the monument is by way of various highways including south from Albuquerque 37 miles on I-25 to Belen, then southeast 21 miles on State Route 47, and east 22 miles on U.S. Route 60 to Mountainair. Abó is 9 miles west of Mountainair on Route 60; Quarai is 8 miles north of Mountainair on Route 55; and Gran Quivira (Las Humanas) is 26 miles south of Mountainair on route 55. Further information: Superintendent, P.O. Box 496, Mountainair, NM 87036. Telephone (505) 847-2585.

SALT RIVER BAY NATIONAL HISTORICAL PARK & ECOLOGICAL PRESERVE

SALT RIVER BAY NATIONAL HISTORICAL PARK & ECOLOGICAL PRESERVE, consisting of 912 acres on St. Croix Island in the U.S. Virgin Islands, West Indies, was established in 1992 to protect outstanding cultural and natural values. As of this writing, the park-preserve is not open to the public. It is cooperatively managed by the Virgin Islands and U.S. federal governments.

The Salt River Bay area contains traces of pre-Columbian native Caribbean settlements. These included three ethnic groups that in sequence moved northward from South America into the West Indies. The earliest were a pottery-making people called the Igneri. Next came the Taino, who arrived around A.D. 600 and were farming people who lived in small coastal villages. The third were the Island Caribs, who arrived around 1400. They killed all the Taino males and captured the women and children who were then assimilated into what became the Carib-Taino culture. There are burial grounds that date from A.D. 665 to 1015. A ceremonial plaza dating from the thirteenth or fourteenth century, the site of an important Indian village, and middens (refuse dumps) are the park's most significant archaeological resources.

Christopher Columbus dropped anchor here on November 14, 1493, on his second transatlantic voyage to the New World. After his visit, which was on behalf of the Spanish Crown, the king of Spain ordered that all native West Indians be put to death, as punishment for their rebellion against Spanish rule. By the end of the sixteenth century, Santa Cruz (Holy Cross) had virtually no remaining inhabitants. During the seventeenth century, Spain, Britain, Holland, and France fought over ownership of the island. Construction of an earthen fort at Salt River Bay was initiated by the British in 1641, completed by the Dutch in 1642, and captured by the French in 1650. France renamed the island St. Croix and retained ownership until 1733. At that time, the Danish West India & Guinea Company purchased it and constructed a customs house and gun battery in an attempt to curtail smuggling. Traces of these structures remain, and are reminders of the Danish sugar-based colony that thrived on St. Croix for 150 years (see also Christiansted National Historic Site). After sugar-beet production in other parts of the world caused a sharp decline in St. Croix's industry, the United States purchased what became the U.S. Virgin Islands, in 1917.

The park-preserve also protects an ecologically rich marine and terrestrial tropical area that includes an unusual underwater limestone canyon, coral reefs, a tidal estuary with beds of sea grass, a salt pond, stands of mangroves, a freshwater marsh, and a variety of canyon and upland woodlands.

Roland Wauer, who was the key author of the National Park Service's document "Alternatives for Salt River," wrote about these ecological resources ("Treasure Island: Salt River Bay, St. Croix, a new national park unit, preserves natural and historical riches," Sept.-Oct. 1992, *National Parks* magazine):

> The diversity of wildlife is due in part to a chain of relatively intact natural habitats, from upland forest to marine corals. Most similar systems in the Caribbean are missing important links, which development has either degraded or eliminated. But here on St. Croix, inland slopes contain thorn woodland habitat on their crests, and deciduous forests grow on cooler hillsides and within a few canyon bottoms.

Rainwater flows from these forests and slopes into Salt River. . . .
The Salt River floodplain still contains adequate moisture to support
a freshwater marsh of cattails, sedges, and grasses. Huge swamp ferns
. . . grow under the canopy of the outer mangroves.

Below the marsh, a forest begins that is made up of stands of button-
woods, white, black, and red mangroves. At the edge of the estuary,
great tangles of red mangrove roots support algae and form spectacular
nursery areas for St. Croix's abundant fish, shellfish, and crustaceans.
A system of fresh to brackish to salt water flora and fauna filters out
pollutants so that the estuary beyond is enriched with nontoxic nutrients on which the young marine life depends.

As the flow continues seaward, it passes over the sea grass beds and
their abundant marine life, nourishing these valuable habitats. The
flow continues past the capes toward the coral gardens and reefs.
These habitats support a diverse collection of marine life and provide
valuable spawning and nursery areas for many species of fish and
crustaceans. Beyond the barrier reef, the submarine canyon forms a
long northsouth trench, whose steep walls are covered with a variety
of deep-water corals and sponges.

There are more than a hundred species of birds known to reside,
breed, or migrate through the Salt River Bay area. Among them are red-billed
tropicbirds; brown boobies; brown pelicans; magnificent frigatebirds; several
species of herons, including tricolored, great and snowy egrets; the rare West
Indian whistling duck; ospreys; clapper rails; a variety of shorebirds, including black-necked stilts; the rare white-crowned pigeon; common ground-
doves; Antillean crested hummingbirds; pearly-eyed thrashers; bananaquits;
and a large number of warblers and vireos that winter in or migrate through
the area.

There are 28 federally and locally listed endangered species of fauna
and flora in the park-preserve, among which are the hawksbill and green sea
turtles, and the large swamp fern. The marine waters of the park-preserve, that
comprise roughly two-thirds of the acreage, provide rich habitat for marine
life, including such beautiful tropical fish as the queen angelfish, several kinds
of butterflyfish, and sargeant majors.

Eight years of litigation, brought by the Virgin Islands Conservation
Society and supported by court-admissible legal briefs filed by several other environmental groups including the National Parks and Conservation Association
(NPCA), fortunately led to a favorable federal district court decision in 1994.
The court declared invalid a coastal zone management permit that would have
allowed a major development company to construct a large resort and marina
complex on one-quarter of the park-preserve's acreage. This was an especially

gratifying victory for park protection, because NPCA had been instrumental in helping to build public support for establishment of the park-preserve and in helping to draft the park-preserve's enabling legislation in Congress.

IF YOU GO: Further information: Superintendent, 2100 Church St., #100, St. Croix, VI 00822-4611. Telephone (809) 773-1460.

SAN ANTONIO MISSIONS NATIONAL HISTORICAL PARK

SAN ANTONIO MISSIONS NATIONAL HISTORICAL PARK comprises 825 acres near the San Antonio River in southern Texas. It was established in 1978 in order to provide for the preservation, restoration, and interpretation of the Spanish missions of Concepción, San José, San Juan, and Espada, including historically associated features. The historic resources within the park that have survived the past 250 years are protected through the combined efforts of the National Park Service, the Roman Catholic Archdiocese of San Antonio, the San Antonio Conservation Society, state and local governments, and the public, including the local residents. By formal agreement, the Archdiocese of San Antonio and the National Park Service encourage visitor enjoyment of these sites, while ensuring there is no interference with the traditional religious services at the four active parishes.

The first mission in the San Antonio area was *Mission San Antonio de Valero*, begun in 1718. It was subsequently relocated and a new structure was begun in 1755—a building made famous by the battle of the Alamo, the 1836 conflict in which Texas fought for independence from Mexico. The Alamo is now a shrine within a state park, in the city of San Antonio.

Of the four mission churches in the national historical park, the first to be founded was *Mission San José y San Miguel de Aguayo*, in 1720. While this mission was initially established in eastern Texas, nomadic Indian raids and pressures from the French in adjacent Louisiana forced its abandonment. It was then successfully established farther west, here in the San Antonio River valley, by Fray Antonio Margil de Jesús.

European-introduced diseases, such as smallpox, ravaged much of the initial Indian mission population in 1739, but by the late 1760s, the numbers of resident Coahuiltecan Indians climbed to the mission's all-time peak of around 350 individuals. San José developed into the largest of the Texas missions and became a major cultural center. A visitor in 1777 referred to San José as "the Queen of the Missions."

The present stone church was built from 1768-1782, with the labor of the Indians. Of the park's four churches, San José is architecturally the most ornamented. It has Romanesque forms and an elaborately carved baroque facade; a single massive, 75-foot-tall corner bell tower; a circular stairway to the bells; a domed and barrel-vaulted ceiling above the nave; and an exquisitely detailed baroque window. According to church legend, this window was designed by Mexican sculptor Pedro Huizar, in memory of his sweetheart, Rosa, who died during a sea voyage on her way to join him at the mission.

Adjoining the church was a *convento* where, as at the other missions, there were quarters for the Franciscans, a refectory (dining room) and kitchen, storerooms, a patio, cloisters, and workrooms and classrooms where the Indians were instructed in a wide range of religious and secular subjects, such as the tenets of Catholic Christianity, the Spanish language, and Spanish arts, crafts, and other vocational skills.

Surrounding this complex was a large compound enclosed by a high stone wall, in which were built a variety of rooms housing the Indians, a few Spanish soldiers, and a granary. This fortified community provided protection from periodic raids of nomadic Comanche and Apache bands. Outside the fortified compound were orchards, pastures, and farmlands. Grazing lands for herds of sheep, goats, cattle, and other livestock were some distance away at the mission's ranch.

Reoccurring epidemics of smallpox and other diseases periodically swept through the mission populations, taking a heavy toll of the Indians in the 1780s and 1790s. Others were killed during Comanche and Apache raids, while still others left the missions to return to their old lifestyle. Consequently, the Indian population at San José, as at other missions, plummeted between 1768 and 1791, to less than a third of its high point. The decline continued, with fewer than 50 Indians by 1815. By 1824, all of the Texas missions were fully secularized, with the churches turned over to secular clergy and the missions' communal lands redistributed to the Indians.

About two miles north of Mission San José is *Mission Nuestra Señora de la Purísima Concepción de Acuña*. This mission was established in eastern Texas in an attempt to convert and minister to the Tejas Indians of that area. It was relocated to the San Antonio River valley in 1731. The present stone church, with its massive twin bell towers, was completed in 1755 in Romanesque and colonial baroque styles of architecture. This building has never been extensively restored, and it looks much as it did over two centuries ago when it served the Coahuiltecan Indians. Even some of the original colorful interior designs on the walls can still be seen. Mission Concepción became a major center for religious ceremonies and festivals.

About 2.5 miles south of San José is *Mission San Juan Capistrano*. As with missions Concepción and Espada, it was originally founded in east Texas, then relocated to this more favorable area in 1731. This church has a corner stairstep-shaped bell tower (*espadana*) with two bells on the first level and one above. Within this mission's compound, the Indians were instructed in Spanish arts, crafts, and other skills, as at the other missions. But San Juan was especially known for its extensive agricultural lands that supplied produce to the surrounding region.

IF YOU GO: A one-third-of-a-mile interpretive nature trail at San Juan offers visitors the chance to see a part of the original river channel in a natural setting.

Mission San Jose, San Antonio Missions National Historical Park [NPS]

Finally, about two miles south of San Juan is the *Mission San Francisco de la Espada*, the southernmost of the San Antonio mission chain. It originated as the earliest of the east Texas missions (1690), but as with missions Concepción and San Juan, Mission Espada was moved to the San Antonio area in 1731. The present stone church was completed in 1756, and was within a strongly fortified wall that successfully protected the community from Indian raids. The church, with the exception of the entrance and bell towers, subsequently fell into ruins, but was carefully rebuilt by a priest in the mid-nineteenth century. The flat roof rests upon large beams and corbels, and the front door is framed by a Moorish-like circular arch with four converging arcs (quatrefoil). The original bell tower (*espadana*) remains.

The orchards and farmlands of the missions were irrigated with water from the San Antonio River that was brought by gravity-flow *acequias* (canals or ditches). The Moors introduced the *acequia* to arid parts of Spain during their long reign beginning in the eighth century A.D. From there the Spaniards brought the concept to New Spain (Mexico). The San Antonio missions' water delivery system was once a 15-mile network of ditches. Each mission had its own *acequia* system consisting of a dam, ditches, and sometimes an aqueduct. The *Acequiá de Espada* that served Mission Espada's needs is still functioning today and includes a working dam and aqueduct.

In 1995, *Rancho de las Cabras*, the historic ranch serving Mission Espada, became part of San Antonio Missions National Historical Park. Located near present day Floresville, Texas, the site contains subterranean remains of the ranch headquarters and associated cultural features. Rancho de las Cabras was a critical link in the mission economy. With as many as 1,200 head of cattle and 4,000 sheep and goats, the mission herds provided abundant food for the mission inhabitants, as well as resources for trade.

In 1996, the park's new 12,000-square-foot visitor center next to Mission San José was completed. This expansive facility contains an exhibit area, interactive videos, a theater, and a sales outlet. Mission San José also contains the nationally recognized Spanish Colonial Bookstore and Los Compadres Giftshop. Two publications, *San Antonio Missions National Historical Park*, by Luis Torres (Southwest Parks and Monuments Association) and *The Missions of San Antonio*, by Mary Ann Noonan Guerra (Alamo Press), are popular sales items available in the park.

The route that connects the four missions can be confusing to visitors. Signs along the route will help guide you, and directions can be obtained from the park staff and from most commercial establishments. Planning your route before you begin will save time and minimize traffic problems. The city bus system is an alternative to your vehicle.

When the San Antonio River rises, the major route south of Mission San José is closed to traffic. Information on alternate routes can be obtained at each mission.

San Antonio Missions National Historical Park is open daily, except on Thanksgiving, Christmas, and New Year's Day. The Park Service warns visitors to stay on sidewalks to avoid fire ants and requests that visitors be respectful of the priests, parishioners, and their church services and related activities.
IF YOU GO: Lodging and meals are available throughout the San Antonio area including many establishments near the park. Camping and picnic facilities are located in the vicinity of the park. Further information: Superintendent, San Antonio Missions National Historical Park, 2202 Roosevelt Ave., San Antonio, TX 78210. Telephone (210) 229-5701.

SAN FRANCISCO MARITIME NATIONAL HISTORICAL PARK

SAN FRANCISCO MARITIME NATIONAL HISTORICAL PARK, established in 1988, comprises 50 acres along the northern waterfront of San Francisco, California. It protects and interprets the seafaring history of the Pacific Coast of the United States, and includes a fleet of historic sailing ships and smaller craft, a maritime museum with artifacts and other exhibits, and a library with research collections.

The square-rigged sailing ship *Balclutha* is one of the primary attractions of the park. Launched in 1886 from near Glasgow, Scotland, she set sail from Cardiff, Wales, on her 140-day maiden voyage to San Francisco, where her cargo of Welsh coal was exchanged for California wheat. She carried two more loads of coal to the city by the bay, also bringing Scotch whiskey and an assortment of other goods. For three years beginning in 1899, this great ship, sailing under the Hawaiian Kingdom flag, delivered lumber from the Pacific Northwest to Australia. In 1904, she ran aground, was bought by the Alaska Packers Association, repaired, renamed the *Star of Alaska,* and transported Alaskan canned salmon to San Francisco.

In 1930, *Balclutha* went into retirement, but was soon purchased by a movie company for use in the film, *Mutiny on the Bounty,* as the renamed

Pacific Queen. In 1954, she was purchased by the San Francisco Maritime Museum, was acquired by the National Park Service in 1978, and once again given the original name *Balclutha* and designated in 1988 as a national historic landmark.

Other vessels in the park's fleet include a three-masted, lumber-carrying schooner, the *C.A. Thayer*, built in 1895; a walkingbeam San Francisco ferry, the *Eureka*, dating from 1890 and the largest of its kind serving the bay at the time; a scow schooner, the *Alma*, launched in 1891; and the 1914 paddle-wheel tug *Eppleton Hall*. The *Alma* was one of 300 to 400 flat-bottomed scows that plied the waters of San Francisco Bay and the Sacramento/San Joaquin delta's shallow river channels. They carried great loads of hay, wheat, onions, and potatoes from the agricultural lands inland; lumber from the mountains; and even coal that was brought by ocean-going vessels from Australia and Britain. These and other craft are docked at the Hyde Street Pier, at the north end of Hyde Street, adjacent to Fisherman's Wharf. There are daily ranger-led tours, interpretive films, and demonstrations.

The park's Maritime Museum, fronting on Aquatic Park at the north end of Polk Street, exhibits a tremendous array of artifacts, historical photographs, paintings, parts of ships, and ship models. To the west of the museum is the J. Porter Shaw Library, open certain hours, Tuesday through Saturday. It is located in the Fort Mason Center and contains more than 22,000 volumes and extensive collections of historical documents, photographs, and ship plans. The park also has a Maritime store at Hyde Street Pier, where books, games, posters, ship models, and other items may be purchased. On the last week in August, the Festival of the Sea is held, featuring living history demonstrations, musical programs, and dray rides in Aquatic Park.

Lodging and meals are abundantly available in San Francisco, some of which are within walking distance of the park and Fisherman's Wharf. Access is recommended by public transportation, since parking is often unavailable in the vicinity of Fisherman's Wharf.

IF YOU GO: The Hyde Street cable car line ends at the park, and there are several bus lines serving the area (public transportation information: 673-MUNI). Further information on the park: Superintendent, Bldg. E, Room 265, Lower Fort Mason, San Francisco, CA 94123. Telephone (415) 556-3002.

SAN JUAN ISLAND NATIONAL HISTORICAL PARK

SAN JUAN ISLAND NATIONAL HISTORICAL PARK, encompassing 1,752 acres in the San Juan Islands of northwestern Washington state, was established in 1966 to protect and interpret the military sites of a long-running dispute between the United States and Great Britain over the ownership of San Juan Island.

The controversy actually began in 1846, when a treaty set the international boundary between the United States and Canada along latitude 49 N, west to the Strait of Georgia, then angling southward and out through the Strait of Juan de Fuca to the Pacific Ocean. This decision was unclear, however, as to exactly where the boundary lay in the vicinity of San Juan Island. Both nations claimed this island and both encouraged settlement by their own citizens, to lend legitimacy to their respective claims.

The stalemate came to a head in June 1859, when Lyman Cutlar, a U.S. farmer, shot and killed a British hog that had trespassed into his garden. Tempers flared and tensions quickly mounted. A company of U.S. troops under George Pickett was sent to the island and subsequently reinforced, while a small fleet of British warships assembled offshore. In the end, common sense prevailed and direct military conflict was avoided. U.S. Army infantry and British royal marines set up camps at opposite ends of the island and awaited diplomatic settlement of the dispute.

Fortunately, no human blood was spilled in what came to be called the "Pig War." The matter was submitted to international arbitration, and in 1872 Germany's Kaiser Wilhelm I ruled that the water boundary lay through Haro Strait, west of San Juan Island. Thus, this island and the rest of the San Juans have thereafter belonged to the United States.

The two-unit park protects the remains of earthworks and the quarters of the American encampment at the southern end of the island; and the restored British guardhouse, barracks, and other structures on the northwest shore of the island.

Two informative publications are *Pig War Islands* by David Richardson (Orcas Publishing Company); and *Pickett: Leader of the Charge* by Edward G. Longacre (White Mane Publishing Company, Inc.). For visitors interested in the birds of the area, there is *Birding in the San Juan Islands* by Mark G. Lewis and Fred A. Sharpe (The Mountaineers).

IF YOU GO: The park's visitor centers are located at Friday Harbor, American Camp, and English Camp (summer only). Interpretive exhibits and programs, historical reenactments, and walks are provided. The visitor centers are closed on federal holidays from mid-November through April. There are also hiking trails and picnicking facilities in the park. Lodging and meals are available in Friday Harbor and elsewhere on the island. Access is by way of Washington state ferry from Anacortes, WA, and from Sidney, British Columbia, or by scheduled airline flights from Seattle, Anacortes, and Bellingham, WA. Further information: Superintendent, P.O. Box 429, Friday Harbor, WA 98250. Telephone (360) 378-2240.

SAN JUAN NATIONAL HISTORIC SITE

SAN JUAN NATIONAL HISTORIC SITE, consisting of 75 acres, was established in 1949 to protect and interpret the massive fortifications begun by Spain in the sixteenth century and expanded and improved in the late eighteenth century. They were built to guard the harbor and colonial city of San

Juan that is situated on a small island adjacent to the mainland of Puerto Rico, in the West Indies. The forts of *El Morro, San Cristóbal*, and *El Cañuelo,* and the walls encircling Viejo San Juan (Old San Juan), are the oldest European-style military defenses in the territorial United States. They have also been designated as a World Heritage Site by the United Nations.

San Juan was founded in 1521 as a Spanish colonial outpost in the Caribbean Sea, which had been claimed by Spain as its exclusive domain by right of conquest and by papal decree. One of six major fortification complexes in the Caribbean region was built at San Juan to help defend Spanish interests from attacks by British, French, and Dutch ships. The first meaningful fortification at San Juan was a round, stone tower built in the late 1530s on the rocky headland (*el morro*) at the mouth of the harbor.

With increasing frequency of enemy raids upon Spanish towns and ships in the Caribbean, additional fortifications, called "hornworks," were constructed around the headland in the 1590s. As ultimately built, *Castillo de San Felipe del Morro* (Castle St. Philip of the Headland) became a massive, six-tiered sandstone fortress that contained gun platforms, bastions for batteries of cannons, storerooms, gun rooms, quarters for the troops, an assembly courtyard, a prison, a chapel, a dry moat, ramps, stairs, tunnels, and a number of *garitas* (round sentry boxes) attached to outer corners of the walls and bastions. Among the military action this fort experienced was during the Spanish-American War when the United States attacked San Juan in 1898, resulting in Puerto Rico being ceded to the United States.

Castillo de San Cristóbal (Castle of St. Christopher) was mostly constructed from 1765 to 1785. It is located about a mile east of El Morro and is the largest Spanish fortress in the Western Hemisphere. Whereas El Morro was built primarily to protect the harbor, San Cristóbal's main purpose was to guard the city against attack on land from the east. With more than 450 cannons, it performed well when 7,000 British troops attempted to seize San Juan in 1797. This fort saw action again when one of its guns fired the opening shot of the Spanish-American War in Puerto Rico.

Sprawled across 27 acres, San Cristóbal is an outstanding example of the military's "defense-in-depth" concept, by which the various elements of a fortress are interdependent—each reinforced by other parts and the whole containing several defensive barriers. A massive gun platform (cavalier) is the highest part of the structure, below which is the hornwork that bristled with armament. A dry moat separates the latter from the next barriers—the ravelin and the counterguard. And beyond those defenses is an open expanse called the *plaza de armas* that extends out to the apex of the fortress, called the fan (*el Abanico*). Other gun batteries faced the Atlantic Ocean.

El Cañuelo, also called *San Juan de la Cruz* (St. John of the Cross) is a small stone fort built in the 1660s to help defend the main channel of the harbor and the mouth of Bayamon River that links San Juan with towns inland. The fort is on the west shore of the harbor, and as of this writing, it is closed to visitors.

El Morro and San Cristóbal are open daily except on Christmas. There are interpretive exhibits, programs, tours, and publications at both forts. Self-guiding maps are available in English and Spanish. The Park Service warns visitors to use care when walking the fortress ramparts, tunnels, ramps, and stairways. Weathered stone surfaces are uneven and are slippery when wet. Sturdy walking shoes are recommended. Special care should be taken of children in the forts, especially that they not be allowed to climb on or approach too closely to hazardous places.

Other points of interest in Old San Juan (outside the national historic site) include the *Alcaldía* (the old city hall) dating from 1602; *Casa Blanca*, a museum of sixteenth- and seventeenth-century art and furnishings; San Juan's oldest fort, *La Fortaleza*, and now the governor's residence; *San Juan Cathedral*, dating from 1540; *San José Church*, the second oldest church in the Western Hemisphere (1532-1539); *Ballaja Barracks*, which houses the Museum of the Americas and features folk art; and *La Casa del Libro* (the House of the Book), a museum containing five centuries of the art and history of books.

IF YOU GO: Lodging and meals are available in San Juan and at resorts elsewhere in Puerto Rico. Further information on the national historic site: Superintendent, Fort Cristóbal, Calle Norzagaray, Viejo San Juan, PR 00901-2094. Telephone (809) 729-6777.

SCOTTS BLUFF NATIONAL MONUMENT

SCOTTS BLUFF NATIONAL MONUMENT, encompassing 3,003 acres, was established in 1919 to protect a prominent natural landmark in the North Platte River valley, on the high plains of western Nebraska. The imposing, weather-sculpted sandstone formation was initially named *Me-a-pa-te*, "the hill that is difficult to go around," by the Indian tribes who shared this region for thousands of years with vast herds of buffalo (bison) and other wildlife.

The first Euro-Americans to pass the bluff were seven fur traders returning from John Jacob Astor's trading post in the Pacific Northwest, in December 1812. By the 1820s, caravans of fur traders were traveling up and down the North Platte valley. One trader, William Ashley, and his trappers, having encountered serious hostilities with Indians in the Upper Missouri River region, shifted southward to the North Platte route and on into the heavily beaver-populated valleys of the central Rocky Mountains.

In 1828, Hiram Scott, a fur trader and clerk with the Rocky Mountain Fur Company, was on his way back to St. Louis when he died near the bluff. The circumstances of his death are unknown, but a commonly held story relates that Scott became ill and his colleagues abandoned him. The next year when they returned, they found Scott's skeleton nearby. Subsequently, the bluff was named in his memory.

In 1837, artist Alfred J. Miller, who made the first sketch of the bluff, wrote:

At a distance as we approached it the appearance was that of an immense fortification with bastions, towers, battlements, embrazures [sic], scarps and counterscarps.

The 1830s witnessed the peak of fur trapping and trading in the Rocky Mountains. Eastbound caravans were heavily laden with thousands of beaver pelts. Shallow-draft bullboats, made of buffalo hides stretched over a wooden frame, were also used to transport furs downriver. When the demand for furs declined, some of the former trappers became guides for a number of Christian missionary parties bound for the Oregon Territory in the late 1830s.

One of the first missionaries, Dr. Marcus Whitman, was a major proponent of emigration to Oregon (See Whitman Mission National Historic Site). As a result of his efforts, an expedition of more than one thousand men, women, and children left Independence, Missouri, in May 1843 and reached Scotts Bluff in July. A hunting party for the expedition encountered a herd of buffalo near Scotts Bluff that a chronicler described:

. . . without any exageration [sic] must have numbered a million. The pounding of their hooves on the hard prairie sounded like the roaring of a mighty ocean, surging over the land and sweeping everything before it. . . . it took the heard [sic] two entire days to pass, even at quite a rapid gait. . . .

In 1845, the number of pioneer families braving the incredible hardships along the 2,000 miles of what soon came to be called the Oregon Trail had increased to the point that at least 5,000 emigrants and 500 oxen-drawn wagons made their way along the banks of the North Platte River. In 1847, 142 pioneering Mormons, under the leadership of Brigham Young, arrived in the Valley of the Great Salt Lake. By the end of the next year more than 4,000 of the Mormon faithful had joined them.

In 1848, the discovery of gold in California triggered the next phase of westward emigration—the flood of the Forty-niners on what now became the Oregon-California Trail. Most of these travelers were young men in search of fortunes. In 1849, between 20,000 and 30,000 gold seekers set out for California, and it is estimated that 5,000 of them died along the way.

Scotts Bluff National Monument, Nebraska [NPS]

Prior to 1850, the overland trail near Scotts Bluff had swung southward away from the river, went through Robidoux Pass, then re-entered the river valley and continued westward into Wyoming. However, someone was able to improve the route through Mitchell Pass, between Scotts Bluff and South Bluff, enough to allow wagon traffic. There is no documentation to prove it, but it is generally believed that soldiers from Fort Laramie had done this work in order to save almost a full day's travel time.

By 1852, most emigrants were using the Mitchell Pass shortcut. Tens of thousands of emigrants in their prairie schooners passed Scotts Bluff—some 50,000 California-bound travelers in 1852 alone. The increase in traffic on the overland roads resulted in heightened tensions between the Plains Indians and the emigrants. By 1854, a U.S. military buildup in the region required shipping out great quantities of supplies. Bullwhackers prodded the six- or eight-oxen teams that pulled the heavy freight wagons across the plains and up the North Platte through the pass at Scotts Bluff.

Mail services also ran through the pass. The Central Overland and Pike's Peak Express Company was operating by 1860 between Missouri and the Pacific Coast. In 1860 and 1861, the short-lived Pony Express provided 11-day mail service between St. Joseph, Missouri, and Sacramento, California. Riders changed to fresh ponies at stations located about 15 miles apart, and there were stations just a few miles to the east and to the west of Scotts Bluff.

In 1861, the installation of a coast-to-coast telegraph line through Mitchell Pass brought an end to the mission of the Pony Express. In the same year, the Butterfield Overland Mail's stagecoach service was temporarily shifted to the north, and for a few months daily coach service traveled through Mitchell Pass.

During the Indian Wars, a number of military outposts were established in the region. One such post was Fort Mitchell, located about two miles northwest of Mitchell Pass. Built in 1864, the 150-man garrison participated in skirmishes at Horse Creek and Mud Springs, but was abandoned in 1867. Today, the site is marked by the Nebraska State Historical Society.

In 1869, the Union Pacific, crossing the plains and passing just to the south of Scotts Bluff, connected with the Central Pacific from California at Promontory Summit, Utah (see Golden Spike National Historic Site). The completion of the transcontinental railroad brought an end to the Oregon-California Trail.

Scotts Bluff itself rises to 4,649 feet in elevation. The bluff stands 700 feet above the ruggedly eroded badlands at the northeast foot of the monument and is 800 feet above the North Platte River. The precipice is actually an eroded remnant of once-extensive sedimentary layers laid down millions of years ago. Most of those strata have been worn away, leaving only such reminders as Scotts Bluff, South Bluff, and other prominent landforms in the surrounding area (see the text on Chimney Rock National Historic Site).

The bluff is composed primarily of Tertiary Period non-marine silt, sand, and gravel washed down when the Rocky Mountains were formed 60 million years ago. The lower two-thirds of Scotts Bluff is composed of river-deposited sandy clays that are easily visible in the badlands. These siltstone and mudstone layers are known as the Brule Formation of the White River Group. The sedimentary layers are interlaced with thin layers of compacted volcanic ash.

The upper one-third of the bluff consists largely of tan and gray sandstone layers of the Gering and Monroe Creek-Harrison formations of the Arikaree Group. The Gering consists of thinly stratified, fine-grained sandstone, intertwined with a number of narrow bands of volcanic ash. Above the Gering are the massive Monroe Creek-Harrison sandstones that are laced with calcite-cemented concretions. The bluff's more resistant and protective cap-rock is made up of patches of these hard concretions.

Fossils are contained in all of these formations, but are especially abundant in the Brule Formation. They are evidence of long-extinct mid-Tertiary animals that inhabited this region some 30 to 40 million years ago. Among them were ancient forms of deer, rhinoceroses, saber-tooth cats, horses, camels, and oreodonts that combined some characteristics of the pig, deer, and camel.

Today, wildlife is abundant at Scotts Bluff National Monument. Among the most commonly seen mammals are whitetail and mule deer, coyotes, red foxes, longtail weasels, porcupines, raccoons, striped skunks, cottontails, blacktail prairie dogs, fox squirrels, and kangaroo rats. Several species of snakes also inhabit Scotts Bluff, including the prairie rattlesnake and the bull snake.

Many birds make Scotts Bluff their home, including double-crested cormorants, great blue herons, Canada geese, mallards and other ducks, occasional sandhill cranes along the river, bald and golden eagles, prairie falcons, red-tailed hawks, the introduced ring-necked pheasant, bobwhites, great horned and burrowing owls, black-billed magpies, rock and house wrens, Townsend's solitaires, brown thrashers, black-headed and blue grosbeaks, indigo and lazuli buntings, rufous-sided towhees, lark and numerous other sparrows, lark buntings, meadowlarks, redwings, orchard and northern orioles, pine siskins, and American goldfinches.

Among the monument's flora are ponderosa pine and Rocky Mountain juniper on the cooler, damper north slopes; cottonwood, willow, boxelder, green ash, and American elm in riparian woodlands; skunkbush, rabbitbrush, fringed and sand sagebrush, winterfat, western snowberry, four-wing saltbush, yucca, prickly pear cactus, western wallflower, prairie coneflower, purple locoweed and other members of the pea family; and a number of beautiful grasses, including western wheatgrass, sideoats grama, little bluestem, needle-and-thread, downy brome, and prairie reedgrass.

The monument provides a visitor center, in which is located the Oregon Trail Museum. Exhibits describe the historic trails, the geology of the area, fossil specimens, and archaeological artifacts, as well as the photographs and paintings of William Henry Jackson. (Jackson was the first person to photograph Yellowstone). An interpretive slide program on the Oregon Trail and a wide assortment of publications are also available at the museum. An excellent source on the history of the monument is the National Park Service's handbook *Scotts Bluff* by Merrill J. Mattes.

A paved road allows vehicles to drive from the visitor center to the summit where short walking trails lead to the North Overlook, which provides a panoramic view of the badlands and the North Platte River valley, and to the South Overlook, with its view of Mitchell Pass and South Bluff. The Saddle Rock Trail allows hikers to climb the 1.6 miles from the visitor center up to the summit of Scotts Bluff, while the shorter Oregon Trail pathway will take visitors out to view the remnants of the trail. The monument does not allow overnight camping, but there is a picnic area. Lodging, camping facilities, and meals are available in Gering and Scottsbluff.

IF YOU GO: The monument is located on State Highway 92, three miles west of Gering; and five miles southwest of Scottsbluff, which is located on U.S. Route 26. The Park Service strongly advises visitors to stay on the trails on and up to the summit, as the rock formations are unstable, crumbly, and potentially hazardous, and to be alert for rattlesnakes during the warmer months. Further information: Superintendent, P.O. Box 27, Gering, NE 69341. Telephone (308) 436-4340.

SITKA NATIONAL HISTORICAL PARK

SITKA NATIONAL HISTORICAL PARK, comprising 106 acres in two units in and adjacent to the city of Sitka, on Baranof Island in southeast Alaska, was established as a national monument in 1910 and renamed a national historical park in 1972. It protects and interprets the Russian Bishop's House, and the site of a fortification and battle of 1804 that was the last Tlingit Indian effort attempting to prevent Russian colonization of this part of North America. The park also exhibits 19 beautifully carved Tlingit and Haida totem poles and other arts and crafts, as well as protecting a scenic area of temperate rainforest.

In 1779, the Russian American Company, under the direction of Aleksandr Baranov, set up a Russian fur-trading outpost. The Redoubt St. Michael, located at a site seven miles north of today's Sitka, was to profit from the hunting of sea otters and fur seals populating the ocean waters of southeast Alaska. In 1802, the native Tlingit Indians attacked and wiped out the fledgling colony. The Russians returned two years later with four shiploads of nearly 1,000 Russian and Aleut Indian reinforcements, and defeated the 700 Tlingits. New Archangel, as Sitka was initially called, was the capital of Russian America and developed into the shipping hub for the company's trade in furs, fish, and lumber.

By the mid-nineteenth century, the fur seal and sea-otter populations had plummeted dramatically because of overhunting. This caused a significant decline in the local economy, and in 1867, Russia sold Alaska to the United States.

Today, one of the park's units protects and interprets the Russian Bishop's House, at Lincoln and Monastery streets, in downtown Sitka. This log building, which was the church's official residence for the bishop of Sitka for over a century, has been sensitively restored to its 1852 appearance. It provides interpretive exhibits of the Russian colonial period, the Russian American Company, the Russian Orthodox Church, and the history of the bishop's house. St. Michael's Cathedral (not within the park but nearby on Lincoln Street) is a replica of the original onion-steepled church dating from 1848, which was destroyed by fire in 1966. Fortunately, many of the cherished and beautiful old icons and other religious treasures were rescued from the blaze and may now be seen in the new structure that was consecrated in 1978.

The other unit of the park contains the site of the Tlingit fort where the Indians were defeated by the Russians and their allies, the Aleuts. This unit also protects a heavily forested peninsula bordered by Sitka Sound and bisected by the Indian River. There are about two miles of trails winding through the park. The delightful Totem Trail winds through the serene, lush rainforest of large Sitka spruces and western hemlocks, passing many fascinating and beautifully carved, tall Tlingit and Haida totems, and leading visitors to the site of the fort on the shore of the sound.

In addition to the grand old spruces and hemlocks, there is also the European mountain-ash, with its clusters of beautiful orange berries, while Sitka, red, and green alders grow along the riverbanks. Other species of flora of the park include currants, red elderberry, trailing raspberry, blueberry, huckleberry, salmonberry, rusty menziesia, foamflower, devil's club, fireweed, northern yarrow, cow parsnip, very large skunk cabbages, shy maidens, three kinds of twisted-stalks, false lily-of-the-valley (deerheart), Merten's coral-root orchid, bunchberry, Siberian spring beauty, rattlesnake root, and a number of buttercups. In this lush environment, graceful ferns are plentiful, including sword, licorice, lady, shield, oak, and bracken.

Sitka National Historical Park exhibits nineteen Tlingit and Haida totem poles. [Larry Ulrich]

Mammals of the park and vicinity include the Sitka blacktail deer, mink, martens, river otters, and occasionally one of the large Alaska brown bears. Offshore are Steller's sea lions, harbor seals, humpback whales, and orcas (killer whales). Among the birds are common, Pacific, and red-throated loons; red-necked and horned grebes; sandhill cranes; Canada geese; a variety of ducks including white-winged and surf scoters, harlequin, oldsquaws, Barrow's and common goldeneyes, buffleheads, and common and red-breasted mergansers; black oystercatchers; glaucous-winged and herring gulls; bald eagles (abundant); blue grouse; great horned owls; rufous hummingbirds; belted kingfishers; Steller's jays; northwestern crows; common ravens; chestnut-backed chickadees; brown creepers; winter wrens; golden- and ruby-crowned kinglets; Swainson's, hermit, and varied thrushes—whose liquid songs drift magically through the forest; yellow, yellow-rumped, and Townsend's warblers; red crossbills; pine grosbeaks; common redpolls; and dark-eyed juncoes. An exciting asset of the park are Indian River's spectacular runs of king, Coho, chum, and pink salmon.

The park's visitor center presents interpretive exhibits and programs on Tlingit history and cultural traditions. The building also houses the Southeast Alaska Indian Cultural Center, in which artists produce beautiful carvings of silver and wood, basketry, and weavings.

Adjacent to the park is the state-run Sheldon Jackson Museum (for information: [907] 747-8981), providing outstanding interpretive exhibits of the native American culture of Alaska. This facility contains one of the very finest collections anywhere of Alaskan cultural material.

An excellent and informative publication is *Sitka,* by Penny Rennick and L.J. Campbell (The Alaska Geographic Society).

Camping is not allowed in the park, but picnic facilities are provided. Lodging and meals are available in Sitka. The main park unit is about a half-mile from Sitka's business district, and may be reached on foot by following Lincoln Street to the park entrance. There are also taxis and buses available to take visitors to the park.

IF YOU GO: Access to Sitka is by way of scheduled airline flights from Seattle and from elsewhere in Alaska; or by boat, including the Alaska state ferry system and cruise ships. Further information: Superintendent, P.O. Box 738, Sitka, AK 99835. Telephone (907) 747-6281.

STATUE OF LIBERTY NATIONAL MONUMENT

STATUE OF LIBERTY NATIONAL MONUMENT, consisting of nearly 40 acres on Liberty and Ellis islands in New York Harbor, was established in 1924, to protect and interpret the Statue of Liberty. At first, the Statue of Liberty was under the care of the War Department, then transferred in 1933 to the National Park Service. All of Liberty Island came to the Park Service in

1937, and the monument was expanded in 1965 to include Ellis Island, which now features the outstanding Ellis Island Immigration Museum.

The colossal 151-foot-tall statue of a woman with upraised torch stands majestically on her 154-foot pedestal. For over a century, she has been an inspiring and cherished symbol of liberty and hope for millions of people from around the world who have sought and continue to seek freedom and new opportunities in America. She is also a powerful symbol for Americans, representing the freedom and privileges we enjoy.

The concept of a great monument signifying liberty—America's independence—was initially discussed in 1865 in Paris, France, by distinguished legal scholar and expert on United States constitutional law and history, Edouard René Lefebvre de Laboulaye. He and other Frenchmen viewed admiringly how the United States of America was achieving what had eluded France—a balance between freedom, on the one hand, and political, legal, and economic stability, on the other. In contrast to the dictatorial monarchies of Europe and the short-lived republics of France, the United States' republican form of government provided an enviable model. Laboulaye wanted to create an enduring monument that would symbolize the ideal of those principles of freedom and stability, and that would also represent the friendship between France and America.

Laboulaye discussed his dream with 31-year-old sculptor, Frédéric-Auguste Bartholdi. At Laboulaye's urging, Bartholdi sailed to the United States in 1871 to "find a happy idea, a plan that will excite public enthusiasm," in Laboulaye's words. Bartholdi was greatly influenced by colossal works in Egypt. Also, at that time, the image of a female figure holding aloft a flame or some other object was frequently used by artists. When he arrived at New York Harbor—America's largest port—on his first of four trips to the United States, he immediately concluded that his grand statue should be placed there, so it could welcome those arriving in America by way of this great harbor.

From 1871 to 1884, a monumental and complicated program of design and construction was carried out, while fund-raising campaigns were launched that were initially more successful in France than in America. Eventually the needed funds were raised on both sides of the Atlantic from corporations and individuals including small contributions from schoolchildren. Models of the statue were first created, each larger than the previous one—beginning with a four-foot-tall clay figure, then a plaster enlargement nine feet high, another of 37 feet, and finally a full-scale plaster enlargement in sections totaling 151 feet in height. The forms of these segments then had to be transferred to 300 sheets of pure copper that were hammered and pressed (*repoussé*) into wooden molds. These 88 tons of copper segments became the statue's relatively lightweight, durable, and strong skin.

The statue was first assembled in 1884, rising above a Paris neighborhood of ancient rooftops and narrow streets, adjacent to the construction shops of Gaget, Gauthier, & Comp[ie]. Supporting the skin was an intricate internal iron skeleton of columns, beams, and braces, each skin section being independently supported. This ingenious structure was created by French engineer, Gustave Eiffel, designer of the Eiffel Tower in Paris. It was then disassembled for shipment to America. Meanwhile, in New York it had been decided that the statue's pedestal should be placed on top of Bedloe's (now Liberty) Island's 1812 Fort Wood. This massive stone masonry structure, in the shape of an eleven-pointed star, would give Liberty and her pedestal a grand platform—a stage from which to rise to an even greater height.

Then came the task of designing the pedestal. After several ideas were produced and rejected, American architect, Richard Morris Hunt, offered a design that was accepted as appropriate—a concrete structure faced with granite masonry. It was completed in April 1886, finally ready for the statue that had made the transatlantic voyage on the French naval ship, *Isère*, in 1885, and that took three months to finally be assembled, piece by piece, upon the pedestal.

Liberty Enlightening the World was unveiled amid grand celebrations on a foggy damp day, October 28, 1886. A flotilla of boats of all shapes and sizes filled New York Harbor. A parade marched in the streets of Manhattan. President Grover Cleveland presided over official ceremonies. And a 21-gun salute boomed out from the harbor batteries. The president affirmed that this colossal gift from France was emphatic evidence of "the kinship of republics [France and America] and conveys to us the assurance that in our efforts to commend to mankind the excellence of a government resting upon popular will, we will have beyond the American continent a steadfast ally."

The grand statue soon came to mean even more than a celebration of French-American friendship. Liberty quickly became a symbol of this great nation—a welcoming symbol of hope and the opportunity of a better life to oppressed and persecuted peoples from all over the world. As the poem by Emma Lazarus, written in 1883 and now displayed on a bronze plaque in the museum, says in part:

> From her beacon-hand
> Glows world-wide welcome; her mild eyes command
> The air-bridged harbor that twin cities frame.
> "Keep, ancient lands, your storied pomp!" cries she
> With silent lips. "Give me your tired, your poor,
> Your huddled masses yearning to breathe free,
> The wretched refuse of your teeming shore.
> Send these, the homeless, tempest-tost to me,
> I lift my lamp beside the golden door!"

A museum located within old Fort Wood provides exhibits on how the statue was constructed and on immigration. Visitors may view New York Harbor from the promenade, colonnade, and from higher levels atop the pedestal. But a 22-story climb inside the statue offers an unforgettable view from within the crown. For this, visitors should not underestimate the stamina

Great Hall at Ellis Island, Statue of Liberty National Monument [NPS]

needed to climb the 162 steps from pedestal to crown.

For a more detailed and comprehensive history of immigration to the United States, the **Ellis Island** unit of the national monument presents the outstanding Ellis Island Immigration Museum. For visitors ranging from prospective citizens and new Americans, to those with generations of roots in America, this exhibition is an unforgettable and deeply moving experience.

From 1892 to 1954, more than *12 million* men, women, and children passed through the processing and holding facilities on this island. Of that total, most were questioned, their travel documents checked, and their medical condition examined for contagious diseases and a variety of disabilities. Among conditions that barred immigrants were trachoma (a then-incurable eye disease that led to blindness and death), cholera, tuberculosis, epilepsy, insanity, and physical disabilities. While questioning of an immigrant normally took only five or ten minutes, frequently with the aid of a language interpreter, the process of standing in long lines and patiently waiting often took an *average* of five or six hours. Inspectors worked long, grueling hours, processing as many as 5,000 immigrants daily during the peak years.

One immigrant wrote, "Let no one believe that landing is a pleasant experience." But for persons surviving the immigration ordeal, ahead lay the freedom of a grand new land and the wondrous chance to attain a dream.

The island is named for the first owner, Samuel Ellis, in the 1780s. In 1808, it was bought by the federal government from New York State and Fort Gibson was built there, just prior to the outbreak of the War of 1812. It was one of a number of New York Harbor fortifications against possible attack by the British. From the 1830s to 1890, the island was used as a military munitions dump.

In 1890, Ellis Island was chosen as the location of a new federal Immigration Station for the Port of New York (the previous one was a place called Castle Garden). A number of buildings were erected, including a large main structure housing an inspection hall that opened in 1892. Five years later, the complex caught fire and burned to the ground. A new and larger Ellis Island Immigration Station was opened in 1900. The centerpiece of this complex was the large Immigration Inspection Center and its cavernous Registry Room. This building is an ornate French Renaissance-style, limestone-trimmed brick structure that won the gold medal for its architectural excellence at the Paris Exhibition in 1900. Other buildings housed such facilities as a dormitory for detainees, kitchens and a dining hall, a small hospital, a bathhouse, baggage station, and power plant.

Planners had designed the station to process a half million immigrants annually, at a time when half that number were arriving. Yet, in 1907, just over a million persons arrived on overcrowded ships and went through the immigration inspection process here—the highest number in the history of Ellis Island. Of that total, about one in five immigrants was detained for days or even weeks, being put up in overcrowded dormitories. There were many medical detentions, women and children were detained until their welfare appeared assured by a relative in the United States, and there were persons awaiting a hearing before the Board of Special Inquiry.

Anti-immigration public reaction to the veritable flood of newcomers to American soil reached a peak in 1917, as the United States entered World War I. This negative reaction caused Congress to enact a law requiring immigrants to pass a literacy test. Some outspoken critics of immigration policy characterized immigrants as dangerous criminals and as an impoverished and diseased burden upon American society. With such hysteria over immigration, Ellis Island's purpose shifted from primarily an immigration processing depot to a deportation center for alien suspects. In 1921, Congress passed a Quota Act—thus ending America's welcoming open-door policy and substituting a system of limited quotas for each nationality. Quotas were further reduced three years later, under provisions of the National Origins Act, a system that was finally eliminated in 1965. This restrictive law was especially directed against immigrants from southern and eastern Europe who were deemed by critics as "less desirable." Also under this law, prospective immigrants were now to be investigated in American consular offices before they could depart from their country of origin.

During the years 1892 to 1931, the two countries from which came by far the greatest number of immigrants were Italy, with over 2.5 million, and Russia, with nearly 1.9 million. Hungary, Austria, Germany, England, and Ireland ranked next, descending in sequence from over 850,000 down to 520,000.

The number of immigrants dwindled dramatically from the 1920s to the early 1950s. Finally, in November 1954, Ellis Island's immigration facility was closed and abandoned. In the early 1960s, a National Park Service study was carried out to determine the appropriateness and feasibility of bringing Ellis Island into the National Park System. The favorable recommendation led President Lyndon B. Johnson to issue a presidential proclamation adding the island to the Statue of Liberty National Monument in 1965.

In 1982, President Ronald Reagan prompted a major fund-raising campaign to restore both the Main Building on Ellis Island and the Statue of Liberty. The Statue of Liberty-Ellis Island Foundation, Inc., was founded to raise what became one of the most ambitious historic restoration programs in U.S. history, involving more than 20 million individual and corporate donors. A major part of meticulously restoring the Main Building on Ellis Island was the creation of the magnificent Ellis Island Immigration Museum.

The museum presents a fascinating and powerful array of exhibits that feature historic photographs, documents, maps, objects of clothing, jewelry, tools, household items, and other personal possessions that immigrants of many nations brought to America with them. There are two theaters in which the award-winning documentary film, *Island of Hope, Island of Tears*, is presented. Taped interviews with immigrants and ethnic music are also on file (appointments are necessary to hear these). And the exhibition's educational facilities feature an innovative learning center for schoolchildren, for which reservations are required. Ellis Island also presents the American Immigration Wall of Honor, containing over 500,000 names. It is the largest such wall in the world.

At this writing, there is renewed public interest in America to once again reform the immigration process. As the late Congresswoman Barbara Jordan, former chair of Congress' U.S. Commission on Immigration Reform, wrote in *The New York Times* (Sept. 11, 1995):

> Congress is considering legislation to curb illegal immigration and set priorities for legal admissions. . . . Newspapers carry immigration-related articles almost daily, in contrast to just a few years ago when hardly any appeared.
>
> This attention is not misplaced. . . .
>
> Legitimate concern about weaknesses in our immigration policy should not, however, obfuscate what remains the essential point: the United States has been and should continue to be a nation of immigrants. A well-regulated system of legal immigration is in our national interest. . . .
>
> The United States has united immigrants and their descendants around a commitment to democratic ideals and constitutional principles. People from an extraordinary range of ethnic and religious backgrounds have embraced these ideals.
>
> There is a word for this process: Americanization . . . becoming one of us. But that does not mean conformity. We are more than a melt-

ing pot; we are a kaleidoscope, where every turn of history refracts new light on the old promise. . . .

Interest in naturalization has never been greater; applications for citizenship exceed in number and proportion any previous period in our history. . . .

Reforming our immigration policy is the best way to revitalize our commitment to immigration and to immigrants. It is literally a matter of who we are as a nation, and who we become as a people.

Statue of Liberty National Monument is a powerful statement and a constant reminder of who we have been as a people, "who we are as a nation and who we become as a people."

Among excellent books and publications are *Liberty: The Statue and the American Dream* by Leslie Allen (The Statue of Liberty-Ellis Island Foundation, Inc., 1985); *Statue of Liberty: The Story Behind the Scenery®* by Paul Weinbaum (KC Publications, 1988); and *Ellis Island: The Official Souvenir Guide* by B. Colin Hamblin (ARA Leisure Services, Inc., 1992).

The Main Building on Ellis Island provides a food service for visitors, along with a gift shop offering publications and other items relating to the immigration theme. Lodging and restaurants are abundantly available in New York City and adjacent northern New Jersey.

IF YOU GO: Visitors to the Statue of Liberty and Ellis Island arrive on the Circle Line-Statue of Liberty Ferry that runs daily at regular intervals from Battery Park, at the southern tip of Manhattan, in New York City, and from Liberty State Park, in New Jersey. The national monument is closed on Christmas Day. Circle Line ferry information: (212) 269-5755. Further information on the national monument: Superintendent, Liberty Island, New York, NY 10004. Telephone (212) 363-3200.

THOMAS STONE NATIONAL HISTORIC SITE

THOMAS STONE NATIONAL HISTORIC SITE consists of 328 acres in southern Maryland. It was authorized in 1978 to commemorate Thomas Stone, who was a signer of the U.S. Declaration of Independence and was a delegate to the Continental Congress (1775-1778 and 1783-1784). The site also protects and interprets "Habre-de-Venture," a red-brick, Georgian-style mansion dating from 1771, near Port Tobacco, on the north shore of the lower Potomac River. It was Stone's home from 1743 to 1787.

The site offers self-guided and ranger-led tours, a brief audiovisual program, and occasional special cultural events. It is open daily, except on Thanksgiving, Christmas, and New Year's Day.

IF YOU GO: Lodging and meals are available in La Plata and elsewhere in southern Maryland, as well as in the Washington, D.C., metropolitan area. Access from U.S. Route 301 at La Plata is by way of State Route 6 and a right turn onto Rose Hill Road to the site entrance; or from State Route 210 southbound from Washington, D.C., a left turn onto State Route 225 eastbound, and a right turn onto Rose Hill Road to the site entrance. Further information: Thomas Stone National Historic Site, Superintendent, 6655 Rosehill Rd., Port Tobacco, MD 20677. Telephone (301) 934-6027.

TIMUCUAN ECOLOGICAL & HISTORIC PRESERVE

TIMUCUAN ECOLOGICAL & HISTORIC PRESERVE, encompassing 46,000 acres in northeast Jacksonville, Florida, was established in 1988 and named for the Indians who occupied the area at the time of European contact in the sixteenth century. (Timucuan is generally pronounced with the accent on the second syllable.) The preserve was established to protect and interpret wetlands, and historic and pre-Columbian sites. The area includes a variety of natural habitats: maritime forest, wooded wetland "islands" referred to as uplands, salt marsh, and tidal streams and estuaries of the St. Johns and Nassau rivers.

In addition to evidence of several thousand years of Indian occupation of the area, the preserve also contains the remains of Spanish, French, and English colonial sites, as well as historic structures and grounds of the American period. Great numbers of people from Africa also made their homes in the Timucuan area and worked as slaves. As the National Park Service says, "these people maintained a distinct and enduring African-American culture which has become a valuable part of our American heritage."

At Kingsley Plantation, to the north of the St. Johns River, there is a visitor center, with interpretive exhibits and programs, a demonstration garden, several well-preserved antebellum buildings, and the ruins of 25 tabby slave cabins (tabby is a building material made from ground-up oyster shells mixed with mud). Also north of the river is the 400-acre Cedar Point Area, from which is a beautiful view of Kingsley Plantation across the Intracoastal Waterway. At this writing (late 1996), the National Parks Service is constructing hiking trails in this area.

In the preserve's 600-acre Theodore Roosevelt Area, along the south side of the St. Johns River, visitors may enjoy weekend interpretive programs and hiking the trails that wind through maritime hammock forest and lead to the edge of a salt marsh. Other exhibits and information about significant natural and cultural resources can be found in the preserve's main visitor center at Fort Caroline National Memorial, which is located within the Theodore Roosevelt Area of the preserve (see Fort Caroline).

Among the trees of the preserve are the dominant slash pine and water oak, along with less common turkey oak and pignut hickory, and the occasional southern magnolia. Spanish moss (a member of the pineapple family) and resurrection ferns festoon the branches of the oaks, adding a fascinating aura of mystery to the woodland scenes. Among common shrubs are beautyberry, with its purplish berries; yaupon, from which the Timucuan Indians brewed a cleansing tea; and azaleas that bloom beautifully in the spring. Wildflowers include the showy orchis and greenfly orchid, the latter being an epiphytic species (living on another plant but not as a parasite) that grows in association with the epiphytic resurrection fern.

Mammals of the preserve include bobcats, raccoons, armadillos, marsh rabbits, river otters, gray squirrels, dolphins, and porpoises. Among the many species of birds are brown pelicans; great blue and green-backed herons; snowy and great egrets; wood storks; numerous waterfowl, including wood ducks; bald eagles and ospreys; common ground-doves; barred owls; belted kingfishers; red-bellied and pileated woodpeckers; blue jays; tufted titmice; brown-headed nuthatches; Carolina wrens; catbirds; mockingbirds; brown thrashers; numerous warblers, such as yellow-rumped, parula, palm, pine, yellowthroat, yellow-throated, prothonotary, Swainson's, black-and-white, and hooded; cardinals; painted buntings; and red-winged blackbirds.

A common amphibian is the green treefrog. Reptiles include alligators; diamondback terrapins; gopher tortoises; fence lizards; and snakes, such as king, indigo, ribbon, rat, and the poisonous cottonmouth (water moccasin) and eastern diamondback rattlesnake. Visitors are cautioned to be especially alert for the latter two. There are also ticks, mosquitoes, and biting flies.

Since much of the upland parts of the preserve remain in private ownership, the Park Service asks visitors to be respectful of private property rights and obtain permission from owners before venturing onto non-public lands.
IF YOU GO: There are no camping or picnicking facilities in the preserve. Lodging and meals are available in Jacksonville. Further information on the preserve, including specific access directions: Superintendent, 13165 Mount Pleasant Rd., Jacksonville, FL 32225. Telephone (904) 641-7155.

TUMACÁCORI NATIONAL HISTORICAL PARK

TUMACÁCORI NATIONAL HISTORICAL PARK comprises 46 acres in three separate units in the Santa Cruz River valley of southern Arizona. It was initially established in 1908 as a single-unit national monument to protect the remains of the early nineteenth-century Spanish Franciscan mission church of *San José de Tumacácori*. In 1990, the monument was changed to a national historical park and expanded to protect the adobe ruins of the mid-eighteenth century Jesuit mission church of *Los Santos Ángeles de Guevavi* and the Jesuit *visita* of *San Cayetano de Calabazas*.

When the Spaniards laid claim to the desert region of what is now southern Arizona and the northern Mexican state of Sonora, Jesuit missionary, Padre Eusebio Francisco Kino, set out in 1687 to convert the O'odham, or Pima Indians to Roman Catholic Christianity. For nearly a quarter century,

Padre Kino established over two dozen mission churches and *visitas* (without a resident priest) at villages of the O'odham. He and his colleagues introduced not only their religious beliefs to the O'odhams, but also taught them the Spanish language and Spanish methods of such things as architectural design and construction, wood carving, crafts, music, the use of new tools, horticulture, and the raising of livestock such as sheep, cattle, and horses that were new to these native people.

Padre Kino first visited the O'odham village of Guevavi in 1691. An initial small church was built by 1703, and a series of short-tenured missionaries served on and off over the next several decades. It was not until 1751 that construction of the larger mission church of *Los Santos Ángeles de Guevavi* was begun by Padre Joseph Garrucho. It was a structure measuring roughly 50 feet long by 15 feet wide with thick adobe walls. A flat roof was supported on large pine logs called *vigas.* Adjoining the church was the *convento,* containing the cells (small, sparsely furnished sleeping rooms), a refectory (dining room) and kitchen, workrooms, and a garden patio. The ruins of this church are protected in the park's Guevavi unit.

The year 1751 was also when gradually escalating resentments over the Spaniards' often harsh, even brutal, treatment of the O'odham people erupted in a four-month Pima Rebellion. Priests were killed or chased away and churches and other symbols of Christianity were plundered. After the revolt was put down by the Spanish military, some of the missionaries gradually returned to resume their ministry.

In 1756, with the relocation of nearly 80 O'odham Indians to a new community near the Santa Cruz River, the church of *San Cayetano de Calabazas* became a *visita* (without a resident priest) of Guevavi mission church. The eroded adobe ruins of this edifice are protected in the park's Calabazas unit.

The village of Tumacácori and the earliest church were located on the east bank of the Santa Cruz River (as were Guevavi and Calabazas), and historians assume that the Indian revolt plundered this mission facility. Shortly after the revolt, Tumacácori and a *presidio* for the military forces were built on the west bank of the river. By 1757, a new adobe church for Tumacácori was built, serving as a *visita* of Guevavi mission. The low ruins of this first church of *San José de Tumacácori* are just east of the remains of the later church, in the Tumacácori unit of the park.

In 1767, the Spanish Crown decreed the removal of the Jesuits from the Spanish territory of *Nueva España.* A full year after their expulsion, missionaries of the Franciscan order began taking over the religious duties. Fray Juan Crisóstomo Gil de Bernabé, who went first to Guevavi, soon moved his headquarters to Tumacácori.

During these years, however, there were devastating epidemics of European-introduced diseases such as smallpox that swept through the Indian population at the villages of Guevavi and Tumacácori. There were also repeated Apache Indian raids upon the O'odham people and the Hispanic missionaries, settlers, and soldiers. The soldiers were generally no match for the nomadic Apache's guerrilla warfare, in which they would make sudden raids on the people and their livestock and other property, and then as quickly melt back into the rugged wilds of the surrounding forested Santa Rita Mountains and other familiar hideouts. As a result of these pressures, Guevavi was finally abandoned in 1776, followed by Calabazas in 1787.

In about 1800, as Apache raids slackened off somewhat, construction began on a much larger church of *San José de Tumacácori*, under the direction of Franciscan Fray Narciso Gutiérrez. The following year, Apaches swooped down and wiped out nearly all of the mission's valued livestock. Because of the difficulty of obtaining adequate funds, work on the great adobe structure proceeded sporadically—stretching over a period of 22 years. The church's nave measured 75 feet long, but because of the severe shortage of money, more ambitious architectural plans had to be eliminated or scaled down. A flat roof supported on beams replaced plans for barrel vaulting. The projected transept was cut from the plans, while a dome that would have been centered above the transept was positioned instead over the sanctuary and above the altar. Plans to place another dome atop the massive bell tower were never carried out.

In 1821, following the independence of Mexico, funds for the missions that had previously come from Spain were cut off. Construction on the region's churches was consequently curtailed even further. When Spanish priests were ordered by Mexico to leave, the construction of Tumacácori's church ended, leaving the bell tower unfinished.

With the resulting shortage of priests, this church became only a satellite operation, with visiting priests continuing to serve parishioners until 1848. A harsh winter combined with a string of devastating Apache raids finally forced the remaining O'odham residents to move from Tumacácori to the community and mission of *San Xavier del Bac*, to the north near Tucson. This beautiful Spanish Baroque church is still in use today. Six years after abandonment of Tumacácori, southern Arizona south of the Gila River became part of the United States of America, under the terms of the Gadsden Purchase.

Especially excellent publications are *Tumacácori National Historical Park* by Susan Lamb (Southwest Parks and Monuments Association); *Tumacácori: From Rancher'a to National Monument* by Nicholas J. Bleser (Southwest Parks and Monuments Association); *Juan Bautista de Anza National Historic Trail* by Don Garate (Southwest Parks and Monuments Association); and *The Missions of Northern Sonora: A 1935 Field Documentation*, edited by Buford Pickens, photographs by George Alexander Grant (University of Arizona Press).

The park's Tumacácori unit is the only one presently open to the public. A visitor center offers interpretive exhibits and publications. A self-guiding path winds through the church and there is a patio garden adjacent to the visitor center where mission-period flora are growing. Ranger-guided tours are offered December to April on a scheduled basis and by appointment in the summer months. Living-history presentations of mission life are offered by appointments to school groups and other organizations. On weekends throughout the year, historic crafts demonstrators show how to make tortillas, paper flowers, piñatas, O'odham baskets, and Mexican pottery.

IF YOU GO: There is no camping allowed in the park, but a small picnic area is provided. Lodging and meals are available in Nogales, Tubac, Green Valley, and Tucson. To reach this unit of the park, visitors drive 45 miles south of Tucson or 19 miles north of Nogales on the Mexican border, by way of I-19 and exit 29. Further information: Superintendent, P.O. Box 67, Tumacácori, AZ 85640. Telephone (520) 398-2341.

WHITMAN MISSION NATIONAL HISTORIC SITE

WHITMAN MISSION NATIONAL HISTORIC SITE consists of 98 acres in the Walla Walla River valley of southeastern Washington State. It was established in 1936 to protect and interpret the site of a Christian missionary station that was founded in 1836, in an attempt to convert the native Cayuse Indians to Christianity and to the white man's lifestyle.

In 1835, the American Board of Commissioners for Foreign Missions, representing a number of Protestant churches, sent medical doctor Marcus Whitman and the Rev. Samuel Parker to the Oregon country to select sites for establishing a missionary program to minister to the Indians of the region. Dr. Whitman soon returned to the East Coast to encourage recruitment of additional emigrants. Shortly after he married Narcissa Prentiss, in February 1836, they headed west, accompanied by the Reverend Henry and Eliza Spalding and William Gray.

Beyond the Mississippi, the pioneers blazed what soon came to be known as the Oregon Trail. They traveled by covered wagon up the Platte and North Platte rivers, passing the prominent natural landmark of Scotts Bluff (see Scotts Bluff National Monument), and descended the Snake River country of what became the state of Idaho. While the Spaldings went off to found a mission among the Nez Perce Indians (see Nez Perce National Historical Park), the Whitmans went on into the Oregon country to establish their mission among the welcoming Cayuse Indians, at a beautiful place called *Waiilatpu* ("place of the people of the rye grass"). And Narcissa and Eliza are remembered in history as the first women to brave the discomforts and dangers of the overland journey across North America. Their courage and success inspired many families to follow their lead and go west to begin a new life in Oregon.

As the program got underway, the missionaries learned the language of the Indians and worked out phonetic equivalents in written English. But Whitman soon encountered what was for him a frustrating hindrance to his Christianizing efforts. The Cayuse, needing to obtain supplies of meat and fish, would head off on nomadic expeditions into the buffalo country, to the salmon fisheries and elsewhere. Consequently, they would be away from *Waiilatpu* for part of the year. Whitman tried in vain to urge the Indians to settle down and plant crops, to become sedentary farmers, instead of continuing their ancient hunting and gathering traditions. They refused.

As other missionaries arrived and other mission stations were set up, Whitman Mission gradually expanded from the initial house to include a large mission house built of adobe, a blacksmith shop, a gristmill, and a structure that subsequently served as an "emigrant house" for Oregon Trail travelers needing shelter, food, or medical attention. The Whitmans also farmed part of the land, planting crops and fruit trees.

The Cayuse not only persisted in following their nomadic food gathering, but also showed little enthusiasm for the white man's religious beliefs and forms of worship. Tensions built between the missionaries and the Indians. Funding for the program declined. And in 1842, the mission board voted to close down the Whitman and Spalding missions. Not willing to accept the board's decision, Whitman and a colleague immediately set out across the continent, braving the perils of blizzards and other winter conditions. They traveled by way of Taos, New Mexico, Bent's Fort (see Bent's Old Fort National Historic Site), and St. Louis, on their way to Boston. Whitman won approval to continue the mission program, and he traveled back to Oregon as the physician and one of the guides for a wagon train of emigrants in 1843. This wagon train was the first to go all the way to the Columbia River.

Over the next several years of missionary work, the Cayuse became increasingly restive, partly in response to a rapidly growing influx of white emigrants and partly over cultural differences and growing pressures for them to accept the white man's ways. The Cayuse, in short, saw their own way of life being seriously threatened.

Then in 1847, a disaster struck. An epidemic of measles virus, brought by a wagon train of emigrants, ravaged the Cayuse who had little or no natural immunity against this scourge. The epidemic proved fatal to half the tribal population. To make matters even worse, Whitman's efforts at administering medication, while helpful to the white children, proved of no value to the Indian children. This fact fueled the Indians' fears that the white man was out to eradicate the Cayuse people, so that the white settlers could take over their ancient lands. On November 29, 1847, a second disaster struck when a group of Cayuse warriors stormed Whitman Mission with tomahawks and rifles and killed Marcus and Narcissa and 11 others including two teen-age boys. This violent end to the mission effectively terminated Protestant missionary programs in the Oregon country. The tragedy did spur efforts to gain territorial status for Oregon, however, and in 1848 the U.S. Congress established the Oregon Territory.

None of the mission buildings remains, but a self-guiding walkway loops by the sites of the main mission house, the original house, the gristmill, the emigrant house, and blacksmith shop. A longer path loops by the Whitman Memorial, a 27-foot-tall obelisk that was erected in 1897. It stands upon a hill where Narcissa sometimes awaited her husband's return from visits among the Cayuse. The site's visitor center provides a brief orientation program, publications, and exhibits of artifacts and other displays. During the summer, there is a variety of cultural demonstration programs.

Most of the trees scattered around the site are non-native species, such as American and London sycamores, eastern cottonwood, silver poplar, black locust, red and silver maples, and blue spruce. Among the birds are American bitterns, great blue herons, Canada geese, wood ducks, golden eagles, ospreys, harriers and other hawks, the non-native ring-necked pheasant, black-billed magpies, cedar and Bohemian waxwings, and redwings.

Whitman Mission National Historic Site, Washington [NPS]

Three informative publications are *Whitman Mission National Historic Site* by Erwin Thompson (National Park Service); *Marcus and Narcissa Whitman and the Opening of Old Oregon*, 2 volumes, by Clifford Drury (Northwest Interpretive Association, Whitman Mission National Historic Site); and *The Cayuse Indians* by Robert Ruby and John Brown (Northwest Interpretive Association, Whitman Mission National Historic Site).

IF YOU GO: Camping is not allowed at the site, but a picnic area is provided near the visitor center. Lodging and meals are available in Walla Walla. Access to the site is by way of U.S. Route 12, seven miles west of Walla Walla. The site is closed on Thanksgiving, Christmas, and New Year's Day. Further information: Superintendent, Route 2, Box 247, Walla Walla, WA 99362. Telephone (509) 529-2761 for recorded information and (509) 522-6357 for more information.

PART 2

WAR FOR INDEPENDENCE (REVOLUTIONARY WAR)

▬ ▬ ▬ ▬ ▬ ▬ ▬ ▬ ▬ ▬ ▬ ▬

Historical Sequence of War for Independence
Battles and Other Events

Minute Man—April 1775
Moores Creek—February 1776
Fort Stanwix—August 1777
Saratoga—October 1777
Valley Forge—Winter 1777–1778
Morristown—Winter 1779–1780
Vincennes—February 1779
Kings Mountain—October 1780
Cowpens—January 1781
Guilford Courthouse—March 1781
Ninety Six—May–June 1781
Yorktown (see Colonial N H Park)—October 1781

COWPENS NATIONAL BATTLEFIELD

COWPENS NATIONAL BATTLEFIELD, consisting of 841 acres in north-western South Carolina, was established in 1929 as a national battlefield site under the War Department, was transferred to the National Park Service in 1933, and renamed as a national battlefield in 1972. It protects and interprets the site of a spectacular War for Independence (Revolutionary War) victory of patriot Continental Army forces and frontier militiamen over a larger regiment of pro-British loyalists, at a frontier livestock pasturing area known as the Cowpens, on January 17, 1781.

The Cowpens battle followed by just over 100 days the stunning triumph of American patriots over loyalists at Kings Mountain, South Carolina (see Kings Mountain National Military Park). It occurred when brilliant military leader, General Daniel Morgan, and his men were trying to outrun the rapidly pursuing British Legion under the command of Banastre Tarleton. A

Cowpens National Battlefield, South Carolina [David Muench]

year earlier, Tarleton had participated with General Charles Earl Cornwallis in the British capture of Charleston and Camden, South Carolina. It was now his assigned task to pursue, harass, and, if possible, defeat General Morgan's troops. And pursue, he did—coming suddenly within only six miles of the patriots, as they were camped and eating breakfast at a place called Thicketty Creek.

When scouts announced that the British forces were rapidly advancing, General Morgan was confronted with a difficult choice: whether to push ahead and attempt a crossing of Broad River or dig in for a fight. Rather than risk being caught in a vulnerable position as they forded the river, he concluded that it was preferable to take what little time they had to get organized and fight the enemy at an open expanse that sloped down in the direction from which the British troops were marching. General Morgan placed his 900 men in three lines of defense stretching across Green River Road, and awaited the arrival of the 1,100-man British Legion.

The initial encounter occurred in the pre-dawn darkness of January 17, 1781, when the British suddenly came upon Morgan's front line of crack rifle sharpshooters, who brought down 15 of the British cavalry in the initial skirmish. British battle lines were immediately formed and—still in the darkness—they proceeded to advance against the Americans.

Morgan's second line of defense, the militia, opened fire and brought down many including British officers. The loyalists continued their advance, now pushing into Morgan's third line, the Continentals. At this point the battle exploded in intensity. Confusion in orders caused the whole line of the Continentals to commence a retreat. Fortunately, General Morgan saw the problem in the nick of time and quickly turned the soldiers around to fire at virtually point-blank range into the advancing enemy. The element of surprise in this rapid turnaround was immediately reinforced by the patriot militia flanking on one side and the cavalry on the other. The triple-barreled assault caused the outnumbering British forces to turn and run. While the decisive American victory left 12 Americans killed and 60 wounded, the British ended the conflict with

110 dead, more than 200 wounded, and some 500 men taken captive.

Although the British had begun their strategy of conquering the South with their takeover of Charleston and Camden, South Carolina, a series of American victories such as Cowpens pushed the loyalists toward their final southern surrender at Yorktown (see Colonial National Historical Park).

Today, the visitor center at Cowpens National Battlefield provides interpretive exhibits; programs—including a presentation, "Daybreak at the Cowpens"—and publications. The park also features an interpretive trail that leads visitors through some of the key battle sites, and a loop road winds around the perimeter of the battlefield with a number of interpretive stops. The park is open daily, except on Thanksgiving, Christmas, and New Year's Day. Camping is not allowed, but there is a picnic area.

IF YOU GO: Lodging and meals are available in Spartanburg, Gaffney, and elsewhere in the region. Access is by way of State Route 11 (the Cherokee Foothills Scenic Highway), 11 miles northwest of I-85 at Gaffney; or two miles east on Route 11 from U.S. Route 221 at Chesnee. Further information: Superintendent, P.O. Box 308, Chesnee, SC 29323. Telephone (864) 461-2828.

FORT STANWIX NATIONAL MONUMENT

FORT STANWIX NATIONAL MONUMENT comprises 15 acres in central upstate New York. It was established in 1935 to protect and interpret the site of an unsuccessful siege upon an 800-man American garrison by 1,700 British soldiers, loyalists, and allied Indians, in August 1777, during the War for Independence (Revolutionary War).

British Colonel Barry St. Leger was heading eastward from Lake Ontario, down the Mohawk River valley, to join General John Burgoyne and General Sir William Howe. Their grand strategy was to take control of the Lake Champlain-Hudson River corridor between Canada and New York City. This control would have effectively split apart the northern American colonies of New York and New England.

But on August 3, St. Leger paused to try and capture Fort Stanwix, a former British outpost now in the hands of the Americans. American Colonel Peter Gansevoort refused to surrender. Then began a nearly three-week siege by St. Leger's troops. While this attack was going on, a 900-man American militia was marching westward up the Mohawk, intending to reinforce the Fort Stanwix defenders. St. Leger heard about the advancing reinforcements and sent part of his forces to block the Americans, trapping them in an ambush in which many on both sides were killed or wounded in bloody hand-to-hand combat, in what came to be known as the Battle of Oriskany.

As this battle raged, Colonel Gansevoort sent some of his men out of the fort to provide assistance. These soldiers raided the virtually undefended British and Indian camps and ran off with their supplies of food and clothing, leaving the encampments in total shambles. As the siege of Fort Stanwix continued, and as supplies of ammunition and food declined in the fort, Colonel Gansevoort succeeded in sending word to the American forces in Albany of their urgent need for help. As an exaggerated rumor spread to the British command that a much larger force of Americans, under the command of General Benedict Arnold, was heading for the fort, hundreds of Indian allies abandoned their alliance with the British. The loyalists also took off. In a short time, St. Leger was stripped of two-thirds of his fighting force. Consequently, on August 22, he reluctantly gave the order to retreat to Canada. Two days later, General Arnold and his men arrived at Fort Stanwix. Just over six weeks later, Arnold helped defeat British forces at the Battle of Saratoga (see Saratoga National Historical Park).

Today, the national monument features the reconstructed log-and-earth fort. A visitor center is located in the fort's west barracks, while interpretive exhibits are housed in the west casemate, and a gift shop with interpretive publications is in the southwest casemate. A casemate was a log structure that was sheltered in the walls of the fort, providing protection for the officers' and enlisted soldiers' quarters from the enemy's artillery bombardments. The monument provides living-history reenactments from May to September.

IF YOU GO: Lodging and meals are available in and around Rome. Access from the New York Thruway (I-90) is by way of exit 33, and continuing on State Route 365 into downtown Rome. Several other state routes, including 26 and 46, pass close to the monument. Within a block of the monument entrance is a municipal parking garage on W. Liberty St. The monument is open daily, except on Thanksgiving, Christmas, and New Year's Day. Further information: Superintendent, 112 E. Park St., Rome, NY 13440. Telephone (315) 336-2090.

GEORGE ROGERS CLARK NATIONAL HISTORICAL PARK

GEORGE ROGERS CLARK NATIONAL HISTORICAL PARK consists of 26 acres on the east bank of the Wabash River in Vincennes, in southwestern Indiana. It was established in 1966 to celebrate and interpret the military prowess and accomplishments of Lieutenant Colonel George Rogers Clark, including the capture of Britain's Fort Sackville, in Vincennes, on February 25, 1779. Clark's military genius and strategies ultimately made it possible to add the vast region that came to be called the Old Northwest Territory.

According to the National Park Service,

> George Rogers Clark had a combination of qualities commonly found in heroes of romantic novels and adventure films but rarely met with in real life. . . . He had the gifts of a magnetic leader and persuasive orator, and he was a master of psychological warfare like few other men of his time. Most importantly, he understood Indian customs and habits of thought. . . . It was largely because of his tireless exertion and

George Rogers Clark National Historical Park, Indiana [NPS]

the extraordinary force of his personality that the western frontier was
held in the face of odds that seemed to call for retreat. . . .

And a retreat back east of the Appalachians was what many of the
earliest settlers in Kentucky were doing, as a result of horrific Indian raids
during the late 1770s. These adventurous pioneers had learned a profound les-
son during their brief stay in Kentucky: Dying in Kentucky was becoming easier than living in Kentucky. That was the precise message the Indians were
delivering with each bloody act against the white man's settlements and isolated cabins.

This guerrilla warfare was receiving the backing of the Indians' British
allies. For the English, these attacks were designed to destroy the Americans'
challenge to unlimited British authority over the region west of the
Appalachians. Guns, knives, and ammunition were supplied to members of
successful Indian raiding parties who brought the scalps of their American victims or who delivered prisoners to the British posts north of the Ohio River.

Officials of the Commonwealth of Virginia would be the ones who
responded to this crisis. During 1776, Virginia had claimed Kentucky as a
county within the commonwealth's jurisdiction. Virginia's Governor, Patrick
Henry, and the Virginia legislature dealt directly with Clark, who had been
chosen by the Kentuckians as their official representative. Clark presented his
plans for a major military offensive campaign against the British. He proposed
capturing at least four key British posts: Kaskaskia, located about 50 miles
south of St. Louis; Cahokia, directly across the Mississippi River from St.
Louis; Vincennes, on the Wabash River about 80 miles north of the junction
of the Wabash and Ohio rivers; and Detroit, located on the Detroit River.
Agreeing to Clark's proposal, Virginia officials commissioned him a lieutenant
colonel and authorized him to assemble a military force.

With volunteers mainly from Virginia and Kentucky, Clark and his
army of an estimated 180 men headed first for Kaskaskia. They took possession

of this key outpost on July 4, 1778. Two days later, Cahokia also fell into American hands. The French residents of these Mississippi Valley towns were encouraged to join the Americans, once they learned of France's recent alliance with the United States. Continued diplomacy won over the French of Vincennes, who listened to their pastor, Father Pierre Gibault. The Catholic priest convinced the Vincennes residents of the advantages of switching their loyalty from the British to the Americans.

Clark's series of accomplishments would be dealt a serious setback once the British at Detroit learned of the American takeover of the three outposts. British Lieutenant Governor Henry Hamilton marched southward with a unit composed of members from the King's 8th Regiment, loyal French militiamen, and pro-British Indian warriors. When this overwhelming group of approximately 500 men arrived in Vincennes on December 17, 1778, the local French residents were quickly coerced into renouncing their recent allegiance with the Americans.

Hamilton followed the custom of that time by making a winter headquarters, to await weather that would be more favorable for a march to Kaskaskia, where Clark and his men were spending the winter. Meanwhile, a St. Louis merchant, Francis Vigo, had been in Vincennes soon after the British takeover. He returned to Kaskaskia and alerted Clark to the danger awaiting the Americans. Vigo provided vital military intelligence, as well as provisions. The young American leader was thus ready to go on the offensive.

An 18-day march from Kaskaskia to Vincennes would expose Clark and his 170 American and French soldiers to mud, muck, mire, and chest-deep freezing waters. They would endure extreme hunger, exhaustion, and anxiety as they journeyed nearly 180 miles through the heart of enemy territory. Extraordinary leadership skills were needed of the 26-year-old commander, if he hoped to complete his mission. Constantly alert for any hazards, Clark succeeded in convincing his men to follow him through the hellish conditions and the high waters.

The standoff would come at about 8 p.m., February 23, 1779, as their heroic efforts culminated in the opening assault upon Fort Sackville. The attack lasted two days. British surrender occurred at 10 a.m., February 25. During the 38-hour siege, only one American was slightly wounded, while an estimated half-dozen British soldiers were seriously injured. No fatalities were reported among the American, French, or British men who participated in the battle.

George Rogers Clark's bold military actions during the War for Independence continuously challenged British claims to and eroded its control over the frontier region west of the Appalachians. Clark's possession of three important posts north of the Ohio River gave the United States a firm foothold in the region, along with a basis to argue successfully that the U.S.-Canadian border should *not* be placed along the Ohio River.

The Treaty of Paris formally ended the War for Independence in 1783. That treaty provided that the U.S.-Canadian border was to be located where it is today. The territory north of the Ohio River and east of the

Mississippi River became known as the Northwest Territory and subsequently as the Old Northwest Territory. Eventually, the land was divided into the states of Ohio, Indiana, Illinois, Michigan, Wisconsin, and the eastern part of Minnesota.

Today, the conquest of the Old Northwest Territory is the theme of the George Rogers Clark National Historical Park. The park's most prominent feature is the impressive Clark Memorial, a circular, Greek-style structure surrounded by 16 Doric columns. The design was created by architect Frederick Hirons. The building contains a larger-than-life bronze statue of Clark. Seven murals on the interior walls graphically portray the rigors of Clark's winter campaign against the British. An adjacent visitor center provides interpretive exhibits, an audiovisual program, and publications.

Among the publications on Clark are: *Conquest of the Country Northwest of the Ohio River, 1778-1783,* and *Life of Gen. George Rogers Clark* by William Hayden English (Heritage Books); and *George Rogers Clark and the War in the West* by Lowell H. Harrison (The University Press of Kentucky). **IF YOU GO:** Lodging and meals are available in Vincennes. Access to the park is by way of the Willow Street exit from U.S. Route 41; or by way of the Sixth Street exit from U.S. Route 50. The park, which is located at 401 South Second Street, is open daily except on Thanksgiving, Christmas, and New Year's Day. Further information: Superintendent, 401 S. Second St., Vincennes, IN 47591. Telephone (812) 882-1776.

GUILFORD COURTHOUSE NATIONAL MILITARY PARK

GUILFORD COURTHOUSE NATIONAL MILITARY PARK, consisting of 220 acres in north-central North Carolina, was established in 1917 under the War Department and was transferred to the National Park Service in 1933. It protects and interprets the site of the two-hour, hard-fought War for Independence (Revolutionary War) battle, on March 15, 1781. Over 4,400 American soldiers dealt the British regiments a heavy blow, inflicting substantial losses on the redcoats, before the patriots were forced to retreat in the face of a withering barrage of cannon fire.

The war in the South, under the command of General Charles Earl Cornwallis, had initially gone well in 1780 for the pro-British loyalists. Georgia had been brought back under British control, followed by victories at Charleston and Camden, South Carolina. These accomplishments were part of Cornwallis' strategy of putting the stalemated struggles with American forces in the North on hold and concentrating on reconquering the South, from Georgia to Virginia.

The British grand scheme began to fall apart, however, with two major defeats: Kings Mountain (see Kings Mountain National Military Park) in October 1780, and the Cowpens (see Cowpens National Battlefield) in January 1781.

Then came Guilford Courthouse. General Nathanael Greene, the commander of the Continental Army's Southern Department, had already succeeded in forcing the British to divide up their troops into several parts. He concluded that General Cornwallis would now attempt a renewed effort to defeat General Daniel Morgan's American forces that had triumphed at the Cowpens in western South Carolina, and would also try to block American reinforcements from reaching General Greene's army.

For several weeks, Greene outran Cornwallis' troops in a wild chase to Virginia that was often in bone-chilling snow and rain. With North Carolina free of Greene, the weary British withdrew to seek loyalist reinforcements. Greene returned to North Carolina and by mid-March arrived at Guilford Courthouse, where he was reinforced by the arrival of North Carolina and Virginia militia and other troops.

On March 15, the Americans were finally prepared to face and fight the advancing British. General Greene placed his military might in three lines of defense reaching across the road up which Cornwallis' troops were advancing. Late in the afternoon, the British encountered the first American line of North Carolina militia poised behind a split-rail fence. Cornwallis' men advanced uphill across open fields to the rousing rhythm of bagpipes and drums. Volleys of weapons fire were exchanged, resulting in some British losses. But the redcoats regrouped and continued their advance.

When the British troops encountered Greene's Virginia militiamen forming the second line of defense, the two sides battled back and forth in the dense underbrush of the forest. Once again the redcoats, with their bayonets swinging and thrusting, succeeded in overwhelming the patriots' defenses and continued their steady advance.

As Cornwallis' men became embroiled in savagely battling both foot soldiers and now also the cavalry, they were suddenly confronted with the possibility of defeat. Cornwallis chose to attempt a rescue of his army from the Americans' third line of defense by ordering his artillery to direct their cannon fire right into the midst of an attack where both American and British troops were locked in combat. This risky tactic succeeded in pushing the American infantry back and allowing more British soldiers to join the battle.

Now the Americans were suddenly faced with the likely prospect of defeat. Consequently, Greene reluctantly gave the order for his troops to withdraw. Yet, in spite of the Americans' loss of the battlefield that day, their casualties were only a fraction of those that overwhelmed the British regiments.

Of the battle, Greene subsequently wrote:

> The battle was long, obstinate, and bloody. We were obliged to give up the ground and lost our artillery, but the enemy have been so soundly beaten that they dare not move towards us since the action, notwithstanding we lay within ten miles of him for two days. Except the ground and the artillery, they have gained no advantage. On the contrary, they are little short of being ruined.

Guilford Courthouse National Military Park, North Carolina [NPS]

While Cornwallis thereafter decided to continue his strategy of pushing northward to reconquer Virginia for the British, Greene wisely let other American forces confront Cornwallis in Virginia. Meanwhile, Greene set off to take back South Carolina from the British. Seven months after Cornwallis' victory at Guilford Courthouse, he was forced to surrender at Yorktown, Virginia (see Colonial National Historical Park).

Two worthy publications are *Another Such Victory* by Thomas E. Baker (Eastern Acorn Press) and *The Monuments at Guilford Courthouse National Military Park* by Thomas E. Baker (Eastern Acorn Press).

Today, the visitor center at Guilford Courthouse National Military Park provides interpretive exhibits, programs, and publications. A tour road winds through the park, with a number of interpretive stops. In several places, trails lead to special points of interest. Dotted here and there are commemorative monuments; among them are the impressive equestrian statue of General Nathanael Greene, a granite shaft rising from the Americans' third line of defense, and the exquisite statue celebrating the kindness of Kerrenhappuch Norman Turner, who traveled by horseback all the way from Maryland to help nurse her son who had been wounded in the fighting. The park is open daily, except on Christmas and New Year's Day.

IF YOU GO: Camping is not allowed in the park; lodging, meals, and campground facilities are available in Greensboro, NC. The park is in northwest Greensboro, off U.S. Route 220 on New Garden Rd. Further information: Superintendent, 2332 New Garden Road, Greensboro, NC 27410. Telephone (910) 288-1776.

KINGS MOUNTAIN NATIONAL MILITARY PARK

KINGS MOUNTAIN NATIONAL MILITARY PARK, consisting of 3,945 acres in northwestern South Carolina, was established in 1931 under the War Department and transferred to the National Park Service in 1933. It protects and interprets the site of a pivotal War for Independence (Revolutionary War) victory in the South of American patriots over pro-British loyalist troops, on October 7, 1780.

The first five years of the war had resulted in a stalemate between American and British military forces in the North. But when the pro-British loyalists began implementing a plan to take control of the southern states, the tide turned in their favor. In May 1780, after British General Charles Earl Cornwallis had captured the major American army forces at Charleston, many South Carolinians, including some who had previously supported American independence, now expressed their allegiance to the British Crown. In August 1780, the British scored another major triumph over the Americans' Continental Army at Camden, South Carolina. It seemed that the British were on an invincible roll. To help defend the Carolinas, Cornwallis ordered British Major Patrick Ferguson and his battalion of soldiers to guard the upcountry of the western Carolinas against attacks by the partisan militia groups.

In September 1780, the overmountain militia forces, which had been harassed by the British military, marched southward from Sycamore Shoals on the Watauga River (at today's Elizabethton, Tennessee), crossed over the snow-covered Appalachian Mountains between Grandfather Mountain and Mount Mitchell, and came to Quaker Meadows (near today's Morganton, North Carolina) where they were joined by several hundred reinforcements of the frontier militias of North and South Carolina.

When Major Ferguson learned of the approaching patriot forces, he decided to move his 1,100 troops from their encampment at Gilbert Town (near today's Rutherfordton, North Carolina) southeast to Kings Mountain, just over the line in South Carolina, and closer to General Cornwallis' main assemblage of troops. He arrived at this 60-foot-high, craggy, forested spur ridge of the southern Appalachians on October 6. The flat summit of the ridge appeared to offer an ideal defensive eyrie, on which to secretly await the patriot forces and keep a sharp lookout on their movements as they approached.

Word quickly reached the advancing American patriots confirming that the loyalists were on Kings Mountain. The weather was miserable as these men, freshly reinforced with 400 South Carolina soldiers, pushed ahead through a night of torrentially soaking rain, and arrived in the vicinity of the mist-shrouded mountain on the afternoon of October 7. As the 900 patriot forces began encircling the mountain, they encountered some of Ferguson's soldiers keeping watch below the mountain. Soon loyalist regiments on the slopes of the mountain opened fire, while from the edge of the summit above, loyalists unleashed a barrage of firepower. Fortunately for the American troops, the thickly forested slopes provided adequate cover from the hail of bullets.

Kings Mountain, South Carolina [David Muench]

Twice the loyalists succeeded in staving off an assault of the mountain by two attacking regiments. But finally, with the support of additional regiments, the American patriots succeeded in reaching the summit. The fury of combat was intense, with muskets and bayonets creating a killing field on and below the mountain. One of the attackers later described the mountain as resembling an erupting volcano: "There flashed along its summit, and around its sides, one long sulphurous blaze."

Ferguson himself was mounted on his horse, giving commands to his soldiers as they fought fiercely. When he was brought down by several bullets and soon died, his next-in-command raised a white flag of surrender in an attempt to end the slaughtering; yet, loyalists' pleas for surrender went unheeded for at least another hour, as the militiamen continued their bloody assault. According to the National Park Service,

> For some time American Whigs (the American patriots) slew American Tories: Ferguson had been the only British soldier on either side of the relentless battle. The "back water men," whom Ferguson had scorned, had slain 225 Loyalists, wounded 163, and taken 716 prisoners, with a loss to themselves of 28 killed and 62 wounded.

Nor did the brutality and killing of Americans versus Americans stop there. On the trek with prisoners to be handed over to the Continental Army, some of the prisoners were beaten, injured, and even killed. Further retaliatory atrocities occurred along the way when a group of military commanders named themselves as jurors to try and convict some of the "obnoxious" loyalists. The trial resulted in nine prisoners being found guilty of crimes committed against innocent men and women. These men were summarily hanged.

In spite of these incidents, the battle of Kings Mountain proved to be a major turning point in the war in the South. Cornwallis uncharacteristically reacted to Ferguson's defeat by scurrying southward, and he held up for three months his plans for further military initiatives. This delay proved to be a major bonus for the Americans' Continental Army—giving its strategists time to assemble a new plan of attack against loyalists.

In December 1780, General Nathanael Greene took over the leadership of the Continental Army's Southern Department and he proceeded to put Cornwallis on the defensive—a position of weakness that ultimately led the British commander to surrender at Yorktown, Virginia, on October 19, 1781 (see Colonial National Historical Park). Thus, loyalists' defeat by the American Patriot militias at Kings Mountain was a crucial turn of events that triggered the downhill slide of British control of the South.

Today, the park's visitor center offers interpretive exhibits, programs, and publications. A self-guiding interpretive walking tour of the battlefield and trail loops around the mountain and then climbs over the mountain summit. Visitors are cautioned that parts of this loop trail are fairly steep—a fact that can help visitors grasp something of how challenging it was for the patriots to dislodge the loyalists from their perch. The park also hosts two annual weekend living-history encampments—one in May and the other nearest October 7. The park is open daily, except on Thanksgiving, Christmas, and New Year's Day.

An informative publication is *Kings Mountain and Its Heroes by Lyman C. Draper*. (See also Overmountain Victory National Historic Trail [National Trails].)

IF YOU GO: Camping and picnicking are not allowed in the park, but facilities for both are available in the adjacent Kings Mountain State Park. Lodging and meals are available in Kings Mountain and Shelby, NC, in York and Gaffney, SC, and elsewhere in the region. Access is by way of the State Route 216 exit from I-85. The park is ten miles from Kings Mountain, NC, on route 216. Further information: Superintendent, P.O. Box 40, Kings Mountain, NC 28086. Telephone (803) 936-7921.

MINUTE MAN NATIONAL HISTORICAL PARK

MINUTE MAN NATIONAL HISTORICAL PARK, encompassing 935 acres along the road between Lexington and Concord, in eastern Massachusetts, was established in 1959 as a national historic site and given its present designation later that same year. It protects and interprets the area in which fighting broke out between the British redcoats and Massachusetts colonial militiamen and minutemen, in April 1775—the first military action of

Minuteman National Historical Park, Concord, Massachusetts [David Muench]

the War for Independence (Revolutionary War).

Paul Revere and others on horseback had sped the warning throughout the countryside beyond Boston that the British soldiers were rapidly on their way to Concord, where Massachusetts militia had hidden large caches of arms, ammunition, and other supplies. The British were setting out to destroy or seize those caches.

As the sun rose on the morning of April 19, the patriot minutemen were out in force and organizing a defense throughout the area. One group of 77 local minutemen was at Lexington Green. Captain John Parker and his men had formed into two lines on the village green, anticipating they would simply stand and watch the redcoats march on by toward Concord. As long as the British did not harm persons or property, the colonials had no wish to trigger a military confrontation.

British Major John Pitcairn, leading nearly ten times the number of men as he now encountered, had just commanded his soldiers not to fire their weapons, but to merely "Keep your ranks and surround them." At that fateful moment, a shot rang out from the sidelines (by whom no one knows). Without orders, the British troops opened fire at the militiamen, some of whom apparently had their backs turned as they had begun to walk from the green moments earlier. While some of the patriots tried to get off a few shots, the gunfire forced most of them to run for cover among the surrounding houses.

While the British came away with no casualties in the Lexington confrontation, eight minutemen were killed and ten others were wounded. Word of this skirmish sped ahead of the redcoats to militiamen at Concord.

Militiamen were waiting at Concord, but assessing that they were substantially outnumbered, they withdrew. Under the command of Colonel James Barrett, the men crossed over the Concord River and climbed to a strategic hill. An argument ensued among the patriots as to whether or not they should attack the British troops, many arguing against bloodshed. By now, more militiamen were arriving, and their numbers had swelled to around 400. Suddenly, a column of black smoke billowed up from town, and a consensus quickly formed to not stand by and watch the British burn down Concord.

So, the patriots marched down to North Bridge, where 100 redcoats were positioned to guard the other end of the arched span. The British fired. Two colonial minutemen lay dead at the west end of the bridge. Patriot Major John Buttrick then yelled to the stunned militiamen, "Fire! For God's sake, fire!" They then unleashed a volley of shots into the redcoats. Two British soldiers were killed, nine were wounded, and the rest turned and fled into Concord. This short battle was immortalized by Ralph Waldo Emerson as "the shot heard 'round the world."

The British began the 20-mile march back to Boston. All along the route, increasing numbers of minutemen and militia harassed the line of redcoats. As the afternoon wore on, the colonials' numbers reached a peak of about 3,500 men. At Meriam's Corner, Brooks Hill, Bloody Angle, and Fiske Hill, the patriots besieged the British. As the British neared Lexington, at Fiske Hill, one officer described their plight: " . . . when we arrived a mile from Lexington, our ammunition began to fail and the light companies were so fatigued with flanking they were scarcely able to act . . . so we began to run rather than retreat in order."

Today, visitors to the park may begin a tour at one of the two visitor centers—North Bridge Visitor Center, near the reconstructed (1956) bridge over the Concord River, at which stands the bronze "Minute Man" statue, created by sculptor Daniel Chester French; or Battle Road Visitor Center, about a mile west of Lexington Green. Both centers provide interpretive exhibits, films, and publications.

Located between the two visitor centers are a number of important points of interest along Battle Road. In addition to the major sites, mentioned above, where the patriots clashed with British soldiers, the park also protects and interprets such other historical features as The Wayside, home of muster master of the Concord militia, Samuel Whitney, and later the home of several famous literary figures, including novelist and short-story writer, Nathaniel Hawthorne (*The Scarlet Letter*) and Louisa May Alcott (*Little Women*), and the Hartwell Tavern, dating from 1733.

The park provides living-history demonstrations (notably the Battle at North Bridge, on the third Monday in April). There are several short trails, including the mile loop around Fiske Hill, where the panicked British troops tried and failed to regroup. The Battle Road Visitor Center is open daily from mid-April through October, and the North Bridge Visitor Center is open daily, except on Thanksgiving, Christmas, and New Year's Day.

IF YOU GO: Lodging and meals are available in Concord, Lexington, and elsewhere around Boston. Access from I-95 is by way of exit 30B into Lexington; or from I-495 onto State Route 2 to Concord. The North Bridge Visitor Center is off Liberty St., in Concord; and the Battle Road Visitor Center is off State Route 2A, in Lexington. Further information: Superintendent, 174 Liberty Street, Concord, MA 01742. Telephone (508) 369-6993.

MOORES CREEK NATIONAL BATTLEFIELD

MOORES CREEK NATIONAL BATTLEFIELD, consisting of 86 acres in southeastern North Carolina, was established in 1926 as a national military park under the War Department, was transferred to the National Park Service in 1933, and renamed as a national battlefield in 1980. It protects and interprets the site of a small but significant battle in the War for Independence (Revolutionary War), on February 27, 1776, between North Carolina patriots and pro-British loyalist troops at Moores Creek Bridge—the only crossing over the lower stretch of this 35-foot-wide river, bordered by swampland and dense bottomland forest.

The loyalist troops had planned to march to the coast by way of the west bank of the Cape Fear River—crossing Moores Creek on the bridge—to meet and join forces with British soldiers due to arrive by ship. Together these military units were to have defeated the patriots' rebellion and taken control of the colony of North Carolina. But the patriots, with 150 men under the command of Colonel Alexander Lillington and 850 men under Colonel Richard Caswell, pulled off a crucial strategical coup by seizing control of Moores Creek Bridge, which the 1,600 loyalists would have to cross to reach the coast and their British reinforcements. When the loyalists learned that they had lost the race to reach the bridge, they decided to attack the patriots who were camped on both sides of the river.

During the night of February 26-27, the loyalists began their march to the bridge—a trek that was hampered by both the darkness and the difficult swampy bushwacking. Also during that night, the patriots who were based on the north bank of the river crossed the bridge and joined the other troops behind defensive earthworks near the river's south bank. The men ripped up the bridge's planking and covered its girders with grease to slow down the loyalists' use of this vital crossing.

At dawn, the loyalists began their attack by scrambling over what remained of Moores Creek Bridge and came within 30 paces of the patriots' protective earthworks. With overwhelming artillery and musketry fire power, virtually the entire advance unit of loyalist troops was wiped out. Within just a few minutes, the bloody encounter was over and the remaining loyalists retreated. While about 30 of their soldiers were killed and another 40 injured, the triumphant patriots lost only one man.

Diorama depicting loyalists crossing Moores Creek Bridge, North Carolina [NPS]

According to the National Park Service,

> Though the battle was a small one, the implications were large. The victory demonstrated the surprising patriot strength in the countryside, discouraged the growth of loyalist sentiment in the Carolinas, and spurred revolutionary feeling throughout the colonies.

The historian, Edward Channing, has suggested that had the loyalists been successful in the southern colonies at places such as Moores Creek Bridge, during the early months of 1776, the British might have been able to squelch not only the North Carolina patriots' rebellion, but could conceivably have also blocked the revolution that led to America's independence.

The national battlefield today protects the site of the battle of Moores Creek Bridge, a segment of historic Negro Head Point Road, and a reconstructed encirclement of defensive earthworks. The visitor center provides interpretive exhibits and programs. Several trails wind through the park, including a short spur to the site of Moores Creek Bridge. The reconstructed bridge is merely to help give some idea of what the historic bridge was like and is not intended as a footbridge. Visitors are also urged to walk carefully near the riverbank, as it may be slippery, and to be alert for poisonous snakes. **IF YOU GO:** Lodging and meals are available in Wilmington and elsewhere in the vicinity. A picnic area is provided in the park, but camping is not permitted. Access to the battlefield is 20 miles northwest of Wilmington, NC, by way of U.S. Route 421, or I-40, then west on State Route 210 to the park entrance. The park is open daily, except on Christmas and New Year's Day. Further information: Superintendent, P.O. Box 69, Currie, NC 28435. Telephone (910) 283-5591.

MORRISTOWN NATIONAL HISTORICAL PARK

MORRISTOWN NATIONAL HISTORICAL PARK, encompassing 1,670 acres in four units in and near Morristown, in northern New Jersey, was established in 1933. It protects and interprets the quarters of the Continental Army in 1777 and in the brutal winter of 1779–1780, during the War for Independence (Revolutionary War). The park features the site of Fort Nonsense, built in 1777; the 1779–1780 winter headquarters of General George Washington in the Ford family mansion in Morristown; the winter of 1779-1780 winter encampment for some 10,000 soldiers at Jockey Hollow; and the New Jersey Brigade's winter encampment area.

Following military triumphs at Trenton and Princeton, New Jersey, General Washington's Continental Army of 5,000 men hunkered down next to the village of Morristown in January 1777, for a needed and welcome lull between battles with the British redcoats. Here the troops were relatively secure in a location chosen by Washington for its excellent defensive advantage of surrounding ridges of the Watchung Mountains; and here Washington and his officers, struggling against great odds, re-inspired and rebuilt the depleted army.

Among the nearly overwhelming challenges that weakened and threatened to destroy the army were soldiers whose periods of enlistment ended or who deserted and headed home; the inexperience of many new recruits and militiamen, such as farmers and other civilians, who knew little or nothing about warfare and military discipline; the sheer challenge of coping with the rigors of winter's bitter cold and snow away from the comforts of home; the frequent shortages of food and adequate clothing; and illnesses that weakened or took the lives of many soldiers. A near-disaster occurred with an outbreak of smallpox. When the disease threatened to engulf the American army, General Washington immediately ordered that all soldiers and civilians in the vicinity be given smallpox inoculations. At that time, inoculating against this dread disease was deemed nearly as great a health risk as smallpox itself. Yet, Washington had no choice but at least to make a desperate effort to save his army. Morristown's two churches were converted to hospitals for treating the afflicted, and the epidemic was finally brought to an end.

As winter melted into spring 1777, General Washington busied his men with construction of a fortified hilltop redoubt, surrounded by defensive earthworks. Although the fortification was apparently built to help protect the army's strategic encampment area, legend suggests that the general may really have had it built to keep his troops busy and less likely to be bored and depressed. Because of this legend, the hill subsequently became known as Fort Nonsense.

By spring 1777, the winter's military training discipline and addition of new recruits, plus Washington's own inspiring leadership, had paid off. The greatly strengthened 8,000-man army was now far better prepared to take on the British forces. But no battle ensued as the redcoats avoided a confrontation in New Jersey and returned to their base in New York. They then sailed south to capture and occupy the then-American capital city of Philadelphia, while Washington's army struggled to survive the winter of 1777-1778 at Valley Forge, near Philadelphia (see Valley Forge National Historical Park).

After more encounters with the British troops, General Washington decided to return to the relative strategic security of Morristown, from which to monitor British troop activities in and around New York, during the winter of 1779-1780. In December, the Continental Army's veteran brigades arrived from many directions. The soldiers and junior officers began building log huts for their barracks in the area called Jockey Hollow, a few miles southwest of Morristown. General Washington took up residence and set up his command headquarters at the beautiful mansion of the widow of Jacob Ford, Jr., in Morristown. The other senior commanders lodged in various houses in and near the village.

Everything was being organized to make the best of winter. But the fierce ice-and-snow storm that greeted General Washington on his arrival in Morristown, on December 1, turned out to be a harbinger of wild weather to come. That winter was the worst of the eighteenth century. At least 20 major snowstorms roared through the region, repeatedly paralyzing transportation, cutting off vital supply routes for the army, and making it even more difficult than usual to obtain essential provisions such as basic foods, clothing, and military supplies. The storms often caused lengthy delays in resupplying the army, when the soldiers had "nothing to eat from morning to night again," and when "men naked as Lazarus" were "begging for clothing." The bitter cold and dampness penetrated the log huts. As a result of inadequate clothing and bedding, the men suffered the effects of frozen hands and feet, many of them becoming unfit for military service. Morale of the troops and officers plunged to the depths of despair.

It was not only the winter weather that made obtaining urgently needed supplies difficult and at times impossible. The Continental Congress remained steadfastly unconvinced of the seriousness of the crisis and consequently would do nothing to help alleviate the hardships. And to make matters worse, rampant inflation made buying provisions virtually out of the question.

Faced with a crisis of this magnitude, General Washington finally appealed to the state of New Jersey and its counties for help. In his words, New Jersey responded generously and "saved the army from dissolution, or starving."

By the spring of 1780, France officially pledged to enter the war in support of America's desperate struggle for independence from Britain. Before French assistance could arrive, however, a combined British and German force was marching from New York into northern New Jersey. General Washington immediately dispatched six brigades from Morristown to head off the enemy's offensive. On June 23, the Continentals clashed with the redcoats and forced them to retreat. Shortly after this American success, all remaining troops left the Morristown encampments. The long ordeal, in which the British might have won the war without firing a shot, was finally over, and the Americans went on to win independence.

Today, the national historical park's visitor center at the Jockey Hollow Encampment unit (Telephone [201] 543-4030) provides interpretive exhibits, programs, and publications. Roads loop through this area of the park. There are interpretive stops at such places as the Henry Wick farmhouse that served as headquarters for General Arthur St. Clair; the encampment site of the Pennsylvania Brigade where once many rows of rustic huts dotted the land-scape; and the parade ground where the troops spent long hours in training.

From the Jockey Hollow unit, a stretch of the Patriots Path leads visi-tors on foot southwestward to the nearby New Jersey Brigade Encampment unit of the park (there is no motor-vehicle access). To the northeast of Jockey Hollow, Western Avenue leads to the Fort Nonsense unit; and from there visi-tors may drive on to the Washington's Headquarters & Museum unit, by way of Western Ave., then right onto Washington St., and left onto Morris St. at Morristown Green, to the park unit entrance. (All routes between the park units are well signed.)

Guided tours of the mansion are provided. All park buildings are closed on Thanksgiving, Christmas, and New Year's Day, and some buildings are also closed during the winter months. The park also provides 27 miles of delightful trails for hiking. Some of these are available for horseback riding. In winter, some of the trails (ungroomed) are ideal for cross-country skiing.

IF YOU GO: Camping is not permitted in the park. Lodging and meals are available in Morristown and elsewhere in the vicinity. Access to the park from I-287 southbound is by way of exit 36 to most directly reach the Washington's Headquarters unit; and exit 26B to reach the Jockey Hollow unit; or I-287 north-bound by way of the Route 202/N. Maple Ave. exit to Jockey Hollow; and exit 36A to Washington's Headquarters. Further information: Superintendent, Washington Place, Morristown, NJ 07960. Telephone (201) 539-2085.

NINETY SIX NATIONAL HISTORIC SITE

NINETY SIX NATIONAL HISTORIC SITE, comprising 989 acres in western South Carolina, was established in 1976 to protect and interpret the site of an early and mid-eighteenth century crossroads settlement of a dozen or so houses. The area became the focus of conflict during the War for Independence (Revolutionary War) in 1781, between American patriots and pro-British loyalists.

The British forces under General Charles Earl Cornwallis had begun a strategy of conquering the South by a series of victories—in Savannah, Georgia, and Charleston and Camden, South Carolina. But then, in 1781, American patriots achieved major triumphs at Kings Mountain (see Kings Mountain National Military Park) and the Cowpens (see Cowpens National

Re-created Encampment, Ninety Six National Historic Site, South Carolina [NPS]

Battlefield). Also in 1781, Cornwallis fought American General Nathanael Greene at Guilford Courthouse (see Guilford Courthouse National Military Park) and succeeded in driving off the Americans. Yet, in spite of this latter victory, the British losses at that bloody engagement had forced Cornwallis to pull back his troops to the Carolina coast.

As for General Greene, he decided not to chase after Cornwallis' army, but instead laid out a strategy for conquering a number of southern backcountry British outposts. Consequently, in May 1781, Greene and his army of over 1,000 men targeted the key British military outpost Ninety Six. There were 550 pro-British loyalists garrisoned there, behind the defenses of a stockade and a star-shaped fort.

The patriot Continental Army's siege of Ninety Six began on May 22, 1781, as the military engineers started constructing a network of trenchwork around the British fortifications. By early June, as the trenches and rifle tower were being completed, Greene received word that a large British force was being dispatched to reinforce the enemy troops at Ninety Six. The patriots quickly initiated their attack on June 18. But when Greene's men reached the star fort, they were repulsed by a brutal counterattack that resulted in many casualties and injuries for both the patriots and loyalists. The village was destroyed in the siege.

Since the British reinforcements were rapidly closing in, Greene realized he lacked the time needed to reorganize his forces for a renewed attack. Consequently, he retreated across the Saluda River before the British could chase after them. Although Greene lost the battle against Ninety Six, the

British soon left the outpost. They destroyed what remained of its buildings as they departed, on their way to a location closer to the South Carolina coast and farther from the harassing patriots.

To quote the Park Service:

> No one is certain how the village [of Ninety Six] got its name. One explanation is that traders out of Charleston thought this stopping place was 96 miles from the Cherokee town of Keowee, in the Blue Ridge foothills.

Today, the national historic site's visitor center provides interpretive exhibits, programs, and publications. From the center, a one-mile interpretive trail leads the visitor to such points of interest as the patriots' earthwork siege lines, the site of the loyalists' star fort, the location of the stockaded village, and the reconstructed stockade fort. The park is open daily, except on Thanksgiving, Christmas, and New Year's Day.

IF YOU GO: Lodging and meals are available in Greenwood, SC, and elsewhere in the region. Access is from State Route 248, two miles south of Ninety Six, SC. Further information: Superintendent, P.O. Box 496, Ninety Six, SC 29666. Telephone (864) 543-4068.

SARATOGA NATIONAL HISTORICAL PARK

SARATOGA NATIONAL HISTORICAL PARK consists of 3,392 acres on the west bank of the Hudson River, in eastern New York State, north of Albany. It was established in 1938 to protect and interpret the site of the American patriots' stunning victory in 1777 over British forces—a victory that became the major turning point in the War for Independence (Revolutionary War).

British General John Burgoyne devised a military strategy by which he planned to divide and conquer America's north colonies by taking control of the Lake Champlain-Hudson River corridor—from British Canada south to New York City. His strategy called for his own troops to march south from Canada, while Colonel Barry St. Leger was to push east from Lake Ontario and down the Mohawk Valley to the Hudson River. Had they come together, these two combined forces might possibly have produced a victory for Britain.

At first, General Burgoyne's strategy went well as he and 9,000 men, consisting of about 4,200 British regulars, 4,000 Germans, some Canadians, and Indian allies, headed south from Canada in June. They captured Crown Point on June 26, overwhelmed the American garrison at Fort Ticonderoga on July 6, and then pushed on south.

But a significant element of Burgoyne's grand scheme went wrong. St. Leger's soldiers never made their march all the way down the Mohawk Valley to Albany. Instead, his troops found the way blocked by Americans at Fort

Stanwix (see Fort Stanwix National Monument) and then, under threat of attack from a force of Americans coming to the aid of the fort, St. Leger retreated to Canada.

In spite of this disappointment, Burgoyne chose to take a chance and push on south, and on September 13, his troops crossed over to the west bank of the Hudson at Saratoga (where Schuylerville is today). Continuing on south a few miles, Burgoyne's men, now reduced to around 4,000, suddenly encountered 9,000 Americans under the newly appointed commander of the Northern American army, General Horatio Gates. The general's 21-year-old Polish military engineer, Colonel Thaddeus Kosciuszko (see Thaddeus Kosciuszko National Memorial), had wisely selected and fortified with artillery the strategic heights and earth-and-log redoubts commanding the Hudson River and the river road. The army's military encampment was established on Bemis Heights.

General Burgoyne decided to attack the American position, advancing in three columns, on September 19. Two columns of troops headed directly toward the Americans and clashed with them in an open area on the Freeman Farm. This bloody battle raged for over three hours. Just as the British soldiers were beginning to wither under the deadly pounding of the Americans' musket and rifle fire, 550 German troops, which had marched down the river road and then swung westward to the Americans' right flank, arrived just in time to prevent a British defeat.

Burgoyne pulled his troops back and dug in about a mile north of the American front line. Here he attempted to await the expected arrival of General Henry Clinton's reinforcements coming up the river. But as he waited, his situation steadily deteriorated. New England militia severed his connection with Canada, cutting off the escape route northward. British supplies were diminishing. Foraging excursions were often attacked by American troops. Indians, who had been cooperating with the British, were now abandoning their alliance. In the meantime, the American military was gaining in strength and numbers, increasing to around 13,000 men. After nearly three weeks of waiting in vain for Clinton's arrival, Burgoyne's situation had become desperate.

Faced by increasingly grim prospects, Burgoyne made the fateful decision to mount a second attack on the Americans. On October 7, about 1,500 of his men, armed with artillery, moved toward the American's left flank and deployed themselves in a wheat field of the Barber Farm. The Americans then responded by attacking in three columns. The British line was hit again and again, but managed to regroup. Then the flanks were pounded hard in the fierce fighting and were forced to fall back. Before the British could recover, American General Benedict Arnold, who had disputed with General Gates and had been relieved of his command, took it upon himself to join the fighting. American troops, spurred on by Arnold, slammed into the British center. Burgoyne's men then retreated to defensive fortifications on the Freeman Farm. Other American troops overwhelmed German soldiers who were defending the log breastwork fortification known as the Breymann Redoubt, destroying Burgoyne's right flank.

Hudson River Valley, Saratoga National Historical Park [David Muench]

Under the cover of that night's darkness, the British forces withdrew behind their earth-and-log fortification above the river—the Great Redoubt. The following night, Burgoyne's men retreated farther north, to the town of Saratoga, where they were then surrounded by the American army and were forced to surrender on October 17. The British had suffered 1,000 casualties, while the Americans lost fewer than half the British total and now had a powerful fighting force of about 15,000 to 20,000 men. General Gates allowed Burgoyne's men to march away with the "Honors of War," leaving behind all their firearms, and General Burgoyne promising that the troops would be sent back across the Atlantic—never again to take up arms against America.

This spectacularly decisive American triumph at Saratoga was a major turning point in the War for Independence.

Today Saratoga National Historical Park's visitor center provides interpretive exhibits, programs, and publications. From there, a nine-mile tour road winds through the park, with interpretive stops at such places as the Freeman Farm overlook; the John Neilson Farm on Bemis Heights, with the restored farmhouse that was used as quarters for General Benedict Arnold and other American officers; the site of the Americans' river fortifications that so effectively blocked the British advance southward along the Hudson; the Barber Farm wheat field; the Breymann Redoubt; the location of Burgoyne's headquarters; and the British fortification—the Great Redoubt.

There are several trails and historic routes in the park, including the four-mile Wilkinson National Recreation Trail that takes off from the visitor center. Hikers are cautioned that some of the trails are rough walking, as on fairly steep parts of the one-mile Fraser Burial Site loop. Visitors are also cautioned to be on the alert for poison ivy, which is common in the park. In winter, the trails become excellent (ungroomed) cross-country skiing routes that reveal the magic of the season.

In addition to the wealth of historical values, the park also protects a rich variety of natural habitats. Prominent among the trees are white pine, American sycamore, American elm, beech, northern red oak—some of which are of large size—paper and yellow birches, and red and sugar maples. Wildflowers include bloodroot, round-lobed hepatica, wild lily-of-the-valley, partridgeberry, pearly everlasting, false Solomon's seal, starflower, wintergreen, several cinquefoils, marsh marigold, yellow trout lily, yellow and orange hawkweeds, wild yellow lily, cardinal flower, columbine, pink lady's slipper, steeplebush, wake-robin, blue flag, several violets, St. Johnswort, a number of goldenrod species, black-eyed susan, Jack-in-the-pulpit, Indian pipe, and beechdrops.

Among the native mammals are whitetail deer, a resident population of coyotes, red foxes, longtail and shortail weasels, raccoons, porcupines, beavers, muskrats, woodchucks, striped skunks, cottontails, gray and red squirrels, and eastern chipmunks. And a few of the many species of birds that inhabit or migrate through this part of the Hudson River valley are great blue and green-backed herons, Canada geese, many varieties of ducks, ring-billed and herring gulls, an occasional bald eagle, redtail and other hawks, ruffed grouse, wild turkeys (sometimes flocks of 20 to 25 are seen), great horned and other owls, belted kingfishers, pileated and other woodpeckers, blue jays, black-capped chickadees, house wrens, wood and hermit thrushes, catbirds, mockingbirds, brown thrashers, numerous warblers including yellowthroat and redstart, rose-breasted grosbeaks, cardinals, indigo buntings, sparrows such as tree and white-throated, bobolinks, eastern meadowlarks, redwings, northern orioles, and scarlet tanagers.

IF YOU GO: Camping is not permitted in the park, but there are two picnic areas. Lodging and meals are available in Stillwater, Schuylerville, Saratoga Springs, Albany, Glens Falls, and elsewhere in the region. Access to the park entrances is by way of U.S. Route 4 and State Route 32, about 30 miles north of Albany. The visitor center is open daily, except on Thanksgiving, Christmas, and New Year's Day. Park roads are open from early April through November, as weather permits. Further information: Superintendent, 648 Route 32, Stillwater, NY 12170. Telephone (518) 664-9821.

SPRINGFIELD ARMORY NATIONAL HISTORIC SITE

SPRINGFIELD ARMORY NATIONAL HISTORIC SITE, consisting of 55 acres in Springfield, Massachusetts, was established in 1978 to protect and interpret the site of the major manufacturer of small firearms for U.S. infantrymen, from 1794 to 1968.

Springfield was selected by General George Washington as the location of the nation's first arsenal, in 1777. Over the many decades, the armory produced weapons that were widely renowned for their precision and dependability. Among the best known were the Springfield rifle (M1903) used in World War I by the United States Army, and the M1 rifle used during World War II. Many advances in firearms technology were achieved at this armory as well.

Today, one of the armory buildings houses a museum of interpretive exhibits of firearms and the history of small firearms production. Interpretive programs and publications are also provided. The site is open daily between Memorial Day and Labor Day, and on Mondays during the rest of the year. It is closed on Thanksgiving, Christmas, and New Year's Day.

IF YOU GO: Lodging and meals are available in the Springfield area. Access from I-91 northbound is by way of the Broad St. exit (#4), turning right onto State St., left onto Federal St., left into Springfield Technical Community College, and proceeding on the road to the left to the site. Access from I-91 southbound is by way of the Broad St. exit (#5), turning left at the bottom of the off-ramp and left at the stoplight onto Columbus Ave; then right onto State St., left onto Federal St., left into the college, and proceeding on the road to the left to the site. Further information: Springfield Armory National Historic Site, 1 Armory Square, Springfield, MA 01105. Telephone (413) 734-8551.

THADDEUS KOSCIUSZKO NATIONAL MEMORIAL

THADDEUS KOSCIUSZKO NATIONAL MEMORIAL, protecting and interpreting the house at Pine and Third streets in Philadelphia, Pennsylvania, was established in 1972 to celebrate the life and accomplishments of the Polish-born hero of the War for Independence (Revolutionary War.).

The memorial consists of the modest, restored brick townhouse, dating from 1775, in which Kosciuszko rented a room in 1797-1798. He is remembered for his skillfully selecting and fortifying with artillery the strategic heights and redoubts above the Hudson River and the river road, about 30 miles north of Albany, New York. At the age of 21, his military engineering genius provided the American patriot forces, under the command of General Horatio Gates, the advantage of holding this critically important high ground around Bemis Heights against the southward advance of the British soldiers, under General John Burgoyne. The Americans won a decisive victory over the British that led to their surrender in October 1777, which proved to be a major turning point in the war against the British (see Saratoga National Historical Park). Kosciuszko was promoted to the distinguished rank of the Continental Army's chief engineer.

IF YOU GO: The national memorial provides a few exhibits and a short slide program (in Polish, as well as English). The park unit is open daily, except on Thanksgiving, Christmas, and New Year's Day. Lodging and meals are available in the Philadelphia metropolitan area. The memorial is located just three blocks from the Independence National Historical Park visitor center. Further information: Superintendent, 313 Walnut St., Philadelphia, PA 19106. Telephone (215) 597-9618.

VALLEY FORGE NATIONAL HISTORICAL PARK

VALLEY FORGE NATIONAL HISTORICAL PARK comprises 3,468 acres along the Schuylkill River in southeastern Pennsylvania. It was established in 1976 to protect and interpret the Continental Army's encampment site during the winter of 1777–1778, in the War for Independence (Revolutionary War). The name, Valley Forge, came from an old iron forge on the banks of Valley Creek.

In August 1777, an army of 18,500 veteran British troops, under the command of General Sir William Howe, landed at the northern end of Chesapeake Bay. Its goal was to capture Philadelphia—the American patriot capital and seat of the Continental Congress. The Americans' Continental Army of 10,500 men, under the command of General George Washington, was outmaneuvered and defeated at the Battle of Brandywine on September 11 (a site protected in Brandywine Battlefield [state] Park). This defeat opened the way for the British capture and occupation of Philadelphia. General Washington attempted to retake the city quickly with a surprise attack on British troops at the Battle of Germantown on October 4, but the Americans failed to achieve a victory.

Consequently, on December 19, 12,000 discouraged, war-weary, scantily clothed, ill-fed, and poorly equipped American troops struggled onto the defensible, but wind-swept heights at Valley Forge above the Schuylkill River, a few miles northwest of Philadelphia.

Upon arriving at Valley Forge, the soldiers immediately set to work constructing hundreds of rustic huts. While these structures provided some degree of shelter from winter's fury, they were cold, damp, and crowded. The men had only tattered clothing, many had no shoes, and their food was mostly a mixture of bland flour and water, with occasional bread and meat—hardly a diet sufficient to build up and maintain the strength of a fighting force.

Here on the gently rolling hills of Mount Joy and Mount Misery, the soldiers endured the sufferings and deprivations in the cold, snowy, and windy winter weather. No battle was fought at Valley Forge, yet at least 2,000 men died from exposure to cold, dampness, and disease. Pneumonia, scabies, dysentery, frostbite, typhus, and typhoid ravaged the troops. Some 4,000 men were unfit for military service during the worst of the winter ordeal.

General Washington wrote of the rough ordeal:

> To see men without clothes to cover their nakedness, without blankets to lie upon, without shoes . . . without a house or hut to cover them until those could be built, and submitting without a murmur, is a proof of patience and obedience which, in my opinion, can scarcely be paralleled.

Under Washington's inspiring moral and military leadership and the capable and disciplined training program of Prussian drillmaster, General Friedrich von Steuben, the soldiers' self-esteem and military skills were greatly

General George Washington's headquarters, Valley Forge National Historical Park [Don R. Naimoli]

enhanced. It was at Valley Forge that America's Army was drawn from 13 independent units into one uniform army, capable of defeating the British.

Why were the American troops so desperately short of all the supplies an armed force should have? Not from poverty in the American colonies, but, as historian Samuel Eliot Morison explains (*The Oxford History of the American People*), from "selfishness, mismanagement, and difficulties in transportation." The basic problem was that businessmen and farmers were mostly unwilling to risk providing clothing, blankets, food, and other supplies in exchange for a Continental voucher that might never be honored.

At Valley Forge, the procurement and distribution of supplies were vastly improved under the newly appointed Quartermaster General, Nathanael Greene. As the winter finally warmed into spring, General Washington's men were well fed and clothed, ready to leave Valley Forge and pursue the British troops as they left Philadelphia on June 19, 1778, and marched toward New York. According to the National Park Service,

> . . . for Washington, his men, and the nation to which they sought to give birth, a decisive victory had been won—a victory not of weapons but of will. The spirit of Valley Forge was now a part of the army, and because of it the prospects for final victory were considerably brighter.

Visitors touring the national historical park today can grasp something of the immense human suffering that occurred in this place, as well as feel enormous pride for the patience, perseverance, and faith with which these men managed to overcome crushing misery. They all could have just succumbed and given up. But they did not, and they went on to win the war for America's independence.

The park's visitor center provides interpretive exhibits and publications, and a small auditorium nearby presents an interpretive film. From May to September, the park sponsors some living-history programs. From the visitor center, a self-guided interpretive drive (an audiotape may be purchased) leads visitors to a number of reconstructed huts at the site of the first in a series of brigades; the Outer Line Defenses; the impressive National Memorial Arch, dating from 1917, that celebrates the "patience and fidelity" of General Washington's soldiers; and the bronze equestrian statue honoring General Anthony Wayne, commander of Pennsylvania soldiers.

The drive then follows a winding stretch of Valley Creek down to General Washington's headquarters, the Isaac Potts House—an attractive two-story stone house near the banks of the Schuylkill River; then winds onto Mount Joy, passing the sites of Redoubt 4, the Inner Line Defenses, Redoubt 3, and Artillery Park—the latter where cannons were stored, maintained, and where artillery crews were trained under the command of Brigadier General Henry Knox; the stone farmhouse that served as General James Varnum's quarters, and statue commemorating General von Steuben; and finally the Valley Forge Historical Society's museum located on a privately owned tract within the park.

A six-mile bicycle and foot path follows alongside much of the park road. On the north side of the river, there are ten miles of trails, a picnic area, and the Schuylkill River Trail.

Two informative publications are *Campaign to Valley Forge, July 1, 1777-December 19, 1777* by John F. Reed (Pioneer Press): and *Birthplace of an Army, A Study of the Valley Encampment* by John B.B. Trussell, Jr. (Pennsylvania Historical and Museum Commission).

IF YOU GO: Lodging and meals are available near the park, and in communities throughout the Philadelphia metropolitan area. Access is by way of the Valley Forge exit (#24) from either direction on the Pennsylvania Turnpike (I-76 from the west and I276 fron the east), then taking the right turn after the toll booth onto North Gulph Rd. and following signs into the park; by way of the Mall Blvd. exit from the Schuylkill Expressway (I-76) westbound from Philadelphia, then turning right onto Mall Blvd. at the stop light. The park is open daily, except on Christmas. Further information: Superintendent, P.O. Box 953, Valley Forge, PA 19482. Telephone (610) 783-1077.

PART 3

WAR OF 1812, MEXICAN-AMERICAN WAR, ETC.

CASTLE CLINTON NATIONAL MONUMENT

CASTLE CLINTON NATIONAL MONUMENT, comprising one acre in Battery Park at the southern tip of Manhattan, in New York City, was transferred to the National Park Service in 1946. It protects and interprets a structure dating from 1811 that was one of a number of fortified military defense installations for New York City and harbor against the possibility of British attack during the War of 1812. Castle Clinton was subsequently used as a public entertainment facility and was then an immigration processing depot serving some eight million prospective new American citizens, from 1855 to 1890.

The national monument provides interpretive exhibits, programs, tours, and publications. The monument is open daily, except on Thanksgiving, Christmas, and New Year's Day. Nearby, the Circle Line (Telephone [212] 563-3590) operates the ferry service from Battery Park across the harbor to the Statue of Liberty and Ellis Island (see Statue of Liberty National Monument).
IF YOU GO: Lodging and meals are available in and around New York City. Access to Battery Park is by way of public transportation (subway and bus) or by taxi. As there is little likelihood of available parking anywhere nearby, driving to the monument is not recommended. Further information: Superintendent, Manhattan Sites, 26 Wall St., New York, NY 10005. Telephone (212) 344-7220.

FORT McHENRY NATIONAL MONUMENT AND HISTORIC SHRINE

FORT McHENRY NATIONAL MONUMENT AND HISTORIC SHRINE, consisting of 341 acres in Baltimore, Maryland, was transferred from the U.S. military to the National Park Service in 1940. It protects and interprets the massive fort that was successfully defended against intense bombardment by British warships on September 13–14, 1814, during the War of 1812.

Construction of this red-brick, star-shaped masonry fort was undertaken in the late 1790s. It was named for James McHenry, secretary of war under the administrations of George Washington and John Adams. It was garrisoned with 1,000 men and bristled with over 50 cannons to guard the mouth of Baltimore Harbor.

In August 1814, a 20-warship British fleet, under the command of Admiral Alexander Cochrane, had sailed into Chesapeake Bay to let off 3,400 veteran soldiers under General Robert Ross for an attack on the new American capital city of Washington. The British troops broke through minimal defenses and burned the White House, the Capitol, and other national government buildings (see The White House). Ross and his men triumphantly returned to the ships, which then sailed on north for an attack upon Baltimore.

While General Ross' British troops were being put ashore at North Point, to attempt a march around to the less well protected landward side of the city, five of Admiral Cochrane's ships, armed with rockets and mortar bombs, moved into range and commenced a battering assault on the fort. Explosions boomed and crashed, pounding down. However, not only did his bombardment fail to drive out Major George Armistead and his garrison, but it inflicted relatively little damage upon the fort itself.

Meanwhile, General Ross and his troops were encountering stiff resistance from the Maryland militia. In fact, they were quickly forced to fall back to North Point after failing to defeat the over 15,000 militiamen in an area of extensive defensive earthworks and palisades known as Rodgers Bastion.

Just after midnight, in the rainy early hours of September 14, the British ships began unleashing a second and even heavier assault upon the fort. The spectacular and terrifying orange and yellow glow of exploding rockets, traceries of shell fuses, and cannon fire lit up the underside of low rain clouds. This relentless bombardment continued unabated through the rest of the night.

Ironically, two Americans happened to be aboard one of the British ships—Colonel John Skinner and a young lawyer, Francis Scott Key. They had been sent out to a "flag-of-truce" vessel to negotiate for the release of a hostage—a medical doctor who was being held captive by the British. The doctor was released, but the British were now holding Skinner and Key. So it was that these men had a ringside seat through the 25 hours of the siege on Fort McHenry and related military tactics in the effort to attack Baltimore.

When the gray dawn's early light finally came and the British ceased their attack, Key and Skinner saw the Stars and Stripes—the huge 42- by 30-foot American flag—still waving above the fort. Key immediately jotted down a few poetic lines describing his excitement over the glorious triumph of the courageous Americans who had defended the great fort, which had survived the onslaught with little damage and with the loss of only four lives.

Key then expanded upon his initial jottings, and several days later a Baltimore newspaper published his poem under the heading, "Defense of Fort McHenry." It was next given a new title, "The Star-Spangled Banner;" was reprinted in many newspapers from New England to Georgia; and the words were then set to the music of "To Anacreon in Heaven." Finally, 117 years later, "The Star-Spangled Banner" became America's official national anthem.

Fort McHenry National Monument and Historic Shrine, Baltimore, Maryland [NPS]

The fort today has a visitor center with interpretive exhibits, a film, and publications. A self-guiding walk through the fort features such points of interest as the ravelin, a V-shaped defensive structure at the fort's entrance, called the Sally Port; bombproof shelters; the parade ground and the location of the original flagpole, from which the famous flag was still waving after the British siege; one of the five outward-projecting bastions that give the fort its star shape; soldiers' barracks and officers' quarters; cannons; the powder magazine, into which a British mortar bomb landed but thankfully failed to explode; and what remains of the encircling dry moat.

Fort McHenry was subsequently used during the Civil War. While it was never involved in a battle, there are a number of modifications to and uses of the fort dating from this period.

The National Park Service warns against climbing on the fort's walls, cannons, and other potentially hazardous places and objects, and advises being especially careful that children do not risk their safety.

During the summer months, the national monument presents guided tours and special Flag Day (June 14) and Defender's Day (September 7) programs, as well as volunteer Fort McHenry Guard living-history reenactments.

There is a pathway along the seawall that is popular for walking and jogging, and the monument also provides a picnic area. Lodging and meals are available in and around Baltimore.

IF YOU GO: Access from I-95 is by way of the Key Highway/Fort McHenry National Monument (#55) exit, then following the blue-and-green signs along Key Highway, to a right turn onto Lawrence Street, and left onto Fort Avenue to the national monument. Access from the Inner Harbor area is by way of Light Street southbound, to a left turn onto Key Highway, and following the blue-and-green signs to a right turn onto Lawrence Street and left onto Fort Avenue to the national monument. Further information: Superintendent, Fort McHenry National Monument and Historic Shrine, Baltimore, MD 21230. Telephone (410) 962-4299.

FORT WASHINGTON PARK

FORT WASHINGTON PARK, comprising 341 acres on the Maryland shore of the Potomac River, about six miles downriver from Washington, D.C., was transferred from the War Department to the National Park Service in 1939. It was returned to the military for use during World War II, and was again transferred to the Park Service in 1946. The park protects and interprets a United States military fortification that dates from 1824 to protect the Potomac River access to the nation's capital. It was strengthened during the Civil War and periodically during the late nineteenth century, and was used for training and other functions during World War II.

This strategic site, on a bluff overlooking the river between Piscataway and Swan creeks, was originally selected as the site of a smaller fort, Fort Warburton, that was completed in 1809. On August 19, 1814, during the War of 1812 between Britain and the United States, British troops invaded defenseless Washington, D.C., from the northeast, and set fire to the U.S. Capitol, the White House, and other public buildings (see The White House). The next day, British warships proceeded up the Potomac River. To prevent a British takeover of the fort, the American garrison blew it up as they departed.

When the Civil War broke out in 1861, and Virginia, across the Potomac from Fort Washington, seceded from the Union, a massive masonry fortification that was completed in 1824 assumed new significance. At the time, the fort was the only fortification near the nation's capital. But soon, an encircling network of earthen forts and artillery batteries was established to guard Washington from all directions (see Fort Circle Parks). Fort Washington never saw any military action during the Civil War or afterward. But its defenses and weaponry were periodically enhanced and strengthened over the years. For example, in the 1880s, Fort Washington was strengthened with some concrete reinforcements and with installation of longer range, rifled cannons and more powerful mortars that were capable of penetrating armor plating of enemy warships.

Today, Fort Washington presents the story of evolving and improving military fortification strategies and technology. A visitor center provides interpretive exhibits, an audiovisual program, and publications. On spring, summer, and autumn weekends, various living-history reenactments and demonstrations are presented—portraying the Civil War era and the life of a nineteenth-century U.S. Army garrison. For information on these programs: Telephone (301) 763-4600. Several trails lead visitors through the park— notably along the Potomac shore. Visitors should be alert for poison ivy. When touring the fort and batteries, visitors are cautioned not to climb onto the parapet and other hazardous places, and to watch carefully that children do not climb around on the fort or cannons. The park is open daily, except on Christmas and New Year's Day.

Camping is not permitted in the park, but picnic areas are provided, some of which may be reserved in advance by contacting the park. Lodging and meals are available throughout the Washington metropolitan area, including at freeway interchanges. **IF YOU GO:** Access from the Capital Beltway (I-95) is by way of Exit 3 and south on State Route 210 (Indian Head Highway), and a right turn onto Fort Washington Road to the park entrance. Further information: Fort Washington Park, Superintendent, National Capital Parks-East, 1900 Anacostia Dr., SE, Washington, D.C. 20020. Telephone (301) 763-4600.

Fort Washington Park [Vicki Paris/NPCA]

PALO ALTO BATTLEFIELD NATIONAL HISTORIC SITE

PALO ALTO BATTLEFIELD NATIONAL HISTORIC SITE consists of 3,400 acres just north of Brownsville, Texas. It was authorized in 1978 to protect and interpret—from both Mexican and American perspectives—the site of the Battle of Palo Alto, on the plains of Palo Alto, near the Rio Grande in south Texas, on May 8, 1846. It was the first territorial-dispute confrontation of the Mexican-American War in 1846–1848. It ended in the triumph of U.S. General Zachary Taylor's 2,300 men over the 4,000 Mexican troops commanded by General Mariano Arista. As of this writing, the land within the park boundary is privately owned and not open to public visitation.

Although the American soldiers were substantially outnumbered, the Mexicans' dozen cannons, many of which were nearly 100 years old, were no match for the ten superior, modern, American siege guns, a howitzer, and other cannons that were easily able to outpace the Mexican artillery in both speed and range. General Taylor unleashed a devastating "rain of metal," forcing the Mexican soldiers to remain at such a great distance that they were unable to open fire with their own muskets.

The Mexicans' cavalry then attempted to dash around and cut off the Americans' vital supply line, but this classic military tactic was slowed down as the horsemen slogged through a marshy area before being attacked by two successful U.S. infantry charges.

For part of the afternoon, thick smoke obscured the battlefield. The smoke spread out from a fire that had been ignited by smoldering cannon wadding, and was whipped into life by a breeze off the Gulf of Mexico. Both sides took advantage of the forced lull in fighting to reposition their troops behind the smokescreen.

When the battle resumed, the Mexican troops gained the offensive for awhile, until a battery of U.S. horse-drawn cannons charged in and blew apart the Mexicans' advancing infantry and cavalry forces; massive, point-blank American artillery fire forced the Mexicans' retreat and the end of this battle. While estimates of Mexican casualties were believed to have been between 125 and 400 killed, plus between 100 and 400 injured, only 9 Americans lost their lives and 43 were wounded.

The following day, the two forces confronted each other again, in the Battle of Resaca de la Palma. Fierce and bloody hand-to-hand fighting, supplemented by cavalry charges, finally forced the greatly diminished Mexican military force to retreat southward across the Rio Grande. In the following months, American forces battled southward—to Veracruz on the Gulf of Mexico coast of Mexico, and then inland to Mexico City, where Mexican leaders reluctantly negotiated a peace agreement in 1847. And what began on the Palo Alto Battlefield ultimately led to Mexico being forced to give up half its land area to the United States, under the 1848 Treaty of Guadalupe Hidalgo. By this treaty, the United States gained the territories of California and New Mexico (including what is now Arizona), an area of over 500,000 square miles.

IF YOU GO: Because the national historic site, at this writing, is not open to visitors, there is no access or interpretive program. Further information: Superintendent, P.O. Drawer 1832, Brownsville, TX 78522. Telephone (210) 548-2788.

PERRY'S VICTORY AND INTERNATIONAL PEACE MEMORIAL

PERRY'S VICTORY AND INTERNATIONAL PEACE MEMORIAL comprises nearly 26 acres and was established in 1936. The park is located in northern Ohio on the Lake Erie island of South Bass, near Sandusky and Port Clinton. It commemorates Commodore Oliver Hazard Perry's victory on Lake Erie, in one of the most decisive naval battles in the War of 1812, and the resulting international peace between the United States and Canada.

Early in the War of 1812, British ships controlled Lake Erie, an important lifeline for American troops and supplies in the Old Northwest. On September 10, 1813, about ten miles northwest of South Bass Island, this stranglehold was broken when nine vessels under the command of Commodore Perry won a decisive victory over six British warships under the command of Robert Heriott Barclay. The battle began at 11:45 a.m. and at first went badly for the Americans. By 2:30 p.m., Perry's flagship *Lawrence* was a floating wreck—every gun was disabled and the crew had suffered 80 percent casualties. But Perry did not give up. He transferred his command to the *Niagara,* which was relatively undamaged, and set sail directly for the enemy line. The British countered Perry's move. The largest ships on each side collided and became helplessly entangled. In 15 minutes, the Battle of Lake Erie was over, prompting Perry to summarize, "We have met the enemy and they are ours."

Since the end of the War of 1812, peaceful relations have existed between the United States and Canada, and with Great Britain prior to that. Canada and the United States share the world's longest undefended border, of more than 4,000 miles. The lessons of peace through negotiation and arbitration are still honored through the 1817 Rush-Bagot Agreement, one of the first disarmament treaties, which remains in effect today.

The park is best known for the granite memorial shaft built between 1912 and 1915 that rises 352 feet above its 45-foot-wide base. Visitors may ride an elevator from the second floor of the memorial to an open-air observation platform 317 feet

Perry's Victory and International Peace Memorial, on South Bass Island, Lake Erie [NPS]

above Lake Erie (fee charged). The memorial is open daily from mid-May to early October, and by appointment the rest of the year. A small visitor center on the street level presents exhibits on the War of 1812 and Perry's Memorial, as well as offering a variety of publications. During summer weekends, costumed living-history demonstrations are given on the grounds.

Lodging and meals are available on the island in season; lodging reservations are advised. Full services are also available in mainland communities. South Bass Island State Park offers 130 sites with primitive camping on the island.

IF YOU GO: In season, automobile and passenger ferries operate from Catawba Point and passenger-only ferries from Port Clinton. There is year-round air service to the island from the Port Clinton and Sandusky airports. Further information: Superintendent, P.O. Box 549, Put-in-Bay, Ohio 43456. Telephone (419) 285-2184.

PART 4

U.S. MILITARY VERSUS NATIVE AMERICANS (INDIANS) (NINETEENTH-CENTURY FORTS AND BATTLEFIELDS)

BIG HOLE NATIONAL BATTLEFIELD

BIG HOLE NATIONAL BATTLEFIELD, consisting of 655 acres in the Big Hole Valley of southwestern Montana, was established as a military reserve in 1883, only seven years after the Battle of Big Hole. The battlefield was then named as a national monument in 1910, was transferred from the War Department to the National Park Service in 1933, and was renamed as a national battlefield in 1963. It protects and interprets the site of the Battle of Big Hole, which was part of a larger conflict known as the Nez Perce War of 1877. Big Hole National Battlefield also stands as a memorial to soldiers, volunteers, and the Nez Perce who died here, fighting for what they believed was right.

Tension between the Nez Perce and the U.S. government had grown after 1863. In 1855, the tribe had agreed to occupy a reservation of about 12,000 square miles in Idaho. But in 1860, gold was discovered on the reservation, and in 1863 the government tried to force a new treaty on the Nez Perce, reducing the reservation to about 1,200 square miles. Part of the tribe agreed to live within the new reservation boundaries, but others resisted and continued to live as they had, within the confines of the larger reservation, until 1877.

In the spring of that year, the U.S. Army was called upon to force the Nez Perce onto the smaller reservation. Although the majority of the Nez Perce were reluctantly complying, violence broke out when several young men avenged the death of one of their fathers by murdering several white settlers. Attempts to avoid war failed, and the Battle of White Bird Canyon became the first of many battles and skirmishes between the non-treaty Nez Perce and the U.S. Army.

The Nez Perce fled to the east, hoping to leave the war and the Army troops behind them when they crossed into Montana Territory. On August 7, 1877, they set up camp in the Big Hole Valley, certain that the pursuing Army would not leave Idaho. Unknown to them, Colonel John Gibbon was

Big Hole National Battlefield, Montana [NPS]

marching west from Fort Shaw, Montana, accompanied by 161 officers and
soldiers, plus 34 civilian volunteers from the Bitterroot Valley. The military
men intended to intercept the non-treaty Nez Perce.

Before dawn on August 9, the soldiers silently positioned themselves
adjacent to the sleeping Nez Perce camp. Their orders were to wait for a signal,
then attack in an organized front. Before everyone was ready, an old Nez Perce
man, checking on his horses, stumbled onto the hiding soldiers and volunteers. The volunteers immediately shot the man, and the battle commenced.

In the initial attack, confusion reigned in the Nez Perce camp. Soon,
however, some of the Indian men began to return fire while women and children ran for cover. The Nez Perce forced Gibbon to call a retreat, and the soldiers and volunteers moved back to a wooded knoll, where they dug rifle pits
and protective trenches. Nez Perce snipers held the soldiers under siege while
other Nez Perce buried the dead, packed their belongings, and began heading
to the southeast. The following day, after a cold and terrifying night under
sniper fire, the soldiers watched the last of the Nez Perce join their fleeing families and friends.

The Nez Perce continued their trek, and the U.S. Army, gaining reinforcements as the weeks passed, continued to pursue them. About 40 miles
south of the Canadian border, the Nez Perce were surrounded by military
forces. After a five-day standoff in the Bear Paw Mountains, most of the people agreed to end the fighting. About 200 Nez Perce escaped into Canada.
Those who remained had been promised safe return to the reservation in
Idaho, but were sent instead to Oklahoma (Indian) Territory, where about a
quarter of the war survivors died. Some of the survivors were finally permitted
to return to Idaho in 1885. Nez Perce Chief Joseph and his family were sent
to eastern Washington state.

Today, the visitor center provides interpretive exhibits, an introductory audiovisual program, and publications. During the summer, there are ranger-guided tours of the battlefield and self-guided touring all year on park trails. The national battlefield is open daily, except on Thanksgiving, Christmas, and New Year's Day.

Camping is not allowed in the national battlefield, but several national forest and private campgrounds are nearby. A picnic area is provided at the trailhead parking area.

IF YOU GO: Lodging and meals are available in Wisdom, Dillon, Butte, Hamilton, and Missoula, MT, and in Salmon, ID. Access from I-15, near Dillon, is north on State Route 278 to Wisdom, and then ten miles west on State Route 43 to the battlefield entrance. From Butte, take I-15 south to Divide, then continue on State Route 43 through Wisdom to the battlefield. From I-90, access west of Butte is by way of State Route 1, and left onto County Route 273, then cross Mill Creek Pass and continue on State Route 43 through Wisdom to the battlefield. From U.S. Route 93 at Lost Trails Pass, it is 17 miles east to the battlefield on State Route 43. Further information: Superintendent, P.O. Box 237, Wisdom, MT 59761. Telephone (406) 689-3155.

FORT BOWIE NATIONAL HISTORIC SITE

FORT BOWIE NATIONAL HISTORIC SITE comprises 1,000 acres in Apache Pass, between the Chiricahua and Dos Cabezas mountains 25 miles southeast of Willcox, Arizona. It was designated in 1972 to protect and interpret the site and stabilized ruins of a U.S. military fort that was established in 1862 to guard Apache Springs, keeping it available for troops heading east to fight Confederates in New Mexico. It was also to protect this strategic stretch of the U.S. mail and immigrant road to California against attacks by the Chiricahua Apache Indians.

For several hundred years, this region had been the homeland of these nomadic Apaches. Under the Gadsden Purchase of 1854, the United States purchased from Mexico nearly 30 million acres of what is now southern Arizona and New Mexico. Two years later, a military route was laid out through Apache Pass to take advantage of a vital water supply from a year-round spring. Thus began a period of steadily increasing traffic by the white man into and through the Apache homeland.

A Butterfield Overland Mail station was constructed near the spring—a source of water that had long been used by the Indians. The mule- and horse-drawn, nine-passenger Butterfield stagecoaches began carrying passengers and the mail between St. Louis and San Francisco in 1858, a journey that took from three to four weeks.

For several years, there were no major conflicts between the Apaches and the stationkeepers. But violence broke out in 1861, triggered by the abduction of a child during an Apache raid. This act was falsely blamed on a band of Chiricahua Apaches, and a detachment of U.S. military troops, under the command of Lieutenant George N. Bascom, was dispatched to the vicinity of Apache Pass. The volatile situation rapidly escalated, with hostages taken and killed by the Indians, prisoners taken by the military, and Butterfield stagecoaches and freight caravans attacked by the Indians. This bloody encounter, which came to be called the Bascom Affair, opened up a long period of warfare between the Chiricahua Apaches and the white settlers.

The following year, with the Civil War in full swing, a detachment of about 96 Union soldiers of the California Column were dispatched to the Rio Grande to head off Confederate troops who were attempting to gain control of New Mexico and Arizona. As the Union soldiers reached Apache Pass, over 100 Apaches suddenly opened fire on them. In both of two encounters, howitzer fire power overwhelmed the Indians and forced them to retreat.

As a result of this Battle of Apache Pass, the U.S. military ordered the construction of a fort at the pass, to protect the strategic route and the important source of water. In this same year, men of the California Volunteers began building simple defensive breastworks; rustic adobe, stone, and log living quarters; and other military post structures, some of which were primitively dug into the hillside.

Living conditions at this first fort were described as deplorable. In 1864, orders were given to build more suitable facilities at a better site nearby. Unfortunately, it took several more years before construction of the second fort actually began. In 1869, the garrison was finally able to move into the initial new adobe-and-wood quarters that were laid out around a parade ground. Over the next few years, additional buildings were added to the military post. The most ornate of these was a two-story, wood-frame, Victorian-style house, erected in 1884 for the commanding officer.

Although the number of soldiers stationed at Fort Bowie reached a peak of approximately 300 in 1886, the average numbered around 100. In the early years, coinciding with the Civil War, California and New Mexico Volunteers guarded the pass, while regular U.S. military troops served at the fort after the war. Periodic battles and skirmishes occurred with the Apaches, who were masters at guerrilla warfare. They naturally knew the lay of the land like the palms of their hands, in the neighboring rugged mountains and canyons, and were consequently able to make lightning-like attacks upon wagon trains, stagecoaches, and military patrols, and then slip as quickly back into their secret hideaways, eluding their pursuers.

The military began engaging the help of a few cooperative Indians in tracking down the warriors. This breakthrough finally enabled the soldiers to halt this frustrating warfare. A peace agreement was negotiated in 1872, under which an Indian reservation was designated, taking in the Chiricahua Mountains. Four years later, Indian raids resumed, whereupon the Chiricahua band was ordered to move about 100 miles to the northwest, onto the San Carlos reservation. Another few years were devoted to capturing or bringing about the surrender of these "renegades," and Fort Bowie's troops were in the forefront of that effort.

The final conflict began in 1885, when more than 100 of the Chiricahuas, under leaders Geronimo and Naiche, left the reservation and dashed into Mexico. Units from Fort Bowie assisted in forcing the surrender of Geronimo's band in September 1886. These captives were sent into exile in Florida, where they joined other Chiricahuas from the San Carlos reservation. After nearly a quarter century of conflict between the native Americans fighting fiercely for their homeland and for their survival and the U.S. military fighting to protect the white man's westward expansion across the United States, the warfare was finally at an end in this corner of the country.

Fort Bowie, Arizona [NPS]

When the Southern Pacific Railroad was completed through Arizona in 1880, passing within about a dozen miles to the north of Apache Pass, the old route ceased to be a major transportation corridor. The fort's remaining troops were transferred to another post in 1894 and Fort Bowie was abandoned.

Today, a 1.5-mile trail leads from Apache Pass Road up to the ruins of the fort. Visitors may return by the same pathway or may hike a three-mile trail along the old Butterfield stage road. Even though water is available at the site, visitors are urged to carry a supply of water, especially in late spring, summer, and early autumn, and to dress so as to be shielded from the intense heat of the sun. A visitor center provides interpretive exhibits, programs, and publications. The center is open daily, except on Christmas.

Two excellent publications are *Fort Bowie National Historic Site* by Mark Gardner (Southwest Parks and Monuments Association); and *A Clash of Cultures, Fort Bowie and the Chiricahua Apaches* by Robert M. Utley (U.S. Government Printing Office).

IF YOU GO: Camping is not allowed, but there is a small picnic area. Overnight lodging and meals are available in Willcox, Benson, and Tucson, AZ; and in Lordsburg, NM. Access from I-10 at Willcox is 22 miles southeast on State Route 186, then left on Apache Pass Road (a gravel road) for about nine miles to the trailhead to the site; from I-10 at Bowie, it is 12 miles south on the gravel road to the trailhead; or from Chiricahua National Monument, it is four miles on State Route 181, nine miles northwest on State Route 186, and right onto the Apache Pass Road for about nine miles to the trailhead. Further information: Manager, P.O. Box 158, Bowie, AZ 85605. Telephone (520) 847-2500.

FORT DAVIS NATIONAL HISTORIC SITE

FORT DAVIS NATIONAL HISTORIC SITE, consisting of 460 acres at the foot of the Davis Mountains in West Texas, was established in 1963 to protect the most impressive and best preserved historic U.S. military fort in the Southwest, dating from 1854 to 1891.

In 1845, Texas had been annexed to the United States, and shortly thereafter had been admitted as the 28th state of the Union. The United States had then used a border-crossing incident at the Rio Grande by Mexican cavalrymen, and their killing of several American dragoons, as the excuse for declaring war on Mexico. As a result of the Mexican-American War of 1846–1848, Mexico had ceded to the United States its claims to a vast region, including Texas, New Mexico (including Arizona), and California.

This new region had immediately begun to attract immigrants by the thousands. When the region was brought into the United States, new transcontinental routes were built through the Southwest. A major stretch of one such southern wagon train and stagecoach road cut through West Texas, from San Antonio to El Paso. To provide military protection against rapidly escalating Indian hostilities along this segment of road, it was decided that a fort should be established at a strategic location in the vicinity of the Davis Mountains. It would be one of several forts in the region to contend with Comanche raids upon travelers and ranchers to the east of the mountains, and with the Mescalero Apache depredations to the west.

In 1854, U.S. Major General Perifor F. Smith chose a site for the fort in sheltered Limpia Canyon, at the southeastern edge of the mountains. The fort was named in honor of then-U.S. Secretary of War, Jefferson Davis, who subsequently became the President of the Confederate States of America. Under the command of Lieutenant Colonel Washington Seawell, this initial fortification consisted of some 60 rustic, pine-log structures. Two years later, a half-dozen stone barracks had been built at the mouth of the canyon, providing vastly better quarters for the enlisted soldiers.

At the outset, the infantrymen served as military escorts for mail stagecoaches and freight wagon trains. With the secession of Texas and other southern states from the Union at the outbreak of the Civil War in 1861, the U.S. military abandoned Fort Davis and the other West Texas forts along the El Paso road. Later that year, these military facilities were taken over by Confederate forces. When the Confederacy failed in its attempt to take control of New Mexico in 1862 (see Pecos National Historical Park), the Confederates abandoned the West Texas forts. Apaches then burned down a number of the Fort Davis buildings. A black U.S. cavalry regiment, under the command of Lieutenant Colonel Wesley Merritt, was sent to West Texas in 1867, two years after the end of the Civil War, to reconstruct and garrison Fort Davis.

This second fort was located at a new site just beyond the mouth of Limpia Canyon. Some of the buildings were constructed of stone, while others were of adobe. Along one side of the post's parade ground were the barracks for enlisted soldiers. Along the other side was officers' row—a line of 13 houses. Both the barracks and officers' quarters were attractively embellished with columned porches fronting on the parade ground. By the time many of the post's more than 50 structures were finally built in the 1880s, the facility had grown to accommodate a dozen companies of infantrymen and cavalry. Other structures included the post headquarters, stables and corrals, a quartermaster storehouse, bakery, granary, chapel, guardhouse, hospital, the post trader's building, and a telegraph office.

During the 1870s, Apache hostilities across southwestern Texas were escalating. In 1880, Apache leader Victorio and his band of 150 warriors, who had been hiding out in the remote and rugged mountains across the Rio Grande in Mexico, launched a string of attacks to the

Officers' Row, Fort Davis National Historic Site, West Texas [Larry Ulrich]

west of the Davis Mountains. Fort Davis' Troop H, the African American cavalry regiment that was also called the "Buffalo Soldiers," under the command of Colonel Benjamin H. Grierson, had already been dispatched to try to prevent Victorio's band from returning to the United States and attacking travelers and ranchers in the region. As soon as the Apaches reappeared, the Fort Davis cavalrymen took off in hot pursuit. After a number of encounters, the Indians rode into an ambush, from which they were able to flee back into Mexico. Mexican troops finally succeeded in trapping them and killing Victorio and most of his warriors.

Except for an occasional skirmish with a few persistent "renegades," the Indian wars of West Texas were over. In 1885, the honored men of Troop H were transferred to the Arizona Territory, where they helped defeat Geronimo's band of Chiricahua Apaches (see Fort Bowie National Historic Site).

Today, more than 20 of the fort's original structures have been restored. The visitor center and museum provide interpretive exhibits, an audiovisual program, and publications. There is a self-guiding tour through the grounds and several buildings that have been authentically refurnished. Among these is an enlisted men's barracks, two officers' quarters, and the commissary. During the summer, there are living-history demonstrations at the barracks, the commanding and officers' quarters, and elsewhere, as well as guided tours by costumed interpreters. A number of trails offer opportunities to explore other parts of the area. The site is open daily, except on Thanksgiving, Christmas, and New Year's Day.

An excellent publication is *Fort Davis: The Men of Troop H* by Scott Thybony (Southwest Parks and Monuments Association).

IF YOU GO: Camping is not allowed in the national historic site, but a campground is available in the adjacent Davis Mountains State Park. The site does provide a tree-shaded picnic area. Lodging and meals are available at an attractive lodge in the state park, as well as in the towns of Fort Davis, Marfa, Alpine, and Fort Stockton. Access is from I-10 at Balmorhea, south on State Route 17; from I-10 at Kent, south on State Route 118; from U.S. Route 90 at Alpine, about 24 miles north on Route 17; or from Route 90 at Marfa, about 21 miles north on route 118. Further information: Superintendent, P.O. Box 1456, Fort Davis, TX 79734. Telephone (915) 426-3224.

FORT LARAMIE NATIONAL HISTORIC SITE

FORT LARAMIE NATIONAL HISTORIC SITE, consisting of 832 acres near the junction of the Laramie and Platte rivers in southeastern Wyoming, was established as a national monument in 1938 and changed to a national historic site in 1960. It protects and interprets the site of a fur-trading post dating from 1834, a major stop for emigrants at Mile 650 on the Oregon Trail in the 1840s and 1850s, and a key U.S. military fort from 1849 to 1890.

The first structure to be built on the banks of the Laramie River was a small palisaded trading post, named Fort William and built by fur traders William Sublette and Robert Campbell. Two years later, the American Fur Company bought the post and quickly expanded it into the major trading center in the region. The original wood structure was soon replaced with a more substantial, fortified adobe complex, renamed Fort John on the Laramie and more commonly called Fort Laramie. During the first several years, trappers traded their caravan loads of beaver and other fur pelts at the post. By the late 1830s, the popularity of fashionable top hats made of beaver fur had declined in favor of silk top hats. But by then, buffalo robes had come into great demand and comprised the bulk of the post's business.

Fort Laramie was also serving as an increasingly popular stopping place, at which thousands of emigrants, men seeking their fortunes in the gold and silver mines of the West, and other travelers could pause, replenish their supplies, repair harnesses and other equipment, and refresh themselves, before pushing westward through the wilderness to Oregon, California, and elsewhere. As this mounting tide of migration swept across the continent, some of the Northern Plains Indians—the Sioux, Cheyenne, and other tribes—became increasingly alarmed by the white man's influx into their traditional lands and interference with their nomadic lifestyle. Hostilities multiplied as this major cultural conflict escalated. Indian warriors attacked wagon trains, in desperate attempts to discourage the white man from migrating into and through their world.

In response to this rising violence, the U.S. military purchased Fort Laramie in 1849 and converted the post to a major army fort, strategically situated on the Oregon Trail. A new and much more extensive, unpalisaded facility was laid out around a large parade ground, to accommodate a company of infantrymen and two companies of cavalrymen. Initially, there were barracks for enlisted soldiers, the officers' quarters, the post headquarters, the quartermaster's storehouse, a bakery, stables, and other buildings.

During the 1850s and 1860s, the fort's soldiers provided military escorts, patrols, and other protection for emigrant and freight wagon caravans and for the U.S. mail coaches traveling the trail. While the soldiers were involved in periodic skirmishes with hostile Indian bands, much of their time was devoted to military drills and other discipline-enhancing activities. Only once did the fort come under attack. A band of 30 Indians rushed into the parade ground and made off with the soldiers' horses, just after a group of cavalrymen had dismounted.

Fort Laramie was also the site of a series of peace negotiations between the Sioux Indians and representatives of the U.S. government. In 1851, close to 10,000 Indians gathered near the fort. Government negotiators obtained a promise from the Indians that they would cease their hostilities toward the white man's wagon trains and other traffic on the Oregon Trail, in exchange for receiving an annuity of $50,000. Disagreements quickly arose among the various Indian leaders, the treaty pledges were rejected by some of them, and a new round of hostilities occurred in the early 1860s. The situation was exacerbated by the increasing numbers of wagon trains, many of which were rolling through one of the Sioux' traditional nomadic hunting regions, on the way to the gold and silver mining areas in Montana.

The Fort Laramie Treaty of 1868 attempted to resolve the Indians' concerns, but the terms of this new document were violated when prospectors discovered gold in 1874, triggering a gold rush into the Black Hills in what is now western South Dakota. These scenic mountains were not only sacred to the Sioux people, but they were in the heart of the region that had been guaranteed to the Indians under the treaty. The Indians were understandably unwilling to sell their mountains to the government, and some of the Sioux warriors preferred to fight, rather than give up this treasured area. Fort Laramie then became a major military base of operations in the ensuing Great Sioux Campaign of 1876. In the following years, the fort's soldiers fought a number of battles and skirmishes that gradually forced the Indians out of the mountains and onto government-designated reservations. Once the threat of Indian hostilities ended, the military post was finally abandoned in 1890 and was sold off by the government.

Today, while many of the fort's original structures are no longer standing, 11 have been restored. Visitors may enjoy a self-guided tour of the grounds and buildings, and during the summer months, costumed guides provide living-history re-enactments. The visitor center, which offers interpretive exhibits, audiovisual programs, and publications, is located in the commissary storehouse, dating from 1884. The old bakery is nearby, and the guardhouse stands just above the banks of the Laramie River.

Facing the parade ground are two attractive structures—"Old Bedlam," a beautifully restored, two-story, balconied house dating from 1849, that provided quarters for unmarried officers and that subsequently also was partly used for awhile as the fort's headquarters; and the commanding officer's house, dating from 1870. Both of these buildings have been authentically refurnished to portray the fort's history.

Other restored buildings include the surgeon's house, refurnished in Victorian decor; the lieutenant colonel's quarters; the magazine, where most firearms and ammunition were stored; the trader's store; and the cavalry barracks.

The ruins and foundations of other buildings include the large infantry barracks that extended along one side of the parade ground; the post headquarters, dating from 1885; other barracks and officers' houses; and the site of old Fort John. The national historic site is open daily, except on Thanksgiving, Christmas, and New Year's Day.

Camping is not allowed on the site, but a small picnic area is available. Lodging, camping, and meals are available in the towns of Fort Laramie, Lingle, Torrington, Guernsey, and Cheyenne, WY; and Scottsbluff, NE.
IF YOU GO: Access from Cheyenne at I-80 is 82 miles north on I-25, then about 30 miles east on U.S. Route 26 to the town of Fort Laramie, and southwest 3 miles on State Route 160 to the site; or from Scottsbluff (see Scotts Bluff National Monument) it is about 50 miles west on U.S. Route 26 to Fort Laramie and 3 miles on State Route 160 to the site. Further information: Superintendent, Fort Laramie, WY 82212. Telephone (307) 837-2221.

FORT LARNED NATIONAL HISTORIC SITE

FORT LARNED NATIONAL HISTORIC SITE, consisting of 718 acres on the Pawnee Fork, a few miles upstream from its junction with the Arkansas River in southwestern Kansas, was established in 1966. It protects and interprets this historically significant U.S. Army post, located midway on the historic Santa Fe Trail (see Santa Fe National Historic Trail) and dating from 1860 to 1878. Named for U.S. Army paymaster-general Colonel Benjamin F. Larned, it was built to help provide military protection from Indian raids upon the U.S. mail coaches, as well as commercial traffic and military supply wagon trains on the trail that ran between Independence, Missouri, and Santa Fe, New Mexico.

Rustic prairie sod-and-adobe buildings were quickly constructed around a spacious central quadrangle that was the post's parade ground. These initial structures, which included an officers' quarters, a barracks and storehouse, a hospital, and guardhouse, served the post for about five years.

From 1861 to 1868, the fort also served as an agency for the U.S. Indian Bureau, which tried to avoid or resolve conflicts through peace-seeking

Fort Larned National Historic Site, Kansas [NPS]

negotiations between the Indian tribes and the white man; and which handed out annuities, such as food, clothing, blankets, tools, and utensils, under the terms of treaties, as part of the often unsuccessful strategy to give incentives for peace.

With the outbreak of the Civil War, in 1861, Fort Larned's regular army soldiers were transferred to join other Union forces in the eastern states. Volunteer state and territorial recruits from Kansas, Colorado, and elsewhere in the region were assigned to the fort. In the beginning, there were only relatively minor hostilities by the Plains Indians, who were concerned about the steadily escalating numbers of emigrants moving through or settling their traditional nomadic buffalo (bison) hunting grounds.

As more and more caravans traveled the Santa Fe and other trails, the greater became the Indians' fears, frustration, and anger, until full-blown warfare erupted in 1864. Arapahoes, Cheyennes, Comanches, and Kiowas—all nomadic Plains tribes—went on the rampage. Like wildfire racing across the prairie, Indians on horseback made lightning-quick raids upon wagon trains and stagecoaches that lacked military protection. The War Department issued orders prohibiting travel westward on the Santa Fe Trail from Fort Larned to Fort Union (see Fort Union National Monument) unless accompanied by an armed escort. Retaliatory strikes by the military often only served to stir up the Indians to greater determination to fight.

Peace treaties were negotiated and broken. Uprisings resumed as new waves of emigrants moved westward after the end of the Civil War in 1865. The military retaliated again, followed by renewed efforts to negotiate a lasting peace.

Also, after the Civil War and the return of regular army soldiers to the fort, the original sod-and-adobe buildings, which had necessitated constant upkeep against the forces of the prairie weather and which were characterized as "shabby, vermin-breeding" structures, were replaced in 1867–1868 with nine far more substantial, more comfortable, and more attractive buildings. They were built of sandstone and many were embellished with columned porches. Three officers' quarters faced one side of the parade ground, barracks were lined along another side, and shops, a commissary, and a quartermaster storehouse were on the other two sides.

In the decade following the completion of the fort's reconstruction, there were continuing Indian hostilities. During the 1867–1869 Indian War, in which the Treaty of Medicine Lodge was no sooner signed than it was violated, Fort Larned became the most important military post in the region. When the Cheyenne Indians raided several wagon trains on the Santa Fe Trail, the Arapahoes, Comanches, and Kiowas joined in the new outbreak of hostilities, erupting from Kansas south into the Indian Territory (now mostly Oklahoma) and Texas. Troops garrisoned at Fort Larned were dispatched with other military units to quell the uprisings. The military campaign, under the command of Lieutenant Colonel George A. Custer, led to the Cheyennes' defeat in the Battle of Washita on November 27, 1868—a defeat that brought an end to organized warfare by the Indians in the region around Fort Larned.

The fort's final assignment was to provide military protection for the laborers building the Santa Fe Railway across the Great Plains to the Southwest. With completion of the railroad, the Santa Fe Trail was made obsolete, and Fort Larned, which had been established to protect the trail, was closed in 1878.

Today, there is a visitor center in one of the barracks buildings, providing interpretive exhibits, an audiovisual program, and publications. A self-guiding tour leads through the restored barracks; the post hospital that occupied one end of a barracks building; a structure that housed the post's bakery, blacksmith shop, and a room used for carpentry, painting, and other activities; the new commissary that also housed a schoolroom; the commissary, a part of which was also for a time used as the arsenal and powder magazine; the quartermaster storehouse for military supplies; and two of the officers' quarters.

The site also presents living-history programs, and a trail leads through an area of restored native shortgrass prairie habitat. Among wildlife species of the area are prairie dogs, coyotes, burrowing owls, and numerous other bird species.

No camping is allowed, but there is a picnic area. The site is open daily, except on Thanksgiving, Christmas, and New Year's Day.

Two especially informative publications are *Fort Larned National Historic Site* by Robert M. Utley (Southwest Parks and Monuments Association); and *Fort Larned* by Leo E. Oliva (Kansas State Historical Society). **IF YOU GO:** Lodging and meals are available in the town of Larned. Access is by way of State Route 156, six miles west of Larned. Further information: Superintendent, Route 3, Larned, KS 67550. Telephone (316) 285-6911.

FORT SCOTT NATIONAL HISTORIC SITE

FORT SCOTT NATIONAL HISTORIC SITE, comprising 16 acres in eastern Kansas, was established in 1979 to protect and interpret the restored and reconstructed buildings of this eastern Great Plains frontier military post, dating from 1842 to 1853. The fort was named for U.S. Army General Winfield Scott. It was one of a chain of nine military posts guarding the so-called "permanent Indian frontier"—extending from Minnesota to Louisiana. To the east of this military line was the white man's declared domain, while to the west and reaching across the vast buffalo (bison) grasslands was the declared Indian territory, occupied by both the nomadic Plains tribes and eastern tribes relocated by the U.S. government.

The U.S. Army had agreed to vacate its Fort Wayne in the Cherokee Indian country and established a new fort farther west. In the spring of 1842, Captain Benjamin D. Moore, of the First United States Dragoons, and his medical officer, J.R. Motte, selected the strategic site on a bluff overlooking the junction of the Marmation River and Mill Creek, tributaries of the Osage and Missouri rivers. This place was also where the mid-continent's deciduous forests gave way to the vast tallgrass prairie of the eastern Great Plains.

The soldiers began by felling trees and putting up a number of rustic log huts. Under the supervision of the quartermaster officer, Captain Thomas Swords, the soldiers soon began constructing permanent buildings. There was no protective fortification or stockade around Fort Scott. Instead, the post was laid out like a village around a central parade ground. On one side of this open quadrangle were spacious two-story houses, graced with columned verandas. On the other sides were the post hospital, similarly embellished with verandas; barracks for the dragoons and infantrymen; stables for the dragoons' horses; and a guardhouse. Built farther back from the parade ground were the quartermaster storehouse, where all the post's military supplies were kept; the post headquarters; the bakery; blacksmith shop; and other structures.

Forts like this were originally established to enforce "the permanent Indian frontier." By 1843, however, the Fort Scott dragoons, mounted on their horses, were joining the dragoons of Fort Leavenworth to the north on the Mis-souri River and riding across the Great Plains to provide armed escort protection for commercial trade on the Santa Fe Trail, between Missouri and New Mexico. The next year, Company A of the Fort Scott dragoons, proudly uniformed and mounted on their black horses, again joined with Fort Leaven-worth, under the command of Colonel Stephen W. Kearny, and made a major showing of American military force, westward up the Oregon Trail to the Rocky Mountains, looping southward to New Mexico, and back across the Great Plains on the Santa Fe Trail. This three-month, 2,200-mile expedition was intended not only to help protect emigrant wagon trains and commercial caravans from Indian raids, but to provide an emphatic United States presence to help discourage British and Mexican territorial ambitions over this vast region.

In 1846, dragoons and infantrymen from Fort Scott and the other frontier forts along the Great Plains fought in the Mexican-American War of 1846–1848. Some of these men were under the command of General Zachary Taylor and General Winfield Scott in Texas and Mexico, while others served in Brigadier General Stephen W. Kearny's Army of the West that conquered New Mexico and went on to California, ultimately defeating Mexican troops there, as well.

After the war with Mexico and the addition of some 500,000 square miles to the United States, the policy of a "permanent Indian frontier" was officially scuttled. In 1853, Fort Scott itself was abandoned and the buildings were sold off. Some became private homes, and others were converted to hotels and other businesses.

U.S. Army soldiers returned to Fort Scott in the late 1850s to quell the confrontations in statehood-seeking Kansas, between pro-slavery and free-state advocates. The town of Fort Scott was caught up in this volatile conflict, dubbed "Bleeding Kansas," that erupted along the eastern border in fights, gunfire, and murder. Kansas ultimately joined the Union as a free state in 1861. The Civil War broke out later that year, and Fort Scott served as a major regional military supply center during the war. Up to 1,000 men, including Indians and African Americans, were garrisoned at the reactivated fort. In fact, the First Kansas Colored Regiment was the first such unit to serve in the Union army. Its soldiers fought with honor in the military campaigns of Kansas, Arkansas, and the Indian Territory (now mostly Oklahoma). Civil War soldiers finally abandoned Fort Scott in 1865.

Today, the national historic site's visitor center, located in the restored post hospital building, provides interpretive exhibits, an audiovisual program, and publications. Other exhibits are presented in the reconstructed dragoon barracks and in one of the restored officers' quarters. The park also presents living-history reenactments, as well as a self-guiding tour of the fort's 20 buildings.

Camping is not permitted, but there is a picnic area. Adjacent to this is one of two parts of the site being restored to natural tallgrass prairie habitat. Fort Scott is open daily, except on Thanksgiving, Christmas, and New Year's Day.

An especially interesting publication is *Fort Scott National Historic Site* by Robert M. Utley (Southwest Parks and Monuments Association).

IF YOU GO: Lodging and meals are available in the town of Fort Scott. Access is from U.S. Routes 69 and 54, which intersect at Fort Scott, and the site is in the center of town on Old Fort Boulevard. Further information: Super-intendent, Old Fort Blvd., Fort Scott, KS 66701. Telephone (316) 223-0310.

FORT SMITH NATIONAL HISTORIC SITE

FORT SMITH NATIONAL HISTORIC SITE, consisting of 75 acres on a bluff above the confluence of the Poteau and Arkansas rivers in downtown Fort Smith, in western Arkansas, was established in 1961 to protect and interpret the historic structures and remains of two nineteenth-century forts and a former federal court. The fort was named for the commander of all United

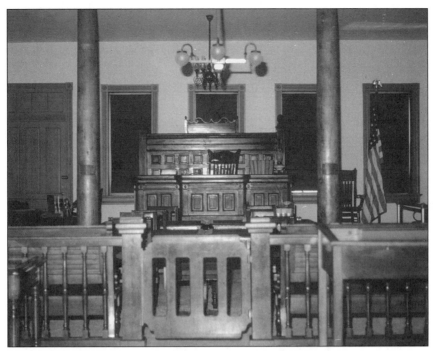

Courtroom, Fort Smith National Historic Site, Arkansas [NPS]

States military forces west of the Mississippi River when the fort was founded.

Built in 1817, the initial fortification was a small log-and-stone stockade measuring 132 feet on each side. Under the command of Major William Bradford, the fort's company of the United States Rifle Regiment was assigned here to maintain peaceful relations between the native Osage Indians of the area, the Cherokee Indian emigrants who were being forced to move from their traditional homeland farther east, and the white settlers moving into this region.

Because of successful negotiations leading to the Treaty of Fort Smith in 1822, most of the potentially divisive issues between the Osages and Cherokees were peacefully resolved, along with a promise that the white man would not settle on the Indian lands. Two years later, Fort Smith was abandoned by the military in favor of establishing a new installation, called Fort Gibson, some 80 miles northwestward up the Arkansas River.

Beginning in 1829, the U.S. government became increasingly more aggressive in carrying out its policy of forcing eastern Indian tribes to give up their ancestral homelands in the southeastern states and move farther west. Cherokees, Chickasaws, Choctaws, Creeks, and Seminoles were relocated by the thousands, in a campaign of ethnic cleansing called "The Great Experiment," and which the Cherokees referred to as "The Trail of Tears" (see Trail of Tears National Historic Trail).

As white settlers witnessed the increasing influx of these Indian refugees pouring into their region in and around Arkansas, they became fearful and asked for federal military protection. Consequently, in 1838, the U.S. Army began building a second Fort Smith near the ruins of the original. Plans this time called for a larger, more secure fortification from which to counter Indian hostilities. There was a massive stone wall that surrounded the officers' quarters, the enlisted men's barracks, the quartermaster storehouse, and commissary storehouse.

By 1845, however, it was evident that the Indians of this area were not going to go on a rampage. Fort Smith was converted to a supply center. During the Mexican-American War of 1846–1848, Arkansas Volunteers occupied the fort; and during the Civil War, Confederate troops initially took command of the fort, followed by occupancy with Union soldiers.

In 1865, a Grand Council of Indians was held at the fort that prepared the way for treaties the following year, under the terms of which the government stripped the Indian tribes of nearly half the acreage that had been their reservations before the Civil War.

In 1871, Fort Smith was too far east to serve well as a supply center, and the military abandoned it. In 1872, the Federal Court for the Western District of Arkansas took over. Most of the criminal cases under its jurisdiction came from the Indian Territory (now mostly Oklahoma). While tribal courts had authority to hear Indian cases, they lacked judicial jurisdiction to hear and decide upon cases involving whites. Consequently, many white criminals fled onto Indian reservations where they could not be extradited or arrested and brought to trial. The federal court at Fort Smith was given special territorial authority to fill this judicial need.

From 1875 to 1896, the judge presiding over this court was the Honorable Isaac C. Parker. In the words of the National Park Service:

> Parker was a tireless, incorruptible defender of justice and a strong supporter of Indian rights. He had no illusions that he could obstruct the advance of white civilization, nor did he want to, but he was determined that whatever fate lay in store for the Indians, they would not be set upon by ruffians operating outside the law.

New courts were set up in the Indian Territory to hear the growing number of cases and, gradually, Judge Parker's jurisdiction diminished until 1896, when Congress ended his court's territorial responsibilities.

Today, the national historic site's visitor center is located in the red-brick, two-story barracks-courthouse-jail building that dates from 1849. It provides interpretive exhibits, an audiovisual program, and publications. The stone commissary storehouse, completed in 1846, is also still standing. Other points of interest are the foundations of the original fort, and the sites of the second fort's officers' quarters and quartermaster storehouse. On the walk over to Belle Point, visitors are urged to carefully cross two sets of railroad tracks by way of a pedestrian pathway. Both the Poteau and Arkansas rivers are hazardous for swimming, and visitors are warned that snakes inhabit tall grassy places. The national historic site is open daily, except on Thanksgiving, Christmas, and New Year's Day.

IF YOU GO: Lodging and meals are available in the city of Fort Smith. Access is from U.S. Route 64 (Garrison Ave.), south two blocks on 4th St., then west (right) onto Parker Ave. to the site. Further information: Superintendent, P.O. Box 1406, Fort Smith, AR 72902. Telephone (501) 783-3961.

FORT UNION NATIONAL MONUMENT

FORT UNION NATIONAL MONUMENT, comprising 720 acres at the western edge of the Great Plains in northeastern New Mexico, was established in 1954 to protect and interpret the ruins of the largest nineteenth-century U.S. military installation in the frontier Southwest.

In 1846 during the Mexican-American War, U.S. troops seized New Mexico (including what is now Arizona) from Mexico. For several years, there were scattered, small army units stationed at towns along the Rio Grande to give their residents protection from raids by hostile bands of Indians. Fort Union was established in July 1851, several miles north of the junction of the two main branches of the Santa Fe Trail. Several reasons are commonly given for its establishment, including a desire on the part of the new district commander, Colonel Edwin V. Sumner, to remove the troops from the "morally degrading" influences of Santa Fe. The most likely reason was economics, however, and Sumner moved numerous New Mexico garrisons out of leased quarters and directed that self-sufficient operations, such as troop-constructed buildings and "post farms," be initiated. Problems with Comanche, Ute, and Jicarilla Apache tribesmen along the southernmost reaches of the Trail constituted another reason for a post away from the Sangre de Cristos and out on the Great Plains. From such a point, troops could more readily patrol the area and react to trouble in a more timely manner than had been the case.

This was the first of three consecutive forts in the area. Its original rustic log structures served the companies of dragoons and other mounted soldiers for ten years, as these troops were repeatedly dispatched to fight hostile bands of Jicarilla Apaches, Comanches, and others who were raiding villages and attacking wagon trains and other travelers on the Santa Fe Trail (see Santa Fe National Historic Trail).

With the outbreak of the Civil War in 1861, many of the regular army troops were reassigned to join Union forces in the eastern states, while New Mexico and Colorado recruits took on duty at Fort Union. Colonel Edward R.S. Canby, now commander of new Mexico's military operation, was certain that confederate forces would attempt to seize the Southwest and Colorado's gold-rich Rocky Mountains. Consequently, he dispatched soldiers from the fort to secure the Santa Fe Trail, which was the essential supply line into the region from the east. Canby also ordered that a new and stronger fort be built—a star-shaped earthen defensive fortification.

The anticipated Confederate invasion was defeated at the Battle of Glorieta Pass, in March 1862, when some of Fort Union's men slipped around the battle area under the cover of darkness and, in a classic military maneuver, destroyed the Confederates' entire supply train (see Pecos National Historical Park). Soon after the Confederate threat was eliminated, the second Fort Union was abandoned.

The following year, the next commander of federal forces in New Mexico, General James H. Carleton, ordered construction of the third and by far the largest fort—the adobe ruins and stone foundations of which are still visible today. It took six years to build this complex, which was comprised of two major parts. There was the military post, with nine officers' homes along one side of the parade ground; the company quarters across the quadrangle; and two post corrals, around which additional quarters were added when the fort was enlarged in 1875, from four to six companies of soldiers.

And there was the fort's extensive quartermaster depot that included spacious officers' quarters, storage buildings, shops, quarters for the many civilian employees, and corrals for the great numbers of horses and mules.

During the Civil War and continuing for a decade afterward, Fort Union soldiers persistently waged campaigns to put an end to the raids and other hostilities by Apaches, Arapahoes, Cheyennes, Comanches, Kiowas, and Navajos. These Plains Indian wars finally came to a conclusion in 1875 (see also the text on Fort Larned National Historic Site).

The supply depot continued in operation until 1879, at which time construction of the Santa Fe Railway, extending westward across the Great Plains, passed by the fort. The railroad soon made the old Santa Fe Trail obsolete, which in turn signaled the end for Fort Union. Slowly the Fort Union depot operation was dismantled, and in 1883 ceased operations altogether, along with the arsenal. The garrison at Fort Union stood alone. The post spread its elbows and assimilated the former depot structures.

Virtually every historian has dated Fort Union's death warrant as 1879, the year the railroad passed by at Watrous, yet the post remained active for an additional 11 years. What happened during that voided decade that contains 25 percent of Fort Union's history? One of the current museum exhibits claims the post was "reduced to caretaker status." The official National Park Service handbook marks the era with the brief statement, "Fort Union had outlived its usefulness."

In actuality, Fort Union remained active until 1891 because it had not "outlived its usefulness." To be sure, the strategic and logistical considerations that had thrust importance upon it were gone. Indian raiding was a thing of the past on the Great Plains. Wagons no longer plied the old overland routes. What Fort Union did offer, however, was an established point near the railroad at which to house and garrison troops. With the complete implementation of the reservation system, the army's frontier mission became one of "watch and wait," maintaining troops in the region in anticipation of just the sort of outbreaks that occurred in southwestern New Mexico and Arizona in the mid-1880s. The policy was only part of the reason so many posts like Fort Union survived the decade. Simple economics dictated that they remain in use. The army desired the consolidation of the former small frontier garrisons into larger ones that would be strategically positioned around the big reservations and convenient to rapid rail transportation. The dollars, however, simply weren't there. Only toward the end of the century did the army successfully obtain funding for construction of the designated permanent posts. When that became reality, posts like Fort Union had truly "outlived" their usefulness.

Today, a visitor center provides interpretive exhibits, programs, and publications. From the center is a self-guiding walking tour of the fort's post and depot ruins. Among points of special interest are the nine post officers' quarters, including the post commander's house; the quarters of four post companies of soldiers; the guardhouse and military prison; the three duplex supply depot officers' quarters; the quartermaster's office; the commissary office; storehouses where military supplies for this and other forts in the region were stored; the mechanics and transportation corrals; the Fort Union hospital that had a capacity of at least 60 patients, a fort surgeon, and nine other staff; and a large network of Santa Fe Trail ruts.

The monument presents living-history reenactments and special programs, and it is open daily, except on Christmas and New Year's Day.

Several interesting publications are *Fort Union: A Photo History* by T. J. Sperry (Southwest Parks and Monuments Association); *Fort Union and the Frontier Army in the Southwest* by Leo E. Oliva (National Park Service); *Fort Union* by Robert M. Utley (U.S. Government Printing Office); and *Fort Union and the Santa Fe Trail* by Robert M. Utley (Texas Western Press).

IF YOU GO: Camping is not allowed, but there is a picnic area. Lodging and meals are available in Las Vegas, NM, located 26 miles from the monument. Access from I-25 is by way of the Fort Union National Monument/State Route 161 exit 366, proceeding north eight miles to the monument. Further information: Superintendent, P.O. Box 127, Watrous, NM 87753. Telephone (505) 425-8025.

HORSESHOE BEND NATIONAL MILITARY PARK

HORSESHOE BEND NATIONAL MILITARY PARK, consisting of 2,040 acres along the Horseshoe Bend of the Tallapoosa River, in eastern Alabama, was established in 1956. It protects and interprets the area of battle where over 3,500 Tennessee militiamen, U.S. infantrymen, and Indian allies, under the command of Major General Andrew Jackson, overwhelmed and crushed the 1,000 Red Stick warriors of the Upper Creek Indians, on March 27, 1814. This bloody fight brought to a close the long-festering Creek Indian War, wresting from the Indians some 20 million acres in Alabama and Georgia.

The Creek Indian War started in 1813, when the Upper Creeks, also known as the Red Sticks because of the red war sticks or clubs they used, became angry with the Lower Creeks, whom they viewed as giving up too much of their traditional land to white settlers and giving up their sacred customs.

When the Red Sticks slaughtered 250 white settlers at Fort Mims, in Alabama (not yet in the Union), the state of Tennessee authorized a 3,500-man volunteer militia, under the command of General Jackson, to seek revenge and pursue the Indians; and, in Jackson's words, to experience "the glory of prostrating those hell hounds." Beginning their march southward into Alabama in October, they attacked and killed 200 Red Sticks in one village, shooting them "like dogs," according to a chronicler. At another village, there were more killings. Roughly a thousand Red Sticks managed to escape and race south to Tohopeka, a village within the 100-acre Horseshoe Bend. This place was surrounded on three sides by the Tallapoosa River and fortified across the neck of the peninsula by a five-to-eight-foot-tall, zigzagged barricade, pierced through with holes for firing rifles.

Jackson and his 2,000 infantrymen and U.S. regulars began their siege of the Horseshoe Bend enclosure, on March 27, by firing their two small cannons into the barricade. So sturdy was the defensive structure that the artillery did relatively minor damage. Meanwhile, 700 cavalrymen and nearly as many Cherokee Indian allies fanned out around the far bank of the river, opposite Horseshoe Bend, to cut off the Red Sticks' escape. The militiamen finally gave up trying to blast through the barricade, and courageously stormed over the top. In the intense hand-to-hand combat that ensued for the next few hours, as described by one of the soldiers, "Arrows and spears and balls were flying; swords and tomahawks were gleaming in the sun and the whole peninsula rang with the yell of savages and the groans of the dying."

At least 800 Red Stick warriors perished, while 350 women and children were taken captive. Their chief, Menaw, and a few of his warriors managed to escape. Jackson lost 49 soldiers, while 150 were wounded. Jackson's victory brought the end of the Upper Creeks' rebellion. The few survivors were left with no choice but to surrender to the white man and to cede to the United States what soon became much of the territory and then the state of Alabama, as well as some of Georgia.

Andrew Jackson's victory at Horseshoe Bend was also his first major thrust into national prominence that ultimately led him to the U.S. Presidency in 1829. As President of the United States, Jackson promoted passage by Congress of the Indian Removal Bill; his signature in 1830 forced Indians east of the Mississippi River to relocate to the Indian Territory (subsequently the state of Oklahoma and part of Kansas). This forced removal in turn cleared the way for the white man's settlement of the Creek Nation's former vast homeland.

Today, the park's visitor center provides interpretive exhibits, an audiovisual program, and publications. A three-mile tour drive winds through the park, looping through Horseshoe Bend and the Tohopeka Village site. An overlook up on Cotton Patch Hill, near the visitor center, offers a view across the battlefield. There are a number of interpretive stops along the drive, including the barricade site and the village site. A 2.8-mile interpretive historic-and-nature trail loops from the overlook down through the battlefield and along the river. Hikers are urged to be alert for poisonous snakes, fire ants that can inflict a painful bite, and poison ivy, and to be careful along the riverbank. The park sometimes offers living-history demonstrations, with the park's major living-history event held annually on the last weekend in March. It is open daily, except on Thanksgiving, Christmas, and New Year's Day.

IF YOU GO: Camping is not allowed in the park, but a campground is provided at nearby Wind Creek State Park, six miles south of Alexander City.

Museum diorama, Horseshoe Bend National Military Park, Alabama [NPS]

There are two picnic areas in the national military park: one near the visitor center and the other across the State Route 49 bridge, next to a park boat-launching ramp on the river. Lodging and meals are available in Dadeville and Alexander City. Access from Birmingham is nearly 95 miles southeast on U.S. Route 280 to Dadeville, and then 12 miles north on State Route 49 to the park. Further information: Superintendent, 11288 Horseshoe Bend Rd., Daviston, AL 36256. Telephone (205) 234-7111.

LITTLE BIGHORN BATTLEFIELD NATIONAL MONUMENT

LITTLE BIGHORN BATTLEFIELD NATIONAL MONUMENT consists of 765 acres in two units, on the Crow Indian Reservation in southeastern Montana. It was established as a national cemetery in 1879, was transferred from the War Department to the National Park Service in 1940, was named the Custer Battlefield National Monument in 1946, and changed to its present name in 1991. It protects and interprets the site of the Battle of the Little Bighorn in 1876, in which 263 men of Lieutenant Colonel George Armstrong Custer's battalion and others of the U.S. Seventh Cavalry were killed by 1,500 to 2,000 Lakota, Cheyenne, and Arapaho warriors.

The Battle of the Little Bighorn, also called Custer's Last Stand, was one of the last clashes in the long cultural collision over control of the vast northern Great Plains region that today includes most of Wyoming, Montana, and North and South Dakota. On the one hand, these northern Plains Indians were frantically fighting to hold onto their treasured traditional homelands and to protect and maintain their ancient nomadic lifestyle. On the other hand, the newcomers from the white man's America to the east were equally intent upon expanding the United States westward across the continent by developing wagon roads and then railroads, establishing ranches and towns, and exploiting the material wealth of the gold and silver mines in the wilderness West.

There had been a number of efforts to resolve conflicts through negotiated peace agreements, such as the Fort Laramie Treaty of 1868 (see Fort Laramie National Historic Site). Under this treaty, in exchange for peace, the U.S. government pledged to give the Lakota and Cheyenne people a major expanse of the Dakota Territory (subsequently present day western South Dakota), including the Black Hills, and promised to protect these Indians from "all depredations by people of the United States."

But prospectors discovered gold in 1874 in the Black Hills, causing a goldrush by thousands of fortune-seekers into the heart of the land that had been reserved for the Lakota. Reacting to this violation of the treaty, many Lakota and Cheyenne people left the reservation and moved back onto the plains of Montana and Wyoming. The Indians paid no attention to the government's demand for them to return to the Dakota reservation. Consequently, the U.S. military initiated a campaign in the spring of 1876 to force the Indians back.

The Battle of the Little Bighorn was a key part of the strategy to round up the thousands of Lakota and Cheyenne. More than 2,500 army troops were dispatched to the Montana-Wyoming border area from three military forts—Fort Lincoln on the Missouri River, in today's central North Dakota; Fort Fetterman on the North Platte River, in eastern Wyoming; and Fort Ellis, near today's city of Bozeman, Montana.

The Dakota Column included the Seventh Cavalry Regiment, under the command of Lieutenant Colonel Custer. He and his men were ordered to lead forth and follow the Indians' trail into the Little Bighorn Valley, where they were believed to be congregated. All of the other troops from forts Fetterman and Ellis were ordered to converge on the valley simultaneously with Custer's cavalry, and thereby surround the Indians.

The U.S. military strategy assumed that there were only around 800 Indians, and that when they were confronted with the combined troop strength from the three army forts, the Indians would give up rather than engage in a blood-letting battle. This assumption proved gravely off the mark—in fact, there were from 1,500 to 2,000 warriors.

In spite of warnings from Custer's own Arikara and Crow Indian scouts that the Indian trail they were following provided evidence of a far greater number of Indian warriors ahead, the troops continued their march toward Little Bighorn Valley. When Custer's men were discovered by a number of warriors on the morning of June 25, Custer fatefully decided to accelerate his column's advance into the valley, or risk the escape of the Indian encampment, even though he knew the other reinforcements were not to arrive until the following day.

As Custer and his men neared the Little Bighorn River, he sent on ahead a battalion, under the command of Major Marcus Reno, to the Indians' village along the river bottomlands. But these troops quickly halted their attack short of the village, as a large number of warriors came charging toward them. The Custer battalion, in the meantime, followed a large force of mounted warriors to the north, perhaps intending to attack the village from the northern end. Reno's soldiers were then left to fend for themselves. Many were killed in their frantic dash to escape, while the others survived only because the Indians suddenly rode off downstream against Custer.

Custer and his own battalion of 210 men were then apparently riding in the vicinity of the river. They were suddenly attacked and greatly outnumbered by a large force of Lakota warriors. Soon the soldiers were subjected to waves of attacking Indians who were pouring in from every direction, as increasing numbers of warriors joined the battle. The U.S. troops were completely overwhelmed by the Lakota and Cheyenne. Within less than one and a half hours, Custer and all of his battalion were killed. Custer himself was shot in the head and chest. The afternoon's brutal battle above the meandering course of the Little Bighorn River ranks as among the worst defeats in U.S. Army history, and a symbolic victory by the Lakota, Cheyenne, and Arapaho.

As for the cavalrymen of Custer's other two battalions, the troops of Captain Frederick Benteen and the surviving troops of Major Reno had begun riding toward the sounds of battle, intending to help Custer. When they reached a high place above the river, known as Weir Point, they too were confronted by hundreds of warriors. They were quickly turned back and dug in at a more defendable position, where they managed to hold off the Indians, until darkness fell. The next morning, the warriors were back to resume the siege. Later that day, June 26, the Montana Column arrived. As they were approaching, the Indians set fire to the grasslands, creating a smokescreen, behind which they withdrew, thus ending the battle.

Today, the national monument's visitor center provides interpretive exhibits, talks, audiovisual programs, and publications. Guided bus tours and guided walks are also offered during the summer, and there are several trails that lead visitors to points of interest. A short path goes from the visitor center to Last Stand Hill, where marble markers are dotted across the battlefield where Custer's men perished. There is also a granite monument marking the place where, in 1881, the bodies of the enlisted men and attached personnel were placed in a mass grave. (The officers' bodies were earlier sent east for reinternment by relatives.) An Indian memorial to honor the Indians' participation in the battle will soon be erected.

The Entrenchment Trail loops through the Reno-Benteen Defense Site unit of the national monument. It contains interpretive stops that explain how these remaining Seventh Cavalry troops managed to hold off the Indians' persistent attacks, until Montana Column finally arrived.

Visitors walking the trails during the warmer months are warned to keep to the pathways and be alert for rattlesnakes. The monument is open daily, except on Thanksgiving, Christmas, and New Year's Day.

An informative publication is *Little Bighorn Battlefield National Monument* by Mark L. Gardner (Southwest Parks and Monuments Association).

IF YOU GO: Camping is not allowed in the monument. Lodging and meals are available in Crow Agency, Hardin, and Billings, MT; and in Sheridan, WY. Access is from I-90 at the U.S. Route 212 exit, and then east one mile to the monument entrance. Further information: Superintendent, P.O. Box 39, Crow Agency, MT 59022. Telephone (406) 638-2621.

PART 5

CIVIL WAR PARKS

Historical Sequence of Civil War Battles

Fort Sumter—April 1861
Manassas: Battle of First Manassas—July 1861
Wilson's Creek—August 1861
Fort Donelson—February 1862
Pea Ridge—March 1862
Battles of Glorieta Pass (Pecos)—March 1862
Shiloh—April 1862
Fort Pulaski—April 1862
Richmond: Seven Days' Battle—June–July 1862
Manassas: Second Battle—August 1862
Harpers Ferry—September 1862
Antietam—September 1862
Fredericksburg: Battle of Fredericksburg—December 1862
Stones River—December 1862–January 1863
Fredericksburg: Battle of Chancellorsville—May 1863
Gettysburg—July 1863
Vicksburg—May–July 1863
Chickamauga and Chattanooga—September and November 1863
Fredericksburg: Battle of the Wilderness—May 1864
Fredericksburg: Battle of Spotsylvania Court House—May 1864
Richmond: Battle of Cold Harbor—May–June 1864
Brice's Cross Roads—June 1864
Kennesaw Mountain—June 1864
Monocacy—July 1864
Fort Stevens (Fort Circle Parks)—July 1864
Tupelo—July 1864
Petersburg: Battle of the Crater—June 1864–April 1865
Richmond: Capture of Fort Harrison—April 1865
Petersburg: The Siege—April 1865
Richmond: Capture of Richmond—April 1865
Appomattox Court House: Surrender—April 1865

AFRICAN-AMERICAN CIVIL WAR MEMORIAL

AFRICAN-AMERICAN CIVIL WAR MEMORIAL, located in Washington, D.C., was authorized in 1991 and the site was dedicated in 1996 to honor the more than 188,000 African-American soldiers and sailors, as well as their officers—most of whom were white—who served in the Civil War. The names of all those persons being honored are being engraved onto plaques on semi-circular walls standing behind the centerpiece of the memorial, an Ed Hamilton sculpture depicting African Americans—soldiers and sailors on one side, and women and children on the other.

African Americans participated in 449 Civil War military engagements, 39 of which were major battles. Except for General William Tecumseh Sherman's march through Georgia to the sea, they fought in every major battle of the war, from 1863 to 1865. Medals of Honor for special courage were presented to 16 soldiers and four sailors. About 37,000 African Americans died in the war.

Publications on this subject include the magazine article, "Fighting for Freedom" by Linda M. Rancourt (September–October 1996 *National Parks);* and the Pulitzer Prize-winning book, *Marching Toward Freedom: Blacks in the Civil War 1861–1865* by historian James McPherson.

IF YOU GO: Further information: Superintendent, National Capital Parks-Central, 900 Ohio Dr., SW, Washington, D.C. 20242. Telephone (202) 426-6841.

ANDERSONVILLE NATIONAL HISTORIC SITE

ANDERSONVILLE NATIONAL HISTORIC SITE, encompassing 494 acres near Andersonville, Georgia, was established in 1970. It protects and interprets the site of Camp Sumter, the most infamous prisoner-of-war camp of the Civil War. From February 1864 to April 1865, Andersonville held approximately 45,000 Union prisoners of war. Nearly 13,000 of these men died of disease, malnutrition, horribly unsanitary conditions, exposure, overcrowding and inadequate medical care. The site also serves as a national memorial to all Americans ever held captive as prisoners of war.

According to the site's enabling legislation, Congress directed that the park is "to provide an understanding of the overall prisoner-of-war story of the Civil War, to interpret the role of prisoner-of-war camps in history, to commemorate the sacrifice of Americans who lost their lives in such camps, and to preserve the monuments" that are located in the site.

Andersonville consisted of a 27-acre prison camp that was enclosed by a high stockade wall. Fifteen feet inside the wall was a short railing known as the "dead line." Guards had orders to shoot any prisoners who dared to cross into this perimeter zone. Some prisoners chose to escape their miserable existence in the stockade and the possibility of a slow death by purposefully walking past the deadline. Most tried to make the best of the worst possible situation.

POWs prepare rations (re-enactment): out of 45,000 Union prisoners of war held here, nearly 13,000 died. Andersonville National Historic Site, Georgia [NPS]

Prisoners of war throughout America's history have faced hardships and mistreatment. Whether they were subjected to prison ships of the American Revolution, death marches of Bataan and Europe during World War II, or mental torture during the conflicts in Korea and Vietnam, their story is one of sacrifice and courage. Andersonville National Historic Site is a memorial to these people and their story.

As the National Park Service explains:

> POWs have lived for months and years with a crushing sense of doom, seeing their comrades dying from disease, starvation, exposure, misguided bombardments, lack of medical care, and murder by firearm, bludgeon, bayonet, and sword. They have faced forced marches on bare subsistence rations or none at all while exposed to intense heat or cold, brutalized along the way and left to die if too injured or ill to keep up. They have been victims of such war crimes as torture and mutilation, beatings, and forced labor under inhumane conditions.

During the Civil War, more than 211,000 Union soldiers were captured by the Confederates, of whom over 30,000 perished in prison camps such as Andersonville; and more than 462,000 Confederates were captured by the Union, of whom nearly 26,000 died in prison camps.

The national historic site's visitor center provides interpretive exhibits, an audiovisual program, and publications. Due to its mission of interpreting the overall POW story, Congress selected Andersonville for the site of the National Prisoner of War Museum. Group tours, led by park rangers or volunteers, can be arranged with two weeks notice. There are special events periodically, including living-history programs the last weekend of February and the first weekend in October.

An auto tape tour is available at the visitor center for a self-guided drive through the park. There are several short paths, one of which loops around the remains of a star-shaped earthwork fortification—one of several that were placed around the perimeter of the stockade enclosure. Also located within the national historic site is the Andersonville National Cemetery, containing more than 17,000 graves. There are many commemorative monuments in both the cemetery and the prison-camp enclosure. The park is open daily.

An informative publication is *Civil War Series: Andersonville* by W. G. Burnett (Acorn Press).

IF YOU GO: Camping is not permitted, but a picnic area is provided adjacent to the stretch of road between the cemetery and the prison site. Lodging and meals are available in Americus and Montezuma. Access from I-75 near Henderson is by way of State Route 26, 16 miles to Montezuma, and then 10 miles south on State Route 49 to the site; or from I-75 near Cordele, 35 miles west on U.S. Route 280 to Americus, and then north 10 miles on State Route 49. Further information: Superintendent, Route 1, Box 800, Andersonville, GA 31711. Telephone (912) 924-0343.

ANTIETAM NATIONAL BATTLEFIELD

ANTIETAM NATIONAL BATTLEFIELD consists of 3,255 acres, located about 50 miles northwest of Washington, D.C., near the Potomac River, in western Maryland. Established as a national battlefield site in 1890, it was transferred from the War Department to the National Park Service in 1933, and was renamed a national battlefield in 1978. It protects and interprets the site of the Battle of Antietam (or Sharpsburg). Fought on September 17, 1862, it was the culmination of the first invasion of the North by Confederate troops. More soldiers were killed and wounded on that single day than on any other one-day battle of the Civil War.

After the South's triumph at the Battle of Second Manassas, in northern Virginia, August 29–30, 1862 (see Manassas National Battlefield Park), Confederate General Robert E. Lee decided now was the time to launch an invasion into the North. On September 3, Lee began moving his Army of Northern Virginia in a wide arc to the west of the federal capital of Washington, and across the Potomac River into Maryland.

Burnside Bridge across Antietam Creek, Maryland [NPS]

Four days later, Major General George B. McClellan, commander of the Union's Army of the Potomac, ordered his men out of the defenses around Washington, to pursue the Confederates. On September 13, when McClellan's forces stopped at an encampment that the Confederates had occupied several days earlier, a Union soldier happened to find a piece of paper, wrapped around a packet of cigars. On it was written a copy of Lee's Special Order No. 191, laying out the details of the Confederates' Maryland campaign. The treasured document revealed that the Southern commander was dividing his army into five parts. Under Major General Thomas J. ("Stonewall") Jackson, elements were being dispatched to seize the Union garrison at Harpers Ferry; others, under Major General James Longstreet, were moving toward Hagerstown, Maryland. Armed with this military intelligence, McClellan decided to deploy his army between the two Confederate forces and attack them piecemeal.

When General Lee discovered the Union commander's strategy, he ordered his scattered forces to reunite. This was partially accomplished by September 16. Although Lee had only about 40,000 soldiers, to the Union's 87,000, he clearly believed his army could defeat the Northerners, as it had demonstrated at Manassas.

September 17 dawned with a chilly, damp mist enveloping the area around Antietam Creek. It lasted for the first hour or so of daylight, before being burned off by the sunshine. The bloody battle began at first light, to the north of the village of Sharpsburg. Under Major General

Joseph Hooker's artillery, Union forces unleashed a brutal, thunderous barrage into the Confederates' left flank, under the command of General Jackson, whose men were in farmer David Miller's 40-acre cornfield. In Major General Joseph Hooker's words:

> In the time I am writing, every stalk of corn in the northern and greater part of the field was cut as closely as could have been done with a knife, and the slain lay in rows precisely as they had stood in their ranks a few moments before.

For about an hour, Jackson's soldiers were struggling against almost 10,000 charging Union troops who blasted the Southerners with "a terrific storm of shell, canister, and musketry," as Jackson described the horrendous onslaught. The famous Texas Brigade bore the brunt of some of the heaviest fighting. The 1st Texas suffered a staggering 82 percent loss. Of the original 226 men in this unit, 186 had been cut down like the corn stalks around them.

But then a powerful counterattack by Jackson's reinforcements sent the Northerners reeling back. However, more Union reinforcements, Major General Joseph Mansfield's 12th Corps, arrived to drive the Confederates back again. By around 9 a.m., Major General John Sedgwick's division of the 2nd Corps was moving into the West Woods, when Confederate reinforcements struck the Union flank. In a mere 20 minutes, more than 40 percent of Sedgwick's division was either dead or wounded, while the terrified survivors fled from the ghastly slaughtering.

Soon another 2nd Corps division, under Major General William French, following behind Sedgwick, swung to the south. At about 9:30 a.m., these soldiers crossed the open fields of the Roulette Farm and came to an old, sunken farm lane. This roadway was being held by less than 2,000 Confederates under the command of Major General D. H. Hill. As soon as the Union men came within range, the Southerners' weapons exploded into the men in blue, decimating virtually all of those in the front ranks. This initial encounter then expanded into a three-and-a-half-hour fight. Wave after wave of Union troops surged into this scene of utter hell on earth, and were repeatedly thrown back. By 10:30, the final 2nd Corps division, under Major General Israel Richardson, arrived to support French. Finally, a misinterpreted order caused one of the Confederate units to pull out of the fight. Soon the entire Confederate line collapsed.

The fighting along Bloody Lane, as the road has subsequently been named, was some of the most desperately brutal blood-letting of the entire Civil War. In the words of a Confederate officer, the soldiers were "mowed down like grass before the scythe." So enormous was the carnage that part of the lane was carpeted with bodies of the dead, so thick that a person could easily have walked along the road without ever touching the ground.

Farther to the south, another of the day's grim dramas was unfolding. In the morning, Union Major General Ambrose E. Burnside's 9th Corps was ordered to launch a strike against Lee's right flank. But crossing Antietam Creek over the Confederate-held, three-arch stone bridge proved a far tougher challenge than was expected. Hundreds lost their lives as the fight dragged on for hours. An assault finally succeeded in dislodging and driving back the Georgian defenders, who were then gradually pushed northwestward to Sharpsburg.

Just as Lee's right flank was on the verge of being overwhelmed, however, the Confederate division under Major General A.P. Hill, which had been at Harpers Ferry, suddenly arrived from the south and slammed into Gen. Burnside's flank. By late afternoon, the Union soldiers were forced to retreat from the day's awesome killing-field, occupying for the night an area of higher ground above Burnside Bridge.

Close to 4,000 soldiers were killed in the Battle of Antietam that day. Another 18,000 men suffered severe wounds, several thousand of whom soon died from their injuries. The area surrounding the battlefield, in the words of one observer, became "one vast hospital."

Today, the peaceful countryside of the national battlefield and its surroundings belies the awful human suffering and death that overwhelmed this place on that September day. The visitor center provides museum interpretive exhibits, audiovisual programs, and publications. Ranger-guided tours are offered during the summer months. A self-guided driving tour leads through the park, with interpretive stops that highlight the battlefield's main points of historic interest. These latter include the reconstructed Dunker Church; the North Woods; the infamous Miller Cornfield; the sunken farm road, Bloody Lane; Burnside Bridge; and the Antietam National Cemetery.

At the southern end of the national battlefield, Snavely Ford Trail runs from Burnside Bridge southward along the west bank of beautiful, tree-bordered Antietam Creek. The park's visitor center is open daily, except on Thanksgiving, Christmas, and New Year's Day.

An excellent publication is *The Bloodiest Day: The Battle of Antietam* by Ronald H. Bailey (Time-Life Books).

IF YOU GO: Camping is not permitted in the park, but there are campgrounds in the vicinity. A picnic area is located just east of the battlefield, on the south side of Boonsboro Pike (State Route 34). Lodging and meals are available in Hagerstown, MD; Harpers Ferry, WV; and elsewhere in the region. Access from I-70 at Hagerstown is south about ten miles on State Route 65 to the battlefield entrance, which is also less than a mile north of Sharpsburg on the same highway. The park is about midway between Boonsboro, MD, and Shepherdstown, WV, on State Route 34. Further information: Superintendent, P.O. Box 158, Sharpsburg, MD 21782. Telephone (301) 432-5124.

APPOMATTOX COURT HOUSE NATIONAL HISTORICAL PARK

APPOMATTOX COURT HOUSE NATIONAL HISTORICAL PARK, consisting of 1,775 acres in central Virginia, about 90 miles west of Richmond and Petersburg, was authorized as a national battlefield site in 1930. Transferred from the War Department to the National Park Service in 1933, it was renamed as a national historical monument in 1935, and was renamed again as a national historical park in 1954. It protects and interprets the site of reconstructed and restored buildings where Confederate General-in-Chief Robert E. Lee agreed to surrender his 35,000-man Army of Northern Virginia to Union Lieutenant General Ulysses S. Grant, in the village of Appomattox Court House, on April 9, 1865; and where weapons were surrendered on April 12—four long, bloody years to the day after the Civil War erupted.

After General Grant's army captured Petersburg and Richmond (see the texts on Petersburg National Battlefield and Richmond National Battlefield Park), General Lee's discouraged soldiers, who had been deployed along some 37 miles of entrenched positions in defense of those two cities, now withdrew westward, in the hope of obtaining urgently needed food rations and joining up with other Confederate forces. Said one of the Confederate commanders, "An indescribable sadness weighed upon us."

The Union forces soon raced after the retreating Confederates, on a parallel route that would attempt to block the enemy from turning southward to team up with General Joseph E. Johnston's troops in North Carolina. General Lee had anticipated reaching the village of Amelia Court House, being able to provision his starving men with supplies of food, and then marching them southward. But the supply trains were never sent and the desperately needed supplies were not received. Taking advantage of the Confederates' delay, the Union men were now being deployed near Jetersville, to the south of Lee's forces. This Union position effectively cut off the route southward into North Carolina.

April 5 was a gloomy, overcast day of rain that seemed to reflect more bad luck for the Confederate forces, for they were unable to find food supplies from foraging expeditions in the surrounding countryside. Lee saw first hand that his way south was blocked by heavily entrenched Union forces.

On April 6, the Union troops launched a massive assault against Confederate troops in the vicinity of Little Sailor's Creek, overwhelming the men in gray. Of the 6,300 Confederate soldiers engaging in this fight, over 2,500 were killed, wounded, or captured. Confederate casualties in all of that day's grim combat totaled about 8,000 men while Union losses were about 1,200 men. In spite of the disastrous toll, General Lee kept pushing his exhausted and hungry men along the muddy roads.

On April 7, General Grant dispatched a message to General Lee, seeking his surrender. It stated:

Appomattox Court House National Historical Park, Virginia [NPS]

The result of the last week must convince you of the hopelessness of further resistance on the part of the Army of Northern Virginia in this struggle. I feel that it is so, and regard it as my duty to shift from myself the responsibility of any further effusion of blood by asking of you the surrender of that portion of the C.S. Army known as the Army of Northern Virginia.

The Confederate commander replied by asking what General Grant's terms of surrender would be, before considering his proposal. On April 8, the Confederates struggled on. Some of the soldiers were so exhausted and hungry that they could march on no more and just lay down by the roadside. General Grant, meanwhile, dispatched another message to General Lee, saying in part:

In reply I would say that, peace being my great desire, there is but one condition I would insist upon, namely: that the men and officers surrendered shall be disqualified for taking up arms again against the Government of the United States until properly exchanged.

Later that day, Confederate supply trains were captured by Union troops at Appomattox Station. A battle ensued, in which the Confederates were defeated in intense combat. That night, General Lee sent off a reply to the Union commander. It said in part:

To be frank, I do not think the emergency has arisen to call for the surrender of this army, but as the restoration of peace should be the sole object of all, I desired to know whether your proposals would lead to that end. I cannot therefore meet you with a view to surrender the Army of Northern Virginia, but as far as your proposal may affect the C.S. forces under my command and tend to the restoration of peace, I should be pleased to meet you at 10 a.m. tomorrow.

In part, General Grant replied:

The terms upon which peace can be had are well understood. By the South laying down their arms they will hasten the most desirable event, save thousands of human lives, and hundreds of millions of property not yet destroyed.

At dawn on April 9, General Lee's troops launched an assault against Union cavalry that were deployed just west of Appomattox Court House village and blocking the Lynchburg Stage Road. The Rebels overran them, but then waves of Union infantrymen rushed into battle and now closed Lee's escape route to the southwest that had briefly opened. At this point, in the late morning, Lee realized he had no alternative. He ordered that truce flags be sent out. He waited under an apple tree for General Grant to respond. Arrangements were quickly made for the two commanders to meet in the red-brick, white-trim home of Wilmer McLean, in the village of Appomattox Court House. General Lee arrived first, and just past 1:30 p.m., General Grant strode up the steps of the front verandah and into the parlor. The two generals shook hands. Grant proceeded to write out a draft of his terms of surrender. Lee's written response stated:

I have received your letter of this date containing the terms of surren-der of the Army of Northern Va. as proposed by you. As they are sub-stantially the same as those expressed in your letter of the 8th inst., they are accepted. I will proceed to designate the proper officers to carry the stipulations into effect.

The final signed copies were exchanged, thus making official the act of surrender, at about 3 p.m. Soon thereafter, General Grant informed the federal officials in Washington, D.C.:

General Lee surrendered the army of Northern Virginia this after-noon on terms proposed by myself.

On April 12, Lee's army gave up its weapons and the men went on their way home. Ulysses S. Grant declared that "The war is over—the Rebels are our countrymen again." Two evenings later, an assassin's bullet struck down

President Lincoln at Ford's Theatre, in Washington, D.C. (see Ford's Theatre National Historic Site), in an individual's tragic act as self-appointed avenger for the South's defeat in the Civil War.

Other Confederate forces persisted for a while longer: General Johnston's army kept going in North Carolina for another two-and-a-half weeks; others farther west held out, the last ending its actions on June 2. The war was legally at an end on August 20, 1866, when a presidential proclamation declared that "peace, order, tranquillity and civil authority now exist in and throughout the whole of the United States."

Today, Appomattox Court House National Historical Park recreates the setting for the momentous signing of the surrender agreements. The park's visitor center, which is located in the reconstructed county court house, provides interpretive exhibits, and an audiovisual program. Living-history programs are provided in the park during the summer months. There is a bookstore where publications may be obtained. The restored village also features the authentic reconstruction of the Wilmer McLean House; the John Woodson law office, which he opened in 1856; the Francis Meeks store, dating from 1852; Clover Hill Tavern, dating from 1819—the oldest building in the village; the jail, dating from 1870; and several other houses. A walking tour of the village can be expected to take a couple of hours. The park is open daily, except on Martin Luther King, Jr., Day, Presidents Day, Veterans Day, Thanksgiving, Christmas, and New Year's Day.

Two especially informative publications are *The Campaign to Appomattox* by Noah Andre Trudeau (Eastern National Park and Monument Association); and *Pursuit to Appomattox: The Last Battles* by Jerry Korn (Time-Life Books).

IF YOU GO: Camping is not permitted, but a campground is located in nearby Holliday Lake State Park. Picnic facilities are provided along State Route 24 at Appomattox Wayside. Lodging and meals are available in Appomattox, Lynchburg, Richmond, and Petersburg. Access from U.S. Route 460 is by way of State Route 24, three miles northeast of Appomattox. Further information: Superintendent, P.O. Box 218, Appomattox, VA 24522. Telephone (804) 352-8987.

ARLINGTON HOUSE, THE ROBERT E. LEE MEMORIAL

ARLINGTON HOUSE, THE ROBERT E. LEE MEMORIAL, consisting of 28 acres in northern Virginia overlooking the Potomac River and Washington, D.C., was authorized as the Custis-Lee Mansion in 1925. Transferred from the War Department to the National Park Service in 1933, it was established as a memorial to Civil War Confederate General Robert E. Lee in 1955, and was given its present name in 1972. It protects and interprets the grand antebellum home of the Custis and Lee families, in which the future Confederate commander lived for 30 years, prior to the outbreak of the Civil War. The memorial is adjacent to Arlington National Cemetery.

Construction of Arlington House was begun in 1802 and was completed 15 years later. The architect was a young Englishman, George Hadfield, who for a while also directed construction of the U.S. Capitol. The east-facing front of the large, imposing central section of the house is embellished with a great marble-columned portico. Wings of the house extend to the north and south.

On April 17, 1861, Virginia seceded from the Union. Lee resigned from the U.S. Army on April 20, and was appointed commander of Virginia's state forces on April 22. In May 1861, Virginia and Lee joined the Confederacy. In 1862, the federal government confiscated the Arlington estate for failure to pay taxes. A 200-acre part of the property was then designated as a military cemetery in 1864, which was the start of Arlington National Cemetery. In 1882, a lawsuit seeking the return of the estate to the Lee family was successful, but by then the hills around the mansion were covered with thousands of graves. Instead of returning the property, the government paid the family $150,000.

Today, visitors may tour Arlington House, entering by way of the front portico and continuing through many rooms on the first and second floors, including the family parlor, the dining room, bedrooms, the White Parlor, the Morning Room, and the conservatory. It is hoped that the interior of the mansion will eventually be restored to its pre-Civil War Custis-Lee family appearance.

Arlington House is open daily, except on Christmas and New Year's Day. Interpreters are available to give talks and answer questions. Special programs are held to commemorate Lee's birthday, his resignation, and his wedding.

Lodging and meals are available in Arlington and Alexandria, VA; in Washington, D.C.; and elsewhere in the metropolitan area. Visitors are urged to make advance hotel reservations, especially during the popular tourist seasons. Access from Washington is by way of the Arlington Memorial Bridge over the Potomac River, to the Arlington Cemetery visitor-center parking area and then a short walk up to the mansion; from elsewhere in Virginia by way of the George Washington Memorial Parkway; and from D.C. by way of a shuttle bus and by the Metro subway's Blue Line.

IF YOU GO: Further information: Arlington House, The Robert E. Lee Memorial, c/o National Park Service, George Washington Memorial Parkway, Turkey Run Park, McLean, VA 22101. Telephone (703) 557-0613.

Brice's Cross Roads National Battlefield Site, Mississippi [NPS]

BRICE'S CROSS ROADS NATIONAL BATTLEFIELD SITE

BRICE'S CROSS ROADS NATIONAL BATTLEFIELD SITE, comprising one acre in northeastern Mississippi, was established in 1929 and was transferred from the War Department to the National Park Service in 1933. It protects and interprets a small part of the area of a Civil War battle on June 10, 1864, in which Confederate cavalrymen demonstrated great tactical skill. Under the leadership of their commander, Major General Nathan Bedford Forrest, the "Wizard of the Saddle," they succeeded in forcing the Union troops to withdraw.

Union Major General William Tecumseh Sherman was the commander of all Union forces between the Appalachian Mountains and the Mississippi River. As he led his 100,000-man army on the march from Chattanooga, Tennessee, to Atlanta, Georgia (see Kennesaw Mountain National Battlefield Park), he ordered Major General Samuel D. Sturgis and his more than 8,000 soldiers to block a Confederate attempt to sever Sherman's vital military supply line on the Nashville-to-Chattanooga railroad.

On June 1, the Rebels' 3,500-man army, under General Forrest, commenced its march northward toward Tennessee from Tupelo, in northern Mississippi. General Forrest's horsemen had ridden into Alabama, on their way to destroy the railroad line in Tennessee. But then Confederate military intelligence revealed that General Sturgis' Union troops were heading from Memphis, in southwestern Tennessee, into Mississippi. The Confederates dashed back to defend their railroad and cavalry base at Tupelo.

The battle began 18 miles north of Tupelo, on June 10, with the greatly outnumbered Rebel cavalrymen attacking the Union cavalry that was several miles in front of the infantrymen. In the muggy heat of the day, the two cavalry forces clashed in tough hand-to-hand fighting in an area of dense, scrubby-oak woodland. The Union infantrymen were urgently needed and were ordered to speed up their march across flooded streams and dirt roads that had become deeply muddy after the previous week of heavy rain.

As Confederate General Forrest had predicted, the Union foot soldiers arrived on the scene totally exhausted from slogging through the mud and in no condition to fight. At this vulnerable moment for the men in blue, the Rebel force launched its assault, pounding them in intensely brutal hand-to-hand combat, "with the ferocity of wild beasts," as one soldier put it. By late afternoon, General Forrest ordered flanking maneuvers against the Union's right and left. The Northerners fell apart, panicked, and hastily fled from the battlefield. The triumphant Confederates pursued and hounded the retreating Northerners into the night. General Sturgis' humiliated soldiers kept running all the way back to Memphis, convinced that they had been up against a far larger army of Confederates. Casualties totaled more than 2,000 Union men, while the Rebels suffered about 500.

In spite of General Forrest's military genius in implementing battle tactics that devastated a numerically superior army, the Union's Nashville-to-Chattanooga rail supply line was still intact and supplying General Sherman's army on its march through Georgia.

Today, the national battlefield site provides views of much of the surrounding area where the fighting occurred. There are no facilities or personnel at the site, but there are a few interpretive panels and markers. More complete interpretation is provided at the Tupelo visitor center at milepost 266.0 on the Natchez Trace Parkway. The visitor center is open daily, except on Christmas.

An informative publication is *The Battle of Brice's Cross Roads* by Edwin C. Bearss.

IF YOU GO: Lodging and meals are available in Baldwyn, Tupelo, and other towns in the vicinity. Access is by way of U.S. Route 45, about 25 miles north of Tupelo, and then on State Route 370, six miles west of Baldwyn. Further information: c/o Superintendent, Natchez Trace Parkway, 2680 Natchez Trace Parkway, Tupelo, MS 38801. Telephone (601) 680-4025 or 1-(800) 305-7417.

CHICKAMAUGA AND CHATTANOOGA NATIONAL MILITARY PARK

CHICKAMAUGA AND CHATTANOOGA NATIONAL MILITARY PARK, comprising 8,106 acres in northwest Georgia and southeast Tennessee, is the largest Civil War park in the National Park System. It was established in 1890 and transferred from the War Department to the National Park Service in 1933. In two major units and a number of other sites, the park protects and interprets the Civil War battlefield of a significant Confederate victory in the valley of West Chickamauga Creek, Georgia, on September 18–20, 1863, and a major Union triumph in the vicinity of Chattanooga, Tennessee, on November 23–25, 1863.

Flowering dogwood, Chickamauga Battlefield, Georgia [Larry Ulrich]

Two-and-a-half months after the decisive Union victories at Vicksburg, Mississippi (see Vicksburg National Military Park), and at Gettysburg, Pennsylvania (see the text on Gettysburg National Military Park), Union and Confederate forces clashed in some of the most difficult combat conditions of the Civil War. The target was the city of Chattanooga, a strategically important railroad hub and a key access into the heart of the South.

Nine months earlier, Union Major General William S. Rosecrans' Army of the Cumberland had fought Confederate General Braxton Bragg's Army of Tennessee at the Battle of Stones River (see Stones River National Battlefield), forcing the Southerners to withdraw. Now Rosecrans' 60,000-man army was once again on Bragg's heels, pushing the Confederate troops into Chattanooga. General Bragg at first deployed his 43,000 soldiers at a number of Tennessee River crossings, upstream and downstream from the city. But when the Union forces crossed the river farther downstream in early September, threatening to sever the Confederates' supply lines, General Bragg was compelled to withdraw southward to LaFayette, Georgia. Unknown to General Rosecrans, however, was the boosting of Confederate forces with substantial reinforcements that, by mid-September, brought their troop strength to over 66,000 soldiers.

On September 18, the Confederates were deployed along the east bank of Chickamauga Creek (*Chickamauga* is a Cherokee name meaning "river of death"), from which position General Bragg planned to launch an assault against the Union army's left flank, outflank them, and cut them off from Chattanooga. Rosecrans' military intelligence revealed this proposed maneuver and he quickly reinforced his troop strength to block Bragg's move.

The Battle of Chickamauga commenced soon after dawn on September 19. Even though the two armies stretched for four miles and faced each other only a few hundred yards apart, the dense forest and underbrush made it virtually impossible to see one another except at close range. With only limited visibility, the uncoordinated fighting was fierce hand-to-hand combat. As one soldier later said, "The two armies came together like two wild beasts, and each fought as long as it could stand up in a knock-down and drag-out encounter." Each side tried in vain to push the other back.

On September 20, the Confederate troops resumed their attempt to wedge themselves in between the Union forces and Chattanooga. In spite of heavy assaults, the Southerners were again unable to get around the Union's left flank. An opening suddenly developed in the middle of the Union ranks, however, and Confederate Lieutenant General James Longstreet drove his corps through, splitting the Union forces in two, slamming the right half and causing its men to flee in panic. In less than an hour, the Confederates had succeeded in pushing a mile through the Federal ranks. Union Major General George H. Thomas managed to redeploy some troops on the battlefield onto Snodgrass Hill, where they defended themselves against wave after pounding wave of attacks in a fierce onslaught that continued through the afternoon. Darkness finally gave General Thomas the opportunity to withdraw his troops into Chattanooga.

In one of the Civil War's bloodiest conflicts, the Battle of Chickamauga resulted in heavy casualties on both sides, totaling over 16,000 Union men and 18,000 Confederates. General Rosecrans reported back to Union command headquarters in Washington, D.C.: "We have met with a serious disaster. . . . The enemy overwhelmed us, drove our right, pierced our center, and scattered the troops there." He subsequently expressed doubt that his forces could maintain their position in Chattanooga.

The Southerners followed the demoralized Northerners and proceeded to occupy the strategic heights that rise around Chattanooga. Rebel artillery batteries were emplaced to the east of town on Missionary Ridge, to the southwest on Lookout Mountain, and on an advance position on Orchard Knob, thereby effectively cutting off virtually all supply routes by road, railroad, and the river into Chattanooga. The 40,000 Union soldiers had backed themselves into a trap, where the 40,000-50,000 Confederates, launching a siege, could hope to either starve them or force them to surrender—unless help could somehow slip through from outside.

In response to the Union army's serious predicament, reinforcements were soon on their way. In October, 20,000 troops of the Army of the Potomac, under the command of Major General Joseph Hooker, came from northern Virginia. In mid-November, another 20,000 soldiers, under Major General William Tecumseh Sherman, came from Mississippi. In addition, General Thomas replaced General Rosecrans as the commander of the Union Army of the Cumberland; and Major General Ulysses S. Grant, who had triumphed over the Confederates in the siege of Vicksburg, was promoted by President Abraham Lincoln to head up all the Union forces between the Appalachian Mountains and the Mississippi River.

General Grant arrived in Chattanooga on October 23 and quickly implemented a plan for opening a shorter, more direct, and vital supply line that reached between Chattanooga and Bridgeport, Alabama, 30 miles to the southwest. A month later, with 70,000 soldiers, Grant's offensive commenced. On November 23, Orchard Knob was seized. On the following day, General Hooker's troops successfully assaulted the few Confederates on mist-shrouded Lookout Mountain. And on November 25, Grant dispatched General Thomas' forces to launch an assault against the rifle pits in the Rebels' center, along the northern foot of Missionary Ridge. The latter thrust proved so successful that the Federals—acting without orders—charged on up the steep slope to the ridge crest. This sudden storming of the ridge surprised the Confederates, who had been confident they held an invincible position. This caused their defenses to panic, collapse, and retreat in disarray.

The siege of Chattanooga ended in what has been called the "Miracle of Missionary Ridge." After darkness fell, General Bragg's disorganized forces withdrew southward into Georgia. This victory gave the Union forces control of Chattanooga and eastern Tennessee. Confederate President Jefferson Davis replaced the unpopular Bragg with General Joseph E. Johnston, as commander of the South's troops in Georgia. Union casualties in the Battle of Chattanooga totaled nearly 6,000 men killed, wounded, captured, or missing, while Confederate losses were in excess of 6,000.

Confederate morale had soared following the Chickamauga victory. But in a mere 11 weeks, their morale plunged. Five months later, Chattanooga would become the staging area and supply base for General Sherman's logistically brilliant Atlanta campaign, in the spring of 1864.

Today, the national military park's two visitor centers provide interpretive exhibits, audiovisual programs, and publications. In the Chickamauga Battlefield unit, there is a seven-mile tour drive that is highlighted by eight interpretive stops. The latter include the place where an entire division of Union soldiers was pulled out of line and redeployed to the north and Snodgrass Hill, on which General Thomas' Union troops managed to stave off repeated assaults by the Confederates. A tape-tour of this route is available at the visitor center.

The Point Park unit contains some of the area in which the Union forces successfully seized Lookout Mountain, in the Battle of Chattanooga. A self-guided walking tour from the visitor center features three gun batteries; the 95-foot-tall New York Peace Memorial that consists of a column, on the top of which is a statue of a Union soldier and a Confederate soldier shaking hands beneath a flag—symbolizing national reunification and brotherly love; the Adolph Ochs Museum that presents exhibits on the Battles for Chattanooga and its significance in helping bring about the end of the Civil War; and the Cravens House where the toughest combat on this mountain occurred.

Well-marked trails wind throughout the park, the main one of which is the Bluff Trail that leads visitors from the museum. Some of the park's trails are also open to horseback riding. Several other historic sites are maintained by the National Park Service, including the Orchard Knob Reservation, from which General Grant directed the Union troops' assault of the rifle pits at the base of Missionary Ridge; Bragg Reservation, where General Bragg had his headquarters during the siege of Chattanooga; and other significant sites on Missionary Ridge.

During the summer months, the park also presents a variety of interpretive talks and living-history demonstrations. The park is open daily, except on Christmas.

Informative publications include *The Fight for Chattanooga: Chickamauga to Missionary Ridge* by Jerry Korn (Time-Life Books); *This Terrible Sound: The Battle of Chickamauga* by Peter Cozzens (University of Illinois Press); *The Battle of Chickamauga* by Dr. William G. Robertson (Eastern National Park and Monument Association); and *Mountains Touched with Fire: Chattanooga Besieged* by Wiley Sword (St. Martin's Press).

IF YOU GO: Camping is not permitted in the park. Lodging and meals are available in Chattanooga, TN, and Fort Oglethorpe, GA. Access to the Chickamauga visitor center is south from I-24 at Chattanooga on U.S. Route 27; or west from I-75 by way of State Route 2 to Fort Oglethorpe and then south on U.S. Route 27. Access to the Point Park unit is west of Fort Oglethorpe by way of State Route 2, north on State Routes 193 and 17, and then State Route 58 into the park; or from Chattanooga south on Broad Street, then on State Routes 17 and 58. Further information: Superintendent, P.O. Box 2128, Fort Oglethorpe, GA 30742. Telephone (706) 866-9241.

FORT CIRCLE PARKS

FORT CIRCLE PARKS, located in and around Washington, D.C., protect and interpret 17 of the many Civil War fortification sites that were established to protect the Federal capital.

When the Civil War broke out, in April 1861, there was only one obsolete fortification guarding Washington, located a dozen miles down the Potomac River, on the Maryland shore (see Fort Washington Park). After the Battle of First Manassas (see the text on Manassas National Battlefield Park), the commander of the Union Army of the Potomac, Major General George B. McClellan, ordered Major General John G. Barnard, of the army's Corps of Engineers, to build a series of new forts. By the end of the war, in 1865, there were 68 forts and 93 batteries ringing the city and bristling with cannons and mortars. In addition, there were 20 miles of trenches and other earthworks for the Union infantry and 30 miles of military roads.

The forts were built by piling up earthworks, with one- to one-and-a-half-foot-thick parapets that provided a thick defense against possible enemy attack. Inside these ramparts were various types of cannons and other artillery set up on platforms. Also within each fort were structures sheltering the soldiers and protecting the ammunition and gunpowder. A dry moat, armed with an abatis of outward-angled sharp stakes, surrounded each fort. All trees and shrubs were cleared for a couple of miles in front of each fort, so that advancing enemy troops would be out in the open, with no cover to hide behind.

Only once during the Civil War did the Confederates challenge Washington's defenses. After being delayed in the Battle of Monocacy (see Monocacy National Battlefield), Confederate troops, under the command of Lieutenant General Jubal A. Early, attacked Fort Stevens, near the northern corner of the District of Columbia, on July 11–12, 1864. Union defenders repulsed this daring assault, and the Rebels quickly withdrew and crossed the Potomac, back into the Confederacy.

Today, **Fort Stevens** is partially reconstructed. Living-history ceremonies are periodically held at this fort site. It is administered under Rock Creek Park, as are Battery Kemble, Fort Bayard, Fort Reno, Fort DeRussy in Rock Creek Park, Fort Slocum, Fort Totten, and Fort Bunker Hill. Access to Fort Stevens is at Quackenbos and 13th streets, NW, just west of Georgia Avenue and just north of Military Road. Fort DeRussy site is in Rock Creek Park, just northeast of the junction of Military Road and Oregon Avenue, NW. Further information on interpreter-led tours, etc.: Rock Creek Park Nature Center, 5000 Glover Rd., NW, Washington, D.C. 20015. Telephone (202) 426-6829.

On the hilltops rising to the southeast of the Anacostia River are the sites of another array of forts. These were designed to offer protection to Capitol Hill, naval facilities along the Anacostia, and the Eleventh Avenue Bridge across the river. These parks, which are under the National Capital Parks-East, are Fort Mahan, Fort Chaplin, Fort Dupont, Fort Davis, Battery Ricketts adjacent to Fort Stanton, Fort Carroll, and Fort Greble.

Fort Dupont is located in Fort Dupont Park, just off Alabama Avenue, SE. This park provides a wide variety of activities such as interpretive nature walks, hiking and biking trails, Civil War programs, musical and environmental programs, and sports events and youth programs. Picnic areas are available. This park encompasses 376 acres of gently rolling forested terrain, with oak, beech, maple, pine and other species of trees. Among the mammals inhabiting the park are gray squirrels, opossums, raccoons, and rabbits. Further information on living-history demonstrations and interpretive exhibits, etc.: Fort Dupont Activity Center, at Minnesota Avenue and Randle Circle, SE, Washington, D.C. Telephone (202) 426-7723.

Fort Foote, on a bluff above the Potomac River just south of the District of Columbia, in Maryland, displays the heaviest type of cannon used during the Civil War. Fort Foote is in Fort Foote Park, Maryland, reached from I-95, exiting onto Oxon Hill Road, and then turning onto Fort Foote Road. Further information on guided tours, etc.: c/o Fort Washington Park, Superintendent, National Capital Parks-East, 1900 Anacostia Dr., SE, Washington, D.C. 20020. Telephone (301) 763-4600.

Fort Marcy, on the high bluffs above the Potomac River in Virginia, near Little Falls, across from the northwest corner of the District of Columbia, is located within the George Washington Memorial Parkway. Fort Marcy is reached by way of the Memorial parkway, turning off to the fort just north of the Fairfax County line, in Virginia. For further information on guided interpretive tours, etc.: Superintendent, George Washington Memorial Parkway, Turkey Run Park, McLean, VA 22101. Telephone (703) 285-2601.

Another fortification site in Virginia, **Fort Ward**, is the Washington area's most complete reconstruction of a Civil War fort. It is maintained by the City of Alexandria and is located in Fort Ward Park, just off Braddock Rd., between State Route 402 and the I-395 underpass. Further information: Fort Ward, 4301 W. Braddock Rd., Alexandria, VA 22300. Telephone (703) 838-4848.

Lodging and meals are available in the Washington metropolitan area. During popular tourist seasons, accommodations are in great demand, and advance reservations are highly recommended.

IF YOU GO: Further information on the Fort Circle Parks: National Capital Parks, National Capital Region Headquarters, 1100 Ohio Dr., SW, Washington, D.C. 20242. Telephone (202) 619-7222.

FORT DONELSON NATIONAL BATTLEFIELD

FORT DONELSON NATIONAL BATTLEFIELD, comprising 536 acres on the west bank of the Cumberland River, in north-middle Tennessee, was established as a national military park in 1926, was transferred from the War Department to the National Park Service in 1933, and was renamed as a national battlefield in 1985. It protects and interprets the site of the first significant Union army victory in the Civil War—the surrender of Fort Donelson by Confederate forces, in February 1862.

Confederate forces had previously triumphed over the Union military at Manassas, in Virginia (see Manassas National Battlefield Park), in July 1861; and at Wilson's Creek, in Missouri (see Wilson's Creek National Battlefield), in August 1861. Since then, there had been no decisive military encounters, until the Union army command decided to attack what seemed to be two possibly vulnerable Confederate defenses in northwestern Tennessee: Fort Henry, guarding the Tennessee River, and Fort Donelson, guarding the Cumberland River. These forts were vital military facilities in the Confederacy's line of western defenses that reached from the Appalachian Mountains to the Mississippi River. Both forts were on tributaries of the Ohio River that provided routes of access into the Confederacy.

On February 6, 1862, a fleet of four Union ironclad gunboats, under the command of naval Flag Officer Andrew H. Foote, had bombarded Fort Henry into surrender, with the majority of the garrison escaping to Fort Donelson, about 12 miles to the east.

On February 11, Brigadier General Ulysses S. Grant and his soldiers set out for Fort Donelson and surrounded it on the landward side on the following day. This 15-acre fort, larger and stronger than Fort Henry, was situated on a high bluff overlooking the Cumberland River, its defenses bristling with a dozen cannons. Around the landward side were three miles of earth-and-log breastworks and other defensive structures. Within the fort were 100 log huts. At least 15,000 soldiers were garrisoned there, including the 2,500 from Fort Henry.

On February 14, the Navy's armored gunboats, which had been so successful at Fort Henry, moved into position to start a similar bombardment of this fort. But the Confederate cannons pounded the ironclads, forcing them to back out of range. The next day, the Confederates, fearing they would be starved into surrender by General Grant's encircling troops, tried to break through the Union lines and escape. An intense battle ensued, with the Northerners appearing unable to hold the right end of their line tight against the Confederates. But, spurred on by Grant, the Union men redoubled their efforts, thereby blocking the Confederates' escape. Grant then ordered the left end of his encircling Union forces to launch an attack upon the fort's breastworks, which had few defenders since most of them had been thrown into the effort to break out and escape. When these Union soldiers began advancing into the breastworks and threatening to capture the fort itself, the Confederates were forced to abort their escape plan and concentrate upon defending the fort.

That night, as part of a new strategy toward surrendering the fort, 2,000 Southerners and the fort's top two commanders escaped by crossing the Cumberland River, while a cavalry unit and some infantrymen managed to slip away by land. Left in command of the remaining Confederates was Brigadier General Simon B. Buckner. He now sought to work out the stipulations of an agreement under which he would surrender. But General Grant replied by saying, "No terms except an unconditional and immediate surrender can be accepted." Ulysses S. Grant, now a hero in the North, earned his nickname, "Unconditional Surrender" Grant. General Buckner, while condemning Grant's answer as "ungenerous and unchivalrous," surrendered the fort and its approximately 15,000 Confederate soldiers to the union commander.

The restored Dover Hotel is located on Petty Street in the town of Dover. This is where Buckner officially surrendered to Grant. The North's casualties in the battle totaled over 2,800 men dead and wounded; the South's totaled 1,500. As a result of this defeat, Confederate forces retreated from Kentucky and a major part of central Tennessee.

Today, there is a visitor center that provides interpretive exhibits, an audiovisual program, and publications. A self-guided tour drive leads to a number of historic points of interest, including the site of the fort; river batteries, from which Confederate cannons chased off the Union's ironclad gunboats; the site of General Buckner's last effort to defend the fort against General Grant's attack; and a monument erected in 1933 to honor the Confederate soldiers who fought and died in this battle. An interpretive trail network also connects historic points of interest in the park. Visitors are cautioned to be alert for poisonous snakes and poison ivy, and to walk carefully near the riverbanks. Fort Donelson National Cemetery is adjacent to the park. The national battlefield is open daily, except on Christmas.

An excellent publication with information on the battle at Fort Donelson is *The Road to Shiloh: Early Battles in the West* by David Nevin (Time-Life Books).

IF YOU GO: Camping is not permitted (except for organized youth-group camping, as pre-arranged with the park staff), but there is a picnic area. Lodging and meals are available in Dover, Clarksville, and Paris, TN. Access by way of U.S. Route 79 is 31 miles west of Clarksville and 31 miles east of Paris. Further information: Superintendent, P.O. Box 434, Dover, TN 37058. Telephone (615) 232-5706.

Fort Point and the Golden Gate Bridge [NPS]

FORT POINT NATIONAL HISTORIC SITE

FORT POINT NATIONAL HISTORIC SITE consists of 29 acres beneath the southern end of the Golden Gate Bridge, in San Francisco, California. It was established in 1970 to protect and interpret this mid-nineteenth-century coastal defense fortification that was built—at the narrowest point of the entrance to San Francisco Bay—to guard the bay and its important commercial harbor from foreign invasion.

The imposing brick-and-granite fort was constructed by the U.S. Army Corps of Engineers between 1853 and 1861, and rushed to completion at the start of the Civil War. It is located on the site of an earlier fort, the Spanish *Castillo de San Joaquin,* dating from 1794. The fortification was occupied throughout the Civil War by a U.S. artillery regiment, but Fort Point's cannons were never called upon to fire a shot at an enemy. As the more accurate and more powerful rifled cannon was introduced, replacing the smooth-bore cannon in military warfare, brick fortifications such as Fort Point quickly became obsolete. The last troops left here in 1886 and the last cannons were removed by 1900.

For many years, the U.S. Army continued to use Fort Point as a training and storage facility. From 1933 to 1937, it served as a base of operations for construction of the Golden Gate Bridge. During World War II, the facility was occupied by about a hundred soldiers manning rapid-fire guns and searchlights that were mounted atop the fort to guard a submarine net strung across the mouth of San Francisco Bay.

Today, visitors may see interpretive exhibits of nineteenth-century armaments and military life and a brief audiovisual program on the fort's history, attend a ranger-guided tour of the fort, and participate in a cannon drill demonstration. Other exhibits include "Women in U.S. Military History," "The African-American Soldier Experience," and photographs of the construction of the Golden Gate Bridge. On winter evenings, candlelight tours are offered. Fort Point rangers also lead natural history hikes on the surrounding coastal bluffs. Advance reservations are required for school and other group programs at Fort Point. A bookstore is located in the fort, with publications on such topics as coastal defenses, the Civil War, women's roles in the 1800s, and African-American history. There are walking and bicycling trails connecting Fort Point with the Coastal Trail, the Golden Gate Promenade, and the Golden Gate Bridge.

A major attraction of the site is the magnificent view of the Golden Gate—with San Francisco and the bay to the east, the Pacific Ocean to the west, the ruggedly scenic Marin Headlands to the north, ships and boats often passing by, and the massive Golden Gate Bridge directly overhead and spanning across to Marin County. Fort Point is also adjacent to the historic Presidio of San Francisco, now part of Golden Gate National Recreation Area (see the text on the latter).

The National Park Service advises visitors to Fort Point to dress warmly and anticipate cool breezes off the ocean. In summer, a chilly fog bank frequently pours through the Golden Gate. The national historic site is open Wednesdays through Sundays, and is closed on Thanksgiving, Christmas, and New Year's Day.

Camping is not allowed on the site, but picnic facilities are provided. Lodging and meals are available in San Francisco. Especially during the peak summer season, advance lodging reservations are highly recommended. **IF YOU GO:** Access from U.S. Route 101 northbound is by way of the last exit before the Golden Gate Bridge toll plaza, turning left onto Lincoln Avenue, left onto Long Avenue, and following this road along the shoreline to Fort Point. Access from U.S. Route 101 southbound is by way of the first exit immediately after the Golden Gate Bridge toll plaza, making a left turn onto Lincoln Avenue, left onto Long Avenue, and proceeding to the site. Further information: Site Supervisor, P.O. Box 29333, Presidio of San Francisco, San Francisco, CA 94129. Telephone (415) 556-1693.

Fort Pulaski National Monument, Georgia [NPS]

FORT PULASKI NATIONAL MONUMENT

FORT PULASKI NATIONAL MONUMENT, comprising 5,365 acres on low-lying, marshy Cockspur and McQueen's islands at the mouth of the Savannah River, at the northern end of Georgia's Atlantic coast, was established in 1924 and was transferred from the War Department to the National Park Service in 1933. It protects and interprets a massive brick fort, construction of which began in 1829 and was essentially completed by 1847. The fortification provided protection for the city of Savannah, about 15 miles upriver.

Fort Pulaski, named in honor of Polish Count Casimir Pulaski, an American hero in the War for Independence, was one of a series of 30 United States coastal defensive fortifications, built after the War of 1812 and reaching from Maine to Louisiana, and Fort Scott in California. On April 10–11, 1862, at the end of the first year of the Civil War, Union batteries of cannons, positioned on nearby Tybee Island, waged a 30-hour bombardment of the fort. This siege caused extensive damage to part of the structure and ended with the fort's surrender by its Confederate defenders.

The attack on this fortification was part of the overall Union military strategy of seizing back the string of coastal forts that had fallen to Confederate control with the outbreak of the Civil War. Previously, Fort Pulaski had been considered one of the "most spectacular harbor defense structures" in the United States—partly for its sturdy construction and partly because of its location just out of harmful range of traditional smoothbore cannons and mortars that had low muzzle velocity and poor accuracy.

The Union artillery barrage against the fort was directed by Engineer Captain Quincy Adams Gillmore. He was a strong advocate of the recently invented rifled cannon, with its greatly enhanced fire power and accuracy. Confederate Colonel Charles H. Olmstead, who was commander of the fort's 384 defenders, had received assurances from General Robert E. Lee that the Union cannons being set up along the shore of Tybee Island "cannot breach your walls at that distance." Consequently, even though Fort Pulaski's garrison was aware of the Union soldiers struggling to establish gun emplacements a mile away, there was little worry that the cannon shells could ever arc across Tybee Roads channel and inflict any serious harm upon the massive walls.

The siege commenced early on April 10 and soon began destroying the Confederate cannons along the southeast parapet. By the day's end, not only were all those artillery pieces knocked out of action, but the wall of that nearest angle of the fort had been reduced to half its original 72-foot thickness. Clearly, the Confederates were in a significantly weakened position.

At dawn on April 11, the Union artillery resumed the siege, with the attack continuing to tear down the section of outer wall. By midday, the southeast angle had been breached in two places. At about 2 p.m., a shell exploded near the entrance to the northwest. With some 40,000 pounds of gunpowder stored just behind that wall, Colonel Olmstead quickly realized the gravity of his situation. At 2:30 p.m., he raised a white flag of surrender.

In spite of the ferocity of the battle, in which the Union guns fired over 5,000 projectiles, only one Confederate was mortally injured and only a single Union artilleryman was killed. In a mere two days, the whole series of supposedly impregnable forts around the Atlantic and Gulf coasts of America had suddenly been made obsolete. Worldwide, defense strategy was forever changed.

Today, the national monument's visitor center provides interpretive exhibits, an audiovisual program, and publications. A self-guided walk leads from the visitor center over the water-filled moat, across the moat-bordered, triangular area of land called the demilune, and across a drawbridge into the fort. Within the great structure, points of special interest include the northwest powder magazine that was at risk of being blown sky high by Union artillery, the section of wall at the southeast corner that was demolished by Union batteries (the breach was repaired soon after Union troops took over the fort); and the commanding officer's room, in which Fort Pulaski was officially surrendered to the Union forces.

A pathway leads visitors on the top of the dike system that encircles the fort. Another path goes to the John Wesley Memorial, the founder of Methodism who landed in America on this island in 1736. Visitors are cautioned not to climb around on the walls of the fort and other historic features such as the mounds. As there are eastern diamondback rattlers as well as species of non-poisonous snakes on the island during the warmer months, it is advisable to be alert and stay on the paths and trails. An alligator is occasionally seen in the moat system. Among the mammals are whitetail deer, mink, river otters, bobcats, raccoons, opossums, and marsh rabbits. Many kinds of birds either reside in or migrate through the area. Because of the marshy habitat around the fort, mosquitoes, gnats, and other insects are evident in spring and summer.

IF YOU GO: The national monument is open daily, except on Christmas. Camping is not permitted, but the monument provides a picnic area. Lodging and meals are available in the city of Tybee Island and in Savannah, GA. Access is 15 miles east of Savannah, by way of U.S. Route 80. Further information: Superintendent, P.O. Box 30757, Savannah, GA 31410. Telephone (912) 786-5787.

FORT SUMTER NATIONAL MONUMENT

FORT SUMTER NATIONAL MONUMENT, taking in 194 acres in two units at the mouth of Charleston Harbor, South Carolina, was established in 1948. It protects and interprets Fort Sumter, where the first military conflict of the Civil War occurred on April 12–13, 1861. The monument also protects nearby Fort Moultrie, which helped defeat Union troops at Fort Sumter, and where 85 years earlier American patriots had triumphed over British troops, on June 28, 1776, in one of the early battles of the War for Independence (Revolutionary War).

The original Fort Moultrie, located on Sullivan's Island at the north side of the mouth of Charleston Harbor, was still being built when its 31 cannons went into action against nine British warships that were attempting to sail into the harbor to capture the city of Charleston. The fort was named after the battle, in honor of its commanding officer, William Moultrie.

A second Fort Moultrie was completed in 1798, as one of 20 new U.S. coastal fortifications. After falling into ruin, a hurricane destroyed what remained of the structure in 1804. By 1809, a third U.S. military fort was constructed and it was this brick fortification that was involved at the start of the Civil War.

When South Carolina became the first state to secede from the Union, on December 20, 1860, the U.S. garrison abandoned Fort Moultrie and was secretly moved across the harbor entrance on December 26, to the larger and stronger, although still-unfinished, Fort Sumter. Construction of this massive red-brick installation had begun in 1828, as one of a chain of enhanced U.S. coastal fortifications after the War of 1812.

On December 27, South Carolina volunteer militiamen took over Fort Moultrie, along with two other harbor forts. U.S. President James Buchanan refused to accede to South Carolina's demands that the U.S. government leave Charleston Harbor. During the first three months of 1861, Confederate soldiers worked to strengthen the harbor batteries and other defenses.

When Abraham Lincoln took over the U.S. presidency on March 4, 1861, he proclaimed that "The power confided to me will be used to hold, occupy, and possess the property and places belonging to the Government." He then ordered that non-military supplies for Major Robert Anderson and his 85 men at Fort Sumter be dispatched by merchant ships under the guard of U.S. warships. On April 10, the commander of Confederate forces at Charleston, Brigadier General Pierre G.T. Beauregard, was ordered by the Confederacy's President Jefferson Davis to attack Fort Sumter if the U.S. command refused to surrender—" . . . if this is refused," said President Davis, "proceed . . . to reduce it."

When Major Anderson refused to give up, Confederate artillery opened fire just before dawn on April 12 and rained down an intense bombardment. Some of these shots were fired from Fort Moultrie. Considering the fierceness of the attack, the fort sustained relatively modest damage. But April 13 was different. The horrendous barrage unleashed by Confederate guns pounded the fort. Some cannonballs were heated red hot, and some of these fiery missiles slammed into the officers' quarters, setting a blaze that quickly spread into the enlisted men's barracks and threatened to reach a powder magazine. By midday, Fort Sumter's soldiers were having difficulty loading and firing their artillery because of the thick, choking smoke, but managed to get off a few more rounds. By late in the day, the Union troops agreed to surrender, and by early evening the attack was halted. The miracle of this battle was that, even though over 3,000 shots were fired at the fort during the two-day bombardment, not even one man in the U.S. garrison was killed.

On the following day, Major Anderson and his men left Charleston Harbor aboard a ship bound for the north. With the Confederacy's rebellion and the defeat of Union troops at Fort Sumter, the flame of the Civil War had been ignited. For nearly four years, Confederate forces occupied the fort and successfully defended it against a number of Union attempts to retake it. Exactly four years from the day that Anderson had surrendered the battered fortress to the Confederates, however, he returned. Now retired from military service, he participated in the ceremony of raising the same United States flag over the fort that had been lowered on April 14, 1861.

Today, there are interpretive museum exhibits in the fort, along with an audiovisual program, publications, and a self-guided walking tour that includes casemates (gunrooms), ruins of enlisted men's barracks and officers' quarters, and the parade ground. The fort is open daily, except on Christmas.

Fort Sumter National Monument, South Carolina [NPS]

IF YOU GO: Access to the Fort Sumter unit of the national monument is by boat (fee) from the City Marina, on Lockwood Drive, in Charleston; and from Patriots Point, in Mt. Pleasant (boat schedules: Fort Sumter Tours, Inc., 17 Lockwood Dr., Charleston, SC 29401. Telephone [803] 722-1691). Fort Moultrie also has a visitor center. This monument unit is open daily, except on Christmas. Access from Charleston is by way of U.S. Route 17N (business route) to Mt. Pleasant; a right turn onto State Route 703; at Sullivan's Island, a right turn onto Middle St., and proceeding two miles to the fort. Lodging and meals are available in and around Charleston and in Mt. Pleasant. Further information on the monument: Superintendent, 1214 Middle St., Sullivan's Island, SC 29482. Telephone (803) 883-3123.

FREDERICKSBURG AND SPOTSYLVANIA COUNTY BATTLEFIELDS MEMORIAL NATIONAL MILITARY PARK

FREDERICKSBURG AND SPOTSYLVANIA COUNTY BATTLE-FIELDS MEMORIAL NATIONAL MILITARY PARK, comprising 8,400 acres in numerous scattered units in and near Fredericksburg, Virginia, was established in 1927 and was transferred from the War Department to the National Park Service in 1933. It protects and interprets four significant

Civil War battlefields: Fredericksburg, December 11–13, 1862; Chancellorsville, April 27–May 6, 1863; the Wilderness, May 5–6, 1863; and Spotsylvania Court House, May 8–21, 1864. The park also includes Chatham Manor, Old Salem Church, and the building in which General Thomas J. ("Stonewall") Jackson died.

After the Army of the Potomac's failure to pursue and annihilate the Confederates following the horrendously bloody one-day Battle of Antietam, in September 1862 (see Antietam National Battlefield), President Abraham Lincoln, in November, fired the army's commander, Major General George B. McClellan, and replaced him with Major General Ambrose E. Burnside—ordering him to move speedily against General Robert E. Lee's Confederate Army of Northern Virginia.

The Battle of Fredericksburg

As a new strategy for trying to attack the Confederate capital, General Burnside deployed most of his army about midway between Washington, D.C., and Richmond, on the north bank of the Rappahannock River, across from Fredericksburg. Bridges over the Rappahannock had been destroyed earlier by the Confederates; now the Union troops had to await the weather-delayed arrival of pontoons (small boats that supported a wooden roadway) with which to bridge the river. Not until a week after the troops' arrival did the pontoons finally appear. Another two weeks slipped away before the soldiers crossed into Fredericksburg. These delays provided General Lee's 78,000 men with ample time to shift infantry and artillery to Fredericksburg and firmly establish themselves on the ridges and hills around the city—most notably on Marye's Heights and Prospect Hill. A Union colonel wrote to his wife: "I can't think that we will move across here. The loss of life would be terrible."

Several hours before dawn, on December 11, the 50th New York Engineers commenced assembling the pontoon bridge across the icy Rappahannock. This task proceeded well under the cover of darkness; but then, even though a thick mist shrouded the river, the first light of dawn began making easy Confederate sniper targets of the workers assembling the span. As shots rang out, the pontoniers were forced to run for cover. Union infantrymen fired back from the north bank of the river, but the mist was too thick for them to see the marksmen who were shooting from buildings along the waterfront.

The engineers repeatedly tried to resume their work, but each time they were chased back to shore. Some of them were killed, as the morning wore on. Around noon, General Burnside ordered close to 150 of his army's cannons to open fire in a two-hour bombardment of Fredericksburg. As a result of some 8,000 rounds of artillery fire, many buildings in town were heavily damaged and a pall of smoke billowed up and hung over the city. Once the thundering assault ended, the engineers felt safe to continue their work. But once again shots rang out and the men had to scramble to safety.

Chatham Manor, a Union army headquarters during the Civil War, Fredericksburg and Spotsylvania County Battlefields Memorial/National Military Park, Virginia [Russ Butcher]

By now, Burnside was becoming really frustrated. He next ordered troops to cross the river in individual pontoons that had not yet been assembled as part of the bridge and to storm Fredericksburg. This successful tactic led to the capture of some Confederate snipers, and by nightfall, four brigades of Union troops occupied the city. That night, six pontoon bridges were finally completed. It is not known why Burnside failed to dispatch many of his other soldiers across the bridge and into Fredericksburg that night. But early on December 12, much of Burnside's army was finally able to cross. As the Union men went on a rampage looting and vandalizing the city, Burnside significantly underestimated the Confederate troop strength and its strategic deployment on and around the ridges and hills encircling Fredericksburg.

The battle finally began in earnest on the morning of December 13. Major General George G. Meade's 4,500-man division of Pennsylvania Reserves assaulted Jackson's divisions that were waiting on Prospect Hill. Nearly three miles south of town by midday, the Union soldiers were initially gaining the upper hand, as the men in blue penetrated deeply into Confederate Major General A.P. Hill's ranks. But the tide suddenly turned, as Jackson ordered forward two other divisions that had been at the ready, behind Hill's men. A fierce counterattack ensued, and with no backup positioned to help General Meade, the greatly outnumbered Union troops were forced to retreat.

At about the same time as Meade's midday battle on Prospect Hill, Major General Edwin V. Sumner's grand division was ordered to launch an attack against Confederate Major General James Longstreet's defenders of Marye's Heights, at the west edge of town. While General Burnside was aware that the hilltop was bristling with batteries of cannons and infantry, he was unaware of what lay at the base of the hill, along a sunken road and out of sight behind the breastwork of a stone wall. As the first brigade of Union men received the dreaded command, "Forward!," they started their charge from town and then across the 400-yard expanse of open ground. Part way across, they were suddenly mowed down and shredded by a massive volley of musket fire that exploded from the brigade of Confederate Brigadier General T.R.R. Cobb's infantrymen, hidden behind the massive stone wall. The open expanse was rapidly covered with bodies, as the Union soldiers reeled and writhed under the storm of bullets and the pounding artillery fire from the hilltop above.

From noon until dark, wave after wave of Union brigades were ordered to charge across the deadly killing field, in an effort to overwhelm the soldiers behind the wall and capture the heights. But each, in turn, suffered the same brutal fate. The slaughter continued, with not even one Union man ever reaching the wall. One of General Burnside's commanding officers grieved, "Oh, great God! See how our men, our poor fellows, are falling!" Even Confederate General Longstreet was moved to write that ". . . the dead were piled sometimes three deep. And when morning broke, the spectacle that we saw upon the battlefield was one of the most distressing I have ever witnessed. I thought, as I saw the Federals come again and again to their death, that they deserve success if courage and daring could entitle soldiers to victory."

Burnside's attempt to take Marye's Heights certainly ranked as one of the worst military disasters of the Civil War. As a newspaper reporter wrote, after witnessing six fatal charges by the Union divisions: "It can hardly be in human nature for men to show more valor or generals to manifest less judgment."

Reeling from this devastating defeat, the Union army withdrew back across the Rappahannock in a cold, drenching rainstorm, on the night of December 15. Union casualties totaled more than 12,000 men—and most of those fell on that open ground in front of the stone wall. The Confederates lost less than half as many soldiers. Following the slaughter, the Union army's morale plunged to a new low. In January 1863, President Lincoln once again named a new commander—firing Burnside and appointing General Joseph Hooker to lead the Army of the Potomac's 135,000 men in the coming battle.

The Battle of Chancellorsville

As the winter mellowed into the spring of 1863, General Hooker devised a plan for attacking the Confederates on both flanks of their troops' deployment along the south bank of the Rappahannock, in the vicinity of Fredericksburg. The major thrust would be thrown against General Lee's left flank and rear. So confident was Hooker that his dual attack would succeed in squashing the enemy's soldiers in a powerful Union vise, that he said, "My plans are perfect. When I start to carry them out, may God have mercy on Bobby Lee; for I shall have none."

On April 27, approximately 70,000 Union troops were dispatched northwestward, along the north bank of the Rappahannock, while a smaller force marched downriver. On the 29th, both Union forces crossed the river, unopposed. Intelligence revealed to General Lee that the Northerners' main thrust was moving toward his left flank. Consequently, he sent the majority of his troops toward Chancellorsville, while leaving a small force behind to guard Fredericksburg.

Just before noon on May 1, the large Union force, which had now turned southwestward and was heading toward Fredericksburg, clashed with soldiers under the direction of General "Stonewall" Jackson. General Hooker suddenly lost his confidence, gave up the offensive, and ordered his men to retreat and establish a line of defense in the vicinity of Chancellorsville. That evening, Lee and Jackson, puzzled over Hooker's retreat, devised a plan—a courageous gamble—for taking the offensive and attacking Hooker's vulnerable right flank.

On the morning of May 2, Jackson's 25,000-man Confederate force began the 12-mile flanking march. These soldiers and their supply wagons were strung out for 12 miles along woods roads that wound through a dense pine, cedar, and oak forest called the Wilderness. Hooker's military intelligence reported the Confederate activity, but the Union commander mistakenly assumed that Lee's troops were retreating. A captured Confederate soldier even blurted out, ". . . wait till Jackson gets around on your right," but his warning went unheeded.

In the late afternoon, Jackson's men began their assault, accompanied by the Confederates' now familiar blood-curdling Rebel yell. The Union troops were caught completely by surprise. In the words of the Union commander, Major General Oliver O. Howard, the Southerners unleashed their assault "with all the fury of the wildest hailstorm." Jackson prompted his men to keep pursuing the fleeing Northerners. Hooker sent in reinforcements in a desperate effort to stop the Confederates. Jackson, too, called up his reinforcements, under Major General A.P. Hill, to help keep the offensive's momentum rolling along.

But just as the battle was going successfully for the Confederates, Jackson was accidentally wounded at night, in a valley freed by his own soldiers; was taken back to a field surgeon, who amputated his left arm; and died of pneumonia eight days later. General Hill was injured in the leg and was also taken out of action. With the loss of two top commanders, the Confederates were forced to cease their attack until the following morning. This lull gave the Union troops a chance to reorganize.

On May 3, Lee, having named Major General J.E.B. Stuart to replace Jackson, resumed the attack against the Union army's superior numbers. Some of the battle's fiercest fighting occurred on this day. For example, after Union troops were ordered to abandon a clearing on a small hill, known as Hazel Grove, Confederates took over the strategic site and set up cannons that unleashed a barrage of artillery fire on Union soldiers in the Chancellorsville vicinity, forcing them to abandon another knoll, called Fairview. The Confederates' artillery fire also pounded on Chancellor House, which was being used as the Union headquarters. General Hooker was on the inn's porch when a cannon shot smashed into a porch pillar that he was leaning against and knocked him unconscious.

Another fight ensued late in the afternoon, near the red-brick, unadorned Salem Church, halfway between Fredericksburg and Chancellors-ville. A 22,000-man Union force that had captured Fredericksburg earlier that day was marching west when it was suddenly shredded as the soldiers attacked the Confederates. As described by a Union survivor of the onslaught, "A tremendous roar of musketry met us from the unseen enemy. . . . Men tumbled from our ranks dead, and others fell helpless with wounds." The withering attack was finally halted when darkness fell. The next evening, these Union troops also began retreating to the Rappahannock. And on May 5, made even more miserable by a driving rainstorm, Hooker's defeated and demoralized soldiers trudged back across the river. Casualties from this battle totaled more than 17,000 Union men killed, injured, or missing; while the Confederates' casualties reached nearly 13,000.

Emboldened by yet another victory of the Army of Northern Virginia, Lee soon set in motion a second military campaign into the North, leading to the Battle of Gettysburg (see Gettysburg National Military Park).

The Battle of the Wilderness

After the Union victory at Chattanooga, Tennessee, in November 1863 (see the text on Chickamauga and Chattanooga National Military Park), a major focus of the Civil War shifted back to just west of Fredericksburg, Virginia. Major General Ulysses S. Grant, who led the Union to victory at Chattanooga, was promoted to lieutenant general. He was to oversee and coordinate all Union military strategies, and to give direction, as needed, to Major General George G. Meade's 118,000-man Army of the Potomac.

In May 1864, as Grant launched a campaign in Virginia against General Lee's 65,000 Confederate troops, several other campaigns were being simultaneously set in motion, including Major General William Tecumseh Sherman's Atlanta campaign. Grant's aim was to relentlessly squeeze the Confederates.

Two days of savage fighting between the armies occurred on May 5 and 6, 1864, in the Wilderness—an area of dense, scrubby second-growth pines, cedars, and oaks, about ten miles west of Fredericksburg. A virtually impenetrable tangle challenged the two armies as they clashed back and forth in ferocious hand-to-hand combat. Fires erupted that created smoke, further reducing the visibility and adding to the utter chaos of the conflict. One soldier described the bedlam: "I do not think I have ever seen a battle-field where there was more destruction and more horrors than that of the Wilderness." Union casualties reached close to 18,000 men, while the Confederates sustained over 8,000 killed, wounded, and captured.

In spite of the punishing toll, Grant refused to retreat. He ordered his forces on southward in a campaign that would fight a string of battles in Virginia. Previous Union generals in Virginia campaigns—McClellan, Burnside, and Hooker—had each, in turn, retreated after encountering General Robert E. Lee. But Grant had set out to wear Lee's forces down, to hammer away and gradually reduce the Rebels' troop strength.

The Battle of Spotsylvania Court House

After the Wilderness, General Grant ordered his Union troops to quickly maneuver eastward at night, circling around the Confederates' right flank, to reach a key crossroads junction at Spotsylvania Court House.

On May 7, General Lee reached Spotsylvania just a hair's-breadth ahead of the Union forces, which had been delayed by a skirmish with intercepting Confederate cavalrymen. By the time the Union forces reached the Spotsylvania crossroads, the Rebels were being rapidly deployed. Seven miles of heavily armed breastworks were soon laid out. The Union troops were thus forced to engage in another fierce battle. In fact, some of the most brutal combat of the entire Civil War took place at a U-shaped salient known as the "mule shoe."

Commencing on May 12, at just after 4:30 a.m., 20,000 Union soldiers launched a frontal attack in thick fog directly into the Confederate ranks, at what was deemed a weak part of their defenses. The men in blue greatly outnumbered the Rebels and soon overwhelmed them. The Confederates desperately counterattacked, as the Union thrust into the breached Rebel ranks. More Union troops were dispatched into the battle, followed by reinforcements for the Confederates, and still more Union troops, until the jutting angle erupted in an orgy of the most savage, hand-to-hand warfare. Bayonets and knives, and even clubs, rocks, and bare fists were used as weapons in the terrible bedlam. For *20 hours*, the savage slaughtering raged on—all made worse by the pouring rain and deepening mud. The conflict continued with diminished fury until after midnight, when the Southerners finally backed away to form a new line of defense.

One Union soldier described the sight of the slaughtered and wounded men he witnessed the next day: "The trench on the Rebel side . . . was filled with their dead piled together in every way with their wounded. The sight was terrible and ghastly." For all of that horrendous day's carnage and for the fighting over the next two weeks, there were no measurable gains by either army. Just a stalemate and the grim, cruel, staggering slaughter.

Following the battles of The Wilderness and Spotsylvania Court House, the area surrounding Fredericksburg became an enormous "hospital" where surgeons worked round-the-clock to attend to the 20,000 wounded Union and Confederate soldiers. One observer wrote, "Go into the hospitals. Armless, legless men, wounds of every description. Men on the hard floor, lying in one position all day, unable to stir till the nurse comes to their aid. Hard it is to see them suffer, and not be able to relieve them."

Today, the peace and beauty of Fredericksburg and Spotsylvania National Military Park mask the unimaginable violence, destruction, human suffering, and killing that stained the lands red with human blood in the four battles. The park has two visitor centers. One is located in the Fredericksburg Battlefield unit, near the stone wall at the foot of Marye's Heights, at 1013 Lafayette Blvd., in Fredericksburg; the other is at Chancellorsville, eight miles west of I-95 on State Route 3.

Other interpretive facilities include exhibit shelters in the Wilderness Battlefield and Spotsylvania Court House Battlefield. Park headquarters occupies part of the historic red-brick, Georgian-style mansion Chatham Manor, atop Stafford Heights, across the Rappahannock River from downtown Fredericksburg. This grand old structure was an early eighteenth-century plantation house, and subsequently served as a Union army headquarters and field hospital during the Civil War. The park provides walking tours and living-history talks during the summer months.

Among the informative publications on this park are three in the Civil War Series of the Eastern National Park and Monument Association: *The Battle of Fredericksburg* by William Marvel; *The Battle of Chancellorsville* by Gary Gallagher; and *The Battles of Wilderness and Spotsylvania* by Gordon Rhea. Also excellent is *Rebels Resurgent: Fredericksburg to Chancellorsville* by William K. Goolrick (Time-Life Books).

IF YOU GO: Camping is not permitted in the park, but there are facilities in the Fredericksburg vicinity. Picnic sites are provided in all four battlefield units, as well as at Chatham Manor and at the Stonewall Jackson Shrine. Lodging and meals are available in Fredericksburg. Access from a number of directions includes State Route 3, east from I-95 into Fredericksburg and west on the same route from I-95 to the Chancellorsville and Wilderness battlefield units. One of the accesses to Spotsylvania Court House Battlefield is by way of State Route 613, southeast from State Route 3, just east of the Wilderness Battlefield. Further information: Superintendent, 120 Chatham Lane, Fredericksburg, VA 22405. Telephone (540) 371-0802.

GETTYSBURG NATIONAL MILITARY PARK

GETTYSBURG NATIONAL MILITARY PARK, consisting of 5,900 acres in southern Pennsylvania, was established in 1895 and was transferred from the War Department to the National Park Service in 1933. It protects and interprets the Civil War's famous Battle of Gettysburg on July 1–3, 1863, in which the Union army decisively defeated the Confederates in their second invasion of the North.

During the second half of June, Confederate General Robert E. Lee's Army of Northern Virginia confidently crossed the Potomac River, from the Confederacy into the North, on his Pennsylvania Campaign. On June 28, President Abraham Lincoln once again replaced the commander of the Union's Army of the Potomac, removing Major General Joseph Hooker and naming Major General George G. Meade. On that same day, Lee's military intelligence suddenly revealed that the 93,000-man Union army was already north of the Potomac, crossing Maryland, and was rapidly closing on the Confederates. He immediately ordered his 70,000 troops, who were scattered in several places in southern Pennsylvania, to hastily come together in the vicinity of Gettysburg—a strategically situated crossroads community.

On July 1, the two armies first clashed just to the north and west of town in fierce fighting, with heavy casualties on both sides. Reinforcements were rushed in. For much of the day, the men in blue put up a courageous defense of their positions, in spite of the fact that they were greatly outnumbered at this early stage of the battle. By late in the day, however, the Confederates were finally able to push the Union soldiers southward around and through Gettysburg. General Lee had ordered his men to take control of the hills just south of town "if practicable"; but the Rebels failed to take advantage of the opportunity. Instead, the Union troops took the high ground and established a new defensive position on Cemetery Hill. During the night, many thousands of additional troops on both sides arrived at the battlefield, while Union reinforcements were being deployed all along the heights of Cemetery Ridge and Culp's Hill, just south of Gettysburg.

On the second day of battle, there were delays throughout the morning and early afternoon, with no attacks by either army. On the Union side, one of General Meade's officers, Major General Daniel E. Sickles, took a huge gamble. Rather than positioning his men along the southern end of Cemetery Ridge, as General Meade had ordered, he took it upon himself to march his 10,000-man force westward, in mid-afternoon, from Cemetery Ridge to what appeared to him to be a strategically advantageous location, but that proved to be an isolated and vulnerable position. It was on a low, flat-topped ridge, situated halfway across the slightly less than milewide valley, between Union-held Cemetery Ridge to the east and Confederate-held Seminary Ridge to the west. Sickles' men were deployed along nearly a mile of the Emmitsburg Road, anchored at the south in a peach orchard, with more units extending southeastward from there, through a wheatfield and ending at a boulder-jumbled place called Devil's Den.

Sickles' unauthorized advance came as a major shock to both the Union and Confederate commanders. Confederate Major General Lafayette McLaws was ordered by General Lee to place his troops across the Emmitsburg Road, and this brought his soldiers unknowingly within only about 600 yards in front of Sickles' forces. McLaws had been assured he would encounter little or no enemy troops across the valley, but as he later related, "The view presented astonished me, as the enemy was massed in my front, and extended to my right and left as far as I could see." When General Meade learned of Sickles' advance position, he was furious and immediately rode up and confronted him. But just as Sickles offered to take his corps back, heavy weapons fire exploded close by—and it was too late to withdraw.

Confederate Lieutenant General James Longstreet had questioned the wisdom of General Lee's plan to launch an all-out offensive against the well-entrenched Union force along Cemetery Ridge. But by late afternoon, Longstreet had to begin carrying out Lee's orders. He directed his two divisions, under Major Generals John B. Hood and McLaws.

General Hood's men went first and their thrust nearly succeeded in giving the Southerners control of Little Round Top, just south of Cemetery Ridge. As it happened, the Army of the Potomac's chief engineer, Brigadier General Gouverneur K. Warren, foresaw the danger and quickly got men onto the summit—arriving there a mere ten minutes ahead of the Rebels. A fierce and bloody fight erupted for control of the rocky promontory, as the Confederates stormed up the hillsides. Among the Union defenders who came to aid Warren was the 20th Maine Regiment, under the command of Colonel Joshua Chamberlain (who subsequently served as governor of Maine). These troops poured a hail of gunfire into the Confederates. Casualties soared. According to one of the Maine soldiers, the desperate battle for Little Round Top was "a terrible medley of cries, shouts, cheers, groans, prayers, curses, bursting shells, whizzing rifle bullets and clanging steel. The air seemed to be alive with lead." The struggle finally ended in a Confederate retreat.

Just below Little Round Top, brutal fighting raged in the labyrinthine Devil's Den and marshy Plum Run area—the latter thereafter referred to as the "Valley of Death" because of the savagery of combat and heavy loss of life that occurred there. An officer who witnessed the killing field from the summit of Little Round Top described the awesome spectacle as "full of smoke and fire, and literally swarming with riderless horses and fighting, fleeing and pursuing men. The wild cries of charging lines, the rattle of musketry, the booming of artillery and the shrieks of the wounded were the orchestral accompaniments of a scene like very hell itself." When the fierce hand-to-hand struggle finally ended, the Confederates controlled

Cemetery Hill, Gettysburg National Military Park [David Muench]

Devil's Den. Both sides sustained heavy casualties—the Union defenders lost over a third of their 2,200-man force.

As Hood's troops were engaged in the Devil's Den fight, McLaws' division unleashed its assault eastward upon Sickles' troops in the area of the peach orchard and wheatfield—letting loose with the by-now infamous, terrifying Confederate yell that accompanied their charges. As Sickles, on horseback, tried to keep his men from falling back, he was hit by a cannonball that virtually severed his right leg just above the knee. Quick-acting aides applied a tourniquet to stop the bleeding, until a surgeon could complete the amputation. Although Sickles lost his leg to the day's battle, he continued in future years to argue that his decision to advance his soldiers had been the correct action. But given the fact that his men took such a terrible beating and that the survivors were ultimately forced to retreat to Cemetery Ridge strongly suggests he may have been wrong.

As one Union soldier subsequently described the brutal battle in the area of the peach orchard and wheatfield,

> . . . the screaming and bursting of shells, canister and shrapnel as they tore through the struggling masses of humanity, the death screams of

wounded animals, the groans of their human companions, wounded and dying and trampled under foot by hurrying batteries, riderless horses and the moving lines of battle, all combined an indescribable roar of discordant elements—in fact a perfect hell on earth, never, perhaps to be equaled, certainly not to be surpassed, nor ever to be forgotten in a man's lifetime.

But for the courageous resistance of Sickles' soldiers, in the seesawing battle that raged back and forth across the wheatfield, the Confederates just might have gained the upper hand over the Union defenders along the southern end of Cemetery Ridge. As it was, the Rebels were slowed in their rush to reach the ridge—and that gave General Meade the time needed to shift troops from the northern end of the ridge and from Culp's Hill, to strengthen the defenses farther south. So, who knows? Just maybe Sickles was right about advancing his soldiers and thus sacrificing many of his men and his leg for the Union cause on that bloody day.

As General McLaws' division was getting the best of Sickles' men, Lieutenant General A.P. Hill unleashed brigade after brigade of his Confederate division, led by Major General Richard H. Anderson. Watching the men in gray as they roared forward into the Union ranks, a soldier on Cemetery Ridge observed, "on they came like the fury of a whirlwind." For a while, it seemed as though some of General Anderson's troops, who briefly reached the crest of Cemetery Hill, might succeed in holding on there. But without reinforcements, those not killed, seriously wounded, or taken captive were forced to retreat. The onrushing tide of Confederates was finally halted and forced back across the valley. Generals Longstreet and Hill's three divisions had failed, in three hours of intense warfare, to defeat the Union—and lost nearly a third of their men in the effort.

The day's horrendous fighting was not quite over. In the twilight of 7 p.m., as Anderson's men were withdrawing, two other Confederate divisions, under Major Generals Jubal A. Early and Edward "Allegheny" Johnson, were trying to seize two strategic hills on the Union's right flank. The Union's troop strength on Culp's and Cemetery hills had been too significantly depleted during the afternoon to provide reinforcements farther south. The Confederates succeeded in reaching the summit of Cemetery Hill, only to be driven back down in darkness, with the arrival of Union reinforcements.

That night, General Meade met with his top officers. Unanimously they agreed their forces should remain deployed where they were and fight to defend their strategic positions, rather than either retreat or launch an offensive against the Confederates on Seminary Ridge. As for General Lee, he decided to resume his aggressive strategy—confident his army would ultimately crush the enemy and bring a decisive end to the battle and the war.

At just past 1 p.m. on July 3, Lee gave Longstreet the order to begin the major assault of the battle. Confederate artillery opened fire on Union positions. For nearly two hours, an intense artillery dual filled the air with deafening thunder, blinding flashes of cannon fire and explosions, and great swirling clouds of gray smoke that obscured much of the battlefield. The cannons were finally silenced on both sides. While Longstreet vigorously protested to Lee against sending his brave soldiers on a frontal attack that would expose them to the enemy's massed cannons and rifle marksmen, he reluctantly gave the command for Major Generals George E. Pickett and Isaac Trimble and Brigadier General J. Johnston Pettigrew to unleash an assault by their infantry against the Union army's center on Cemetery Ridge.

As the men charged eastward, across the gently rolling fields, Union artillery explosions blasted bloody holes in the long gray lines. Once they crossed the Emmitsburg Road, the 12,000 Southerners surged into the range of a deadly, flaming blizzard of lead and iron erupting from the Union's 2nd Corps, under the command of Major General Winfield Scott Hancock. The Confederates were mowed down like wheat with a huge scythe—slaughtered by the relentless, brutal, terrifying volleys that decimated the Rebels' rapidly thinning ranks. At one point, some of the Southerners managed to pause long enough to let loose a volley of their own that forced a Union artillery regiment to abandon its big guns and flee for cover. Confederate Major General Lewis Armistead yelled out to his soldiers to keep pushing forward. But just as the brave commander reached out for one of the cannons, he fell, wounded.

With some 300 of Armistead's men either killed, seriously injured, or taken captive, the high-water mark of the Confederate assault came and went, along a jog in a stone wall called "the Angle," just below Cemetery Ridge. Surviving Southerners fled back across the blood-soaked valley.

Pickett was devastated by the immensity of the carnage and the enormity of the defeat. He rode back to report: "General Lee, I have no division now." Of the 12,000 men who charged toward Cemetery Ridge that day, about 7,000 of them—roughly 60 percent—were killed, injured, or captured. And in the three-day Battle of Gettysburg, the Confederates sustained a staggering 23,000 casualties, while the Union army similarly suffered 23,000 men killed, wounded, or captured.

General Meade opposed launching an offensive against the Confederates deployed along Seminary Ridge. So, the Union forces let the Southerners begin their retreat. Meade delayed but then cautiously pursued the Rebels, hoping to attack them before they crossed the Potomac back into Virginia. But by the time the Northerners attacked on July 14, the enemy was for the time being safely back in the Confederacy, thus ending the Pennsylvania Campaign.

The Union victory at Gettysburg, combined with the Union triumph at Vicksburg on the Mississippi (see Vicksburg National Military Park) was the major turning point in the Civil War—in favor of the North. The Confederate Army of Northern Virginia had suffered irreparable losses, with one-third of 75,000 Confederates participating either killed, wounded, captured, or missing. The Union force was able to replace its Gettysburg casualties with substantial reserves, and would become an even more powerful army than before.

To help bolster the North's will to carry on the war against secession, President Lincoln took the opportunity, on November 19, 1863, at the dedication of a national cemetery for the Union dead in the Battle of Gettysburg, to deliver the stirring words of his Gettysburg Address. In part it says:

> Four score and seven years ago our fathers brought forth on this continent a new nation, conceived in Liberty, and dedicated to the proposition that all men are created equal.

> Now we are engaged in a great civil war, testing whether that nation, or any nation so conceived and so dedicated, can long endure. We are met on a great battlefield of that war. We have come to dedicate a portion of that field as a final resting place for those who here gave their lives that that nation might live. It is altogether fitting and proper that we should do this.

> . . . It is for us the living . . . to be dedicated here to the unfinished work which they who fought here have thus far so nobly advanced. It is . . . for us to be here dedicated to the great task remaining before us—that from these honored dead we take increased devotion to that cause for which they gave the last full measure of devotion—that we here highly resolve that these dead shall not have died in vain—that this nation, under God, shall have a new birth of freedom—and that government of the people, by the people, for the people, shall not perish from the earth.

Today, Gettysburg National Military Park's visitor center provides interpretive exhibits, audiovisual programs, and publications. Just to the south of the visitor center is the Cyclorama Center, exhibiting a huge circular painting of Pickett's Charge, which is highlighted by a light-and-sound program. A self-guided tour drive winds through the park, with interpretive stops highlighting key places and events of the battle. Among the stops are McPherson and Oak ridges, to the northwest of Gettysburg, where the two armies first clashed on July 1; the North Carolina and Virginia memorials on Seminary Ridge, where Southerners participating in Pickett's Charge launched their offensive on July 3; Little Round Top; the wheatfield and peach orchard; the architecturally imposing Pennsylvania Memorial; and the high water mark, where a one-mile trail loops through the area, in which Confederate General Armistead and 300 of his infantrymen entered "the Angle."

The soldiers' National Cemetery is adjacent to the park. Among the scores of other monuments scattered throughout the park and cemetery are the equestrian bronze statues of Union General Meade and Confederate General Lee; the prominent column of the New York State Monument; the Mississippi Monument that graphically portrays in bronze a Southern soldier's bravery in battle; the bronze statue of Union General Warren, whose quick response saved Little Round Top; and the memorial in honor of President Lincoln's Gettysburg Address. Also adjacent to the park is the Eisenhower National Historic Site (see the text on the site) that celebrates the 34th President of the United States.

The park offers interpreter-led talks and walks, living-history reenactments, and other programs. The visitor center and Cyclorama Center are open daily, except on Thanksgiving, Christmas, and New Year's Day.

Among the worthy publications on the battle and the park are *Gettysburg: The Story Behind the Scenery*® by William C. Davis (KC Publications); *Gettysburg: The Final Fury* by Bruce Catton (Doubleday and Co.); *Gettysburg: The Confederate High Tide* by Champ Clark (Time-Life Books).

IF YOU GO: Camping in the park is not permitted, except for organized youth groups (information: [717] 334-0909). There are picnic facilities. Lodging and meals are available in Gettysburg and elsewhere in the vicinity. Access from a variety of routes includes U.S. Route 30, between I-83 at York and I-81; or by way of U.S. Route 15, between I-70 and I-76 (the Pennsylvania Turnpike). The visitor center is located on State Route 134 (the Taneytown Road), just south of its junction with U.S. Business Route 15 (the Emmitsburg Road). Further information: Superintendent, 97 Taneytown Road, Gettysburg, PA 17325. Telephone (717) 334-1124.

KENNESAW MOUNTAIN NATIONAL BATTLEFIELD PARK

KENNESAW MOUNTAIN NATIONAL BATTLEFIELD PARK, consisting of 2,884 acres in northwestern Georgia, was established as a national battlefield in 1917, was transferred from the War Department to the National Park Service in 1933, and was renamed as a national battlefield park in 1935. It protects and interprets the area of a fierce Civil War battle, on June 27, 1864, during the march of Union forces toward the capture of Atlanta.

In the spring of 1864, the Union commander-in-chief, Lieutenant General Ulysses S. Grant, had directed that all the Union armies commence a broadly coordinated offensive against the Confederate forces. While he was personally overseeing the Virginia campaign he ordered Major General William Tecumseh Sherman to leave Chattanooga, Tennessee, and lead his 100,000-man army into Georgia against the 65,000-man Confederate Army of Tennessee, under the command of General Joseph E. Johnston. In Grant's words, Sherman's forces were to break up the Rebel forces and "go into the interior of the enemy's country as far as you can go, inflicting all the damage you can upon their war resources."

On May 6, Sherman's troops began their march southeastward into northwestern Georgia, seeking to destroy the Confederates' supply lines from Atlanta and to ultimately wipe out the military manufacturing and strategic railroad center itself. As Sherman said later, "Atlanta was too important a place in the hands of the enemy to be left undisturbed, with its magazines, stores, arsenals, workshops, foundries, and more especially its railroads, which converged there."

As the Union soldiers steadily advanced, they kept encountering General Johnston's entrenched forces. Sherman repeatedly devoted some of his troops to minor combat tactics in an effort to keep the enemy in place, while sending other soldiers on flanking maneuvers. These maneuvers were designed to circle around behind the Confederates and sever the Rebels' railroad supply lines from Atlanta. This series of encounters and maneuvers, without major fighting, again and again caused the Southerners to withdraw back and back, to head off the threat from behind.

By the third week of June, the Union forces had succeeded in pushing the Confederates southeastward, until they were only 20 miles to the northwest of Atlanta. The Rebel troops once again dug themselves in—this time establishing massive defenses that were located on and around a steep-sloped, densely forested, rocky, double-peaked ridge known as Kennesaw Mountain. The Confederates built miles of a network of defensive earthen-and-log breastworks, stretching across all the immediately surrounding ravines that extend outward from the base of the mountain. These fortifications bristled with big guns as well as musketry, emplaced to pound the men in blue, as they came marching toward this last important summit, before the relatively level plain extending on to Atlanta.

At 8 a.m., on June 27, with the goal of wiping out the Confederates, the Union troops opened fire upon the entrenched enemy with at least 200 cannons. This thundering siege lasted for an hour, and was followed by an infantry attack. When the Union soldiers came into range, the Confederate artillerymen and infantrymen opened fire, unleashing a bloody slaughter. This frontal attack on the Confederates' strategically well-placed position on and around the mountain came up against far greater Southern resistance than General Sherman had expected. Two Union assaults were driven back. The worst of the encounters was brutally intense combat in part of the Southerners' zigzagging breastworks that was subsequently called the "Dead Angle." As the battle's fighting ended by midday, casualties totaled over 3,000 Union men and around 500 Confederates. The Union frontal attack had proved utterly futile—the defenses were simply too strong. But then, the Northerners, having only been delayed by the entrenched Confederates, continued their march toward Atlanta. The siege of the city commenced in August, with Atlanta seized by Sherman's forces on September 2. Most of the city was burned in November, as the union forces set off on their ravaging "March to the Sea."

Today, the beauty and peace of Kennesaw Mountain make it hard for visitors to imagine the terrifying violence, intense human suffering, and death that took place on that hot, humid June day. The park's visitor center provides interpretive exhibits, an audiovisual program, and publications. Living-history programs are presented during the summer months. There are self-guided tour drives and walks, with a series of stops at key points of interest.

One of the interpretive stops is at the observation overlook that offers broad panoramas of the surrounding countryside. Trails lead to the summit of the mountain, and then continue southward along the crest of Little Kennesaw Mountain to a spur of the ridge called Pigeon Hill, where Confederate troops were deployed and from which they successfully fought off Union attacks. Trails lead farther south to Cheatham Hill, on which the battle's fiercest, bloodiest fighting occurred. A spur park road leads to this site, as well. A loop trail continues on south to Kolb's Farm, at the southern end of the park, where skirmishing occurred five days before the main battle. The log house of this farm, dating from 1836, was used briefly as a Union headquarters, and has since been restored to its historic appearance. The house is not open to the public. It is also reached by way of the park tour drive. The park is open daily, except on Christmas and New Year's Day.

An informative description of the Battle of Kennesaw Mountain is in the publication *Battles for Atlanta: Sherman Moves East* by Ronald H. Bailey (Time-Life Books).

Camping is not permitted, but the park provides two picnic areas—one near the visitor center and the other near the north end of Cheatham Hill Road. Lodging and meals are available in Marietta, Kennesaw, and Atlanta.

IF YOU GO: Access from I-75 is by way of Exit 116 and then four miles, following signs to the park. Access is also northwest from Marietta by way of Kennesaw Avenue, Old U.S. Route 41, and Stilesboro Road, to the visitor center, at the north end of the park; west from Marietta by way of Whitlock Avenue and either Burnt Hickory Road to the Pigeon Hill area of the park, or Dallas Highway to the Cheatham Hill area; or southwest from Marietta by way of Powder Springs Road to Kolb's Farm site. Further information: Superintendent, 900 Kennesaw Mountain Dr., Kennesaw, GA 30152. Telephone (770) 427-4686.

MANASSAS NATIONAL BATTLEFIELD PARK

MANASSAS NATIONAL BATTLEFIELD PARK comprises 5,071 acres in northern Virginia. It was established in 1940 to protect and interpret the Civil War's Battles of First and Second Manassas, on July 21, 1861, and August 28–30, 1862, respectively, both of which were won by the Confederate forces.

After the Confederacy's capture of Fort Sumter on April 13, 1861 (see Fort Sumter National Monument), public outrage and political pressure quickly mounted in the North to strike back and avenge the South's military aggression in the bold takeover of this major federal fortification at the mouth of Charleston Harbor, South Carolina. Two days after the fall of this fort into Confederate hands, President Abraham Lincoln issued a call for 75,000 militiamen from the Northern states to come forward and help put down the Confederacy's "insurrection." While the response was initially slow, thousands of volunteers signed up and began pouring into the nation's capital.

In the South, meanwhile, there was an appeal for 100,000 volunteers, and eager men reported for service to help fight for Southern independence. Richmond, Virginia, the newly chosen capital of the Confederate States, was a mere 110 miles south of Washington, D.C. With war clouds gathering, it was logical to assume that the initial major land battle between the North and South would occur somewhere between the two capital cities.

By July 8, the Union army had grown to 35,000 soldiers—up to then, the largest military force ever assembled in North America. Although the army's commanders were convinced that the mostly inexperienced troops were nowhere near ready to fight effectively, orders were nevertheless given by President Lincoln on July 10 to commence a military campaign against the Confederacy in northern Virginia. As for the South's soldiers, most of them were as inexperienced as the Union men.

The Battle of First Manassas (Bull Run)

Confederate President Jefferson Davis, with his military advisor, General Robert E. Lee—a former United States Army officer—rejected Brigadier General Pierre G.T. Beauregard's plan to take the offensive against Union forces, since Confederate soldiers lacked adequate strength and training. Instead, they adopted a strong defensive strategy, to block a possible Union advance upon Richmond. Beauregard established a defensive line with his 22,000 soldiers, along the south bank of the creek known as Bull Run. This was a key place from which to protect the nearby strategically important Manassas Junction, where two railroad lines merged—one running south to Gordonsville, where another line continued to Richmond.

The Union commander, Brigadier General Irvin McDowell, began moving his 35,000 soldiers southwestward from Washington, D.C., and Alexandria, Virginia, on July 16. The troops suffered under the intensely oppressive midsummer heat and humidity, and from the choking dust that

Stone House, Manassas National Battlefield Park, Virginia [David Muench]

their numbers stirred up as they trudged along the turnpikes and side roads of the Virginia farming country.

The first encounter between the two armies occurred on July 18, along Bull Run. Even though Union division commander Brigadier General Daniel Tyler had been expressly instructed *not* to cause an engagement, he took it upon himself to advance with some of his soldiers for a closer look at the situation along the stream, near the shallow crossing called Blackburn's Ford. At first, Tyler failed to detect anything more than just a few scattered Confederate pickets near Bull Run. Being impatient to attempt a crossing and push on to capture the railroad junction, he ordered some of his men to advance farther toward the north bank of the stream and launch an attack.

Suddenly, these soldiers found themselves caught in a massive fusillade from the well-hidden enemy. Tyler had, in fact, encountered a far larger force than he had bargained for. Three brigades of General Beauregard's troops were deployed along that stretch of the meandering waterway. Before the withering firepower subsided, the Union soldiers were forced to flee in terror from what was an inauspicious prelude to the battle.

General McDowell spent the next two days seeking a way around Beauregard's strong defenses. Ultimately he came up with a plan to encircle and attack the northern end of the Confederate line. Two divisions of his army crossed Bull Run on the morning of July 21 at Sudley Ford, six miles upstream from Blackburn's Ford. Beauregard had discounted this ford as one the Union army would not likely use due to the confusing nature of the dirt roads leading to it. Consequently, he had not thought it important to deploy any of his troops that far north.

Meanwhile, on July 19 and 20, Confederate reinforcements from the Shenandoah Valley began to arrive at Manassas Junction by the trainload. These 9,000 men in four brigades were under the command of General Joseph E. Johnston, who was the highest ranking officer to resign from the U.S. Army and join the Confederate army. This was also the first time in history that a railroad was used to transport military personnel for strategic purposes.

On the morning of July 21, McDowell's advancing column was confronted by a small Confederate brigade in the vicinity of Matthews Hill. The Southerners opened fire as soon as the Northerners were within range, inflicting some casualties and bringing the advancing forces to a halt. Before the Union troops could deploy, the Confederates suddenly charged, catching their opponents off guard and creating much confusion in the Union ranks.

This initial clash bought time for Confederate reinforcements to reach the field and enter the fight, but even with these additional troops, the Southerners remained greatly outnumbered by about three to one. As one survivor describes this fierce fight: "It was a whirlwind of bullets. Our men fell constantly. The deadly missiles rained like hail among the boughs and trees."

This was a terrible, cruel slaughter for both sides. By noon, the Southerners, under threat of massive envelopment, retreated in disorder southward from the hill. One of the Union brigades pursued the Rebels, as other Union units were crossing Bull Run. At this point in the battle, the Northerners appeared to have the upper hand. McDowell, astride his horse, even yelled out to his men: "Victory! Victory! The day is ours!"

The Confederates fell back to another rise of ground called Henry (House) Hill. After the large number of casualties in the morning's conflict, 11,000 of the Union troops reorganized themselves at the base of this hill, before advancing. This delay helped the roughly 6,000 Confederate soldiers get themselves defensively repositioned as well. The Union troops, outnumbering their opponents, were now poised to advance up the slope with their powerful artillery, to be followed closely by infantry, who were to charge the enemy with bayonets fixed.

In early afternoon, McDowell ordered two artillery units, under the command of Captains Charles Griffin and James B. Ricketts, to move their horse-drawn cannons up the hillside. When Griffin received the command, he voiced grave concern that his battery would be advancing against the enemy without the support of reliable, battle-tested infantry. Griffin's concerns went unheeded. The turning point in the Battle of First Manassas (Bull Run) came, in fact, when the inexperienced 11th New York Fire Zouaves arrived late and suddenly came under a fierce volley of fire from the 33rd Virginia Infantry. Just as Griffin had feared, many of the New York soldiers fled back down the hillside, after a number of their regiment had been mowed down by this first Confederate volley, while others retreated well behind the batteries they were supposed to have been defending.

The commander of the 33rd Virginia, Colonel Arthur Cummings, on his own initiative, then ordered and led a charge on the unsupported Union battery. Why didn't the big guns immediately open fire upon the advancing Rebels? The Union army's Chief of Artillery, Major William F. Barry, was so certain that the approaching men were friendly reinforcements that he ordered Griffin not to fire his guns. Griffin, on the other hand, was convinced they were the enemy. This momentary ambiguity, largely due to similarities in the uniforms worn on both sides, proved a costly error. It allowed the advancing Confederates to get within musket range of the battery, at which point they opened fire. Battery horses not shot stampeded away, the surviving artillery-men abandoned their guns and, along with the remaining Zouaves and other infantry, fled in terror from the hillside.

This disaster for the Northerners was only the beginning of the end. Other Confederate units now joined in, while fresh Union reinforcements were also sent up the hill. The battle see-sawed back and forth over the summit of Henry Hill for another couple of hours. The big guns, which the Union troops had been forced to abandon, changed hands several times. Heavy casualties escalated on both sides—resulting both from the battle itself and from the oppressive heat and choking dust and smoke stirred up by the intense fighting.

By the close of this ghastly afternoon, the exhausted Union forces were falling apart—fragmented in confused disarray—and at a time when the Confederates were still sending in fresh reinforcements. In an act of bold, crucial timing, General Beauregard ordered the whole Confederate line to charge. In the face of this daring onslaught, the Northerners panicked and began retreating in terror in every direction back across Bull Run. Some ran for their lives, while others were far too exhausted to do more than trudge slowly off the battlefield. For a while, the Southern units continued to pursue and harass the fleeing Union army. But by early evening, Beauregard called back his own battle-fatigued forces.

On July 22, in the midst of a heavy rainfall, the depressed, trauma-tized, and bedraggled Union men struggled back to Washington—many in the company of some Congressmen, their families, other politicians, and festive onlookers who had come out behind the Union forces, in hopes of witnessing a Northern victory. The Confederates, meanwhile, wildly celebrated their second significant victory of the Civil War. Casualties from this brutal conflict totaled nearly 2,000 Confederate soldiers and more than 3,000 Union men, killed, wounded, and missing. Because of the defeat, General-in-Chief Winfield Scott replaced McDowell with Major General George B. McClellan. This bloody battle also largely dispelled prevailing notions on both sides that war was somehow a romantic endeavor and that this war would soon be over. Both sides were now filled with a sober determination to get serious about training their armies and fighting on to victory.

The Battle of Second Manassas

The Civil War at Manassas fast-forwards to just over 13 months later, to August 28–30, 1862 (see the texts on the intervening major battles of Wilson's Creek, Fort Donelson, Pea Ridge, Shiloh, Fort Pulaski, and the Peninsular Campaign of Richmond). In the Peninsular Campaign, the Union Army of the Potomac and the Confederate Army of Northern Virginia pounded each other mercilessly during the wettest spring in living memory in Virginia. Then in August, the North and South clashed again on the gently rolling northern Virginia countryside near Manassas Junction.

The Union forces in northern Virginia were now reorganized as the Army of Virginia, commanded by Major General John Pope. When Confederate Commander-in-Chief, General Robert E. Lee, learned that Major General George B. McClellan's Army of the Potomac was evacuating Harrison's Landing on the James River, where it had been deployed since the conclusion of the Peninsular Campaign in early July, to join Pope, he ordered Major General Thomas J. ("Stonewall") Jackson on a campaign to attack and "suppress" Pope's 63,000-man force before McClellan's 120,000-man army could arrive. If the two Union forces were able to unite, their combined troop strength would be more than twice General Lee's Confederate numbers.

In a classic military maneuver, Jackson's 24,000 troops swung, in a 50-mile arc, around and behind Pope's forces and captured the Union supply depot at Manassas Junction, also severing communications and the supply line to Washington, D.C. After helping themselves to some of the spoils, the Confederates torched the remaining supplies and wagons and then moved northward about five miles—toward the old battlefield of First Manassas. Outraged by the Confederates pillaging his supplies, Pope immediately led his troops toward Manassas to "bag" Jackson, as he boasted. But Pope badly underestimated Lee's ability to concentrate his forces.

On the evening of August 28, Jackson attacked part of Pope's army near Groveton, making his location known. At dawn the following morning, Union forces launched a series of attacks on Jackson's line, now concealed in the woods along a stretch of an unfinished railroad grade. The Union thrusts were largely uncoordinated and while some briefly broke through the Confederate front line, Jackson's reserve units managed to recover the ground and repulse the Northerners. A late afternoon assault, carried out by a Union division under the command of one-armed Major General Philip Kearny, drove back and nearly shattered Jackson's left flank at Sudley. This success also proved short-lived, as Pope neglected to provide reinforcements for Kearny.

The Union commander had hoped to defeat Jackson before his reinforcements had time to arrive on the battlefield. But unknown to General Pope, the 30,000 Confederates under General Lee and Major General James Longstreet had already arrived and were being deployed for attack by the close of August 29. Emboldened by his sporadic successes of the 29th, Pope predicted that his Union soldiers would quickly grasp victory, reporting, "We fought a terrific battle here yesterday. The enemy is still in our front, but badly used up."

By noon of August 30, Pope had still not realized that Longstreet's fresh Confederate divisions were in place on Jackson's right, poised to clamp shut on the Northerners like a giant vise. Pope remained under the impression that Jackson was in retreat. As he ordered 10,000 troops forward, he quickly learned that the Confederates were not withdrawing at all. The Union attack ran headlong in a massive firestorm, especially in an area called the "Deep Cut," where Confederates had the advantage of being shielded in the railroad cut and wooded places. As one Southerner later recalled: "What a slaughter! What a slaughter of men that was! They were so thick it was just impossible to miss them."

Only a half-hour later, amid clouds of choking gunsmoke and a deadly blizzard of bullets and thundering artillery fire, the surviving Union men were forced to withdraw. The Union's massive assault had utterly failed. And at that moment, Lee took full advantage of Pope's vulnerability, ordering Longstreet to launch a powerful counterattack. A wave of 30,000 Confederates charged forward, pouring massive artillery fire into the exposed left flank of the Union forces, followed by Longstreet's infantry that slammed into the Northerners' left flank. As Jackson witnessed this successful assault, he ordered his men forward. Within minutes of launching this double-barreled assault, some of Pope's units were either overwhelmed or completely destroyed. As one Union soldier later described the Confederates pouring across Chinn Ridge, the Rebels roared along "like demons emerging from the earth."

At the close of this bloody, awful day on this killing field, General Pope somehow managed to assemble a line of defense on Henry (House) Hill where the Union soldiers were able to hold off repeated Rebel attacks. After this ferocious battle, Pope led his badly battered army—which had come perilously close to being completely annihilated—back to the protective defenses around Washington. Casualties in this second battle at Manassas totaled nearly 24,000 men. The Union army sustained over 1,700 soldiers killed and more than 8,400 wounded, with another 4,000 taken captive; the Confederates suffered more than 1,500 killed and over 7,800 wounded.

Within three months of General McClellan's Army of the Potomac being within a mere half-dozen miles of the Confederate capital, General Lee's Army of Northern Virginia had suddenly triumphed over the Union forces. For the Confederate commander, this victory—at the peak of the Confederacy's power—invited an invasion of the North and the prospect of a Confederate triumph there, as well.

Today, a visitor center on Henry Hill provides interpretive exhibits, audio-visual programs, and publications. A mile-long, self-guided walking trail with interpretive panels and taped messages leads from the visitor center to some of the key points on the battlefield of First Manassas (Bull Run). It includes the Henry House; the grave of Mrs. Henry, the battle's only civilian casualty; a memorial to the "Patriots who fell at Bull Run, July 21, 1861"; an equestrian monument of General Jackson; and Union artillery positions seized by the Confederates. A 1.4-mile loop trail runs along Bull Run from the Stone Bridge where the Confederates faced a Union diversionary attack. Another trail can be found at Sudley Springs.

An interpretive facility on Stuart's Hill, site of General Lee's head-quarters at Second Manassas, offers orientation to this battle during the summer months, and a 12-mile driving tour covers the far more extensive expanse of the Second Manassas battlefield. The tour contains interpretive stops at such highlights as Battery Heights; the Stone House; Sudley, scene of repeated Union attacks on August 29 against Jackson's left flank; the unfinished railroad that gave Jackson's men excellent cover; "Deep Cut"; Groveton Confederate Cemetery and nearby Dogan House, the only other original structure existing in the park; Chinn Ridge; and Henry Hill.

In addition to numerous hiking trails, the park maintains extensive equestrian trails for those with their own horses. The National Park Service cautions visitors to be careful when crossing, and turning on or off any of the public highways that pass through the park, particularly the busy Warrenton Turnpike (U.S. Route 29) and the Manassas-Sudley Road (State Route 234). The park is open daily, except on Christmas.

Informative descriptions of the Manassas battles are in the publications *First Blood: Fort Sumter to Bull Run* by William C. Davis; *Lee Takes Command: From Seven Days to Second Bull Run* by The Editors (Time-Life Books); *Battle at Bull Run* by William C. Davis (Louisiana State University Press); *Return to Bull Run* by John J. Hennessy (Simon & Schuster); and *Bull Run Remembers* by Joseph Mills Hanson (Prince William County Historical Commission).

IF YOU GO: Camping is not permitted in the park, but a picnic area is provided near the "Dogan Ridge" interpretive stop, located off State Route 234 north of U.S. Route 29. Food and lodging, as well as camping facilities, are available in the immediate vicinity of the park. Access is 26 miles southwest of Washington, D.C., via I-66. Take Exit 47 off I-66 and follow State Route 234 north one-half mile from the interchange to the visitor center entrance on the right. Further information: Superintendent, 12521 Lee Highway, Manassas, VA 20109. Telephone (703) 754-1861.

MONOCACY NATIONAL BATTLEFIELD

MONOCACY NATIONAL BATTLEFIELD, comprising 1,647 acres near Frederick, Maryland, 35 miles northwest of Washington, D.C., was authorized as a national military park in 1934, was renamed as a national battlefield in 1976, and was opened to visitation in 1991. It protects and interprets the site of a Civil War battle that occurred on July 9, 1864, in which Confederate forces defeated Union troops. But the main result of this conflict was to delay the Southerners, thus giving the Northerners time to assemble adequate defenses for the federal capital, Washington, D.C.

Also known as "The Battle that Saved Washington," the Battle of Monocacy took place during Confederate General Jubal A. Early's bold raid toward Washington. This was the third and final attempt to bring the war into the North—Antietam, 1862, and Gettysburg, 1863, were the two previous attempts—(see Antietam National Battlefield and Gettysburg National Military Park).

In June 1864, Confederate General Robert E. Lee ordered General Early and his 18,000 troops into the Shenandoah Valley. From there they were to proceed northward to threaten Washington, D.C., and Baltimore, Maryland, in an attempt to divert Union forces away from Lee's front at Petersburg, Virginia (see Petersburg National Battlefield). By July 2, Early had reached Winchester, in northwestern Virginia. A few days later, the Confed-erates destroyed federal military supplies at Harpers Ferry, West Virginia (see the text on Harpers Ferry National Historical Park). By July 6, Early and his men were at Shepherdstown, crossing the Potomac River into Maryland, and were soon proceeding eastward over South Mountain toward Frederick.

Meanwhile, Union Major General Lew Wallace, who had been training recruits in Baltimore, learned that a large enemy force was advancing through Maryland. Alerted by the president of the Baltimore & Ohio Railroad, Wallace was initially unsure whether the Confederates were heading for Washington or Baltimore; nor did he know the strength of the approaching troops. Wallace only knew that he must at least attempt to delay the Confederates until reinforcements could reach either city.

By the morning of July 9, Wallace had positioned 5,800 soldiers near Frederick, concentrating a majority of his troops at Monocacy Junction, where the road to Washington (Georgetown Pike) crossed the railroad to Baltimore. Here were two blockhouses, while the higher east bank of the Monocacy River provided a strong defensive position. In addition, this location afforded Wallace a clear view of the city of Frederick, three miles away, permitting him to determine the direction and strength of the approaching Southerners.

As General Early's troops moved out of Frederick along the road to Washington, they began encountering the determined resistance of General Wallace's men near Monocacy Junction. Noting the Union's strong defensive position along this road, the Confederates refrained from unleashing a direct frontal assault. Instead, Early sent an infantry division, under General John Gordon, to the southwest, to cross over the river below the Union left flank. Some of Wallace's troops were shifted to meet this attack. After crossing the Monocacy, the Confederates hit the Union line hard. It was during this action that the day's heaviest casualties occurred. As one Southerner said, "It made our hearts ache to look over the battlefield and see so many of our dear friends, comrades and beloved officers, killed and wounded."

After tenaciously maintaining their position throughout the afternoon, the Union troops were eventually forced from the field by outnumbering Confederate forces. The Union troops began their retreat toward Baltimore, leaving the battlefield to the Confederate victors. Union casualties totaled over 1,200 soldiers, while the Confederates lost between 700 and 900 men. But even though the battle was won by the Southerners, Wallace viewed it as a strategic victory, since he had succeeded in delaying Early's march to Washington by one vitally important day, providing sufficient time for reinforcements to reach and establish adequate defenses for the federal capital.

On July 10, General Early's troops resumed their advance on Washington. They got as far as Fort Stevens in the northern part of the District of Columbia (see the text on Fort Circle Parks), but were then easily repulsed by Union troops that had arrived just in time to reinforce the city's defenses. Had the Confederates been able to seize and occupy the federal capital, the political and psychological impacts upon the North and upon the Lincoln administration could have been catastrophic. As it was, Early's troops crossed over the Potomac and returned to Virginia by July 14.

Today, the national battlefield's visitor center provides interpretive exhibits, an audiovisual program, and publications. There is a half-mile trail adjacent to the visitor center, as well as a four-mile self-guided battlefield driving tour, for which a brochure is available. The visitor center is located on State Route 355, two-tenths of a mile south of the Monocacy River. It is open daily from Memorial Day weekend through Labor Day weekend; and from Wednesdays through Sundays during the rest of the year. The center is closed on Thanksgiving, Christmas, and New Year's Day.

IF YOU GO: Camping is not permitted and the park does not provide a picnic area. Lodging and meals are available in Frederick. Access is by way of either I-70 or I-270, three miles south of Frederick. Further information: Superintendent, 4801 Urbana Pike, Frederick, MD 21704. Telephone (301) 662-3515.

PEA RIDGE NATIONAL MILITARY PARK

PEA RIDGE NATIONAL MILITARY PARK, consisting of 4,300 acres in northwestern Arkansas, was authorized in 1956 to protect and interpret the site of and commemorate the Civil War battle fought March 7–8, 1862, that helped Union forces gain control of Missouri.

A slave-holding border state, Missouri was essential to the Union strategy of dividing the Confederacy by seizing control of the Mississippi River. Union Brigadier General Nathanial Lyon's campaign to break up Major General Sterling Price's pro-Confederate Missouri State Guard was thwarted at the Battle of Wilson's Creek, August 10, 1861 (see Wilson's Creek National Battlefield).

Brigadier General Samuel R. Curtis was appointed to command the Federal Southwestern District of Missouri on Christmas Day, 1861. In February 1862, Curtis' army of 10,500 chased Price and about 5,200 ill-equipped Missouri State Guard troops south into Arkansas along Telegraph or Wire Road. Formerly a part of the Trail of Tears (see Trail of Tears National Historic Trail) and Butterfield Overland Stage route, Telegraph Road played an important role during the Pea Ridge Campaign.

Reaching Arkansas, Price joined forces with General Benjamin McCulloch in the Boston Mountains, south of Fayetteville. Curtis established a base camp on the bluffs overlooking the north bank of Little Sugar Creek. Confederate Major General Earl Van Dorn assumed command of all the troops with McCulloch and Price, and on March 4, 1862, marched north to destroy Curtis and invade Missouri. During the night of March 6–7, Van Dorn marched his army northeast behind Curtis, hoping to launch a

Cannon and Elkhorn Tavern, Pea Ridge National Military Park, Arkansas [Larry Ulrich]

surprise attack on the rear of the Union army. However, forced marches in bitterly cold weather with little food left the Confederate army fatigued and widely separated, with McCulloch's troops lagging several miles behind.

Attempting to rejoin Van Dorn and Price by marching a shorter distance around the west end of Big Mountain, McCulloch's column, including two regiments of Cherokee Indians, was fired upon by Union artillery. The Confederate delays gave Curtis time to turn his army around and carry the fight to Van Dorn. In the ensuing battle, McCulloch and his successor General James McIntosh were killed. Several lesser ranking officers were captured. By nightfall, Union troops pushed the exhausted Confederates off the battlefield.

Meanwhile, Van Dorn and Price attacked the Union 4th Division east of the Big Mountain. The heaviest fighting occurred near a two-story hostelry locally known as Elkhorn Tavern and the critical Union supply line along Telegraph Road. Curtis counterattacked the next day. Under cover of a massive artillery bombardment, Union infantry charged the Confederates and pushed the last survivors off the battlefield.

An informative publication is *Pea Ridge: Civil War Campaign in the West* by William Shea and Earl Hess.

Today, the park's visitor center includes a museum, two slide programs, and a bookstore. Visitors may drive the seven-mile tour road with ten stops including exhibits and push-button messages. A recorded tape tour is available. The tour includes both the Leetown battlefield and the Elkhorn Tavern battlefield as well as the reconstructed tavern that is open for tours from Memorial Day through October. Ten miles of hiking trails and an eleven-mile equestrian trail wind through the park.

IF YOU GO: The park is open daily, except on Thanksgiving, Christmas, and New Year's Day. Camping facilities are provided at nearby Beaver Lake. Lodging is available in Rogers and Bentonville. The park is located ten miles north of Rogers, Arkansas, on U.S. 62. Further information: Superintendent, P.O. Box 700, Pea Ridge, AR 72751. Telephone (501) 451-8122.

PETERSBURG NATIONAL BATTLEFIELD

PETERSBURG NATIONAL BATTLEFIELD consists of 2,735 acres in five main units in southern Virginia. Established as a national military park in 1926, it was transferred from the War Department to the National Park Service in 1933, and was renamed as a national battlefield in 1962. It protects and interprets several Civil War sites involving the Union army's grim, nearly ten-month campaign to capture the Confederates' key railroad center of Petersburg—a siege that ran from June 19, 1864, to April 2, 1865.

As Union Lieutenant General Ulysses S. Grant, commander-in-chief of all the federal forces, was overseeing military operations in Virginia toward the capture of Petersburg and Richmond, other coordinated military efforts were occurring. Among these were Grant's order to Union forces to block Confederate plans to sever the railroad between Nashville and Chattanooga, Tennessee, which was the vital military supply line for federal forces in Georgia (see Brice's Cross Roads National Battlefield Site and Tupelo National Battlefield); and his order for other federal army forces to march into Georgia and capture Atlanta and other cities.

In Virginia, Grant knew the extreme importance of seizing Petersburg. As he said, "The key to taking Richmond is Petersburg," since it was a major transportation hub. Confederate General Robert E. Lee also knew the significance of Petersburg and what would happen if the Union should capture it: "We must destroy this army of Grant's," he said, "before he gets to the James River. If he gets there it will become a siege and then it will be a mere question of time."

The Union army did cross the James, reached and encircled Petersburg, and launched its months-long siege. At the start, there were more than 15,000 Union troops, and just over 2,000 Confederate defenders. Lee had not understood Grant's real purpose in crossing the James River. Consequently, he had failed to shift some of his army from Richmond to Petersburg.

At 7 p.m. on June 15, Union soldiers, under the command of Major General William F. "Baldy" Smith, began attacking the Rebel defenses—a ten-mile-long series of fortifications around the southeast, south, and southwest sides of Petersburg known as the Dimmock Line. Within a short time that evening, the Union troops had succeeded in seizing over a mile of Confederate batteries. Even though "Petersburg at that hour was clearly at the mercy of the Federal commander," as Confederate General Pierre G.T. Beauregard said, Smith was especially cautious and chose to keep his exhausted men where they were, rather than ordering a night assault.

When the numerically superior Union troops resumed their attack the following day, the Confederates were successful in driving back a series of uncoordinated, piecemeal Union thrusts. On June 17, the Union forces managed some further advances and Lee shifted the Army of Northern Virginia to Petersburg. Then early on June 18, Beauregard occupied new works slightly closer to Petersburg. When the Union soldiers launched an attack, they were shocked to find that the trenches were empty. Uncoordinated Union advances toward the redeployed Rebels, now reinforced with soldiers of Lee's Army of Northern Virginia, were defeated and thrown back. The Union assaults collapsed and many Northerners were slaughtered and wounded, as they were exposed to the defenders' weapons fire.

During those first four days of combat, Union casualties totaled more than 10,000 soldiers, while the Confederates lost 4,000. As a result of the Confederate retreat into Petersburg, the Union forces held the advantage, as they attacked the city, its Rebel defenders, and its civilian population. While many residents remained in the city, the woodlands, farmlands, and houses for miles around the besieged city were "filled with women and children and old men who have fled from their homes," wrote a newspaper reporter. The Union army also seized two railroads and several roads leading into the city.

One Union regiment, comprised mostly of Pennsylvania coal miners, devised the idea of digging a tunnel under the Rebels' entrenched lines and detonating a huge explosion that would destroy an artillery position and open a gap in their defenses. It took the men three weeks to construct the tunnel that extended over 500 feet from the Union lines to directly under the Confederate trenches. At the end of the tunnel, the miners laid over 300 kegs of gunpowder. On July 30, just after dawn, the explosion was set off. It was described by one witness: "Without form or shape, full of red flames and carried on a bed of lightning flashes, [it] . . . spread out like an immense mushroom whose stem seemed to be of fire and its head of smoke." But then the Union troops rushed, not around, but into the huge crater formed by the explosion, and total bedlam prevailed as some 10,000 men-in-blue were targeted for a horrendous massacre by Confederate artillery and musket fire. Many men perished in the entrapping crater. Even veteran General Grant called this "the saddest affair I have witnessed in this war."

It was this Battle of the Crater that caused the Union commander to cease trying to storm the entrenched Rebels and, instead, to concentrate on the long siege of the city. The Northerners steadily encircled Petersburg and continued to sever the Confederates' supply lines. By October, they had encircled more of the area around the city. Although military activities slowed during the bitter-cold winter months, the Union army, with its 30-mile siege line from Richmond to Petersburg, kept up relentless pressure every day with mortar shelling, small arms fire, and minor skirmishing.

By February 1865, there were 110,000 Union troops in front of Petersburg. These men were being kept well supplied by way of the recently constructed, 21-mile U.S. Military Railroad from City Point, to the northeast at the junction of the Appomattox and James rivers. By contrast, there were only 60,000 hungry and cold Confederate soldiers huddled in miserable trenches and fortifications. Many Southerners deserted the Confederate military. By March, General Lee was frantically trying to figure out how his soldiers could break out of the trap by an attack on General Grant's forces at Fort Stedman, cutting through the Union lines and from there hoping to gain control of the Union's military railroad.

On March 25, the Rebels actually succeeded in breaking out and attacking and capturing Fort Stedman. But they were soon defeated by a powerful Union counterattack. Four days later, 22,000 Federal troops, under Major General Philip H. Sheridan, were dispatched by Grant to sever the last major supply line to Petersburg—the South Side Railroad. To head off this threat, General Lee sent 10,000 cavalry and infantry units, under Major General George E. Pickett. The two armies clashed at a crossroads known as Five Forks, about 10 miles southwest of Petersburg. On April 1, Federal cavalry and infantry overwhelmed the Confederates, capturing 2,000 Rebels.

The following day, Grant's forces launched an all-out assault, a massive bombardment of Petersburg, and the city was evacuated by the Confederate military that night, thus ending the siege. Petersburg and Richmond were

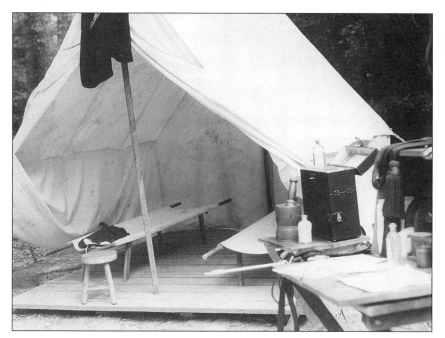

Field hospital, surgeon's tent (interpretive living-history encampment), Petersburg National Battlefield, Virginia [Russ Butcher]

abandoned simultaneously (see Richmond National Battlefield Park) and this led to the Confederates' surrender at Appomattox Court House (see Appomattox Court House National Historical Park).

Today, Petersburg National Battlefield has a visitor center, located in the park's main unit, just off State Route 36, about two and one-half miles east of downtown Petersburg. The center provides interpretive exhibits, an audiovisual program, and publications. A four-mile tour drive leads from the visitor center, with stops at such highlights as two Confederate batteries that were captured by African-American soldiers; Fort Stedman, which was captured by Confederate soldiers who were then soon overwhelmed by a powerful Union counterattack; and the crater that was created by the powerful Union explosion detonated beneath a Confederate fortification.

Other park units are linked together by a 16-mile tour drive, extending from the south and west of Petersburg. This route highlights a number of Union and Confederate forts, the Poplar Grove National Cemetery, and Five Forks Battlefield, where Union troops succeeded in clearing the way to sever the last major supply route into Petersburg.

Eight miles to the northeast of Petersburg, in the city of Hopewell, Virginia, is the City Point unit of the park. This became a bustling supply center and terminus of the railroad serving the Union troops around Petersburg. City Point was also General Grant's command center for the war effort.

Among interesting publications are *The Siege of Petersburg* by Noah Andre Trudeau (Eastern National Park and Monument Association); and *The Siege of Petersburg* by Joseph P. Cullen (Eastern Acorn Press). Also excellent is *Death in the Trenches: Grant at Petersburg* by William C. Davis (Time-Life Books).

During the summer months, the national battlefield offers living-history programs of the life of Civil War soldiers, as well as the firing of artillery. The park also provides hiking and biking trails of certain historic sites, and is open daily, except on winter holidays. Camping is not permitted in the national battlefield, but there are picnic facilities. Lodging and meals are available in Petersburg and elsewhere in the vicinity.

IF YOU GO: Access is by way of State Route 36 to both the main park unit and the City Point unit. The Five Forks unit is reached from I-85 by way of the Dinwiddie Courthouse exit, following the signs to Dinwiddie Courthouse Road (State Route 627) which leads in five miles northwestward to the park unit. Further information: Superintendent, P.O. Box 549, Petersburg, VA 23804. Telephone (804) 732-3531 .

RICHMOND NATIONAL BATTLEFIELD PARK

RICHMOND NATIONAL BATTLEFIELD PARK consists of 771 acres in 11 scattered units in and around Richmond, Virginia. It was established in 1936 to protect and interpret a number of Civil War battle sites, in which the Union army targeted the Army of Northern Virginia and the Confederacy's capital city. There were two major campaigns: Major General George B. McClellan's Peninsular (or Peninsula) Campaign, in 1862; and Lieutenant General Ulysses S. Grant's Virginia Campaign, in 1864–1865.

Since the start of the Civil War, in April 1861, capture of the capital of the Confederate States was viewed as a primary goal of the Union military and political strategy. Seizing Richmond would almost certainly have a major psychological impact upon the Confederacy's political morale, and it definitely would have a major impact upon the South's economic and military viability, since the city was a key manufacturing and military supply center.

After the serious setback for the Union army at the Battle of First Manassas, in July 1861 (see Manassas National Battlefield Park), the newly named commander of the Union forces, General McClellan, spent the winter of 1861–1862 assembling and disciplining the 120,000-man Army of the Potomac. The initial strategy for the summer of 1862 was to seize Richmond. Rather than marching directly overland from Washington, D.C., McClellan decided to launch his assault by bringing his forces by water, down the Potomac River and onto Chesapeake Bay, to the eastern Virginia peninsula between the York and James rivers and advancing up from there to the Confederate capital. Part of McClellan's plan was to have reinforcements, under Major General Irvin McDowell, march from northern Virginia to join McClellan's troops and to also have a fleet of Union naval gunboats bombard Richmond from the James River—thus launching a three-pronged attack on Richmond.

The Peninsular Campaign of 1862

Implementation of the Peninsular Campaign got underway on March 17, with one of the largest amphibious movements of military forces up to that time in history. More than 400 vessels were called into service, including schooners, brigs, sloops, steamboats, and even ferry boats and barges—almost anything that would float. In addition to the soldiers, there were 27,000 mules, horses, and cattle; over 3,000 wagons; several hundred cannons and other artillery; 700 ambulances; and tons of rations and other supplies. The Union forces sailed down the Potomac and onto Chesapeake Bay, disembarking at Fort Monroe, at the tip of the peninsula. This was a fortification that never fell into Confederate hands during the war. On their way up the peninsula, the Federals seized Yorktown and Williamsburg from Confederate defenders.

During most of the month of April, and continuing on through much of May and June, rain fell heavily on Virginia, saturating the land, overflowing rivers and streams, and turning the dirt roads into rivers of mud. Both the Union and Confederate troops camped on and slogged slowly through the soggy ground. Bridges kept washing out and constantly had to be repaired or replaced. And in the midst of this miserably muddy mess, horse- and mule-drawn wagons and other wheeled conveyances were continually getting mired down and stuck. As slow as was the Union army's advance toward Richmond, the soldiers somehow managed to make steady progress.

The Union naval fleet of five gunboats, which was to have sailed up the James River to assist in the attack on Richmond, was attacked and blocked in a fierce four-hour battle at Fort Darling. This Confederate fortification was perched atop 90-foot-high Drewry's Bluff, seven miles downriver from Richmond. Rebel batteries, deployed at the fort, blasted away at the Union boats and forced them to retreat back down the river. With naval bombardment of Richmond no longer possible, General McClellan was now forced to proceed without this part of the battle plan.

A second key part of the grand strategy that McClellan had been counting on was the plan to have General McDowell's forces march southward from northern Virginia, to reinforce McClellan's troops. As a result of successful Confederate actions in the Shenandoah Valley that seemed to pose a threat to the security of Washington, D.C., President Abraham Lincoln sent a message to McClellan on May 24, saying, "I have been compelled to suspend McDowell's movements to join you." This was a major setback for McClellan, whose troops had been struggling for so many weeks through the mud and rain to get into position for a major offensive against Richmond's defenders. Suddenly his position was placed in jeopardy, with his troops now deployed along both banks of the rain-swollen, swampy Chickahominy River—within striking distance of Richmond.

When the Confederate commander, General Joseph E. Johnston, learned that McDowell's troops would not be meeting up with McClellan's he decided to launch an attack on May 31 upon the Union forces, at a place called Seven Pines (not in today's park). A savage and confused battle ensued, in which there were thousands of casualties. After a day and a half, the Union men managed to throw off the enemy. One of the casualties was the Confederates' General Johnston, who was severely injured. President Jefferson Davis quickly appointed a new commander, General Robert E. Lee, to head up what now became known as the Army of Northern Virginia.

The Seven Days' Battles of 1862

Then, on June 26, 1862, at swampy Beaver Dam Creek, began the Seven Days' Battles, with Confederates sustaining heavy losses as they hurled themselves against 30,000 Union troops, who were under the command of Brigadier General Fitz-John Porter. Amid a terrible slaughter by Union artillery and small arms fire, the Rebels were finally forced to retreat. That night, Porter's soldiers pulled back five miles to higher ground around Gaines' Mill.

On the 27th, the 55,000-man Confederate army unleashed a blistering and bloody assault against the Union army. In the **Battle of Gaines' Mill**, with bayonets at the ready, the Southerners smashed right into and breached the Northerners' front line, causing many of the Union soldiers to panic and run to the rear. This was General Lee's first real victory in the Peninsular Campaign. That night, Porter moved his men again—south across the Chickahominy, after a day of a grimly horrendous toll of dead, dying, and injured soldiers on both sides.

In the words of a Southern surgeon, Spencer G. Welch:

> The most saddening sight was the wounded at the hospitals, which were in various places on the battlefield. Not only are the houses full, but even the yards are covered with them. There are so many that most of them are much neglected.

(As reprinted in the book, *In Hospital and Camp: The Civil War through the Eyes of Its Doctors and Nurses*, compiled by Harold Elk Straubing (Stackpole Books).)

General McClellan felt bitter that the government leaders in Washington had not provided him with additional forces. He sent a message to President Lincoln, in which he said:

> I have lost this battle because my force was too small . . . and I say it with the earnestness of a general who feels in his heart the loss of every brave man who has been needlessly sacrificed today. I know that a few thousand men would have changed this battle from a defeat into a victory. As it is, the government can not and must not hold me responsible.

Drewry's Bluff, Richmond National Battlefield Park [NPS]

On June 28, McClellan, believing that his army was greatly outnumbered (an assumption that actually proved false) and that it was, therefore, on the verge of being defeated, ordered his men to retreat southward, on the way to Harrison's Landing on the James River. General Lee suspected that the Union men were in full retreat toward the river, and decided to take a gamble by ordering several units of his army to attack the retreating Union army from the rear and on its flanks. Lee's commanders moved more slowly and cautiously in pursuing the Northerners than Lee wished, but finally an assault began on the afternoon of June 30.

The Southerners broke through the center of the Army of the Potomac's line. In this **Battle of Glendale** (or Frayser's Farm), Brigadier Generals Joseph Hooker and one-armed Philip Kearny ordered their units to fill the breach and help hold the Union line against the savage fighting—much of which was brutal, hand-to-hand combat. That night, the retreat proceeded, with some Federal units, including General Porter's, taking control of Malvern Hill, while others were deployed under the shield of Union naval gunboats at Harrison's Landing.

General Lee decided to gamble once again in what he saw as his last chance to defeat McClellan's army, before it escaped down the James River. The uncoordinated and wasteful attack was launched on the afternoon of July 1, against the Northerners deployed on and around Malvern Hill. As chronicled by General Porter, late in the day:

. . . the enemy opened with artillery from nearly the whole front, and
soon after pressed forward in columns of infantry. . . . As if moved by
a reckless disregard of life equal to that displayed at Gaines' Mill, with
a determination to capture our army or destroy it by driving us into
the river, brigade after brigade rushed at our batteries; but the artillery
. . . mowed them down with shrapnel, grape, and canister, while our
infantry, withholding their fire until the enemy were in short range,
scattered the remnants of their columns. . . .

In this **Battle of Malvern Hill**, the Rebels' attempt to defeat the
Union forces with this frontal attack was a complete fiasco, and left the killing
field covered with dead, dying, and wounded. The Confederates suffered more
than 5,000 casualties, and the Union forces sustained nearly 3,000. As one
Southern general observed: "It was not war—it was murder."

Thus ended the Seven Days' Battles, which had caused nearly 16,000
Union casualties out of their total force of 115,000 soldiers; and the Confederate army of 88,000 men lost over 20,000. The Peninsular Campaign, that ran
from mid-March to early July, had ended indecisively. The Union army failed
to seize Richmond; and the Confederate army, while pushing the Northerners
away from the Confederate capital for now, failed to defeat the Union troops.
The brutal combat and heavy losses made it abundantly clear to the North
and South that this war was not likely to be easily won by either side anytime
soon. The next military actions relating to Richmond now fast-forward nearly
two years.

The Battle of Cold Harbor of 1864

The Union and Confederate armies had fought some of the bloodiest
encounters of the Civil War, from May 5–24, 1864, at the battles of the
Wilderness and Spotsylvania (see Fredericksburg and Spotsylvania National
Military Park), followed by the Battle of North Anna River, only 25 miles
north of Richmond. After the latter conflict, in which the Union troops barely
escaped from a powerfully fortified trap set by General Lee's soldiers, Union
commander-in-chief, Lieutenant General Ulysses S. Grant, continued to pursue the goal of attacking the Confederate capital.

The next battle took place from May 30 to June 12, 1864, only eight
miles to the northeast of Richmond, in the vicinity of a strategic crossroads
known as Cold Harbor (the name of a tavern), between the Pamunkey and
Chickahominy rivers. A number of confrontations occurred on May 31 and
June 1. A day's delay in Union troop deployments gave the Rebels extra time
to enhance their defenses along the numerous creeks, ravines, and other
advantageous terrain in the area. A journalist wrote that the Confederate
entrenchments "are intricate, zigzagged lines within lines, lines protecting
flanks of lines, lines built to enfilade opposing lines . . . each laid out with
some definite design."

Without the benefit of the usual military intelligence indicating the enemy's position and strength, Grant launched a frontal attack right into the powerfully deployed Confederate positions, commencing at 4:30 a.m. on June 3. As the Union advanced, the Rebel troops suddenly rose into view from behind their massive earthworks and let loose with a flaming, deafening, withering blast from their massed artillery and muskets—hammering the Union ranks mercilessly, in a firestorm of lead and iron. In roughly a single hour, the conflict was at an end, leaving close to 6,000 Union men dead or wounded on the battlefield. One horrified participant observed that, "In that little period of time more men fell bleeding as they advanced than in any other like period of time throughout the war."

Although no further significant attacks occurred from either side, the two armies remained deployed in the trenches for another week. Union casualties for the whole battle totaled close to 13,000 men, while the Confederates' losses were several thousand. General Lee's Southerners never again achieved so large a victory. Following the Battle of Cold Harbor, General Grant made major changes in his Virginia Campaign strategy, now placing greater emphasis upon military sieges. Toward that end, he ordered his soldiers to swing eastward around Richmond, cross the James River, and launch a siege upon the key railroad hub of Petersburg, 23 miles south of the Confederate capital (see the text on Petersburg National Battlefield).

The Capture of Fort Harrison in 1864

In September 1864, as Grant's army was gradually tightening its noose around Petersburg, the commander-in-chief ordered a surprise attack on one of the Confederate fortifications, Fort Harrison, about seven miles south of Richmond. On September 29, the early morning assault against the fort was designed to discourage Lee from sending some of his men to reinforce Rebel troop strength in the Shenandoah Valley, in northern Virginia. Although heavily armed, the fort was lightly manned. Consequently, the Union division succeeded in seizing this important fortification.

The next day, the Confederates attempted to storm the fort and take it back, but the Union troops in the meantime had received reinforcements and were able to repulse the pounding attacks, causing heavy Rebel losses. As a result, the Southerners withdrew some of their outer line of defenses and established a new network of entrenchments closer to Richmond. This also weakened some of their defenses around Petersburg.

The Capture of Richmond in 1865

On April 2, 1865, as the Union forces succeeded in capturing Petersburg, after the nearly ten-month siege of that city, the order quickly went out from Confederate President Jefferson Davis for all civilians to be evacuated from Richmond. Absolute bedlam and lawlessness took hold of the population of 100,000 residents, refugees, battle-wounded, prisoners, and others. Many people loaded what possessions they could onto any available wheeled conveyances—from carts and wagons to carriages—and sped across the city, scrambled to get across the congested bottleneck of Mayo Bridge spanning the James River, and fled away to the south. Many others couldn't escape from the city and gathered, terrified, on the lawn surrounding the capitol building.

To make matters far worse, Confederate leaders ordered the burning of warehouses, arsenals, and other supplies so that these assets would not fall into Union hands. On the night of April 2–3, huge fires erupted and roared out of control in the warehouse district by the river, turning the night sky red and the once-proud city into a nightmarish inferno. Winds came up during the night that spread the conflagration from building to building. About 15 percent of the city burned.

As Joseph P. Cullen has described the utter devastation, in the National Park Service's handbook *Richmond Battlefields*:

> The blaze from the Shockhoe Warehouse . . ., where 10,000 hogshead of tobacco was put to the torch, flew skyward as if shot from a huge blowtorch. The flames quickly spread to the Franklin Paper Mills and the Gallego Flour Mills, 10 stories high. Higher and higher they soared, and then widened until it seemed a red hot sea of fire would engulf the whole city.

> . . . Powder magazines and arsenals let go with a whooshing boom. Thousands of bullets and shells tore through buildings and ploughed up the streets. Shells exploded high in the smoke cascading a metal spray over the area, followed by a rattle of bursting cartridges in one great metallic roar. Just before daybreak a deafening explosion from the James River signalled the destruction of the Confederate warships and the Navy Yard.

> Richmond was now one vast inferno of flame, noise, smoke, and trembling earth. The roaring fire swept northwestward from the riverfront, hungrily devouring the two railroad depots, all the banks, flour and paper mills, and hotels, warehouses, stores, and houses by the hundreds.

Union troops soon took control of the city. By the next evening, most of the city's business and industrial district had been destroyed. As Cullen wrote:

> The stars shone down that night on the smouldering ruins of more than 700 buildings. Gaunt chimneys stood naked against the black velvet sky. A Federal officer, picking his way through thousands of pieces of white granite columns and marble facades that littered the streets . . . noted that the silence of death brooded over the city.

President Abraham Lincoln visited the city on April 4. As he walked through the grim ruins in the former capital of the Confederacy, former slaves came to greet the president, some even kneeling before him, in gratitude for ending slavery.

A week later, the Confederates surrendered at Appomattox Court House (see Appomattox Court House National Historical Park), finally drawing the curtain down on the Civil War.

Today, Richmond National Battlefield Park's visitor center, at 3215 E. Broad Street, Richmond, provides interpretive exhibits, audiovisual programs, and publications. The center is at the site of one of the Confederacy's most extensive hospital complexes—Chimborazo General. This facility was built in 1861 and served more than 75,000 sick and wounded Confederates. The buildings no longer exist—only the grassy expanse of Chimborazo Park, adjacent to the visitor center, overlooking the James River.

Other park interpretive facilities include the Cold Harbor visitor contact station, located just off State Route 156, to the northeast of Richmond; and the Fort Harrison orientation center, at the Fort Harrison unit (open seasonally), on Battlefield Park Road, off State Route 5, between Richmond and the I-295 interchange. Short interpretive trails are provided at Chickahominy Bluffs, Cold Harbor, Gaines' Mill, Malvern Hill, Fort Harrison, Fort Brady, and Drewry's Bluff units. The ten park units and visitor center are reached by way of an 80-mile connecting drive—mostly on U.S. and state routes. There is a self-guided tour (tapes are available at the visitor center). The park's battlefield units are open daily; and the visitor center is open daily, except on Thanksgiving, Christmas, and New Year's Day.

Four especially informative publications are *Bloody Roads South: The Wilderness to Cold Harbor, May-June 1864* by Noah Andre Trudeau (Little Brown and Company); *Forward to Richmond: McClellan's Peninsular Campaign* by Ronald H. Bailey (Time-Life Books); *The Killing Ground: Wilderness to Cold Harbor* by Gregory Jaynes (Time-Life Books); and *To the Gates of Richmond: The Peninsula Campaign* by Stephen W. Sears (Ticknor & Fields).

Camping is not permitted, but a picnic area is provided near Fort Harrison. Lodging and meals are available in and around Richmond.

IF YOU GO: Access to the visitor center is from various routes, including from I-95 northbound, by way of Exit 74C and swinging onto 17th Street (southbound), turning left onto Broad Street and continuing to 33rd Street, and then a right turn into the visitor center parking area; or I-95 southbound by way of Exit 74B, onto Franklin Street, a right turn onto 14th Street and a right turn onto Broad Street, and continuing to the visitor center. For further information on the park and directions for reaching the various park units: Superintendent, 3215 E. Broad St., Richmond, VA 23223. Telephone (804) 226-1981.

SHILOH NATIONAL MILITARY PARK

SHILOH NATIONAL MILITARY PARK, encompassing 3,962 acres surrounding Pittsburg Landing on the Tennessee River in southwestern Tennessee, was established in 1894 and was transferred from the War Department to the National Park Service in 1933. It protects and interprets over 90 percent of the battle lines of the Civil War's first major western engagement, on April 6–7, 1862, that was won by the Union forces. The park also includes a significant Woodland/Mississippian cultural site—Shiloh Indian Mounds National Historic Landmark.

Here on April 6, Major General Ulysses S. Grant's unsuspecting troops, encamped on the lower Tennessee River's west bank, were jolted by an overwhelming Confederate assault. A bloody and bitterly fought two-day battle raged back and forth across this landscape, before the Southerners' attack was repulsed, and Union forces could again turn their attention to capturing the critical railroad junction at Corinth, Mississippi.

Earlier that year, in February, a river route into the South's heartland had been opened with Grant's capture of Forts Henry and Donelson, guarding the Cumberland and Tennessee rivers (see the text on Fort Donelson National Battlefield). In concert with a fleet of Union naval gunboats, the Union army could now move at will all the way to the shallows of Mussel Shoals, Alabama.

On the morning of April 6, while Grant was downriver at his headquarters, a large wave of Confederates, under the command of General Albert Sydney Johnston, exploded onto the scene, sending the Union men scrambling to turn the frenzied chaos into a semblance of order. The Southerners' repeated assaults succeeded in driving the Northerners back steadily during the early morning. But by midmorning, the Union troops succeeded in establishing a line of defense along a sunken wagon road and fence. Here both sides fought savagely, as the Union troops managed to hold their position until late afternoon. The Confederates, who unleashed 11 individual attacks against the 6,000 Union soldiers, called this place the "Hornets' Nest," because of the intensity of the fighting that occurred there.

By the end of the afternoon, after 2,200 Union soldiers had been surrounded and captured, Grant's forces were redeployed for the night along a new defense line, located just north of a ravine called Dill Branch, adjacent to Pittsburg Landing. Aggressive assaults by the Confederates that day had pushed the Union forces back nearly three miles.

During this first day of the battle, Johnston was mortally wounded—the highest ranking American ever killed on a battlefield. Brigadier General Pierre G.T. Beauregard, who previously led Confederate troops in the Battle of First Manassas (see Manassas National Battlefield Park), now assumed command at Shiloh.

On the torrentially rainy and windy night of April 6–7, as Union gunboats relentlessly bombarded Confederate positions, some 25,000 fresh

Grant's Last Line, Shiloh National Military Park, Tennessee [David Muench]

troops of the Army of the Ohio, under the command of General Don Carlos Buell, and other reinforcements arrived at Pittsburg Landing. In that miserable night, there were an estimated 2,000 men killed and 10,000 wounded, in some places lying in piles together. A very few overworked surgeons, under primitive field conditions, struggled, amid mounting piles of amputated arms and legs, to alleviate a little of the awesome suffering of the wounded.

Early on April 7, Grant and Buell's combined forces struck back hard at the Confederates, pounding them again and again, and steadily driving them back across the now muddy land that the Union soldiers had been forced to give up just the day before. The fighting finally led the exhausted Confederates to simply give up and retreat back to the south. The horrendous slaughter on this grim killing field claimed over 13,000 casualties out of the Union's 62,000 soldiers; and 25 percent of the Confederates' approximately 44,000-man force was killed, wounded, or missing. So many bodies covered the battlefield that General Grant said:

> I saw an open field over which the Confederates had made repeated charges the day before, so covered with dead that it would have been possible to walk across the clearing in any direction stepping on dead bodies without a foot touching the ground.

Of the wounded and dying, one soldier remarked that "Their groans and cries were heart-rending." And even veteran General William Tecumseh Sherman, who was one of General Grant's most brilliant commanders, was sobered by the sickening brutality of this conflict. "The scenes on this field," he said, "would have cured anybody of war." But out of the bloodshed, the Confederate defeat ultimately opened the way for Union control of the biggest river in the region, the Mississippi.

Amid today's peaceful setting, it is difficult to imagine the magnitude of the carnage and suffering that occurred here on those two ghastly days. A visitor center provides interpretive exhibits and a half-hour film. Publications are available at a bookstore. There is a self-guided, eight-mile tour drive that winds through the park, highlighted by a series of interpretive stops. The latter include General Grant's last line of defense; the Hornets' Nest, where the Union men courageously held their defenses; Water Oak Pond, where Confederate soldiers launched a final desperate and bloody counterattack; a rebuilt Shiloh Church completed in 1949, the original of which was a Methodist meeting house (*Shiloh* is a Hebrew word meaning "place of peace"); and the site of the Union field-tent hospital, one of the first such facilities in the Civil War.

As for the medical treatment of the Confederates, New York surgeon William G. Stevenson, who was forced into medical service for the enemy, later wrote in his book, *Thirteen Months in the Rebel Army:*

> During the week following the battle the wounded were brought in [to Corinth, MS] by hundreds, and surgeons were overtasked. About 5,000 wounded men, demanding instant and constant attendance, made a call too great to be met successfully. A much larger proportion of amputations was performed than would have been necessary if the wounds could have received earlier attention. On account of exposure, many wounds were gangrenous when the patients reached the hospital. In these cases delay was fatal, and an operation almost equally so, as tetanus often followed speedily. Where amputation was performed, eight out of ten died.

Nor was there any anesthesia to help deaden the pain, other than maybe a swig or two of whiskey.

A national cemetery is within the park, at Pittsburg Landing. Visitors are cautioned to walk carefully near steep riverbanks. Interpretive talks and living-history reenactments and demonstrations are presented at various times, from late spring through autumn, as weather permits. The park is open daily, except on Christmas.

Two informative publications are *Shiloh—in Hell Before Night* by James Lee McDonough (University of Tennessee Press); and *The Road to Shiloh: Early Battles in the West* by David Nevin (Time-Life Books).

IF YOU GO: Camping is not permitted, but a picnic area is located in the park, just off State Route 22. Lodging and meals are available in Savannah and

Adamsville, TN; at Pickwick Landing State Park, TN; and in Corinth, MS. Access by way of U.S. Route 64 is four miles west of Savannah or four miles east of Adamsville; then south six miles on Tennessee State Route 22. Or access from Corinth is northeast by way of Mississippi State Route 2 and Tennessee State Route 22. Further information: Superintendent, Route 1, Box 9, Shiloh, TN 38376. Telephone (901) 689-5696.

STONES RIVER NATIONAL BATTLEFIELD

STONES RIVER NATIONAL BATTLEFIELD consists of 509 acres in central Tennessee. It was established as a national military park in 1927, was transferred from the War Department to the National Park Service in 1933, and was renamed as a national battlefield in 1960. It protects and interprets the site of one of the bloodiest and most intense conflicts of the Civil War, from December 31, 1862, to January 2, 1863. Although the battle was not a decisive victory for the North, it did result in the Confederacy giving up rich and valuable agricultural lands and withdrawing farther from central Tennessee, thereby helping to open the way for the North to invade the Deep South.

Early in 1862, Union troops captured Fort Donelson on Tennessee's Cumberland River (see Fort Donelson National Battlefield) and achieved a victory at the bloody Battle of Shiloh (see Shiloh National Military Park). In the autumn, Confederate Major General Braxton Bragg gathered his 38,000 soldiers at the central Tennessee town of Murfreesboro, to set up a winter encampment. Union Major General William Rosecrans tailed General Bragg from Kentucky south into Tennessee, and on December 26, he led the 44,000 troops of his Army of the Cumberland southeast from Nashville. His plan was to defeat Bragg's forces at Murfreesboro, on the way to seizing Chattanooga, in the southeastern corner of the state. The Union army set up its own encampment about a half-mile from the Confederates and prepared for battle.

On the frosty dawn of December 31, the Battle of Stones River (or Murfreesboro) began when the Confederates suddenly launched a powerful assault, with massive artillery and small arms fire against the Northerners' right flank, that caught the Union men off guard. As one Confederate soldier later said, "We swooped down on those Yankees like a whirl-a-gust of woodpeckers in a hailstorm." This fierce attack pushed the Union troops back and back and back again, with some difficult fighting amid dense stands of scrubby red cedar trees. By mid-morning, the Union forces had been rolled back nearly three miles, before they were able to stop the enemy's offensive and establish a new line of defense.

The key focus of the Northerners' new deployment was a small rocky knoll topped with trees, known as "the Round Forest," on which cannons were positioned, along with a force of infantrymen. Just before midday, the Confederates launched an attack. As 800 Rebels charged across a cotton

Hazen Monument (built 1863), Stones River National Battlefield, Tennessee [NPS]

field, the Union's hilltop artillery and small arms fire unleashed a deadly blizzard that killed or injured over 250 of the enemy. A few minutes later, another brigade of Southerners attempted to break through the withering barrage to reach the knoll, but these men were also beaten back with a loss of 50 percent of their numbers. Later that afternoon, two more waves of Confederate soldiers tried to brave the onslaught, amid similar staggering losses, but to no avail. With the afternoon's deafening thunder of volley after deadly volley being hurled down from the knoll and causing such a horrendous massacre, is it any wonder that the Confederates named this place "Hell's Half Acre"?

After the afternoon's final assault, the Southerners withdrew to their encampment. The next day, New Year's Day, 1863, both armies regrouped and avoided conflict, each side hoping the other would withdraw. On January 2, General Rosecrans kept his Union forces deployed in their strategically successful positions, while General Bragg was surprised to find that the Northerners had not already departed. Finally, late that afternoon, Bragg ordered 4,500 soldiers, under the command of Major General John C. Breckinridge, to launch an assault against the Union's left flank that was deployed on higher ground just east of the river. Breckinridge, who had previously been vice president of the United States, strenuously objected to Bragg's order sending his division against such well-defended high ground. But Bragg stubbornly stood by his decision.

The high ground was solidly under Union control, with infantry-men massed across the hilltop and 58 cannons stationed behind them on a rise, on the west side of the river. As the Confederates came charging across an open field, the Union soldiers opened fire, causing many Southern casualties. Yet, the survivors of these volleys kept coming. With their bayonets unsheathed, they charged on up the hill to the Union ranks, causing them to turn and dash down the far side. As the Rebels kept pursuing the men in blue, the Union artillery unleashed a thunderous barrage that halted the Confederates' attack, devastated their ranks, and then forced the survivors into dazed retreat. In just under one and a half hours, the Confederates had sustained casualties totaling more than 1,800 killed, wounded, or missing.

The next morning, the Confederates' intelligence sources revealed to General Bragg that Union reinforcements had arrived to bolster General Rosecrans' army—thus making it prudent, in Bragg's words, for "my withdrawal from so unequal a contest." Consequently, the Southerners, in a miserable, cold, soaking rainstorm, began their demoralized retreat from the battlefield that night. In a mere three days of terrible bloodletting, 23,000 soldiers had been killed, wounded, taken captive, or were missing—over 13,000 Union men and 10,000 Confederates.

Visiting the peaceful battlefield today, visitors find it difficult to imagine that such a brutal slaughter—one of the worst in the Civil War—actually occurred here. A visitor center provides interpretive exhibits, an audiovisual program, and publications. A tour drive loops through the park, with a series of stops that highlight historic points of interest. These stops include "the Round Forest"; the Hazen Brigade Monument—one of the oldest Civil War monuments; and the high ground above the river, where Union artillery finally persuaded the Confederates to give up and withdraw. The park offers a number of short trails that loop through parts of the battlefield. There are also ranger-led walks and talks, and living-history programs during the summer months and on the battle's anniversary. The National Park Service cautions visitors to be alert for poison ivy and ticks. Stones River is not safe for swimming or even wading.

Stones River National Cemetery is also located within the national battlefield.

From January to June 1863, after the Battle of Stones River, Union troops built Fortress Rosecrans, a sod-covered earthen fort to defend a military supply depot, from which arms, equipment, and food were distributed. The 200-acre fort was never fired upon, and it was finally abandoned in 1866, after the war. Today, under the care of the national battlefield, only 3,000 of the original 14,000 feet of earthworks remain; and of the four original interior redoubts, only Reboubt Brannan remains. An interpretive trail winds through this unit of the national battlefield.

Informative descriptions of the Battle of Stones River are provided in *The Struggle for Tennessee: Tupelo to Stones River* by James Street, Jr. (Time-

Life Books); and *The Battle of Stones River* by Peter Cozzens (Eastern National Park and Monument Association).

Camping is not permitted within the park, but there are camping facilities in the vicinity. A small picnic area is provided. Lodging and meals are available in Murfreesboro, Nashville, and other cities in central Tennessee. **IF YOU GO:** Access by way of I-24 is about 30 miles from downtown Nashville, to Exit 78B, then east two miles on State Route 96 and left (north) on U.S. Route 41, following signs to the battlefield entrance. Further information: Superintendent, 3501 Old Nashville Highway, Murfreesboro, TN 37129. Telephone (615) 893-9501.

TUPELO NATIONAL BATTLEFIELD

TUPELO NATIONAL BATTLEFIELD consists of one acre within the city of Tupelo, in northeastern Mississippi. Established in 1929, it was transferred from the War Department to the National Park Service in 1933, and was renamed as a national battlefield in 1961. It protects and interprets a small part of the area where a Civil War battle was fought, on July 14, 1864.

A month earlier, Confederate Major General Nathan Bedford Forrest had brilliantly led his cavalrymen in a victory over a numerically superior Union cavalry and infantry force at the Battle of Brice's Cross Roads (see Brice's Cross Roads National Battlefield Site), a few miles to the north of Tupelo, Mississippi. Union Major General William Tecumseh Sherman, in command of all Union forces between the Appalachian Mountains and the Mississippi River, had dispatched Union troops from Tennessee to block Forrest's plans to sever Sherman's vital military supply line on the Nashville-to-Chattanooga railroad.

Now Sherman ordered another sweep into Mississippi to end the threat to the railroad that was carrying war supplies to his army in Georgia. He directed Major General Andrew Jackson Smith to launch another attack against Forrest, the man he called "the very devil." In Sherman's words: "Go out and follow Forrest to the death, if it costs 10,000 lives and breaks the Treasury. There will never be peace in Tennessee until Forrest is dead."

General Smith's 14,000 Union soldiers left LaGrange, Tennessee, on July 5, under orders to "pursue Forrest on foot, devastating the land over which he passed or may pass. . . . If we do not punish Forrest and the people now, the whole effect of our past conquests will be lost."

After laying waste to a ten-mile-wide swath of northern Mississippi, the Union forces suddenly turned and headed for the largely undefended railroad town of Tupelo, to wreak havoc upon the Confederates' vital Mobile & Ohio Railroad and Forrest's cavalry base. Advance cavalrymen reached Tupelo by midday on July 13 and began tearing up stretches of the rail line. But the Confederates' military intelligence had revealed that the Union troops had suddenly turned toward Tupelo, instead of continuing south a few miles to where Forrest had gathered most of his soldiers. The 9,000 Confederates then rushed northward to challenge the men in blue. During the night, the Union soldiers dug themselves in with entrenched fortifications along the base of a ridge that extends from northwest to southwest of Tupelo. At 7 a.m., July 14, the Confederates launched a frontal assault on the Union forces. The men in gray were thrown back. A number of subsequent attacks were similarly repulsed, inflicting heavy casualties on the Rebels. As Forrest said later, the Union position was "impregnable," and after three hours of intense Union cannon and rifle fire in the morning there was a lull in the battle. Then the Confederate troops tried again, only to be thrown back once more. After the Rebels made a last unsuccessful attack in the evening, General Smith decided to withdraw, since his food and ammunition supplies were running low and many of the soldiers were suffering from the intensely muggy mid-summer heat.

On July 15, the Confederates hounded the Union troops as they withdrew northward. Another brutal clash occurred at the Federals' rear, and as Forrest was organizing these tactical efforts, he was shot in the foot. The Southerners soon ended their pursuit and withdrew, as the Northerners continued their march back into Tennessee. Casualties totaled more than 1,300 Confederates killed, wounded, or missing; the Union army suffered half that number. Even though Smith's forces had not been able to pursue Forrest "to the death," he was successful then and in subsequent encounters later that year in keeping Forrest from severing Sherman's supply line in Tennessee. In reality, the action by Smith in Mississippi succeeded in assisting Sherman's battles with the Confederate forces in Georgia—illustrating the tremendous value of well-coordinated military strategies.

IF YOU GO: Today, the national battlefield provides a number of interpretive panels and markers. The site is just over a mile east of the Natchez Trace Parkway. More complete interpretation is available at the Tupelo visitor center, at milepost 266.0 on the nearby Natchez Trace Parkway. The visitor center is open daily, except on Christmas. Lodging and meals are available in Tupelo. Access is by way of State Route 6, just over a mile west of its junction with U.S. Route 45. Further information: c/o Superintendent, Natchez Trace Parkway, 2680 Natchez Trace Parkway, Tupelo, MS 38801. Telephone (601) 680-4025 or 1-(800) 305-7417.

VICKSBURG NATIONAL MILITARY PARK

VICKSBURG NATIONAL MILITARY PARK, encompassing 1,625 acres in western Mississippi, was established in 1899 and was transferred from the War Department to the National Park Service in 1933. It protects and interprets the site of the 47-day Civil War siege that culminated in the Confederate surrender of Vicksburg, on July 4, 1863.

After Union forces, under Brigadier General Ulysses S. Grant and assisted by naval ironclad gunboats, gained control of the Tennessee and Cumberland rivers in February 1862 (see the text on Fort Donelson National Battlefield); and after Grant, then promoted to major general, defeated Confederate forces at the Battle of Shiloh, in April 1862 (see the text on Shiloh National Military Park), one of the highest priorities in the Civil War was to wrest control of the mighty Mississippi River from the Confederates.

Since the outbreak of the war in 1861, the Southerners had built a network of fortifications to help guard this vital transportation corridor. But Union forces had been capturing these outposts one after another, from Illinois to the Gulf of Mexico, except for the last two. By the end of the summer of 1862, Port Hudson in Louisiana and the larger and far more significant Vicksburg remained in Southern hands. President Abraham Lincoln characterized Vicksburg as the "key" and that "the war can never be brought to a close until that key is in our pocket." Beginning in the spring of 1862, the Union army and navy had repeatedly been trying and failing to seize this citadel. The Confederates called it the "Gibraltar of the Confederacy," named for its strategic position atop 200-foot bluffs at a sharp bend in the river.

So it was that Grant and his 45,000-man Army of the Tennessee, in October 1862, were ordered to eliminate the Confederate resistance along the lower Mississippi. Also in October, Confederate Lieutenant General John C. Pemberton was ordered to defend Vicksburg with his 40,000-man army by whatever means possible.

During the winter of 1862–1863, Grant finally implemented a plan for crossing the Mississippi from the Louisiana side, after a series of unsuccessful amphibious "bayou expeditions" through the swamps and dense forests adjacent to the river. Ferrying his troops across the Mississippi, about 30 miles downriver from Vicksburg, occurred without opposition, from April 30 to May 1. While the majority of Pemberton's forces were deployed at Vicksburg, there were smaller Confederate units scattered across the state, to the east and south of the city. Grant deemed it wise to defeat these forces first, before they could move to reinforce the Vicksburg defenders. In rapid succession, the Union troops defeated 8,000 Rebels at the Battle of Port Gibson, on May 1; forced Confederates to retreat at the Battle of Raymond, on May 12; and defeated 6,000 Rebels at the Battle of Jackson, on May 14. Grant's men then swung westward toward Vicksburg and were challenged by 23,000 of General Pemberton's soldiers who had been hastily dispatched from the city defenses to block the Union advance.

At the Battle of Champion Hill, on May 16, the Northerners relentlessly pounded against the Southerners' resolute resistance, in what a commander described as "one of the most obstinate and murderous conflicts of the war." Hour after grueling hour, "Cannons thundered 'til the heavens seemed bursting," wrote a newspaper reporter. "Dead men, and wounded, lay strewed [*sic*] everywhere." After sustaining horrendous casualties, totaling 4,000 dead, injured, and those taken captive, the Confederates finally withdrew westward

Iowa Monument, Vicksburg [David Muench]

and established a new defensive position along the Big Black River, closer to
Vicksburg. Grant's soldiers pursued and attacked them again, on May 17, this
time forcing them back to Vicksburg's fortifications. The next day, the Union
forces reached Vicksburg.

On May 19, the Northerners launched frontal attacks on Vicksburg,
in an unsuccessful attempt to break through the Confederate defenses. On
May 22, they tried again to attack the defensive earthworks, with a series of
massed infantry assaults that were successfully repulsed by the defenders. General Grant finally gave the order to begin a formal siege of the city that was to
continue without letup until July 4. While batteries of cannons were emplaced
and bombarded the Rebel fortifications and city from land, Rear Admiral
David D. Porter's naval ironclad gunboats hammered at the city from the river.
Day and night the artillery shelling thunderously poured down its destruction
upon the city. Communications were severed. Food and other needed domestic and military supplies were blocked. Confederate reinforcements were kept
away. And to assure the Union army's success, reinforcements were called in—
by the end of June, Grant's military strength had swelled to more than 70,000
soldiers.

In an effort to avoid the relentless and dangerous artillery explosions
that rained down on the city, residents abandoned their homes and sought
shelter in makeshift caves dug into the hills. By the end of June, Confederate
soldiers were forced to live largely on dried beans, peas, and pea bread, supplemented by small quantities of mule meat. Many residents fared even more
poorly. Finally, General Pemberton recognized the seriousness of his plight and
that he really had little choice but to seek a negotiated surrender.

Consequently, on July 3, he agreed to meet with General Grant. As the Union leader had done at Fort Donelson, he demanded nothing less than unconditional surrender. He soon relented slightly, in the face of Pemberton's refusal to surrender without some sort of concession. Finally, on the morning of July 4, the nearly 30,000 Confederates moved out of their defenses and stacked their firearms, as the Stars and Stripes replaced the Confederate flag over the county courthouse.

Five days later, Port Hudson also surrendered, so that the entire length of the Mississippi was now under Union control—thereby splitting the Confederacy, with most of Louisiana, Arkansas, and Texas to the west severed from the eight other Confederate states. Ulysses S. Grant was an instant hero in the North, lifting him ultimately to the Presidency of the United States. The Vicksburg victory, furthermore, coincided with another major Union triumph—the Battle of Gettysburg in Pennsylvania (see Gettysburg National Military Park). Not only were these two battles major triumphs for the Federal forces, but taken together, they produced a profound psychological turning point in the Civil War.

Today, a visitor center provides interpretive exhibits, an audiovisual program, and publications. The park's 16-mile, self-guided tour drive (a tape tour is available at the visitor center) winds through the battlefield. A series of stops highlights many of the historically significant places and events. They include the Shirley House, the only remaining Civil War-era building in the park, and the Third Louisiana Redan, one of the key Confederate fortifications. Other stops include the site of the Stockade Redan attack; Fort Hill; the Great Redoubt; Fort Garrott, near the south end of the park; and Hovey's Approach, a restored portion of two Union approach trenches. Among the many monuments erected in the park are the imposing Greek Revival-style Illinois Monument; the Mississippi Monument; and the Naval Monument, a tall obelisk commemorating the Union naval support that was indispensable to Grant's capture of Vicksburg. The Vicksburg National Cemetery is within the park. Visitors walking in the park are cautioned to be alert for poison ivy and fire ants, the latter capable of inflicting a painful bite. The park is open daily, except on Christmas.

Four especially informative publications are: *The Vicksburg Campaign* (3 volumes) by Edwin C. Bearss (Morningside); *Vicksburg: 47 Days of Siege* by A.A. Hoehling (Stackpole Books); *Vicksburg: Southern City Under Siege* (Historic New Orleans Collection); and *War on the Mississippi: Grant's Vicksburg Campaign* by Jerry Korn (Time-Life Books).

IF YOU GO: Camping is not permitted in the park, but there is a picnic area. Lodging and meals are available along Clay Street, in Vicksburg, just outside the park. Access is by way of Clay Street (U.S. Route 80), which is reached from the W. Clay Street exit 4-B from I-20. Further information: Superintendent, 3201 Clay St., Vicksburg, MS 39180. Telephone (601) 636-0583.

WILSON'S CREEK NATIONAL BATTLEFIELD

WILSON'S CREEK NATIONAL BATTLEFIELD, consisting of 1,750 acres in southwestern Missouri, was established as a national battlefield park in 1960 and renamed as a national battlefield in 1970. It protects and interprets the site of the first major Civil War battle west of the Mississippi, on August 10, 1861.

After the defeat of the Union forces at the Battle of First Manassas (Bull Run), in Virginia, on July 21, 1861 (see Manassas National Battlefield Park), President Abraham Lincoln signed an act of Congress ordering the creation of a one-million-man Army of the Potomac, under the command of newly appointed Major General George B. McClellan.

Missouri was one of three border states (along with Kentucky and Maryland) that teetered between remaining loyal to the Union and seceding to join the Confederacy. Several key transportation routes connected Missouri with the west coast, including the Santa Fe and Oregon trails, and significant navigable rivers, notably the Missouri and Mississippi, flowed through or adjacent to the state—giving it prominent strategic importance. Consequently, both the North and the South considered Missouri of great value.

There were sizable military units in Missouri as the Civil War got under way—Union troops and pro-Confederate soldiers were both prepared to take up arms and fight. And fight they did. On the night of August 9–10, 1861, Brigadier General Nathaniel Lyon, without obtaining troop reinforcements that he desired from St. Louis, opted to risk sending his approximately 6,000 men against the 12,000 Confederates, who were under the command of Brigadier General Benjamin McCulloch. The pending battle was about ten miles from the town of Springfield, in the southwestern corner of the state, where there was strong support for seceding from the Union and joining the Confederacy.

Lyon divided his troops into two units—4,000 of his own men and another 1,200 under Colonel Franz Sigel. Lyon's strategy was to send Sigel's soldiers around the Confederates' right flank and attack from the rear. Meanwhile, he would direct his own unit to attack from the north. The object was to catch the Confederates by surprise with an assault at 5 a.m., in the half-light of dawn. Sigel's attack from the south was to be coordinated with Lyon's, so that the Rebels would be crushed in a vise, while they were being awakened from their sleep.

The element of surprise worked well and the Union troops rushed on to seize and occupy the top of a ridge that came to be known as Bloody Hill. At the southern end of the battlefield, meanwhile, Sigel's force fell apart when the men mistook the Confederacy's Third Louisiana unit for Union reinforcements of the First Iowa Infantry, which were dressed in gray, rather than the usual Union blue. Consequently Sigel's troops were holding their weapons fire, when suddenly the enemy opened fire with a massive and brutal volley that left many casualties as the survivors fled. With the Union troops to the south

Wilson's Creek National Battlefield, Missouri [U.S. Dept. of the
Interior/NPS/Wilson's Creek National Battlefield]

no longer a threat, the Confederate soldiers now concentrated all their attention upon Lyon's troops on Bloody Hill.

For a while, the Union men held their lines securely on the ridgetop.
A regiment of Texas cavalrymen rode their horses westward around Lyon's
troops' right flank, distracting the Union men just long enough, in the midst
of the raging battle of gunfire, to give the Confederate infantrymen a chance
to back off and reorganize for another fierce assault. This time, the Southerners unleashed some 6,000 soldiers against the hill defenders. Initially, the
Union position held, in the face of intense, up-close combat and a blizzard of
bullets. Casualties dropped all over the hill, amid the terrifying onslaught.
Again and again, the Confederates threw themselves up the slope in an effort
to dislodge the greatly outnumbered Northerners. For a time, the artillery and
rifle fire from the summit forced the Southerners to retreat and reorganize for
another try.

Unfortunately for the Union troops, their commander, General
Lyons, who had so effectively and courageously spirited his men into battle
against great odds and was leading them in a charge against the enemy, was
suddenly shot and killed. In addition, Union ammunition supplies were running low. And the soldiers themselves were simply exhausted from the rigors of
the hours of battle since dawn and from the oppressive heat and humidity.
The Union men finally gave up Bloody Hill, where so many lives were lost,
and retreated. Union casualties totaled around 1,300 killed, wounded, and

missing, and the Confederate losses totaled over 1,200. While the Confederate sympathizers triumphed over the Union soldiers that day, Missouri ultimately remained loyal to the Union.

Today, a visitor center provides interpretive exhibits, an audiovisual program, and publications. A 4.9-mile, self-guided drive loops through the park, along which are interpretive stops, such as Bloody Hill; Gibson's Mill, near which the Union troops staged their successful dawn attack on the sleeping Confederates; and the Ray House. The latter building, dating from 1852, is the only structure in the park that survives from the time of the Civil War battle. It is named for John A. Ray, a U.S. postmaster prior to and during the Civil War. It also served as a Confederate hospital during and after this battle.

The park offers guided tours seasonally of the Ray House and Bloody Hill, and there are also living-history demonstrations in the spring, summer, and autumn. A number of trails lead to or connect various historic points of interest. The national battlefield is open daily, except on Thanksgiving, Christmas, and New Year's Day.

IF YOU GO: Camping is not allowed in the park, but there is a picnic area. Lodging and meals are available in Springfield, and meals in Republic. Access from I-44 is by way of Exit 70, south on State Route MM, across U.S. Route 60 and about three-quarters-of-a-mile to State Route ZZ, and finally a left turn (east) onto Farm Road 182 to the battlefield entrance. Further information: Superintendent, Route 2, Box 75, Republic, MO 65738 Telephone (417) 732-2662.

PART 6

TWENTIETH-CENTURY MILITARY PARKS

KOREAN WAR VETERANS MEMORIAL

KOREAN WAR VETERANS MEMORIAL, consisting of just over two acres near the Lincoln Memorial, in Washington, D.C., was authorized by the U.S. Congress in 1986 and dedicated in 1995. It commemorates the commitment and sacrifice of many Americans and individuals from other countries who served the cause of freedom in the defense of the Republic of South Korea in the Korean War, which was fought from 1950 to 1953.

On June 25, 1950, the North Korean army suddenly crossed the 38th Parallel into South Korea. Following the United Nations Security Council's approval of dispatching troops to oppose the military aggression, 15 countries sent their forces, and five others provided medical support. The United States supplied 90 percent of the U.N. troop strength, and American generals provided overall leadership.

During the three years, nearly a million Chinese communist soldiers aided the North Koreans, while the Soviet Union provided money and supplies for North Korea. More than 56,000 U.S. military personnel lost their lives during the war. Of those, more than 33,000 were listed as killed in action, while another 2,700 died in captivity, and 8,000 U.S. soldiers were listed as missing in action. Another 103,000 soldiers were wounded. The war finally ended with the signing of the armistice on July 27, 1953, which established the boundary between South and North Korea.

The design concept for the Korean War Veterans Memorial was the result of a national competition and was produced in 1989 by a group of architects from State College, Pennsylvania. In 1991, the U.S. Army Corps of Engineers chose Cooper-Lecky Architects, of Washington, D.C., to complete the memorial. Sculptor Frank Gaylord, of Barre, Vermont, created the 19 seven-foot-tall stainless steel sculptures of foot soldiers that are "walking" across the field of service toward a flagpole, from which waves the Stars and Stripes. The figures represent Caucasian, African American, Hispanic, Asian,

Korean War Veterans Memorial, Washington, D.C. [Vicki Paris/NPCA]

and Native American soldiers; and 14 represent the U.S. Army, three the U.S. Marine Corps, one U.S. Navy Medic, and one U.S. Air Forward Observer.

A polished granite wall, created by Louis Nelson Associates of New York City, presents a mural of etched intermingled photographic images of 2,500 soldiers that were derived from archival records of the war. Beyond the flagpole is a grove of linden trees framing the 30-foot-diameter, circular Pool of Remembrance—a tranquil place for contemplative thought and relaxation. **IF YOU GO:** The memorial is staffed by park rangers daily, except on Christmas. Interpretive publications are available at the bookshop on the chamber level of the Lincoln Memorial, which is a short walk from the Korean War memorial. See the texts on the Lincoln Memorial and nearby Vietnam Veterans Memorial for access to this part of The Mall. Further information: Korean War Veterans Memorial, Superintendent, National Capital Parks-Central, 900 Ohio Drive, SW, Washington, DC 20240.

MANZANAR NATIONAL HISTORIC SITE

MANZANAR NATIONAL HISTORIC SITE, consisting of 500 acres in the Owens Valley of eastern California, was established in 1992 to protect and interpret one of the ten World War II relocation camps, the Manzanar War Relocation Center, in which Japanese-American citizens and legal resident aliens were interned from 1942 to 1945 by the U.S. government.

On February 19, 1942, President Franklin D. Roosevelt signed an executive order providing for the mandatory "evacuation" of more than 110,000 Japanese-Americans residing on the West Coast, of whom over 60 percent were American citizens. At its peak of operation, Manzanar held captive more than 10,000 people.

While the view of the eastern face of the Sierra Nevada is highly scenic from the Owens Valley, Manzanar is in the "rain-shadow" of the mountain range and is, therefore, in a sandy, extremely arid, wind-blown desert region. The camp itself consisted of 576 one-story, 20-by-100-foot hastily erected barracks divided into 36 blocks. Each barrack was partitioned into either four or five rooms. An entire family, including children, was often crammed into either a 20-by-20-foot or 20-by-24-foot room. Other buildings in each block included laundry and ironing rooms, the large mess hall, showers, and latrines. The camp was surrounded by barbed-wire fencing and guard towers manned by sentries. Blowing dust penetrated everywhere, while evacuees endured baking heat in summer and bitter cold in winter. Life was utterly miserable, and during those war years, there was never any assurance that this hell-on-earth would ever come to an end.

Today, the site contains three historic structures: a police post, a sentry post, and a large structure that once served as the camp's gymnasium and auditorium. Some of the camp's streets can still be seen. There are some remnants of former rock gardens, many building foundations, and the camp cemetery.

In 1980, Congress set up a Commission on Wartime Relocation and Internment of Civilians to review the circumstances that led to the issuance of the executive order in 1942, to examine the order's impact upon U.S. citizens and permanent resident aliens, and to make recommendations. The commission's report, *Personal Justice Denied*, stated that:

> The personal injustice of excluding, removing, and detaining loyal American citizens is manifest. Such events are extraordinary and unique in American history.

In 1988, President Ronald Reagan signed legislation that offered an apology and provided for the payment of $20,000 to each individual interned at centers such as Manzanar. In the words of David J. Simon, of the National Parks and Conservation Association, "Manzanar is a symbolic reminder that a nation of laws needs constantly to honor the concept of freedom and the rights of its citizens."

The park is under development and has no facilities or staff on site. The grounds, privately owned, are open during daylight hours only. No overnight camping is allowed. Camp roads are rough, and driving on site can result in getting stuck in washes or sandpits. Lodging and meals are available in Lone Pine.
IF YOU GO: The site is located adjacent to U.S. Route 395, five miles south of Independence and ten miles north of Lone Pine. Further information: Superintendent, P.O. Box 426, Independence, CA 93526. Telephone (619) 878-2932.

USS *ARIZONA* MEMORIAL

USS *ARIZONA* MEMORIAL, located in Pearl Harbor, on the Island of O'ahu, Hawai'i, was established in 1980. It is a floating memorial marking the place where the USS *Arizona* was sunk during the Japanese air attack on December 7, 1941. The site is owned by the U.S. Navy and is administered by the National Park Service.

When 343 Japanese bombers, fighters, and torpedo aircraft suddenly swooped in and launched an assault upon the U.S. naval base at Pearl
Harbor, at 7:55 a.m., the battleships, destroyers, and other warships of the
Pacific Fleet were strung out in the harbor, anchored in pairs side by side. As
bombs and aerial torpedoes fell on the ships, the Japanese had perfect targets.
The element of surprise was complete, in the early morning mist. It was a full
three minutes before the naval air commander broadcast the blunt announce-
ment: "AIR RAID, PEARL HARBOR—THIS IS NO DRILL."

The warlords of Japan had feared the U.S. naval fleet could hinder
their plans of conquest. Consequently, without issuing a declaration of war,
the Japanese launched their surprise assault to destroy what they viewed as the
menacing fleet of warships based halfway across the Pacific Ocean toward Asia.
The United States reacted swiftly—on December 8, Congress declared war on
Japan. This action, in turn, caused Germany and Italy to declare war on the
United States, on December 11. Thus was the United States suddenly thrust
right into the middle of the rapidly growing global conflict.

On that bloody day, described by President Franklin D. Roosevelt as
"a day that shall live in infamy," the Japanese attack killed 2,403 American
sailors, marines, soldiers, and civilians, and wounded 1,178 others. The battle-
ship USS *Arizona* was bombed beyond the possibility of repair; the *Oklahoma*
was blown apart and capsized; four other battleships were sent to the bottom
of the harbor or were deliberately run aground to keep them from sinking,
and three destroyers and other ships were seriously damaged.

Fortunately, three of the Pacific Fleet's aircraft carriers, the *Enterprise*,
Lexington, and *Saratoga*, were not anchored in Pearl Harbor that fateful morning, but were out at sea. Eventually, all except two of the targeted battleships
were salvaged, repaired, and returned to military service. As for the USS
Arizona, it and the remains of its 1,177-man crew and officers lie at the bottom
of the harbor, directly beneath the moored memorial. Inside the memorial
structure, visitors view interpretive exhibits and programs about the attack.

The U.S. Navy provides boat access from Halawa Landing to the
memorial. The site is open daily, except on Thanksgiving, Christmas, and New
Year's Day. Lodging and meals are available nearby at the Honolulu
International Airport and in Honolulu.

IF YOU GO: Access from Waikiki and Honolulu is west by way of highway
H-1, passing the airport and taking the Arizona Memorial/Stadium exit. There
is also bus service (#20) from Waikiki and Honolulu. Further information:
Superintendent, One Arizona Memorial Place, Honolulu, HI 96818.
Telephone (808) 422-2771.

VIETNAM VETERANS MEMORIAL

VIETNAM VETERANS MEMORIAL, consisting of two acres at the western
end of the Constitution Gardens, just to the northeast of the Lincoln
Memorial, in Washington, D.C., was authorized by Congress in 1980 to

honor all the men and women of the Armed Services of the United States who served in the Vietnam War from 1963 to 1973. The two 246.75-foot-long walls of polished black granite from India extend outward like great enveloping triangular wings, from a 125°, 12-foot angle at the vertex. The walls are inscribed with 58,132 names of the persons who died or remain missing.

The memorial was designed by Maya Ying Lin, the winner of a national competition. At the time, she was a 21-year-old architectural student at Yale University. Her goal was to create a peaceful, contemplative place—a park within a park. The mirrored surface of the granite reflects the surroundings of trees and monuments, as well as the persons reading the inscribed names.

In January 1982, the decision was made to add a figurative bronze sculpture portraying American soldiers in Vietnam. Washington, D.C., sculptor Frederick Hart designed the life-size statue, The Three Servicemen, that was completed in 1984. The $7 million needed to create the Vietnam Veterans Memorial was obtained entirely from private contributions—from 275,000 individuals and from corporations, foundations, veterans groups, and other organizations.

Rangers at the memorial kiosk provide directions and computer printouts with such information as a soldier's date of birth, date of casualty, and branch of military service. Permits are required for holding First Amendment and other activities. The memorial is open for visitation daily.
IF YOU GO: Lodging and meals are available in Washington, D.C., and adjacent Virginia and Maryland. Advance hotel reservations are highly recommended during the popular tourist seasons. The memorial is located adjacent to Constitution Avenue and 23rd Street, NW. The Tourmobile and The Old Town Trolley offer service to the memorial. The nearest Metro subway stop is at Foggy Bottom station, on the Blue and Orange lines, at 23rd and I ('Eye') streets, NW. Further information: Superintendent, National Capital Parks-Central, 900 Ohio Dr., SW, Washington, DC 20242. Telephone (202) 485-9880.

Vietnam Veterans Memorial, Washington, DC [NPS]

War in the Pacific National Historical Park [William Clark/NPS]

WAR IN THE PACIFIC NATIONAL HISTORICAL PARK

WAR IN THE PACIFIC NATIONAL HISTORICAL PARK, comprising 1,960 acres in seven separate units, is located in or near the villages of Asan, Piti, and Agat, on the west side of the Island of Guam, in the North Mariana Islands in the Western Pacific Ocean. The park was established in 1978 "to commemorate the bravery and sacrifice of those participating in the campaigns of the Pacific Theater of World War II and to conserve and interpret outstanding natural, scenic, and historic values and objects on the island of Guam."

In 1944, these sites were blood-soaked battlefields where American and Japanese marines and soldiers fought. By visiting each park unit, you can trace the 21-day battle that began on the beaches, spread inland into Guam's rugged terrain, and swept across the island. Memorials dedicated to the Chamorro people and the American armed forces, honoring those who served and lost their lives during the war years on Guam, are located in the park.

The T. Stell Newman Visitor Center, located on Marine Drive in Asan, presents museum exhibits, war memorabilia, and audio-visual programs interpreting the causes and effects of the outbreak of the Pacific war leading up to the end of World War II. Special programs on the war years of Guam and Saipan are shown upon request. Park rangers are available to assist with any questions visitors may have.

Guam's warm climate, sandy beaches, and turquoise waters beckon visitors to discover the island's rich heritage. Guam offers recreational opportunities that include hiking historic trails, wind surfing, fishing, snorkeling, and scuba diving.

The Arizona Memorial Museum Association, a nonprofit organization whose purpose is to assist the interpretive programs of the park, operates a bookstore with educational materials on the Pacific war, Guam, and Micronesia. This sales outlet is in the visitor center.

IF YOU GO: Camping is not permitted, but the park does provide picnic facilities. Lodging and meals are available nearby. Further information: Superintendent, P.O. Box FA, Agana, Guam 96932. Telephone (671) 472-7240.

PART 7

PARKS CELEBRATING U.S. PRESIDENTS

ABRAHAM LINCOLN BIRTHPLACE NATIONAL HISTORIC SITE

ABRAHAM LINCOLN BIRTHPLACE NATIONAL HISTORIC SITE, consisting of 116 acres in the richly forested hills of central Kentucky, was established as a national park under the War Department in 1916, was transferred to the National Park Service in 1933, and was renamed as a national historic site in 1959. It commemorates the birth and birthplace of the sixteenth president of the United States.

The one-room log cabin that is on exhibit was originally thought to have been the structure in which Lincoln was born, on February 12, 1809. Subsequent research has cast some doubt on the validity of that assumption. Yet, the nineteenth-century cabin is at least representative of the Lincoln family home. This humble little cabin is preserved at Lincoln's Sinking Spring Farm birthplace, enshrined within a contrastingly imposing marble-and-granite neoclassical memorial building that was completed in 1911. As a visitor views this peaceful rural area, it seems hard to believe that a man born into such a humble environment could eventually become the president of the United States—the man who would lead this nation through the hostilities and trauma of civil war and would initiate the process of binding up the nation's wounds toward a "just and lasting peace."

A visitor center at the site provides interpretive exhibits, programs, and publications on Abraham Lincoln. There are hiking trails that loop through the site, inviting visitors to explore the historic farm area—the enshrined cabin, Sinking Spring which provided water for the Lincoln family, and some of the beautiful forest. Among the trees are white and northern red oaks, shagbark hickory, black walnut, and sassafras. Mammals include red foxes, raccoons, opossums, rabbits, and gray squirrels. The many species of birds include red-headed and other woodpeckers, blue jays, tufted titmice, white-breasted nuthatches, several kinds of wrens, wood thrushes, numerous species of warblers that migrate through in spring and autumn, cardinals, and American goldfinches.

Abraham Lincoln Birthplace National Historic Site, Kentucky [NPS]

While camping is not permitted within the site, a picnic area is provided, adjacent to an environmental study area. Lodging and meals are available in Hodgenville, Elizabethtown, and other communities in the surrounding area.

An excellent publication on this and other National Park System units commemorating the life and accomplishments of Abraham Lincoln is *Lincoln Parks: The Story Behind the Scenery®* by Larry Waldron (KC Publications). (See also Lincoln Boyhood National Memorial, Lincoln Home National Historic Site, Ford's Theatre, and the Lincoln Memorial.)

IF YOU GO: Access to the site, which is open daily except on Thanksgiving and Christmas, is three miles south of Hodgenville by way of U.S. Route 31E/State Route 61; and is 12 miles south of the junction of routes 31E/61, I-65, and U.S. Route 62. The site is about 50 miles northeast of Mammoth Cave National Park. Further information: Superintendent, 2995 Lincoln Farm Road, Hodgenville, KY 42748. Telephone (502) 358-3137.

ADAMS NATIONAL HISTORIC SITE

ADAMS NATIONAL HISTORIC SITE, comprising nearly 10 acres in Quincy, Massachusetts, was established as the Adams Mansion National Historic Site in 1946 and changed to its present name in 1952. It protects and interprets the home of the second and sixth presidents of the United States— John Adams and John Quincy Adams, and other members of this illustrious family. The site also includes the two houses that were the birthplaces of the two presidents.

Peacefield, as John Adams called the home, or The Old House, as referred to by other family members, was originally a small structure dating from 1731. John and his wife, Abigail, bought the house in 1787 and expand-

Adams National Historic Site, Massachusetts [David Muench]

ed it to nearly twice the size. After being occupied by four generations of scholarly, distinguished Adamses, until 1927, it was generously given to the National Park Service, complete with its furnishings and outstanding collections of books, documents, and porcelain.

The site has a visitor center that provides interpretive exhibits, programs, and publications. And it is here that visitors obtain passes to tour the three historic buildings (the tour includes trolley transportation from the visitor center to each place). The center is closed on the weekends from November 11 through April 18, but is otherwise open daily. Lodging and meals are available in Quincy, Boston, and other eastern Massachusetts cities. **IF YOU GO:** Access from Boston is by way of I-93 south, the Route 3 South exit, and proceeding on Route 3 to the Washington Street exit; then following signs to the Quincy "T" Station, which route becomes the Burgin Parkway and proceeding through six sets of traffic lights; at the seventh light, a right turn onto Dimmock Street and going one block, then right onto Hancock Street to the visitor center at 1250 Hancock—located in the Galleria at Presidents Place (parking at the rear of the building, left off Hancock). Further information: Superintendent, P.O. Box 531, Quincy, MA 02269. Telephone (617) 770-1175.

ANDREW JOHNSON NATIONAL HISTORIC SITE

ANDREW JOHNSON NATIONAL HISTORIC SITE, consisting of 16 acres in Greeneville, Tennessee, was established as a national monument in 1935 and changed to a national historic site in 1963. It protects and interprets the two homes and the tailor's shop of the 17th president of the United States, who served from 1865–1869. The site also includes the Andrew Johnson National Cemetery, in which the former president is buried.

A few hours after President Abraham Lincoln died from an assassin's bullet, on April 15, 1865, Andrew Johnson was sworn in as president. Born in 1808, in Raleigh, North Carolina, Andrew was only four years old when his father died. To help support the family, he skipped school and at an early age became a tailor's apprentice. When he was 17, the family moved to the eastern Tennessee town of Greeneville, where he became a successful tailor. The following year, he met and married Eliza McCardle.

Although Johnson received virtually no formal education, his wife and friends took turns reading books to him while he worked at his trade. He joined a debating society at Greeneville College, which enhanced his public speaking ability and which subsequently greatly benefited his career in politics.

At the age of 20, Johnson was elected to serve as an alderman in Greeneville. At 25, Johnson was elected the town's mayor, and then served as representative and then as a senator in the Tennessee state legislature. At the age of 34, his political rise continued with election to the first of five terms in the U.S. House of Representatives. From the age of 44, he served two terms as governor of Tennessee. Then at 48, he moved another rung up the political ladder, to occupy a seat in the U.S. Senate.

While a senator in 1860, he delivered a major speech on the Senate floor. Even though he was a Southern slaveholder, he spoke out forcefully against the secession of the Southern proslavery states from the Union. As a result of his support for maintaining the Union and against the "rebellious" secessionist actions of the South, including his own state of Tennessee, President Lincoln named Johnson as a special advisor during the Civil War on Southern affairs. After Union forces had recovered much of Tennessee from Confederate control, the president appointed Johnson to be that state's military governor. He then became Lincoln's vice-president, and at the age of 56 took over the presidency after Lincoln was assassinated.

As president, Johnson was faced with the enormous challenge of trying to lead the nation in its post-Civil War healing and rebuilding. Unfortunately, his attempts to bring the South back into the Union as if those states had never seceded were strongly opposed by Congress, which even voted to block giving seats to elected representatives. The two-thirds majority of Congress also overrode a number of presidential vetoes, thereby authorizing the right of former Southern slaves to vote and establishing military rule over the South.

This battle between Congress and the White House led to impeachment proceedings against President Johnson—a strategy that failed by only a single vote in the Senate's trial. Ironically, after Andrew Johnson's presidency, he was elected as a U.S. Senator, where he served for six months, until his death on July 31, 1875.

An informative reference is *The Presidency of Andrew Johnson* by Albert Castel (The Regents Press of Kansas).

The national historic site provides a visitor center, located at College and Depot streets. It presents interpretive exhibits, programs, and publications, and it also contains Johnson's tailor's shop. Across College Street is the house where he lived from his twenties to age 42. The red-brick house, the Homestead, which was his home from then until his death, is located on Main Street, between Summer and McKee streets. Guided interpretive tours are provided at the Homestead. The Andrew Johnson National Cemetery, where Johnson's grave is located, is just off U.S. Route 321, on Monument Avenue. **IF YOU GO:** Lodging and meals are available in Greeneville. Access to the site is from several directions, including from I-81 southbound by way of State Route 70; from I-81 northbound by way of U.S. Route 11E; or from I-40 at Newport, TN, by way of U.S. Route 321. The site is open daily, except on Christmas. Further information: Superintendent, P.O. Box 1088, Greeneville, TN 37744. Telephone (423) 638-3551.

EISENHOWER NATIONAL HISTORIC SITE

EISENHOWER NATIONAL HISTORIC SITE, consisting of 690 acres near Gettysburg, Pennsylvania, was established in 1967 to protect the home of the 34th president of the United States, serving from 1953 to 1961, and interpret his life and work.

Dwight David Eisenhower was born in 1890. A graduate of West Point, he served in the Philippines under General Douglas MacArthur in the 1930s. During World War II, he commanded the Allied landing in North Africa in 1942. As the supreme Allied commander in Europe, he led the successful invasion of Normandy, France, against the German military in 1944. In 1945, General Eisenhower accepted the German surrender, ending World War II in Europe.

Resigning from his heroic military service, Eisenhower won the Republican party's nomination and was elected president in 1952. As president, Eisenhower ended the Korean War, launched the space program, and created the nation's Interstate Highway system. He sought to end the Cold

Eisenhower National Historic Site, Gettysburg, Pennsylvania [NPS]

War only to have improved relations with the Soviet Union dashed with the ill-fated U-2 spy plane incident.

From 1955, the Gettysburg farm was a treasured retreat for President and Mrs. Eisenhower during his presidency, with world leaders such as De Gaulle, Churchill, and Krushchev visiting. It was their retirement home after leaving The White House.

Visitors begin interpretive tours from the Eisenhower Tour Center, in the lobby of the Gettysburg National Military Park visitor center. A shuttle service takes visitors to the farm, where a brief orientation program and exhibits are available, prior to a self-guiding tour of the home and grounds. The site is open daily from April through October, and is closed Mondays and Tuesdays from November through March; on Thanksgiving, Christmas, and New Year's Day; and during four weeks in winter.

An informative publication is *Eisenhower, Soldier and President* by Stephen E. Ambrose (Simon and Schuster).

IF YOU GO: Lodging and meals are available in Gettysburg and other communities in the area. Access to Gettysburg National Military Park visitor center is by way of State Route 134 (Taneytown Rd.), near its junction with U.S. Business Route 15. Further information: Eisenhower National Historic Site, 97 Taneytown Rd., Gettysburg, PA 17325. Telephone (717) 338-9114.

FORD'S THEATRE NATIONAL HISTORIC SITE

FORD'S THEATRE NATIONAL HISTORIC SITE, consisting of one-third of an acre at 511 and 516 Tenth Street, NW, in downtown Washington, D.C., was established to protect and interpret the theater where Abraham Lincoln, the 16th president of the United States, was shot by an assassin on the evening of April 14, 1865; and the house across the street where he died the following morning. The federal government purchased the theater building in 1866 and the house where Lincoln died in 1896. Both structures were transferred to the National Park Service in 1933 and were combined as Ford's Theatre National Historic Site in 1970.

The theater has since been carefully restored to its appearance on that fateful night in 1865, when the president was shot at point-blank range in the back of his head by John Wilkes Booth, a Confederate sympathizer who favored slavery. Lincoln and his wife, Mary, had been watching the play, *Our American Cousin.*

Not only is the theater now a museum, but it is an active facility where the nonprofit Ford's Theatre Society performs ethnically and culturally varied, contemporary plays that reflect America's diversity. The basement of the theater building contains interpretive exhibits on Lincoln's life and accomplishments, and a bookstore.

The William Petersen house across the street from the theater is where the president was taken after being mortally wounded. The president's wife, son Robert, and most of Lincoln's cabinet members spent the night there, while the Secretary of War interrogated witnesses to the shooting. At 7:22 a.m., April 15, Abraham Lincoln died, just six days after the Confederacy's General Robert E. Lee surrendered to U.S. General Ulysses S. Grant at Appomattox Court House, in Virginia, thus finally bringing the "just and lasting peace" that President Lincoln had so fervently sought.

Booth, meanwhile, escaped from the theater, breaking a leg on his way, and fled south into Virginia, where he was caught and killed on April 26.

An excellent publication on this and other National Park System units commemorating the life and accomplishments of Abraham Lincoln is *Lincoln Parks: The Story Behind the Scenery®* by Larry Waldron (KC Publications). (See also Abraham Lincoln Birthplace National Historic Site, Lincoln Boyhood National Memorial, Lincoln Home National Historic Site, and the Lincoln Memorial.)

Excellent 15-minute interpretive talks on the assassination and the theater are presented from the stage daily by the National Park Service. The theater is not open to visitors when the stage is being prepared for a play, when there are rehearsals, or during matinee performances. For information on performances and tickets, the box-office phone is (202) 347-4833. The Lincoln Museum exhibits are open daily, except on Christmas.

Lodging and meals are abundantly available in the Washington metropolitan area. Advance reservations for lodging are highly recommended, especially during the popular tourist seasons. Parking (fee) is available nearby.
IF YOU GO: Further information: Superintendent, National Capital Parks—Central, 900 Ohio Dr., SW, Washington, DC 20242. Telephone (202) 426-6924.

FRANKLIN DELANO ROOSEVELT MEMORIAL

FRANKLIN DELANO ROOSEVELT MEMORIAL is located on seven-and-a-half acres by the Tidal Basin in West Potomac Park, in Washington, D.C. It was dedicated in 1997 to honor the accomplishments of the 32nd president of the United States (1933–1945). The memorial contains four outdoor galleries that portray FDR's four terms in office. Granite walls, inscriptions, bronze sculptures, waterfalls, and ornamental landscaping combine to give visitors a feeling of being in a secluded garden. Among the inscriptions are Roosevelt's words on the environment: "Men and nature must work hand in hand. The throwing out of balance of the resources of nature throws out of balance also the lives of man."
IF YOU GO: Access to the FDR Memorial is by way of Indendence Avenue (between the Washington Monument and the Lincoln Memorial), following signs to the site on the west bank of the Tidal Basin. There is limited parking in the vicinity. The Tourmobile provides transportation. The closest Metro subway stop is Smithsonian on the Orange and Blue lines. Further information: Superintendent, National Capital Parks-Central, 900 Ohio Dr., SW, Washington, D.C. 20242. Telephone (202) 426-6841.

GENERAL GRANT NATIONAL MEMORIAL

GENERAL GRANT NATIONAL MEMORIAL, consisting of three-fourths of an acre at West 122nd Street and Riverside Drive, at the northern end of Manhattan in New York City, is a mausoleum that was designed by John H. Duncan. It was dedicated in 1897, was transferred to the federal government in 1958, and was added to the National Park System in 1959. In 1966, Allyn Cox created a series of murals portraying General Ulysses S. Grant's Union military triumphs over Confederate forces that brought about the end of the Civil War. It was Grant who accepted Lee's surrender at Appomattox, in April 1865. Grant's Tomb is the largest mausoleum in the country. The imposing granite structure rises 150 feet high and overlooks the Hudson River from Riverside Park.

Grant was also the 18th president of the United States, serving from 1869 to 1877. Among his acts at the White House was signing into law the bill establishing Yellowstone—the world's first national park—on March 1, 1872. (See also Ulysses S. Grant National Historic Site.)

The memorial presents interpretive exhibits and talks. It is open Wednesdays through Sundays, and is closed on Thanksgiving, Christmas, and New Year's Day, as well as on certain Wednesdays that follow a national holiday on a Monday or Tuesday.

IF YOU GO: Lodging and meals are available in New York City and the surrounding area. Access by private motor vehicle is by way of the Henry Hudson Parkway, with parking near the memorial. The IRT #1 subway stops at 116th and 125th streets; and there is bus service by way of 125th Street. Further information: Superintendent, 122nd St. and Riverside Dr., New York, NY 10027. Telephone (212) 666-1640.

GEORGE WASHINGTON BIRTHPLACE NATIONAL MONUMENT

GEORGE WASHINGTON BIRTHPLACE NATIONAL MONUMENT encompasses 538 acres along the shore of Popes Creek, a tributary of the lower Potomac River, in Virginia. It was established in 1930 to protect and interpret the eighteenth-century tobacco farm where the celebrated Revolutionary War general and first president of the United States was born and spent his childhood. The park features a mansion and gardens, as well as Washington family tombs.

The national monument offers interpretive exhibits, programs and tours. There are also trails and self-guided nature walks. The National Park Service cautions visitors to be alert for ticks. Picnicking is permitted, but camping is not. Campsites are provided six miles from the monument, at Westmoreland State Park. The monument is open daily, except on Christmas and New Year's Day.

IF YOU GO: Lodging and meals are available in Fredericksburg and other communities in the vicinity of the monument. Access from I-95 is by way of

State Route 3, 38 miles east of Fredericksburg. Further information: Superintendent, RR1, Box 717, Washington's Birthplace, VA 22443. Telephone (804) 224-1732.

GEORGE WASHINGTON MEMORIAL PARKWAY

GEORGE WASHINGTON MEMORIAL PARKWAY, comprising 7,159 acres along the Potomac River in Virginia, runs downriver from near Great Falls to George Washington's home at Mount Vernon. It was authorized by Congress in 1930 for development and was transferred in 1933 to the National Park Service. In 1989, the Maryland stretch, from near Chain Bridge to just beyond I-495, was redesignated as the Clara Barton Parkway.

From north to south, George Washington Memorial Parkway comes first to Turkey Run Park, where there are scenic views from the palisades of the Potomac and where the parkway headquarters is located. (Also under the parkway's administration are Arlington House, Clara Barton National Historic Site, Glen Echo Park, Great Falls Park, Lyndon Baines Johnson Memorial Grove on the Potomac, and Theodore Roosevelt Island.)

Farther south, after passing beneath the approach to Francis Scott Key Bridge, is the parking area for the pedestrian bridge to Theodore Roosevelt Island. The parkway soon runs across Columbia Island, on which is located the Lyndon Baines Johnson Memorial Grove on the Potomac, Columbia Island Marina, and the Navy and Marine Memorial—a bronze sculpture of a graceful flock of gulls and ocean waves that was designed by Ernesto Bagni del Piatta in 1922. Just north of Washington National Airport is Gravelly Point, a recreation site that provides an excellent view of Washington across the river. Adjacent to this point is an inlet of the river known as Roaches Run Waterfowl Sanctuary. This popular bird-watching area was set aside as a wildlife refuge in 1934 and is inhabited by many kinds of ducks and other birds.

South of the airport, the parkway passes Daingerfield Island, on which are hiking paths and other recreational facilities, and the Washington Sailing Marina. The route continues through the historic downtown of the city of Alexandria, by way of Washington Street. The parkway continues southward, passing Belle Haven Marina and the wild expanse of Dyke Marsh, which is important habitat for such birds as egrets, herons, rails, and ducks. Toward the south end of the parkway is Fort Hunt, where visitors may view batteries that guarded the river approach from 1898 to 1918. From here there is a view across the Potomac of Fort Washington (see Fort Washington Park).

Picnic facilities, hiking and bicycling paths, boat ramps and other marina facilities, and interpretive exhibits and programs are provided within the parkway area. The paved Mount Vernon Trail runs for 18.5 miles from Theodore Roosevelt Island to Mount Vernon. This hiking and bicycling route winds along the Potomac River shore and provides many vistas of

Washington. Camping is not allowed within the parkway area; lodging and meals are available throughout the Washington, D.C., metropolitan area. Since lodging may be difficult to obtain during peak tourist seasons, advance reservations are recommended.

IF YOU GO: Access to the parkway from Maryland, north of Washington, is by way of Exit 14 from I-495 (the Capital Beltway). Access from Washington is from State Route 123 at Chain Bridge; Theodore Roosevelt Bridge; Arlington Memorial Bridge; or the 14th Street (I-395) Bridge. Further information: Superintendent, George Washington Memorial Parkway, Turkey Run Park, McLean, VA 22101. Telephone (703) 285-2598.

HARRY S TRUMAN NATIONAL HISTORIC SITE

HARRY S TRUMAN NATIONAL HISTORIC SITE, consisting of one acre in and near Independence, Missouri, was established in 1983 to protect and interpret the 14-room Victorian-style home of the 33rd president of the United States, who served from 1945 to 1953. In 1994, the Harry S Truman Farm Home, in Grandview, was added to the national historic site.

Harry Truman was born in Lamar, Missouri, in 1884. When he was six years old, his parents moved the family away from the 600-acre Grandview farm, so that he and his younger brother and sister could attend school. After the family home was destroyed by fire in 1894, a new house was built, which is the structure that stands on the property today.

In 1906, at the age of 22, Truman was asked to leave a job at a Kansas City bank to help his father and brother run the farm. When his father died eight years later, Truman took over the management of the farming enterprise that included plowing, sowing, reaping, bailing hay, and milking cows.

In World War I, Harry Truman served in the U.S. Army in France, rising to the rank of first lieutenant. Soon after his discharge from military service in 1919, he married his childhood sweetheart, Bess Wallace, and they initially shared her family home, at 219 North Delaware in Independence, with Bess's mother and grandmother. Their daughter, Margaret, was born here. This house was Truman's beloved home until his death in 1972.

In the early 1920s, he served as a county administrator and attended law school, which he never finished. Truman's political career took a giant leap forward in 1934, when he was elected to the United States Senate. He was reelected to this seat in 1940, but then successfully ran for the vice-presidency with Franklin D. Roosevelt in 1944. On Roosevelt's death in 1945, Harry Truman assumed the presidency, and in 1948 was elected president.

Although a man of humble beginnings, as president he tackled head-on numerous challenging and complex national and international issues. Among his actions were the decision to drop atomic bombs on Japan—an act that hastened the end of World War II in 1945; promoting creation of the North Atlantic Treaty Organization (NATO); successful implementation of

Truman's "White House," Harry S Truman National Historic Site, Independence, Missouri [NPS]

the Marshall Plan that greatly aided Europe's recovery from the devastation of the war; the Truman Doctrine, which helped Greece, Turkey, and other countries successfully fend off the threat of communist aggression; and winning United Nations approval for the use of U.S.-led, allied "police-keeping" forces against North Korea's military invasion of South Korea in 1950.

President Truman was called "a most uncommon man." As president he practiced the principal of leadership, characterized by the saying, "The buck stops here." When given an opportunity to run for a third term in The White House, he chose instead to return to the simpler life in Missouri, saying that "I have had all of Washington I want." As ex-president, he wrote his two-volume memoirs and promoted establishment of the presidential library.

Among interesting references are *Harry S Truman* by Margaret Truman (William Morrow); and *Mr. Citizen* by Harry S Truman (Geis Associates).

Visitors are encouraged to begin their tour of the national historic site at the Truman Home Ticket and Information Center, at Truman Road and Main Street. Tickets are issued each day on a first-come, first-served basis, and the National Park Service recommends that visitors arrive early to avoid a possibly lengthy delay for a tour of the Truman Home. The center, which offers an audiovisual introduction to the site, is open daily, except on Thanksgiving, Christmas, and New Year's Day. Lodging and meals are available in Independence and other communities in the area.

Other Truman-related places in the vicinity include the Harry S Truman Library, which contains exhibits and many of Truman's presidential papers; the Harry S Truman Railroad Station, where some 10,000 people welcomed the Trumans home in 1953; the Jackson County Courthouse, where he began his political career; and the surrounding neighborhood, which is designated as a national historical landmark district. Also, in Lamar, 122 miles to the

south of Independence, is the Harry S Truman Birthplace State Historical Site.
IF YOU GO: Access to the national historic site's Truman Home unit is north
from I-70 on Noland Rd., then left (west) onto Truman Road to the ticket
center and home; or east on Truman Road from I-435. Access to the Truman
Farm Home unit is south from I-435 on Route 71, then right (west) onto
Blue Ridge Blvd., about a mile to the farm on the left. Further information:
Superintendent, 223 N. Main St., Independence, MO 64050. Telephone
(816) 254-9929.

HERBERT HOOVER NATIONAL HISTORIC SITE

HERBERT HOOVER NATIONAL HISTORIC SITE, consisting of 186
acres in the farming community of West Branch, Iowa, was established in
1965 to protect and interpret properties relating to the life of the 31st president of the United States, who served from 1929 to 1933.

The site includes Herbert Hoover's birthplace—a small, two-room
cottage at Downey and Penn streets, dating from 1871 and where Hoover was
born three years later. The 14- by 20-foot structure was restored in 1939 and
contains furniture belonging to his parents. Also on the national historic site
are a blacksmith shop like the one that was owned by Herbert's father; a one-
room schoolhouse dating from 1853 that was initially a Quaker meetinghouse;
a newer and larger meetinghouse, where the Hoovers worshipped; the Herbert
Hoover Presidential Library-Museum, run by the National Archives and
Records Administration; and the graves of President and Mrs. Hoover. The
park area includes an expanse of restored native tallgrass prairie and a stretch
of the West Branch Wapsinonoc Creek.

When Herbert Hoover was nine years old, he, his older brother, and
his younger sister were orphaned. A year later, he moved to Oregon to live with
an uncle. At age 17, he was in the first class entering Stanford University's school
of engineering, where he majored in geology and from which he graduated in
1895. He subsequently worked for mining companies in Colorado, Australia,
and China, becoming a junior partner in an international firm by age 27.

During World War I, Hoover was placed in charge of a number of
war-relief programs to help feed millions of people in more than 30 nations.
Following that war, President Woodrow Wilson named him director general of a
U.S. relief and rehabilitation program. At age 47, he was appointed Secretary of
Commerce—a post he held through the Harding and Coolidge administrations.

In 1928, Hoover won the presidential election for the Republican
Party. Following the October 29, 1929, stock market crash that triggered the
great depression of the 1930s, the federal government's efforts under the
Hoover Administration to reduce the disastrous impacts on the nation's econo-
my proved woefully inadequate. As a result, the voters elected the Democrat
Franklin D. Roosevelt, in 1932.

Hoover continued devoting his efforts to public service, focusing on
Stanford University's Hoover Institution on War, Revolution, and Peace; rec-

Herbert Hoover's birthplace, Iowa [NPS]

ommending to the Truman administration strategies for avoiding post-World War II famine; and chairing commissions in 1947 and 1953, seeking ways to improve the workings and efficiency of the federal government's executive branch.

An informative account of Hoover's life is the book, *An Uncommon Man: The Triumph of Herbert Hoover* by Richard Norton Smith (Simon & Schuster).

The site's visitor center provides interpretive exhibits, programs, and publications, as well as paths and walking tours. There are blacksmithing demonstrations in the summer, and when winter conditions are favorable, visitors may enjoy the area on cross-country skis. The site is open daily, except on Thanksgiving, Christmas, and New Year's Day. Camping is not allowed, but a picnic area is provided. Lodging and meals are available in West Branch, Iowa City, Davenport, and elsewhere in the surrounding area.

IF YOU GO: Access to the site is 40 miles west of Davenport or 10 miles east of Iowa City, at I-80 exit 254, then a half-mile north to the visitor center at Main Street and Parkside Drive. Further information: Superintendent, P.O. Box 607, West Branch, IA. 52358. Telephone (319) 643-2541.

HOME OF FRANKLIN D. ROOSEVELT NATIONAL HISTORIC SITE

HOME OF FRANKLIN D. ROOSEVELT NATIONAL HISTORIC SITE consists of 290 acres overlooking the Hudson River, in Hyde Park, New York. It was established in 1945 to protect and interpret the spacious mansion and presidential library of the 32nd president of the United States, who served from 1933 to 1945.

Franklin Roosevelt was born in 1882 and raised in this grand home. He graduated from Harvard in 1902 and attended Columbia Law School. In

Hyde Park, Home of FDR National Historic Site, Hyde Park, New York [NPS]

1905, he married Eleanor, and it was here in this home that they raised their five children. At the age of 28, he was elected to the New York State Senate, serving there until President Woodrow Wilson appointed him assistant secretary of the U.S. Navy in 1913. In 1920, he made an unsuccessful bid for the vice-presidency, and then went into private law practice. The following year, he was stricken with polio that cruelly paralyzed his legs. With great personal courage and perseverance, Roosevelt learned to walk with braces and a cane, determined to get on with his life.

In 1928 and again in 1930, Franklin Roosevelt was elected governor of New York State. In 1932, as the Democratic Party's national standard bearer, he won election to the U.S. presidency, easily defeating incumbent Herbert Hoover who was blamed for the federal government's inadequate response to the devastating impacts of the great depression triggered by the 1929 stock market crash.

President Roosevelt sought and obtained emergency powers to deal more effectively with the crisis. He proclaimed the New Deal and set in motion numerous nationally funded projects, such as the Civilian Conservation Corps (CCC), designed to help provide jobs and put America back to work—thereby refueling the economy. FDR's actions also focused increasing federal regulation upon private businesses, as well as levying new and higher progressive income and excess-profits taxes designed to bring about an unprecedented redistribution of wealth. And the FDR administration promoted regulations that gave labor enhanced leverage in organizing into unions and collective bargaining. Roosevelt served longer in the White House than any previous or subsequent president—being elected to four terms. He died in office in 1945.

Tours of the mansion are provided, and there are exhibits in the library. The Tourist Information Center provides publications. President and Mrs. Roosevelt are buried in the Rose Garden. The site is open daily, except on Tuesdays and Wednesdays from November through March, and on

Thanksgiving, Christmas, and New Year's Day.

IF YOU GO: Lodging and meals are available in Hyde Park, Poughkeepsie, and other communities in the area. Access to the site is by way of U.S. Route 9, just to the north of Poughkeepsie, in Hyde Park. Further information: Superintendent, Roosevelt-Vanderbilt National Historic Sites, 519 Albany Post Rd., Hyde Park, NY 12538. Telephone (914) 229-9115.

JAMES A. GARFIELD NATIONAL HISTORIC SITE

JAMES A. GARFIELD NATIONAL HISTORIC SITE, consisting of just over seven acres in Mentor, in northeastern Ohio, was established to protect and interpret the property, known as "Lawnfield," relating to the life of the 20th president of the United States. Garfield served in the White House for only a few months in 1881, before being shot by an assassin and dying two months later. As of this writing, the 30-room, Victorian-style home is closed for renovation and is expected to reopen in 1998.

Born in 1831, Garfield worked as a canal bargeman, carpenter, farmer, preacher, professor, college president, and an attorney. He was elected to the Ohio state senate in 1859; then served in the Union army during the Civil War, fighting in the battles of Shiloh and Chickamauga (see Shiloh and Chickamauga and Chattanooga national military parks). As a result of his bravery and skill in the Chickamauga battle, he was promoted to major general.

Lawnfield is the site of the first successful "front porch" presidential political campaign (1880), where more than 17,000 people from across the

First presidential memorial library c. 1891, James A. Garfield National Historic Site, Ohio [NPS]

country came to see Garfield speak. It also became the first presidential memorial library.

An informative publication is *Garfield* by Allan Peskins (Kent State University Press).

The site's visitor center is located in the carriage house that dates from 1893. It provides interpretive exhibits, audiovisual programs on Garfield's life and brief presidency, and publications. There are also wayside exhibits interpreting the buildings and property. Lawnfield has been a museum since 1936. Although the National Park Service owns the property, it is administered by the Western Reserve Historical Society. The site is open on Tuesdays through Sundays, except on national holidays such as Thanksgiving, Christmas, and New Year's Day.

IF YOU GO: Lodging and meals are available in Mentor and other cities along the Lake Erie shore, northeast of Cleveland. Access from I-90 westbound is by way of the Mentor-Kirtland/Route 306 exit; then a right turn onto State Route 306, proceeding north two miles; then right onto U.S. Route 20 (Mentor Avenue), and proceeding east two miles to Lawnfield, on the left (north side of the highway). From I-90 eastbound, take the Mentor-Kirtland/Route 306 exit; then a left turn onto State Route 306 and proceed as above. Further information: Curator, Lawnfield, 8095 Mentor Ave., Mentor, OH, 44060. Telephone (216) 255-8722.

JIMMY CARTER NATIONAL HISTORIC SITE

JIMMY CARTER NATIONAL HISTORIC SITE consists of 70 acres in the southwest Georgia town of Plains. It was established in 1987 to protect and interpret the boyhood home, high school, and residence of the 39th president of the United States, serving from 1977 to 1981.

The site typifies the small-town, rural culture of the South that is deeply rooted in agriculture, church, and school. The values fostered by this cultural environment fundamentally influenced Jimmy Carter's views on life and his attitude toward people. Born in 1924, Carter attended the U.S. Naval Academy and served in the navy's nuclear submarine program. When his father died in 1953, Carter returned to Plains to run the family's businesses that included growing, buying, and selling peanuts.

Jimmy Carter entered politics by serving in the Georgia state senate, and in 1970 was elected governor. Winning the election to the presidency at age 53, President Carter was instrumental in encouraging negotiations that resulted in a peace agreement between Israel and Egypt. This was an effort that typified his belief in the importance of trying to resolve conflicts through negotiations and mediation. His work as an international mediator for peace has continued in the years since his presidency ended in 1980.

Three books worthy of mention are *Why Not the Best?* and *Turning Point* by Jimmy Carter and *Everything to Gain* by Jimmy and Rosalynn Carter.

While president, Carter also advanced the cause of environmental protection. The latter prominently included establishment of extensive new national parklands in Alaska, which he initially set aside as national monuments with his presidential proclamation of December 11, 1978.

The Carter residence and boyhood home are not open to the public. The visitor center, which is located in the former railroad station and Carter presidential campaign headquarters, offers some interpretive exhibits by the Plains Historical Trust. These portray the Carter presidency, as well as aspects of this Southern town's farming and railroad history. There are also self-guiding tours of the town. The site is open daily, except on Thanksgiving, Christmas, and New Year's Day.

A picnic area is located at the Georgia Welcome Center, and camping facilities are located near the site. Lodging and meals are available in Plains, Americus, and other towns in the vicinity.

IF YOU GO: Access to the site is by way of U.S. Route 280: 44 miles west of I-75 and 17 miles east of State Route 520. Further information: Superintendent, P.O. Box 392, 300 N. Broad St., Plains, GA 31780. Telephone (912) 824-3413.

JOHN FITZGERALD KENNEDY NATIONAL HISTORIC SITE

JOHN FITZGERALD KENNEDY NATIONAL HISTORIC SITE, at 83 Beals Street, in the Boston suburb of Brookline, Massachusetts, was established in 1967. It protects and interprets the 1917 birthplace and early childhood home of the 35th president of the United States, who served from 1961 to 1963.

Graduating from Harvard in 1940, Jack Kennedy served in the U.S. Navy in World War II; authored the Pulitzer Prize-winning book, *Profiles in Courage*; was elected to the U.S. House of Representatives, beginning in 1947, and to two terms in the U.S. Senate, beginning in 1952. In 1960, Kennedy won the Democratic nomination and was elected to the presidency. Among the highlights of his brief tenure in the White House were his successful insistence that the Soviet Union remove its missiles from Cuba, his support of civil rights, expanded health care for senior citizens, and strong support for enhanced environmental protection including expansion of the National Park System.

On November 22, 1963, President Kennedy was assassinated in Dallas, Texas. Many of the human and environmental welfare goals advocated by Kennedy were implemented by President Lyndon B. Johnson, Kennedy's vice-president and successor.

The National Park Service offers interpretive tours of the house. The site is open daily, except on Thanksgiving, Christmas, and New Year's Day. A walking tour of the surrounding neighborhood includes the house to which the Kennedy family moved in 1921, as well as schools and the church Kennedy attended.

IF YOU GO: Lodging and meals are available throughout the Boston metropolitan area. Access is by way of the Allston-Cambridge-Brighton exit from the Massachusetts Turnpike Extension, then proceeding on Cambridge St. (toward Allston), left onto Harvard St., and left onto Beals St. to #83. Further information: John Fitzgerald Kennedy National Historic Site, 83 Beals St., Brookline, MA 02146. Telephone (617) 566-7937

LINCOLN BOYHOOD NATIONAL MEMORIAL

LINCOLN BOYHOOD NATIONAL MEMORIAL encompasses 200 acres in the forested hills of southern Indiana. Established in 1962, it protects and interprets the site of the Lincoln family farm, where Abraham Lincoln, the 16th president of the United States, lived most of his formative years—from age 7 to 21.

Lincoln's father, Thomas, a farmer, carpenter, and furniture-maker, was previously forced off several farms in Kentucky because of land-title disputes. So, in December 1816, the family moved north, across the Ohio River into Indiana (just then being admitted into the Union as the nineteenth state). The family soon began creating a new home on government-surveyed land on which Thomas Lincoln had previously filed a claim. With the assistance of helpful neighbors, the Lincolns carved their new home out of the heavily forested wilderness—clearing the site, building a log cabin, and planting crops. Here there were no more threats of land ownership disputes; and here, too, there was no slavery, a fact that appealed to the Lincolns.

When Lincoln was only nine years old and his sister Sarah only 11, their mother, Nancy, at age 34, died of poisoning called "milksick," caused by drinking the milk or eating the butter from a cow that had eaten a plant known as white snakeroot. The following year, their father married a widow, Sarah Bush Johnston, who had three children of her own. She was a cheerful and capable stepmother to Abraham and Sarah, treating them as lovingly as her own children.

Although Lincoln briefly attended school near the farm, he later observed that "There was absolutely nothing to excite ambition for education." Nevertheless, he developed a deep desire for learning and enjoyed reading books such as *Robinson Crusoe, Pilgrim's Progress, Aesop's Fables, The Life of George Washington*, and the Bible. He also became well known for his humorous storytelling.

In 1828, when Lincoln turned 19, he was 6' 4" tall and weighed 200 pounds. Also that year, his sister, who had been married for just over a year, died in childbirth. Greatly saddened by her loss, he later that year hired on for a three-month adventure helping a friend navigate a flatboat loaded with livestock and agricultural produce down the Ohio and Mississippi rivers to New Orleans.

Lincoln soon became interested in the law. He visited courtrooms, watched cases being argued, and discussed the law with attorneys and judges,

Lincoln Boyhood National Memorial, Indiana [David Muench]

as he studied everything from property law to the U.S. Constitution. In 1830, Lincoln's father decided to sell their Indiana farm and move the family westward onto the fertile prairie lands of Illinois. Abraham lived in Illinois for the next 30 years, working his way into the political and legal professions that led ultimately to the White House in Washington.

Lincoln Boyhood National Memorial features a recreated rustic cabin and other structures, providing the setting for a living-history demonstration program that helps visitors see what life was like for the Lincolns. The memorial's visitor center provides interpretive exhibits, programs, and publications; and the exterior of this building presents a number of beautiful bas-relief panels that portray aspects of Lincoln's life. Trails, including an interpretive nature trail, loop through the memorial property.

An excellent publication on the national memorial and other National Park System units commemorating Abraham Lincoln is *Lincoln Parks: The Story Behind the Scenery* by Larry Waldron (KC Publications). (See also Abraham Lincoln Birthplace National Historic Site, Lincoln Home National Historic Site, Ford's Theatre National Historic Site, and the Lincoln Memorial.)

Camping is not permitted within the memorial, but a campground is located in a nearby state park. Limited picnicking facilities are provided. Lodging and meals are available in Dale, Santa Claus, Huntingburg, Jasper, and Evansville, Indiana; Owensboro and Louisville, Kentucky; and elsewhere in the surrounding area.

IF YOU GO: Access is two miles east of Gentryville, IN, on State Route 162; and four miles south of I-64 at Dale by way of U.S. Route 231 to Route 162. The national memorial is open daily except for Thanksgiving, Christmas, and New Year's Day. Further information: Superintendent, P.O. Box 1816, Lincoln City, IN 47552. Telephone (812) 937-4541.

LINCOLN HOME NATIONAL HISTORIC SITE

LINCOLN HOME NATIONAL HISTORIC SITE, consisting of 12 acres in the central Illinois city of Springfield, was established in 1972 to protect and interpret the house that was the Abraham Lincoln family home from 1844 to 1861. Lincoln was the 16th president of the United States, from 1861 to 1865.

Prior to buying the house, Lincoln had been elected to the House of Representatives of the Illinois state legislature in 1834, was reelected in 1836, and had begun his successful legal career in 1837. In 1839, after some rocky romantic ups and downs, he met a woman with whom he fell deeply in love —Mary Todd. Because of criticism from some of her family, he broke off their engagement, but then descended into such overwhelming depression that he was unable to focus on his work. He described himself as "the most miserable man living." But fortunately, he and Mary resumed their relationship, and in November 1842, they were married. Their first son, Robert, was born the next August. In the spring of 1844, they bought the Springfield house, which at that time had only one story.

As Lincoln's profession flourished and as his family grew, with Mary giving birth to three more sons, a second floor was added to the house. In 1846, Lincoln was elected to and served one term in the U.S. House of Representatives. In 1858, in an unsuccessful bid for a seat in the U.S. Senate, he gained national exposure from his public debates with incumbent Senator Stephen A. Douglas over the divisive issue of slavery, which Lincoln passionately opposed. As he said: "I hate it because of the monstrous injustice of slavery itself."

In 1860, with the country sharply divided over the question of slavery, presidential candidates Lincoln and Douglas squared off again. But this time, Lincoln, the Republican Party candidate, easily defeated his opponent. On February 11, 1861, the day before his fifty-second birthday, the president-elect, who had begun his life in a rustic little log cabin in Kentucky, thanked all his friends in Springfield for their help, climbed aboard a train, and headed east to take up residence in the White House in Washington, where he successfully faced the enormous challenge of the Civil War.

An excellent publication on the national historic site and other National Park System units commemorating Abraham Lincoln is *Lincoln Parks: The Story Behind the Scenery* by Larry Waldron (KC Publications). (See also Abraham Lincoln Birthplace National Historic Site, Lincoln Boyhood National Memorial, Ford's Theatre National Historic Site, and the Lincoln Memorial.)

The national historic site is located in downtown Springfield, with its visitor center at 426 South Seventh Street and the historic home at Eighth and Jackson streets. Interpretive exhibits, programs, and publications are provided at the visitor center. There are also tours of the Lincoln Home and periodic tours of the four-block historic neighborhood.

Lincoln Home National Historic Site, Springfield, Illinois [David Muench]

IF YOU GO: The site is open daily, except on Thanksgiving, Christmas, and New Year's Day. Lodging and meals are available in and around Springfield. The city of Springfield is located at the junction of I-55 and U.S. Route 36. Further information: Superintendent, 413 South Eighth St., Springfield, IL 62701. Telephone (217) 492-4150.

LINCOLN MEMORIAL

LINCOLN MEMORIAL, consisting of 109 acres overlooking the Potomac River in Washington, D.C., was authorized by Congress in 1911, and was designed by architect Henry Bacon to be similar to the ancient Parthenon on the Acropolis in Athens, Greece. It was dedicated in 1922 to honor the memory and accomplishments of Abraham Lincoln, the 16th president of the United States, from 1861 to 1865.

Lincoln began his eventful life in a humble little log cabin in the rural hill country of Kentucky and rose to become one of the most celebrated presidents in U.S. history. He was committed to the abolition of slavery and to the preservation of the Union. As president, he faced the enormous challenge of a nation divided against itself in the Civil War. Before an assassin's bullet tragically ended his life, Lincoln had signed the Emancipation Proclamation, on January 1, 1863, outlawing slavery; he had successfully led the nation through the bloody civil conflict; he had signed the 13th Amendment to the U.S. Constitution which made slavery unconstitutional; and he saw that amendment ratified by the required three-fourths majority of the states.

This inspiring memorial to the Great Emancipator houses a magnificent, 19-foot seated, white-marble statue of Lincoln, created by sculptor

Lincoln Memorial, Washington, D.C. [David Muench]

Daniel Chester French and his assisting stone carvers. The sheltering memorial building is embellished with 36 Doric columns, representing the 36 states of the United States at the time of President Lincoln's death. The names of those states are carved into the marble frieze just above the columns, and the names of all 48 states at the time of the memorial's dedication are carved into the marble above the frieze. A plaque mounted on the memorial recognizes the subsequent admission into the Union of the states of Alaska and Hawai'i. Carved into the interior marble walls are the eloquent words of Lincoln's Gettysburg Address and his Second Inaugural Address.

For a singularly unforgettable experience, climb the marble steps and look eastward up the length of the Reflecting Pool toward the towering obelisk of the Washington Monument, with the U.S. Capitol beyond. Then turn and pass between the tall columns into the subdued lighting of the memorial's interior and look up at the great seated figure of Abraham Lincoln, with its troubled facial expression reflecting the huge burden of worries and heartbreak over the Civil War.

Since the dedication of the memorial, attended by some 50,000 people, this hallowed place has been a popular forum for many celebrations and civil rights events. Among the latter was the Reverend Martin Luther King's "I Have a Dream" speech in 1963, delivered from the steps of the memorial.

An excellent publication on this and other National Park System units commemorating the life and accomplishments of Abraham Lincoln is *Lincoln Parks: The Story Behind the Scenery*® by Larry Waldron (KC Publications). (See also Abraham Lincoln Birthplace National Historic Site, Lincoln Boyhood National Memorial, Lincoln Home National Historic Site, and Ford's Theatre National Historic Site.)

National Park Service interpreters are on duty at the memorial daily, except on Christmas, from 8 a.m. to midnight. An exhibit on "Lincoln's Legacy" is located on the ground floor level of the memorial. A bookstore is located on the memorial's chamber level. Park Service permits are required for holding First Amendment and other special functions.

Lodging and meals are abundantly available in downtown Washington; across the Potomac in Arlington and Alexandria, Virginia; and elsewhere in the Washington metropolitan area. Advance reservations for lodging are highly recommended.

IF YOU GO: Access to the Lincoln Memorial is by way of Constitution Avenue and 23rd Street, NW; and from Virginia by way of the Arlington Memorial Bridge. The closest Metro subway stop is Foggy Bottom, at 23rd and I ("Eye") streets, NW, by way of the Orange and Blue lines. The Tourmobile provides transportation services to the memorial. Further information on the Lincoln Memorial: Superintendent, National Capital Parks-Central, 900 Ohio Drive, SW, Washington, DC 20242. Telephone (202) 426-6841.

LYNDON BAINES JOHNSON MEMORIAL GROVE ON THE POTOMAC

LYNDON BAINES JOHNSON MEMORIAL GROVE ON THE POTOMAC, consisting of 17 acres in Lady Bird Johnson Park, is located on Columbia Island in the Potomac River, near the Virginia shore in Washington, D.C. It was dedicated in 1974 to honor the 36th president of the United States.

With a view across the river to the nation's capital, visitors may enjoy walking in a grove of white pines and dogwoods and reading some of President Johnson's words inscribed into a large block of Texas granite. Paths leading to the grove wind through beautiful plantings of flowers and shrubs. In springtime, azaleas, rhododendrons, and other flowering shrubs bloom, while daffodils by the thousands explode in a crescendo of dazzling golden-yellow—all a living memorial to the president's wife, Lady Bird, who worked so hard to encourage the beautification of America, during the Johnson years in the White House, from 1963 to 1969.

The park and its grove are adjacent to the George Washington Memorial Parkway, just upriver from George Mason Bridge (14th Street Bridge: I-395, westbound). Parking is available at Columbia Island Marina. Camping is not permitted, but a picnic area is provided. Lodging and meals are available in Arlington and Alexandria, Virginia; in Washington, D.C.; and elsewhere in the metropolitan area. Advance reservations for lodging are advised, especially during times of high visitation to the Nation's Capital.

IF YOU GO: Further information on the grove: Superintendent, c/o George Washington Memorial Parkway, Turkey Run Park, McLean, VA 22101. Telephone (703) 285-2598.

LYNDON B. JOHNSON NATIONAL HISTORICAL PARK

LYNDON B. JOHNSON NATIONAL HISTORICAL PARK, comprising 1,572 acres in the central Texas hill country west of Austin, was established in 1969 as a national historic site and became a national historical park in 1980. It protects and interprets the birthplace, boyhood home, and ranch area of the 36th president of the United States (1963-1969). The park also includes his grandparents' log house and the Johnson family cemetery.

The park is located in two areas: LBJ's boyhood home and his grandparents' settlement complex in Johnson City; and LBJ's birthplace and the LBJ Ranch along the Pedernales River, about 14 miles west of Johnson City. The latter part of the park is cooperatively managed by the federal and state park agencies. North of the river, the National Park Service administers the birthplace and ranch. South of the river, the Texas Parks and Wildlife Department administers the Lyndon B. Johnson State Historical Park, containing the visitor center that serves both parks.

The LBJ birthplace, near the eastern edge of the ranch, is a modest little ranch house that has been reconstructed. The LBJ boyhood home is a comfortable little white house, on 9th Street in Johnson City, that has been restored. This is where LBJ lived from age 5 to 19, with his parents, his brother, and two sisters. From his mother, Rebekah, during these formative years, he learned the importance of education and of compassion for human needs of those less fortunate. From his father, Sam, who served in the state legislature, he began to learn about politics—its agrarian liberal tradition and its practical workings.

At the LBJ Ranch, with its large, rambling ranch house, which became the Texas White House, the visitor can sense President Johnson's enormous power and energy that was rooted in this beautiful and productive land, where he worked the ranch and raised prize cattle. This was a place of renewal where he frequently returned during his 32 years as congressman, senator, and president. As the National Park Service says, "Here a man who loved action could set a task, get it going, and get it done. It was a healing place far removed from the turbulence of Washington."

The parks' main visitor center is located near the main entrance off U.S. Route 290, in the Lyndon B. Johnson State Historical Park. It contains interpretive exhibits, programs, and publications. And it is from here that one to one-and-a-half-hour bus tours of the parks begin. (Tours may be shorter during periods of inclement weather or when summer heat and humidity are high.) Included on the tour are the ranch house complex, the showbarn, LBJ's birthplace, Junction School, and the family cemetery where LBJ's grave is located.

In Johnson City, there is a small visitor center across G Street from the LBJ boyhood home. From the visitor center, there is also a half-mile walking path that leads visitors through the Johnson settlement to Sam Ealy Johnson's log house, an exhibit center, and other ranch buildings.

While camping is not permitted within the national and state parks, a picnic area is provided near the main visitor center in the state park. Lodging and meals are available in Johnson City, Fredericksburg, and Austin.

Sam Ealy Johnson Log House, LBJ National Historical Park, Texas [Larry Ulrich]

The LBJ Ranch area is open daily, except on Christmas; and the Johnson City park area is open daily, except on Christmas and New Year's Day. **IF YOU GO:** Access to both parts of the park is by way of U.S. Route 290, between Austin and Fredericksburg. Johnson City is 50 miles west of Austin, and the LBJ Ranch is about 14 miles west of Johnson City and 16 miles east of Fredericksburg. Further information: Superintendent, P.O. Box 329, Johnson City, TX 78636. Telephone (210) 868-7128.

MARTIN VAN BUREN NATIONAL HISTORIC SITE

MARTIN VAN BUREN NATIONAL HISTORIC SITE consists of 39 acres near Kinderhook, New York. Established in 1974, it protects and interprets Lindenwald, the elegant retirement home of the 8th president of the United States, who served from 1837 to 1841.

Van Buren was born in 1782 in Kinderhook. He served in the New York state senate and as the state's attorney general before being elected to the U.S. Senate in 1821. After serving two terms, he was then elected governor of New York in 1828. The following year, he was named secretary of state in the Andrew Jackson administration, and in 1832 won the vice-presidency. In 1836, Van Buren won the presidential election and served during a period of nationwide depression.

The site provides interpretive tours of the spacious mansion, which has been restored to its mid-nineteenth century appearance. A visitor center provides interpretive exhibits, programs, and publications. The site is open daily from mid-April through October, and is closed on Mondays and Tuesdays from November 1 through December 5, on Thanksgiving, and from December 6 to mid-April.

IF YOU GO: Lodging and meals are available in Kinderhook, Albany, and elsewhere in the area. Access is two miles south of Kinderhook on State Route 9H; or on I-90 between the Berkshire stretch of the Massachusetts Turnpike and Albany, exiting south onto U.S. Route 9 and going about five miles to State Route 9H, then five miles on Route 9H. Further information: Superintendent, P.O. Box 545, Kinderhook, NY 12106. Telephone (518) 758-9689.

MOUNT RUSHMORE NATIONAL MEMORIAL

MOUNT RUSHMORE NATIONAL MEMORIAL, consisting of 1,278 acres in the scenic Black Hills of western South Dakota, was dedicated in 1925 and protects and interprets the enormous sculpted heads of former U.S. Presidents George Washington, Thomas Jefferson, Abraham Lincoln, and Theodore Roosevelt. It took sculptor Gutzon Borglum and his crew of assistants, 14 years (from 1927 to 1941) to carve these likenesses from the granite pegmatite face of Mount Rushmore.

Initially, plans called for only three heads—Washington, Jefferson, and Lincoln. But space allowed for another, and Theodore Roosevelt was chosen. The project was repeatedly plagued with problems of inclement weather, public criticism, and shortage of funds. For a lack of private contributions, no work was accomplished in 1928. It resumed in 1929 only after Congress passed legislation establishing the Mount Rushmore Memorial Commission and providing $250,000 in federal funding to be matched with private donations. But then came the stock market crash and the depression, resulting in a drastic reduction in private contributions. This resulted in periods of work stoppage on the mountain. Finally, in 1934, Congress ended the matching requirement and authorized direct appropriations of federal funds that carried the project to completion seven years later.

Rough models were made first, beginning with Washington, on a scale of an inch on the model to a foot up on the mountain. The completed faces measure about 60 feet in height. The heads were carved with an intricate system of measuring known as "pointing," enabling measurements on the model to be expanded twelve times and calculated on the mountain's granite surface. The nose and other facial features were located through the measurement of these numbered points. Drilling, blasting, and stonecutting could then proceed. While a few of Borglum's assistants were skilled stonecarvers, some were miners, loggers, and others who were trained on the job. When it came to the nuances of sculpting, Borglum carefully scrutinized each detail in the context of the whole from various perspectives and under different lightings, to make certain the carvings would look correct. Former South Dakota governor and U.S. senator William J. Bulow, writing, in the January 11, 1947, *Saturday Evening Post*, said that "It takes a genius to figure out the proper perspective so that the carvings will look right from the point from which the human eye beholds them. Gutzon Borglum was that genius."

Construction, 1941, of Mount Rushmore National Memorial, South Dakota [NPS]

Three informative publications are *Mount Rushmore: The Story Behind the Scenery®* written by Lincoln Borglum, the son of the sculptor (KC Publications); *Mount Rushmore* by Gilbert C. Fite (University of Oklahoma Press); and *The Carving of Mount Rushmore* by Rex Alan Smith (Abbeville). Lincoln Borglum was his father's assistant throughout much of the project, and after his father's death became the first superintendent of the national memorial.

The park unit has a visitor center that provides interpretive exhibits, programs, and publications. There are also summer evening interpretive programs. The visitor center is open daily, except on Christmas. Climbing Mount Rushmore is not permitted. Camping is not allowed in the national memorial, but national forest and state park campgrounds are nearby. Lodging and meals are available in Keystone, Hill City, Rapid City, and elsewhere in the Black Hills. Meals are also available in the memorial during the summer months, provided by the concessionaire. **IF YOU GO:** Access is two miles from Keystone on State Route 244, or 25 miles from Rapid City on U.S. Route 16. Further information: Superintendent, P.O. Box 268, Keystone, SD 57751. Telephone (605) 574-2523.

SAGAMORE HILL NATIONAL HISTORIC SITE

SAGAMORE HILL NATIONAL HISTORIC SITE, comprising 83 acres near Oyster Bay, on the north shore of Long Island, New York, was established in 1962 to protect and interpret the large estate that was the home of Theodore Roosevelt, the 26th president of the United States.

Soon after graduating from Harvard, Teddy Roosevelt assisted in designing the grand, three-story, 23-room mansion at Sagamore Hill that became his primary residence from 1886 to 1919 and that was also the Summer White House during his presidency, from 1901 to 1909. Visitors may see the furnishings and many of his personal possessions; they can also sense something of this dynamic man's passion for the conservation of wildlife and the natural environment, his love of horses and books, and his years in politics.

The very appearance of this substantial home reflects the tremendous strength and drive of a man who cared passionately about life and living, and who derived immense inspiration from the natural environment. He committed the power of his presidency to conserving the forests, wildlife, and other natural resources of America, at a time when profligate waste and unbridled exploitation, with little or no thought for the future, were the rule of the day. New national forests and parks and the first national monuments were established during his years in the White House. Much of his inspiration came from his western North Dakota ranchland, where he came to love the wildness of the West. He was a hunter, yet he understood the urgent need to conserve wildlife, whose populations were being decimated by greed and mindless slaughterings across the continent.

Visitors may tour Roosevelt's home and Old Orchard Home, built by his son, General Theodore Roosevelt, Jr., which provides interpretive exhibits, a film, and publications on his life, presidency, and family. The site is open daily, except on Thanksgiving, Christmas, and New Year's Day. A small food concession is open during the summer.

(See also the other National Park System units commemorating Theodore Roosevelt: Theodore Roosevelt Birthplace National Historic Site, Theodore Roosevelt Inaugural National Historic Site, and Theodore Roosevelt Island. Theodore Roosevelt National Park is described in *Exploring Our National Parks and Monuments* by Devereux Butcher, revised by Russell D. Butcher, Ninth Edition, 1995.)

IF YOU GO: Lodging and meals are available in Oyster Bay, East Norwich, and elsewhere on Long Island and in New York City. Access is by way of Exit 41 north from the Long Island Expressway or Exit 35 north from Northern State Parkway, and north on State Route 106 to Oyster Bay. At the third stoplight in the town of Oyster Bay, turn right onto E. Main Street and follow signs to Sagamore Hill, three miles east on Cove Neck Road, to 20 Sagamore Hill Road. Trains run from Pennsylvania Station in New York City to the station in Oyster Bay, from which taxis take visitors to the site. Further information: Superintendent, 20 Sagamore Hill Rd., Oyster Bay, NY 11771. Telephone (516) 922-4788.

THEODORE ROOSEVELT BIRTHPLACE NATIONAL HISTORIC SITE

THEODORE ROOSEVELT BIRTHPLACE NATIONAL HISTORIC SITE consists of a tenth of an acre at 28 East 20th Street, in New York City. It was established in 1962 to protect and interpret the birthplace of the 26th president of the United States.

A brownstone house at this site was the Roosevelt family home from 1854 to 1872. TR was born here on October 27, 1858. The original house was torn down in 1916. The present reconstruction was built in 1923. The site offers guided tours of the rooms, with their Victorian period furnishings. There are also interpretive exhibits and programs. Concerts are presented on Saturday afternoons. The site is closed on Mondays and Tuesdays, as well as on national holidays such as Thanksgiving, Christmas, and New Year's Day.

(See also the other National Park System units commemorating Theodore Roosevelt: Sagamore Hill National Historic Site, Theodore Roosevelt Inaugural National Historic Site, and Theodore Roosevelt Island. Theodore Roosevelt National Park is described in *Exploring Our National Parks and Monuments*, Ninth Edition, 1995.)

IF YOU GO: Lodging and meals are abundantly available on Manhattan and elsewhere in the New York City area. Access is by way of the 14th and 23rd street subway stops (N, R, and #6 lines); or by taxi. Parking in the vicinity of the site is virtually impossible to find. Further information: Superintendent, 28 E. 20th St., New York, NY 10003. Telephone (212) 260-1616.

THEODORE ROOSEVELT INAUGURAL NATIONAL HISTORIC SITE

THEODORE ROOSEVELT INAUGURAL NATIONAL HISTORIC SITE protects the historic house museum at 641 Delaware Avenue in Buffalo, New York. It was established in 1966 to commemorate the place where the 26th president of the United States took the oath of office, on September 14, 1901, at the age of 42. The swearing-in ceremony was held in the library of the home of Ansley Wilcox, a friend and political associate of Theodore Roosevelt, after President William McKinley's death. McKinley had been shot while visiting the Pan-American Exposition in Buffalo.

The site offers interpretive exhibits and an introductory slide program. It is open Monday through Friday from 9 a.m. to 5 p.m. and weekends from 12 p.m. to 5 p.m. (January through March the site is closed on Saturday.) Special events throughout the year include walking and bus tours, Teddy Bear Picnic, a re-enactment of the September 14 inaugural ceremony, and Victorian Christmas.

(See also the other National Park System units commemorating Theodore Roosevelt: Sagamore Hill National Historic Site, Theodore

Library, Theodore Roosevelt Inaugural National Historic Site, New York [NPS]

Roosevelt Birthplace National Historic Site, and Theodore Roosevelt Island. Theodore Roosevelt National Park is presented in the companion volume, *Exploring Our National Parks and Monuments*, Ninth Edition, 1995.)
IF YOU GO: Lodging and meals are available in Buffalo. Access is a mile north of downtown Buffalo. Further information: Superintendent, 641 Delaware Avenue, Buffalo, NY 14202. Telephone (716) 884-0095.

THEODORE ROOSEVELT ISLAND

THEODORE ROOSEVELT ISLAND consists of 88 acres of wild forest, marsh, and swamp in the Potomac River, in Washington, D.C., close to the Virginia shore. Its protection was authorized by Congress in 1932 and it was transferred to the National Park Service in 1933.

A 17-foot-tall bronze statue of the 26th president of the United States, created in 1967 by sculptor Paul Manship rises impressively from a terrace. There are also two fountains and four granite panels containing excerpts from Teddy Roosevelt's inspired writings on conservation, manhood, youth, and government. One of his statements is that "The Nation behaves well if it treats the natural resources as assets which it must turn over to the next generation increased and not impaired in value." Beyond the formal terrace, which was designed by Eric Gugler, is the rich river bottomland forest of the island. It is protected and dedicated to the memory and accomplishments of President Roosevelt, who did so much to advance natural resource conservation and park protection in America during his years in the White House, from 1901 to 1909. It is a peaceful place, except where Theodore Roosevelt Bridge crosses the lower end of the island and when commercial jet aircraft fly low overhead, as they come in and out of Washington National Airport.

Access to the island is by way of a footbridge from the Virginia shore, reached from a parking area adjacent to the northbound lanes of the George

Washington Memorial Parkway. Another enjoyable way to reach the island is to paddle a canoe there. A canoe rental business is located just upstream, below the Washington end of Francis Scott Key Bridge. Trails wind through two-and-a-half miles of the island, beneath a variety of trees. Some of the many species are American sycamore, tuliptree, sassafras, sweetgum, several oaks, river birch, eastern redbud, black tupelo, and red maple.

Among the island's mammals are red and gray foxes, muskrats, opossums, raccoons, eastern cottontails, chipmunks, and gray and flying squirrels. Birds that reside on or visit the island include black-crowned night-herons, great blue and green-backed herons, wood ducks and other waterfowl, bald eagles, ospreys, barred owls, belted kingfishers, pileated and red-bellied woodpeckers, blue jays, tufted titmice, Carolina wrens, wood thrushes, many kinds of warblers such as prothonotary and yellowthroat, and cardinals.

(See also the texts on the other National Park System units commemorating Theodore Roosevelt: Sagamore Hill National Historic Site, Theodore Roosevelt Birthplace National Historic Site, and Theodore Roosevelt Inaugural National Historic Site. Theodore Roosevelt National Park is described in *Exploring Our National Parks and Monuments*, Ninth Edition, 1995.)

IF YOU GO: The island is open daily during the day. There are guided tours. Camping is not permitted. Lodging and meals are available in Arlington and Alexandria, VA; in Washington, DC; and elsewhere in the metropolitan area. Advance reservations are advised, especially during times of high visitation to the nation's capital. Further information on the island: Superintendent, c/o George Washington Memorial Parkway, Turkey Run Park, McLean, VA 22101. Telephone (703) 285-2598.

THOMAS JEFFERSON MEMORIAL

THOMAS JEFFERSON MEMORIAL, consisting of 18 acres facing north across the Tidal Basin in Potomac Park, adjacent to the Potomac River in Washington, D.C., was authorized by Congress in 1934. It was designed mostly by architect John Russell Pope, with final implementation by Daniel Higgins and Otto Eggers. The memorial was dedicated in 1943 to the memory and accomplishments of the scholarly Thomas Jefferson, author of the Declaration of Independence and the third president of the United States, from 1801 to 1809.

The circular marble structure is crowned by a low dome and is encircled by a colonnade of classical Ionic columns. A colonnaded portico fronts on the Tidal Basin. In the rotunda stands a 19-foot-tall bronze statue of President Jefferson, created by sculptor Rudulph Evans. On the rotunda's encircling inner wall are excerpts from documents written by Thomas Jefferson, including words from the Declaration of Independence and the Virginia Statute for Religious Freedom.

Thomas Jefferson Memorial, Washington, D.C. [David Muench]

The memorial's architecture is also a fitting reflection of Jefferson's architectural designs for his own Virginia home, Monticello, which was completed at the end of his presidency, in 1809; and for the initial buildings of the University of Virginia, which Jefferson helped establish and which opened in 1825. The Jefferson Memorial is, in fact, basically similar to the university's rotunda building.

One of Washington's most exquisitely beautiful scenes occurs during late March and early April, when the pink-blossoming Japanese cherry trees burst into bloom around the Tidal Basin and magically frame the memorial.

National Park Service interpreters give talks about Thomas Jefferson and the memorial daily, except on Christmas. During the week of the Cherry Blossom Festival, around the first week of April, interpreters lead scheduled walks in the vicinity of the Tidal Basin. The memorial is also the forum for some First Amendment and other special functions, for which permits are required.

Lodging and meals are abundantly available in downtown Washington, as well as across the Potomac in Arlington and Alexandria, Virginia, and elsewhere in the metropolitan area. Advance reservations for lodging during the Cherry Blossom Festival and other popular visitation seasons are recommended. **IF YOU GO:** Access to the memorial is by way of Independence Avenue (between the Washington Monument and the Lincoln Memorial along the south side of the Mall), following signs to the Thomas Jefferson Memorial. The Tourmobile provides transportation services to the memorial. There is limited parking at the memorial. The closest Metro subway stop is Smithsonian, on the Orange and Blue lines. Further information about the Jefferson Memorial: Superintendent, National Capital Parks-Central, 900 Ohio Drive, SW, Washington, DC 20242. Telephone (202) 426-6841.

ULYSSES S. GRANT NATIONAL HISTORIC SITE

ULYSSES S. GRANT NATIONAL HISTORIC SITE, comprising about nine-and-a-half acres in suburban St. Louis, Missouri, was established in 1989 to interpret the lives of Ulysses S. Grant and his wife, Julia Dent Grant and to protect their home, called White Haven. General Grant had a profound impact on the Civil War and played an integral part in the ultimate Union victory. In 1868, he was elected as the 18th president of the United States, and served two terms.

IF YOU GO: The national historic site, is open daily, except on Thanksgiving, Christmas, and New Year's Day. Lodging and meals are available in and around St. Louis. The site is located at 7400 Grant Road. Further information: Superintendent, 7400 Grant Rd., St. Louis, MO 63123. Telephone (314) 842-3298.

WASHINGTON MONUMENT

WASHINGTON MONUMENT, comprising 106 acres midway between the U.S. Capitol and the Lincoln Memorial, in Washington, D.C., is a graceful, towering, 555-foot-tall marble obelisk dedicated to the memory and accomplishments of George Washington, the first president of the United States, from 1789 to 1797. He was the successful commander-in-chief of American forces in the War for Independence (Revolutionary War) and served as the presiding officer of the Constitutional Convention in 1787 that ratified the U.S. Constitution.

Legislation to authorize building a monument to honor President Washington was first initiated by the Continental Congress in 1783. Plans for its construction received new urgency after his death in 1799. Finally, a non-

"White Haven," Ulysses S. Grant National Historic Site, Missouri [NPS]

profit organization, the Washington National Monument Society, was founded to raise funds and build a monument. Architect Robert Mills won a design competition, with a proposal for a giant obelisk, around the base of which was also to have been a circular building intended to exhibit statues of important persons in U.S. history. In 1848, Congress authorized the project to proceed.

By 1854, construction reached 150 feet and was then suddenly halted over a controversy concerning a commemorative stone that was a papal gift of the Roman Catholic Church in Rome. While the disputed stone was stolen by protesters and never used, construction was further delayed during the Civil War and did not resume until 1879. The 3,300-pound marble capstone and an aluminum pyramid were lifted into place in 1884 and the structure was completed without the building at its base. The majestic, yet simple, obelisk was dedicated in 1885. In 1933, the monument was transferred to the National Park Service.

Visitors may take the elevator to the 500-foot level, where two windows in each of four directions offer panoramas of the city. Encircling the obelisk's base are 50 American flags, representing the 50 states of the Union. A ticket system is in effect from early April to Labor Day. Free tickets for timed entry may be obtained from the Ticketmaster booth, located east of the monument on 15th Street, or may be purchased in advance for a small fee by calling 1(800) 505-5040. After 8 p.m., tickets are not needed. Summer hours for the monument are from 8 a.m. to 11:45 p.m.; and for the rest of the year they are from 8 a.m. to 4:45 p.m.

Lodging and meals are available in downtown Washington as well as across the Potomac in Arlington and Alexandria, Virginia, and elsewhere in the Washington metropolitan area. Advance reservations for lodging are highly recommended, especially during popular tourist seasons. A snackbar is located east of the monument, on 15th Street.

IF YOU GO: Park Service interpreters are on duty at the monument daily, except on Christmas. First Amendment and other special functions are periodically held at the monument, for which a permit is required. The monument site is bounded by 15th and 17th streets, and Constitution and Independence avenues. There is limited parking nearby. The closest Metro subway stops are Smithsonian and Federal Triangle, on the Orange and Blue lines. The Tourmobile provides transportation services to the Washington Monument. Further information: Superintendent, National Capital Parks-Central, 900 Ohio Dr., SW, Washington, DC 20242. Telephone (202) 426-6841.

THE WHITE HOUSE

THE WHITE HOUSE, located on 18 acres between Lafayette Square and the Mall, at 1600 Pennsylvania Avenue in Washington, D.C., has been the focus of the presidency for about two centuries and the home of all U.S. presidents after George Washington. Tours of the mansion are under the jurisdiction of the National Park Service.

The White House was designed by architect James Hoban and is patterned after Irish Georgian-style country mansions. Construction began in 1793. Stonemasons were hired from Scotland, and the sandstone was quarried in Virginia and shipped by boat up the Potomac River to Washington. Kilns were set up on the White House grounds for the production of millions of bricks for the mansion and other federal government buildings. And the lumber for flooring, doors, and framing of doors and windows came mostly from Virginia and North Carolina.

In November 1800, toward the end of his term as the second president, John Adams moved into the not-yet-completed President's House, as the structure was officially called for many years. A few years later, disaster struck. During James Madison's presidency, British troops, under the command of General Robert Ross, set fire to the mansion on the evening of August 24, 1814—retaliating for destruction of governmental buildings by American soldiers in British Canada, during the War of 1812 between the United States and Britain. Ross even supervised the stacking up of the mansion's elegant furnishings before igniting what became a raging inferno. Other national government buildings were torched as well, before the British troops moved northward to Baltimore and their futile attack of Fort McHenry (see the text on Fort McHenry National Monument and Historic Shrine), where the national anthem, "The Star Spangled Banner," was written and where Ross was killed.

Reconstruction of the burned-out shell of the President's House was started the following year and was completed in 1817, just a few months after the next president, James Monroe, took office. The mansion's columned north portico was completed in 1824 and the curved and columned south portico was completed five years later. Not until 1833 did the house have running water, and not until 1853 was there a central heating system.

In 1857, a glass conservatory was erected adjacent to the west end of what, from the mid-nineteenth century, was officially called the Executive Mansion. Twenty years later, the popular conservatory of greenery was greatly enlarged, provided with walkways and places to sit, and joined to the State Dining Room of the mansion.

Washington Monument, Washington, D.C.
[David Muench]

Electric lighting replaced gaslights in 1891. When President Theodore Roosevelt moved into the great house in 1901, he officially changed its name to the long-popular White House. In 1902, federal funds were authorized by Congress to make repairs and to build an executive office building off the west end of the mansion in place of the conservatory. By 1909, further expansion of the executive offices was carried out, including the creation of the president's Oval Office. Executive office space was again expanded in 1934, in response to a constantly growing White House staff.

To overcome Washington's often oppressively muggy summer heat, air conditioning was installed in the early 1930s. In 1948, a second-floor balcony was added to the south portico; and from 1948 to 1952, the entire interior of the White House was gutted to the outer walls, steel beams were installed, and the structure completely renovated. During this interval, President Harry Truman occupied the Blair House across Pennsylvania Avenue.

During recent presidencies, major efforts have been made to enhance the White House with historic furniture and paintings. And in the early 1990s, the mansion's exterior was revitalized. Nearly thirty layers of paint were stripped off the sandstone, while carvers repaired stone ornamentation of the porticos' column capitals, the exquisite carvings around the front door, and other details that had long been neglected.

Among historical publications on the White House are *The President's House: A History* by William Seale; *The White House, An Historic Guide*; and *The Living White House* (all published by the White House Historical Association, 740 Jackson Place, NW, Washington, DC 20560). There is also *Inside the White House: America's Most Famous Home—the First 200 Years* by Betty Boyd Caroli *(Reader's Digest)*.

Self-guided tours of the state and ground floors of the mansion are available for visitors. Except for handicapped visitors, who enter by way of the north portico and front door onto the state floor, touring begins on the ground floor. Here are located the Library, containing books on history, the sciences, and other subjects—all by American authors; the Vermeil Room, named for its collection of gilded silver; the China Room, in which are displayed china and glassware used by various presidents; and the beautiful oval Diplomatic Reception Room, featuring French wallpaper that portrays such places as Niagara Falls, the Natural Bridge in Virginia, and Boston Harbor. On the state floor, visitors walk through the spacious East Room, the mansion's largest room which is often the focus of press conferences, receptions, and special ceremonies. Next is the Green Room, for small receptions; the exquisite oval Blue Room that is frequently used by presidents for receiving guests; the little Red Room that is a favorite with first ladies for receptions; and, finally, the elegant State Dining Room. Carved into the fireplace mantel are the hopeful words of President John Adams: "I Pray Heaven to Bestow the Best of Blessings on THIS HOUSE and All that shall hereafter Inhabit it. May none but Honest and Wise Men ever rule under this Roof."

1600 Pennsylvania Avenue [NPS]

Visitors may generally tour the White House on Tuesdays through Saturdays, from 10 a.m. to noon. The mansion is closed during official functions and programs and on certain holidays such as Thanksgiving, Christmas, and New Year's Day. Wheelchairs are available for handicapped visitors at the Northeast Gate on Pennsylvania Avenue (no tickets are required for handicapped visitors and those accompanying them). For all other visitors, tour tickets are not required between Labor Day weekend and Memorial Day week, and visitors may simply go to the East Gate of the White House. For the rest of the year, free tickets are available at booths on the Ellipse just south of the White House. They are issued on a first-come, first-served basis (from 8 a.m. until that day's supply runs out). They cannot be reserved and each visitor must pick up his or her own ticket. Each ticket indicates when the tour will begin on the Ellipse for the ranger-escorted walk from there to the East Gate.

Lodging and meals are available in Washington and elsewhere in the metropolitan area, but advance reservations for hotel accommodations are strongly advised, especially during peak tourist seasons.

IF YOU GO: The White House is located south across Pennsylvania Avenue from Lafayette Square, and north of the Ellipse and the Washington Monument, between 15th and 17th streets. The nearest Metro subway station is Farragut West, just a block to the northwest at 17th and H streets. There is also surface public transportation. Further information: National Park Service, National Capital Region, 1100 Ohio Dr., SW, Washington, DC 20242. Telephone (202) 456-7041 (regarding tour schedules) or (202) 755-7799.

WILLIAM HOWARD TAFT NATIONAL HISTORIC SITE

WILLIAM HOWARD TAFT NATIONAL HISTORIC SITE comprises three acres at 2038 Auburn Avenue, in Cincinnati, Ohio. It was established in 1969 to protect and interpret the restored childhood home of the 27th president of the United States, from 1909 to 1913, and the tenth Chief Justice of the U.S. Supreme Court, from 1921 to 1930.

Taft was born in 1857 in this two-story, Greek-revival-style brick house. He was described as a happy, outgoing child and was an excellent student in school. He graduated from Yale University and Cincinnati Law School; and in 1886, he married Helen ("Nellie") Herron.

In 1887, at the age of 30, Taft became an Ohio Superior Court judge. Three years later, he was appointed U.S. Solicitor General. From 1892 to 1900, he served on the Sixth U.S. Circuit Court of Appeals; and from 1896 to 1900 was also dean of the Cincinnati Law School. From 1904 to 1908, he served as Secretary of War in the Theodore Roosevelt administration. In 1908, he won the presidential election.

Following his four-year term in the White House, Taft taught constitutional law at Yale University and was chief justice of the Supreme Court for nine years. While serving on the court, he wrote that "The court, next to my wife and children, is the nearest thing to my heart in life."

Four rooms of the Taft home have been restored to their 1860s appearance of Taft's childhood. Family portraits, many books, and some furniture belonged to the Taft family, while other furnishings are period antiques. Other rooms contain interpretive exhibits on Taft's life and accomplishments. The house is open daily for guided tours, except on Thanksgiving, Christmas, and New Year's Day.

IF YOU GO: Lodging and meals are available in Cincinnati. Access from I-71 northbound is by way of Exit 2 (stay in the right lane), then left at the first stoplight and up Dorchester Ave., and right onto Auburn Ave., a half-block to the site; or from I-71, southbound by way of Exit 3, then right onto William Howard Taft Rd., and left onto Auburn Ave., a half-mile to the site. There is a parking area nearby, off Southern Ave. Further information: Superintendent, 2038 Auburn Ave., Cincinnati, OH 45219. Telephone (513) 684-3262.

PART 8

PARKS CELEBRATING WOMEN IN U.S. HISTORY

CLARA BARTON NATIONAL HISTORIC SITE

CLARA BARTON NATIONAL HISTORIC SITE, consisting of an acre in Glen Echo, Maryland, less than three miles northwest of the District of Columbia, was established in 1974 to protect and interpret the history of the early American Red Cross (ARC) through the life and times of its founder, Clara Barton (1821–1912). The Clara Barton home, dating from 1891, was the headquarters of ARC from 1897 to 1904.

During the Civil War, from 1861 to 1865, Clara Barton volunteered to help wounded soldiers at the battles of Second Manassas, Antietam, Fredericksburg, the Wilderness, and Spotsylvania. In her words:

> Men have worshipped war till it has cost a million times more than the whole earth is worth. . . . Deck it as you will, war is Hell. . . . Only the desire to soften some of its hardships and allay some of its miseries ever induced me . . . to face its pestilent and unholy breath.

Following the Civil War, she continued her charitable endeavors, such as setting up a program to locate missing soldiers and pushing for the establishment of a national cemetery at Andersonville prison, in Georgia, to identify the graves of nearly 13,000 Union soldiers who perished as prisoners of war there (see Andersonville National Historic Site).

In 1870, Clara Barton began working with the International Red Cross in France and Germany; and from 1881 to 1904, she served as president of the American Red Cross, assisting in relief efforts of natural disasters such as hurricanes and floods.

She also spoke out in support of the enfranchisement of the former slaves and regarding the rights of women. Concerning the latter, Clara Barton said:

> I believe I must have been born believing in the full right of women to all privileges and positions which nature and justice accord her common with other human beings. Perfectly equal rights—human rights. There was never any question in my mind in regard to this.

Home of Clara Barton, founder of the American Red Cross, Maryland [Vicki Paris]

Today, at the Clara Barton home, there are interpretive exhibits, audio-visual programs (with advance reservations), and guided tours of the house. Advance arrangements are required for group tours of ten or more visitors. The site is open daily, except on Thanksgiving, Christmas, and New Year's Day, and is shown only by guided tour.

A small picnic area is provided at the site. Lodging and meals are available in Glen Echo and elsewhere in the Washington, D.C., metropolitan area. **IF YOU GO:** Access is by way of MacArthur Bvd. from Washington, about three miles to the northwest of the D.C.-Maryland line; then turning left onto Oxford Rd. and continuing to the parking area between the house and Glen Echo Park (see the text on this park unit). Access from Washington is also by way of Massachusetts Avenue (in D.C. and continuing into Maryland), then left (west) onto Goldsboro Road (State Route 614), right onto MacArthur Blvd., and left onto Oxford Rd. Access from I-495 (the Capital Beltway) is by way of the Clara Barton Parkway along the Potomac River to Glen Echo, and following Glen Echo Park and Clara Barton National Historic Site signs to Oxford Rd. Further information: Clara Barton National Historic Site, 5801 Oxford Rd., Glen Echo, MD 20812. Telephone (301) 492-6245.

ELEANOR ROOSEVELT NATIONAL HISTORIC SITE

ELEANOR ROOSEVELT NATIONAL HISTORIC SITE, comprising 180 acres in Hyde Park, New York, was established in 1977 to protect and interpret Eleanor Roosevelt's retreat, Val-Kill Cottage, and surrounding property. Val-Kill was a popular Roosevelt family picnicking and swimming place from the 1920s to 1945. The cottage was originally a factory building in which, in the

Val-Kill Cottage, Eleanor Roosevelt National Historic Site, New York [NPS]

1920s and 1930s, Mrs. Roosevelt promoted a program for local craftsmen for weaving and the making of furniture and pewter items. Much of the furniture in the cottage was made here by craftsmen.

From the death of her husband, President Franklin D. Roosevelt, until her own death in 1962, Mrs. Roosevelt relaxed and worked at Val-Kill Cottage, and en-tertained foreign dignitaries and guests from around the United States. And here she enjoyed the natural beauty of the surrounding woods, fields, marshes, and ponds.

Today, guided tours of the home are provided (group tour reserva-tions: [914] 229-9115). A brief audiovisual program is also shown. The site is open daily from May to October, on weekends during the rest of the year, and is closed on Thanksgiving, Christmas, and New Year's Day.

IF YOU GO: Lodging and meals are available in Hyde Park. Access is two miles east on U.S. Route 9G from the Home of Franklin D. Roosevelt Nat-ional Historic Site (see the text on this park unit). Shuttle service (fee) is provid-ed from the Roosevelt Home to Eleanor Roosevelt NHS. Further information: Eleanor Roosevelt NHS, c/o Superintendent, Roosevelt-Vanderbilt National His-toric Sites, 519 Albany Post Rd., Hyde Park, NY 12538. Telephone (914) 229-9115.

WOMEN'S RIGHTS NATIONAL HISTORICAL PARK

WOMEN'S RIGHTS NATIONAL HISTORICAL PARK, consisting of five-and-a-half acres in several units in Seneca Falls and Waterloo in western New York State, was established in 1980 to commemorate the long struggle for women's rights and equality. In Seneca Falls, the park protects and interprets a number of properties, including the home of Elizabeth Cady Stanton, a writer and activist who led the formal start of the women's equal rights movement at the First Women's Rights Convention, in 1848, and the remains of the Wesleyan Methodist Chapel where that convention was held; in Waterloo, the M'Clintock House, in which the Declaration of Sentiments was written; and the Hunt House (privately owned), where the equal rights leadership met to plan the convention.

At the time of the Women's Rights Convention, women were clearly held in an inferior status to men. Unmarried women, for instance, were mostly not permitted to earn a living except as teachers, domestics, seamstresses, and mill workers. Nor were they allowed to attend college, hold public office, speak in public, or vote in political elections. Married women were barred from owning their own property, making contracts, filing lawsuits, divorcing an abusive husband, or gaining custody of their children.

In July 1848, a group of equal rights advocates, including Elizabeth Cady Stanton, Lucretia Mott, Martha Wright, Mary Ann M'Clintock, and Jane Hunt, put together a listing of grievances that were patterned after the Declaration of Independence. It condemned the lack of justice and fairness in many walks of life, including marriage and the family, education, employment, property rights—and the right to vote.

The First Women's Rights Convention began on July 19. The more than 300 participants discussed women's social, economic, and political conditions; demanded full, equal rights with men; and the delegates signed the Declaration of Sentiments, which said: "We hold these truths to be self-evident: that all men and women are created equal . . ."

Nearly two weeks following this historic event, a second convention was held in Rochester, New York. In 1850, another, attended by 1,000 participants, took place in Worcester, Massachusetts, followed by more such gatherings throughout the decade. In 1860, lobbying by Elizabeth Cady Stanton and Quaker teacher Susan B. Anthony led to revision of New York State law, permitting a wife to own her own property, retain her earnings and inheritances, make contracts, file lawsuits, and share child custody. Nine years later, Wyoming became the first U.S. territory to allow women to vote in political elections. But in 1875, the U.S. Supreme Court upheld the right of states to bar women from voting.

In 1890, Wyoming came into the Union as the first state allowing women's suffrage, followed shortly by Colorado and Idaho. It was not until 1918 that a women's suffrage amendment to the U.S. Constitution was introduced in Congress, authored by Jeanette Rankin (R-MT)—the first woman elected to the U.S. Congress. The amendment was approved (proposed) by Congress in 1919. In 1920, the U.S. Constitution's Nineteenth Amendment, also known as the Susan B. Anthony Amendment, in honor of her leadership, was ratified—72 years after that first women's rights convention in Seneca Falls. The amendment states that, "The right of citizens of the United States to vote shall not be denied or abridged by the United States or by any State on account of sex."

In 1963, Congress passed the Equal Pay Act, which was the first federal law mandating equal compensation for men and women in the federal government's work force. In the following year, Congress passed a Civil Rights Act banning job discrimination because of sex or race. Progress has continued since then toward achieving for women in America "all the rights and privileges which belong to them as citizens," as stated by the women's movement leaders in 1848. The struggle for equality is continually being promoted in many areas—for women seeking better education, enhanced political influence, employment equality, and health and legal reforms.

Today, visitors to the national historical park should begin at the visitor center, at 136 Fall Street (U.S. Route 20), in Seneca Falls. The center provides interpretive exhibits, an orientation film, videos, and publications. Adjacent to the center is Declaration Park, in which a granite water-wall features the inscribed words of the Declaration of Sentiments. Just to the east of the

M'Clintock House, Women's Rights National Historical Park, Waterloo, New York [NPS]

park are the protected remains of the Wesleyan Chapel. The restored, white-clapboard Elizabeth Cady Stanton House is located at 32 Washington Street and is open for guided tours in summer and for tours on a limited basis during the rest of the year.

In Waterloo, the two-story, red-brick M'Clintock House is located on E. Williams Street, between Virginia and Church streets; and the white-columned, two-story, red-brick Hunt House (not open to the public) is located east of downtown Waterloo, on E. Main Street (U.S. Route 20). The national historical park is open daily, except on Thanksgiving, Christmas, and New Year's Day.

Other places of special interest include the National Women's Hall of Fame, at 76 Fall Street, Seneca Falls (Telephone [315] 568-8060) and the Hall of Fame's Washington, D.C., office, at 406 Skyhill Road, Alexandria, VA 22314 (Telephone [703] 370-3334); the Seneca Falls Urban Cultural Park visitor center, at Fall and State streets; and the Seneca Falls Historical Society, at 55 Cayuga Street. Lodging and meals are available in Seneca Falls, Waterloo, and elsewhere in the area.

IF YOU GO: Access from I-90 (the New York State Thruway) is by way of Exit 41, then south four miles on State Route 414, and left (east) two miles on U.S. Route 20 to the visitor center, at the intersection of Fall and Clinton streets in Seneca Falls. Further information: Superintendent, 136 Fall St., Seneca Falls, NY 13148. Telephone (315) 568-2991.

PART 9

PARKS CELEBRATING AFRICAN AMERICANS IN U.S. HISTORY

BOOKER T. WASHINGTON NATIONAL MONUMENT

BOOKER T. WASHINGTON NATIONAL MONUMENT, consisting of 224 acres in the southern Virginia piedmont, was established in 1957 to honor the memory and accomplishments of Booker T. Washington (1856–1915), an African American who rose from humble beginnings as a child-slave valued at $400. He pursued his education after the Emancipation Proclamation of April 1865 at the conclusion of the Civil War, and attended Hampton Institute, a secondary school in Virginia, where he earned his way by performing menial labor. The monument protects and interprets the historic James Burroughs farm, where Washington was born and spent his childhood as a young slave.

As an adult, Washington became a teacher at the age of 23 at the Hampton Institute, from which he had graduated with honors. At the age of 25, he became the principal of Tuskegee Institute, in Tuskegee, Alabama (see Tuskegee Institute National Historic Site). Washington and his students themselves constructed the institute's initial building—even making their own bricks. In the process, they also practiced one of Washington's fundamental beliefs: hard work teaches self-reliance and builds character. Washington ultimately came to be known as America's leading black educator.

Although, in 1895, Washington expressed the view that it was acceptable for the races to be socially separate—"as separate as the fingers" on the hand, "yet one as the hand in all things essential to mutual progress"—it is also known that Washington secretly gave money to antisegregation activities. In his later years, Washington spoke out forcefully against racism and segregation. In the words of the National Park Service, "Booker T. Washington is best remembered for helping black Americans rise up from the economic slavery that held them down long after they were legally free citizens."

Today, the national monument's visitor center provides interpretive exhibits, an audiovisual program, and publications. A walk on the Plantation

Trail leads visitors to a number of reconstructed farm buildings in the historic part of the monument. The longer Jack-O-Lantern Heritage Trail winds through a wooded expanse of the farm. The monument is open daily, except on Thanksgiving, Christmas, and New Year's Day.

Camping is not permitted in the national monument, but a picnic facility is provided near the site's parking area. Lodging and meals are available in Roanoke, Rocky Mount, and elsewhere in the vicinity.

IF YOU GO: Access from I-81 is by way of I-581; and then 22 miles south from Roanoke on U.S. Route 220 to State Route 122 (the Booker T. Washington Highway); and continuing on the latter to the park entrance. From the Blue Ridge Parkway, access is by way of State Route 43 south to State Route 122 at Bedford; then continuing on the latter to the monument entrance. Further information: Superintendent, 12130 Booker T. Washington Highway, Hardy, VA 24101. Telephone (540) 721-2094.

BOSTON AFRICAN AMERICAN NATIONAL HISTORIC SITE

BOSTON AFRICAN AMERICAN NATIONAL HISTORIC SITE, established in 1980, focuses upon 14 pre-Civil War, privately owned properties relating to African history and culture in the vicinity of Beacon Hill, in Boston, Massachusetts. These properties are linked together by a 1.6-mile-long walking tour known as the Black Heritage Trail. The site information office is located at 46 Joy Street.

While most of the buildings on this route are private residences not open to the public and may be viewed only from the outside, two of the sites are open to visitors: the African Meeting House and the Abiel Smith School.

Another site features the Robert Gould Shaw and 54th Regiment Memorial. The latter commemorates the 54th Regiment of Massachusetts Volunteer Infantry that participated in the Civil War and was the first black regiment to be recruited for the Union army. This regiment, under the command of a young white officer, Colonel Robert Gould Shaw, is remembered for its courageous assault upon Fort Wagner, as part of the strategy for capturing the Confederate-held city of Charleston, South Carolina. In that fierce battle, Colonel Shaw and many of his soldiers were killed. One of the black soldiers, Sergeant William Carney, was wounded three times as he struggled to keep the American flag from falling into Confederate hands. For his valor, Carney became the first African American to receive the Congressional Medal of Honor.

The memorial, which was dedicated in 1897, is a high-relief bronze sculpture that portrays the regiment and which was designed by August Saint-Gaudens. It is located in Boston Common, across from the State House, on Beacon Street.

African Meeting House, Boston African American N H Site [courtesy of the Society for the Preservation of New England Antiquities]

After the memorial, the second stop along the route is the George Middleton House, at 5–7 Pinckney Street. Dating from 1797, it is the oldest extant home on Beacon Hill built by African Americans, and is named for George Middleton (1735–1815), a liveryman who served in the War for Independence (Revolutionary War) and apparently led the black company known as the "Bucks for America."

The third site is the Phillips School at Pinckney and Anderson streets. The three-story, red-brick building, dating from 1824, was initially open only to white male students. In 1855, this became one of the first schools in Boston to contain an interracial student body.

The fourth stop is the John J. Smith House, at 86 Pinckney Street, and is named for John J. Smith (1820–1906), whose barber shop was a focal point for abolitionist activities and a rendezvous for fugitive slaves. During the Civil War, Smith served in Washington, D.C. as a recruiting officer for the all-black 5th Cavalry of the Union army. Following the war, he was elected to the Massachusetts House of Representatives, in 1868, 1869, and 1872. In 1878, he was named to the Boston Common Council, and he lived in this house from 1878 to 1893.

The next site is the Charles Street Meeting House, at Charles and Mt. Vernon streets, which dates from 1807. Before the Civil War, this structure served as a church with segregated seating. From 1876 to 1939, the edifice served as the African Methodist Episcopal Church.

Site 6 is the Lewis and Harriet Hayden House, at 66 Phillips Street, dating from 1833. Lewis Hayden (1816–1889) was born a slave in Kentucky, fled to Detroit by way of the "Underground Railroad," moved to Boston with his wife, Harriet, and quickly became a leader in the abolitionist movement. Hayden's home became a focus of his activities toward abolishing slavery. In 1853, the Vigilance Committee, an abolitionist group, acquired the house.

The John Coburn House, at 2 Phillips Street, dates from 1844, and is named for John Coburn (1811–1873). He served as treasurer of the New England Freedom Association, which was a petitioner in the Boston desegregation effort, and was a member of the Boston Vigilance Committee.

Sites 8 to 12 are the five Smith Court Residences, representative of eighteenth-century black Bostonian homes, at 3–10 Smith Court.

Finally, there are the two properties that are open to the public: the Abiel Smith School, at 46 Joy Street, and the African Meeting House, at 8 Smith Court. The primary and grammar school was built in 1834 and was devoted to the education of many of Boston's black children, until Massachusetts outlawed segregation in public schools in 1855. The Abiel Smith School closed, as students then entered the city's public school system.

The African Meeting House, dating from 1806, is the oldest extant black church building still standing in the United States. The meeting house was not only a place for holding religious services, but also for antislavery and other political gatherings. The New England Anti-Slavery Society was founded here in 1832. In 1972, the building was purchased by the Museum of African American History, with the interior now restored to its 1854 design.

The Black Heritage Trail is offered as a self-guided walking tour, while guided tours are provided daily from Memorial Day to Labor Day, and by special arrangement during the rest of the year. The site office is open five days a week; it is closed on Thanksgiving, Christmas, and New Year's Day.

IF YOU GO: Lodging and meals are available throughout the Boston metropolitan area. Access from the Massachusetts Turnpike is by way of the Prudential-Copley Square exit to Stuart Street and left onto State Route 28

(Charles Street) to Boston Common. As parking is usually virtually impossible to find in downtown Boston, visitors may prefer to take mass transit, by way of the MBTA Red or Green Line to Park Street Station. Further information: Site Manager, National Park Service, 46 Joy Street, Boston, MA 02114. Telephone (617) 720-0753.

BROWN v. BOARD OF EDUCATION NATIONAL HISTORIC SITE

BROWN v. BOARD OF EDUCATION NATIONAL HISTORIC SITE was established in 1992 to commemorate the landmark 1954 U.S. Supreme Court decision of *Brown v. Board of Education* that outlawed racial school segregation. At this writing, the site is scheduled to be open to visitors once the refurbishing of the Monroe Elementary School, in Topeka, Kansas, is complete. There will be interpretive exhibits and programs presenting the struggle in America to achieve equal rights in education.

On May 17, 1954, the nine justices of the Supreme Court voted unanimously to overturn the "separate but equal" doctrine set forth in the court's 1896 decision of *Plessy v. Ferguson.* The ruling in that case upheld the view that accommodations for blacks and whites could be separate, if they were equal. While that case involved passenger segregation on railroads, the doctrine was eventually applied to many other areas, including public education.

The Topeka school case was first heard by the U.S. District Court for Kansas, in 1951. That court ruled against the plaintiffs who included Oliver Brown. However, District Court Judge Walter Huxman subsequently explained that the court's ruling was intended to force the U.S. Supreme Court to a decision on the matter. "If it weren't for *Plessy v. Ferguson,*" he said, "we surely would have found the law unconstitutional. But there was no way around it—the Supreme Court had to overrule itself."

Attorneys for the National Association for the Advancement of Colored People (NAACP) promptly began preparing for the appeal. Other cases similar to *Brown* were being filed in Washington, D.C., Virginia, South Carolina, and Delaware. All these cases had initially been focusing upon the issue of unequal funding between black and white education. Attention now shifted to the claim that segregation was unconstitutional—a violation of the equal protection clause of the U.S. Constitution's Fourteenth Amendment. In December 1952, the Supreme Court decided to consolidate the five cases and hear them together.

Chief Justice Earl Warren wrote the unanimous opinion, stating that "separate educational facilities are inherently unequal." In the courts opinion's summary Warren wrote:

Monroe School, Topeka, Kansas, out of which came the historic *Brown v. Board of Education* Supreme Court case [NPS]

To separate them from others of similar age and qualifications solely because of their race generates a feeling of inferiority as to their status in the community that may affect their hearts and minds in a way unlikely ever to be undone.

Although the site is not open to the public at this time (1997), interpretive talks about the school and the Supreme Court case are provided with advance arrangements.

IF YOU GO: Further information: *Brown v. Board of Education* National Historic Site, 424 S. Kansas Ave., Suite 332, Topeka, KS 66603. Telephone (913) 354-4273.

FREDERICK DOUGLASS NATIONAL HISTORIC SITE

FREDERICK DOUGLASS NATIONAL HISTORIC SITE, consisting of eight acres at 1411 W Street, SE, Washington, D.C., was established in 1962 to honor the legacy and accomplishments of Frederick Douglass (1818–1895), an African American who was born a slave and escaped to freedom at the age of 20. It also protects and interprets Cedar Hill, an 1850s brick house that was Douglass' home from 1877 to 1895.

As an adult, Douglass was a major proponent of the abolition of slavery; advocated women's rights; was an author and owner-editor of an antislavery newspaper; was a fluent speaker in a number of languages; and was an eloquent and highly regarded nineteenth-century African-American orator. Douglass also served as minister to Haiti for the U.S. government. And in his senior years, at his home at Cedar Hill, he was admired as the "Sage of Anacostia" (named after the nearby river), a tribute to his keen, intellectual spirit.

Today, the site's visitor center provides interpretive exhibits, an audio-visual program, and a bookstore with publications on Douglass and African-American culture. Visitors may tour the house and see the Douglass furnishings, books, and other possessions. Cedar Hill is open daily, except on Thanksgiving, Christmas, and New Year's Day. Reservations are required for groups of ten or more.

There are three publications by Douglass: *Life and Times of Frederick Douglass: Written by Himself* (reprint, Collier); *My Bondage and My Freedom* (reprint, Chelsea); and *Narrative of the Life of Frederick Douglass, An American Slave, Written by Himself* (reprint, Harvard University Press).

IF YOU GO: Lodging and meals are available throughout the Washington, D.C., metropolitan area. Access to the site from the I-495/I-95 Beltway is

Cedar Hill, Frederick Douglass National Historic Site [Vicki Paris/NPCA]

by way of Exit 3, north onto Indian Head Highway, which becomes South Capitol Street; then right onto W Street to the site's parking lot. On public transit, from the Howard Road Green Line Metro stop, ride the Mt. Rainier B-2 bus to the site. Further information: Frederick Douglass National Historic Site, 1411 W Street, SE, Washington, DC 20020. Telephone (202) 426-5961.

GEORGE WASHINGTON CARVER NATIONAL MONUMENT

GEORGE WASHINGTON CARVER NATIONAL MONUMENT, comprising 210 acres near Joplin, in southwestern Missouri, was established in 1943 to honor the memory and accomplishments of George Washington Carver (1864–1943). He was an African American who was born a slave and became exceptionally proficient in painting, music, mathematics, and the natural sciences. He was widely acclaimed as an educator, botanist, and agronomist. The national monument also protects and interprets the site where he was born; the surrounding farm, where he learned to love and study the natural environment; and the Carver Family Cemetery.

George Washington Carver was born in a one-room log cabin on the Moses Carver Farm. Soon after his birth, he and his mother were kidnapped in a Confederate guerrilla raid during the Civil War. He was located and returned to Moses and Susan Carver, a white couple who raised him as one of their own family. In George's childhood years, he explored "the woods alone in order to collect my floral beauties and put them in my little garden I had hidden in brush. . . ." He was nicknamed "the Plant Doctor," because of the flowering plants that thrived under his nurturing care. When Carver finally left the farm, his active interest in the natural environment had already given him the perspective of a naturalist and the inquiring mind of a research scientist, while retaining a child's "sense of wonder" about nature. As he said "My work, my life, must be in the spirit of a little child seeking only to know the truth and follow it."

Carver began his career as a research botanist at Iowa Agricultural College (now Iowa State University). He then joined Booker T. Washington at his Tuskegee Institute, in Alabama (see Booker T. Washington National Monument and Tuskegee Institute National Historic Site), where Carver taught botany and agriculture.

Dr. Carver first came to national attention with his agricultural chemistry research that led to the extraction of many products from peanut, sweet potato, and soybean plants. In his desire to help the poor one-horse black farmers, Carver encouraged them to abandon the growing of soil-exhausting cotton, and to cultivate instead such soil-enriching, protein-rich crops as peanuts and soybeans. Dr. Carver's research, writing, and teaching were always carried out with his intense desire "to be of the greatest good to the greatest number of 'my people.'"

Prairie Days at George Washington Carver National Monument, Missouri [NPS]

As the National Park Service says:

Throughout his career, he refused to respect the "boundaries" between science, art, and religion, drawing from one realm to strengthen concepts in another. Perhaps his greatest gift was a talent for drawing others into the spirit of his research. . . . It is not so much his specific achievements as the humane philosophy behind them that define the man. His work was always done with its potential benefit to people in mind. His practical and benevolent approach to science was based on a profound religious faith to which he attributed all his accomplishments. Always modest about his success, he saw himself as a vehicle through which the natural bounty of the land could be better understood and used for the good of all people.

Today, the national monument's visitor center provides interpretive exhibits, audiovisual programs, and publications. On most weekends, special programs, films, and/or tours are offered. There is a self-guiding tour of the main points of interest along the three-quarter-mile Carver Trail. Near the visitor center is the Carver Bust, sculpted by Audrey Corwin and where visitors may hear Dr. Carver's poem, "Equipment," in which he expresses his conviction that we can all attain the goals of life that we set ourselves to pursuing.

Other stops along the trail include the birthplace site; the Boy Carver Statue, sculpted by Robert Amendola; Carver Spring; Williams Spring and Pond; the 1881 Moses Carver House; the site of a grove of persimmon trees planted by Moses Carver; the Carver Family Cemetery; and an area of tallgrass prairie that is being restored to a natural condition. Visitors are cautioned to be alert for poison ivy along the trail. The monument is open daily, except on Thanksgiving, Christmas, and New Year's Day.

Camping is not permitted in the monument, but a picnic area is provided. Lodging and meals are available in Neosho and Joplin, and meals are available in Diamond.

IF YOU GO: Access to the monument from I-44 is by way of Exit 18, then south on U.S. Route Alternate-71 to the town of Diamond, west two miles on County Route V, and south about a mile on Carver Road (County Route 16Q) to the monument entrance. Further information: Superintendent, 5646 Carver Road, Diamond, MO 64840. Telephone (417) 325-4151.

MAGGIE L. WALKER NATIONAL HISTORIC SITE

MAGGIE L. WALKER NATIONAL HISTORIC SITE, consisting of one acre at 110 1/2 E. Leigh Street, in Richmond, Virginia, was established in 1978 to honor the memory and accomplishments of Maggie L. Walker. She established in 1903 one of the first African-American-owned banks in the United States and was the first American woman to become a bank president. She was also a prominent leader of Richmond's black community. The site also protects and interprets the Maggie L. Walker House, a restored red-brick townhouse with original Walker furnishings.

Guided tours are provided through the house, where there are exhibits portraying her life and achievements. A video is shown to visitors upon request. The site is open on Wednesdays through Sundays, except on Thanksgiving, Christmas, and New Year's Day. Groups of five or more visitors are required to make advance reservations.

An informative publication is *Maggie L. Walker: Her Life and Deeds* by Wendell P. Dabney (Eastern National Park and Monument Association).

IF YOU GO: Lodging and meals are available in Richmond. Access from I-95 is by way of Exit 76A or 76B, then continue to Leigh Street. Further information: Maggie L. Walker NHS, c/o Superintendent, Richmond National Battlefield Park, 3215 E. Broad St., Richmond, VA 23223. Telephone (804) 780-1380.

Maggie L. Walker c. 1900 [NPS]

MARTIN LUTHER KING, JR., NATIONAL HISTORIC SITE

MARTIN LUTHER KING, JR., NATIONAL HISTORIC SITE, comprising 23 acres on a five-block stretch of Auburn Avenue, in Atlanta, Georgia, was established in 1980 to honor the memory and accomplishments of Dr. Martin Luther King, Jr. (1929–1968). It protects and interprets the birthplace, church, and grave of the African-American civil rights leader—revered as the most eloquent and successful advocate of racial equality of his time.

Martin Luther King, Jr., was born on January 15, 1929, at 501 Auburn Avenue, in Atlanta. He was the second of three children and attended all-black schools. By age 27, he had earned a Ph.D. in theology from Boston University. In 1954, King was named to the pastorate of the Dexter Avenue Baptist Church, in Montgomery, Alabama. In 1955, after a black woman, Rosa Parks, refused to sit in the back of a bus and was arrested, King was chosen to head the Montgomery Improvement Association—a group established to defend Ms. Parks and to lead a boycott against the bus company.

By 1960, with civil rights travels and other activities consuming the majority of his time, King resigned from the church in Alabama. He then accepted the presidency of a new organization, the Southern Christian Leadership Conference, devoted to the nonviolent advancement of civil rights. Over the next several years, King organized boycotts and other demonstrations in Georgia, Alabama, and elsewhere, in a more aggressive push for equal rights for African-American citizens. In response to these acts of civil disobedience, a number of black homes, businesses, and churches were bombed; civil rights workers were killed; and King was arrested and served a jail sentence.

In 1963, more than 250,000 people held a March on Washington, sponsored by groups such as the Southern Christian Leadership Conference, the National Association for the Advancement of Colored People, the Student Non-Violent Coordinating Committee, the Urban League, the American Negro Labor Council, the National Council of Churches, the National Catholic Conference, and the American Jewish Council. After leaders of the groups met with President John F. Kennedy, King delivered his captivating "I Have a Dream" speech from the steps of the Lincoln Memorial.

In part he said:

> I have a dream that one day on the red hills of Georgia, sons of former slaves and the sons of former slave owners will be able to sit down together at a table of brotherhood. . . . I have a dream that my four little children will one day live in a nation where they will not be judged by the color of their skin, but by the content of their character. This is our hope. This is the faith that I go back to the

South with. With this faith we will be able to hew out of the mountain of despair a stone of hope.

In 1964, after successful lobbying by King and his followers, Congress passed and President Lyndon B. Johnson signed into law the omnibus civil rights bill that banned discrimination across a broad range of areas, including employment, voting, and public accommodations. In 1965, a voting rights act was passed and signed.

On April 4, 1968, while Dr. King was in Memphis, Tennessee, lending his support to a sanitation workers' strike, an assassin fatally shot the civil rights leader.

As John Hope Franklin says of Martin Luther King, Jr., in the National Park Service's brochure on the national historic site:

He raised the discussion of human rights to a new level, and he developed techniques and approaches that made activism in civil rights a viable policy by which stated goals could be achieved. He discovered, however, that it was far easier to secure basic civil and voting rights—as difficult as that was—than to remove from a society the racial prejudices and discriminatory practices by which it had lived for centuries. But by his teachings and example, he infused his own and succeeding generations with a commitment to racial equality and a zeal to work diligently for it. That legacy was second in importance only to the goals that he achieved in his own time.

Several books authored by Dr. King are: *Stride Toward Freedom; Why We Can't Wait;* and *Where Do We Go From Here?*

Today, visitors to the national historic site may begin at the northeast corner of Auburn Avenue and Jackson Street by stopping at the visitor kiosk, where park personnel offer information and where a schedule of activities is available. Scheduled guided tours begin at the historic Bryant-Graves House, dating from 1893 to 1895, at 522 Auburn Avenue, between Hogue and Howell streets. This house now serves as a National Park Service information station. It is named for two prominent African Americans: Rev. Peter James Bryant and developer Antoine Graves. At 501 Auburn Avenue is the Martin Luther King, Jr., Birth Home, dating from 1895. This Queen Anne-style house has been restored to the period when King lived there, from his birth in 1929 to 1941, when the family moved to another house.

Other structures and sites include the Ebenezer Baptist Church, at 407–413 Auburn Avenue, dating from 1914 to 1922, where King followed his grandfather's and father's footsteps as co-pastor, from 1960 to 1968; King's memorial tomb, near the church; and the Martin Luther King, Jr., Center for Nonviolent Social Change, Inc., founded in 1968 to continue Dr. King's work toward achieving social and economic equality.

Adjacent to the national historic site is a three-unit, 68-acre historic preservation district that includes a number of other buildings that were part of Atlanta's African-American economic and cultural center, "Sweet Auburn," during most of the twentieth century.

IF YOU GO: Lodging and meals are available in and around Atlanta. Access to the national historic site from I-75/85 northbound is by way of the Edgewood/Auburn Avenue exit; from I-75/85 southbound by way of the Butler Street exit; and following the signs to the site. Parking is available only in the lot reached from Edgewood Avenue. Further information: Superintendent, 526 Auburn Ave., NE, Atlanta, GA 30312. Telephone (404) 331-5190.

MARY McLEOD BETHUNE COUNCIL HOUSE NATIONAL HISTORIC SITE

MARY McLEOD BETHUNE COUNCIL HOUSE NATIONAL HISTORIC SITE, comprising seven-tenths of an acre, was established in 1982 to honor the memory and accomplishments of Mary McLeod Bethune (1875–1955), an American who rose from modest beginnings to become a distinguished educator, political activist, organizer, and adviser to four presidents of the United States. Founder of Bethune-Cookman College and the National Council of Negro Women, Dr. Bethune worked tirelessly to influence legislation affecting African Americans and women and to develop programs that sought to alleviate economic and social injustice.

The site, which served as her home from 1943 to 1949, also protects and interprets the three-story Victorian townhouse that she acquired to serve as the first headquarters of the National Council of Negro Women from 1943 to 1966.

Bethune realized the significance of education in the emerging civil rights struggle. In 1904, she founded the Daytona Educational and Industrial School for Negro Girls, in Daytona Beach, Florida (subsequently becoming the Bethune-Cookman College).

Presidents Calvin Coolidge and Herbert Hoover appointed Bethune to serve on the National Child Welfare Commission. In 1935, President Franklin D. Roosevelt named her to be a special adviser on minority affairs. When Roosevelt later selected her to direct the National Youth Administration's Division of Negro Affairs, she became the first black woman to head a federal agency. In 1936, she brought together an ad hoc group of black officials—the so-called "Black Cabinet"—which offered suggestions to President Roosevelt on how to provide African Americans with a fair share of the Roosevelt Administration's New Deal social welfare programs.

Appropriately, the house that once served as headquarters for the National Council of Negro Women contains the National Archives for Black Women's History. The Archives is the only site in the United States solely dedi-

Mary McLeod Bethune, educator, political activist, and adviser to four presidents [NPS]

cated to this purpose. The archival holdings include the personal papers of African-American women and the records of their organizations. In addition, there is a photographic collection of more than 3,500 images that document African-American women's activities in the twentieth century. Scholars and researchers from across the country and abroad continue to use the archives. It serves as a catalyst for stimulating research in African-American women's history.

As Mary McLeod Bethune wrote in "Legacy" (1955):

I leave you love. I leave you hope. I leave you the challenge of developing confidence in one another. I leave you a thirst for education. I leave you respect for the use of power. I leave you faith. I leave you racial dignity. I leave you also a desire to live harmoniously with your fellow man. I leave you finally a responsibility to our young people.

These words are inscribed on the base of a 12-foot-tall bronze statue of Mary McLeod Bethune that stands in Lincoln Park, on E. Capitol Street, between 11th and 13th streets, NE, Washington, D.C.

The site provides interpretive exhibits, audiovisual programs, and a bookshop. There are also lectures, workshops, and guided tours for groups of ten or more persons. The archives are available for reference use by appointment. The site is open daily, except on federal holidays.

The Bethune Council House is one of a series of sites along the Washington, D.C., Black History National Recreation Trail. A self-guiding pamphlet on the trail is available by contacting the National Park Service's public affairs office: (202) 619-7222.

Lodging and meals are available throughout the Washington, D.C., metropolitan area. For lodging, advance reservations are advised, especially during peak tourist periods.

IF YOU GO: Access to the site is just south of Logan Circle on Vermont Avenue, in Washington, D.C. Further information: Mary McLeod Bethune Council House, 1318 Vermont Ave., NW, Washington, DC 20005. Telephone (202) 332-1233.

TUSKEGEE INSTITUTE NATIONAL HISTORIC SITE

TUSKEGEE INSTITUTE NATIONAL HISTORIC SITE, consisting of 57 acres adjacent to the city of Tuskegee, in eastern Alabama, was established in 1974 to celebrate the founding in 1881 of Tuskegee Institute as well as its goals and accomplishments.

The school, which began as the Tuskegee Normal and Industrial Institute, held classes for its first 30 students in a run-down church and shanty. The founding principal, Booker T. Washington (see Booker T. Washington National Monument), was born a slave. He established three main goals for his institute. A first objective was to promote teacher training so that graduates would "return to the plantation districts and show the people there how to put new ideas into farming as well as into the intellectual and moral and religious life of the people." A second objective was to promote occupational training so that students would learn practical skills in agricultural and industrial fields. While at Tuskegee, students actually helped construct the institute's buildings and raise food for the school at the institute's farm. A third objective was to promote high moral standards and good manners.

Among the professors that Washington hired was another man who was born a slave, George Washington Carver (see George Washington Carver National Monument). As a member of the institute's faculty for 47 years,

Carver taught, wrote, and carried on an extensive research program in his laboratory. Not only did his work help to bring fame to Tuskegee, but also earned him an international reputation as a leading American research scientist. The institute honored his accomplishments by establishing the George Washington Carver Museum in 1938. The memory of the professor-scientist is also honored by the Carver Research Foundation.

From its modest beginnings, the institute has grown to include more than 160 buildings and over 5,000 students. Many of the buildings were constructed during Booker T. Washington's lifetime, and most of those were built by the students themselves—even down to the firing of the bricks. Architect R.R. Taylor, a member of the institute's faculty and the first African American to graduate (in 1892) from the Massachusetts Institute of Technology, designed most of Tuskegee's buildings and supervised the students in their work of construction.

Visitors to the campus today may tour on foot or by car. The visitor orientation center is located in the Carver Museum, where audiovisual programs and publications are provided. Guided tours are offered at The Oaks, the historic Booker T. Washington home. While a walking tour of the campus is encouraged, visitors are urged to be respectful of the institute's activities and the students' privacy. Both the Carver Museum and The Oaks are administered by the National Park Service, while the remaining historic district is jointly administered by Tuskegee Institute and the Park Service.

IF YOU GO: Lodging and meals are available at the junction of I-85 and Notasula Highway. Access to the institute from I-85 is by way of the State Route 81 exit south; then turning right onto Old Montgomery Road and following signs to the visitor orientation center. Further information: Superintendent, P.O. Drawer 10, Tuskegee, AL 36088. Telephone (205) 727-6390.

PART 10

PARKS CELEBRATING WRITERS, ARTISTS, MUSICIANS, ETC.

■■ ■■ ■■ ■■ ■■ ■■ ■■ ■■ ■■ ■■ ■■

CARL SANDBURG HOME NATIONAL HISTORIC SITE

CARL SANDBURG HOME NATIONAL HISTORIC SITE, comprising 263 acres near Flat Rock, in western North Carolina, was authorized in 1968 to honor the memory and literary accomplishments of poet-author Carl Sandburg (1878–1967). The site also protects and interprets the Sandburg farm, Connemara, where he resided for the last 22 years of his life.

Sandburg was born the son of Swedish immigrants, on January 6, 1878, in the small prairie town of Galesburg, Illinois. Some of his subsequent writings reflected his youth in the Midwest, with its austerity, down-to-earth values, and emphasis on the work ethic. His outlook on life was further influenced by his travels all over the United States and by his active participation in social and political reform efforts.

As the National Park Service says,

> Sandburg was to emerge as one of the great 20th-century voices of the evolving American experience. This "poet laureate" of the people sang of pioneers, cowboys, lumberjacks, railroad section gangs, and steamboat crews. He observed and commemorated the American people, their folk wisdom, heroes, ballads, hopes, and worth.

When Sandburg returned home to Galesburg, Illinois in 1898, at the age of 20, he attended Lombard College and began writing poetry. His first book of poetry, *Chicago Poems*, was published in 1916. For a number of years, he was a newspaper writer, including 13 years with the Chicago *Daily News*. In 1926, his two-volume biography, *Abraham Lincoln: The Prairie Years*, was published. In 1932, he resigned from his newspaper work and turned full-time to his literary career of writing biographical and autobiographical works, a novel, children's books, and poetry and prose on such subjects as history and American folk music.

Carl Sandburg [W. C. Burton]

Sandburg and his wife Lilian ("Paula") lived for a few years in Harbert, Michigan, where he wrote the four-volume *Abraham Lincoln: The War Years,* for which he received the 1940 Pulitzer Prize for history. It was here also that his wife and daughter Helga started raising a prize-winning herd of Chikaming dairy goats. Because of these goats, the Sandburgs decided to head south to a warmer climate; in 1945, they moved to a farm in western North Carolina. For the following two decades, the man of letters derived special inspiration from the farm, Connemara. Here he continued to write prolifically. His novel, *Remembrance Rock,* set forth the American narrative, from the Anglo-Europeans' landing at Plymouth Rock through World War II.

In 1951, Sandburg's *Complete Poems* earned him the Pulitzer Prize for poetry. Two years later, his autobiography, *Always the Young Strangers,* was published. While her husband kept busy writing, Mrs. Sandburg, assisted by their daughters, Helga and Janet, ran the farm and continued to raise her prize-winning herd of goats.

After Carl Sandburg's death on July 22, 1967, The New York *Post's* eulogy said:

> Carl Sandburg was the poet of the American dream and the American reality. His poetry has the freedom of prose, his prose the quality of poetry, and through it all ran what has been called the sense of being American.

Carl Sandburg Home, North Carolina [NPS]

Today, the national historic site's visitor center occupies the ground floor of the three-story, white-clapboard Sandburg home. The center provides orientation and interpretive exhibits; audiovisual programs, including a short orientation film; and an 11-minute taped interview with Sandburg in 1954 by the well-known radio news commentator Edward R. Murrow. The center is open daily except on Christmas.

Visitors may walk around the farm to see such structures as the main goat barn and milkhouse; the farm manager's house; the Swedish House, where Sandburg stored books, magazines, and other research materials; and the pump houses. The site also provides five miles of trails that wind through the property.

Among the many books about Sandburg are *Carl Sandburg, A Biography,* by Penelope Niven; *Carl Sandburg Home,* by Sandburg's granddaughter, Paula Steichen (National Park Handbook #117); and *My Connemara,* by Paula Steichen (Eastern Acorn Press). Many of Sandburg's poems are published in *Carl Sandburg Selected Poems* (Gramercy Books).

IF YOU GO: Camping is not permitted on the property. Lodging and meals are available in Flat Rock, Hendersonville, Saluda, Tryon, and elsewhere in the area. Access is by way of I-26 southbound about 30 miles from Asheville, take exit 22 and follow signs to U.S. Route 25, and turn left onto Little River Road to the site; or by way of U.S. Route 25 from Greenville, SC, about 37 miles. Further information: Superintendent, 1928 Little River Rd., Flat Rock, NC 28731. Telephone (704) 693-4178.]

EDGAR ALLAN POE NATIONAL HISTORIC SITE

EDGAR ALLAN POE NATIONAL HISTORIC SITE, comprising about half an acre at 532 North 7th Street, Philadelphia, Pennsylvania, was established in 1978 to commemorate the life and writings of the American author, poet, editor, and critic Edgar Allan Poe (1809–1849).

At the age of 18, he published his first collection of poems, and at 26, he became the editor of the *Southern Literary Messenger*, in Richmond, Virginia. Thus began his career as editor, critic, and contributor of writings for a number of literary publications. The following year, he married Virginia Clemm and, with her mother, they moved from Richmond to New York City and then to Philadelphia. They resided there from 1843 to 1844 at the red-brick, three-story building in today's national historic site. It was while in Philadelphia that Poe reached his greatest success as editor and critic, and as writer of murder mysteries and other stories. Among his most famous tales were "The Gold Bug," "The Fall of the House of Usher," "The Tell-Tale Heart," "The Man of the Crowd," "The Purloined Letter," "The Murders in the Rue Morgue," "The Black Cat," and "The Pit and the Pendulum."

In 1844, they moved back to New York, where he owned his own journal for a brief time. Three years later, his wife died of tuberculosis. Following Virginia's death, Poe's mental and physical health declined, and he died in 1849 in Baltimore.

In the words of the National Park Service:

Edgar Poe . . . has probably had a greater influence than any other American writer. Although Poe's tales and poems range from masterful to ludicrous, Poe exerted his most significant influence as a man who understood the temper of his times, and foreshadowed so much of the future of literature . . . A review of his more than seventy pieces of fiction testifies not merely to his range, but also to the significant popular genres he created or made his own which today form the staples of American fiction.

Poe's greatest influence comes about in the murder mystery. He can be said to have invented it when he published "The Murders in the Rue Morgue." Although murders in fiction existed before Poe, his preoccupation with the ingenious solution of the crime established in his tales of ratiocination (the process of exact thinking) changed the emphasis from the acts to getting the facts.

Today, the national historic site is a complex of three buildings including Poe's home and two neighboring structures containing interpretive exhibits and an audiovisual program. With hours that fluctuate seasonally, the site is open daily, except on Thanksgiving, Christmas, and New Year's Day.

IF YOU GO: Lodging and meals are available throughout the Philadelphia metropolitan area. The site is located approximately one mile north of Independence Hall (see Independence National Historical Park). Access from I-95 northbound is by way of the "Historic Area" exit, turning left at the bottom of the ramp onto Delaware Avenue (some sections are called "Columbus Ave."), proceeding about one-and-a-half miles, turning left onto Spring Garden Street, and continuing to 7th Street; or from I-95 southbound is by way of the "Independence Hall/Historic Area" exit, turning right at the bottom of the ramp onto Callowhill Street, proceeding to 7th Street, turning right onto 7th , and continuing to Spring Garden Street. On-street parking is sometimes available.

Access from I-76 (the Schuylkill Expressway) eastbound is by way of I-676 East, toward "Central Philadelphia," proceeding to the 8th Street exit and proceeding straight at the first traffic light, turning left at the second traffic light, and continuing two blocks to Spring Garden Street.

Public transit access includes the Market-Frankford subway east to 8th and Market streets, walking one block east to 7th Street, and taking the #47 bus to 7th and Spring Garden streets. Further information: Superintendent, 313 Walnut Street, Philadelphia, PA 19106. Telephone (215) 597-8780.

EUGENE O'NEILL NATIONAL HISTORIC SITE

EUGENE O'NEILL NATIONAL HISTORIC SITE, comprising 13 acres near Danville, California, was designated in 1976 to commemorate the famous playwright Eugene O'Neill (1888–1953) and his contribution to American theater. He wrote such plays as *Emperor Jones, Anna Christie, Mourning Becomes Electra,* and *Strange Interlude.* At this site, O'Neill wrote of his own family tragedies in *Long Day's Journey Into Night* and *A Moon for the Misbegotten,* his last play. Eugene O'Neill was the recipient of four Pulitzer Prizes and is, to this time, the only American playwright to receive the Nobel Prize for literature (1936).

The National Park Service protects and interprets the site, which includes Tao House, O'Neill's home from 1937 to 1944. Ranger-led tours are provided to visitors on Wednesdays through Sundays throughout the year, except on Thanksgiving, Christmas, and New Year's Day. Reservations for tours are required and may be made by contacting the park.

An informative publication is *Eugene O'Neill at Tao House,* by Travis Bogard (Southwest Parks and Monuments Association). The playwright's works are published in the three-volume *Complete Plays of Eugene O'Neill,* edited by Travis Bogard (The Library of America).

IF YOU GO: Lodging and meals are available in Danville, San Ramon, Pleasanton, Walnut Creek, and to the west in the San Francisco Bay Area. Access to the park's shuttle pick-up site from I-680 is by way of the Diablo Road exit in Danville. Further information and reservations: Superintendent, P.O. Box 280, Danville, CA 94526. Telephone (510) 838-0249.

FREDERICK LAW OLMSTED NATIONAL HISTORIC SITE

FREDERICK LAW OLMSTED NATIONAL HISTORIC SITE consists of just under two acres at 99 Warren Street in Brookline, a suburb of Boston, Massachusetts. It was established in 1979 to honor the memory and accomplishments of the nineteenth-century father of landscape architecture in America and prominent designer of urban parks, Frederick Law Olmsted (1822–1903). The site also protects and interprets Olmsted's home and office, known as Fairsted.

In 1883, Olmsted moved from New York City to a farmhouse in Brookline where he created the nation's first comprehensive professional landscape architecture practice. His office was the nucleus of a complex of offices and other facilities. Olmsted's sons, John Charles (1852–1920) and Frederick, Jr. (1870–1957), were both trained in landscape design and worked for the firm—John Charles as manager, following the senior Olmsted's retirement in 1895, and Frederick, Jr., as a partner.

Frederick Law Olmsted developed an early appreciation for the "great simple country" from his travels through the countryside in New England. With less than a year of college studies, he decided to go out and explore and experience the world. He served as an engineer's apprentice, devoted four years as a "scientific farmer," and in 1850 went on a walking tour of Europe, studying the landscaping of estate grounds and parks.

The New York Times assigned Olmsted to report on impacts of slavery on the economy of the South, a trip that resulted in the publication of his book, *Journey in the Seaboard Slave States*. The following year, he was chosen to oversee construction of New York City's Central Park. He teamed up with architect Calvert Vaux to create "a multi-faceted pleasure ground" from 840 acres of rocky ground, swampy wetlands, hog farms, and slaughterhouses.

For the next four decades, Olmsted's fame soared. He received commissions to design dozens of city and state parks; the grounds for educational and hospital institutions; parkways; private estates, including the George Vanderbilt estate, "Biltmore," in North Carolina; residential subdivisions, such as the Chicago suburb of Riverside; the Boston Park System's five-mile "emerald necklace" of connected parklands, ponds, riverway, and parkways; the U.S. Capitol grounds, in Washington D.C.; and the site of the 1893 Chicago World's Fair. The grounds of Olmsted's own home at Fairsted were beautifully landscaped to show how the "ideal suburban lifestyle" could be picturesquely created.

In the words of the National Park Service:

> America was experiencing unprecedented growth in the mid-19th century, making the transition from a rural people to a complex urban society. . . . Olmsted and others saw the need for preserving green and open spaces where people could escape city pressures,

places that nourished body and spirit. . . . Unable to separate his love and respect for the land from his belief in democracy, Olmsted saw parks as bastions of the democratic ideals of community and equality. . . . With other reformers, he pushed for protection of the Yosemite Valley. His 1864 report on the park was the first systematic justification for public protection of natural areas, emphasizing the duty of a democratic society to ensure that the "body of the people" have access to natural beauty.

Today, visitors to the national historic site may tour the Olmsted home, office, and attractively landscaped grounds. Interpretive exhibits, an audiovisual program, and publications on landscape architecture are provided. The site is open on Fridays through Sundays, except on Christmas and New Year's Day. Group tours are provided with advance reservations.

Lodging and meals are available in Brookline and elsewhere in the Boston metropolitan area. Access from I-95 is by way of State Route 9 East (Brookline/Boston) exit, proceeding on Route 9 just beyond the Brookline Reservoir on the right, and then turning right onto Warren Street, and continuing to the site, on the right, at the junction of Warren and Dudley streets. Or from I-93 (the Southeast Expressway), proceeding west on the Massachusetts Turnpike, taking the Brighton-Harvard Street exit, following Harvard Street to a right turn onto Boylston Street (State Route 9), proceeding to a left turn onto Warren Street and to the site. Further Information: Superintendent, 99 Warren St., Brookline, MA 02146. Telephone (617) 566-1689.

GLEN ECHO PARK

GLEN ECHO PARK comprises nine acres in Glen Echo, Maryland, about two-and-a-half miles northwest of Washington, D.C. It was acquired by the National Park Service in 1971, with the leadership of a group of public-spirited citizens who were instrumental in helping bring the park into public ownership and assure the protection of this historic place and its continued use as a park that emphasizes the arts and cultural education.

Glen Echo began in 1891 as a National Chautauqua Assembly—a center where people came to learn about and participate in the arts, literature, languages, and the sciences. The center started with great enthusiasm. But when one of the program directors died of pneumonia and it was rumored that he had succumbed to malaria, people were afraid to attend the center's programs, and it was forced to close after that first season.

In 1899, the property was taken over by the Glen Echo Company, which established a major amusement park that was popular for the following six decades. There were roller-coaster rides, a Dentzel carousel, a bumper-car pavilion, a large pool, a hall of mirrors, and ballroom attractions. By 1968, the popularity of the amusement attractions had significantly declined and Glen Echo was closed after that season.

Between the time the facility closed and 1971, when a land exchange enabled the federal acquisition of the property, many of the rides had been sold, including the carousel. But then a group of interested persons organized a fundraising campaign that succeeded in buying back this historic merry-go-round.

The National Park Service met with community leaders, artists, teachers, and special interest organizations to discuss the potential for Glen Echo Park. As a result, once again Glen Echo has become a Chautauqua Assembly-like learning center, where artists, students, teachers, and park visitors come together, exchange ideas, and learn from one another, in a setting of historic buildings from the Chautauqua and amusement park past.

Today, visitors are urged to stop at the historic stone tower/gallery to obtain information on park activities. The gallery is open in the afternoon, Tuesdays through Sundays. Visits to resident artists' studios is also encouraged, and there are four annual art and educational class sessions that are available for enrollment. In addition, the park provides Sunday concerts, workshops, demonstrations, and festivals, from mid-May through September. The carousel operates in the afternoon, Wednesdays, Thursdays, and weekends, from May through September. The park is open daily.

Adjacent to the park is the Clara Barton National Historic Site (see the text on this unit of the National Park System).

Picnic facilities are provided at the park. Lodging and meals are available in Glen Echo and elsewhere in the Washington, D.C., metropolitan area. Advanced reservations are advised for the peak tourists seasons.

IF YOU GO: Access to the park is by way of MacArthur Boulevard from Washington, about three miles to the northwest of the D.C.-Maryland line; then turning left onto Oxford Road and continuing to the parking area. Access from Washington is also by way of Massachusetts Avenue (in D.C. and continuing into Maryland), then left (west) onto Goldsboro Road (State Route 614), right onto MacArthur Boulevard, and left onto Oxford Road. Access from I-495 (the Capital Beltway) is by way of the Clara Barton Parkway along the Potomac River to Glen Echo, and following Glen Echo Park signs to Oxford Road. Further information: Glen Echo Park, MacArthur Blvd., Glen Echo, MD 20812. Telephone (301) 492-6282.

Hampton National Historic Site, Maryland [NPS]

HAMPTON NATIONAL HISTORIC SITE

HAMPTON NATIONAL HISTORIC SITE, comprising 63 acres at 535 Hampton Lane, in Towson, Maryland, was given to the National Park Service in 1948 to protect and interpret an elaborate late-eighteenth-century mansion, originally called Hampton Hall, that was built between 1783 and 1790. The lavish home of Captain Charles Ridgely, and of six other generations of this prominent Maryland family for more than 150 years, was once surrounded by a 24,000-acre estate that was served by a large number of slaves and indentured servants. It boasted a complex of outbuildings, grand trees, extensive English-style formal gardens, vineyards, orchards, expansive pastures and fields, and prize-winning thoroughbred racehorses.

The three-story mansion, topped by an imposing cupola, is an ostentatiously ornate takeoff from the typically more conservative Georgian architectural style of that time. The interior of the grand home is furnished to reflect the period from the late eighteenth to the late nineteenth centuries. Visitors today may see many of the original Ridgely family possessions, including elegant furniture, carpets, china, chandeliers, and family pictures.

Tours of the mansion are offered, while visitors may enjoy self-guided tours of the gardens, farm, stables, and other parts of the property. There are also a gift shop and tea room. The grounds of the site are open daily, except on Thanksgiving, Christmas, and New Year's Day.

An informative publication is *A Guidebook to Hampton National Historic Site* by Lynne Dakin Hastings (Historic Hampton, Inc.).

IF YOU GO: Lodging and meals are available in Towson and elsewhere in the vicinity. Access from I-95 is by way of the exit onto Dulaney Valley Road (State Route 146) and then a right turn onto Hampton Lane to the site. Further information: Superintendent, 535 Hampton Lane, Towson, MD 21286. Telephone (410) 962-0688.

John Muir Home, in California, where he lived from 1890 to 1914 [Jack Harris/NPS]

JOHN MUIR NATIONAL HISTORIC SITE

JOHN MUIR NATIONAL HISTORIC SITE consists of 334 acres at 4202 Alhambra Avenue, in Martinez, California. It was established in 1964 to commemorate the life, writings, and environmental-protection efforts of John Muir, the Scottish-born, late-nineteenth and early-twentieth-century advocate of wilderness and park protection. The site also protects and interprets Muir's two-story, cupola-topped, 17-room, Victorian, Italianate-style mansion, dating from 1882. This was his home from 1890 until his death in 1914. The site also preserves the two-story, Monterey-style adobe home of Vicente Martinez, son of Ignacio, for whom the town of Martinez is named. The Martinez Adobe, dating from 1849, presents information on local history and of land use in California.

John Muir urged others to do what he had a passion for: "Climb the mountains and get their good tidings. Nature's peace will flow into you as sunshine flows into trees."

When he was not climbing the heights of the Sierra Nevada or other wilderness places, he was writing books and articles for magazines such as *Century* and *The Atlantic*, in an effort to help inspire others with his enthusiasm for wilderness and the importance of protecting scenic wilderness areas for their own sake and for future generations to enjoy.

As Muir hiked the Sierra wilderness, he was deeply distressed to see how vast hordes of sheep were ravaging the delicate high-mountain meadows. He referred to those destructive herds as "hoofed locusts." Such human impacts upon the natural ecosystems of the mountains led Muir to strongly advocate the establishment of parks where grazing, logging, and other extractive resource uses would not be permitted. He was largely responsible for the establishment of Yosemite National Park, in California, protecting not only the famous Yosemite Valley, but much of the High Sierra that he especially loved.

In 1892, Muir helped to found the San Francisco-based conservation organization, the Sierra Club. Unfortunately, his and the club's bitterest environmental defeat came at Yosemite National Park in 1913, with approval of the construction of Hetch Hetchy Dam. That power-generation facility for the city of San Francisco inundated the park's other irreplaceable and spectacularly scenic valley that was second only to Yosemite Valley.

As Ariel Rubissow writes in *John Muir National Historic Site* (Southwest Parks and Monuments Association):

> Muir's influence on the birth and growth of an American conservation ethic was both public and private. His charisma, humor, and uncompromising integrity won him the support of all kinds of people, from President Theodore Roosevelt and Ralph Waldo Emerson to the many young men and women who later followed in his footsteps. With their support and the energy of his pen and imagination, Muir played a major role in preserving the unique lands that now form the heart of America's vast national park system. . . .

Among the books on and by John Muir are: *The American Conservation Movement: John Muir and His Legacy* by Stephen R. Fox (reprint, University of Wisconsin Press); and by John Muir: *The Mountains of California* and *Our National Parks.* All of Muir's books are available through Sierra Club Books, under the auspices of the John Muir Library.

Exhibits on John Muir and the Sierra Club and an audiovisual program on Muir's life and environmental philosophy are presented at the site. There are guided tours (starting at 2 p.m.) and self-guiding tours on

Wednesdays through Sundays (between 10 a.m. and 4:30 p.m.). Advance reservations are required for groups of ten or more persons. The site is closed on Thanksgiving, Christmas, and New Year's Day.

IF YOU GO: Camping is not allowed on the site, but a picnic facility is available. Lodging and meals are available in Martinez, Concord, and the San Francisco Bay Area. Access is by way of the Alhambra Avenue exit from State Route 4 (the site is at the foot of the off-ramp, to the north of route 4). Further information: Superintendent, 4202 Alhambra Ave., Martinez, CA 94553. Telephone (510) 228-8860.

LONGFELLOW NATIONAL HISTORIC SITE

LONGFELLOW NATIONAL HISTORIC SITE, consisting of two acres at 105 Brattle Street, in Cambridge, Massachusetts, was established in 1972 to commemorate the life and works of the famous American poet, Henry Wadsworth Longfellow (1807–1882). The site also protects and interprets the elegant red-brick, Georgian-style house, dating from 1759, where Longfellow lived for 45 years, while teaching at Harvard. Earlier, George Washington headquartered at this house during the British siege of Boston, in 1775–1976.

Longfellow initially rented two rooms in the Brattle Street house, but when he married Frances Elizabeth Appleton in 1843, the bride's father bought the house as a gift for the newlyweds. The Longfellows' marriage has been described as an extremely happy one. Frances, who was a literary and art critic, gave birth to their six children; but tragically she died of burns from a fire in 1861. The grieving poet found solace in his writing, his children, and his friends, who included such other prominent literary figures as Ralph Waldo Emerson and Nathaniel Hawthorne.

Today, visitors to the Longfellow house may see his study and the desk where he wrote many of his works including *Evangeline: A Tale of Acadie* (1847), *The Song of Hiawatha* (1855), and *Tales of a Wayside Inn* (1863, 1872, and 1873). Although Longfellow was a complex man, much of his writing expressed the virtue of simplicity and uncomplicated solutions to facing life's challenges. One of Longfellow's poems, "The Psalm of Life," offers advice on overcoming difficulties by keeping busy, reaching for our inner strength, holding onto hope, and being patient:

Henry W. Longfellow, 1868, photographed by Julia Margaret Cameron [NPS]

Longfellow's house, Cambridge, Massachusetts [NPS/Longfellow National
Historic Site]

> Let us, then, be up and doing,
> With a heart for any fate;
> Still achieving, still pursuing,
> Learn to labor and to wait.

Ranger-guided tours of the house are offered several times each day.
Summer concerts are presented in the garden (weather permitting) on every
other Sunday, beginning in mid-June. The national historic site is open daily,
except on Thanksgiving, Christmas, and New Year's Day.

IF YOU GO: Lodging and meals are available in Cambridge and elsewhere in
the Boston metropolitan area. For visitors wishing to avoid driving and parking in Cambridge, they may park beneath Boston Common, ride the Red Line
subway to Harvard Square, and walk down Brattle Street just over half-a-mile
to the site. Further information: Superintendent, 105 Brattle St., Cambridge,
MA 02138. Telephone (617) 876-4491.

NEW ORLEANS JAZZ NATIONAL HISTORICAL PARK

NEW ORLEANS JAZZ NATIONAL HISTORICAL PARK, located in New Orleans, Louisiana, was established in 1994 to commemorate the history of jazz—a uniquely American musical form that had its roots in this city. The park's purpose is also to encourage the preservation and interpretation of jazz's evolution in New Orleans. In the park's enabling legislation, Congress described jazz as "a rare and invaluable national treasure of international importance" that is the "most widely recognized indigenous art form" in the United States. New Orleans Jazz Park, which is to be managed in conjunction with Jean Lafitte National Historical Park and Preserve (see the text on this park), will likely be less land-based than programmatic. As of this writing (1996), no properties have been acquired by the National Park Service.

Ironically, none of the sites in New Orleans associated with jazz was even placed on the National Register of Historic Places by the time this park was established. One explanation for this omission may be that by the time this form of music became really popular and deserving of being recorded by the then-just-budding recording industry, many of its best jazz musicians had moved away to seek jobs in the North in such places as Chicago. As John McDonough wrote in his article, "Crescent City Cadence" *(National Parks,* May/June 1995):

> The coordinates of art and technology would meet in Richmond, Indiana, where the earliest examples of authentic New Orleans jazz were inscribed between 1917 and 1923. Recordings were made by musicians who had left the city behind for points north, carrying with them the mature polyphonic forms of classic New Orleans jazz. The early evolution and development of the music in New Orleans left no recordings, no paper trail of score sheets, and no financial records. It all lay largely lost and neglected behind an unbreachable wall of historic silence.

Among the places that may become part of the park's interpretive focus are Perseverance Hall, in which some of New Orleans' earliest jazz was presented; Odd Fellows and Masonic Dance Hall-and-Eagle Saloon; Frank Early's Saloon; The Red Onion; Francis Amis Hall, a former Creole dance hall where jazz bands performed; Iroquois Theater, an African-American vaudeville center; and the Tango Belt where the Original Dixieland Jazz Band and the New Orleans Rhythm Kings played before moving north.

As McDonough explained:

> New Orleans was the original multicultural city, and jazz would become perhaps the first enduring monument to genuine American multiculturalism. No race, language, or nationality holds true title,

emotional or otherwise, to the creation of jazz. Though the preponderance of its masters surely have been African American, jazz's roots are entangled in the fusion of black, white, and Creole; African, European, and American; spirituals, rhythm, and melody.

IF YOU GO: For further information on the New Orleans Jazz National Historical Park: Superintendent, Jean Lafitte National Historical Park and Preserve, 419 Rue Decatur, New Orleans, LA 70130. Telephone (504) 589-3882.

SAINT-GAUDENS NATIONAL HISTORIC SITE

SAINT-GAUDENS NATIONAL HISTORIC SITE, comprising 150 acres overlooking the Connecticut River valley, in Cornish, New Hampshire, was established in 1977 to commemorate the life and works of the famous American sculptor Augustus Saint-Gaudens (1848–1907). The site also protects and interprets the sculptor's home, which he named "Aspet" and transformed from a former tavern to an elegant mansion. Saint-Gaudens also converted a barn into his studio. Other studios were subsequently built nearby, as the property became a center for the "Cornish Colony" of painters, musicians, actors, and writers.

Shaw Memorial by Saint-Gaudens [Jeff Ninzel]

"Aspet," home of sculptor Augustus Saint-Gaudens, in Cornish, New Hampshire [NPS]

Among the sculptor's works are the "Farragut Monument" in New York City; the bronze heroic of the "Robert Gould Shaw and 54th Regiment Memorial" on Boston Common (see the text on Boston African American National Historic Site); and the "Adams Memorial" in Rock Creek Church Cemetery, in Washington, D.C. Bronze casts of these sculptures are on exhibit at the site.

Today, visitors are given interpretive tours of the Saint-Gaudens home, the studios, and landscaped grounds. More than 100 of the sculptor's works are on permanent exhibition. Two nature trails offer delightful walks through 100 acres of natural area. A sculptor-in-residence program is located at the Ravine Studio. During the summer months, a series of concerts and changing art exhibits are presented in cooperation with the Saint-Gaudens Memorial. The site is open from Memorial Day weekend through October.

IF YOU GO: Camping is not permitted on the site, but picnic facilities are provided. Lodging and meals are available in Claremont and Lebanon, NH; Windsor, VT; and elsewhere in the area. Access is by way of New Hampshire State Route 12A, nine miles north of Claremont, or two miles from Windsor. Access from I-89 is by way of Exit 20 (West Lebanon), and then taking State Route 12A south to the site. Further information: Superintendent, RR 3, Box 73, Cornish, NH 03745. Telephone (603) 675-2175.

SAINT PAUL'S CHURCH NATIONAL HISTORIC SITE

SAINT PAUL'S CHURCH NATIONAL HISTORIC SITE comprises six acres at 897 S. Columbus Avenue, in Mount Vernon, New York. It was established in 1938 to protect and interpret this eighteenth-century church that is associated with the struggle for freedom of speech and the press in colonial America.

The original Saint Paul's Church edifice was built in 1665. It was made famous in 1733, during the election for Westchester County assemblyman. The county's high sheriff, who had been appointed by New York's British colonial governor, placed a notice of the election on the door of the church, but deliberately neglected to say when on election day voting was to take place. As had previously occurred, the sheriff aimed to show up on the village green adjacent to the church with the governor's candidate at an unannounced time and hold the election without local opponents. The sheriff did not know, however, that a newly formed political action group, calling itself "The People's Party," had plans to at appear the village green with the party's own candidate—and to remain there throughout the day if necessary, to assure being present whenever the sheriff and the governor's candidate chose to arrive.

When the election began, voters lined themselves behind the candidate of their choice—this becoming the first recorded election in colonial America between candidates of opposing political parties. The People's Party's candidate, William Morris, was the winner. The sheriff then attempted to disqualify certain voters, but Morris still had enough votes to defeat the governor's candidate.

A week after the election, the first edition of the New York *Weekly Journal* was produced by a former newspaper apprentice, John Peter Zenger. The newspaper published a thorough account of the sheriff's corrupt political actions; ran satirical attacks upon governmental officials, including the governor, who considered themselves above the law; and praised the virtues of freedom of speech and the press. In retaliation, the governor ordered Zenger jailed and had him tried for what he viewed as libelous writings. Zenger's defense was that he had the right to publish information that was "notoriously" factual. A jury found Zenger innocent of the charge of libel. Not only did this historic court decision set a significant precedent in New York for the protection of the press from governmental interference, but the Zenger trial provided a compelling reason for nationally ensuring freedom of the press, as subsequently embodied in the First Amendment of the U.S. Constitution's Bill of Rights.

A new stone church building, replacing the original wood structure, was completed in 1787. Today, the national historic site features that building, along with the former parish hall that now houses a museum. Visitors may tour the church, museum, and associated cemetery. Publications are available at the museum's gift shop.

The site is open on Saturday afternoons, except when a Saturday is prior to a national holiday on the following Monday; on Tuesdays through Fridays by appointment; and is closed on Thanksgiving, Christmas, and New Year's Day. Lodging and meals are available in Mount Vernon, New Rochelle, and New York City.

IF YOU GO: Access from I-95 (the New England Thruway) northbound is by way of the Conner Street exit; turning left and proceeding one stop light; turning left and continuing straight (this street becomes S. Columbus Avenue (State Route 22) to the site. Further information: Superintendent, 897 S. Columbus Ave., Mount Vernon, NY 10550. Telephone (914) 667-4116.

Vanderbilt Mansion, near Hyde Park, New York [NPS]

VANDERBILT MANSION NATIONAL HISTORIC SITE

VANDERBILT MANSION NATIONAL HISTORIC SITE, consisting of 211 acres at 519 Albany Post Road, just north of Hyde Park, New York, was established in 1940 to protect and interpret this nineteenth-century palatial home. The ostentatious Italian Renaissance-style mansion, overlooking the Hudson River Valley, was built by millionaire Frederick W. Vanderbilt. It is an outstanding example of opulent estates built by men who made enormous fortunes during America's late-nineteenth-century era of rapid economic growth in finance and industry. Prior to Vanderbilt's purchase of the property, it had long been the site of horticultural experimentation and gardening that included a wealth of beautiful exotic and rare plants and trees.

Today, the site has a visitor center, located in the pavilion close by the mansion, that provides interpretive exhibits and an audiovisual program. Tours of the mansion and grounds begin at the center. The site is open daily from April through October, and on Thursdays through Mondays from November through March. It is closed on Thanksgiving, Christmas, and New Year's Day. **IF YOU GO:** Lodging and meals are available in Hyde Park, Poughkeepsie, and elsewhere in the area. Access is by way of U.S. Route 9, eight miles north of Poughkeepsie or 18 miles south of Rhinebeck. Further information: Superintendent, Roosevelt-Vanderbilt National Historic Sites, 519 Albany Post Rd., Hyde Park, NY 12538. Telephone (914) 229-7821.

WEIR FARM NATIONAL HISTORIC SITE

WEIR FARM NATIONAL HISTORIC SITE, comprising 60 acres in the southwestern Connecticut towns of Ridgefield and Wilton, was established in 1990. It protects and interprets the summer home and workplace of American Impressionist painter, J. Alden Weir (1852–1919), who purchased the property in 1882 for ten dollars and a painting. The farm became one of Weir's primary sources of inspiration, and it has provided continuous inspiration to artists ever since.

Weir Farm [NPS]

Weir lived and painted here for nearly 40 years. He expanded the "quiet plain little house among the rocks" several times, built an art studio, and kept working to improve the aesthetic quality of the farm's landscape. The National Park Service writes:

> The farm became, in a sense, a big sprawling palette, its buildings, stone walls, woods, and gardens all elements in the painter's evolving composition. It also inspired and suggested subject matter for much of Weir's work and offered countless excursions, both recreational and creative, to his wide circle of friends that included many leading figures in American art.

J. Alden Weir also devoted much of his time to teaching and helping young artists. Among his artist friends who visited the farm were John Twachtman and Childe Hassam, who in 1897 helped form a prominent exhibition group known as the "Ten American Painters."

In 1931, noted sculptor Mahonri Young (1877-1957) married Weir's daughter Dorothy and came to live and work at the farm. He built his own studio next to Weir's, to accommodate large-scale sculpture. Dorothy, herself a painter who had trained with her father, used his studio for her own work after Weir's death in 1919.

Since Mahonri Young's death in 1957, the tradition of artists living and working at Weir Farm has been carried on by Sperry and Doris Andrews, both painters. The Andrewses recognized this as a place of extraordinary significance to American art and were instrumental in preserving the landscape and its artistic legacy for the visiting public and future generations of artists.

Weir Farm, Connecticut [NPS]

Today, a visitor center is located in Burlingham House, an old farm house on the property once occupied by another of Weir's daughters, Cora Weir Burlingham. An orientation video, visitor desk, and changing exhibits are offered here. Guided tours of the Weir Studio, Weir Garden and Young Studio are offered Wednesdays through Saturdays at 10 a.m. The Weir Farm Heritage Trust, a nonprofit organization working in partnership with the National Park Service, offers lectures, art classes, workshops, and special exhibits. Additionally, the trust sponsors a program for professional artists, the Visiting Artists Program, which continues the tradition of Weir Farm's landscape-inspiring art.

Of particular interest to park visitors is the self-guided Weir Farm Historic Painting Sites Trail. Visitors are able to visit 12 sites at the farm and compare reproductions of paintings to the actual landscape views that inspired them. This is perhaps the best way to experience one of Weir Farm's greatest treasures, the landscape of American Impressionism.

Several publications are deserving of mention: *J. Alden Weir: An American Impressionist* by Doreen Bolger (University of Delaware Press); *The Life and Letters of J. Alden Weir* by Dorothy Weir Young (Yale University Press); and *J. Alden Weir: A Place of His Own* by Hildegard Cummings, Helen K. Fusscas, and Susan G. Larkin (William Benton Museum of Art, University of Connecticut).

IF YOU GO: Lodging and meals are available in Ridgefield and other communities in the surrounding area. Access to the site from I-95 and the Merritt Parkway is by way of their exits onto U.S. Route 7 northbound; or from I-84 by way of exit 3 or U.S. Route 7 southbound; proceed to State Route 102 West to Old Branchville Road to Nod Hill Road. For information on special Weir Farm Heritage Trust programs, classes, and exhibits: Telephone (203) 761-9945. Further information: 735 Nod Hill Road, Wilton, CT 06897. Telephone (203) 834-1896.

Wolf Trap Farm Park for the Performing Arts, Virginia [NPS]

WOLF TRAP FARM PARK FOR THE PERFORMING ARTS

WOLF TRAP FARM PARK FOR THE PERFORMING ARTS, consisting of 130 acres near Vienna, Virginia, and about eight miles west of Washington, D.C., was established in 1966, specifically designed to promote the performing arts. The park and its Filene Center were the generous gift of Catherine Filene Shouse. She wished to preserve this former farm as a place where visitors could be inspired by the natural beauty and tranquillity of the surrounding woods, a stream, and fields and where audiences could be inspired by the human creativity of the performing arts.

The Filene Center opened in 1971 and quickly earned a reputation as a "world-class entertainment facility." But then on April 4, 1982, a fire burned the center to the ground. While performances were being held under a large tent, the facility was rebuilt and opened in 1984. In the words of the National Park Service:

> On stage—dance, opera, symphony orchestras, jazz, pop, musicals, country-western, or bluegrass—the performing artists and their creative skills are paramount here, whether the evening's performance is a grand-scale production or an entertaining country group.

Wolf Trap Farm Park, which is open daily, except on Christmas, is a partnership between the National Park Service and the Wolf Trap Foundation for the Performing Arts. The Park Service protects and manages the park, and provides interpretive programs and backstage tours. The Park Service also sponsors performances and workshops for children, at the Theatre-in-the-

Woods, in July and August. For information on the Theatre-in-the-Woods free performances, and reservations, phone (703) 255-1827.

The Wolf Trap Foundation arranges the schedule of Filene Center's summer performances and festivals, while the Park Service is responsible for maintaining the technical operation, including scenery changes, lighting control, special effects, and sound reinforcement. For information on off-season backstage tours and pre-performance talks, phone (703) 255-1800.

The foundation also owns and provides year-round programming for The Barns of Wolf Trap—two reconstructed, early-eighteenth-century barns that are located close by the park. The Barns information: Telephone (703) 938-2404.

Camping is not permitted in the park, but visitors may picnic on grassy areas and at tables provided in the special events area. Lodging and meals are available in Vienna, Reston, McLean, Arlington, and Alexandria, VA; in Washington, D.C.; and elsewhere in the metropolitan area. Advance lodging reservations are strongly advised for the peak tourist seasons. Access to the park from downtown Washington, D.C., is by way of any of the bridges across the Potomac River (Key Bridge, Theodore Roosevelt/U.S. Route 50 Bridge, Arlington Memorial Bridge, or George Mason/I-395 Bridge); then north on the George Washington Memorial Parkway and onto the Capital Beltway (I-495) southbound into Virginia; taking Exit 11B (Tysons Corner/Route 123) and proceeding a short way on State Route 123; then onto State Route 7 westbound and a left turn onto Towlston Road; and continuing a mile to the park entrance.

For visitors attending Filene Center performances, access is also by way of the Dulles Toll Road, up to two hours prior to the start of such performances. The toll road is reached by way of Exit 12B from the Capital Beltway (I-495) or Exit 67 from I-66, and proceeding to the toll road's Exit 6 (Wolf Trap exit).

IF YOU GO: Tickets are required for most of the performances. For information on programs: Wolf Trap Foundation for the Performing Arts, 1624 Trap Rd., Vienna, VA 22182. Telephone (703) 255-1900 or (703) 255-1860. For further park information: Director, Wolf Trap Farm Park for the Performing Arts, 1551 Trap Rd., Vienna, VA 22182. Telephone (703) 255-1800.

PART 11

PARKS CELEBRATING TECHNOLOGY AND INDUSTRIAL AMERICA

DAYTON AVIATION HERITAGE NATIONAL HISTORICAL PARK

DAYTON AVIATION HERITAGE NATIONAL HISTORICAL PARK,
located in Dayton, Ohio, was authorized in 1992 to protect and interpret the
aviation history relating to Orville and Wilbur Wright, and their successful
aviation research, inventions, and development.
(See also Wright Brothers National Memorial.)
In addition, the park celebrates the life and
writings of the African-American poet Paul
Laurence Dunbar, who was a friend of the
Wright brothers.

As of this writing (1997), the National
Park Service provides no visitor services or facilities. Cooperating sites that are open to visitation
include the Wright Cycle Company shop, which
the Wright brothers opened in 1892, after
which they soon moved into serious research
and experimentation in the field of aeronautics;
the Huffman Prairie Flying Field and Wright
Brothers Memorial Hill, at Wright-Patterson Air
Force Base; the Wright Flyer III at the Carillon
Historical Park (fee); and the Paul Laurence
Dunbar House State Memorial (fee). There is
also a driving tour of 45 aviation-associated sites
in the Dayton area, for which a guidebook is
available at Dayton bookstores.

1905 Wright Flier III, in Wright Hall
at Carillon Historical Park [NPS]

IF YOU GO: Lodging and meals are available
in and around Dayton. Further information:
Superintendent, Dayton Aviation Heritage
National Historical Park, P.O. Box 9280, Wright
Brothers Station, Dayton, OH 45409. Telephone
(513) 223-0020.

Wright Cycle Company [NPS]

EDISON NATIONAL HISTORIC SITE

EDISON NATIONAL HISTORIC SITE consists of 21 acres at Main Street and Lakeside Avenue, in West Orange, New Jersey. It was initially partly established as the Edison Home National Historic Site in 1955 and partly established as the Edison Laboratory National Monument in 1956; the two separate units were combined as Edison National Historic Site in 1962. The park commemorates the life and technological accomplishments of the famous inventor, Thomas A. Edison (1847–1931).

As a child, Edison was educated at home by his mother, and by ten years of age, he had become passionately interested in chemistry. As a teenager, he built his own laboratory. He was only 22 when he received a patent for an invention in 1869—the first of more than a thousand patents issued to him by the U.S. government. In the 1870s, Edison developed many inventions in the field of electricity. Among these were his automatic repeating telegraph that was clearer and faster than previous telegraphs; his phonograph; his telephone transmitter; and the first reliable incandescent light bulb. In the early 1880s, Edison created an electric power transmission system that he placed in New York City's financial district to operate hundreds of his light bulbs. In 1887, the inventor moved to new research laboratories at what is now the laboratory unit of the national historic site. A major invention that was created at the new facilities, where he employed more than 50 assistants, was the first motion picture camera.

As the National Park Service says:

> To Edison, no problem was unsolvable, even when the leading theo-reticians of the day said otherwise. It was simply a matter of intense application until he could "bring out the secrets of nature and apply them for the happiness of man." A combination of patient empirical work, his own inspired guesses, and the important contributions of his scientists and technicians resulted in the astonishing success of Edison's labs.

A mile away from Edison's research laboratories is the 23-room Victorian mansion known as Glenmont. The grand three-story home is fur-nished essentially as it was when Edison and his second wife, Mina, lived there. It is filled with their furniture, memorabilia, and other personal posses-sions. Beautifully landscaped grounds surround the mansion.

Today, the site has a visitor center at the laboratory unit that provides interpretive exhibits, an audiovisual program, and publications. The interior of the laboratories and Glenmont are open for guided tours only (daily at the laboratory and Wednesdays through Sundays at the mansion). Passes for Glenmont tours are available at the visitor center. Non-family tours require advance reservations. The national historic site is open daily, except on Thanksgiving, Christmas, and New Year's Day.

IF YOU GO: Lodging and meals are available in West Orange and elsewhere in the surrounding area. Access from I-280 westbound is by way of Exit 10 or eastbound by way of Exit 9, and following the signs to the site. Further information: Superintendent, Main St. and Lakeside Ave., West Orange, NJ 07052. Telephone (201) 736-0550.

HOPEWELL FURNACE NATIONAL HISTORIC SITE

HOPEWELL FURNACE NATIONAL HISTORIC SITE, comprising 848 acres at 2 Mark Bird Lane in Elverson, Pennsylvania, was established as Hopewell Village National Historic Site in 1938 and was changed to its present name in 1985. It protects and interprets an outstanding example of a nineteenth-century rural iron plantation that operated from 1771 to 1883. Among the buildings are the blast furnace, the casthouse, and the ironmaster's mansion.

The plantation was founded by ironmaster Mark Bird. To make cast iron or molded products, Hopewell Furnace used iron ore, limestone (to eliminate impurities in the ore during smelting), and charcoal. The furnace was powered by a water wheel. Soon after its founding, this furnace provided George Washington's Continental Army with cannons, shot, and shell during the War for Independence (Revolutionary War). The postwar depression and a flood in 1786 put Bird out of business. After subsequent hard times and closings under new owners, Clement Brooke restarted the operation in 1816.

Hopewell Furnace National Historic Site, Pennsylvania [NPS]

From then until 1844, Hopewell Furnace produced tens-of-thousands of cast-iron and woodburning stoves, as well as a variety of cookware, such as kettles, pots, and pans. The furnace was kept roaring-hot 24 hours per day, with the tenant workers laboring in 12-hour shifts. The equivalent of an acre of hardwood forest, converted into charcoal, was consumed daily. This wood yielded over 700 bushels of charcoal, to process six or seven tons of ore.

Following the Panic of 1837, the nation's economic prosperity declined, which in turn caused the demand for the furnace's products to shrink. Because of transportation and technological advances in the iron industry, small furnaces like Hopewell could no longer compete. After the summer of 1883, Hopewell Furnace closed down for the final time.

Today, the site has a visitor center that provides interpretive exhibits, an audiovisual program, and publications. Visitors may tour such highlights of the site as the furnace, casthouse, ironmaster's mansion, blacksmith shop, company store, charcoal cooling shed, barn, and tenants' quarters. During the summer months, the site presents a variety of living-history programs of Hopewell Village activities. The National Park Service urges visitors not to climb on unstable anthracite furnace ruins, fences, or other historic structures. Hiking trails winding through the northern part of the site connect with the French Creek State Park's trail network. The site is open daily, except on Martin Luther King, Jr., Day, Presidents' Day, Veterans Day, Thanksgiving, Christmas, and New Year's Day.

Camping is not permitted on the site, but there are campgrounds in the adjacent state park. Lodging and meals are available in Pottstown, Reading, and throughout the Philadelphia metropolitan area.

IF YOU GO: Access from I-76 (the Pennsylvania Turnpike) westbound is 16 miles by way of Exit 23 (Downingtown), proceeding north on State Route 100, left (west) onto State Route 23, and right (north) onto State Route 345 to the site entrance; or from I-76 eastbound, it is 10 miles by way of Exit 22 (Morgantown), proceeding east on State Route 23, and left (north) onto State Route 345 to the site entrance. Further information: Superintendent, 2 Mark Bird Ln., Elverson, PA 19520. Telephone (610) 582-8773.

KEWEENAW NATIONAL HISTORICAL PARK

KEWEENAW NATIONAL HISTORICAL PARK is located on the Keweenaw Peninsula, in Michigan's Upper Peninsula. It was authorized in 1992 to commemorate and interpret the copper mining history in this area. The Keweenaw Peninsula is the only known place in the world where commercially abundant deposits of pure, native copper occurred. The mining history of this area dates back some 7,000 years, and is "the oldest known metal mining heritage in the western hemisphere," according to the National Park Service. Historically, mine shafts on the Keweenaw reached more than 9,000 feet below ground. The park consists of two units: one encompassing Calumet's historic business district and the other in the adjacent town of Laurium's historic residential district. Much of these units will remain in private ownership—the Park Service will acquire only certain properties to preserve and interpret key structures.

The National Park Service does not yet have its own visitor services established, as of this writing (1997). Visitors are urged to stop at the Keweenaw Tourism Office, located at the intersection of U.S. Route 41 and State Route 26 in Calumet, for directions to parking and the location of the historic buildings and sites in Calumet and Laurium. Among the commercial points of interest are the Calumet & Hecla (C&H) Mining Company's general offices building, dating from 1897, at 100 Red Jacket Road; across the street is the C&H Library (1897) that once held the third-largest collection of books in the state of Michigan. Nearby are the C&H Bath House (1911); the C&H Roundhouse (1888), which was the maintenance building for steam engines and other railroad equipment; and the company machine and blacksmith shops.

In the heart of the town's business district are such structures as the Red Jacket Town Hall and Opera House (1886), at 340 Sixth Street, a 1,000-seat facility that was paid for with fees from Calumet's more than 70 saloons (tours: Telephone [906] 337-2610); the Red Jacket Fire Station (1898), across from the theater that now presents the Upper Peninsula Fire Fighters' Memorial Museum; Marco Curto's Saloon (1895), at 322 Sixth Street; and several historic churches including St. Anne's (1900) and St. Paul's (1903). The Coppertown Museum provides an overview of the C&H history (Telephone [906] 337-4534). During the summer, a trackless trolley serves this unit of the park.

In Laurium, historically and architecturally significant residences (now privately owned) include the Gipp house, at 434 Hecla, in which the nationally renowned Notre Dame football player George Gipp was born; the Joseph Latowski house (1900), at 434 Kearsarge, which was the elegant home of the president of the Laurium Mining Company; the Colonel William H. Thielman house (1902), at 404 Kearsarge, the Queen Anne-style home of a partner in the Armstrong-Thieltman Lumber Company; the Captain Thomas Hoatson house (1908), at 320 Tamarack, home of the founder of the Calumet & Arizona Mining Company and the most impressive home in the area (now the Laurium Manor Inn, a bed-and-breakfast that offers daily tours on the hour, from noon to 3 p.m. (phone [906] 337-2549); the Norman Macdonald house (1906), at 305 Tamarack, home of a major investor in the Calumet & Arizona Mining Company—this structure contains seven bedrooms and a ballroom; and the Johnson Vivian, Jr., house (1896), at 240 Pewabic, where Vivian created beautifully landscaped grounds and built a conservatory onto the house. Since these and other buildings on the tour are privately owned, the Keweenaw Tourism Council and National Park Service request that visitors respect privacy of the owners.

There are a number of cooperating sites elsewhere on the Keweenaw Peninsula. These include the Quincy Mine Hoist (the largest steam hoist in the world) & Underground Mine, located just north of Hancock, on U.S. Route 41 (underground tours are provided from Memorial Day to Labor Day—phone [906] 482-3101); the Houghton County Historical Museum, in the former mill office of the C&H Mining Company, on State Route 26 in Lake Linden, between Hancock and Calumet (open June to September; Telephone [906] 296-4121); the Seaman Mineralogical Museum (Michigan's official minerals museum) where visitors may learn about the geological processes that produced the world's most extensive known concentration of pure native copper (located on the fifth floor of Michigan Technological University's Electrical Energy Resources Center, in Houghton, and open weekdays all year from 9 a.m. to 4:30 p.m.; Saturdays from noon to 4 p.m., except in the winter; phone [906] 487-2572); and the Keweenaw County Historical Museum, at Eagle Harbor (located along State Route 26, between Calumet and Copper Harbor; open afternoons daily, from June to September; phone [906] 289-4990), presenting information on Lake Superior shipping that was historically the vital lifeline to the Keweenaw peninsula.

At the southwest corner of the Keweenaw Peninsula is the magnificently scenic Porcupine Mountains Wilderness State Park, containing virgin-growth, mixed coniferous and deciduous forests, glacier-sculpted mountains, the exquisitely beautiful Lake of the Clouds, and a stretch of Lake Superior shoreline. This gem of a park is located about 15 miles west of Ontonagon, on State Route 107 (Telephone [906] 885-5275).

Lodging and meals are available in Houghton, Hancock, Eagle Harbor, and Copper Harbor. Campgrounds are provided in Hancock; F.J. McLain State Park, about ten miles west of Calumet; and Fort Wilkins State Park at Copper Harbor.

IF YOU GO: Access is by way of U.S. Route 41, through Houghton and Hancock to Calumet and Laurium, and on to Copper Harbor. Further information: Keweenaw Tourism Council, P.O. Box 336, Houghton, MI 49931. Telephone 1(800) 338-7982 or (906) 337-4579. Or: Keweenaw National Historical Park, P.O. Box 471, Calumet, MI 49913. Telephone (906) 337-3168.

LOWELL NATIONAL HISTORICAL PARK

LOWELL NATIONAL HISTORICAL PARK, comprising 137 acres in Lowell, Massachusetts, was authorized in 1978 to commemorate the history of the Industrial Revolution in America. The park protects historic nineteenth-century cotton textile mill complexes, over five miles of a canal network, and housing for the mill workers. It interprets the transition from a farm to factory economy in the northeastern United States, immigrant labor history, and the development of industrial technology.

The visitor center, located at 246 Market Street, provides interpretive exhibits, an audiovisual program, and publications. In addition to self-guided touring, the park provides year-round guided tours on foot and by historic trolleys (fee); and daily guided tours on canal barges (fee), from July 1 to Columbus Day, in October. The Mogan Cultural Center presents the Working People Exhibit and is open Tuesdays through Saturdays, from July 1 to Columbus Day. There are also the Suffolk Mill Turbine Exhibit; the Boott Cotton Mills Museum, with an operating weaving room containing 88 operating looms; the Tsongas Industrial History Center; the New England Folklife Center of Lowell; and the Lowell Heritage State Park's Waterpower Exhibit. During the last week of July, the three-day Lowell Folk Festival is presented—one of many special events held during the year. The park is open daily, except on Thanksgiving, Christmas, and New Year's Day.

Lodging and meals are available in the Lowell area (the visitor center has a guide to restaurants in the vicinity of the park.)

IF YOU GO: Access to the park from either I-495 or U.S. Route 3 is by way of the Lowell Connector, exiting onto Thorndike Street northbound, and continuing for about a half-mile; then turning right onto Dutton Street, and proceeding to a park visitors' parking lot. Further information: Superintendent, 169 Merrimack St., Lowell, MA 01852. Telephone (508) 459-1000.

SAUGUS IRON WORKS NATIONAL HISTORIC SITE

SAUGUS IRON WORKS NATIONAL HISTORIC SITE, consisting of eight acres at 244 Central Street, in Saugus, Massachusetts, was established in 1969 to protect and interpret the location of the first integrated ironworks in North America which operated from 1646 to about 1668. The site features the reconstructed blast furnace, forge, rolling and slitting mill, and a restored house dating from the 1600s.

The idea of an iron works in New England was promoted by John Winthrop, Jr., son of the governor of the Massachusetts Bay Colony. Winthrop needed investors to provide capital to start up his venture, and these he found in England. He created a "Company of Undertakers of the Iron Works in New England," for which he recruited about two dozen company shareholders and 62 ironworkers and other laborers from England and Scotland. In Massachusetts, he obtained a grant to the rights of iron ore deposits within the colony, along with the use of lands and water, the latter providing power to drive the iron-making operation.

The iron ore smelting process—which substituted gabbro, a dense rock, for the traditional limestone, to help eliminate impurities in the bog iron ore—used large quantities of charcoal, derived from acres of hardwood trees, to fuel the furnace. The intense heat in the furnace, which was operated round the clock, converted the ore to a liquid form of iron, some of which was made

Saugus Iron Works, Massachusetts [Richard Merrill/NPS]

into finished products, such as kettles, pots, and pans, while much of the rest was made into bars. The brittle cast-iron bars were then taken to the forge, where machinery was operated with power generated by water turning a number of waterwheels. Here the bars were changed to more malleable wrought iron "merchant bars." The slitting mill further processed wrought iron—flattening and slitting the bars into "flats" and "rod" stock for nails. In 1650, only about a dozen mills in the world had this advanced technology.

In addition to the iron works operation, there was also a community, known as Hammersmith, that was run by the company for its employees. Facilities included housing and a company farm. The Iron Works House, dating from 1646, was the town's business and social center.

Today, visitors may tour the national historic site's museum, which provides interpretive exhibits and a brief audiovisual program. Publications are available in a gift shop located in the visitor contact station at the entrance to the site. There are guided and self-guided interpretive tours, and living-history programs and demonstrations at the furnace, forge, and slitting mill, as well as an operating blacksmith shop. The site also includes the seventeenth-century Iron Works House; an herb garden representative of the seventeenth century; and a nature trail, with a marsh section and a woodland section along the east bank of the Saugus River, where visitors may see some of the flora and fauna of the area. Visitors are urged to be careful around the waterwheels and other historic structures. The site is open daily, except on Thanksgiving, Christmas, and New Year's Day.

Camping is not permitted on the site (there is a campground at Harold Parker State Forest, a few miles to the north by way of State Route 114), but picnic facilities are provided. Lodging and meals are available along nearby U.S. Route 1.

IF YOU GO: Access from I-95 (north or south) is by way of the Walnut Street exit (number 43) in Lynnfield, and following the brown signs for the national historic site for five miles to the Saugus Iron Works. Access from U.S. Route 1 northbound is by way of the Main Street exit in Saugus and following the site signs through Saugus Center to the parking lot; or from U.S. Route 1 southbound by way of the Walnut Street exit eastbound and following the site signs to the parking lot. Further information: Superintendent, 244 Central St., Saugus, MA 01906. Telephone (617) 233-0050.

STEAMTOWN NATIONAL HISTORIC SITE

STEAMTOWN NATIONAL HISTORIC SITE comprises about 50 acres at 150 S. Washington Avenue, in Scranton, Pennsylvania. It was authorized in 1986 to interpret the century of steam-engine-powered railroad history in the United States, from the mid-nineteenth to the mid-twentieth century.

The site takes in the historic Delaware, Lackawanna & Western Railroad switching yard, featuring such related structures as the locomotive maintenance shop, a 13-stall roundhouse, and an older 3-stall roundhouse section. The mighty coal-burning, smoke-belching steam locomotives were serviced in the two roundhouses. The National Park Service has assembled and is restoring a collection of 28 steam locomotives and nearly 75 passenger, freight, and other railroad cars. The park's visitor center and a theater present interpretive exhibits and programs. There are guided tours of the main roundhouse, in which steam engines are being maintained. Among the collection's locomotives are a Canadian Pacific 4-6-2 (the numbers referring to the configuration of the wheels), a Baldwin Locomotive Works 0-6-0, and one of the most awesome

Steamtown National Historic Site, Pennsylvania [Ken Ganz/NPS]

Steamtown National Historic Site [Ken Ganz/NPS]

steam engines ever made—a 4-8-8-4 Union Pacific Railroad "Big Boy." These leviathans measured over 132 feet in length and reached speeds of more than 80 miles per hour.

The park contains a Railroad History Museum where visitors learn about the people who ran the trains, such as the porters, ticket agents, engineers, and dining-car chefs and stewards. The Technology Museum is where visitors learn how steam locomotives function and how steam-engine technology changed and improved over the decades.

From spring through autumn, the park also features steam-train excursions, ranging from a short ride to the Scranton Iron Furnaces (in which most of the iron rails for the railroads in the U.S. were manufactured in the late nineteenth century) to a two-and-a-half-hour weekend journey to Moscow, Pennsylvania (reservations suggested: [717] 340-5204).

Lodging and meals are available in Scranton, including the Lackawanna Station Hotel, at 700 Lackawanna Avenue, which used to be the grand train station, dating from 1908.

IF YOU GO: Access to the site is by way of a number of major routes, including I-80 west from the New York City area, to I-380 westbound to I-81 southbound to exit 53, from here proceeding on the Central Scranton Expressway to the first traffic light, then turning left and continuing seven blocks, and finally, a left turn into the national historic site. If driving west on I-84, proceed to I-81 southbound to exit 53, and then as above. If heading east on I-80, take I-81 northbound to exit 53, and then as above. The park is open daily, except on Thanksgiving, Christmas, and New Year's Day. Further information: Superintendent, 150 S. Washington Ave., Scranton, PA 18503. Telephone (717) 340-5200.

WRIGHT BROTHERS NATIONAL MEMORIAL

WRIGHT BROTHERS NATIONAL MEMORIAL, consisting of 431 acres on the northeast coast of North Carolina, was established in 1927 as Kill Devil Hill Monument National Memorial. It was transferred from the War Department to the National Park Service in 1933, and was renamed Wright Brothers National Memorial in 1959. It commemorates the first sustained flight in a heavier-than-air flying machine that was successfully flown on a stretch of beach near the Kill Devil Hills, by the Atlantic Ocean, in 1903. As pilot Orville Wright described that historic flight: "It was the first [flight] in history in which a machine carrying a man had raised itself by its own power into the air in full flight, had sailed forward without reduction of speed, and finally landed at a point as high as that from which it started."

The brothers, Wilbur and Orville Wright, opened a bicycle shop in Dayton, Ohio, in 1892, but they soon set their sights on broader horizons. (See also Dayton Aviation Heritage National Historical Park.) In 1896, Samuel Langley's success in launching powered flying-machine models, and the death in a flying accident of a famous experimenter with gliders, spurred the Wright brothers into their own aeronautical research.

Beginning in 1899, they devoted four years toward the pursuit of their goal of mastering flight. The brothers were confident that solutions to lift and propulsion merely required fine tuning. On the other hand, they believed that lateral control, which had not yet been achieved, should depend upon the pilot, rather than on "inherent stability," as was commonly believed at the time. Wilbur Wright discovered that flight could be stabilized by warping the wings so they could be rotated—a concept inspired by his observation of birds in flight. They tried out the idea of wing-warping with a five-foot biplane kite.

In 1900, the brothers created a 17-foot glider, and went to Kitty Hawk, North Carolina, to see how it would perform. The wings produced less lift than they had anticipated, and the glider was operated mostly from the ground as a kite. Encouraged by the limited success of the glider, the brothers went back to Dayton and were determined to persist. The next year, they redesigned their craft by lengthening the wingspread to 22 feet and by increasing the camber—the arching curvature of an airfoil, from the wing's leading edge to the trailing edge—in an effort to solve the lift problem, and tested it at their new flight test location at Kill Devil Hills, near Kitty Hawk. But the lift was still far less than needed, and the glider pitched and tossed and climbed into stalls. Further difficulties came close to causing the brothers to become very discouraged. But rather than give up, they decided to construct a wind tunnel, from which they developed their own research data.

In 1902, they produced a new machine that incorporated some of the Wrights' own research. The wings were enlarged to 32 feet, while a fixed vertical tail was added to counteract adverse yaw. The brothers carried out some 400 glides, but there were still some flaws that included a tendency for the machine to slide sideways during a turn and send the craft spinning to the ground. This problem was eventually solved when Orville came up with the idea of using a movable tail and Wilbur decided to link the tail movement to the wing warping function. Six hundred more glide tests that year convinced them that they had finally succeeded in producing the first real airplane.

In 1903, the Wright brothers tackled the challenge of developing a source of power for their flying machine. Because there was no lightweight engine available, they concentrated on developing their own. In the process, they also developed the first workable airplane propeller—a direct outgrowth of their own research. They then returned to the beach in North Carolina so they could install the 12-horsepower engine on the new 40-foot wingspan aircraft, *The Flyer*. The engine powered two pusher propellers. Other glitches slowed their progress, such as broken propeller shafts and a stubborn engine. On December 14, Wilbur piloted the plane, but oversteered, causing the craft to climb steeply, stall, and dive into the sand. Repairs were made and then finally on December 17, Orville and Wilbur Wright took turns at the controls and flew four flights, the last of which was airborne for nearly a minute, covering more than 850 feet. As the National Park Service says:

> This was the real thing, transcending the powered hops and glides others had achieved. The Wright machine had flown. But it would not fly again; after the last flight it was caught by a gust of wind, rolled over, and damaged beyond easy repair. Their flying season over, the Wrights sent their father a matter-of-fact telegram reporting the modest numbers behind their epochal achievement.

Today, the national memorial has a visitor center that provides interpretive exhibits, programs, and publications. There are reproductions of the 1902 glider and the 1903 *Flyer*. The park is open daily, except on Christmas.

Camping is not permitted in the national memorial, but campgrounds are located in nearby Cape Hatteras National Seashore. Lodging and meals are available in Kitty Hawk, Kill Devil Hills, Nags Head, and Elizabeth City.

IF YOU GO: Access is 50 miles from Elizabeth City by way of U.S. Route 158; or about 70 miles south from I-664 in Norfolk, VA. Further information: Superintendent, Wright Brothers National Memorial, c/o Cape Hatteras National Seashore, Route 1, Box 675, Manteo, NC 27954. Telephone (919) 441-7430.

PART 12

NATIONAL CAPITAL PARKS (not listed elsewhere)

CONSTITUTION GARDENS

CONSTITUTION GARDENS consists of 52 acres located between the Lincoln Memorial and the Washington Monument, and between Constitution Avenue and the Reflecting Pool. It was dedicated as a formal park in 1976, as a memorial to the nation's founders. A presidential proclamation in 1986 also made the gardens "a Living Legacy dedicated to the commemoration of the United States Constitution."

The site on which the gardens are now located was originally part of a wider Potomac River. Landfill projects during the late nineteenth century moved the riverbank to the west. During World Wars I and II, temporary military structures occupied the site—the last of which was finally removed in 1971. The following year, President Richard M. Nixon ordered the creation of a formal park. In 1974, the international architectural and engineering firm, Skidmore, Owings & Merrill, began designing and building the gardens, which include a six-and-a-half-acre artificial lake with a one-acre island.

In 1978, Congress authorized the establishment of a memorial on the lake's island, in honor of the 56 signers of the Declaration of Independence. The Signers' Memorial was designed by EDAW, Inc., and is made up of 56 low granite stones, arranged in a half-circle around a cobblestone plaza, in 13 groups representing the 13 original states. Each stone bears the signer's signature, his profession, and his home. The memorial was dedicated in 1982. In the words of the National Park Service:

> As a Living Legacy, Constitution Gardens has become a tribute to the successful experiment in government begun by the Founders; it is a quiet, contemplative spot, in the midst of a bustling capital.

Today, Constitution Gardens is a beautiful, peaceful place to walk or sit and enjoy the flowers, trees, and water—a place in which to reflect on the blessings this nation offers that derived from the Founders' foresight and wisdom, from the Declaration of Independence, and from the U.S. Constitution.

IF YOU GO: Lodging and meals are available in Washington, D.C.; in Arlington and Alexandria, Virginia; and elsewhere in the metropolitan area. Advance lodging reservations are advised, especially for the peak tourist seasons. Although parking is often unavailable, there is time-limited parking near the Washington Monument off Constitution Avenue, between 15th and 17th streets; and other time-limited parking along Constitution Avenue and along Jefferson and Madison drives. The Tourmobile stops near the base of the Washington Monument and at the Lincoln Memorial (see the texts on these sites). Also close by the gardens are the Vietnam Veterans Memorial and the Korean War Memorial (see the texts on these sites). The nearest Metro subway stop is Smithsonian, on the Blue and Orange lines. Further information on the Constitution Gardens: Superintendent, National Capital Parks-Central, 900 Ohio Dr., SW, Washington, DC 20242. Telephone (202) 485-9880.

KENILWORTH AQUATIC GARDENS

KENILWORTH AQUATIC GARDENS consists of 12 acres located along the banks of the Anacostia River, at Anacostia Avenue and Douglas Street, NE, in Washington, D.C. It was established in 1938 to continue the extraordinary propagation and display of aquatic plants, such as water lilies and lotuses, that grow in the gardens' 44 ponds.

Civil War veteran Walter B. Shaw purchased this area in 1880, when it was a farm along the river. He had become interested in water lilies in his home state of Maine, and he created a number of ponds, began raising these plants, and became a major supplier to Washington florists. During the 1920s, his daughter, Helen Fowler, expanded the operation, and visitors came to enjoy walks around the ponds.

Today, visitors may enjoy walking through the gardens and observing the aquatic plantlife that includes some 70 species of water lilies from all over the world, as well as bordering marsh habitat. Many species of birds, such as ducks and rails, and a number of mammals live in the wetlands habitats of the ponds, marshes, and the Anacostia estuary. June and July are the best months to see the many varieties of day-blooming water lilies; and July and August are the best time to see other day- and night-blooming species, along with an array of fascinating tropical plants.

The one-and-one-half-mile River Trail winds through part of the 73-acre remnants of the river wetlands and landfill known as Kenilworth Park. Some areas of this park have been developed for outdoor recreational activities such as soccer and rugby. Picnic facilities are also available in the park. Kenilworth Park is, in turn, part of the larger Anacostia Park that extends from Kenilworth Aquatic Gardens downstream, taking in more than five miles of shoreline along each bank of the river. The name Anacostia is derived from a little-known group of native Americans, the Nacotchtank Indians, or the Anacostians, as they were subsequently called. Just across the river from the

Kenilworth Aquatic Gardens is the National Arboretum, reached by way of U.S. Route 50 or U.S. Route 1.

The Kenilworth Aquatic Gardens visitor center provides interpretive exhibits and a bookstore. Ranger-guided tours are offered on summer weekends, from Memorial Day to Labor Day. Reservations are required for interpretive and educational programs. The park is open daily, except on Thanksgiving, Christmas, and New Year's Day.

Lodging and meals are widely available throughout the Washington metropolitan area. Reservations for lodging are highly recommended, especially during the popular tourist seasons.

IF YOU GO: Kenilworth Aquatic Gardens are located off I-295 (Kenilworth Avenue) at Douglas Street and Anacostia Avenue, NE. The closest Metro subway stop is Deanwood on the Orange Line. Further information: Kenilworth Aquatic Gardens, National Park Service, 1900 Anacostia Dr., SE, Washington, D.C. 20020. Telephone (202) 426-6905.

NATIONAL MALL

NATIONAL MALL, consisting of 146 acres extending from the Washington Monument eastward to the U.S. Capitol, in Washington, D.C., was conceived as a park in 1790, as part of French engineer Pierre L'Enfant's grand design for the nation's capital. Rows of American elm trees gracefully spread their branches above much of the Mall, while open lawn stretches the length of the park. The Mall was transferred from the Office of Public Buildings and Public Parks of the National Capital to the National Park Service in 1933.

A number of museums front on the open space, including the National Museum of American History; the National Museum of Natural History; the National Sculpture Garden and Ice Rink; the National Gallery of Art (west and east buildings); the Freer Gallery of Art; the National Museum of African Art; the Arts and Industries Building; the Hirshhorn Museum and Sculpture Garden; and the National Air and Space Museum. Adjacent to the east end of the Mall is the Reflecting Pool, with the imposing, dome-crowned Capitol rising from Capitol Hill beyond. Adjacent to the west end of the Mall is the graceful, 555-foot-tall marble obelisk that is dedicated to the memory of George Washington (see Washington Monument). Westward beyond the monument lies the long Reflecting Pool, extending to the columned Lincoln Memorial (see Lincoln Memorial) that overlooks the Potomac River to the west. This whole complex of parkland and monumental buildings is one of the most visually exciting cityscapes in the world, providing enormous inspiration for the millions of visitors and Washington area residents who come each year.

The National Mall is popular with walkers, joggers, and others seeking casual recreational pleasures. Permits are required for First Amendment activities and other special events.

Lodging and meals are available in downtown Washington; across the Potomac in Alexandria and Arlington, Virginia; and elsewhere in the metropolitan area. Advance lodging reservations are advised, especially during the peak tourist seasons.

IF YOU GO: Access is by way of Constitution or Independence avenues, between 14th and 3rd streets. There is a Metro subway stop in the Mall (Smithsonian, near the Smithsonian Institution). Further information: Superintendent, National Capital Parks-Central, 900 Ohio Dr., SW, Washington, DC 20242. Telephone (202) 426-6841.

PENNSYLVANIA AVENUE NATIONAL HISTORIC SITE

PENNSYLVANIA AVENUE NATIONAL HISTORIC SITE consists of a part of Pennsylvania Avenue and architecturally and historically important areas along the avenue, between the White House and the U.S. Capitol. This site includes several blocks of Washington, D.C.'s commercial district, with theaters, stores, museums, and hotels; the Federal Bureau of Investigation; and the Federal Triangle of national government buildings, including the National Archives and the Old Post Office Tower.

Scheduled tours of the national historic site are provided by Architour, which is a nonprofit educational organization (phone [202] 265-6454). Lodging and meals are available in downtown Washington and elsewhere in the metropolitan area. Advance lodging reservations are advised, especially for peak tourist seasons. This part of Pennsylvania Avenue lies between 1st and 15th streets, NW. Access is from numerous directions, including Constitution Avenue (U.S. Routes 1 and 50). The nearest Metro subway stops are in the Federal Triangle (Federal Triangle and Archives stops).

IF YOU GO: Further information: Pennsylvania Avenue Development Corporation, 331 Pennsylvania Ave., NW, Suite 1220 North, Washington, D.C. 20004. Telephone (202) 426-6720.

ROCK CREEK PARK

ROCK CREEK PARK, consisting of 1,754 acres in Washington, D.C., was established in 1890 and was transferred from the War Department to the National Park Service in 1933. It protects one of the most extensive urban parks in America. It is largely a densely forested "wilderness" slicing through the middle of the nation's capital. The majority of the park extends southward from the D.C.-Maryland line to the National Zoological Park (the Washington Zoo), while a much narrower stretch continues on down to the junction of Rock Creek and the Potomac River.

Soon after the end of the Civil War, the idea for this park began with a search for a new location for the President's House (The White House), in a park-like setting on higher ground, in Washington, D.C. The secretary of war gave the search assignment to Major Nathaniel Michel, who devoted most of his attention to researching areas for a possible park. Although the plan for moving the site for the President's House was never acted upon, Michel proposed that the valley of Rock Creek be set aside as a park. He considered it remarkable that an area of such extraordinary natural beauty was so close to the offices of the national government. Michel's plan initially failed to win enough votes for its passage by Congress; two decades later, however, the measure finally did obtain congressional approval. President Benjamin Harrison signed the bill in 1890—within just a few days of the establishment of Sequoia, Kings Canyon, and Yosemite national parks.

In 1917, the U.S. Army's Board of Control contracted with the landscape design firm, the Olmsted Brothers, Inc., founded by Frederick Law Olmsted (see the text on Frederick Law Olmsted National Historic Site), to produce a plan for protecting and developing the park.

Rock Creek valley is predominantly covered with a forest of deciduous trees. Among the species are tulip tree; beech; red maple; sassafras; flowering dogwood; eastern redbud; American sycamore; and a number of oaks, including southern and northern red, black, scarlet, chestnut, willow, and white. In autumn, the woods turn many shades of yellow, orange, and red.

The park contains a great variety of native spring wildflowers that include Mayapple, bluets, spring beauty, bloodroot, trailing arbutus, Dutchman's breeches, round-lobed hepatica, showy orchis, rattlesnake orchid, whorled pogonia, and extensive areas of naturalized daffodils that cover some of the slopes in the lower end of the park.

Mammals of Rock Creek valley include red and gray foxes, raccoons, flying and eastern gray squirrels, opossums, and eastern cottontails. The park's lengthy list of resident, breeding, and migratory birds includes turkey vultures; mourning doves; barred owls; belted kingfishers; common flickers; pileated, red-bellied, downy, and other woodpeckers; blue jays; crows; Carolina chickadees; tufted titmice; white-breasted nuthatches; brown creepers; Carolina wrens; mockingbirds; catbirds; brown thrashers; wood thrushes; red-eyed vireos;

Rock Creek Park, Washington, D.C. [Vicki Paris/NPCA]

Rock Creek Park is one of the nation's largest urban parks. [Bill Clark]

many species of warblers, such as black-and-white, prothonotary, yellow, chestnut-sided, yellowthroat, American redstart, and ovenbird; scarlet tanagers; cardinals; American goldfinches; rufous-sided towhees; and a number of sparrows, including chipping, white-throated, and song. In spring, the woods are filled with a concert of bird songs and calls.

Hiking trails and bridle paths wind throughout the wooded valley, and a signed bicycle route runs the length of the park. In any season, it is a pleasure to follow the trails—to experience a sense of wonder and feel the wildness that can take the visitor so far away from the fast pace of city life. In springtime, it is the magic of unfolding foliage, the blooming of flowers, and the myriad songs of birds. In summer, it is a sense of mystery in the deep shade beneath the forest canopy. In autumn, it is the foliage colors and the fragrance of dry leaves. And in winter, it is the beauty of the forest when decked out in a mantle of white. Rock Creek Park is in the midst of a big city, but it is a world apart, providing inspiration and recreation to its visitors while protecting the natural environment as habitat for wildlife.

An 18-hole golf course, playing fields, and tennis courts are also available. (Golf course information: [202] 882-7332; playing field reservations: [202] 767-8363; and tennis court reservations: [202] 722-5949.) Nature walks and hikes are offered. The Rock Creek Park Horse Center, near the visitor center, offers horse rentals and riding lessons. (Horse center information: [202] 362-0117.)

The park's major information facility, Rock Creek Nature Center, presents interpretive exhibits, programs, and publications, as well as a natural history library that is open to the public. Reservations for school group visits to the center are recommended. The center is open daily, from Memorial Day to Labor Day; otherwise closed on Mondays, Tuesdays, and holidays. (Nature center and planetarium information: [202] 426-6829.)

One of the park's historic features is Pierce Mill, a restored stone gristmill that provides an opportunity for visitors to hear the rumble of the great millstones, as they grind corn and wheat into flour; and to watch the gears, drive shafts, and other parts as they are being operated by the force of falling water that turns the water wheel. This mill is the only one remaining of a number along Rock Creek that once served farmers, from the late eighteenth to early twentieth centuries. The flour ground at Pierce Mill is available for purchase. The mill provides a visitor center with exhibits and a bookstore. (Mill information: [202] 426-6908.)

The Art Barn, located near the gristmill, is a historic carriage house. It displays the works of local artists, and is operated by the Art Barn Association, in cooperation with the National Park Service. (Art Barn information: [202] 244-2482.)

Other historic sites in the park include Fort DeRussy, located off the bike path at Oregon Avenue and Military Road; and Fort Bayard, located at River Road and Western Avenue, NW. These two forts were among the ring of fortifications built by the Union army during the Civil War, to help protect the city of Washington from attack by the Confederate forces (see Fort Circle Parks.) Another significant structure is the Old Stone House—the oldest house in Washington, where visitors may learn about the D.C. area's eighteenth-century history. Located in nearby Georgetown, there are exhibits and a bookstore. (Old Stone House information: [202] 426-6851.)

Camping is not permitted in Rock Creek Park. There are 30 picnic areas scattered throughout the park, some of which may be reserved for groups (phone [202] 673-7646). Lodging and meals are available throughout the

Pierce Mill, Rock Creek Park [Jack Rottier/NPS]

Washington, D.C., metropolitan area. Advance reservations are advised for the peak tourist seasons. Access is by way of a number of streets and roads, including Military Road, just south of which are the nature center, planetarium, and horse center, all located on Glover Road.

Public transportation to the nature center is by way of the Friendship Heights Metro stop, transferring the E2 bus to Glover and Military roads. Other accesses lead off from Connecticut Avenue, which runs mostly to the west of the park; and 16th Street, to the east. Tilden Street branches right from Connecticut and Piney Branch Parkway from 16th—both of which lead down to Pierce Mill and the Art Barn. Old Stone House is reached from M Street in Georgetown, between 30th and 31st streets.

IF YOU GO: Further information: Superintendent, Rock Creek Park, 3545 Williamsburg Lane, NW, Washington, D.C. 20008. Telephone (202) 282-1063.

PART 13

NATIONAL RECREATION AREAS AND URBAN PARKS

AMISTAD NATIONAL RECREATION AREA

AMISTAD NATIONAL RECREATION AREA, consisting of 57,292 acres along the border of Texas and Mexico, was administered by the National Park Service beginning in 1965 under a cooperative agreement with the United States Section, International Boundary and Water Commission, the U.S. and Mexico, and was then authorized in 1990 as a national recreation area. This international recreation area takes in the man-made reservoir—which is navigable for 74 miles—that was created when the six-mile-long Amistad Dam was completed in 1969, backing water up the Rio Grande for 74 miles, up the Pecos River for 14 miles, and up the Devils River for 25

Rock Shelter, Devils River, Amistad National Recreation Area [NPS]

Rock Shelter, Devils River, Amistad National Recreation Area [NPS]

miles. Amistad National Recreation Area also protects prehistoric rock art sites that are considered by archaeologists to be some the best in the world.

Visitor activities include boating, water-skiing, fishing, and hiking. There are marinas and boat ramps, as well as boat- and houseboat-rentals. In addition to the recreational values, Amistad also contains evidence that Indians have lived in this area continuously for some 10,000 years prior to the initial European exploration of the region in the sixteenth century. Archaeologically significant sites, including rock art, have been found within the national recreation area, along the Rio Grande, Devils, and Pecos rivers. The area headquarters and primary information center are open daily, except on Thanksgiving, Christmas, and New Year's Day. There are a number of other information offices, as well as information kiosks and panels in the area.

Picnicking and camping facilities are provided at a number of places; and backcountry camping from boats only is permitted along the lakeshore.

Panther Cave rock art, Amistad National Recreation Area [NPS]

Food, boat rentals, and supplies are available at Lake Amistad Resort and Marina, and at Rough Canyon Marina. Lodging and meals are available in Del Rio and on U.S. Route 90.

IF YOU GO: Access to the national recreation area headquarters is just west of Del Rio on U.S. Route 90. The nearest lake access points are about six miles from headquarters. Further information: Superintendent, HCR 3, Box 5-J, Del Rio, TX 78840. Telephone (210) 775-7491.

BIGHORN CANYON NATIONAL RECREATION AREA

BIGHORN CANYON NATIONAL RECREATION AREA, comprising 120,296 acres extending from southern Montana into northern Wyoming, was established in 1966 and encompasses the 71-mile-long reservoir Bighorn Lake, behind Yellowtail Dam on the Bighorn River. Fifty-five miles of the lake are within the scenically spectacular, sheer-walled Bighorn Canyon.

View south from Pretty Eagle, Bighorn Canyon, Montana and Wyoming [NPS]

Visitor activities include motorboating, water-skiing, swimming, hiking, bird-watching, and fishing. The national recreation area has the Bighorn Visitor Center, at Lovell, Wyoming, and the Yellowtail Dam Visitor Center, Fort Smith, Montana, where information is available and interpretive programs are presented. Marinas, located at the north and south ends of the lake, are open from Memorial Day through Labor Day. River-guide services are available in Fort Smith.

Facilities for camping aboard boats are provided at each end of the lake. Lodging and meals outside the national recreation area are available in Lovell, and Fort Smith and Hardin, Montana. Access from I-90 at Hardin is 44 miles south on State Route 313 to Yellowtail Dam at the north end; and from I-90 on U.S. Route 14 west 34 miles, then right onto U.S. Route 14A, about 40 miles to the south end.

IF YOU GO: Further information: Bighorn Canyon NRA, P.O. Box 7458, Fort Smith, MT 59035. Telephone (406) 666-2412.

CATOCTIN MOUNTAIN PARK

CATOCTIN MOUNTAIN PARK, comprising 5,770 acres in northern Maryland, was first set aside as part of the Catoctin Recreational Demonstration Area in 1935, a 10,000-acre area that was under the management of the National Park Service and the Maryland Park Service. It was changed to its present name in 1954. It protects and interprets a scenic expanse of gentle mountain topography that is richly covered in a predominantly deciduous forest. Adjacent to the park is Cunningham Falls State Park, run by the Maryland Forest, Park, and Wildlife Service.

Scenic drives wind through both parks, and 25 miles of hiking trails invite visitors to explore the forests, reach waterfalls, and climb to rocky, panoramic overlooks atop the mountain. Some of the trails provide cross-country skiing and snow-shoeing routes in winter, when the mountain is decked out in white.

Among the tree species of Catoctin Mountain are eastern hemlock; tulip tree; sassafras; hickories, such as shagbark and bitternut; beech; a number of oaks, including white, chestnut, northern red, black, and scarlet; river birch; black locust; and red maple. Among the great variety of wildflowers, there are Jack-in-the-pulpit, spring beauty, bloodroot, round-lobed hepatica, yellow trout-lily, trilliums, and violets.

Mammals of the mountain include whitetail deer, longtail weasels, raccoons, striped skunks, red and gray foxes, eastern chipmunks, chickarees, flying and gray squirrels, and an occasional black bear. Among the many species of birds that live in or migrate through the area are a number of hawks, including red-tailed, broad-winged, Cooper's, and sharp-shinned; ruffed grouse; barred and great horned owls; pileated, red-bellied, and downy wood-peckers; blue jays; ravens; chickadees; tufted titmice; white-breasted nuthatch-es; Carolina wrens; wood thrushes; kinglets; a great variety of warblers, such as black-and-white, yellow, magnolia, yellow-rumped, black-throated green, blackburnian, chestnut-sided, ovenbird, hooded, Canada, and American red-start; northern orioles; scarlet tanagers; cardinals; rose-breasted and evening grosbeaks; rufous-sided towhees; and white-crowned and song sparrows.

This area was once part of the homeland of small tribes of Indians who lived off the land as gatherers, hunters, anglers, and small-scale farmers. The mountain provided rhyolite, an important resource in making stone tools. The name Catoctin apparently came from the tribal name Kittocton. In the early 1700s, the white man began settling in the nearby Monocacy River valley. Among the newcomers were lumberjacks and charcoal-makers, who supplied wood for and worked at the Catoctin Iron Furnace, which was operated from 1776 to 1904. (The remnants of this commercial enterprise are located in the southern end of the park.) Others working in the woods gathered chestnut and oak bark for its tannin, for use in Monocacy valley tanneries. The forests of Catoctin Mountain, as on mountain ridges throughout the Appalachian region, were clear-cut or burned off for these and other of man's uses. Mountain valleys were also cleared for farmland, and the remains of stone walls and farmhouse cellar holes are still visible here and there in today's woodlands, which have grown back in the decades since the earlier exploitation.

Catoctin Mountain Park has a visitor center that provides interpretive exhibits, programs, and publications. Seasonal interpretive activities include walks, campfire programs, cross-country skiing seminars, and talks about the whiskey-making industry. The park and visitor center are open all year.

An informative publication is *Maryland's Catoctin Mountain Parks* by John Means (The McDonald & Woodward Publishing Company). Cunningham Falls State Park's headquarters is located in the William Houck area. For information on this park, its camping facilities, Hunting Creek Lake recreation, and other facilities, phone (301) 271-7574.

Picnic and camping facilities are provided in both parks. The youth-group camping area Poplar Grove requires advance reservations with the National Park Service. Lodging and meals are available in Thurmont, Frederick, Emmitsburg, and Hagerstown, Maryland; and Gettysburg, Pennsylvania.

IF YOU GO: Access is by way of I-270 from the Washington, D.C., area to Frederick; then U.S. Route 15 about 13 miles; and west three miles on State Route 77 to Catoctin Mountain Park entrance to the right (north) and just beyond to the left (south) to the state park entrance. Access from Baltimore is by way of I-70 to Frederick, then north on U.S. Route 15, as above. From Gettysburg, it is about 17 miles south on U.S. Route 15 to State Route 77. Further information: Superintendent, Catoctin Mountain Park, 6602 Foxville Rd., Thurmont, MD 21788. Telephone (301) 663-9343.

View from Chimney Rock, Catoctin Mountain Park, Maryland [NPS]

CHATTAHOOCHEE RIVER NATIONAL RECREATION AREA

CHATTAHOOCHEE RIVER NATIONAL RECREATION AREA comprises 9,256 acres in 16 land units scattered along a 48-mile stretch of the Chattahoochee River, to the north and east of Atlanta, Georgia. It was established in 1978 to protect places of exceptional recreational, ecological, and historic value. Visitor activities include canoeing, boating (boat rentals), fishing, hiking (50 miles of trails), horseback riding, and bird-watching. Native American archaeological sites, nineteenth-century historic sites, and a rich variety of ecologically valuable habitats are located within the area.

Visitor contact stations are located at the national recreation area headquarters Island Ford unit and at the Paces Mill unit, providing orientation, interpretive information, and publications. Shuttle-bus service is provided between Paces Mill, Powers Island, and Johnson Ferry unit canoe- and boat-rental sites. (For information on rentals and related services that are primarily available from Memorial Day weekend through Labor Day weekend, contact Chattahoochee Outdoor Center, [770] 395-6851). The national recreation area is open daily, except on Christmas.

There are numerous picnic sites, but no camping facilities are provided in the recreation area. Lodging, camping, and meals are available in the adjacent Atlanta metropolitan area.

IF YOU GO: There are a number of access routes to the various units of the national recreation area, many of which lead from I-285 and I-75. Further information on access and on Chattahoochee River National Recreation Area: Superintendent, 1978 Island Ford Parkway, Atlanta, GA 30350. Telephone (770) 399-8070.

CHICKASAW NATIONAL RECREATION AREA

CHICKASAW NATIONAL RECREATION AREA, comprising 9,931 acres in the gently rolling hill country of south-central Oklahoma, was authorized initially as the Sulphur Springs Reservation in 1902. In 1906, it was redesignated as Platt National Park and then combined with Arbuckle National Recreation Area and given its present name in 1976. Named for the Chickasaw Indian Nation, the area protects low, partly wooded and partly prairie-covered hills, beautiful streams, freshwater and mineral springs, and several lakes, including the sprawling reservoir Lake of the Arbuckles.

This country is believed to have been inhabited for perhaps the past 7,000 years, with ancient peoples coming for the healing properties of the mineral springs. Subsequently, the Caddos, Comanches, and Choctaws came for the waters; and in 1855, the area became part of the Chickasaw Nation. The white man began settling this region in the late 1800s, establishing a town around what became known as Pavilion Springs. To help prevent the degradation of the springs by uncontrolled use, the Choctaw and Chickasaw nations sold 640 acres of their lands to the U.S. government for the establishment of a protective reservation.

Today, visitors to the national recreation area may enjoy the paved loop drive through the area's historic Platt District and backcountry roads in the vicinity of Lake of the Arbuckles. Some 18 miles of trails offer delightful hikes to several of the springs and along Travertine and Rock creeks, as well as along the shore of Lake of the Arbuckles.

The recreation area straddles the transition between eastern woodlands and the open prairie grasslands, at the eastern edge of the Great Plains. Trees include the Ashe juniper; eastern red cedar; eastern cottonwood; black walnut; bitternut and black hickories; pecan; a number of oaks, including bur, post, chinkapin, and black; American, slippery, and winged elms; mulberries; osage-orange; American sycamore; American and Chickasaw plums; eastern redbud; honeylocust; boxelder; Texas buckeye; Carolina buckthorn; western soapberry; flowering dogwood; common persimmon; and green and Texas ashes. Prickly pear cactus and yucca also grow in drier places.

The area's range of habitat provides a wealth of wildlife species. Among the mammals are whitetail deer, beavers, bobcats, coyotes, red and

Lincoln Bridge over Travertine Creek, Chickasaw [NPS]

gray foxes, raccoons, striped skunks, opossums, armadillos, and red fox squirrels. The many kinds of birds include great blue and green-backed herons, bald eagles, wild turkeys, bobwhite quail, roadrunners, barred and great horned owls, belted kingfishers, blue jays, red-bellied woodpeckers, mockingbirds, scissor-tailed flycatchers, and summer tanagers. Visitors are urged to be careful when walking, since the western diamondback and timber rattlesnakes, and copperheads inhabit the area. Poison ivy is also common in parts of the area.

First pavilion built at Bromide Springs, 1907, Chickasaw [NPS]

Other activities include swimming, motorboating, water-skiing, sailing, and canoeing. Unlike the ban on hunting in national parks and monuments, public hunting is permitted in part of the national recreation area during the designated season. At the Travertine Nature Center, there are interpretive exhibits, audiovisual programs, and a bookstore. The National Park Service offers a variety of ranger-led nature walks and other interpretive programs. The center is open daily except on Christmas and New Year's Day. The national recreation area is open daily.

An excellent publication is *Chickasaw National Recreation Area* by Laurence Parent (Southwest Parks and Monuments Association).

There are three developed campgrounds in the area's historic Platt District and three others around Lake of the Arbuckles (group camping reservations: [405] 622-6677). Picnicking facilities are also provided. Lodging and meals are available in Sulphur, Davis, and Ardmore.

IF YOU GO: Access is by way of U.S. Route 177; or from I-35 by way of State Route 7 eastbound to Sulphur. Further information: Superintendent, P.O. Box 201, Sulphur, OK 73086. Telephone (405) 622-3165.

COULEE DAM NATIONAL RECREATION AREA

COULEE DAM NATIONAL RECREATION AREA consists of 100,390 acres in northeastern Washington state. It was established in 1990 under a cooperative agreement with the U.S. Bureau of Reclamation, Bureau of Indian Affairs, National Park Service, Colville Confederated Tribes, and the Spokane Tribe of Indians. The area encompasses the 130-mile long, man-made reservoir Franklin D. Roosevelt Lake, behind Grand Coulee Dam, on the Columbia River.

Visitor activities include boating, water-skiing, swimming, and fishing. Boat ramps are provided; and boats are available for rent at several lakeside concessionaires. Unlike the ban on public hunting in national parks and monuments, hunting is permitted in the national recreation area during the designated season. The area's visitor center, located at Grand Coulee Dam, is open daily, except on Thanksgiving, Christmas, and New Year's Day. Campgrounds are located at a number of places along the lake. Food service is provided during the summer at Seven Bays Marina and Spring Canyon Campground. Lodgings outside the national recreation area are available in the communities of Coulee Dam, Grand Coulee, and in the city of Spokane. Meals are also available in Kettle Falls, Northport, and Colville.

IF YOU GO: Access from U.S. Route 2 to Coulee Dam is north by way of State Route 155; from U.S. Route 2 to Ft. Spokane and north along the east shore of the lake to Northport is by way of State Route 25; and from Spokane north on U.S. Route 395 to State Route 25 at Kettle Falls. Further information: Coulee Dam National Recreation Area, 1008 Crest Dr., Coulee Dam, WA 99116. Telephone (509) 633-9441.

CURECANTI NATIONAL RECREATION AREA

CURECANTI NATIONAL RECREATION AREA, consisting of 40,526 acres in southwestern Colorado, was established under a memorandum of understanding between the National Park Service and the U.S. Bureau of Reclamation in 1965. The area encompasses three reservoirs—Blue Mesa, Morrow Point, and Crystal—on the Gunnison River. These long, narrow reservoirs are framed by ruggedly scenic canyons, cliffs, and pinnacles.

Blue Mesa Reservoir, which is the largest flat body of water in Colorado, is a boating mecca, and also provides the biggest Kokanee salmon fishery in the country. Morrow Point Reservoir is located in the uppermost stretch of the Black Canyon of the Gunnison, and is accessible only by trail, with lightweight, hand-carried craft such as sea kayaks. Crystal Reservoir, also accessible with hand-carried craft, fills the next stretch of the canyon—just upstream from Black Canyon of the Gunnison National Monument. Even though the latter protects the scenically awesome, undammed part of this narrow, sheer-walled gorge, the upstream dams and their reservoirs have significantly altered the river ecology within the national monument by capturing the river's natural load of sediments, and by altering the river's flow through the monument during the drier seasons.

Visitor activities include boating (boat rentals in summer), water-skiing, windsurfing, swimming (no designated areas), fishing, and hiking on a number of short trails. In winter, there are opportunities for cross-country skiing, winter treks, snowshoe hikes, ice fishing, and snowmobiling. Unlike the ban on public hunting in the national parks and monuments, hunting is permitted in certain areas within the national recreation area during the designated season. Boat tours are provided from Memorial Day to Labor Day (information: [970] 641-0402). There are two marinas and a number of boat-launching ramps.

The national recreation area also contains a 5,000-acre archaeological district, the remains of a 6,000-year-old Indian dwelling, recently discovered fossils of dinosaurs, and a narrow-gauge train exhibit.

The National Park Service provides interpretive programs. There are three visitor centers providing interpretive exhibits and programs: Elk Creek, located on the shore of Blue Mesa Reservoir and which includes a trout-viewing pond in the summer; Lake Fork; and Cimarron, featuring a narrow-gauge railroad exhibit and a Morrow Point Dam overlook. The National Park Service also provides numerous summer interpretive hikes and talks at various locations of the national recreation area; and there are summer evening interpretive programs at the Elk Creek and Lake Fork amphitheaters, and at Stevens Creek amphitheater. The national recreation area is open daily. The three visitor centers are open daily from mid-May through September; the Elk Creek visitor center is open on weekends through the winter, except on federal holidays, and intermittently on weekdays.

An informative publication is *Curecanti National Recreation Area* by Rose Houk (Southwest Parks and Monuments Association).

Picnicking and camping facilities are provided. There are ten campgrounds, as well as backcountry camping boat-in and hike-in sites. A restaurant is located adjacent to Elk Creek marina, open during the summer season. Outside the national recreation area, lodging and meals are available in Gunnison and Montrose.

IF YOU GO: Access is by way of U.S. Route 50, which runs the length of the area, providing outstanding views of Blue Mesa Reservoir and the Dillon Pinnacles. Further information: Superintendent, 102 Elk Creek, Gunnison, CO 81230. Telephone (970) 641-2337.

CUYAHOGA VALLEY NATIONAL RECREATION AREA

CUYAHOGA VALLEY NATIONAL RECREATION AREA, consisting of 33,000 acres between Akron and Cleveland, Ohio, was established in 1974 and has a great variety of natural, historical, and other cultural values in a pastoral setting of the Cuyahoga River valley. Visitor activities include hiking, bird-watching, bicycling, horseback riding, golf, cross-country and downhill skiing, snowshoeing, sledding, and ice-skating. This beautiful, largely wooded valley was sculpted by continental glacial ice thousands of years ago. The valley's human history began some 12,000 years ago with prehistoric hunters and has changed and evolved through time. Today, it presents an aesthetically pleasing diversity of floodplain, valley slopes, mixed deciduous and coniferous woodlands, agricultural fields, and many streams that have carved ravines on their way from upland plateaus to the river.

In addition to numerous trails, as in the Virginia Kendall area, there is the Bike and Hike Trail in and adjacent to the recreation area. Running the length of the national recreation area is the Ohio & Erie Canal Towpath Trail. This major trail follows the historic route of the canal that was completed in 1832 and which provided an important transportation link between Cleveland, on the shore of Lake Erie, and Portsmouth, on the Ohio River. Portions of the canal still contain water, and some of the historic locks and other structures remain. Visitors on the Towpath Trail enjoy views of woodlands, fields, and marshes. This trail is used by hikers; joggers; bicyclists; horseback riders on some stretches; and in winter, cross-country skiers. (Bicyclists are to yield to the other trail users.) Also running the length of the national recreation area is the Cuyahoga Valley Scenic Railroad (fee)—a diesel-locomotive-powered passenger train that follows the historic route of the Valley Railroad that began in the 1870s. It is owned and operated by a private, non-profit organization, and offers a very enjoyable way of experiencing the valley. National Park Service interpreters usually ride the train, presenting information on the natural and cultural history of the valley.

Three information centers provide interpretive exhibits, audiovisual programs, and publications: Canal Visitor Center, at Canal and Hillside roads,

Ohio and Erie Canal Towpath Trail, Cuyahoga Valley, Ohio [NPS]

in Valley View; Happy Days Visitor Center, on State Route 303; and Hunt Farm Visitor Information Center, on Bolanz Road, between Riverview and Akron-Peninsula roads. Both Canal and Hunt Farm centers feature exhibits portraying the history of Cuyahoga Valley. Canal Visitor Center is open daily, except on Thanksgiving, Christmas, and New Year's Day. Happy Days Visitor Center and Hunt Farm Visitor Information Center hours vary seasonally. In addition to the exhibits at the centers, two muse-ums, the Frazee House and the Boston Store, pro-vide exhibits on the history of the valley. The Frazee House explores the early settlement of the valley, while the Boston Store focuses on the early industry of canal boat building.

Musical programs are presented at the Blossom Music Center (fee), which is also the sum-mer home of the Cleveland Symphony Orchestra. The center is owned by the Musical Arts Association. Nearby is the Porthouse Theater (fee), owned by Kent State University, presenting Shakespeare, Broadway musicals, drama, and opera.

Another cultural center is Hale Farm & Village (fee), owned and operated by the Western Reserve Historical Society. A central feature is the Jonathan Hale brick farmstead that dates from 1826. Hale was one of the earliest settlers in the Western Reserve, an area reserved by Connecticut following the War for Independence (Revolutionary War). The farm-and-village recreates the lifestyle of early Ohio residents. It contains historic buildings

Boardwalk at Brandywine Falls, Cuyahoga Valley [Ted Davis/NPS]

from around the region and presents many nineteenth-century crafts, demon-strated by glassblowers, spinners, weavers, potters, blacksmiths, and candle-makers.

Two informative publications are *The Colorful Era of the Ohio Canal* by Margot and James S. Jackson (Cuyahoga Valley Association); and *A Photo Album of Ohio's Canal Era* by Jack Gieck (Kent State University Press).

There are numerous picnic areas, but no camping facilities. Within the national recreation area are the Stanford Youth Hostel in the historic Stanford farmhouse, and the historic inn at Brandywine Falls—formerly a farmhouse that is now a bed-and breakfast inn. Outside the recreation area, lodging and meals are available in Brecksville, Cleveland, and Akron. There are many routes to and through the area.

IF YOU GO: Access from I-80 (the Ohio Turnpike) is by way of Exit 11, continuing northbound on I-77 to the Rockside Road exit, then proceeding east on Rockside just over a mile, turning right (south) onto Canal Road, entering the north end of the recreation area, and proceeding two miles to the Canal Visitor Center, on the right. Further information: Superintendent, 15610 Vaughn Rd., Brecksville, OH 44141. Telephone (216) 650-4636.]

DELAWARE WATER GAP NATIONAL RECREATION AREA

DELAWARE WATER GAP NATIONAL RECREATION AREA, comprising 70,000 acres, was established in 1978. It takes in a relatively unaltered natural area along 40 miles of the middle stretch of the Delaware River, in Pennsylvania and New Jersey, including the famous and scenic Delaware Water Gap, where the river makes an S-turn through Kittatinny Ridge.

The parkland, which includes the "Wild and Scenic River" designa-tion, offers a broad range of cultural, natural, and scenic diversity. The actual gap, located at the southern end of the park, is a distinct notch more than a mile wide, cut through one of the prominent ridges of the Appalachian Mountains by the Delaware River. The national recreation area's landscapes vary from forested areas and rugged mountain terrain and farmland, to swiftly flowing streams, waterfalls, slowly moving stretches of river, and still ponds.

Visitors may enjoy such activities as sightseeing, hiking, boating, canoe-ing, swimming, and fishing. Unlike the ban on public hunting in national parks and monuments, hunting is permitted in the national recreation area dur-ing the designated season. Trails lead throughout the national recreation area, including 25 miles of the Appalachian Trail that runs from Maine to Georgia.

Two visitor centers provide interpretive displays, audiovisual pro-grams, and publications: one located at Kittatinny Point in New Jersey, which is open daily from May through October, and on weekends from November through April; and the other at Dingmans Falls in Pennsylvania, which is open seasonally (call for hours). Interpretive guided walks, evening programs, and children's programs are also offered during July and August. At Millbrook Village (open seasonally), the National Park Service sponsors craft demonstra-

Millbrook Village, Delaware Water Gap National Recreation Area [Dick Frear/NPS]

tions during Millbrook Days. This annual, two-day cultural event, during the first full weekend of October, celebrates nineteenth-century lifestyles in this recreated farming village. The national recreation area is open all year.

Picnicking and camping facilities are provided. There is a concession-operated campground, as well as two group campgrounds. Canoeists on extended trips may camp one night at primitive campsites along the river. Lodging and meals are available in Bushkill, Stroudsburg, and Milford, Pennsylvania; and in Columbia, New Jersey.

IF YOU GO: Access from I-84 is by way of U.S. Route 209 southbound or from I-78 by way of U.S. Route 209 northbound, in Pennsylvania. Further information: Superintendent, Delaware Water Gap NRA, Bushkill, PA 18324. Telephone (717) 588-2451.

GATEWAY NATIONAL RECREATION AREA

GATEWAY NATIONAL RECREATION AREA comprises more than 26,000 acres organized into three primary units in and around New York Harbor, in New York and New Jersey. It was established in 1972 to protect and interpret salt marshes and other wildlife habitats, sandy beaches, urban outdoor recreational facilities, and historic fortifications and airfields located within its boundaries. Gateway and Golden Gate in the San Francisco Bay area (see the text on the latter) were the first urban national recreation areas in the United States.

Gateway NRA consists of the **Jamaica Bay/Breezy Point Unit,** in Queens and Kings counties, New York, and includes among its districts the historic airfield, Floyd Bennett Field, and the bathhouse at Jacob Riis Park—

Van Campen Inn, built c. 1746, Delaware Water Gap [NPS]

both on the National Register of Historic Places (NRHP), as well as the former harbor defense site, Fort Tilden; the **Staten Island Unit,** in Richmond County, New York, which includes a historic military airfield, Miller Field, Great Kills Park, and the recently acquired (1996) Fort Wadsworth (not yet open to visitors, as of this writing); and the **Sandy Hook Unit,** in Monmouth County, New Jersey, which includes Fort Hancock and another NRHP-listed structure—its historic lighthouse. Hoffman and Swinburne islands, in lower New York Harbor, are managed by the Staten Island Unit as important bird-nesting areas and sensitive wildlife habitat, and are not open to the public.

Visitor activities include swimming on lifeguard-protected ocean beaches in season; sunbathing; sports such as tennis, baseball, softball, soccer, football, and cricket (organized league play requires a permit, acquired by contacting the unit involved); miniature golf; kite-flying; archery by permit (contact the unit); bicycling; boating (for boat launching and mooring facility information, call the respective unit); fishing (after-hours parking permits for this activity are available at the units); walking/hiking; jogging/running; bird-watching; environmental education programs; ranger-led walks/hikes and other programs (call the unit for a schedule of upcoming events), horseback riding on designated trails; and special cultural events in the summer. Off-road vehicles are permitted in the Breezy Point District only, and then only by permit during the designated season.

The national recreation area is open to visitors daily until dusk year-round (except by permit). Its complete range of services are provided from Memorial Day through September. The visitor center at Jamaica Bay Wildlife Refuge is open daily, except on Christmas and New Year's Day. There are no swimming beaches in Gateway NRA during the winter months.

Camping facilities are limited to park environmental education programs operated in cooperation with local educational institutions and not-for-profit organizations. A traditional restaurant is located at Canarsie Pier in the Jamaica Bay District, and fast-food services are available in all of the main units. Lodging and meals are available in the adjoining areas of Brooklyn and Queens, in New York, and in the Highlands, in New Jersey.

IF YOU GO: For information, including access by automobile or public transit, phone Jamaica Bay/Breezy Point Unit: (718) 318-4300; Staten Island Unit: (718) 351-7921, and Sandy Hook Unit: (908) 872-5970. Further information on Gateway National Recreation Area: General Superintendent, Floyd Bennett Field, Brooklyn, NY 11234. Telephone (718) 338-3575.

GLEN CANYON NATIONAL RECREATION AREA

GLEN CANYON NATIONAL RECREATION AREA, comprising 1,236,880 acres in northeastern Arizona and southeastern Utah, was established in 1972 and features canyon-framed, 186-mile-long Lake Powell—the reservoir behind Glen Canyon Dam on the Colorado River. The lake's blue waters contrast with the reddish sandstone walls and formations. There are over a hundred side canyons and coves around the 1,960-mile shoreline. Adjacent to the south shore of Lake Powell is the magnificent reddish sandstone bridge known as Rainbow Bridge. Rising 290 feet above the streambed and spanning 278 feet, it is the world's largest natural bridge and is located in Rainbow Bridge National Monument (most easily reached by boat tours from Wahweap and Bullfrog marinas).

Within the national recreation area and extending away from the lake is some of America's most ruggedly beautiful canyon country—including the

Lake Powell, Glen Canyon National Recreation Area [NPS]

Rainbow Bridge, Glen Canyon National Recreation Area [NPS]

scenic Escalante River canyon, its many tributaries, and natural sandstone arches; and the Orange Cliffs area adjoining Canyonlands National Park to the west.

Visitor activities include boating, water-skiing, swimming, scuba diving, fishing, hiking, and tours of the dam. There are marinas, boat-launching ramps, and boat tours and rentals, including houseboats, at Wahweap, Bullfrog, Halls Crossing, and Hite (for information on tours and rentals: phone 1 [800] 528-6154). Unlike the ban on public hunting in the national parks and monuments, hunting is permitted in parts of the national recreation area during the designated season.

Carl Hayden Visitor Center, presenting exhibits, audiovisual programs, and publications on the dam and the national recreation area, is located just to the north of Glen Canyon Dam, and is open daily except Thanksgiving, Christmas, and New Year's Day. Bullfrog Visitor Center is situated on Utah State Route 276, just south of the Bullfrog airstrip, and is open weekends in March and November, daily April through October. National Park Service contact stations are at all of the main developed sites. Ranger-led interpretive programs are provided at Wahweap, from Memorial Day through Labor Day.

There are several excellent publications on Glen Canyon and Lake Powell: *In Pictures Glen Canyon-Lake Powell: The Continuing Story* by Denny Davies (KC Publications); *Glen Canyon-Lake Powell: The Story Behind the Scenery®* by Ronald E. Everhart (KC Publications); *Lake Powell: A Different Light,* photographs by John Telford and text by William Smart (Gibbs-Smith Publisher); and *The Place No One Knew: Glen Canyon on the Colorado,* Eliot Porter photographs of Glen Canyon before Lake Powell (Sierra Club).

Camping and picnicking facilities are provided at a number of locations in the national recreation area, including the National Park Service-run campground at Lees Ferry. Lodging and meals are available at Wahweap,

Bullfrog, Halls Crossing, and Hite. (Information on services and reservations, phone 1 [800] 528-6154). Outside the national recreation area, lodging and meals are available in Page, Arizona.

IF YOU GO: Access to the Arizona part of the national recreation area is by way of U.S. Route 89, through Page. Just north of the dam is the loop road eastward into the Wahweap Lodge area.

Access to Bullfrog, in Utah, is by way of I-70, exiting onto State Route 24 and proceeding 54 miles, then left at Hanksville onto State Route 95 and continuing 26 miles, and right onto State Route 276 for 46 miles to Bullfrog.

Or access from U.S. Route 191 is by way of State Route 95 (passing by Natural Bridges National Monument) and either turning left onto State Route 276 northbound to Halls Crossing, or continuing on Route 95 through Hite and turning left onto Route 276 southbound to Bullfrog. Ferry service between Bullfrog and Halls Crossing is provided across Lake Powell. Further information: Superintendent, P.O. Box 1507, Page, AZ 86040. Telephone (520) 608-6404.

GOLDEN GATE NATIONAL RECREATION AREA

GOLDEN GATE NATIONAL RECREATION AREA, comprising 76,500 acres in San Francisco and in Marin and San Mateo counties, was established in 1972. It is the largest urban park in the world and protects scenic Pacific Ocean beaches; prominent coastal cliffs, bluffs, and headlands; hidden valleys, streams, marshes, and lagoons; peaceful redwood groves, lush riparian woodlands, and sweeping expanses of grasslands and meadows that are splashed with the vibrant colors of springtime wildflowers. There is also a wealth of historical structures and sites—from the rich array of historic structures in the Presidio of San Francisco, at Fort Mason, the former military defense batteries scattered along the coast, and the Cliff House overlooking Seal Rocks; to the former federal penitentiary perched atop Alcatraz Island in San Francisco Bay. The national recreation area is dedicated to the memory of its chief legislative champion, U.S. Congressman Phillip Burton.

Visitor activities include walking, hiking and jogging on the many miles of paths, trails, and old ranch roads that wind throughout many parts of the national recreation area (hikers are cautioned to be alert for places where poison oak grows and to use extra care not to approach too closely to the edge of ocean bluffs that may suddenly slump off). Sunbathing and swimming can be enjoyed at a number of beaches: in **San Francisco**, the four-mile-long strand of Ocean Beach (swimmers are urged to use caution because of the surf and ocean currents), China (Phelan) Beach, and Baker Beach (the latter is considered unsafe for swimming because of the surf and ocean currents), as well as swimming at Aquatic Park. In **Marin County**, Rodeo, Tennessee, Muir, and Stinson beaches all are considered hazardous for swimming; and at Stinson,

**Headlands, Golden Gate National Recreation Area
[Richard Frear]**

swimming is permitted only when lifeguards are on duty, from late May to mid-September. There is picnicking at many facilities, such as at Fort Mason, Crissy Field, Baker Beach, Muir Beach, and Stinson Beach; camping at a number of backpack and group campsites (reservations required) in Marin County; bird-watching throughout the national recreation area; board-sailing at Crissy Field; bicycling on fire roads in the Marin Headlands area; and hang-gliding above the beach and bluffs at Fort Funston.

Among the more popular walks and hikes are the paved Golden Gate Promenade at Crissy Field and the Coastal Trail south of Fort Point and around Land's End, in San Francisco; the five-mile Wolf Ridge loop trail near Rodeo Beach (a breeze is frequently whipping in off the ocean) and the adjoining roughly five-mile Miwok-Bobcat loop trail; the mostly level two-mile Tennessee Trail from the end of the road down to the lagoon and beach in Tennessee Valley; and the western end of the Dipsea Trail near Stinson Beach. The latter sometimes steep trail winds on southeastward through adjacent Mount Tamalpais State Park (information: [415] 388-2070), where there are grand panoramas of the San Francisco Bay region, and two short stretches of the trail within Muir Woods National Monument (information: [415] 388-2595).

Other protected areas adjacent to the national recreation area are Fort Point National Historic Site (see the text on this site); San Francisco Maritime National Historical Park (see the text on this park); Point Reyes National Seashore (information: [415] 663-1092) Samuel P. Taylor State Park (information: [415] 488-9897) and the Audubon Canyon Ranch (information: [415] 868-9244).The latter is owned and operated by the Marin Audubon Society, providing a four-mile trail, offering great bird-watching opportunities in the canyon and at adjacent Bolinas Lagoon, and presenting outdoor education exhibits and programs.

For boat trips out to Alcatraz Island ("The Rock") to tour the former federal prison that operated from 1934 to 1963, there is daily ferry service, provided by the Red and White Fleet (information and reservations: [415] 546-2700), for which a fee and reservations are required and which depart every 45 minutes from Pier 41 at Fisherman's Wharf in San Francisco. There is an absorbing, self-guiding tape-tour of the penitentiary, available at the start of the tour. An excellent publication is *Alcatraz: The Story Behind the Scenery*® by James P. Delgado (KC Publications).

Golden Gate National Recreation Area headquarters is located at Fort Mason, Building 201, in San Francisco. Visitor centers are located there, (415) 556-0560; at the Presidio, (415) 561-4323; at Fort Funston (also serving Phleger Estate, Sweeney Ridge, and Milagra Ridge), (415) 239-2366; at the Marin Headlands, (415) 331-1540; and on Alcatraz, (415) 705-1042.

Also located at Fort Mason is the Fort Mason Center, which is home to over 50 resident, nonprofit organizations—theaters, museums, and galleries, and environmental education programs (information: [415] 441-3400). The Marine Mammal Center, located in the recreation area, is a nonprofit group dedicated to saving injured, sick, and orphaned marine mammals (information: [415] 289-SEAL).

American Youth Hostels offers overnight accommodations in the Marin Headlands area (information and reservations: [415] 331-2777) and at Fort Mason ([415] 771-1065). Other lodgings and meals are abundantly available throughout the San Francisco Bay region. Advance lodging reservations in San Francisco, especially during the summer tourist season, are highly recommended.

IF YOU GO: Further information about the national recreation area and access to the various parts and points of interest: Superintendent, Building 201, Fort Mason, San Francisco, CA 94123. Telephone (415) 556-0561.

Fort Funston, Golden Gate National Recreation Area [NPS]

GREAT FALLS PARK

GREAT FALLS PARK, consisting of 800 acres along the Potomac River in northern Virginia, about eight miles northwest of Washington, D.C., was established in 1966 to protect the Virginia side of the Great Falls of the Potomac. (See the text on the Chesapeake and Ohio Canal, regarding the Maryland side of the falls area).

This park provides outstanding views of Great Falls that include a number of rocky islands and the deeply incised Mather Gorge, in which the river is squeezed between sheer cliffs. The rushing river is especially exciting to watch after periods of heavy rainfall, as it plunges, foams, and roars over the rocks and into the confines of the gorge.

Most of the park is heavily wooded with a predominantly deciduous forest. A network of delightful hiking trails winds throughout the area, including the River Trail that follows the western rim of the gorge. Some of the trail system is open to horseback riding and mountain biking.

The park has a visitor center that provides interpretive exhibits, programs, and publications. A short walk from the visitor center leads to overlooks of the falls. Some of these viewing places date from the early twentieth century, when this area was a privately run amusement park. Today, the National Park Service provides a variety of ranger-guided programs and interpretive walks that help explain the natural and human history of the area.

Another historical feature of the park are the remains of George Washington's dream to build a canal. In 1784, the Patowmack Company was formed to construct a series of five canals in conjunction with the river, to help stimulate trade between the mid-Atlantic states and the Ohio River valley. Construction on this first canal in the United States started in 1785 and was completed 17 years later. The stretches of canal around Little Falls, just above Georgetown, in Washington, D.C., and around Great Falls necessitated a series of locks to lift canal boats up and down in a series of steps between the river level below the falls and the elevation above. This canal system operated for 26 years, carrying a trade in such items as lumber, coal, iron ore, tobacco, corn, flour, and furs. The flatboats were about 75 feet long and about 5 feet wide. It took them approximately three days to travel the entire 190 miles between Cumberland, Maryland, and Georgetown. In 1828, the Chesapeake and Ohio Canal Company, operating its continuous canal between Georgetown and Cumberland along the Maryland shore of the river, bought the Patowmack Company. The C&O Canal was soon put out of business by the Baltimore & Ohio Railroad, which traversed that distance much faster.

Camping is not permitted in the park, but picnic facilities are provided. Lodging and meals are available throughout the Washington, D.C., metropolitan area. Advance lodging reservations are advised, especially for the peak tourist season.

IF YOU GO: Access to the park is by way of State Route 193 (the Georgetown Pike) and then right onto State Route 738 (Old Dominion

Drive) or by way of State Route 738—both options reached from I-495 (the Capital Beltway). Further information: Great Falls Park, c/o Superintendent, George Washington Memorial Parkway, Turkey Run Park, McLean, VA 22101. Telephone (703) 285-2598.

GREENBELT PARK

GREENBELT PARK, comprising 1,175 acres located in Maryland, about four miles northeast of Washington, D.C., was transferred from the Public Housing Authority to the National Park Service in 1950. It protects an area of rich, mixed coniferous and deciduous woodland that provides habitat for native flora and fauna, and that offers a variety of outdoor recreational opportunities for park visitors. Greenbelt Park is traversed by the Baltimore-Washington Parkway, between Good Luck Road and I-495/I-95.

This land was once cleared of the forest that grew here when the early colonists arrived and settled the area. Trees were felled and the land was cleared for cultivating crops such as corn and tobacco. Eventually, the soil fertility became badly depleted and could no longer yield high-quality crops. Erosion scarred the denuded land and carried off much valuable topsoil. But once again the area supports a habitat that contains a rich variety of plant and animal life. Among the mammals of the park are whitetail deer, red and gray foxes, raccoons, beavers, opossums, and gray and flying squirrels. Of the many species of birds, there are mourning doves; barred owls; pileated, red-bellied, downy, and other woodpeckers; blue jays; tufted titmice; white-breasted nuthatches; Carolina wrens; wood thrushes; a number of warblers, including black-and-white, yellow, chestnut-sided, American redstart, and ovenbird; scarlet tanagers; cardinals; rufous-sided towhees; white-throated and song sparrows; and scarlet tanagers.

A network of trails winds throughout the park. Hiking trails include the 1.2-mile Azalea Trail that connects the park's picnic areas and that loops along forest-canopy-shaded creeks and hillsides. The 1.4-mile Dogwood Trail, accessed from a parking area on Park Central Road, loops through another beautiful area and provides interpretive information on the park's ecological values, early human uses of the land, and the recovery from land-use abuses of the past. A shorter loop, the Blueberry Trail, is located in the vicinity of the park's campgrounds. In addition, there are the six-mile perimeter trail that is available for horseback riding (horses are not available in the park), jogging, and hiking. This route leads visitors through some of the most scenic parts of the park.

The park has information centers at headquarters near the park entrance and at the entrance to the campgrounds. The National Park Service offers guided interpretive walks, as well as evening and other programs.

Camping is permitted in the four campground loops in the southern end of the park, while picnic areas are located near park headquarters. Lodging and meals are available in the surrounding metropolitan area, including the suburban communities of Greenbelt and College Park, as well as in Washington, D.C. Advance lodging reservations are advised, especially for the popular tourist seasons.

IF YOU GO: The park is bordered by Good Luck Road on the south, State Route 201 (Kenilworth Avenue) on the west, State Route 193 (Greenbelt Road) to the north, and I-495/I-95 (the Capital Beltway) to the northeast. Access is by way of State Route 193, which can be reached from I-495 by way of Exit 23 onto the parkway, and then taking the next exit onto State Route 193. Further information: Park Manager, Greenbelt Park, Greenbelt, MD 20770. Telephone (301) 344-3948.

LAKE CHELAN NATIONAL RECREATION AREA

LAKE CHELAN NATIONAL RECREATION AREA, comprising 61,887 acres on the east slope of the Cascade Mountains of northern Washington state, was established in 1968 to give protection to the richly scenic Stehekin Valley and the upper five miles of 55-mile-long Lake Chelan. The national recreation area adjoins North Cascades National Park, which extends northward, encompassing some of the most dramatically beautiful high mountain country in America.

Lake Chelan, at 1,500 feet in depth, is the third deepest lake in the United States. It fills a glacier-carved trench that was naturally dammed at the southern end by a terminal moraine of boulders, gravel, and other sediments deposited at the end of a long tongue of Pleistocene glacial ice. In 1927, a power dam was built that raised the lake's level by another 21 feet.

Most visitors arrive either by boat (daily from mid-March to the end of October; less frequently the rest of the year)—a spectacularly beautiful ride toward and into the mountains that takes up to four hours from Chelan to the boat landing at the remote community of Stehekin (Lake Chelan Boat Company, Chelan, WA 98816; phone: [509] 682-2224); or by float plane (Chelan Airways, Chelan, WA 98816; phone: [509] 682-5555).

There is no access to Stehekin by automobile. A small visitor center is located in Stehekin that provides orientation and interpretive exhibits. Ranger-led walks and interpretive programs are offered by the National Park Service from late June through early September. Visitors enjoy such activities as hiking, mountain climbing, horseback riding, boating, fishing, and commercial river rafting. In contrast to the ban on public hunting in the adjacent national park, hunting is permitted in the national recreation area during the designated season.

Of historic interest is the William Buckner family homestead, with its log cabin, barn, and workshop, that was carved out of the wilderness, beginning in 1911.

Among the trees in the national recreation area are ponderosa pine; western larch, the needles of which turn soft gold in the fall; Douglas fir; and bigleaf and vine maples—the latter two turning shades of yellow, orange, and crimson in autumn. Mammals include mountain goats, black bears, whitetail and mule deer, coyotes, mountain lions, bobcats, red foxes, raccoons, porcupines, striped skunks, martens, mink, weasels, chickarees, and chipmunks. A few of the many bird species are great horned and spotted owls; belted kingfishers; pileated woodpeckers; Steller's and gray jays; Clark's nutcrackers; ravens; mountain, black-capped, and chestnut-backed chickadees; red-breasted nuthatches; winter wrens; kinglets; varied thrushes; robins; dippers; black-headed and evening grosbeaks; dark-eyed (Oregon) juncoes, white-crowned sparrows, western tanagers, red crossbills, and rosy finches.

Among the hiking trails are the short Imus Creek interpretive trail, the Lakeshore Trail providing beautiful views of Lake Chelan, and the Agnes Gorge Trail that starts at High Bridge. One of the more challenging hikes is on the MacGregor Mountain Trail, which branches from the short stretch of the Pacific Crest National Scenic Trail, as the latter crosses the northwest corner of the national recreation area.

The spectacular, 312-foot Rainbow Falls (a picnic area is nearby) is located just off the 20-mile-long, unpaved road that climbs from Stehekin, along the dashing waters of the Stehekin River, up to High Bridge, and into the national park, ending at Cottonwood Campground. From mid-May to mid-October, daily shuttle bus service (fee) makes regular runs up and down this road. From Rainbow Falls, Rainbow Creek Trail invites exploration northward; while another hike loops eastward, around Purple Mountain on the Boulder Creek and Purple Creek trails, and back to Stehekin.

Backcountry and trail camping are popular (free permits are required and must be obtained in person, up to 24 hours in advance of the hike's start). Campgrounds are located at Purple Point, on the shore of Lake Chelan; at Harlequin, a short way up the road from Rainbow Falls, near the west bank of the Stehekin River; at Bullion; and at High Bridge. There are other campgrounds to the north, in the national park, and along the shores of Lake Chelan (some reached only by boat).

Lodging and meals are available in Stehekin, but lodging reservations well in advance are highly recommended. Other lodging and meals are available in Chelan.

IF YOU GO: Access from Wenatchee is 40 miles by way of U.S. Route 97 and a short stretch on U.S. Route 97 Alt.; or from Wenatchee on U.S. Route 97 Alt. Further information: Superintendent, 2105 State Route 20, Sedro-Woolley, WA 98284. Telephone (360) 856-5700.

LAKE MEAD NATIONAL RECREATION AREA

LAKE MEAD NATIONAL RECREATION AREA, consisting of 1,501,216 acres, encompasses two reservoirs on the lower Colorado River—Lake Mead, behind Hoover Dam (completed in 1935), and Lake Mohave, behind Davis

Dam (completed in 1953), in southeastern Nevada and northwestern Arizona. The area was initially administered under cooperative agreements between the National Park Service and the U.S. Bureau of Reclamation—in 1937 (as Boulder Dam Recreational Area), and 1947 (as Lake Mead Recreation Area). In 1964 it became the first "national" recreation area established by congressional legislation. It offers a wide range of recreational opportunities, while providing protection for natural, archaeological, and historical resources. There are wild desert expanses, sheer-walled canyons, pine- and juniper-covered high plateaus, and starkly rugged mountains. Much of the area contains spectacular desert and canyon landscapes of varying shades of black, gray, brown, and red that provide a dramatic setting for the blue of the lakes—most notably in and around the lower end of the Grand Canyon—adjoining Grand Canyon National Park.

Visitor activities include motor-boating (boat rentals), water-skiing, canoeing, kayaking, sailing, sailboarding, snorkeling and scuba diving, fishing, swimming, sunbathing, and hiking. Unlike the ban on public hunting in national parks and monuments, hunting is permitted in the national recreation area during the designated season.

The Alan Bible Visitor Center, located just west of the intersection of U.S. Route 93 and Lakeshore Road, just down the hill from Boulder City toward Lake Mead, provides orientation, interpretive exhibits, an audiovisual program, and publications. A small desert botanical garden, just outside the center, helps visitors identify some of the fascinating trees, shrubs, and cacti of the area. Other National Park Service contact stations are located on the shore of Lake Mead at Overton Beach, Echo Bay, Callville Bay, and Las Vegas Bay, and on Lake Mohave at Cottonwood Cove in Nevada; and Willow Beach, Temple Bar, and Katherine, in Arizona. Among the interpretive programs are ranger-led hikes and programs, paddle-wheel tour-boat rides to Hoover Dam, Black Canyon raft trips, and a lectures series in winter.

The best months for hiking are generally from October through April or early May. The National Park Service urges visitors planning a backcountry hike always to leave an itinerary with someone and adhere to it, so that rangers will know where to search, in the event of an emergency. It is always wise to carry water on hikes—a gallon per person per day is recommended. Long-distance hiking is strongly discouraged during the furnace-hot months of late May through September. The Park Service offers a number of interpretive, ranger-led hikes on weekends, during the fall and winter.

There are numerous picnicking facilities, eight campgrounds, and six RV campgrounds in the national recreation area. Groceries, marine, and other supplies are available at the marina camp stores. Boat rentals are available at the marinas. Lodging (five motels) and meals are available at a number of places within the national recreation area. (Concession facilities are listed in a flyer that may be obtained at the visitor center or by writing or phoning the area.) Outside the recreation area, lodging and meals are available in Boulder City, Henderson, Las Vegas, Bullhead City, Laughlin, Overton, and Searchlight.

Black Canyon, Lake Mohave, Lake Mead National Recreation Area [NPS]

Access routes include: in **Nevada**, from northbound I-15, 20 miles northeast on State Route 146; from Las Vegas, about 25 miles by way of State Route 147 southbound; from State Route 147 in North Las Vegas about eight miles by way of Lake Mead Boulevard; from I-15 southeast about 12 miles on State Route 169 through Logandale and Overton; from I-15 eastbound on the road through Nevada's spectacularly scenic Valley of Fire State Park, which adjoins the northernmost arm of the national recreation area; and from U.S. Route 95 at Searchlight eastbound 14 miles on State Route 164 to Cottonwood Cove on Lake Mohave. In **Arizona,** from U.S. Route 93 northeast 28 miles to Temple Bar; from U.S. Route 93 northeast 44 miles to South Cove and Pearce Ferry on Lake Mead; from U.S. Route 93 westbound four miles to Willow Beach on Lake Mohave; and from State Route 68 northbound three miles to Katherine on Lake Mohave. The national recreation area is open daily all year.

Two informative publications are *Lake Mead-Hoover Dam: The Story Behind the Scenery*® by James C. Maxon (KC Publications); and *Lake Mead National Recreation Area,* by Rose Houk (Southwest Parks and Monuments Association).

IF YOU GO: Further information on other backcountry access routes into shoreline areas of the national recreation area; backcountry roads across the Arizona Strip to the Shivwits Plateau country around Mount Dellenbaugh, and Andrus and Whitmore canyons; and on Lake Mead National Recreation Area in general: Superintendent, 601 Nevada Highway, Boulder City, NV 89005. Telephone (702) 293-8990.

Black Canyon, Lake Mead National Recreation Area [NPS]

LAKE MEREDITH NATIONAL RECREATION AREA

LAKE MEREDITH NATIONAL RECREATION AREA comprises 44,977 acres upstream from Sanford Dam on the Canadian River, in the Texas Panhandle. It was established as the Sanford National Recreation Area in 1965, under an administrative agreement with the U.S. Bureau of Reclamation. It was changed to Lake Meredith Recreation Area in 1972 and to its present designation in 1990. The area takes in the manmade reservoir, Lake Meredith, which is framed by scenic rock walls, buttes, and pinnacles. Numerous species of waterfowl and other birds are attracted to the lake and adjacent wetlands habitat.

Visitors enjoy motor-boating, water-skiing, sailing, canoeing, fishing, and even scuba diving. There are boat-launching ramps, a marina, and areas of beach. Unlike the ban on hunting in national parks and monuments, public hunting is permitted in the national recreation area in the designated season. The national recreation area is always open.

An informative publication is *Lake Meredith National Recreation Area* by Laurence Parent (Southwest Parks and Monuments Association).

Nearby is Alibates Flint Quarries National Monument that protects and interprets a pre-Columbian site where people quarried flint for tool-making over a period of 12,000 years, ending around 1870.

IF YOU GO: Camping and picnicking facilities are provided in the national recreation area. Light snacks are provided at the Sanford-Yake marina. Lodging and meals are available in Fritch, Sanford, Borger, Dumas, and Amarillo. Access from Amarillo is by way of State Route 136. Further information: Superintendent, P.O. Box 1460, Fritch, TX 79036. Telephone (807) 857-3151.

OXON HILL FARM/OXON COVE PARK

OXON HILL FARM/OXON COVE PARK consists of 512 acres adjacent to the south end of Washington, D.C., in Maryland. It was established in the mid-1960s to protect and interpret this working farm in the Oxon Hill area along the east bank of the Potomac River—an area that has been valued for its agricultural potential since the seventeenth century.

Large plantations cultivated corn, tobacco, and other crops; and raised cattle, sheep and goats, pigs and hogs, and chickens. Slaves provided much of the labor on these extensive tidewater estates, which were subsequently divided into smaller farms. In 1891, the federal government acquired this area to operate a farm for St. Elizabeth's Hospital, the patients of which helped with the work of farming, as a form of therapy, as well as to grow food for the institution.

Soon after the property was transferred to the National Park Service, Oxon Hill Farm was opened to the public in 1967. In the words of the National Park Service:

> The park opened its gates not as a farm museum or a petting zoo but as a working farm that represented the time when horsepower still came directly from horses. The success of Oxon Hill Farm, as with all small farms, reflects an understanding of agriculture and animals, a love of independence, and a willingness to work hard.

> Buildings on the farm include the two-story farm house, the dairy barn and silo, hay barn, feed shed, stable, tool shed, chicken house, hog house, and root cellar.

Visitors to Oxon Hill may observe a variety of activities or may actually participate in some of the activities, such as working in a garden, milking a cow, churning butter, making ice cream and apple cider, feeding chickens, husking and cracking corn, gathering fresh eggs, or picking pumpkins. There are seasonal opportunities to observe sheep-shearing, wool-spinning, and natural dyeing. Hay rides are sometimes offered. (For some events, including crafts programs, nature walks, and wagon rides, advance reservations are required.) In springtime, the large draft horses are used to plow, disc, and harrow the fields for the planting of crops. In the autumn, these great horses haul the farm produce into storage.

In October, an annual Fall Festival is a popular event that features farming demonstrations, music, and a variety of workshops. The park also hosts annual Halloween and Christmas parties.

Visitors may walk around the farm complex to see the buildings, bookstore, barnyard, and antique farm machinery. Visitors are also encouraged to explore other areas of the park, such as the lower fields or to ride the bike path along the shore of the Potomac River's Oxon Cove.

Oxon Hill Farm, Maryland [Bill Clark]

Oxon Hill Farm is open daily, except on Thanksgiving, Christmas, and New Year's Day. To make reservations, learn about volunteer and educational programs, or obtain information on how to plan for group visits, phone (301) 839-1176. For a recorded message of daily and monthly programs and events, phone (301) 839-1177.

Camping is not permitted in the park, but picnic facilities are provided. Lodging and meals are available in the community of Oxon Hill; across the Potomac in Alexandria, Virginia; in Washington, D.C.; and elsewhere in the metropolitan area. Advance lodging reservations are advised, especially for the peak tourist seasons.

IF YOU GO: Access to Oxon Hill Farm/Oxon Cove Park from I-495/I-95 (the Capital Beltway) is by way of Exit 3A (State Route 210/Indian Head Highway exit); then turning right onto Oxon Hill Road and following the park signs. From Washington, D.C., proceed south on I-295 (Anacostia Freeway), exit onto I-495/I-95 (bearing left away from the river into Maryland), take Exit 3A, and turn right onto Oxon Hill Road to the park entrance. Further information: Site Manager, Oxon Hill Farm, 1900 Anacostia Dr., SE, Washington, DC 20020. Telephone (202) 690-5185.

PRINCE WILLIAM FOREST PARK

PRINCE WILLIAM FOREST PARK, comprising 18,571 acres in northern Virginia, about 30 miles south of Washington, D.C., was initially established as the Chopawamsic Recreation Demonstration Area. It was transferred from the Resettlement Administration to the National Park Service in 1940, and was changed to the Prince William Forest Park in 1948. The park protects a rich, predominantly deciduous forest that contains beautiful creeks, waterfalls, and springs in the Quantico Creek watershed of the Virginia Piedmont region.

A scenic drive loops through the park, and more than 37 miles of hiking trails wind throughout the area. These trails include the two-tenths-of-a-mile Pine Grove Forest Trail, the half-mile Crossing Trail, the 1.3-mile Laurel Trail Loop, and the 1.8-mile Birch Bluff Trail—all in the vicinity of the park's visitor center. The 2.6-mile North Valley Trail follows the banks of Quantico Creek, and the 9.7-mile South Valley Trail follows a long stretch of the creek's South Fork. There is also a network of unpaved roads available for biking and hiking.

As the National Park Service says:

> Quantico Creek and its major tributary, the South Fork, flow through the park collecting water from rain, springs, and small side streams. Together they drain more than 20 square miles within the park. About midway through their courses the creeks cut deep valleys and cascade over steep erosion-resistant rocks as they leave the Piedmont Plateau and enter the Atlantic Coastal Plain.

This rich habitat supports a wide variety of flora and fauna. For instance, among the species of trees are Virginia pine; eastern hemlock; tulip tree; sassafras; American sycamore; sweetgum; bitternut and shagbark hickories; beech; a number of oaks, including white, post, chestnut, northern and southern red, black, and blackjack; river birch; ironwood; eastern redbud; flowering dogwood; and red maple. Shrubs include spicebush, devil's-walking-stick; mountain laurel, and rhododendron. Among the many kinds of wildflowers are Jack-in-the-pulpit, Mayapple, Dutchman's breeches, spring beauty, bloodroot, round-lobed hepatica, trilliums, pink lady's-slipper, showy orchis, violets, and Indian pipe. Ferns include bracken, the decorative Christmas, and the rare walking fern.

Mammals include whitetail deer, beavers, raccoons, opossums, red and gray foxes, and flying and gray squirrels. Of the many kinds of birds there are wild turkeys; barred owls; pileated, red-bellied, and downy woodpeckers; blue jays; Carolina chickadees; tufted titmice; white-breasted nuthatches; Carolina wrens; wood thrushes; numerous species of warblers, including black-and-white, yellow, yellow-rumped, chestnut-sided, prairie, ovenbird, Louisiana waterthrush, yellowthroat, yellow-breasted chat, hooded, and American redstart; northern orioles; scarlet tanagers; cardinals; rufous-sided towhees; and white-throated and song sparrows. Snakes inhabiting the park include copperhead and timber rattlesnake.

In the words of the National Park Service:

> Enter Prince William Forest Park and you know it is a special place. Sunlight filtering through the trees forms luminous freckles on the forest floor. Birds and bubbling streams give shape to nature's music, and the woodsy fragrance of moist vegetation fills the air.

Prince William Forest Park, Virginia [NPS]

This land was not always wild and beautiful. Algonquin Indians lived in this region for thousands of years, until European colonists settled in Virginia, beginning in 1607. Soon the original forests were cut down to make way for the cultivation of crops such as tobacco and corn. Tobacco, in particular, eventually depleted the soil's fertility. Erosion cut gullies into the land and carried away denuded topsoil, redepositing it in Dumfries Harbor in the Potomac River. The original large plantations were given up or were divided into small farms.

Confederate and Union troops skirmished in the area during the Civil War, between 1861 and 1865. In 1889, Cabin Branch pyrite mine, located on Quantico Creek just upstream from its junction with the South Fork, produced pyrite for sulfur that was used in making gunpowder. It operated and brought some economic prosperity to the area through World War I. By the 1930s, with just a few farms remaining, the impoverished land was beginning to recover and a new forest was struggling to cover the soil. In 1936, the Quantico and nearby Chopawamsic watersheds were selected as one of 46 national marginal farmland projects in the United States, in which the lands were slated for restoration and protection.

By 1941, the Civilian Conservation Corps had built roads, bridges, dams, and five rustic cabin camps—the latter serving as urban youth group summer camps. These camps are still being used as group and family retreats (reservations: [703] 221-4706); and are listed on the National Register of Historic Places.

During World War II, the park was closed to the public and became part of a top-secret military facility, as the predecessor to the Central

Intelligence Agency (the Office of Strategic Services), carried out training programs here. In 1948, the property was returned to the National Park Service and renamed Prince William Forest Park.

Today, a visitor center provides interpretive exhibits, programs, and publications. Ranger-led walks and evening programs are offered throughout the year. Group activities are scheduled by contacting the visitor center (703) 221-7181. The visitor center is open daily, except on Christmas and New Year's Day.

Camping facilities are provided at the Oak Ridge Campground, in the western end of the park. There is also the concession-run Travel Trailer Village at the northern edge of the park, just off State Route 234. (Trailer village reservations: phone: [703] 221-2474.) Primitive camping is available in the Chopawamsic Backcountry Area. Group camping is available at Turkey Run Ridge Campground. Permits can be obtained from the visitor center. Lodging and meals are available in Dumfries, Stafford, and elsewhere in the area. Meals are available in Triangle.

IF YOU GO: Access to the park is 32 miles south of Washington, D.C., by way of I-95; taking Exit 150B (State Route 619) west a quarter-mile to the park entrance on the right. From Fredericksburg, it is 22 miles north on I-95 to Exit 150B and left (west) on State Route 619. Further information: Superintendent, 18100 Park Headquarters Rd., Triangle, VA 22172. Telephone (703) 221-7181.

ROSS LAKE NATIONAL RECREATION AREA

ROSS LAKE NATIONAL RECREATION AREA, consisting of 117,574 acres between two parts of North Cascades National Park, in the Cascade Mountains of northern Washington state, was established in 1968. It contains the North Cascades Highway (State Route 20) and three mountain-framed, man-made reservoirs on the Skagit River: 22-mile-long, 12,000-acre Ross Lake that extends northward from 540-foot-high Ross Dam to just beyond the Canadian border; 910-acre Diablo Lake behind Diablo Dam; and 210-acre Gorge Lake behind Gorge Dam. The three hydropower dams were constructed by Seattle City Light between 1919 and 1949. Only Diablo and Gorge lakes are accessible from the highway by automobile. Ross Lake is accessible by automobile only from the Trans-Canada Highway, near Hope, British Columbia, by way of a 38-mile (61-km) gravel road to a boat launch at the upper end of the lake.

Among the visitor activities in the national recreation area are hiking (a number of the trails climb into the national park), mountain climbing, horseback riding, backcountry camping, boating, canoeing, and fishing. North Cascades Visitor Center provides interpretive exhibits, publications, and information on hiking, camping, boating, interpretive walks, and tours of the Seattle City Light facilities. Leading from nearby Newhalem Creek Campground are two short nature trails: Trail of the Cedars and To Know a Tree Trail.

Among the tree species of this part of the national recreation area are lodgepole pine, western hemlock, Douglas fir, western red cedar, and Pacific yew. Because of the heavy rainfall on this western side of the Cascades, many of these trees have grown to a large size over several centuries. Wildlife of the national recreation area include mule (blacktailed) deer, black bears, mountain lions, bobcats, red foxes, raccoons, porcupines, striped skunks, martens, mink, weasels, beavers, river otters, chickarees, and chipmunks. Of the birds, there are bald eagles; great horned, barred, and spotted owls; belted kingfishers; pileated woodpeckers; Steller's and gray jays; Clark's nutcrackers; ravens; black-capped chickadees; red-breasted nuthatches; winter wrens; kinglets; hermit, Swainson's, and varied thrushes; robins; dippers; dark-eyed (Oregon) juncoes; white-crowned sparrows; western tanagers; red crossbills, and rosy finches.

A number of waterfalls plunge down from the high country, including Gorge Creek Falls, on the north side of the highway. Farther east, the route swings southward to an arm of Diablo Lake. From near Colonial Campground, Thunder Woods Nature Trail steeply loops from Thunder Creek Trail through an area of magnificent, huge western red cedars. And from near here, Thunder Creek Trail follows along this beautiful stream and climbs into the heart of the national park's south unit. (Free backcountry permits are required for overnight stays.) The national recreation area is open all year, but the visitor center is open daily from mid-April to mid-November and is open on weekends only during the rest of the year (closed on Thanksgiving, Christmas, and New Year's Day).

In addition to the two campgrounds mentioned above, there is Goodell Campground, just west of the Newhalem Creek area; and a campground near the boat-launching site, at Hozomeen, near the north end of Ross Lake. Lodging within the recreation area is available at Ross Lake Resort, near the southern end of the lake. (Advance reservations are highly recommended well in advance: Ross Lake Resort, Rockport, WA 98283. Phone [206] 386-4437.) This resort is reached either by trail from Ross or Diablo dams, by boat from the launch at the north end of the lake, or by a combination of boats and truck from Diablo Lake. Kayaks, canoes, and motorboats are available for rent; and water taxi service is provided at the resort.

Big Beaver Trail is a popular hike from the resort, as it follows a stretch of the lakeshore, enters a magnificent stand of giant red cedars, and heads up Big Beaver Creek valley, where it eventually climbs into the heart of the national park's north unit. Another delightful walk (and a pleasant respite from highway driving), is the Happy Creek Forest Walk through an area of ancient forest, along the North Cascades Highway, 14 miles east of Newhalem.

IF YOU GO: Lodging and meals outside the national recreation area are available in Marblemount, Concrete, and cities along Puget Sound, to the west; and Winthrop to the east. Access is by way of State Route 20, running east from I-5 to U.S. Route 97. Further information: Superintendent, Ross Lake National Recreation Area, 2105 State Route 20, Sedro-Woolley, WA 98284. Telephone (360) 856-5700.

SANTA MONICA MOUNTAINS NATIONAL RECREATION AREA

SANTA MONICA MOUNTAINS NATIONAL RECREATION AREA
consists of 22,000 acres of federal parklands in a number of scattered sites.
It was established in 1978 to protect some of the key areas of these scenically rugged, canyon-carved, chaparral-covered mountains that stretch west
from Los Angeles and lie adjacent to the Pacific Ocean, in southern
California. Within the overall boundary of the national recreation area,
which takes in the whole of the Santa Monica Mountains, are also a number of significant state and county parks, and other public lands that bring
the total of protected parklands to around 70,000 acres. Also scattered
throughout the area encompassed by the boundary are many private properties, including homes, ranches, and communities. A network of paved
roads winds throughout the area.

Visitor activities include hiking, horseback riding, mountain biking,
surfing, and bird-watching. There are more than 580 miles of trails within the
federal, state, and local parks. A key trail that is still in the process of being completed is the Backbone Trail that will ultimately extend for about 70 miles, connecting a number of the major park areas within the national recreation area.

Among the main sites of the federally owned national recreation area
are Rancho Sierra Vista/Satwiwa, located near the northwest corner of the
recreation area and adjacent to Point Mugu State Park (a number of intercon-
necting trails lead through both the federal and state parks, including the Big
Sycamore Trail); Circle X Ranch; Zuma Canyon-Trancas Canyon; Rocky Oaks;
Castro Crest and Paramount Ranch, both adjacent to Malibu Creek State Park;
Franklin Canyon Ranch, toward the far east end of the recreation area; and
Cheeseboro Canyon-Palo Comado Canyon, the latter encompassing beautiful,
wild, ecologically rich country to the north of U.S. Route 101 freeway.

The Santa Monica Mountains are one of the few east-west-trending
mountain ranges in California. They are relatively young mountains, still
being slowly, inexorably uplifted by the tremendous pressure of massive, col-
liding plates of the earth's surface. Complex faulting and overturning of the
rock strata and formations, eroded by streams, have created a landscape of
great scenic beauty.

Among the rich variety of plantlife making up the chaparral habitat
are fragrant-flowering ceanothus species, chamise, manzanita, toyon
(Christmasberry), and California scrub oak. Grassy valleys are dotted with valley and coast live oaks; while riparian habitat along streams is shaded by
California sycamores and willows. A tremendous variety of wildflowers bloom
in the spring after the winter rains. Usually at the end of the long, dry summers, wildfires play a powerfully rejuvenating force. Seeing the blackened,
charred landscape after a firestorm makes it hard to believe the rebirth of life
just a few months later, following winter rains. An explosion of wildflowers
and rapid resprouting of chaparral shrubs transforms the barren, moon-like
landscape into lush green growth and a rainbow of color.

Santa Monica Mountains National Recreation Area, southern California [NPS]

A representative bird of the chaparral is the wrentit, whose loud, clear song drifts across the shrubby hillsides. Other birds in the area include redtail hawks, California quail, several species of hummingbirds, acorn woodpeckers, ravens, and brown pelicans. Mammals include mule deer, bobcats, coyotes, gray foxes, raccoons, striped skunks, rabbits, and ground squirrels.

A visitor center provides interpretive exhibits and publications. The center is open daily, except on Thanksgiving, Christmas, and New Year's Day. Other interpretive centers include the Satwiwa Native American Indian Culture Center, Malibu Creek State Park visitor center, and Topanga State Park nature center. Among the drives through the national recreation area is the Mulholland Scenic Corridor—a 55-mile scenic road through the heart of the Santa Monica Mountains—from Leo Carrillo State Beach to Griffith Park (the National Park Service urges caution in driving narrow, winding mountain roads, routes that are also used by visitors riding bicycles and motorcycles). There is a variety of year-round cultural events, including summer music concerts. The National Park Service publishes *Outdoors,* a calendar of events. To obtain a free copy, call (818) 597-9192, ext. 201.

An informative publication is *Mountains to Ocean: A Guide to the Santa Monica Mountains National Recreation Area* by Randolph Jorgen (Southwest Parks and Monuments Association).

Most of the campgrounds in the Santa Monica Mountains are located in state parks, on or near beaches. Reservations for state park campsites are made through Destinet, the state's campsite reservation program (phone 1 [800] 444-7275). Happy Hollow Campground is a National Park Service-run facility located in the Circle X Ranch area. For these walk-in camping sites, reservations are issued on a first-come, first-served basis. Lodging and meals are available in the vicinity, from Los Angeles, to Woodland Hills, Calabasas, Agoura Hills, Thousand Oaks, Camarillo, and Ventura. Access is by way of U.S. Route 101 (Ventura Freeway), which borders the mountains to the north; and by way of the Pacific Coast Highway to the south.

IF YOU GO: Further information: Superintendent, 30401 Agoura Rd., Suite 100, Agoura Hills, CA 91302. Telephone (818) 597-9192, ext. 201.

WHISKEYTOWN-SHASTA-TRINITY NATIONAL RECREATION AREA

WHISKEYTOWN-SHASTA-TRINITY NATIONAL RECREATION AREA, consisting of 42,500 acres in the National Park Service-administered Whiskeytown Unit, near Redding, in northern California, was established in 1965 to provide a variety of recreational opportunities. (The Trinity and Shasta units are under the management of the U.S. Forest Service.)

The Whiskeytown Unit includes the man-made reservoir, Whiskeytown Lake, which is popular for sailing (a sailing regatta is held on the lake on Memorial Day weekend), motorboating, water-skiing, canoeing, swimming, fishing, and even scuba diving. In the 40,000 acres of surrounding mountainous backcountry, visitors enjoy hiking, horseback riding, mountain biking, and backcountry camping (free backcountry permits are required). Unlike the ban on hunting in national parks and monuments, public hunting is permitted in the national recreation area during the designated season. The forests of the backcountry include such species as ponderosa and knobcone pines; Douglas fir; California black, valley, and canyon live oaks; and Pacific dogwood. Wildlife of the Whiskeytown Unit includes black bears, mule deer, mountain lions, Canada geese, bald eagles, and ospreys. The backcountry also contains beautiful streams and waterfalls.

The national recreation area's Tower House Historic District dates back to the mid-nineteenth-century California Gold Rush Era. The historic, two-story Camden House, dating from 1852 and presenting a few period furnishings, is open for visitor tours; the district also contains the El Dorado Mine and stamp mill. Information is also provided on the early Wintu Indians who once lived in this part of California, until pioneer settlers moved in with the advent of the mining boom.

The visitor center, which is located eight miles west of Redding, just off State Route 299, at Kennedy Memorial Drive, provides interpretive exhibits on mining history and the Wintu Indians, an interactive computer system for visitor use, and a bookstore. Interpretive activities include evening programs at Oak Bottom Campground, night hikes, and other interpretive walks. There is also an active junior-ranger program.

On September 28, 1963, President John F. Kennedy dedicated Whiskeytown Dam. Today, there is a memorial to the former president that includes an audiotape recording of his dedication speech.

An informative publication is *Whiskeytown National Recreation Area* by Gregory M. Gnesios (Southwest Parks and Monuments Association).

IF YOU GO: Camping and picnicking facilities are provided. (Campground reservations through Destinet: 1 [800] 365-2267.) Lodging and meals are available in Redding and Weaverville. Access is by way of State Route 299, west from Redding, and east from Arcata. Further information: Superintendent, P.O. Box 188, Whiskeytown, CA 96095. Telephone (916) 241-6584.

PART 14

AFFILIATED PARKS

- - - - - - - - - - - -

AMERICAN MEMORIAL PARK

AMERICAN MEMORIAL PARK comprises 133 acres on the shore of Tanapag Harbor, Saipan, in the North Mariana Islands (a commonwealth in political union with the United States), which are part of Micronesia, in the western Pacific Ocean. The park honors the memory of those who died in the Marianas Campaign of World War II. (See also War in the Pacific National Historical Park.) American Memorial Park also provides recreational opportunities, such as boating, swimming, and picnicking. Information: American Memorial Park, P.O. Box 198, CHRB, Saipan, MP 96950. Telephone (670) 234-7207.

BENJAMIN FRANKLIN NATIONAL MEMORIAL

BENJAMIN FRANKLIN NATIONAL MEMORIAL, located in the rotunda of the Franklin Institute, in Philadelphia, Pennsylvania, features the huge seated figure, sculpted by James Earle Fraser, of the American statesman-inventor, Benjamin Franklin (1706–1790). Information: Executive Director, Benjamin Franklin National Memorial, Benjamin Franklin Parkway at 20th Street, Philadelphia, PA 19103. Telephone (215) 448-1329.

BLACKSTONE RIVER VALLEY NATIONAL HERITAGE CORRIDOR

BLACKSTONE RIVER VALLEY NATIONAL HERITAGE CORRIDOR, stretching between Providence, Rhode Island, and Worcester, Massachusetts, commemorates the beginning of the American Industrial Revolution, which had its roots along 46 miles of river and canals in the Blackstone Valley. Villages, mills, and the transportation waterways help to interpret this industrial heritage. Numerous private, local, and state partners are working with the National Park Service to help protect the historic and natural values of the valley. Information: Blackstone River Valley National Heritage Corridor, P.O. Box 730, Uxbridge, MA 01569. Telephone (508) 278-9400.

CHICAGO PORTAGE NATIONAL HISTORIC SITE

CHICAGO PORTAGE NATIONAL HISTORIC SITE, consisting of 91 acres in Lyons, Illinois, protects part of the portage between the Great Lakes and the Mississippi River. The portage was discovered by French explorers Louis Joliet and Jacques Marquette. Information: Director, Chicago Portage NHS, c/o Forest Preserve District of Cook County, 536 N. Harlem Ave., River Forest, IL 60305. Telephone (708) 771-1335.

CHIMNEY ROCK NATIONAL HISTORIC SITE

CHIMNEY ROCK NATIONAL HISTORIC SITE, comprised of 83 acres near Bayard, in western Nebraska, protects Chimney Rock, a 500-foot-high rock spire that was an important landmark for trappers, traders, and thousands of emigrants on their long journey on the Oregon Trail into the West. Information: c/o Scotts Bluff National Monument, P.O. Box 27, Gering, NE 69341. Telephone (308) 436-4340.

DAVID BERGER NATIONAL MEMORIAL

DAVID BERGER NATIONAL MEMORIAL, at 3505 Mayfield Road, in Cleveland Heights, Ohio, honors the memory of the eleven athletes representing Israel who were killed at the 1972 Olympic Games in Munich, Germany. One of the competitors was an American, David Berger. Information: David Berger National Memorial, Jewish Community Center, 3505 Mayfield Rd., Cleveland Heights, OH 44118. Telephone (216) 382-4000.

DELAWARE AND LEHIGH NAVIGATION CANAL NATIONAL HERITAGE CORRIDOR

DELAWARE AND LEHIGH NAVIGATION CANAL NATIONAL HERITAGE CORRIDOR, from Wilkes-Barre to Bristol, Pennsylvania, protects these two nineteenth-century commercial canals and related early railroads that provided transportation routes spurring the development of eastern Pennsylvania's rich anthracite fields. Information: National Park Service-Northeast Area, 200 Chestnut St., Philadelphia, PA 19106. Telephone (215) 448-1329.

FATHER MARQUETTE
NATIONAL MEMORIAL & MUSEUM

FATHER MARQUETTE NATIONAL MEMORIAL & MUSEUM, consisting of 52 acres in St. Ignace, in the Upper Peninsula of Michigan, commemorates the life and accomplishments of Father Jacques Marquette, a French explorer and priest. Information: Parks Division, Michigan Department of Natural Resources, P.O. Box 30028, Lansing, MI 48909.

GLORIA DEI (OLD SWEDES') CHURCH
NATIONAL HISTORIC SITE

GLORIA DEI (OLD SWEDES') CHURCH NATIONAL HISTORIC SITE, located on the shore of the Delaware River, at Delaware Avenue and Christian Street in Philadelphia, protects and interprets the second oldest Swedish church in America, founded in 1677. The present edifice was built around 1700, and is owned and administered by the Corporation of Gloria Dei (Old Swedes') Church. Information: Delaware Avenue and Christian Street, Philadelphia, PA 19106. Telephone (215) 597-8974.

GREEN SPRINGS HISTORIC DISTRICT

GREEN SPRINGS HISTORIC DISTRICT, comprising some 14,000 acres of Virginia's Piedmont region in Louisa County, was designated to focus attention on the outstanding array of manor houses in an unmarred landscape. Much of the land area is protected under conservation easements with the property owners. Information: Green Springs National Historic Landmark District, P.O. Box 1838, Louisa, VA 23093. Telephone (703) 967-9671. A motor-touring brochure with a map of the historic district is available at the National Park Service office, 115 U.S. Route 33 East, Louisa, VA. Telephone (703) 967-9671.

HISTORIC CAMDEN

HISTORIC CAMDEN, in Camden, South Carolina, encompasses this eighteenth-century village. Originally called Fredricksburg Township, it was later named in honor of a member of the British Parliament who championed American colonial rights—Charles Pratt, Lord Camden. Information: Director, Historic Camden, P.O. Box 710, Camden, SC 29020. Telephone (803) 432-9841.

ICE AGE NATIONAL SCIENTIFIC RESERVE

ICE AGE NATIONAL SCIENTIFIC RESERVE, comprising 32,500 acres in nine separate units dotted across the state of Wisconsin, from Lake Michigan to the St. Croix River, protects important glacial landforms and landscapes providing evidence of the Wisconsinan stage of the last ice age, as recently as 12,000 years ago, that covered much of the northern United States with a continental ice sheet. Units that are open to visitation are Kettle Moraine State Forest; Horicon Marsh Wildlife Area; and Devil's Lake, Mill Bluff, and Interstate parks. Information: Wisconsin Department of Natural Resources, P.O. Box 7921, Madison, WI 53707. Telephone (608) 266-2181.

ILLINOIS & MICHIGAN CANAL NATIONAL HERITAGE CORRIDOR

ILLINOIS & MICHIGAN CANAL NATIONAL HERITAGE CORRIDOR, in northeastern Illinois, protects this canal which was completed in 1848 and helped to open the region to the west, including the city of Chicago, to settlement and development. Today, the canal is the center of a system of parks, historic sites, and museums in the area. Information: 30 N. Bluff St., Joliet, IL 60435.

INTERNATIONAL PEACE GARDEN

INTERNATIONAL PEACE GARDEN, located astride the U.S.-Canadian boundary, about a dozen miles north of Dunseith, North Dakota, commemorates the peaceful relationship between the two countries. The area is administered by International Peace Garden, Inc., for North Dakota and Manitoba. Visitor activities include hiking, canoeing, picnicking, camping, self-guided drives and walks, and guided tours arranged in advance. The area features beautiful formal gardens, an arboretum, a bell tower, and peace chapel. The garden is also the home of the International Music Camp and the Legion Athletic Camp. Information: P.O. Box 419, Dunseith, ND 58329. Telephone (701) 263-4390.

JAMESTOWN NATIONAL HISTORIC SITE

JAMESTOWN NATIONAL HISTORIC SITE (see Colonial National Historical Park).

McLOUGHLIN HOUSE NATIONAL HISTORIC SITE

McLOUGHLIN HOUSE NATIONAL HISTORIC SITE, consisting of two-thirds-of-an-acre in Oregon City, Oregon, commemorates the life and accomplishments of nineteenth-century fur trader John McLoughlin—most notable for his efforts, whether deliberate or not, toward securing for the United States most of the Pacific Northwest region then known as the Oregon Country (see Fort Vancouver National Historic Site). The site is owned and operated by the McLoughlin Memorial Association. Information: Superintendent, McLoughlin House National Historic Site, 713 Center St., Oregon City, OR 97045. Telephone (503) 656-5146.

PINELANDS NATIONAL RESERVE

PINELANDS NATIONAL RESERVE, encompassing 1.2 million acres of southern New Jersey Atlantic coastal plains, is a vast, basically undeveloped expanse of ecologically rich pinelands, marshes, bogs, ponds, streams, and rivers. The area contains a tremendously diverse array of flora and fauna, including numerous rare species. Its reserve designation was authorized by Congress in 1978. In 1983, the reserve was given special international recognition for its extraordinary natural values as a part of the South Atlantic Coastal Plain Biosphere Reserve, under the United Nations "Man and Biosphere Program." **Great Egg Harbor National Scenic and Recreation River** was established in 1992 to give enhanced recognition to one of the reserve's major rivers. There are very limited public facilities in this area, in which close cooperation is anticipated between the federal, state, and local government land-management agencies, and private owners. Information: Pinelands National Reserve, c/o National Park Service-Northeast Area, 200 Chestnut St., Philadelphia, PA 19106. Telephone (215) 597-1582.

PORT CHICAGO NAVAL MAGAZINE NATIONAL MEMORIAL

PORT CHICAGO NAVAL MAGAZINE NATIONAL MEMORIAL, on the U.S. Navy's Concord Naval Weapons Station, on the south bank of the Sacramento River, is about 25 miles northeast of San Francisco, California. It honors all those who lost their lives or were injured in the terrible explosion of July 17, 1944; recognizes those who served at the magazine; and commemorates the facility's role during World War II.

The ship-loading pier at Port Chicago could handle two ships simultaneously. On the fateful evening of July 17, the *S.S. Quinault Victory* was being prepared for loading and the *S.S. Bryan* was being loaded, just across the pier's platform from each other. As described by the National Park Service:

> The holds were packed with high explosive and incendiary bombs, depth charges, and ammunition—4,606 tons of munitions in all. There were sixteen rail cars on the pier with another 429 tons. 320 cargo handlers, crewmen, and sailors were working in the area.

> At 10:18 p.m., a hollow ring and the sound of splintering wood erupted from the pier, followed by an explosion that ripped apart the night sky. Witnesses said that a brilliant white flash shot into the air, accompanied by a loud, sharp report. A column of smoke billowed from the pier, and fire glowed orange and yellow. Flashing like fireworks, smaller explosions went off in the cloud as it rose. Within six seconds, a deeper explosion erupted as the contents of the Bryan detonated as one massive bomb. The seismic shock wave was felt as far away as Boulder City, Nevada.

> The Bryan and the structures around the pier were completely disintegrated. A pillar of fire and smoke stretched over two miles into the sky above Port Chicago. The largest remaining pieces of the 7,200-ton ship were the size of a suitcase. . . . The shattered Quinault Victory was spun into the air. . . .

> All 320 men on duty that night were killed instantly. The blast smashed buildings and rail cars near the pier and damaged every building in Port Chicago. . . . The air filled with the sharp cracks and dull thuds of smoldering metal and unexploded shells as they showered back to earth as far as two miles away. . . .

> In addition to those killed, there were 390 wounded. . . . Less than a month after the worst home-front disaster of World War II, Port Chicago was again moving munitions to the troops in the Pacific. . . . Of the 320 men killed in the explosion, 202 were the African-American enlisted men who were assigned the dangerous duty of loading ships.

Results of the explosion: Racial discrimination, as by assigning only African Americans in the Port Chicago ordnance battalion, was soon remedied at this and other facilities of the U.S. Navy. By 1948, racial desegregation became national policy throughout the U.S. Armed Services. And safety standards at munitions-handling facilities such as this were greatly enhanced, with mandatory, formalized training of personnel, and redesigning of munitions for greater safety during handling. For visitor reservations: Office of Public Affairs, Concord Naval Weapons Station: (505) 246-5591. Further information: National Park Service, P.O. Box 280, Danville, CA 94526. Telephone (510) 838-0249.

QUINEBAUG AND SHETUCKET RIVERS VALLEY NATIONAL HERITAGE CORRIDOR

QUINEBAUG AND SHETUCKET RIVERS VALLEY NATIONAL HERITAGE CORRIDOR, including 25 (cooperating) towns in nearly 600 square miles of northeastern Connecticut, was certified by Congress in 1994 as a significant national heritage area. The National Park Service was authorized to provide the state with assistance to develop and implement a Cultural Heritage and Corridor Management Plan to retain, enhance, and interpret the significant lands, waters, and structures of the Quinebaug and Shetucket rivers valley.

The area contains a number of important historical links to the development of the United States as a nation, including native American and colonial archaeological sites; upland farming areas; relatively unspoiled, scenic rural landscapes; and exceptional nineteenth-century mill villages—reflecting the key role the mills of this area played in America's earliest industrial revolutionary period.

In the words of the Park Service's Statement of Significance document, "Because much of the region's rolling countryside has not yet been swallowed up by uncontrolled development does not mean its current bucolic condition will continue. Various development pressures are beginning to be felt, and comprehensive, region-wide planning is needed to protect the area's most important resources for future generations." Further information: c/o Northeast Area, National Park Service, 15 State St., Boston, MA 02109. Telephone (617) 223-5199.

RED HILL PATRICK HENRY NATIONAL MEMORIAL

RED HILL PATRICK HENRY NATIONAL MEMORIAL, in Brookneal, Virginia, protects the law office and grave site on the plantation of the eloquent and fiery eighteenth-century orator and Virginia assemblyman, Patrick Henry. He vigorously advocated that the government of colonial Virginia be granted autonomy from Britain and, as a member of the First Continental Congress, in 1774, supported a "radical" revolutionary stand against British authority over the American colonies—implying that the colonies must be treated as independent states. The memorial includes a museum and a reconstruction of Henry's last home. Information: Red Hill Patrick Henry National Memorial, Rt. 2, Box 127, Brookneal, VA 24528. Telephone (804) 376-2044.

ROOSEVELT CAMPOBELLO INTERNATIONAL PARK

ROOSEVELT CAMPOBELLO INTERNATIONAL PARK, comprising 2,721 acres on Campobello Island, New Brunswick, Canada, protects U.S. President Franklin D. Roosevelt's spacious summer home set amid the natural beauty of coastal bluffs and rocky shores, forest, fields, and bogs. It is a memorial to the 32nd president of the United States, and represents the friendly, peaceful relationship that has long endured between the U.S. and Canada. Information: Executive Secretary, Roosevelt Campobello International Park Commission, P.O. Box 97, Welshpool, Campobello Island, New Brunswick EOG 3HO; or P.O. Box 97, Lubec, ME 04652. Telephone (506) 752-2922.

SEWALL-BELMONT HOUSE NATIONAL HISTORIC SITE

SEWALL-BELMONT HOUSE NATIONAL HISTORIC SITE, consisting of one-third-of-an-acre at 144 Constitution Avenue, NE, in Washington, D.C., protects one of the oldest houses on Capitol Hill. Rebuilt after being damaged by fire in the War of 1812, it has served as the headquarters of the National Woman's Party since 1929. Information: Sewall-Belmont House National Historic Site, 144 Constitution Ave., NE, Washington, DC 20002. Telephone (202) 546-3989.

TOURO SYNAGOGUE NATIONAL HISTORIC SITE

TOURO SYNAGOGUE NATIONAL HISTORIC SITE consists of one-quarter-of-an-acre at 85 Touro Street, in Newport, Rhode Island. It celebrates this small synagogue that was established in 1763 by Jewish settlers who came to Roger Williams' colony of Rhode Island, where religious freedom and tolerance were promoted. The synagogue continues to be used for religious services. (See also Roger Williams National Memorial.) Information: Touro Synagogue National Historic Site, 85 Touro St., Newport, RI 02840. Telephone (401) 847-4794.

PART 15

NATIONAL TRAILS

APPALACHIAN NATIONAL SCENIC TRAIL

APPALACHIAN NATIONAL SCENIC TRAIL, established in 1968, extends for 2,146 miles from Mount Katahdin, in Baxter State Park, Maine; southwestward through the White Mountains of New Hampshire; the Green Mountains of Vermont; along ridges of the Appalachian Mountains, including Shenandoah National Park, Virginia, and Great Smoky Mountains National Park, Tennessee-North Carolina; to Springer Mountain, Georgia. The national scenic trail consists of 165,357 acres.

Activities include hiking, bird-watching, and camping. Shelters are available every ten or twelve miles, with campsites near the shelters. Camping permits are required in Shenandoah and Great Smoky Mountains national parks, and in Baxter State Park. Further information: Appalachian Trail Conference, P.O. Box 807, Harpers Ferry, WV 25425. Telephone (304) 535-6331.

CALIFORNIA NATIONAL HISTORIC TRAIL

CALIFORNIA NATIONAL HISTORIC TRAIL, established in 1992, totals over 5,600 miles of mid-nineteenth-century overland trails from their starting points at St. Joseph and Independence, Missouri, and Council Bluffs, Iowa; and extending westward to California and Oregon. Over these routes trekked one of America's greatest mass migrations of people seeking gold and the promise of a new life in California, in the 1840s and 1850s. The national historic trail is presently in its planning stage by the National Park Service and cooperating trail organizations. Further information: California National Historic Trail, National Park Service, 324 South State St., Suite 250, Salt Lake City, UT 84145. Telephone (801) 539-4094.

ICE AGE NATIONAL SCENIC TRAIL

ICE AGE NATIONAL SCENIC TRAIL, established in 1980, extends 1,000 miles through Wisconsin, winding over geologically significant glacial moraines and linking six of the nine units of the Ice Age National Scientific Reserve (see the text under Affiliated Parks). The trail protects a chain of glacial moraine ridges that were formed when continental glaciers melted and withdrew some 10,000 years ago. Activities include hiking and cross-country skiing, as well as bicycling and snowmobiling on certain stretches. There are presently close to 500 miles of the trail open to the public. Further information: Ice Age National Scenic Trail, National Park Service, 700 Rayovac Dr., Suite 100, Madison, WI 53711. Telephone (608) 264-5610.

JUAN BAUTISTA DE ANZA
NATIONAL HISTORIC TRAIL

JUAN BAUTISTA DE ANZA NATIONAL HISTORIC TRAIL, established in 1990, is a 1,200-mile trail that commemorates the Spanish expedition, under the leadership of Colonel Juan Bautista de Anza, that set forth from Mexico in 1775, in search of an overland route to California. At Tubac, now in southern Arizona, but then in Mexico, 240 colonists gathered and launched their trek. Accompanying them was a mile-long caravan that carried a tremendous array of provisions. There were more than 300 horses, 300 cattle, and 165 pack mules. The six-month journey crossed the awesome desert region of southwestern Arizona and southeastern California, and continued north along the coast of California to the Golden Gate, where the city of San Francisco is today.

At this writing (1997), the route is only in the planning stage. Short segments are open to hikers—including a four-and-a-half-mile trail from Tumacacori National Historical Park (see the text on this park) to Tubac Presidio State Historical Park, a few miles north of Nogales, Arizona; and several miles in Anza-Borrego Desert State Park, in southern California. An excellent publication is *Juan Bautista de Anza National Historic Trail,* by Don Garate (Southwest Parks and Monuments Association). Further information: Juan Bautista de Anza National Historic Trail, National Park Service-Pacific West Area, 600 Harrison St., Suite 600, San Francisco, CA 94123. Telephone (415) 744-3932.

LEWIS AND CLARK NATIONAL HISTORIC TRAIL

LEWIS AND CLARK NATIONAL HISTORIC TRAIL, established in 1978, celebrates the epic, 3,700-mile Lewis and Clark Expedition of 1804–1806, from the Mississippi River to the uncharted wilderness of the American West, to the mouth of the Columbia River, near which they spent a miserable, rainy winter, before returning to the East. Roads, trails, and rivers and other water routes connect the route's historic sites, which are variously managed by federal, state, and local government agencies, and private organizations. National Park System units along the trail are: Jefferson National Expansion Memorial, in St. Louis, Missouri; Knife River Indian Villages

National Historic Site, in North Dakota; Nez Perce National Historical Park, in Montana, Idaho, Oregon, and Washington; and Fort Clatsop National Memorial, in Oregon. (See the texts on these four parks.)

A National Park Service brochure on the trail briefly describes and indicates the location of many places and points of interest across the 11-state region, reaching from the Illinois shore of the Mississippi, up the Missouri River, across the Rocky Mountains in Montana and Idaho, and down the Snake and Columbia rivers to the Pacific Ocean. Further information: Lewis and Clark National Historic Trail, National Park Service, 700 Rayovac Dr., Suite 100, Madison, WI 53711. Telephone (608) 264-5610.

MORMON PIONEER
NATIONAL HISTORIC TRAIL

MORMON PIONEER NATIONAL HISTORIC TRAIL, established in 1978, is a 1,297-mile trail tracing the route on which Brigham Young led his initial group of 159 Mormon pioneers, in 1847, westward through Iowa, Nebraska, and Wyoming, to what became Salt Lake City, Utah, as they fled from religious persecution. More than 70,000 Mormon emigrants trekked west to their new Zion. Today, an automobile tour route, approximating the historic trail, has been marked. A National Park Service brochure on the trail indicates and briefly describes the location of key places and points of interest along the route. The trail is a cooperative effort between the National Park Service, U.S. Bureau of Land Management, U.S. Forest Service, the Mormon Trails Association, state and local government agencies, and other groups and individuals. Further information: Mormon Pioneer National Historic Trail, National Park Service, 324 South State St., Suite 250, Salt Lake City, UT 84145. Telephone (801) 539-4094.

NATCHEZ TRACE NATIONAL SCENIC TRAIL

NATCHEZ TRACE NATIONAL SCENIC TRAIL, established in 1983, reaches 110 miles from Natchez, Mississippi, northeastward to Nashville, Tennessee, closely paralleling the **Natchez Trace Parkway**. The trail and parkway commemorate the historic Natchez Trace pathway, which was used by native Americans, as well as early explorers and pioneers from the east. The trail follows some stretches of the ancient path that lie within the boundaries of the parkway. Several other key parts of the trail, near Natchez and Jackson, Mississippi, and Nashville, Tennessee, are being restored. Activities include hiking, horseback riding, and bird-watching. Bicycling is popular along the parkway. Further information: Natchez Trace National Scenic Trail, c/o Natchez Trace Parkway, RR 1, NT-143, Tupelo, MS 38801. Telephone (601) 842-1572.

NEZ PERCE [NEE-ME-POO]
NATIONAL HISTORIC TRAIL

NEZ PERCE [NEE-ME-POO] NATIONAL HISTORIC TRAIL (see Nez
Perce National Historical Park).

NORTH COUNTRY NATIONAL SCENIC TRAIL

NORTH COUNTRY NATIONAL SCENIC TRAIL, established in 1980,
reaches 3,200 miles, from Crown Point, New York, westward through New
York's Adirondack Mountains, Pennsylvania, Ohio, Michigan, Wisconsin, and
Minnesota, to Lake Sakakawea, amidst the vast Great Plains of North Dakota.
While the trail is largely for hiking, certain stretches are open to horseback riding and cross-country skiing. Nearly half of the trail is presently available for
public use. Camping and other facilities are located along certain portions of
the route, in state parks and national forests. Further information: North
Country National Scenic Trail, National Park Service, 700 Rayovac Dr., Suite
100, Madison, WI 53711. Telephone (608) 264-5610.

OREGON NATIONAL HISTORIC TRAIL

OREGON NATIONAL HISTORIC TRAIL, established in 1978, commemorates this 2,170-mile trail and the fur traders, trappers, early frontiersmen,
goldseekers, missionaries, and 300,000-400,000 emigrants seeking a new
homeland, in the 1840s and 1850s, who traveled westward by covered wagon
from the Midwest to Oregon by way of the Oregon Trail. Extending northwestward from Independence, Missouri, to Oregon City, Oregon, the route
led travelers across the vast expanse of the Great Plains, following the course of
the North Platte River and passing the prominent landmarks of Chimney
Rock (see the text on Chimney Rock National Historic Site) and Scotts Bluff
(see Scotts Bluff National Monument); then across the broad expanses of
Wyoming; down the Snake River valley of southern Idaho; and out to Oregon.
      The trail is cooperatively managed by the National Park Service, the
U.S. Bureau of Land Management, the U.S. Forest Service, state and local
government agencies, and private organizations and individuals. A National
Park Service brochure has a map that indicates and briefly describes some of
the highlights along the Oregon Trail. An excellent publication is *Oregon Trail:
Voyage of Discovery: The Story Behind the Scenery,*® text by Dan Murphy and
photographs by Gary Ladd (KC Publications). Further information: Oregon
National Historic Trail, National Park Service, 324 South State St., Suite 250,
Salt Lake City, UT 84145. Telephone (801) 539-4094.

OVERMOUNTAIN VICTORY NATIONAL HISTORIC TRAIL

OVERMOUNTAIN VICTORY NATIONAL HISTORIC TRAIL, established in 1980, commemorates the 300-mile route followed, in 1780, by bands of War for Independence (Revolutionary War) American patriot backwoods militiamen. These were overmountain men from Tennessee, and other backwoods settlers from what was then the western frontier of North and South Carolina. The British loyalist commander Major Patrick Ferguson had tried to intimidate the western frontier settlers, threatening to "lay waste the country with fire and sword," if they did not put down their firearms and pledge their allegiance to Britain.

The overmountain men were so outraged over this threat that an army of some 900 militiamen was organized that pursued Ferguson's forces; surrounded and furiously attacked them on Kings Mountain, South Carolina; and killed or captured his entire command. (See Kings Mountain National Military Park.) This battle at Kings Mountain was the beginning of the successful conclusion of the War for Independence—leading to independence for the United States of America. In the words of the National Park Service:

> The citizen militia . . . organized to protect their community. Men without formal training or recognized social standing—Ferguson called them mongrels—took hold of their destinies. . . . They relied upon their individual initiative, skills with the rifle, and courage to ensure the success of their cause.

Today, the 220-mile national historic trail runs from Abingdon, Virginia, to Kings Mountain. It crosses the Appalachian National Scenic Trail (see the text) at Yellow Mountain Gap, crosses the Blue Ridge Parkway at Heffner Gap, cuts through Cowpens National Battlefield (see the text), and ends at Kings Mountain National Military Park. Each autumn, there is a two-week commemorative reenactment with costumes and military equipment (information: Overmountain Victory Trail Association [OVTA], P.O. Box 632, Manassas Park, VA 22111). Visitors may hike sections of the trail at Cowpens and Kings Mountain, SC; Sycamore Shoals State Historic Area, TN; Roan Mountain State Park, TN; at Yellow Mountain Gap in Cherokee National Forest, TN; Heffner Gap, NC; and elsewhere. The national historic trail is a cooperative project of the National Park Service, the U.S. Forest Service, the U.S. Army Corps of Engineers, OVTA, local organizations, and state agencies of North and South Carolina, Tennessee, and Virginia. Further information: OVTA, c/o Sycamore Shoals State Historic Area, Elizabethton, TN 37643; and Overmountain Victory National Historic Trail, Southeast Field Area Office, National Park Service, 75 Spring St., SW, Atlanta, GA 30303. Telephone (404) 331-5465.

PONY EXPRESS NATIONAL HISTORIC TRAIL

PONY EXPRESS NATIONAL HISTORIC TRAIL, established in 1992, extends 1,966 miles from St. Joseph, Missouri, to Sacramento, California. It commemorates the Pony Express' mail-delivery service that operated its ten-day runs from April 1860 to October 1861. The trail is presently in the planning phase by the National Park Service, in cooperation with other government agencies and private groups. Further information: Pony Express National Historic Trail, National Park Service, 324 South State St., Suite 250, Salt Lake City, UT 84145. Telephone (801) 539-4094.

POTOMAC HERITAGE
NATIONAL SCENIC TRAIL

POTOMAC HERITAGE NATIONAL SCENIC TRAIL, established in 1983, is projected to run for 700 miles up the Potomac River valley, from the mouth of the Potomac River, in Virginia, through Maryland, and into the Laurel Highlands of Pennsylvania. It includes the 17-mile Mount Vernon Trail, in the George Washington Memorial Parkway (see the text on the parkway), that runs from Mount Vernon, George Washington's historic home, to Washington, D.C.; the 184-mile Chesapeake and Ohio Canal (see the text on this national historical park), that runs from Georgetown, in Washington, D.C., to Cumberland, Maryland; and the 70-mile Laurel Highlands National Recreation Trail, in Pennsylvania. Other segments of the national scenic trail are yet to be designated and planned. Sections not in federal ownership are expected to remain in other governmental or private ownerships, under cooperative management with the National Park Service. Further information: Potomac Heritage National Scenic Trail, National Park Service-National Capital Area, 1100 Ohio Dr., SW, Washington, DC 20242. Telephone (202) 619-7025.

SANTA FE NATIONAL HISTORIC TRAIL

SANTA FE NATIONAL HISTORIC TRAIL, designated in 1987, commemorates this 1,200-mile route that was a cultural and commercial connection, initially between the United States and Mexico, which gained its independence from Spain in 1821.

As the National Park Service says:

> Shortly thereafter, a party of five men led by William Becknell, who had left Franklin, Missouri, to trade "to the westward," encountered a group of Mexican soldiers who guided them to Santa Fe, where they sold their goods. Thus encouraged by Mexican officials, the now-legal commerce turned into a burgeoning [two-way] trade, providing an

economic boon for the economies of Mexico's northern provinces and the State of Missouri. Across 900 miles of what are now the States of Missouri, Kansas, Colorado, Oklahoma, and New Mexico, merchants . . . [led] enormous caravans of [mule- or oxen-pulled] freight wagons, loaded with goods for customers in New Mexico that they traded for silver coin, mules, and wool.

Following the Mexican-American War, of 1846-1848, New Mexico became a territory of the United States. Postwar trade on the trail greatly escalated. Again, in the words of the Park Service:

As human traffic increased, the Plains Indian tribes saw their homelands, subsistence, and lifeways in jeopardy. More and more confrontations occurred between Indians and travelers. To protect trade caravans, the U.S. Army established military posts like Fort Union (1851) and Fort Larned (1860). Ultimately, Indian resistance could not match the well-equipped incursion into their lands.

See also the texts on Bent's Old Fort National Historic Site, Pecos National Historical Park, Fort Union National Monument, and Fort Larned National Historic Site. Trail ruts are still visible within the latter three National Park System units.

At present, there are more than 50 federal, state, county, and municipal governmental agencies, private organizations, and private landowners in partnership with the National Park Service. Interpretive exhibits and programs that the Park Service has been involved with are installed at the Morton County Historical Society Museum, in Elkhart, Kansas; and the Santa Fe Trail Museum, in Trinidad, Colorado. Other exhibits and programs on the trail are presented at the Santa Fe Trail Center, in Larned, Kansas; and the National Frontier Trails Center, in Independence, Missouri. Wayside interpretive exhibits have also been installed by the Park Service in Franklin, Missouri; and in Prairie Village, Kansas; with others to be established soon. The automobile tour route along the trail is marked with signs of the official trail logo.

Two excellent publications are: *Santa Fe Trail National Historic Trail,* by Mark L. Gardner (Southwest Parks and Monuments Association) and *Santa Fe Trail—Voyage of Discovery: The Story Behind the Scenery®* text by Dan Murphy and photographs by Bruce Hucko (KC Publications). For a complete listing of interpretive sites along the trail and other information: Santa Fe National Historic Trail, Long Distance Trails Group Office-Santa Fe, National Park Service, P.O. Box 728, Santa Fe, NM 87504. Telephone (505) 988-6888.

SELMA-TO-MONTGOMERY NATIONAL HISTORIC TRAIL

SELMA-TO-MONTGOMERY NATIONAL HISTORIC TRAIL, authorized in 1996, runs from Selma to Montgomery, Alabama. It commemorates the 54-mile route of the 1965 voting rights march that was planned by Dr. Martin Luther

King, Jr., and the Southern Christian Leadership Conference. It was organized to help emphasize the need for the Voting Rights Act, then pending in Congress.

When the marchers began their journey on March 7, they were immediately blocked at the Edmund Pettus Bridge in Selma by state troopers wielding whips, clubs, and tear gas. Only after President Lyndon B. Johnson ordered federal protection for the marchers were they able to proceed, on March 21, with their three-day trek. On March 25, more than 25,000 people gathered at the state capitol to hear Dr. King speak. Just 134 days later the Voting Rights Act was signed into law.

As of this writing (late 1997), it is expected that planning for the national historic trail will begin soon, the route will be signed, and significant sites along the way will be interpreted. Further information: (404) 562-3175.

TRAIL OF TEARS NATIONAL HISTORIC TRAIL

TRAIL OF TEARS NATIONAL HISTORIC TRAIL, established in 1987, marks two of the routes that, from June 1838 to March 1839, were used in the forced removal of more than 15,000 Cherokee Indians from their ancestral lands in the states of Georgia, Alabama, North Carolina, and Tennessee, to a new homeland west of the Mississippi River, in Indian Territory (Oklahoma).

The first route reached 1,226 miles by water from Chattanooga, Tennessee; down the Tennessee, Ohio, and Mississippi rivers, and up the Arkansas River to beyond Fort Smith, Arkansas; and finally to an area near Tahlequah, Oklahoma. This latter community remains the Cherokee Nation's tribal headquarters today.

The second relocation route extended 826 miles by land, and is marked with signs displaying the official trail logo. The route extends along highways from near Chattanooga, through McMinnville, and Nashville, Tennessee; through Hopkinsville, Kentucky, and Vienna, Illinois; crossing the Mississippi at Cape Girardeau, Illinois; and continuing out through Rolla and Springfield, Missouri, and Fayatteville, Arkansas; to Tahlequah, Oklahoma.

The U.S. government's early-nineteenth-century policy of forced removal of the Cherokees and other tribes resulted from President Thomas Jefferson's proposal to establish a buffer zone between the then-existing United States and the vast territories to the west that were claimed by European nations. This buffer zone just west of the Mississippi was to provide a new homeland for the eastern Indian tribes, and was also to allow for U.S. settlers to move westward into the region being vacated by the Indian tribes.

A witness to this tragic event, U.S. Cavalry veteran, John G. Burnett, years later recalled his still-vivid memories:

> I saw the helpless Cherokees arrested and dragged from their homes, and driven at the bayonet point into the stockades. And in the chill

of a drizzling rain . . . I saw them loaded like cattle or sheep into six hundred and forty-five wagons and started toward the west.

One can never forget the sadness and solemnity of that morning. Chief John Ross led in prayer and when the bugle sounded and the wagons started rolling many of the children rose to their feet and waved their little hands good-by to their mountain homes, knowing they were leaving them forever. Many of these helpless people did not have blankets and many of them had been driven from home bare-footed. . . .

The long painful journey to the west ended . . . , with four-thousand silent graves reaching from the foothills of the Smoky Mountains to what is known as Indian territory in the West.

And covetousness on the part of the white race was the cause of all that the Cherokees had to suffer. . . .The doom of the Cherokee was sealed. Washington, D.C., had decreed that they must be driven West, and their lands given to the white man, and in May 1838 an Army of four thousand regulars, and three thousand volunteer soldiers under command of General Winfield Scott, marched into the Indian country and wrote the blackest chapter on the pages of American History. . . .

Nor were the Cherokees the only tribe forced to give up their homelands, as the National Park Service explains:

Between 1816 and 1840, tribes located between the original states and the Mississippi River, including Cherokees, Chickasaws, Choctaws, Creeks, and Seminoles, signed more than 40 treaties ceding their lands to the U.S. In his 1829 inaugural address, President Andrew Jackson set a policy to relocate eastern Indians. In 1830 it was endorsed, when Congress passed the Indian Removal Act to force those remaining to move west of the Mississippi. Between 1830 and 1850, about 100,000 American Indians living between Michigan, Louisiana, and Florida moved west after the U.S. government coerced treaties or used the U.S. Army against those resisting. Many were treated brutally. An estimated 3,500 Creeks died in Alabama and during the westward journey. Some were transported in chains. . . .

Families were separated, elderly and ill forced out at gunpoint, people given only moments to collect cherished possessions. White looters followed, ransacking homesteads as Cherokees were led away. . . .

A variety of local, state, and national efforts have commenced to preserve and interpret Trail resources. A growing awareness of this important story, and those of other removed tribes, has stimulated interest to nationally recognize this chapter in our Nation's past. The Trail of Tears tells of the Cherokees' ordeal, but many tribes can tell similar stories.

Interpretive exhibits and programs relating to the Trail of Tears are provided at such facilities as the Cherokee National Museum, in Tahlequah, Oklahoma; the Museum of the Cherokee Indian, in Cherokee, North Carolina; at the Trail of Tears Park, in Hopkinsville, Kentucky; and at the Trail of Tears State Park, Missouri. Automobile tour routes, between Charleston, in southeastern Tennessee, and Tahlequah, Oklahoma, are marked with the trail sign, as an aid to visiting trail sites.

Two informative books on the Trail of Tears, in particular, and the removal of some 60,000 Indians from the Southeast, in general, are: *Trail of Tears: The Rise and Fall of the Cherokee Nation* by John Ehle (Anchor Books: Doubleday) and the classic, first published in 1934, *The Five Civilized Tribes: Cherokee, Chickasaw, Choctaw, Creek, Seminole* by Grant Foreman (University of Oklahoma Press).

At this writing (1997), the trail's management plan is in the early stages of being implemented. The trail is a cooperative project involving the National Park Service; other federal, state, and local government agencies; the Cherokee Nation; the Eastern Board of Cherokee Indians; private landowners, and private groups, such as the Trail of Tears Association (1100 N. University, Suite 133, Little Rock, AR 72207. Telephone [501] 666-9032). The Park Service urges visitors to respect private properties. Further information: Trail of Tears National Historic Trail, Long Distance Trails Group Office-Santa Fe, National Park Service, P.O. Box 728, Santa Fe, NM 87504. Telephone (505) 988-6888.

(*Several other national trails are administered by other federal agencies:* Continental Divide National Scenic Trail, Florida National Scenic Trail, and Pacific Coast National Scenic Trail are managed by the U.S. Forest Service; and Iditarod National Historic Trail, in Alaska, is administered by the U.S. Bureau of Land Management.)

PART 16

OTHER NATIONAL PARK SYSTEM AREAS
(described in *Exploring Our National Parks and Monuments*)

▬ ▬ ▬ ▬ ▬ ▬ ▬ ▬ ▬ ▬ ▬

NATIONAL PARKS

Acadia National Park
P.O. Box 177
Bar Harbor, ME 04609
Phone: (207) 288-3338

Arches National Park
P.O. Box 907
Moab, UT 84532
Phone: (801) 259-8161

Badlands National Park
Box 6
Interior, SD 57750
Phone: (605) 433-5361

Big Bend National Park
P.O. Box 129
Big Bend National Park, TX 79834
Phone: (915) 477-2251

Biscayne National Park
Box 1369
Homestead, FL 33090
Phone: (305) 247-7275

Bryce Canyon National Park
Bryce Canyon, UT 84717
Phone: (801) 834-5322

Canyonlands National Park
125 West 200 South
Moab, UT 84532
Phone: (801) 259-7164

Capitol Reef National Park
HC 70, Box 15
Torrey, UT 84775
Phone: (801) 425-3791

Carlsbad Caverns National Park
3225 National Parks Highway
Carlsbad, NM 88220
Phone: (505) 785-2232

Channel Islands National Park
1901 Spinnaker Dr.
Ventura, CA 93001
Phone: (805) 658-5700

Crater Lake National Park
P.O. Box 7
Crater Lake, OR 97604
Phone: (503) 594-2211

Death Valley National Park
P.O. Box 579
Death Valley, CA 92328
Phone: (619) 786-2331

Denali National Park & Preserve
P.O. Box 9
McKinley Park, AK 99755
Phone: (907) 683-2294

Dry Tortugas National Park
40001 State Rd. 9336
Homestead, FL 33034
Phone: (305) 242-7700

Everglades National Park
40001 State Rd. 9336
Homestead, FL 33034
Phone: (305) 242-7700

Gates of the Arctic National Park & Preserve
P.O. Box 74680
Fairbanks, AK 99707
Phone: (907) 456-0281

Glacier Bay National Park & Preserve
P.O. Box 140
Gustavus, AK 99826
Phone: (907) 697-2232

Glacier National Park
West Glacier, MT 59936
Phone: (406) 888-5441

Grand Canyon National Park
P.O. Box 129
Grand Canyon, AZ 86023
Phone: (520) 638-7888

Grand Teton National Park
P.O. Drawer 170
Moose, WY 83012
Phone: (307) 733-2880

Great Basin National Park
Baker, NV 89311
Phone: (702) 234-7331

Great Smoky Mountains National Park
Gatlinburg, TN 37738
Phone: (615) 436-1200

Guadalupe Mountains National Park
HC 60, Box 400
Salt Flat, TX 79847
Phone: (915) 828-3251

Haleakala National Park
P.O. Box 369
Makawao, Maui, HI 96768
Phone: (808) 572-9306

Hawaii Volcanoes National Park
P.O. Box 52
Hawaii Volcanoes National Park, HI 96718
Phone: (808) 967-7311

Hot Springs National Park
P.O. Box 1860
Hot Springs, AR 71902
Phone: (501) 623-1433

Isle Royale National Park
800 E. Lakeshore Dr.
Houghton, MI 49931
Phone: (906) 482-0984

Joshua Tree National Park
74485 National Monument Dr.
Twentynine Palms, CA 92277
Phone: (619) 367-7511

Katmai National Park & Preserve
P.O. Box 7
King Salmon, AK 99613
Phone: (907) 246-3305

Kenai Fjords National Park
P.O. Box 1727
Seward, AK 99664
Phone: (907) 224-3175

Kobuk Valley National Park
P.O. Box 1029
Kotzebue, AK 99752
Phone: (907) 442-3890

Lake Clark National Park & Preserve
4230 University Dr., Suite 311
Anchorage, AK 99508
Phone: (907) 781-2218

Lassen Volcanic National Park
P.O. Box 100
Mineral, CA 96063
Phone: (916) 595-4444

Mammoth Cave National Park
Mammoth Cave, KY 42259
Phone: (502) 758-2328

Mesa Verde National Park
P.O. Box 8, Mesa Verde National
Park, CO 81330
Phone: (970) 529-4461

Mount Rainier National Park
Tahoma Woods, Star Route
Ashford, WA 98304
Phone: (360) 569-2211

National Park of American Samoa
c/o Pacific Area, National Park Service
P.O. Box 50165
Honolulu, HI 96850
Phone: (808) 541-2693

North Cascades National Park
2105 Highway 20
Sedro Woolley, WA 98284
Phone: (360) 856-5700

Olympic National Park
600 E. Park Ave.
Port Angeles, WA 98362
Phone: (360) 452-4501

Petrified Forest National Park
Petrified Forest National Park, AZ 86028
Phone: (520) 524-6228

Redwood National Park
1111 Second St.
Crescent City, CA 95531
Phone: (707) 464-6101

Rocky Mountain National Park
Estes Park, CO 80517
Phone: (970) 586-1206

Saguaro National Park
36933 S. Old Spanish Trail
Tucson, AZ 85730
Phone: (520) 296-8576

**Sequoia and Kings Canyon
National Parks**
Three Rivers, CA 93271
Phone: (209) 565-3341

Shenandoah National Park
Route 4, Box 348
Luray, VA 22835
Phone: (540) 999-2243

Theodore Roosevelt National Park
P.O. Box 7
Medora, ND 58645
Phone: (701) 623-4466

Virgin Islands National Park
6310 Estate Nazareth
St. Thomas, VI 00802
Phone: (809) 775-6238

Voyageurs National Park
3131 Highway 53
International Falls, MN 56649
Phone: (218) 283-9821

Wind Cave National Park
RR 1, Box 190
Hot Springs, SD 57747
Phone: (605) 745-4600

**Wrangell-St. Elias National
Park & Preserve**
P.O. Box 29
Glennallen, AK 99588
Phone: (907) 822-5234

Yellowstone National Park
P.O. Box 168
Yellowstone National Park, WY 82190
Phone: (307) 344-7381

Yosemite National Park
P.O. Box 577
Yosemite National Park, CA 95389
Phone: (209) 372-0200

Zion National Park
Springdale, UT 84767
Phone: (801) 772-3256

NATIONAL MONUMENTS: NATURE

Agate Fossil Beds National Monument
P.O. Box 27
Gering, NE 69341
Phone: (308) 668-2211

Aniakchak National Monument
P.O. Box 7
King Salmon, AK 99613
Phone: (907) 246-3305

Black Canyon of the Gunnison National Monument
2233 E. Main St., Suite A
Montrose, CO 81401
Phone: (970) 249-7036

Buck Island Reef National Monument
P.O. Box 160
Christiansted, St. Croix, VI 00821
Phone: (809) 773-1460

Capulin Volcano National Monument
P.O. Box 40
Capulin, NM 88414
Phone: (505) 278-2201

Cedar Breaks National Monument
82 North 100 East
Cedar City, UT 84720
Phone: (801) 586-9451

Chiricahua National Monument
Dos Cabezas Route, Box 6500
Willcox, AZ 85643
Phone: (520) 824-3560

Colorado National Monument
Fruita, CO 81521
Phone: (970) 858-3617

Congaree Swamp National Monument
200 Caroline Sims Rd.
Hopkins, SC 29061
Phone: (803) 776-4396

Craters of the Moon National Monument
P.O. Box 29
Arco, ID 83213
Phone: (208) 527-3257

Devils Postpile National Monument
c/o Sequoia National Park
Three Rivers, CA 93271
Phone: (209) 565-3341

Devils Tower National Monument
P.O. Box 8
Devils Tower, WY 82714
Phone: (307) 467-5283

Dinosaur National Monument
4545 Highway 40
Dinosaur, CO 81610
Phone: (970) 374-3000

El Malpais National Monument
P.O. Box 939
Grants, NM 87020
Phone: (505) 285-5406

Florissant Fossil Beds National
Monument
P.O. Box 185
Florissant, CO 80816
Phone: (719) 748-3253

Fossil Butte National Monument
P.O. Box 592
Kemmerer, WY 83101
Phone: (307) 877-4455

Great Sand Dunes National
Monument
11500 Highway 150
Mosca, CO 81146
Phone: (719) 378-2312

Hagerman Fossil Beds National
Monument
P.O. Box 570
Hagerman, ID 83332
Phone: (208) 837-4793

Jewel Cave National Monument
RR 1, Box 60AA
Custer, SD 57730
Phone: (605) 673-2288

John Day Fossil Beds National
Monument
420 W. Main St.
John Day, OR 97845
Phone: (503) 987-2333

Lava Beds National Monument
P.O. Box 867
Tulelake, CA 96134
Phone: (916) 667-2282

Muir Woods National Monument
Mill Valley, CA 94941
Phone: (415) 388-2595

Natural Bridges National Monument
P.O. Box 1
Lake Powell, UT 84533
Phone: (801) 692-1234

Oregon Caves National Monument
19000 Caves Highway
Cave Junction, OR 97523
Phone: (503) 592-2100

Organ Pipe Cactus National Monument
Route 1, Box 100
Ajo, AZ 85321
Phone: (520) 387-6849

Pinnacles National Monument
Paicines, CA 95043
Phone: (408) 389-4485

Rainbow Bridge National Monument
c/o Glen Canyon National Recreation Area
P.O. Box 1507
Page, AZ 86040
Phone: (520) 645-2471

Sunset Crater Volcano
National Monument
Route 3, Box 149
Flagstaff, AZ 86004
Phone: (520) 556-7042

Timpanogos Cave National Monument
RR 3, Box 200
American Fork, UT 84003
Phone: (801) 756-5238

White Sands National Monument
P.O. Box 1086
Holloman AFB, NM 88330
Phone: (505) 479-6124

Alibates Flint Quarries
National Monument
P.O. Box 1460
Fritch, TX 79036
Phone: (806) 857-3151

Aztec Ruins National Monument
P.O. Box 640
Aztec, NM 87410
Phone: (505) 334-6174

Bandelier National Monument
HCR 1, Box 1
Los Alamos, NM 87544
Phone: (505) 672-3861

Canyon de Chelly National
Monument
P.O. Box 588
Chinle, AZ 86503
Phone: (520) 674-5436

Cape Krusenstern National
Monument
P.O. Box 1029
Kotzebue, AK 99752
Phone: (907) 442-3890

Casa Grande Ruins National
Monument
1100 Ruins Dr.
Coolidge, AZ 85228
Phone: (520) 723-3172

Effigy Mounds National Monument
151 Highway 76
Harpers Ferry, IA 52146
Phone: (319) 873-3491

Gila Cliff Dwellings National
Monument
Route 11, Box 100
Silver City, NM 88061
Phone: (505) 536-9344

Hovenweep National Monument
McElmo Route, Cortez, CO 81321
Phone: (970) 529-4461

Montezuma Castle National
Monument
P.O. Box 219
Camp Verde, AZ 86322
Phone: (520) 567-3322

Navajo National Monument
HC 71, Box 3
Tonalea, AZ 86044
Phone: (520) 672-2366

Ocmulgee National Monument
1207 Emery Highway
Macon, GA 31201
Phone: (912) 752-8257

Petroglyph National Monument
123 Fourth St., SW
Albuquerque, NM 87102
Phone: (505) 766-8375

Pipestone National Monument
P.O. Box 727
Pipestone, MN 56164
Phone: (507) 825-5464

Poverty Point National Monument
c/o Poverty Point State
Commemorative Area
P.O. Box 248
Epps, LA 71237
Phone: (318) 926-5492

Russell Cave National Monument
3729 County Road 98
Bridgeport, AL 35740
Phone: (205) 495-2672

Tonto National Monument
P.O. Box 707
Roosevelt, AZ 85545
Phone: (520) 467-2241

Tuzigoot National Monument
P.O. Box 219
Camp Verde, AZ 86322
Phone: (520) 634-5564

Walnut Canyon National Monument
Walnut Canyon Rd.
Flagstaff, AZ 86004
Phone: (520) 526-3367

Wupatki National Monument
HC 33, Box 444A
Flagstaff, AZ 86004
Phone: (520) 556-7042

Yucca House
c/o Mesa Verde National Park
P.O. Box 8
Mesa Verde National Park, CO 81330
Phone: (970) 529-4461

NATIONAL HISTORICAL PARKS: ARCHAEOLOGICAL

Chaco Culture National Historical Park
Star Route 4, Box 6500
Bloomfield, NM 87413
Phone: (505) 988-6716

Hopewell Culture National Historical Park
16062 State Route 104
Chillicothe, OH 45601
Phone: (614) 774-1125

NATIONAL PRESERVES

Bering Land Bridge National Preserve
P.O. Box 220
Nome, AK 99762
Phone: (907) 443-2522

Big Cypress National Preserve
HCR 61, Box 110
Ochopee, FL 33943
Phone: (813) 695-4111

Big Thicket National Preserve
3785 Milam
Beaumont, TX 77701
Phone: (409) 839-2689

Little River Canyon National Preserve
P.O. Box 45
Fort Payne, AL 35967
Phone: (205) 997-9239

Mojave National Preserve
222 E. Main St., Suite 202
Barstow, CA 92311
Phone: (619) 255-8726

Noatak National Preserve
P.O. Box 1029
Kotzebue, AK 99752
Phone: (907) 442-3890

Yukon-Charley Rivers National Preserve
P.O. Box 167
Eagle, AK 99738
Phone: (907) 547-2234

NATIONAL SEASHORES AND LAKESHORES

Apostle Islands National Lakeshore
Route 1, Box 4
Bayfield, WI 54814
Phone: (715) 779-3397

Assateague Island National Seashore
7206 National Seashore Ln.
Berlin, MD 21811
Phone: (401) 641-1441

Canaveral National Seashore
308 Julia St.
Titusville, FL 32796
Phone: (407) 267-1110

Cape Cod National Seashore
South Wellfleet, MA 02663
Phone: (508) 255-3421

Cape Hatteras National Seashore
Route 1, Box 675
Manteo, NC 27954
Phone: (919) 473-2111

Cape Lookout National Seashore
131 Charles St.
Harkers Island, NC 28531
Phone: (919) 728-2250

Cumberland Island National Seashore
P.O. Box 806
St. Marys, GA 31558
Phone: (912) 882-4335

Fire Island National Seashore
120 Laurel St.
Patchogue, NY 11772
Phone: (516) 289-4810

Gulf Islands National Seashore
1801 Gulf Breeze Parkway
Gulf Breeze, FL 32561
Phone: (904) 934-2600

Indiana Dunes National Lakeshore
1100 N. Mineral Springs Rd.
Porter, IN 46304
Phone: (219) 926-7561

Padre Island National Seashore
9405 S. Padre Island Dr.
Corpus Christi, TX 78418
Phone: (512) 937-2621

Pictured Rocks National Lakeshore
P.O. Box 40
Munising, MI 49862
Phone: (906) 387-3700

Point Reyes National Seashore
Point Reyes, CA 94956
Phone: (415) 663-1092

Sleeping Bear Dunes National Lakeshore
P.O. Box 277
Empire, MI 49630
Phone: (616) 326-5134

NATIONAL RIVERS AND RIVERWAYS

Alagnak Wild River
c/o Katmai National Park &
Preserve
P.O. Box 7
King Salmon, AK 99613
Phone: (907) 246-3305

Big South Fork National River & Recreation Area
Route 3, Box 401
Oneida, TN 37841
Phone: (615) 879-4890

Bluestone National Scenic River
c/o New River Gorge National River
P.O. Box 246
Glen Jean, WV 25846
Phone: (304) 465-0508

Buffalo National River
P.O. Box 1173
Harrison, AR 72601
Phone: (501) 741-5443

Delaware National Scenic River
c/o Delaware Water Gap National
Recreation Area
Bushkill, PA 18324
Phone: (717) 588-2435

Great Egg Harbor National
Scenic & Rec. River
c/o Northeast Area, National Park Service
200 Chestnut St.
Philadelphia, PA 19106
Phone: (215) 597-1582

Mississippi National River &
Recreation Area
175 E. 5th St., Suite 418
St. Paul, MN 55101
Phone: (612) 290-4160

Missouri National Recreational River
P.O. Box 591
O'Neill, NE 68763
Phone: (402) 336-3970

New River Gorge National River
P.O. Box 246
Glen Jean, WV 25846
Phone: (304) 465-0508

Niobrara National Scenic River
P.O. Box 591
O'Neill, NE 68763
Phone: (402)336-3970

Obed Wild & Scenic River
P.O. Box 429
Wartburg, TN 37887
Phone: (615) 346-6294

Ozark National Scenic Riverways
P.O. Box 490
Van Buren, MO 63965
Phone: (314) 323-4236

Rio Grande Wild & Scenic River
c/o Big Bend National Park
P.O. Box 129
Big Bend National Park, TX 79834
Phone: (915) 477-2251

Saint Croix National Scenic Riverway
P.O. Box 708
St. Croix Falls, WI 54024
Phone: (715) 483-3284

Upper Delaware Scenic & Recreational
River
P.O. Box C
Narrowsburg, NY 12764
Phone: (717) 729-7135

PART 17

POSSIBLE NEW PARKS

▬ ▬ ▬ ▬ ▬ ▬ ▬ ▬ ▬ ▬ ▬ ▬ ▬

The following 37 places are among those that National Parks and Conservation Association (NPCA) has recommended as deserving of enhanced protection as units of the National Park System. They are of unquestioned merit as nationally significant natural and cultural areas. As written in NPCA's *National Park System Plan* (1988): "Many of these areas were elevated to attention by virtue of the fact that inclusion in the national park system would address identified gaps, in the representation of the nation's diverse ecosystems and landscapes. Others would provide additional representation for some themes, yet have such high intrinsic merit as to argue for their eventual management by the National Park Service." (Quotations in the following descriptions are also from NPCA's *Plan* document.)

• **Amicalola River,** Georgia, is "one of only a handful of river systems in the country whose watersheds are essentially undeveloped" and is "highly regarded for its superior whitewater." It is recommended as a national river.

• **Anasazi Culture Sites,** in southwestern Colorado, would bring under federal protection at least seven major, nationally significant pre-Columbian pueblo ruin sites. All seven sites are listed on the National Register of Historic Places and they are recommended as a multi-unit national historical park.

• **Arctic National Wildlife Refuge,** in northeastern Alaska, would be transferred to the National Park Service for enhanced protection of what is described as "the last essentially intact, undisturbed ecosystem in the United States. It is a place of astonishing beauty. . . . The narrow strip of coastal plain is the vital calving grounds of the Porcupine caribou herd, which contain an estimated 180,000 animals." The area was first recommended for national park status in the 1950s. It is recommended as part of a U.S.-Canadian international park, with the adjoining Northern Yukon National Park.

• **Atchafalaya Basin,** Louisiana, is "the largest river swamp system in North America, the most important floodway on the continent, and one of the most commercially important wetlands in the world. . . . The riverway is a place of mysterious, enchanting beauty; its sheer size, mysterious shapes, echoing silence, and bountiful wildlife make it a unique place." It is recommended as a national preserve.

• **Big Sur Coast,** in central California, has long been viewed as deserving of National Park System protection of its magnificently bold coastal scenery, where the Santa Lucia Mountains plunge precipitously into the Pacific Ocean. Although the area contains numerous homes and ranches, there are parts that merit enhanced protection as a unit of the National Park System.

• **Black River,** in North Carolina, is "special among coastal rivers—'a river that had shrugged off man's hand and quietly maintaining its ancient ways.'. . . In addition, the natural environment of the river is healthy and rich." It is recommended as a national wild and scenic river.

• **Blackwater River,** on the eastern shore of Chesapeake Bay in Maryland, is "an ecological system which has no current representation in the national park system." Partly within a national wildlife refuge, the river "winds languidly through marshland, pools, and shallow channels before emptying into Fishing Bay." . . . "Typical of coastal, swampy rivers," it is recommended as a unit of the National Park System.

• **Caddo Culture Mounds Sites,** in Texas and Oklahoma, consists of "six impressive mound complexes associated with the [pre-Columbian] Caddo occupation of the Red River Valley area." They are described as "the best preserved examples of this once-great culture." The dispersed sites are recommended as a national historical park.

• **Cahokia Mounds,** in Illinois, has been recognized as a World Heritage Site by the United Nations and comprise the remains of the central part of "the only prehistoric Indian city north of Mexico." It is recommended as a national historic site or national monument.

• **Caribbean National Forest/Yunque Forest,** in Puerto Rico, consists of 27,846 acres, in the rugged Sierra de Luquillo and contains luxuriant tropical rainforest. Known locally as "El Yunque National Park," the area boasts more than 200 species of native trees (including tree ferns and mountain palms), more than 100 kinds of vertebrate animals, and over 1,100 miles of streams and rivers. It is recommended for enhanced protection as a national park or monument.

• **Casas Grandes Culture Sites,** in southwestern New Mexico, were scattered pre-Columbian adobe villages at the northern frontier of the Mesoamerican Civilization that extended southward through Mexico and Central America. The culture is named for the major urban site of Casas Grandes in Chihuahua, Mexico. Some of the best sites of this cultural heritage, which is not yet represented in the National Park System, are located on the Gray Ranch in the "boot-heel" of New Mexico and are recommended as a multi-unit national monument.

• **Cobscook Bay and Cutler Coast,** in "down east" coastal Maine, consists of 17 miles of wild, spectacularly rugged coastline as well as numerous lakes, bays, coves, peninsulas, and islands. Much of the area is within the Moosehorn National Wildlife Refuge. Featuring rich marine and estuarine ecosystems, the area is recommended as a national park.

• **Thomas Cole House,** in Catskill, New York, commemorates this nineteenth-century landscape painter best known for his work to inspire the

Hudson River School of landscape painting. The house was designated as a national historic landmark in 1965. It is recommended for enhanced protection as a national historic site.

• **Dirty Devil River Canyons,** in south-central Utah, contains magnificent scenic, geological, and wilderness-recreational values. It is recommended as a national park.

• **Emigrant Trail/Black Rock Desert/High Rock Canyon,** in northwestern Nevada, would bring enhanced protection to an important part of the historic Applegate-Lassen Trail—a major westward migration route (1840s–1860s) that emigrants used across an awesomely scenic expanse of high desert and canyon country to California. The trail is listed on the National Register of Historic Places and is recommended as a national monument.

• **Escalante River Canyons,** in south-central Utah, boasts some of the most magnificent canyon scenery and wilderness-recreational values in the country, "characterized by a labyrinth of deep meandering canyons. . . . The canyons contain spectacular natural bridges, arches, eroded alcoves and beautiful streaked walls. . . . Waterfalls, hanging gardens and lush riparian vegetation fill the canyons." The area was urged as worthy of national park status back in the 1930s and the entire Escalante Canyon system is now recommended as a grand national park. **Update:** On September 18, 1996, President Bill Clinton signed a presidential proclamation establishing the 1.7-million-acre Grand Staircase-Escalante National Monument—the largest national monument in the lower 48 states. However, the area is not to be administered by the National Park Service, but remains under the jurisdiction of the Bureau of Land Management. In addition to giving protection to outstanding scenic and ecological values, this designation is intended to block development of large-scale coal resources beneath the Kaiparowits Plateau. At this writing (1997), it is not known whether Andalex, the British-owned, Dutch-registered company that holds rights to mine the coal, will push ahead with its plans or whether it will be possible to negotiate an exchange for values elsewhere.

• **Robert Frost Farm,** near Ripton, Vermont, is where the Pulitzer Prize-winning poet spent 30 summers. "Surrounding the farm are the roads, farmlands and woods which were Frost's favorite haunts and retreats, and the inspiration for much of his New England flavored poetry." The site is part of Middlebury College's Breadloaf School campus and includes some of the adjacent Green Mountain National Forest. It is recommended as a national historic site in close cooperation with the college.

• **Hells Canyon,** on the Snake River in Idaho and Oregon, is considered "the deepest erosion-carved canyon (as distinguished from faulting) on Earth." While most of the dramatically scenic area is within a U.S. Forest Service national recreation area, far more meaningful and urgently needed protection is recommended for the area. This could be accomplished by designating Hells Canyon as a national park.

• **Jemez Mountains/Valles Caldera,** in northern New Mexico, is one of the world's largest calderas—an enormous, collapsed volcano. The caldera is

15 miles across at its widest and is filled with grassy valleys and forested lava domes, and is encircled by a ring of forested mountains that are the remnant of the volcano's once enormous summit that blew apart in massive explosions about a million years ago. Some of the Rio Grande Valley's Pueblo Indians look upon the Jemez Mountains and the caldera as their power center, their source of life. One function of a recommended national park could be to provide these native Americans an opportunity to share with visitors some of their environmentally focused life orientation and philosophy.

• **Kauai,** Hawaii, is a 97,000-acre national park proposal that was initially put forth in the 1960s, encompassing a remarkable part of the Island of Kauai. Deeply incised, jungle-filled canyons and valleys, high mountain "swamps," sheer coastal cliffs, and beautiful beaches are among the incredible scenic splendor of this unique area that is highly recommended as a supremely worthy national park.

• **Aldo Leopold Farm,** near Baraboo, Wisconsin, commemorates one of the fathers of the American conservation movement and author of the book, *A Sand County Almanac.* The farm is recommended as a national historic site.

• **John Marshall House,** in Richmond, Virginia, commemorates "one of the most important and influential figures" in the early history of the United States. His public service culminated as Chief Justice of the U.S. Supreme Court, on which he served for 30 years and for which he wrote a number of landmark decisions. The site was designated as a national historic landmark in 1960 and is recommended as a unit of the National Park System.

• **Micronesia**—Western Pacific islands and atolls (U.S.-administered Pacific Trust Territories)—of the Federated States of Micronesia, is "stunningly beautiful, containing thickly gathered tropical islands and coral reefs that offer [an] excellent opportunity for the establishment of several fine marine parks that would truly be part of an international network." It is recommended that national parks and national historical parks be established "in free association with the native peoples" on the Truk islands, Palau, and in the Northern Mariana Islands.

• **Mimbres Culture Sites,** in southern New Mexico, has long been viewed as worthy of federal protection. The Mimbres culture is noted for its wonderfully abstract black-on-white and polychrome ceramic art, portraying animals as well as human figures and activities. Several of the best pueblo ruin sites are recommended as a multi-unit national monument.

• **Misty Fiords,** in southeast Alaska, is a national monument under U.S. Forest Service management. The area contains magnificent scenic, ecological, geological, and cultural values. "Misty Fiords is a dramatically beautiful land of varying textures and moods; it exemplifies the words 'national park.'" The area easily merits the recommendation as a national park.

• **Mobile-Tensas River Bottomlands,** in southern Alabama, is "a nationally significant wetland, with its integrity still largely intact. An area of 185,000 acres was designated as a national natural landmark in 1974, making it one of the biggest landmarks. These bottomlands are one of the few remaining —and highest quality—areas within themes identified as under-represented in the 1972 NPS *National Park System Plan,* such as: large river systems, eastern deciduous forest, estuaries, streams, lakes and ponds. . . ." This ecologically rich area is recommended as a national preserve.

• **Nipomo Dunes,** in southern California, is "an exemplary candidate for a national seashore." The area comprises the highest dunes on the California coast, along with beautiful beaches, headlands, estuaries, lagoons, and lakes. The area was designated as a national natural landmark in 1974 and is recommended as a national seashore.

• **Oregon Dunes,** between Coos Bay and Florence, Oregon, are the highest dunes on the West Coast. The majority of the area is within a U.S. Forest Service-managed national recreation area. In addition to the magnificent dune complex, there are scenic pine forests and lakes. The area is recommended as worthy of addition to the National Park System, most likely as a national seashore.

• **Owyhee Canyonlands,** in Nevada, Idaho, and Oregon, consists of sagebrush-covered high-desert plateaus that have been "sharply dissected, and a network of canyons varying in depth from 200 to 1,200 feet stretch and radiate from points along miles of river. The meandering nature of the canyon country, with its sharp bends and sheer rock walls, . . . contributes to a sense of isolation and seclusion." The vast *de facto* wilderness is recommended as an expansive national park of "easily several hundred thousand acres."

• **San Rafael Swell and Reef,** in central Utah, contains grand scenic, geological, and wilderness-recreational values and "has long been referred to as 'Utah's sixth national park,' and its resources are easily on a par with Utah's existing five national parks." The area is recommended as a national park.

• **Sawtooth National Recreation Area,** in Idaho, is managed by the U.S. Forest Service and is a stunningly scenic area of mountain peaks rivaling the Tetons in Wyoming. For many decades, the Sawtooth Mountains have been advocated as eminently worthy of national park status. The area continues to be recommended for enhanced protection as a great national park.

• **Shenandoah Valley Civil War Battlefields,** in Virginia, is a key area surprisingly not yet represented in the National Park System. The valley was one of the most hotly contested places in the Civil War, stemming from its strategic location for both Union and Confederate forces and its being an ideal corridor from which the Confederates could attempt to attack the nation's capital. At this writing, legislation is pending in Congress to establish a multi-unit national battlefield park.

• **Siskiyou/Kalmiopsis,** in southwestern Oregon and adjacent California, is a rugged mountainous area, part of which is a lush coastal environment, while farther east it is much drier. The vast wilderness, containing much "priceless old growth forest," boasts a tremendous botanical diversity that is nationally significant. The U.S. Forest Service-managed area is recommended as a national park.

• **Steens Mountain** is a massive, east-facing fault-block mountain rising boldly out of the sagebrush-covered high desert of southeastern Oregon. The highly scenic area is "especially noted for its spectacular wildflower displays, which move up the slopes following the receeding [sic] snow and climax in the upper alpine meadows where they result in seas of color." While the area could qualify as a U.S. Bureau of Land Management wilderness area, it is recommended for enhanced protection as a national park.

• **Tallgrass Prairie,** comprising the 10,894-acre Z Bar/Spring Hill Ranch, is proposed to protect this scenically beautiful, ecologically rich rolling grasslands area and its prairie streams, in the Flint Hills of eastern Kansas. Nearly 200 species of birds and over 30 kinds of mammals have been recorded here, along with numerous varieties of wildflowers and grasses—the tallest of the latter growing to ten feet in height. Over the years, since at least as far back as the 1920s, there have been various proposals for National Park System protection of remaining worthy tallgrass prairie areas in Kansas and Oklahoma. **Update:** In September 1996, the Tallgrass Prairie National Preserve was established by Congress and signed into law by President Bill Clinton. This major achievement finally occurred under the closely cooperative leadership of National Parks and Conservation Association and the National Park Trust. The trust is to continue ownership of most of the property, while the National Park Service, under a special agreement, is to manage the preserve for resource protection and visitation.

Among the area's plantlife are the big and little bluestems, needlegrass, prairie dropseed, switchgrass, and sideoats grama; and many wildflowers such as prairie blazing star, windflower, various species of the pea family, verbena, goldenrods, prairie coneflower, compassplant, and sunflowers. Trees include eastern red cedar, American sycamore, black walnut, shagbark and bitternut hickories, American hornbeam, chinkapin oak, American basswood, and eastern redbud. Of the mammals, there are whitetail deer, bobcats, coyotes, and badgers; while birds include the upland sandpiper (formerly

Tallgrass Prairie, eastern Kansas [Raymond Gehman]

Tallgrass Prairie, eastern Kansas [Raymond Gehman]

called *plover*), greater prairie chicken, bobwhite quail, horned lark, grasshopper and lark sparrows, dickcissal, and meadowlark.

Historical values include a nineteenth-century mansion and a one-room schoolhouse. Both of these structures are listed on the National Register of Historic Places.

The wild grasslands of the highly prized unplowed area offer a wonderful remnant of what was originally some 250 million acres of tallgrass prairie in the eastern Great Plains, stretching from North Dakota to Texas. This ranch had been proposed for more than three decades for addition to the National Park System—originally as a national park. Opposition to federal ownership stalled the plan for years, but ultimately led to the unusual plan, whereby the land is to remain in private ownership, while being managed by the National Park Service. Tallgrass Prairie National Preserve, Rt. 1, Box 14, Strong City, KS 66869. Telephone: (316) 273-8494.

• **Walt Whitman House,** in Camden, New Jersey, commemorates "one of America's most distinguished writers and poets," who initially gained prominence as author of *Leaves of Grass,* and eventually was recognized as the "Poet of Democracy." The house was designated as a national historic landmark in 1962, and is recommended as a national historic site.

• **Wounded Knee,** on the Pine Ridge Indian Reservation in southwestern South Dakota, is the site of the last major encounter, in 1890, between American Indians and the U.S. military. This was "a tragic event which claimed the lives of nearly 300 Indians (more women and children than braves) and 31 American soldiers. . . . The event remains one of the most controversial and emotional of the 400-year struggle between whites and native Americans for control of the land." The area is recommended as a national historic site in close cooperation with the Sioux Nation.

PART 18

THREAT AFTER THREAT

DAMS AND DIVERSIONS

Dinosaur National Monument, in northwestern Colorado and adjacent Utah, is a spectacular land of river-carved canyons. On the warm summer evening we reached the monument's sheer-walled Echo Park at the junction of the Green and Yampa rivers, we watched in awe as the sunshine painted the upper sandstone cliffs and domes high above with the last rich glow of color. The river at our feet reflected the scene in shifting patterns of light and shadow. Except for the distant soothing sound of rapids beyond the mouth of the Canyon of Lodore and the twittering of white-throated swifts darting in and out of the canyon, there was silence.

Yet, we felt sadness. For we knew that the transformation some engineers and politicians had in mind for the free-flowing rivers would fill these magnificent canyons with hundreds of feet of dead storage in two huge reservoirs. The very thought of these schemes cast a pall over the magical beauty of this canyon-embraced scene.

In the late 1930s, the U.S. Bureau of Reclamation explored the canyons of Dinosaur for dam sites and presented plans for Echo Park dam, just below massive Steamboat Rock, and Split Mountain dam farther downstream in Split Mountain Canyon. These were two of more than 20 dams contemplated for the Upper Colorado River Basin. The Bureau admitted there were sites outside the monument that could produce equal if not greater water-storage and power-generation benefits. The Department of the Interior, responsible for planning the Upper Colorado River Storage Project, acknowledged that these two dams were not needed. Yet, despite this conclusion, the issue was subsequently reopened in 1950. While congressional hearings were held and the U.S. Senate actually passed the bill including the Dinosaur dams, the House of Representatives—responding to widespread public opposition led by National Parks Association (original name of National Parks and Conservation Association) and the Sierra Club—fortunately failed to act on the legislation.

Finally in 1956, after six long years of tense controversy, the landmark lobbying campaign against the dams finally paid off, a campaign that was characterized by a University of Colorado political science professor as "the dinosaurs go to Washington." Consequently, Dinosaur National Monument, an area that easily merits full national park status, was spared the fate of another national park—Yosemite, in California.

• Congress tragically ignored the pleas of an earlier generation of park advocates, led by John Muir and his Sierra Club, and in 1913 approved construction of a municipal dam that inundated Hetch Hetchy—a valley second only to Yosemite Valley in scenic grandeur. Even though there were alternative reservoir sites outside Yosemite National Park, nationally significant Hetch Hetchy Valley was sacrificed to meet the demands of the city of San Francisco for water and power. Imagine if today park visitors who crowd into Yosemite Valley could have a choice between *two* magnificent and less crowded valleys. No wonder some have advocated tearing down the dam and restoring Hetch Hetchy!

• It *is* possible to actually remove dams from national parks. For example, in 1992, with strong support from National Parks and Conservation Association, Congress authorized the removal of two dams on the Elwha River in Olympic National Park, in Washington state. This action is part of an effort to restore salmon and trout runs.

• In what has been dubbed the "Hetch Hetchy of the 1980s," another dam—the Cochiti on the Rio Grande in northern New Mexico—flooded much of the once scenic, rapids-filled White Rock Canyon and desecrated the eastern part of Bandelier National Monument. This U.S. Army Corps of Engineers project destroyed wildlife habitat, including valuable roosting places of wintering bald eagles, inundated Indian ruins and hiking trails, killed native trees and other vegetation, and caused an aggressive invasion of exotic plant species. Gone are the exciting boulder-filled rapids—replaced by the ugliness of widely fluctuating dead storage, in an area that was once a pristine wilderness.

• A number of other dam threats have fortunately been defeated. For instance, California hydropower proposals that since the 1920s had threatened inundation of two spectacular parts of Kings Canyon National Park in California—Tehipite Valley on the Middle Fork of the Kings River and Yosemite-like Cedar Grove on the South Fork of the Kings—were ultimately dropped, following years of public opposition.

• A scheme to dam Kentucky's Green River and destroy Mammoth Cave was blocked.

• Glacier View dam, once planned to flood 20,000 acres of prime wildlife habitat in Glacier National Park along Montana's North Fork of the Flathead River, was defeated.

• And in a grand victory in Arizona in the mid-1960s, two proposed Bureau of Reclamation projects—Bridge Canyon and Marble Canyon dams in the Grand Canyon—were rejected. This was one of the biggest battles in the history of the National Park System, with major leadership from the Sierra Club, National Audubon Society, and National Parks and Conservation

Association, as well as enormous help from *The Reader's Digest* and newspaper editorials from coast to coast.

As *The New York Times* editorialized ("Grand Canyon Not for Sale!," Dec. 20, 1964):

The Grand Canyon of the Colorado is one of the world's great scenic marvels, a masterpiece of nature's creative sculpturing of the earth over vast periods of time by wind, rain, frost, and most of all by a free-flowing river. It is a mile-deep open book of the geological ages, with layer upon colorful layer of sandstone, limestone and shale down to the dramatic inner gorge where the river is exposing the oldest known rock on earth.

Under the proposed Pacific Southwest Water Plan, nearly half of this inner gorge of 279-mile-long Grand Canyon would be flooded behind two hydroelectric power dams. . . .

Much has been said by the dam proponents of how small an area of the total canyon would be affected by these dams and reservoirs. Yet it is the very heart, the most significant creative force that gives meaning to the canyon scenery, that would be destroyed. That is the living river.

A grand victory it was! But hold on. That's not the end of the story. The Bureau of Reclamation *did* build the huge Glen Canyon Dam just a few miles upriver from Grand Canyon National Park. It not only flooded a magical canyon that could have become a magnificent new national park, but it also fundamentally altered and impaired the Colorado River within Grand Canyon. When the dam was completed and its floodgates were closed in 1963, the river's flow patterns, turbidity, chemistry, and temperature were radically changed, and its fish and other aquatic life were severely impacted. Peaking-power water releases fluctuated dramatically, causing serious erosion of beaches and embankments, changing shoreline riparian habitat, and creating major difficulties for the popular whitewater rafting trips through the canyon. Canyon-cutting sediments that were formerly carried by the river and constantly replenished the beaches are now trapped behind the dam. Populations of native fish, such as Colorado River squawfish, razorback sucker, and humpback chub, were devastated by the dam's impacts.

A victory? Well, only partly. For while the proposed dams in Grand Canyon were fortunately scuttled, Glen Canyon Dam has caused substantial man-made changes in a place that was supposed to remain forever wild and unimpaired. It is true that the Department of the Interior, Congress, and environmental organizations have been working hard to craft a management plan that will mitigate the unnatural flow-release impacts. But such measures, in the face of such overwhelming ecological changes, are just that: mitigation. The bottom line at the bottom of the Grand Canyon is that the overall ecology of the Colorado River corridor has been so drastically altered within the national park that only relatively minor, albeit welcome, adjustments can be made. And that can hardly be called a victory!

• Grand Canyon is not the only National Park System unit faced with impacts or threats of impacts from upstream dams. You thought Dinosaur National Monument was saved? Well, yes and no. Flaming Gorge Dam was built only 45 miles upstream on the Green River. As with Glen Canyon Dam above Grand Canyon, it has substantially altered the river's flow patterns, turbidity, chemistry, and temperature; impacted fish and other aquatic life; caused erosion of sandbars and other shoreline; changed the ecology of bordering riparian habitat; and the dam's peaking-power water releases have created problems for river trips.

As if this isn't enough, proposals have long been advocated to build dams upstream from Dinosaur on the still essentially free-flowing Yampa River. While it may now be that the economic feasibility of the proposed Cross Mountain and Juniper dams is in doubt, park advocates should remain alert to these and other potential dam plans that would impair this wonderful wild river.

• Black Canyon of the Gunnison National Monument, in southwestern Colorado, has also been impacted by the construction of three dams just upstream in Curecanti National Recreation Area. Seasonal high-water flows no longer occur. Even more serious ecologically is the fact that very little water is allowed through to the national monument during the drier periods—thus seriously threatening the welfare of the river's aquatic life and riparian flora and fauna.

• Then there is Zion National Park, in southwestern Utah—one of the scenically most spectacular parks in the world. There are threats of a number of possible storage projects immediately up-watershed from this park. These include one or more dams on the North Fork of the Virgin, the beautiful river that flows through the Narrows and gives life to the heart of Zion Canyon. Not only is this perennial river an integral visual part of the canyon's remarkable scenic splendor, but it sustains a rich riparian habitat of cottonwood trees and other vegetation, as well. There are also proposals for dams on the East Fork of the Virgin and on Deep and LaVerkin creeks—all flowing into the park.

• In addition to upstream dams and threats of dams affecting parks, there have been some substantially impairing water diversions and threats of diversions—carrying waters away from downstream parks. Death Valley National Park, in the California desert, may someday be deprived of its vital waters that enter the eastern side of the valley as life-giving springs; as well as the Amargosa River, which flows into the southern end of the valley, creating an area of rare desert wetlands. All of these waters in the park may simply cease to flow, if massive pumping of underground aquifers occurs to supply the insatiable appetite for water of America's fastest-growing city— Las Vegas, Nevada.

• Organ Pipe Cactus National Monument, on the Mexican border in southwestern Arizona, is facing increasing impacts from agricultural and urban development across the border in Mexico. Groundwater is being pumped out of the aquifer at more than 200 wells—more than double the rate of natural replenishment. It is assumed that the aquifer extends far under the national monument, and that the downdraw may ultimately impair or destroy a number of springs, including the beautiful desert oasis Quitobaquito, where the endangered desert pupfish resides. Add to this threat the possibility that toxic pesticides and other chemicals used on the agricultural lands across the border may be drifting into the monument and contaminating such fragile places as Quitobaquito and its pupfish.

• So far, the most notorious example of water diversions affecting a national park is Everglades in south Florida. There the natural southwesterly flow of surface waters has been increasingly diverted over many decades through a complex system of canals to serve the needs of growing cities along the east coast of Florida. These large-scale diversions have brought about a sharp decline in the ecological health of the Everglades ecosystem. This decline has dramatically affected the populations of fish and wildlife. In fact, the whole intricate web of life of this rich, but fragile wetlands environment has been severely impaired. The numbers of birds—herons, egrets, ibises, wood storks, and other waders, for instance—dramatically plummeted by the 1990s, to less than ten percent of the populations thriving in the Everglades when the park was established in 1947.

In all these and other water containments and diversions, the issue ultimately boils down to the reality of constantly increasing human needs versus the basic ecological integrity of the parks and their irreplaceable resources. This competition for water raises the underlying question that has, so far, not been very clearly defined: How can the water requirements of the national parks and their ecosystems be adequately protected? As a matter of legal doctrine, the U.S. Supreme Court has affirmed that national parks are legally entitled to have what is termed federal reserved water rights—the theoretical basis for protecting water resources in the parks against threats of depletion.

But as a practical matter, most national parks have not yet had such water rights specifically defined and established. Just how these rights will be determined—how much water will be judged sufficient or essential to fulfill the purposes for which a particular park was established—will be a potentially complex and costly process, with little certainty of the outcome. A Colorado court has ruled, for example, that the only water deemed essential to the purposes of Dinosaur National Monument is the quantity of water minimally needed to operate the original small national monument established to protect the quarry of dinosaur bones. Consequently the monument has no federal reserved water rights relating to the Green and Yampa rivers in the subsequently expanded national monument. Obviously this was the narrowest of legal interpretations, and if it stands as a precedent, the case could spell serious trouble for vital water resources in many parks across the country.

For a far more detailed account of threats to National Park System waters and the concept of federal reserved water rights, an excellent document is National Parks and Conservation Association's *Park Waters in Peril* (1993).

WATER POLLUTION

Add to the decline in Everglades water quantity the decline, as well, in water quality. This impact results from the runoff of pesticides and nutrient-rich chemicals used in the production of sugar cane and other agricultural crops on lands up-watershed from the park. Phosphates and nitrates flowing into the Everglades saw-grass wetlands are already causing a major ecological transformation in areas just north of the park, eliminating the native saw grass and replacing it with the aggressive, non-native cattail. Over time, the park's saw grass also appears destined to be wiped out—unless an answer can be found and implemented before it is too late. In addition to agricultural impacts, there are proposals for oil-and-gas development to the north of the park and adjacent to Big Cypress National Preserve—developments that could cause major pollution were there to be accidents releasing these carcinogenic substances into the wetlands.

Government representatives and environmental leaders of the Everglades Coalition, of which National Parks and Conservation Association is a key member organization, have been struggling to devise achievable, ecologically meaningful solutions by which the decline of the Everglades can be halted and reversed. But progress to date has been painfully slow; in some cases even non-existent. While some welcome measures to somewhat increase the flow of water are being carried out, the problem of agricultural pollution appears virtually intractable—given the political clout of the powerful sugar lobby. Litigation may provide the best chance of help, since negotiations appear to have collapsed.

In spite of all the efforts to seek solutions, the future of Everglades National Park and its fragile ecosystem still hangs in the balance.

Update: On October 12, 1996, President Bill Clinton signed into law a federal water projects bill that included up to $75 million to help restore the quantity and quality of waters flowing into the park. As Vice President Al Gore said at the signing ceremony, "While we have much further to go, today we move closer to making sure that the Everglades are everlasting."

Among numerous other examples of water pollution and threats of pollution affecting national parks are the following:

• Contaminants, leaching for a decade from a town landfill on Mount Desert Island, Maine, are still polluting a creek that flows through Acadia National Park, even after the site was cleaned up. Fish and other aquatic life have been killed.

• The world's oldest national park, Yellowstone, in northwestern Wyoming and adjacent Montana and Idaho, is impaired with contamination from an abandoned heap-leach mine up-watershed from the park. In addition, there is the potential for vastly increased mining on public and private lands adjacent to the park. In fact, as of this writing, the potentially most serious threat to the park's watershed integrity comes from a proposal to mine eight million tons of ore at the New World Mine, a mere three miles away from the park boundary. As *The New York Times* aptly editorialized ("No Mines Near Yellowstone," Aug. 29, 1994):

A calamity threatens Yellowstone, the crown jewel of the American park system. Administration officials say that their hands are tied by archaic laws [the 1872 mining law, etc.] and that there is nothing they can do. . . .

The threat arises from a Canadian conglomerate, Noranda Inc., which plans to hollow out a mountain that sits above Yellowstone, a scant three miles from the park's border. The mountain is said to contain $500 million in gold, silver and copper. The company promises that poisonous wastes from the mine will not seep into the surrounding streams and the park. But the troubled history of Western mining sends a different message entirely: This project poses a clear long-term threat to the water, wildlife and general sanctity of the 2.2 million acre preserve.

There are precedents for drastic action. . . . A buyout may be necessary . . . since the land is now owned by Noranda. This and all other options should be rapidly explored.

Stopping this mine is priority number one.

Update: On August 12, 1996, President Bill Clinton unveiled a plan whereby the company would drop its claim to the gold deposits, in exchange for $65 million in other federal assets. While this plan was only an agreement in principle, it is hoped that such a swap can be worked out, thereby avoiding the risk of harmful mining impacts at Yellowstone. In March 1997, the Clinton administration proposed a $65-million cash payment derived from federal mineral royalties in the state of Montana.

• Sewage from nearby towns in Kentucky is polluting the underground waters of Mammoth Cave—the cave that was saved many years ago from a proposed dam on the Green River.

• A proposed coal mine in Canada may pollute Montana's North Fork of the Flathead along the western edge of Glacier National Park—the river that was spared the fate of dam construction and inundation several decades ago.

• Leaching of acids and heavy metals from mining activities on thousands of acres of mineral claims within Wrangell-St.Elias and other national parks in Alaska is impacting many rivers and streams.

• In the early 1980s, there was the possibility of coal mining on federal lands up-watershed from Zion National Park in Utah. National Parks and Conservation Association strongly opposed any mining in the Kolob Coal Field, since it would be virtually assured to cause severe long-term pollution of the North Fork of the Virgin River and other streams flowing into the park. The Kolob mining proposal seems to have been shelved for now, but park advocates should be alert to any future revival of the idea.

• Mining, agricultural, and urban development along the St. Croix and Lower St. Croix National Scenic Riverways, in Minnesota and Wisconsin, are causing heavy-metal and chemical pollution, as well as sedimentation of the river, and impairing its aquatic life.

• Urban and industrial developments are impacting the ecologically fragile wetlands in Colonial National Historical Park, in Virginia.

• There are many examples of marine pollution or threats of such pollution. For example, with increasing congestion of the shipping lanes and the presence of numerous oil-drilling rigs in the Santa Barbara Channel, there is the heightened possibility of ship collisions and oil rig accidents adjacent to Channel Islands National Park. At risk are the important populations of pinnipeds and other wildlife, marine resources, and the beaches and other shores of these magnificent islands. In 1987, a ship collision in the channel spilled 320,000 gallons of bunker oil into the sea. The huge oil slick fortunately moved away from the park. But next time, the park may not be so lucky.

• In 1988, 12 miles of Olympic National Park's scenic and ecologically outstanding 57-mile-long coastal shore were impacted and some 10,000 seabirds were killed, when an oil barge collision spilled 230,000 gallons of oil into the sea.

• Then in March 1989 came the infamous *Exxon Valdez* oil spill that created a huge disaster in Alaska's Prince William Sound. Two national parks were impacted by oil: Katmai and Kenai Fjords. Beaches and rocky shores were coated with oil; and wildlife was heavily affected, with many thousands of mortalities, as well as unknown degrees of injury through ingesting the carcinogenic substance either directly or indirectly, as when brown bears and bald eagles fed on carcasses of dead, oil-soaked animals. At Katmai the Park Service has described the impacts of the spill as causing "massive environmental damage to the pristine Katmai islands and mainland coast." Over 7,000 dead, oiled birds were recovered, representing only a fraction of the total lost. And the Park Service has stated that, "Despite three seasons of cleanup effort, large quantities of oily mousse, tar, and asphalt-like residues remain along the shores, in the bays, and estuaries of the Katmai coast."

As the Associated Press reported (July 24, 1994), more than five years after the spill,

> Government scientists estimate 300,000 to 645,000 birds were killed outright by the oil, and some devastated bird populations, including common murres and harlequin ducks, are failing to reproduce in areas that were oiled. Young sea otters are dying in unusual numbers in western Prince William Sound, possibly from feeding on mussel beds where oil remains trapped.

GEOTHERMAL DRILLING

• A serious threat to Yellowstone is the potential impairment or destruction of the park's world-famous geothermal attractions: the geysers and hot springs. The Church Universal Triumphant plan to utilize geothermal energy for its world headquarters near the park risks impacting the irreplaceable geothermal features. Even oil- and gas-drilling on lands near the park poses the risk of disrupting underground water flows or releasing hydrostatic pressure that causes the wondrous eruption of the geysers. National Parks and Conservation Association has been a leader in supporting congressional approval of the Old Faithful Protection Act. This legislation would ban geothermal drilling within 15 miles of the park until further research is completed.

• Geothermal drilling adjacent to Crater Lake National Park, in Oregon, poses the risk of impairing the lake's extraordinary water quality. Crater Lake is fed by warm springs at the bottom of the crater.

AIR POLLUTION

Many units of the National Park System are increasingly degraded by air pollution. So serious are elevated levels of acid deposition from acid rain and fog, and so serious is declining visibility in some parks that air pollution is now rated the overall number one most severe external threat to the integrity of the National Park System. Even though air pollution research at most national parks has been inadequately funded, by the 1980s the National Park Service was expressing deep concerns about acid rain and fog impacts at more than 80 parks, and concerns about air pollution in general at more than 100 parks.

Studies at such parks as Sequoia, Kings Canyon, and Yosemite have clearly demonstrated that the most prevalent, observable smog impact has been damage to the foliage of trees. The needles of pines, for instance, become blotched with yellow and brown spots, turn yellow, and die. The obvious result is the weakening of the trees, inviting insect infestations, drought, and disease to hasten their death. At research sites, up to 50 percent of the pines are damaged by air pollutants from the high levels of ozone drifting up from cities in the Central Valley, the Los Angeles Basin, and elsewhere. Assuming pollution damage will continue to occur and steadily increase, will the magnificent conifer forests of these parks ultimately be doomed? Scientific evidence presently yields little reason for optimism.

There is another troubling trend: the decline in populations of amphibians—notably the once-abundant foothills yellow-legged frog that apparently no longer lives in Sequoia and Kings Canyon, and the rapidly dwindling mountain yellow-legged frog. The results of these studies reflect a worldwide decline of frogs, salamanders, and other sensitive amphibians. So, why are the frogs disappearing?

As *The New York Times* editorialized ("What the Frogs Are Telling Us," March 6, 1994):

> . . . scientists at Oregon State University have found that ultraviolet rays do deadly damage to the eggs of frogs and toads that have been

vanishing from the Cascade Mountains of Oregon. This has to be of some interest to another bare-skinned species.

The experimental data seem persuasive. Frog eggs form gelatinous masses, and Oregon's declining species tend to lay them in uncovered shallow water. The Oregon researchers were able to greatly enhance the survival rate of the eggs from Cascade frogs and western toads by shielding them from ultraviolet rays.

What this fails to explain, however, is why the Pacific treefrog, which is also native to Oregon, has escaped the fate of its cousins by laying eggs with greater survival power.

Even so, the Oregon team has provided suggestive evidence that wildlife is affected by the thinning ozone layer. Those vanishing frogs are telling us something.

Research into the frog mystery is continuing at Sequoia and Kings Canyon national parks and elsewhere. Scientists are eager to pinpoint the culprit(s) causing the rapid decline and demise of these fascinating amphibians and to discover how to reverse the trend . . . before it is too late. As the National Park Service has said, "the factors affecting them may be harming other species—including us."

Some other specific air-pollution impacts at national parks include the following:

• At Rocky Mountain National Park, in Colorado, researchers have discovered that seasonally elevated levels of acidification of its lakes and streams from air pollution may prove lethal to sensitive aquatic life.

• At Great Smoky Mountains, in North Carolina-Tennessee, acid fog and rain are causing high rates of acidic deposition. Studies in the 1980s showed that metals and other toxic pollutants are actually accumulating in the foliage of trees, are moving up the food chain, and consequently may be posing a threat to wildlife. Such threats could eventually include a severe decline in the reproductive rates of songbirds, as has been documented in northern Europe. Acid rain there is reportedly causing a lack of calcium in the soil, and scientists now strongly suspect that this calcium deficiency is producing egg defects and thus breeding failures. Streams in the Smokies are "chronically acidified"—that is, nitrogen-saturated—and are causing the decline of sensitive aquatic life.

• At Shenandoah National Park, in Virginia, at least *half* of the streams in the 1980s were already so sensitive to acid rain that total acidification may well occur by the end of the first decade of the twenty-first century. The likely result is that sensitive amphibians and other aquatic life will ultimately be wiped out, unless steps can be taken in time to reverse this trend.

• Acadia National Park, in Maine, is downwind from East Coast and Midwest industrial and urban centers. It is not surprising, therefore, that this exquisite national park is ranked with Santa Monica Mountains National Recreation Area, adjacent to Los Angeles, as among the most heavily impacted by air pollution in the country. Research in the 1980s revealed that "sulfate loadings" were already believed to be significantly above adverse impact levels; that acidification of the lakes, ponds, and streams may be increasing; and that aquatic life is increasingly at risk. Acadia is also showing signs of ozone damage to some sensitive flora. Acadia without aquatic life and some of its plantlife? A dreary prospect, echoing what has been occurring in Europe!

Visibility impairment is another serious form of air quality degradation. Integral vistas, both within parks and extending beyond their boundaries, have been routinely compromised at many parks, including the following:

• At Grand Canyon, in Arizona, the visual magnificence of this world-famous natural wonder is often tragically diminished by air-pollution haze drifting in from cities in Southern California, Nevada, and from farther south in Arizona. During the winter months, when thermal inversions frequently prevail, pollution from the coal-fired power generating station just northeast of the park at Page settles into and is trapped for days within the canyon—obscuring the colors and details of this grand landscape.

• Sequoia, Kings Canyon, and Yosemite vistas are frequently degraded by the invasion of pollution from the rapidly growing cities to the west.

The results of a ten-year study of air pollution in a dozen national parks around the country, as reported in *The New York Times* (June 7, 1994), have revealed that sulfur dioxide pollution has sharply increased, from the mid-1980s to the mid-1990s, at two major national parks in the East: by 37 percent at Shenandoah and by 40 percent at Great Smoky Mountains. According to this University of California at Davis research, the Great Smokies' mean visibility of at least 70 miles back in the 1950s shrank to a mere 12 miles over the subsequent 40 years. Smaller but still significant increases of acidic sulfates were recorded at Grand Canyon, Guadalupe Mountains, Glacier, and Yosemite. Grand Canyon experienced an annual 4 percent increase during the ten-year study period.

Good news came from several parks, including Mesa Verde in southwestern Colorado, which revealed a 25 percent reduction in acidic sulfates. This improvement was the direct result of the installation of pollution-control facilities at major coal-fired power plants upwind from the park, in northwestern New Mexico. Similar cleanup efforts, after many years of delay, are finally underway at the big power plant at Page, Arizona, which will further enhance air quality in the Four Corners region.

NOISE POLLUTION

One of the objectives of national parks is to protect the natural quiet. Yet, some of the parks are being seriously impacted and the natural quiet is being sacrificed to activities that create disturbing noise pollution. As NPCA's former president Paul C. Pritchard has said, "The vast quiet of national parks, which allows distant sounds of water and wind and bird song to be heard, is as important as the clear air that allows spectacular views. Just as we defend the parks against air pollution, we must safeguard them against noise pollution." The sound of small aircraft can be particularly objectionable, since the roar of their engines and rotors penetrates the most remote areas of a park.

• At Grand Canyon, air-tour overflights have long been causing major noise impacts that are a disturbance to on-the-ground visitors. In 1987, Congress finally authorized an aircraft-management plan in an attempt to restore natural quiet to at least some areas of the park. It established "flight-free" zones encompassing 44 percent of the park and prohibited tour flights below the canyon rim. Over the next six years, however, the number of tour flights nearly *doubled*. That number is predicted to double again by the end of the 1990s.

The noise of aircraft, especially of helicopters, penetrates virtually all parts of the canyon. The several flight-free zones are not noise free, since the sound from aircraft spreads outward as it travels downward to the ground. Consequently, the "cone" of sound spreads out from a helicopter or fixed-wing aircraft as it flies through one of the designated flight corridors. And this sound extends far into the flight-free zones. In fact, recent sound monitoring has shown that aircraft noise extends farther into flight-free zones than previously suspected.

With the number of tour flights increasing dramatically, the number of times in a day when aircraft noise disrupts the peace and quiet of the canyon has significantly increased. During the peak summer season, there is more than one flight per minute over the canyon. And that figure appears likely to keep on increasing. The National Park Service's research clearly demonstrates that the 1987 aircraft management plan's objective—the "substantial restoration of natural quiet"—has not been achieved. To the contrary, the situation has worsened, most notably because of an increase in the number of the noisiest aircraft—the helicopters.

National Parks and Conservation Association has been a major participant in Federal Aviation Administration-National Park Service Grand Canyon aircraft overflight meetings over a string of years. The association has urged such actions as creating flight-free zones of adequate size, banning flights at certain times of the day, and providing incentives for air-tour operators to invest in quieter aircraft or quieter technology for their existing aircraft. For example, several of the fixed-wing air-tour operators have retrofitted their airplanes to make them significantly quieter. For aircraft that do not meet certain meaningful quieter noise levels, flights over the canyon or at least over especially sensitive areas should be banned. At Hawaii Volcanoes and Haleakala national parks, there are approximately 60 helicopter tour flights daily, creating noise pollution, as well as visual intrusions, for visitors on the ground during about 50 percent of every daylight hour.

Other parks are being increasingly subjected to the disruptive sounds of air-tour overflights, among them Zion, Canyonlands, Mesa Verde, Glacier, Great Smoky Mountains, Acadia, and national parks in Alaska. It is becoming increasingly obvious that a national policy needs to be established, by which the quality of natural quiet can be protected.

Update: On December 31, 1996, Bruce Babbitt, secretary of the interior, announced new restrictions on air-tour flights over the Grand Canyon. The new rules would ban such flights over roughly 80 percent of the park, up from the current 45 percent. A summer months over-flight curfew would also be in effect from 6 p.m. to 8 a.m., and the plan would limit the number of aircraft that may be engaged in commercial air-tour flights. However, the plan unfortunately failed to include placing an urgently needed cap on the number of flights. Nor did it shift flight routes from above a number of key trails and popular canyon overlooks. In February 1997, the FAA announced that the new rules would not be implemented until at least 1998.

Babbitt and then-Transportation Secretary Federico Peña also announced that proposed air tours over Rocky Mountain National Park, in Colorado, would be prohibited, pending development of a long-term policy for protecting the serenity of all national parks. In early January 1997, a coalition representing 13 air-tour operators filed suit in the U.S. Court of Appeals for the District of Columbia, claiming that the new rules are excessive and unneeded. A few days later, seven environmental groups, including National Parks and Conservation Association, filed a lawsuit with the appellate court, arguing that the plan does not adequately restrict the 90,000 to 100,000 air tours that fly over the park each year. As of this writing (1997), it is not known how this court contest will be resolved.

• In Acadia, the roar of snowmobiles echoes off the mountainsides and carries across the frozen lakes, shattering the winter quiet in large parts of the park.

• In Yellowstone, snowmobile congestion has become a serious management problem, as winter visitation continues to escalate dramatically. Needless to say, the natural quiet in the world's first national park is not something most winter visitors experience.

• At Voyageurs National Park, in northern Minnesota, a controversy has been swirling around the proposal to construct a snowmobile route through the heart of the park's 100,000-acre Kabetogama Peninsula—an area highly deserving of designation as wilderness. At first, it appeared that the National Park Service was ready to carve the projected wilderness into two segments, divided by a "nonwilderness" strip to accommodate the snow machines. Then it seemed hopeful that the Park Service would scuttle the snowmobile route altogether. But as of this writing, it looks as though the proposed wilderness area will be dropped and the snowmobile trail established, after all. If so, this will be a tragic loss for this park, for its natural quiet, and for wildlife, including the magnificent timber wolf.

• In the 1980s, Lassen Volcanic National Park, in northern California, was opened to snowmobiling on a "trial" basis for a couple of years. Fortunately, the National Park Service, with strong backing from NPCA, decided to ban the machines and restore an atmosphere of natural quiet to this park.

• On the North Rim of the Grand Canyon, snowmobiles have never been allowed for recreational use. The natural quiet of that winter wonderland can still be enjoyed on cross-country skis, which is an ideal way in which all of the parks with adequate snow can be enjoyed and quietly savored.

As Harold C. Bryant, Grand Canyon superintendent from 1941-1954, wrote in *National Parks Bulletin* (February 1941), "Noise is nerve-wracking. More and more, man needs [an] opportunity to get away from those things which wear upon his nerves. . . . The appeal of true wilderness is found in quietude . . . as well as in the unspoiled beauty of natural surroundings."

URBAN / SUBURBAN IMPACTS—EXTERNAL

Urban encroachments are affecting many parks. Residential subdivisions and commercial developments are pushing up to park boundaries, which too seldom follow natural topography such as ridgecrest watershed divides, but instead arbitrarily slice straight through the landscape and wildlife habitat. These encroachments often present a sharp visual contrast between parklands and urban development. Such development also typically cuts off natural migration routes for deer and other wildlife, while domestic cats and dogs that roam into adjacent parks may become a threat to native wildlife.

Among units of the National Park System faced with such urban problems are the following:

• Petroglyph National Monument, one of the newest yet most beleaguered units of the park system, at the western edge of Albuquerque, New Mexico, is being hemmed in by real estate subdivisions, as well as threats of highway construction through the national monument and its irreplaceable petroglyphs. Amid the treeless high-desert terrain, the visual impacts of housing developments and roads stand out starkly against the adjacent wild parkland. Ironically, the very city government that had the initial foresight to acquire much of the 17-mile-long petroglyph-patterned lava-rock escarpment and boulders is pushing forward with plans to construct two major highways through the monument. While various local and national environmental groups, including National Parks and Conservation Association, have been strongly opposing these projects, the outcome is still uncertain, as of this writing.

• Saguaro National Park's Rincon Mountain and Tucson Mountain sections bracket the city of Tucson, Arizona, to the east and west. New home construction and housing subdivisions are increasingly pushing against the boundaries. However, some significant efforts to expand both sections of the monument are progressing. A National Parks and Conservation Association-initiated proposal to expand the Rincon Mountain section in the 1980s subsequently gained the support of and was enlarged upon by the Saguaro National Monument-East Expansion Coalition. This coalition was a broad spectrum of local and national environmental groups, horseback riders, mountain bikers, homeowners groups, corporate and individual landowners, the Tucson City Council, the Pima County Board of Supervisors, and the Arizona State Land Department.

Because of this broad consensus and leadership from key members of the Arizona congressional delegation, notably Rep. Jim Kolbe (R-Ariz.), Congress quickly approved the 3,500-acre expansion and has subsequently been appropriating public funds for acquisition of this outstanding saguaro cactus-studded Sonoran Desert area—an area that was previously slated for real estate development.

A similar legislative effort has succeeded in adding a number of key tracts of land to the park's Tucson Mountain section.

• Adjacent to Valley Forge National Historical Park, in southeastern Pennsylvania, a prominent viewshed extending beyond park boundaries is degraded by the visual impacts of a series of large commercial buildings that rise up in sharp contrast to the park's historic and natural features. Other similar structures may be built.

• Antietam National Battlefield, in Maryland, established to protect the site of one of the Civil War's bloodiest battles, encompasses less than half the 7,000-acre battlefield. Urban residential and commercial developments are threatening to wipe out the historic values on the unprotected lands and hem in the existing park. Similar encroaching real estate developments pose a threat to the integrity of Fredericksburg and Spotsylvania County Battlefields National Military Park and Richmond National Battlefield Park, in Virginia. And Gettysburg National Military Park, in Pennsylvania, has already been seriously compromised by commercial developments on lands adjacent to the park.

• At Rocky Mountain National Park, in northern Colorado, large housing subdivisions and other urban developments are increasingly encroaching on park boundaries and severing wildlife migration routes.

• A number of national-park gateway communities, notably Gatlinburg, Tennessee, next to Great Smoky Mountains, and West Yellowstone, Montana, next to Yellowstone, have become unplanned commercial urban centers that provide an unsightly contrast to the natural beauty of the adjacent parklands. There are two good examples, though, in which real estate developments adjacent to parklands have been successfully defeated:

• At the former Pecos National Monument, in northern New Mexico, surrounding ranchland was suddenly slated for a huge urban development scheme—development that would have virtually surrounded the national monument and would have caused enormous visual impacts to the integral viewshed from the monument's ridgetop ruins of the seventeenth- and eighteenth-century Franciscan mission churches and convents and the adjacent ruins of Pecos pueblo.

Fortunately, outstanding investigative news reporting by the Santa Fe *Reporter* brought the massive scheme to widespread public attention in the nick of time. The plan was not only defeated, but the historically and ecologically significant Forked Lightning Ranch was acquired and added to the designated Pecos National Historical Park.

• Adjacent to the Cheeseboro Canyon section of Santa Monica Mountains National Recreation Area, in southern California, private landowner and world-famous entertainer Bob Hope was proposing to build a PGA golf course and 1,250 luxury homes on his 2,308-acre Jordan Ranch. The plans even called for the exchange out of 59 acres of national recreation area land so that an access road could be carved through an area of steep hills to serve the development.

Thanks to the initiative and political courage of Maria VanderKolk, a then-newly elected member of the Ventura County Board of Supervisors, negotiations were held in 1992 that produced an agreement that finally resulted in the sale of the ranch and its magnificent, live oak-covered Palo Comado Canyon to the National Park Service as part of an expanded Cheeseboro Canyon section of the national recreation area. The agreement may also ultimately bring into the park another 2,633 acres of the Ahmanson Ranch, which adjoins the Cheeseboro Canyon area to the east.

National Parks and Conservation Association, which had opposed development of Jordan Ranch and the deal to swap out park acreage for construction of the access road, had viewed the outcome of this threat of urban development with little optimism . . . until Ms. VanderKolk's upset election victory and her successful efforts in promoting negotiations. This is a wonderful example of how one person's political courage can make all the difference in the outcome of an environmental decision—in this case, a decision protecting a scenically beautiful and ecologically rich area for posterity.

URBAN IMPACTS—INTERNAL

Several of the larger national parks are faced with impacts of urbanization within their boundaries. Given the history and logistics of visitation, communities have incrementally grown up over many decades. Two of the most notorious examples are at Grand Canyon and Yosemite.

• On Grand Canyon's South Rim, Grand Canyon Village is an extensive urban development within the park. It includes hotel and motel lodgings, a variety of restaurants and gift shops, a general store, gasoline station, post office, school, visitor center and other interpretive facilities, administrative and other offices, maintenance facilities, and the historic Grand Canyon Railway line and depot. Over the decades, there has been a steady increase in the number of buildings. Even so, there is still a severe shortage of adequate staff housing. Some of the housing is shamefully substandard.

The incremental increase in urban development inside the park appears likely to continue unabated in the decades to come, unless a way can be found to begin shifting housing and some community services to the nearby gateway town of Tusayan. Such an opportunity seems possible, with the plans of a private developer who has proposed a master-planned community near the airport and projected railway spur line and transportation hub. These plans call for housing to be provided for government and concession company employees. If successful, such privately funded housing and other facilities and services would offer the only real hope of slowing down or even reversing the urbanization trend inside Grand Canyon National Park.

• Parts of Yosemite Valley, in Yosemite National Park, in California, are similarly cluttered with buildings, such as hotel, motel, and tent-cabin lodgings, restaurants, stores, and employee housing. In recent years, some changes have been undertaken to begin reducing the urban congestion. New employee housing, park offices, and maintenance and sewage-treatment facilities have been built outside the park on an administrative site at El Portal, down in Merced Canyon.

One of the continuing goals for reducing urban congestion in the valley is to move certain employees and their housing out—unless their jobs are essential in the valley. The basic objective is to place employees and their housing close to their workplace, to reduce the need for commuting to and from their jobs. Such commutes and shuttles only add to the problems of traffic congestion on park roads. Those employees whose jobs are not essential in the valley would be moved to El Portal or to Wawona, near the park's south entrance—thereby allowing for the removal of some housing from the valley.

Other plans at Yosemite Valley call for the reduction in the overall number of lodging units and for some reconfiguration of the lodgings by reducing the sprawl of tent-cabins and increasing somewhat the number of consolidated room units, so that the overall "footprint" of structures would be reduced.

Although a January 1997 flood caused an estimated $100 million in damage, the event may accelerate the relocation of some facilities outside the valley.

TOO MANY CARS

In many parks, large and small, there is a transportation crisis in the form of too many private motor vehicles being driven into the parks during periods of heavy visitation and causing traffic congestion. This situation notably happens during Memorial Day and Labor Day weekends, but also generally occurs during longer stretches of peak visitation. Some limited solutions toward solving the automobile crunch have proven helpful at a few parks. For example:

• At Grand Canyon's South Rim, the West Rim Drive is closed to private automobiles during the summer months and a free shuttle-bus system provides visitor access on this rim drive between Grand Canyon Village and Hermits Rest. In addition, there is an optional shuttle service connecting major points within the village with the campground and visitor center. The latter shuttle has at least marginally helped reduce village traffic congestion, in a park that receives over a million motor vehicles annually.

• In Yosemite Valley, a shuttle service successfully provides transportation between the visitor center area and various trailheads and other places in the east end of the valley that are no longer accessible by private automobile. The National Park Service is studying various transportation options, including an expanded valley-wide shuttle and other peak-season shuttles from the valley to other destinations in the park.

• At the Mariposa Grove of giant sequoias, near Yosemite's south entrance, visitors may no longer drive their cars through the grove, but have the option of either walking or taking an open-air shuttle.

• At Zion, automobile gridlock is an increasing concern. On an average peak-season day, about 1,700 motor vehicles enter the park. Car parking overflows from parking areas, spilling onto the roadsides and creating unsafe traffic congestion, as, for example, at the end of the Zion Canyon road at the start of The Narrows trail. There is currently a peak-season shuttle connecting the gateway town of Springdale with the park's visitor center and other main points of interest. The National Park Service is considering a plan to eliminate cars from Zion Canyon, at least during the main visitation season.

• At Chiricahua National Monument, in Arizona, a shuttle van takes visitors on busy days from the visitor center up to the end of the road so they may hike through the "Wonderland of Rocks" and back down to the visitor center.

• At Bandelier National Monument, in northern New Mexico, the Park Service is studying several transportation options to alleviate peak visitation congestion on the road that dead-ends in Frijoles Canyon at the visitor center, where parking overflows onto roadsides. At busiest times, some visitors are even forced to wait their turn to enter the monument in an unsafe lineup along the adjacent state highway. Some form of shuttle system seems virtually assured.

At both Grand Canyon and Yosemite, planning efforts are underway, as of this writing, for more comprehensive transportation solutions to traffic congestion. While one of those solutions could be the total ban of automobiles in both parks and the creation of some form of mandatory mass-transit system (logistically far more difficult at Yosemite than at the Grand Canyon), there are a number of potential, less costly and simpler measures—as suggested by Earth Island Institute's Yosemite Guardian (YG) and National Parks and Conservation Association. As YG's Garrett De Bell has pointed out:

> The severe overcrowding of Yosemite by automobiles, particularly in
> Yosemite Valley, is a well known problem, but solutions have been

difficult because the issue is so widely misunderstood. The perception is of major overcrowding for most of the year at least in Yosemite Valley. The reality is that only a very few days a year reach the near gridlock situation so frequently publicized by the media. Perhaps 60 days exceed—to varying degrees—the comfortable capacity of the existing road network and available parking and exceed the NPS guidelines in the 1980 Yosemite General Management Plan.

This is both good and bad news.

The bad news is that solutions that would work if the overcrowding were a daily occurrence similar to the commute problems of the Los Angeles area, do not work in a situation that is more comparable to the overcrowding of Times Square on New Year's Eve or a popular restaurant on Mother's Day. . . . The good news is that simple measures can alleviate the most serious problems that exist for the 20 or so days by knocking off the peaks in visitation and shifting some of those visits to the off peak periods.

De Bell goes on to say that some previous solutions have already worked well, such as the existing shuttle services in the valley and at Badger Pass, the creation of a valley bicycle path and bike rental service, and a campground reservation system. Among the array of possible additional solutions that De Bell recommends be implemented, either separately or in combination, are the following:

(1) A tiered fee structure, with higher fees on peak days, much as movie theaters use matinee prices to encourage some movie goers to avoid weekend evening showings.

(2) The "Diamond Lane" concept, providing free or reduced-fee entrance for cars carrying four or more occupants.

(3) Provide an optional reservation system so that day visitors may be assured access when they reach the park. De Bell explains:

Coupled with enforcement of the existing traffic management plan with a somewhat lower maximum number of cars, this is the fairest way (no way is perfect) to treat visitors who may only be able to come on a certain day.

By providing clear, consistent, and widely available public information on the anticipated visitation, this reservation system (in conjunction with the other measures advocated here) could be the least intrusive to the experience of park visitors while providing a fair mechanism to restrict overcrowding.

(4) Carefully regulate the use of buses. Tour buses should be limited in number and size—there can easily be too many buses and bus transportation is not the panacea that some would suggest. For shuttling visitors back and forth between lodging in nearby towns outside the park, vans and small shuttle buses should be encouraged, with incentives such as preferential fees, assured access, and designated parking.

(5) Encourage the California Department of Transportation

(CalTrans) to help develop a regional transportation strategy, including better information (changeable signs, etc.) to offer advance notice to motorists regarding the status of visitation at the park.

A longer range and obviously far more costly solution to automobile congestion is some form of rail transportation, similar to the historic railroad that years ago brought visitors up Merced Canyon to the park. Either conventional or light rail trains could carry visitors of the future up one or more of the transportation corridors to Yosemite.

At the Grand Canyon's South Rim, the logistics of reducing automobile congestion are potentially far easier than at Yosemite. Suggested solutions include the following :

(1) Establish a transportation hub in the gateway town of Tusayan, convenient to the highway, the airport, and the projected rail spur line, to encourage visitors to take some form of mass transit—either train or shuttle bus—into the park.

(2) Inside the park, create an orientation and day-use parking staging area, from which a number of shuttle services would be offered. Shuttles could include a short run out to the nearest point on the canyon rim, for visitors wishing only a brief look at the canyon and then proceed on their way back out of the park; shuttles to key places in Grand Canyon Village; and another shuttle eastward along the canyon rim to Desert View. Overnight campers and lodgers would drive on to the campground or lodgings and then park at the designated place—leaving their vehicles there until ready to leave the park.

Grand Canyon already provides an excellent example of rail service to the park. Re-establishment of the historic steam train service from Williams, Arizona, by Grand Canyon Railway a few years ago, enabled visitors once again to come to the park without the hassle of driving. Even more visitors will have the option of entering the park by rail, once the projected short spur line is built from Tusayan.

Update: Under a new Grand Canyon National Park management plan that began in 1997 and will be completed in 15 years, visitors would no longer drive into the Grand Canyon Village area of the park's South Rim. Under the plan, a system of shuttles, buses, and light rail would bring visitors into the park from a staging area in the gateway community of Tusayan, thereby eliminating traffic congestion in the park.

A fascinating account of historic railroads to the western national parks is Alfred Runte's book *Trains of Discovery.*

In the years ahead, as park visitation continues to climb, innovative solutions—some new and some old—will be needed to resolve the growing problem of too many cars. Some of the ideas suggested for Yosemite and Grand Canyon will likely prove helpful, not only in those parks, but in many others across the country.

VISITOR-USE IMPACTS

In the early years of the national parks, when advocates were trying to devise ways of explaining the wonders and value of these extraordinary places, the National Park Service actually encouraged people to visit the parks. By the early 1920s, visitation had crept up to the then-incredible figure of one million. By the mid-1950s, that figure had multiplied 50 times. Within the next ten years, visits doubled, to 100 million. By the late 1970s, that number had again doubled, reaching 200 million. By 1990, there were 250 million. As of this writing, the total has topped 270 million and seems headed for 300 million or more by the beginning of the twenty-first century.

Granted, the number of National Park System units has also grown during this time—from about 40 parks in the early 1920s to more than 370 parks today. Yet, the dramatic increase in visitation emphasizes how popular the national parks have become. Rather than encouraging people to visit the parks, ways must now be found to save the parks from overuse and to manage visitor use.

With this increasing popularity, visitor-use impacts upon the parks, upon their natural and cultural resources, and upon the quality of visitor experience are generally increasing, as well. Harmful impacts are occurring both because of the sheer numbers of visitors and because of such other factors as inadequate and even diminishing public funds for such programs as trail and other facilities maintenance, resource protection, educational and interpretive programs, research, and use-impacts monitoring.

Visitor uses impair the environment and its natural and cultural values in many ways. From walking, hiking, backpacking, rock climbing, horseback riding, trekking with pack stock, and camping, to mountain biking and motorized vehicle activities, visitor uses all have impacts. In varying degrees, vegetation may be damaged, crushed, or destroyed. Soil may be compacted— reducing its capacity to hold and absorb moisture—an impact that increases the likelihood of soil erosion.

In desert habitats, the fragile, slightly hardened crusty layer of sandy soil is readily disturbed or destroyed—exposing the more fragile underlying soil to the direct impacts of wind and rain. Off-road vehicles easily destroy this protective layer; but even walking on it disrupts this almost sponge-like formation.

In forests and grasslands, the fragile micro-habitats of the soil and litter are home to insects, spiders, and herbivorous invertebrate and vertebrate animal life—many of them vital to the process of breaking down dead organic matter.

In coastal sand dunes and beaches, dune buggies, all-terrain vehicles, four-wheel-drive, and other motor vehicles can inflict enormous impacts upon dune-stabilizing grasses and other vegetation. Even walking on dunes can disrupt the fragile dune ecosystem. Wildlife can also be disturbed or driven away from seashore areas. For example, during the breeding season, the rare piping plover, which nests and rears its young on East Coast beaches, is especially vulnerable to human disturbances. Because of the sharp decline in this shorebird's population, it was federally listed in 1986 as a threatened and endangered species.

In spite of the unpopular inconvenience to beach enthusiasts, visitor-use restrictions have now been established during the bird's breeding season at all the national seashores from Cape Cod to Cape Lookout. There are already indications that the plover is beginning to recover. As NPCA's former Northeast Regional Director Bruce Craig has said, "If the plover can't have a safe haven in the national parks, just how is the species to thrive?"

Yet, as Bill Sharp and Elaine Appleton wrote in their *National Parks* magazine article, "Plight of the Plovers" (March/April 1994):

> The plover controversy, whether viewed at Cape Cod, Fire Island, Gateway, Assateague, or Cape Lookout, places [the National Park Service] . . . in a classic bind between its dual responsibilities to preserve and protect species and to provide for public enjoyment of natural resources. It is a dilemma that defies simple answers and that will challenge the Park Service for years to come.

Of course, many species of wildlife are more tolerant of or less vulnerable to human activities than is the piping plover. But disturbances by visitor activities nevertheless can and do cause behavioral changes in movements, feeding, and breeding patterns; can cause a decline in populations; and can result in changes in the makeup and diversity of wildlife.

Visitor activities and crowding also have a range of social impacts that impair the quality of visitor experience overall. Or the activity of one visitor group can impair the quality of experience of another group. If, for example, too many people are allowed to crowd into a particular place at one time, the quality of experience can definitely be degraded and compromised—whether that is on a short walk from Lake Powell in Glen Canyon National Recreation Area into Rainbow Bridge National Monument to see the world's largest natural sandstone arch; crowding onto Colorado River beaches at the bottom of the Grand Canyon; hiking the John Muir Trail up in the High Sierra wilderness of Yosemite, Kings Canyon, and Sequoia national parks; hiking the Appalachian Trail in Shenandoah; climbing Mount Rainier; hiking out the Bear Valley Trail in Point Reyes National Seashore; or walking The Narrows path at Zion.

Crowds of people do have a significant impact that makes it more difficult to enjoy the natural beauty and serenity of an area. NPCA's former Rocky Mountain Regional Director, Terri Martin, has aptly characterized the Park Service's allowing too many visitors into Rainbow Bridge as like seeing how many people can be jammed into a phone booth. Quality quite definitely is sacrificed to quantity.

By contrast, the number of visitors allowed into scenically spectacular South McKittrick Canyon, in Guadalupe Mountains National Park, in west Texas, is purposely limited by the available car parking near the mouth of the canyon. This limit is designed to help protect the quality of the canyon's resources and the quality of experience in this magical place.

Conflicts between visitor groups can take on many forms. For example, mountain bikers and hikers can get in each others' way, as on one popular trail in Saguaro National Park. Motorboats can seriously impair the experience of canoeing. Snowmobiles can shatter the peaceful experience of cross-country skiing.

Of course it is true that visitors are varyingly tolerant or intolerant of various kinds and degrees of crowding, as well as of different visitor activities. Reactions and responses depend in large measure upon an individual's expectations, norms, and conditioning. The perception of crowding is, after all, a value judgment—a negative evaluation of a particular density of visitor use.

Yet, it is also true that the national parks must be protected against overuse. As one saying goes: We are loving our parks to death. There are often increasingly serious visitor-use impacts that compromise the quality of the resources that the parks were established to protect "unimpaired," for the enjoyment of future generations. It is the responsibility of the National Park Service, therefore, to determine how best to preserve park resources and the quality of experience—to find the best ways to prevent visitor overuse and abuse of this treasured national heritage.

In 1978, Congress directed the National Park Service to establish a "visitor carrying capacity" for each unit of the National Park System. Soon after, National Parks and Conservation Association decided to help by preparing a methodology document on visitor-use management—to develop a management process for evaluating and managing visitor use in the national parks. As NPCA's former president Paul C. Pritchard said:

> We sought to develop a management process that encompasses the physical, environmental, and social aspects of recreational carrying capacity. It had to incorporate scientific principles and natural resources management concepts. It had to be applicable to any unit of the national park system including historic and cultural parks. It had to be applicable to all types of natural resources and environments found within the national park system. It had to be applicable to the types of visitor use and activities appropriate and expected in the range of settings found in the national park system areas. It had to be in a form readily usable by field managers and planners. And it had to be democratic, that is, allow visitation based upon the desire and ability of the individual, not their income or social condition.

The outcome was a two-volume document, produced in collaboration with the University of Maryland and Pennsylvania State University, titled *Visitor Impact Management* (1990). This landmark publication is being used extensively by the National Park Service, as well as by parks elsewhere in the world.

Visitor-use management—the setting of levels of visitation that will not result in harm to the parks' resources and that will not compromise the visitor's experience—is an enormous, but vitally important challenge. In the use of any resources—be they consumptively or non-consumptively used or enjoyed—there is always a limit to growth in use levels. How successful scientists and planners are in ascertaining appropriate carrying capacity will, in turn, determine just how well park resources are really protected unimpaired and will also determine whether the visitor's quality of experience is degraded or enhanced. One of the most important parts of the visitor-impact management process is the need for sound science-enhanced and adequately funded programs of research, the development of adequate baseline data, and monitoring of impacts.

SCIENCE SHORTFALL

While most park visitors might assume that the National Park Service knows all that basically needs to be known about the parks and their resources, the truth is that scientific research and baseline data are woefully inadequate. Only a shockingly minuscule 2.3 percent of the Park Service's budget is earmarked for research. As the 1992 *Science in the National Parks* study put it: "Informed resource management is impossible without science in its broadest sense—that is, the acquisition, analysis, and dissemination of knowledge about natural processes and about the human influences on them."

Many species of flora and fauna could be vanishing right now. Yet, with inadequate or even nonexistent research and information, the Park Service or the Biological Resources Division of the U.S. Geological Survey might not even know what is happening. As reported in Bill Sharp and Elaine Appleton's *National Parks* magazine article, "The Information Gap" (Nov./Dec. 1993), just the listings of species in 40 national parks and monuments in the West were less than 80 percent complete. Only a few parks are preparing systematic inventories. "Over the past decade, a handful of these parks added 1,439 vascular plants, 111 birds, and 15 mammals not previously recorded."

Furthermore, the same article indicated another shortfall: While the larger or more obvious mammals, birds, trees, and wildflowers are generally listed, about half the parks surveyed in 1992 have virtually no research and data on insects and other invertebrates and on non-vascular plants, which are vital parts of a healthy ecosystem. James F. Quinn, of the University of California at Davis, is quoted as saying that, "Lots of parks have no formal biological studies at all. . . .We have little bright spots of knowledge in a sea of ignorance."

A few parks have had relatively substantial research activities, among them Sequoia-Kings Canyon, where fire research and management and air-pollution monitoring have been major focuses for many years. In fact, much of what has been learned at these parks has been used or applied at other parks—notably in fire management. Because of past decades of unnatural fire suppression in the parks, the makeup of forests was changed and fuel overloads were allowed to develop. Some habitats became relatively sterile and static without the periodic function of fire to reduce the fuels (deadwood, fallen trees, etc.) and bring about a renewal of plantlife through the release of minerals and nutrients. Because of the fuel overload, prescribed burning under carefully applied guidelines, which began at Sequoia-Kings Canyon, has spread to many other parks. The pace of carefully reintroducing fire back into the ecosystems, in which it is a major natural ecological process, is regrettably too slow due to insufficient funding. In some areas, even carefully prescribed fires burn hotter than they would have under natural, more frequent, and cooler fires. As a consequence of decades of fire suppression, many park system units, notably in the West, are like volcanoes ready to explode from their fuel overloads.

According to Sharp and Appleton, Channel Islands scientists have been actively studying some 500 of the park's 2,000 species. The park's marine biologist, Gary E. Davis, "is assembling what he calls an early warning system for endangered species and ecosystems at Channel Islands. Rather than waiting for crises to develop for wild populations, Davis gathers information on selected species on a routine basis to construct baseline information," in a long-term ecological monitoring effort. What is happening at this park ought to be happening at parks all across the country.

Thomas J. Stohlgren, a Park Service ecologist and global climate change research coordinator, says that "We have a lot to learn about the plants and animals—what they are, where they are, how healthy they are, and what roles they play. That information affects [or should affect] every important decision we make." The bottom line is that without adequate research, park planners and resource managers can hardly be expected to know how best to manage the parks—for example, how to avoid mistakes like the unfortunate fire-suppression policy of the past, instead promoting and maintaining natural ecological processes, which the national parks are established to protect.

ET CETERA

There are numerous other kinds of problems affecting or threatening to affect the welfare of the national parks. Among them are:

• Private inholdings within some forty units of the park system, many of which should be acquired so that their present or potential development will not adversely impact the surrounding parklands.

• Many historic buildings and other cultural resources are in a seriously deteriorating condition or lack appropriate routine maintenance.

• Livestock trespass is impacting natural ecosystems in a number of areas, including Saguaro, Glacier, and Cape Lookout.

• Exotic species, such as the wild boars in Great Smoky Mountains and Pinnacles, have become major pests. At this writing, a boundary fence is being completed at Pinnacles, which is expected to keep these destructive animals out. Feral burros have likewise been a major problem at Death Valley, Grand Canyon, Bandelier, and elsewhere; but removal programs in recent years have generally been successful. Exotic species, both flora and fauna, pose one of the most serious long-term threats to native species in the national parks (a topic discussed in George Wuerthner's article, "Alien Invasion," *National Parks*, Nov./Dec. 1996).

• There is still the possibility that the Department of Energy may wish to site an enormous, high-level nuclear waste repository in Utah's Canyonlands Basin, only one mile from the boundary of Canyonlands

National Park. This scheme became a matter of intense controversy in the early 1980s, but was then at least temporarily shelved if not permanently discarded. National Parks and Conservation Association, other environmental groups, and the State of Utah vigorously opposed the plan. In fact, NPCA went even further by urging that the original proposal for a Canyonlands National Park, first advocated by former Interior Secretary Stewart L. Udall, be implemented—by expanding the park to extend from rim to rim across the entire basin, much as Grand Canyon National Park reaches from rim to rim. This expansion would include the nuclear waste dump site, as well as appropriately bringing national park protection to the entire Canyonlands Basin.

• Poaching of wildlife and plantlife, including desert cacti, is a perennial problem impairing park resources. One of the affected areas is Organ Pipe Cactus National Monument along the Arizona border with Mexico, where desert trees are being removed for use as firewood across the border. Fossil and petrified-wood collecting also continues to plague parks containing these assets.

• Concession and Park Service structures within the parks have sometimes been inappropriately eye-catching in their design or have been just plain ugly. Other buildings and structures have been made to harmonize with a park's environmental or historical theme. Buildings should be designed to blend as much as possible with the park scene, while being aesthetically pleasing and incorporating the best energy-conserving technologies.

• Concession operations, providing visitor lodgings, dining facilities, gift shops, etc., have sometimes been blatantly commercial in their tone or have neglected to function cooperatively with the Park Service in striving to meet objectives that are in the best interest of park protection. Virtual monopolies have often prevailed, where competition in contract bidding would have produced a healthier business climate. Contracts have sometimes extended over too many years, while fees charged larger concession companies have frequently been far below a fair percentage of profit being made in national parks. At this writing, some of the woes of the existing concession services system will be corrected if Congress passes legislation to remedy the situation.

• Certain recreational activities have been allowed in the parks that are contrary to the fundamental purposes of these places. Among them are speed-boating, snowmobiling, off-road motorized vehicle use, downhill skiing (requiring mechanical ski lifts, etc.), and hang-gliding. Such activities can create significant noise disturbances, tear up the land, and harass wildlife, or become crowd-attracting events. These pursuits should be banned, especially since they are readily available outside the parks.

As national parks advocate T. Destry Jarvis wrote in NPCA's book, *National Parks in Crisis* (1982):

> National park enjoyment, while it hopefully will be physically rewarding, should predominantly be mentally and intellectually stimulating. Wholesome outdoor recreation appropriate to the parks should be encouraged, but organized recreation requiring investment in capital improvements occupying areas whose natural condition or historical significance are more appropriately unintruded upon, and

various amusement and resort-type facilities and features are wholly [sic] inappropriate in the National Park System.

Jarvis also wrote:

The stillest crowded place in America, someone has said, is the rim of the Grand Canyon. To visitors gathered around the tree of trees in Sequoia National Park, the hushed fall of the tiniest of seeds is audible upon the forest floor. These silent moments are never forgotten. In the presence of vast sweeps of Nature's stupendous revelation, there is the inspiration that uplifts the spirit into joy. To a visiting immigrant . . . the Statue of Liberty and the facilities of Ellis Island inspire far more emotion than can be felt from mere bricks and mortar. . . .

While the national parks serve a number of purposes, they are not merely places in which to rest and exercise and learn. The parks are there to kindle an Appreciation of the natural world around us, the man-created heritage of our history, and the inspiration of landscapes in which we may be renewed of spirit.

As environmental author Darwin Lambert once wrote in *National Parks and Conservation Magazine,* (January 1976):

Our National Park System is not a mishmash, it's an interlocking pattern, a living mosaic, an earth-man picture. Fully and truly interpreted and understood, it simultaneously preserves natural life and the human spirit. It thus contributes to the shaping of humanity's future.

If this living mosaic, this earth-man picture, this priceless and irreplaceable heritage is to be protected unimpaired for the renewal of the human spirit and the shaping of humanity's future, an informed and caring citizenry must remain ever vigilant—alert to the threats within and from outside the parks that can blatantly or subtly impact the integrity of these magical places.

MAINTAINING THE STANDARDS

National Parks and Conservation Association has for decades been at the forefront of those advocating high standards for the National Park System (see "National Park Standards"). High standards mean not only maintaining the quality and integrity of each park unit and its natural and cultural resources, but also adding to the system only those places that are worthy of national attention and protection. For years, park advocates have wisely warned against "watering down" the park system with areas that lack inherent qualities of national significance and that could be managed and protected by an alternative jurisdiction, such as a state park system.

In 1995, Congress considered legislation that purported to reform the process by which proposed or possible new parks are evaluated for addition to the National Park System. It would have directed a review of what constitutes adequate representation of the various natural and cultural resources and what priorities there are for adding new parks to the system. It would also have required a review of all existing parks to determine whether any of them may lack adequate merits and should be eliminated.

While these kinds of evaluations can have substantial benefits—if carried out with professional integrity—there is also the potential danger that such a review process can "snowball" and sweep out of the system important existing parks or block worthy proposed parks from being added. The key to such review is the degree of professional integrity that is brought to bear upon that process and upon those participating in it.

If the outcome of such a review were to be based upon such factors as a park's cost, the number of visitors, the lack of visitor accessibility, or the feasibility of managing the area, the basic need to protect irreplaceable values could easily be ignored. Enormous mischief could threaten the integrity of the National Park System, which is not only the pride of America, but has long been the model for nations throughout the world.

Paul C. Pritchard, then-president of National Parks and Conservation Association, said in testimony (February 3, 1995) on the National Park System Reform Act:

> "Cost" is a term that could be interpreted in many different ways and has no clear meaning. Does this refer to the size of the unit's budget, its cost per-visitor, etc.? How do you compare the significance of the site where Lincoln delivered the Gettysburg Address with the site where he was assassinated?
>
> Further, how do you compare today's operating cost with a unit's value in teaching future generations about our national heritage? Finally, do we want our generation to be remembered for knowing the cost of everything and the value of nothing?
>
> We are also troubled by the use of the term "lack of visitor accessibility." What exactly does it mean? Low numbers of visitors? Visitation rates is a misleading criterion. Units like Yosemite and Great Smokies, located near large metropolitan areas, are no more significant in the system than Big Bend or the Alaska units which are more difficult to reach. Further, many of the smaller units simply cannot accommodate a high number of visitors for a variety of reasons, but this does not make them either insignificant or inappropriate. Finally, lower visitation rates at larger natural parks offers Americans an increasingly rare opportunity to experience undisturbed solitude.

The bottom line in any legitimate review process is to assure quality control that is predicated upon the protection unimpaired of nationally significant resources. Anything less could pose one of the single greatest threats to the integrity of this priceless national heritage.

NATIONAL PARKS AND CONSERVATION ASSOCIATION
A Brief History

In 1916, Congress created the National Park Service, in the U.S. Department of the Interior, to administer the then-nearly 40 national parks and monuments. The service's first director, Stephen T. Mather, soon felt that there should be a private organization, independent of the federal government, established to fight for the welfare of the national parks.

Consequently, on May 19, 1919, National Parks Association (NPA), subsequently renamed National Parks and Conservation Association (NPCA), was founded in Washington, D.C. At the helm as executive secretary was Mather's former public relations director, Robert Sterling Yard, who energetically led NPA for 25 years.

The Association's primary missions were then and continue to be to fight against threats to the integrity of the parks; to advocate the highest standards of national significance for the addition of new units to the National Park System and for protectively managing the parks and their natural and cultural resources; and to promote the public understanding and appreciation of the parks and promote educational and inspirational uses of the parks.

One of the biggest political conservation battles of that time erupted in 1920, right after NPA got underway. This was a scheme to build an irrigation reservoir and canals in the southwestern part of Yellowstone National Park, and another proposal to raise the level of Yellowstone Lake, in the heart of the park, to provide for irrigation water in Montana.

As Yard wrote in NPA's *Bulletin* (September 30, 1920) of the danger of setting harmful precedents:

> One thing we certainly know . . . the granting of even one irrigation privilege in any national park will mark the beginning of a swift end; within five years thereafter all our national parks will be controlled by local irrigationists, and complete commercialization inevitably will follow.

Fortunately, these repeatedly proposed projects, which would have exploited the park's waters and inundated thousands of acres of pristine scenery and wildlife habitat, were ultimately defeated. And the fledgling NPA was an important force in the landmark victory.

At about the same time, another controversy developed—over the legal authority previously given to the Water Power Commission (subsequently the Federal Power Commission) to authorize construction of hydropower projects in national parks, as had happened with the inundation of Hetch Hetchy Valley in Yosemite National Park. In the political struggle that ensued over an amendment to the water power law that was intended to rescind the commission's authority, there was only a partial victory. Rather than removing the commission's power over all parks and monuments, the amendment, as approved by Congress, removed it from only the then-existing parks and monuments, but retained its authority over yet-to-be-established parks and monuments. This meant that each new park's enabling legislation would have to specifically exempt that park so it would not fall under the commission's power. While NPA fought hard on this issue, the political clout of the water power interests proved too strong for a complete victory.

In the 1920s, NPA also argued strongly again and again for maintaining high standards in establishing new national parks. As Yard wrote in the *Bulletin* (October 9, 1923):

> Several bills to create local National Parks below the standard quality are expected to be introduced into the next Congress. These bills will offer to "give" the Nation areas which enclose neither scenery of national importance nor sufficient area for fitting administration and the accommodation of park visitors. One such "national park" will open the door to scores of others, inviting wide competition for little local National Parks. We must permit no such precedent. National Park standards must not be lowered.

NPA felt the need to publish "A Statement of the National Policy" on national parks, in the *Bulletin* (December 1, 1923). It said in part:

> National Parks are areas of publicly-owned lands "set aside by the American Government to be maintained untouched by the inroads of modern civilization" . . . because they possess scenic significance of a quality to attract and itself hold national attention; or because they contain extraordinary remains of prehistoric civilization; or because they contain extraordinary examples of natural forests and . . . forms of wild life. . . .

> The historic and popular conception of the National Park System . . . is that of a gallery of masterpieces; necessarily it must be restricted in the future, as it has been in the past, to the noblest examples only, be they few or many, of the various includable kinds.

> While it is conceivable that many other public areas may usefully be conserved, that is one thing and creating a majestic, well-balanced National Parks System is another. The two must not be confused.

NPA also expressed concern about the National Park Service's independence from political interference: "It is the duty of the people to protect the National Park Service from political and other pressures tending to disturb its calm judgment and force its hand. . . ." Many decades later, NPCA is still deeply concerned about this need and has recommended that the agency be removed from the Interior Department and be set up as an independent agency.

In 1925, the Association urged the establishment of new parks, among them Shenandoah and Great Smoky Mountains, in the East; and Carlsbad Caverns, Bryce Canyon, and the area that ultimately became Kings Canyon and an expanded Sequoia, in the West.

In 1926, NPA pushed for expansion of park boundaries at Yellowstone, Grand Canyon, and Rocky Mountain. "The boundaries of the older parks were often established arbitrarily, following ruler lines drawn in far-away offices." Some of the proposed boundaries along the eastern side of Yellowstone would have been shifted from the arbitrary straight line to the natural topography of the crest of the Absaroka Range. The Association continues today to advocate such boundary adjustments for numerous parks.

In 1927, NPA actually urged the deletion of several "national parks" that it viewed as unworthy—including Hot Springs, Platt, and Sully's Hill. The latter was subsequently eliminated and Platt was redesignated finally, in 1976, as part of Chickasaw National Recreation Area.

The Association repeatedly promoted the idea that the national parks are an institution of learning— an "Outdoor University," "a great educational and spiritual reservoir for the nation." John C. Merriam, chairman of NPA's Advisory Board on Educational and Inspirational Uses of National Parks, wrote in a feature article in the *National Parks Bulletin* (July 1927):

> The need of education is never met merely in accumulation of facts. In some of its most important aspects education is essentially inspirational. It is through this form of expression that it exerts the largest influence in stimulation to constructive thought and in forming of ideals. . . . In the presence of these extraordinary aspects of nature [in the national parks], it is possible to widen and deepen our knowledge in such a way that the enlargement of thought or mental vision becomes a permanent condition, making possible fuller understanding of many things which might otherwise seem less striking.

Many new units were added to the Park System in the late 1920s and 1930s. The biggest shift in focus was the establishment of parks primarily for their historical theme and resources—beginning in 1930 with Colonial National Historical Park and George Washington Birthplace National Monument, in Virginia. A number of other historic areas were also transferred from military jurisdiction to the Park Service.

NPA accurately predicted that this new historical category of parks "will rapidly surpass, in the number of units, its world-celebrated scenic" parks. Today, there are approximately 200 historical units out of the total of 367. In addition, a variety of national capital parks were brought under the Park Service's care, including Washington, D.C.'s wooded valley "wilderness" that slices through the heart of the city—Rock Creek Park; and forest-covered Theodore Roosevelt Island in the Potomac River; along with parkways and a number of structures, including the Washington Monument and The White House.

With this substantial new expansion of the Park Service's management responsibilities, NPA expressed concern that the original natural National Parks could ultimately become compromised. NPA President William P. Wharton urged in *National Parks Bulletin* (February 1937) that the great natural parks be segregated under the descriptive title, the National Primeval Parks System. "National Primeval Parks," Wharton said, "should be kept distinct, we believe, not only in name, but also in administration, from all others." While this recommendation was never officially adopted, it reflected the Association's continuing emphasis on maintaining the high standards of the national parks.

In 1937, the *Bulletin* published an article on the then-proposed Everglades National Park. The author described the "vast flocks" and "successive waves" of white ibises and other wading birds:

> . . . the long lines reaching so far across the sky that the extreme tips of each flock appeared to touch the low mainland on the one hand and the distant rim of the Gulf on the other . . . There seemed no end to their incredible numbers! . . . The simple beauty and power of these swift-winged, grotesquely handsome creatures when observed in great flocks places them beside snow-mantled peaks, towering waterfalls and other natural treasures in their wide appeal and high inspirational value Attempt to count them as their headlong flight carries them by overhead.

One hundred, five hundred, one thousand! Two thousand in a single minute! Ten thousand birds winging swiftly! across the space between mainland and key in a five minute interval! As many as fifty and seventy-five thousand ibises crowding every available perch on the key for the duration of a single night.

No wonder NPA pushed hard for establishment of Everglades National Park. And no wonder the Association and the Everglades Coalition are today pushing so hard to restore the severely impaired Everglades ecosystem—where tragically there is now a mere one-tenth or less of the former avian abundance that existed in the 1930s and 1940s.

Of two other national park proposals in 1937, Big Bend in west Texas was finally established in 1944 and Sawtooth in Idaho has never been given park protection. Also in 1937, a new category of Park Service areas was initiated with authorization of Cape Hatteras National Seashore, in North Carolina. Not only a new category, it set a new precedent by allowing public hunting, a precedent that in later decades paved the way for other national seashores and lakeshores, national rivers, and national preserves to be opened to this consumptive use.

In 1938, history repeated itself with a new scheme in Congress to dam Yellowstone Lake and tunnel its raised waters into the Snake River for irrigation projects in Idaho. Fortunately, once again NPA and its allies were victorious in their defense of Yellowstone National Park.

In 1940, after a half-century of controversy, Kings Canyon National Park was established. But in a major compromise with the powerful California power and irrigation interests, two of the most scenic highlights—Tehipite Valley and Cedar Grove—were omitted from the park. Because of this compromise, NPA actually refused to support the park legislation. A few more years elapsed, however, and those spectacular places were added to the park and the water withdrawals were abandoned.

The late Devereux Butcher (father of this author) was hired in 1942 to take over NPA's leadership as executive secretary—a position he held until 1950; then serving as field representative until 1957. One of Butcher's initial priorities was to learn from his mentor, Robert Sterling Yard. They spent many long, fruitful hours together discussing park philosophy and history and the role of National Parks Association in the future.

There had been a period during the early part of World War II when *National Parks Bulletin* ceased to be published. Butcher agreed with Yard that public education must be a major goal of NPA, and in 1942 he started *National Parks Magazine*—a completely redesigned, more aesthetically appealing publication that came out four times a year. During his 15-year editorship, the magazine built upon the Association's earlier years of advocating high standards for new parks, battling against threats to the parks, and running articles to help educate and inspire the membership.

In the December 1938 *National Parks Bulletin*, the Association had published a document called "National Park Standards: A Declaration of Policy," which had been created and adopted by the Camp Fire Club of America in 1929. It was largely based upon the thinking of the Park Service and was subsequently endorsed by over a hundred organizations that were interested in the purpose, use, and protection of the national parks.

In the mid-1940s, Butcher refined and updated these "Standards" and published the document in the magazine. Over the subsequent several decades, the "National Park Standards: For the Establishment and Protection of National Parks and Monuments" was periodically further revised. The most recent version to "crystallize fundamental ideals" was written in 1976 and appears after this chapter. While the document does not address issues specific to other categories of Park System units, the basic ideals for park establishment and management generally apply to all areas within the National Park System.

There were some significant victories over threats to the parks during the 1940s and 1950s—among them the defeat of two proposed dams in Dinosaur National Monument and defeat of a dam adjacent to Glacier National Park, blocking of plans to log off virgin-growth Sitka spruce in Olympic National Park, and defeat of a dam that would have wiped out Mammoth Cave. During this period, relatively few new parks were established. Everglades was finally a reality in 1947, and Effigy Mounds in 1949 and Virgin Islands in 1956 were among the few newcomers.

One of the major controversies of these years broke out between NPA and the National Park Service. It concerned a congressionally authorized ten-year crash facilities-construction program. During and for a few years following World War II, there was virtually no available funding to maintain and expand facilities such as visitor centers, trails, roads, and housing for park personnel. As visitation began to escalate at a record pace in the early 1950s, conditions in the parks had declined so deplorably, with rumors that some parks might even be closed, that Congress finally authorized "Mission 66," an emergency construction program from 1956 to 1966.

NPA's Butcher was, by then, traveling frequently to many of the national parks and monuments. As the emergency construction work got under way, he saw first-hand and photographed many of the projects. Some of the new structures and roads outraged him, and the magazine carried illustrated reports from the field. In those days, of course, there was no National Environmental Policy Act (NEPA), requiring that significant projects be run through environmental-impact statement processes for public review and comment, as is the case today. Criticism was, therefore, usually ignored and the Park Service forged ahead. Architecture of visitor centers and other structures typically failed to reflect historic architectural themes or to reasonably harmonize visually with the natural environment. Many structures looked more suited to an urban setting than a national park.

In the years since Mission 66, the Park Service has tended to swing back to a more sensitive approach to buildings. Some visitor centers, as at Pecos and Point Reyes, are outstanding examples of structures that both blend with their settings and reflect a particular local architectural theme.

During the 1940s and 1950s, NPA also stiffened its opposition to pressures that would open the parks to public hunting. The hunting lobby has periodically tried to gain access to these special havens for people and wildlife. In the 1960s and 1970s, national seashores and lakeshores, national rivers, and national preserves were established—and many of them, including all the preserves, were opened to public hunting, following the earlier Cape Hatteras precedent.

While NPCA and other environmental groups never favored opening any unit of the National Park System to hunting, the powerful politics of this issue has often appeared to offer little or no chance of bringing these important new areas under the protective care of the Park Service unless hunting were allowed. For example, hunting was a key bone of contention over the proposed Mojave National Park in the California desert. When political push came to shove, the hunting provision was retained in the enabling legislation and Congress established instead the Mojave National Preserve. This is a designation that falsely implies a level of protective management that is higher than for a national park, but it is a category that actually authorizes one or more extractive resource uses that are not permitted in a park. The line has still been firmly held, therefore, against opening the national parks and monuments to public hunting. Perhaps someday, when the public's need greatly increases to have more havens for people that are free from conflict with hunting activities, the units of the park system currently open to this consumptive use may be closed.

In 1955, the Student Conservation Program was created under the sponsorship of NPA, to provide a way for high school and college students to volunteer for useful summer employment in the national parks. By 1960, the program had become so successful that it launched forth on its own as the Student Conservation Association. It continues today to administer an outstanding program that helps young people develop an appreciation of the parks and other public lands, and it provides the parks with an invaluable cadre of helping hands.

In the 1970s, NPA's name was changed to National Parks and Conservation Association, reflecting a desire at that time to broaden the focus on environmental issues beyond the national parks.

In 1980, Paul C. Pritchard took the reigns of leadership as NPCA's president. From 1980 to 1997, the Association experienced by far its greatest growth in membership in its 78-year history: from around 23,000 and declining, to 500,000 members and climbing.

In 1981, NPCA held a conference to discuss serious problems affecting the welfare of the National Park System, and the following year published a book on this theme, *National Parks in Crisis.*

In the 1980s and early 1990s, NPCA promoted and sponsored its nationwide March for Parks program, in conjunction with Earth Day in April. Money raised from the hundreds of marches goes entirely into local park projects—specific improvement needs, protection priorities, and educational projects for national, state, and local parks.

In 1988, the landmark nine-volume document, *National Park System Plan,* was issued—with new park and expanded park proposals, threats to park resources, an assessment of research needs, the importance of interpretation to the visitor's quality of experience, and issues relating to the internal organization of the National Park Service.

In 1990, the two-volume *Visitor Impact Management* document was released, and it found favor with the National Park Service because of its important and pragmatic discussions of carrying capacity and visitor-impact management methodology and case studies. This publication has also been welcomed by parks in other parts of the world.

In 1993, *Park Waters in Peril* was released, featuring threats jeopardizing park water resources and presenting a dozen case studies. As with earlier documents mentioned above, this volume's highly professional quality has made it of great value to the Park Service, as well as of educational value to the public.

In 1994, coinciding with NPCA's 75th anniversary, the Association held a major conference in San Francisco: "Citizens Protecting America's Parks: Joining Forces for the Future." As further advocacy of citizen participation, the Association published the book, *Our Endangered Parks: What You Can Do to Protect Our National Heritage.*

Education. Education. Education. That is what NPA/NPCA has been focused on for all these many years, on behalf of protecting the National Park System. That is what its growing number of publications is designed to do—to educate and inspire and lead. And of course, *National Parks* magazine continues its role of educating its readers—with news, editorial opinion, and descriptive feature articles.

In 1983, NPCA began launching a new venture with the creation of the National Park Trust. Its primary mission is the purchase of private inholdings for addition to the surrounding parks, the purchase of important adjacent lands, and the purchase of lands for new units of the park system. By using private moneys in its revolving fund, the Trust can generally act more swiftly to save threatened or key lands than can the federal government. While the Trust is now an independent organization, it cooperates on projects with NPCA.

Since its founding, National Park Trust has acquired a group of historic mining structures in Wrangell-St. Elias National Park & Preserve, in Alaska; purchased a four-acre tract of private land in Acadia National Park, in Maine, that was slated for real estate development; acquired the last privately owned parcel in Ft. Laramie National Historic Site, in Wyoming; purchased a five-acre inholding in Gates of the Arctic National Park, in Alaska, and dismantled a hunting camp that had provided hunters with a convenient base for access into a vast area of the park's wilderness; and acquired two important tracts within Big Cypress National Preserve: 100 acres of valued Florida panther habitat and a lodge that was in disrepair, which has been converted into the preserve's headquarters. Most recently the Trust acquired the Z Bar/Spring Hill Ranch in the Flint Hills of eastern Kansas—an ecologically rich area of grassland, established in 1996 as the Tallgrass Prairie National Preserve. For further information: National Park Trust, 1776 Massachusetts Ave., NW, Washington, D.C. 20016. Telephone (202) 659-0996.

Also during the 1980s, the Association began setting up regional offices, starting in the Pacific Southwest. By 1994, this regional office network blanketed virtually all of the country, thereby greatly increasing NPCA's effectiveness in keeping up with issues and problems in and adjacent to the parks, providing the organization's views and comments on park threats and Park Service planning proposals, seeking the assistance of grassroots volunteers, and communicating with other environmental representatives and the press in each region.

As NPCA and its committed and caring Board of Trustees, staff, and volunteers face the challenges of park protection in the future, the words of the Association's past president Wallace W. Atwood, in 1929, are as timely now as then:

> All who join our Association have the satisfaction that comes only from unselfish acts; they will help carry forward a consistent and progressive program . . . for the preservation and most appropriate utilization of the unique wonderlands of our country. Join and make this work more effective.

Everyone who cares can help make a difference—a difference in determining how well we succeed in passing along the priceless and irreplaceable natural and cultural treasures of the National Park System unimpaired for the generations yet to come. Like candles shining their light in the darkness, each flame, no matter how small, helps to sustain and nurture one of the noblest endeavors in the entire history of mankind—the national parks that began so many years ago at Yellowstone and have spread and blossomed around the world.

NATIONAL PARK STANDARDS FOR THE ESTABLISHMENT AND PROTECTION OF NATIONAL PARKS AND MONUMENTS

This statement of policy is a revision of the Standards originally developed by the Camp Fire Club of America in the 1920s and endorsed by nearly a hundred organizations. Offered to help crystallize fundamental ideals, it is based on the thinking of the National Park Service and a number of individuals and organizations, including National Parks and Conservation Association, since the establishment of the first national park in 1872.

DEFINITIONS

National Parks. National Parks are spacious land and water areas of national significance, established as inviolable sanctuaries for the permanent protection of scenery, wilderness, and native fauna and flora in their ecologically natural condition. National parks are composed of wilderness essentially in a primeval or natural condition, containing scenic and ecological magnificence and of a wide variety of features. Their unequaled quality and unique inspirational beauty distinguish them from all other places, and make imperative their protection, unimpaired for human enjoyment, education, and inspiration in perpetuity. National Parks are established by Act of Congress.

National (Nature) Monuments. National (Nature) Monuments are established to protect specific natural phenomena of such significance that their preservation is in the national interest. They are outstanding examples of their kind, and are given the same degree of federal protection as the national parks. While there are wilderness and magnificent scenery in most of the larger monuments, the primary purpose of these monuments is usually to protect specific geological formations, biological features, or other significant specific aspects of the natural environment. The smaller national monuments differ from the parks in that they usually do not contain as wide a variety of outstanding features. National monuments may be established either by Act of Congress or presidential proclamation, under authority of the Antiquities Act of 1906.

National (Archaeological) Monuments. National monuments with archaeological features as their primary theme are established specifically to protect the structures and other remains of indigenous civilization. They are administered under the same protective principles as apply to other national monuments, and may be established either by Act of Congress or presidential proclamation.

National Historical Parks, (Historical) Monuments, and Historic Sites. National parks, monuments, and sites, commemorating nationally significant historical events and people and containing nationally significant historical structures and sites as their primary theme, are administered under the same protective principles as other units of the National Park System. National historical parks and national historic sites are established by Act of Congress, and national (historical) monuments may be established either by Act of Congress or presidential proclamation.

APPLICATION OF PRINCIPLES

National Parks and Monuments Are of National Importance. An area should be evaluated on the merits of national park or monument status and commitment to federal care by the degree of its value and interest to the nation as a whole. Every proposal for establishing of a new national park, monument, or site should be carefully examined, to assure that places of less than national significance are not added to the National Park System.

Adequate Area Is Needed. National parks and national (nature) monuments are set aside for the enjoyment, scientific study, and permanent protection of the native flora and fauna and other features. Each should be a comprehensive unit embracing an area of sufficient size for effective protective management. Where feasible, parks should ideally encompass complete ecological and scenic units—such as watersheds, with boundaries that avoid slicing arbitrarily through areas of ecological or scenic significance.

Protection Is Based on Scientific and Esthetic Values. Federal guardianship of national parks and national (nature) monuments should be solidly based upon sound scientific research that leads to enhanced understanding and protection of natural ecological processes, wilderness values, water and air quality, and flora and fauna—including rare and endangered species. Adequate research that is relevant to resource protection is absolutely vital to the welfare of the National Park System. Insufficient science-based data and a lack of understanding of what is actually occurring within complex park ecosystems poses a threat to the environmental health and the inspirational value of these priceless parklands. Monitoring of visitor-use impacts upon park resources and upon the quality of visitor experience is also a major research priority.

Congress Intends Enjoyment of Unimpaired Nature. When Congress adopted the National Parks Act of 1916, establishing the National Park Service, it made this agency the guardian of the National Park System, directing it to "conserve the scenery and the natural and historic objects and the wildlife therein, and to provide for the enjoyment of the same in such manner and by such means as will leave them unimpaired for the enjoyment of future generations." Public enjoyment of the natural and cultural features in the national parks and monuments is one of their basic reasons for being. These magnificent places are, in fact, outdoor universities where visitors may learn about and be inspired by the natural and cultural values the parks contain.

Private Inholdings Are Being Acquired. The acquisition of privately owned lands within national parks and national monuments is imperative to facilitate administration and protection, and to prevent intrusion of undesirable developments and activities on them. Such acquisition should be carried out as rapidly as feasible.

Commercial Uses Are Inappropriate. Commercial uses of national park and monument resources are inconsistent with the mission of protecting the parks *unimpaired.* Such extractive resource uses would harm or destroy natural ecological conditions and the natural scenery. Mining, timber harvesting, livestock grazing, and damming of watercourses are among commercial activities that are contrary to the fundamental principals upon which the protective management of the National Park System is based. Where grazing, mining, dams, and other degrading, non-park-related uses and facilities exist, they should be eliminated as soon as feasible.

Amusement Attractions Are Inconsistent. National parks and monuments are not commercial resorts or amusement centers. The introduction of incongruous recreational features diminishes visitors' enjoyment of the basic qualities of the parks. Resort amusement facilities, which are abundantly available elsewhere, detract from the wilderness atmosphere, and impair the quality of experience for visitors seeking inspiration from nature unimpaired.

Interpretation Is the Key to Appreciation. Interpretive programs, including visitor center and museum exhibits, books and other educational literature available for purchase, movie and video presentations, interpretive talks, ranger-led walks, and self-guided tours, are all part of a vital educational service for visitors in the parks and monuments. Trained volunteers assist with many of these programs. Because interpretation leads to understanding, and understanding to appreciation, these programs are vital to the visitor's enjoyment of the parks. An informed and appreciative public is ultimately the strongest advocate for protecting the parks from threats to their integrity.

Protection of Fauna and Flora Is Fundamental. Hunting in national parks and monuments is inconsistent with the idea of providing sanctuary for both people and wildlife, and is prohibited in national parks and monuments. Whenever scientific research shows, however, that a native species has become so abundant as to threaten the health of its habitat or the survival of another species, the National Park Service has authority to reduce its numbers in an ecologically sensitive and scientifically appropriate manner.

Commercial fishing is incompatible with the concept that the national parks and monuments are sanctuaries for native fauna. Commercial fishing is prohibited in most parks, and where it still occurs, it should be eliminated as soon as feasible. Sport fishing, where legal, should ideally emphasize the practice of capture and release. Where stocking is required, it should be carried out only with species that are native to the specific lake or stream.

Indiscriminate cutting of trees and shrubs and other native vegetation is inconsistent with basic park-resource protection. At important scenic overlooks along roads and trails, and at places where visitors may observe outstanding natural or cultural features, discrete thinning of vegetation is sometimes appropriate. In heavy use areas such as campgrounds and picnic areas, the removal of vegetation should always be carried out under ecologically sensitive, trained supervision.

Mechanical Noise Intrudes Upon the Natural Quiet. Low-elevation overflights of helicopters and fixed-wing aircraft create noise that can greatly impair the park visitor's quality of experience on the ground. Since protecting the natural quiet is one of the objectives of national parks and monuments, airtour and other nonessential low-elevation overflights should be banned above the national parks and monuments. Where such tour flights already exist, they should be carefully regulated to minimize intrusive noise impacts upon park visitors. Low altitude flights should, of course, be permitted for emergency search-and-rescue operations and other truly essential park management services.

Because motorized recreation, including the use of snowmobiles, jetskis, and powerboats, can disturb both wildlife and other visitors, these kinds of activities should be and in most places are prohibited in the national parks and monuments. Opportunities for motorized recreation are abundantly available elsewhere. Where these recreational activities are presently permitted in the parks, to be consistent with basic park protection policies they should be eliminated. The use of snowmobiles for emergency search-and-rescue and other essential park-management services should, of course, be permitted.

Roads Should Be Held to a Minimum. Only such roads as are truly essential to provide appropriate access for visitors should be built in national parks and monuments. Roads should be located to intrude as little as possible upon sensitive natural and cultural resources and the scenery. They should be carefully designed and constructed for leisurely driving that offers a feeling of being embraced by the natural environment, rather than speeding through it. Park roads should sensitively follow the natural terrain's contours providing the least possible physical and visual impact upon the environment. Where park roads have been inappropriately situated in ecologically or scenically sensitive places, efforts should be made to remove them. There is mounting concern over the increasing numbers of oversize motor vehicles, such as motor-homes and tour buses, whose size demands invasive public works (wider and straighter roads and larger parking areas) that are inconsistent with the intimacy of existing park roads. If we are not to sacrifice much of the integrity of the parks, ways must be found to accommodate motor vehicular use to the needs of park protection, rather than accommodating the parks to the ever-escalating impact of the motor vehicle.

Buildings Should Be Designed to Harmonize with the Environment. Buildings within national parks and monuments should be designed to be as unobtrusive as possible. Architectural design, materials, and colors should all conspire to minimize the visual impact of park structures, and to harmonize with the surrounding environment. Wherever feasible, buildings should incorporate energy-saving technologies. Structures should be situated so as to impact sensitive park resources and the natural scenery as little as possible. Except for worthy historic buildings, where existing structures occupy ecologically and scenically sensitive sites, every effort should be made to ultimately remove them.

Concession Operations Should Be Only for Essential Services. Concession operations should be granted only for the necessary care of visitors, such as lodging and food services. They should be operated so as not to lower the dignity of the parks and should be restricted to appropriate locations that have a minimal impact upon the natural environment. The parks are not established to provide opportunities for concessionaires to profit from inappropriate crowd-attracting facilities and amusements. A fair proportion of concession profits should be returned directly to the parks for enhanced protective management.

The Violation of One Park Is a Threat to All. Any infraction of these principles in any national park or monument potentially poses a threat to all national parks and monuments. If we are to succeed in truly protecting the integrity and quality of the national parks for the enjoyment of future generations, they must be held uncompromisingly inviolate.

EPILOGUE

The accurate knowledge of what has happened will be
useful, because, according to human probability, similar
things will happen again.

—Thucydides
Fifth century, B.C.

FURTHER READING

Agar, Herbert. *The Price of Union.* Boston: Houghton Mifflin Company, 1950.

Albright, Horace M., and Robert Cahn. *The Birth of the National Park Service: The Founding Years, 1913-33.* Salt Lake City, Utah: Howe Brothers, 1985.

Batty, Peter, and Peter Parish. *The Divided Union: The Story of the Great American War 1861–65.* Topsham, Massachusetts: Salem House Publishers, 1987.

Butcher, Devereux. *Exploring Our National Parks and Monuments* (9th edition, by Russell D. Butcher). Boulder, Colorado: Roberts Rinehart Publishers, 1995.

Champagne, Duane. *Native America: Portrait of the Peoples.* Detroit, Michigan: Visible Ink Press, 1994.

Darling, F. Fraser, and Noel D. Eichhorn. *Man and Nature in the National Parks: Reflections on Policy.* Washington, D.C.: The Conservation Foundation, 1969.

Davis, William C. *Civil War Parks: The Story Behind the Scenery®.* Las Vegas, Nevada: KC Publications, Inc., 1984.

DenDooven, K.C., publisher. *The Story Behind the Scenery®* series on many national parks; and *The Continuing Story: In Pictures* series. Las Vegas, Nevada: KC Publications, Inc.

Drain, Thomas A. *A Sense of Mission: Historic Churches of the Southwest.* (Photography by David Wakely.) San Francisco: Chronicle Books, 1994.

Everhart, William C. *The National Park Service.* New York: Praeger Publishers, 1972.

Fontana, Bernard L. *Entrada: The Legacy of Spain & Mexico in the United States.* Tucson, Arizona: Southwest Parks and Monuments Association, 1994.

Frome, Michael. *Regreening the National Parks.* Tucson, Arizona: The University of Arizona Press, 1992.

Hagmann, Marnie. *Hawaii Parklands: An interpretive companion to Hawaii's national, state, county, and private parks.* Honolulu: Hawai'i Geographic Society, 1988.

Harmon, David (editor). *Mirror of America: Literary Encounters with the National Parks.* Boulder, Colorado: Roberts Rinehart Publishers, 1989.

Ise, John. *Our National Park Policy: A Critical History.* Baltimore, Maryland: The Johns Hopkins Press, 1961, 1967.

Kennedy, Francis H. (editor). *The Civil War Battlefield Guide.* (The Conservation Fund.) Boston: Houghton Mifflin Co., 1990.

Lavender, David. *De Soto, Coronado, Cabrillo: Explorers of the Northern Mystery.* Washington: National Park Service, 1992.

Lawliss, Chuck. *The Civil War Sourcebook: A Traveler's Guide.* New York: Harmony Books, 1991.

Lister, Robert H., and Florence C. Lister. *Those Who Came Before: Southwestern Archeology in the National Park System.* Tucson, Arizona: Southwest Parks and Monuments Association, 1983, 1994.

Miles, John C. *Guardians of the Parks: A History of the National Parks and Conservation Association.* Washington, D.C.: Taylor & Francis, 1995.

Mills, Enos A. *Your National Parks.* Boston: Houghton Mifflin Co., 1917.

Muir, John. *Our National Parks.* 1901. (Reprint.) Madison, Wisconsin: The University of Wisconsin Press, 1981.

National Parks and Conservation Association. *National Park Guides* (8 regional guidebooks). Washington, D.C.: NPCA, 1996.

_____. *National Parks Activist Guide: A Manual for Citizen Action.* Washington, D.C.: NPCA, 1993.

_____. *National Parks in Crisis.* Washington, D.C.: NPCA, 1982.

_____. *Our Endangered Parks: What You Can Do to Protect Our National Heritage.* Washington, D.C.: NPCA, 1994.

_____. *Visitor Impact Management* (2 volumes). Washington, D.C.: NPCA, 1990.

National Park Service. *Management Policies.* Washington, D.C.: NPS, 1988.

_____. *National Parks for the 21st Century: The Vail Agenda.* Washington, D.C.: NPS, 1992.

_____. *The National Parks: Index 1995.* Washington, D.C.: U.S. Government Printing Office, 1995.

_____. *The National Parks: Shaping the System.* Washington, D.C.: U.S. Government Printing Office, 1991.

_____. *Washington, DC: Official National Park Guidebook.* Washington, D.C.: U.S. Government Printing Office, 1989.

O'Shea, Richard. *American Heritage Battle Maps of the Civil War.* (Maps by David Greenspan.) Tulsa, Oklahoma: Council Oak Books, 1992.

Pohanka, Brian C. *Don Troiani's Civil War.* (Excellent reproductions of paintings by Don Troiani.) Mechanicsburg, Pennsylvania: Stackpole Books, 1995.

Robertson, James I., Jr. *Civil War Virginia: Battleground for a Nation.* Charlottesville, Virginia: University Press of Virginia, 1991, 1994.

Runte, Alfred. *National Parks: The American Experience.* Lincoln, Nebraska: The University of Nebraska Press, 1979, 1987.

Sax, Joseph L. *Mountains Without Handrails: Reflections on the National Parks.* Ann Arbor, Michigan: The University of Michigan Press, 1980.

Shankland, Robert. *Steve Mather of the National Parks.* New York: Alfred A. Knopf, 1951.

Smithsonian Institution. *Smithsonian's Great Battles of the Civil War* (8 video volumes). New York: Mastervision, 1992.

_____. *The Smithsonian Guide to Historic America* (12 volumes). New York: Stewart, Tabori & Chang, 1989.

Straubing, Harold Elk. *In Hospital and Camp: The Civil War through the Eyes of Its Doctors and Nurses.* Harrisburg, Pennsylvania: Stackpole Books, 1993.

Tilden, Freeman. *The National Parks.* New York: Alfred A. Knopf, 1968.

Time-Life. *Civil War Journal* (30 videos). Alexandria, Virginia: Time-Life Video, 1993.

_____. *The Civil War* (28 volumes). Alexandria, Virginia: Time-Life Books, 1983-1987.

_____. *How the West Was Lost* (13 videos, on the cultural clash between the Euro-Americans and the indigenous native American peoples that drove most of the latter from their homelands and decimated their cultures). Alexandria, Virginia: Time-Life Video, 1993.

Yard, Robert Sterling. *The Book of the National Parks.* New York: Charles Scribner's Sons, 1919, 1928.

INDEX

Abiel Smith School 342, 344
Abo Pueblo & church 116–118
Abraham Lincoln Birthpl. NHS 297
Acadia NP 478, 482, 485
Acoma Pueblo 33
Adams NHS 298
Adams, John 298
Adams, John Quincy 298
Affiliated parks 437
African Amer. in U.S. History parks 341
African Amer. Soldier exhibit 232
African Meeting House 342–344
African–Amer. Civil War Mem. 210
Alcatraz Island 417, 418
Alcott, Louisa May 162
Aldo Leopold Farm 478
Aleuts 132–133
Allegheny Portage 1
Alvarado, Hernando de 33
American Fur Company 54
American Jewish Council 352
American Mem. Park 437
American Negro Labor Council 352
American Red Cross 335
Amicalola River 465
Amistad NRA 401
Anasazi Culture Sites 465
Andersonville NHS 210
Andersonville N Cemetery 212
Andrew Johnson NHS 299
Anthony, Susan B. 338
Antietam NB 212, 487
Antietam, Battle of 213–215
Anza, Juan Bautista de 446
Apache Pass, Battle of 188
Apaches 117, 122, 143–144, 187–189, 191, 201, 202
Appalachian NST 445
Appleton, Elaine 496–497
Appomattox Court House 216
Arapahoes 195, 202, 205
Arctic N Wildlife Refuge 465
Arikaras 92
Arkansas Post N Mem. 2
Arlington House 219
Arlington N Cemetery 220
Army of No. Virginia 212, 218, 238, 245, 250, 258, 259
Army of Tennessee 223, 251
Army of the Cumberland 225
Army of the Potomac 213, 227, 238, 258, 259
Arnold, Gen. Benedict 152, 170, 171
Assateague NS 494
Assiniboines 55
Atchafalaya Basin 465
Atwood, Wallace W. 517
Audubon, John James 55
Automobile congestion 489

Baltimore & Ohio Railroad 18
Bandelier NM 474, 490, 497
Baranov, Aleksandr 132

Barataria Preserve 80
Barns of Wolf Trap 380
Bartholdi, Frederic-Auguste 135
Barton, Clara 335
Beauregard, Gen. Pierre G.T. 236, 254–7, 264–5, 276
Benjamin Franklin N Mem. 437
Bent's Old Fort 6
Bent, St. Vrain & Co. 6
Bent, Wím & Charles 6, 7
Berger, David 438
Bethune, Mary McLeod 354–355
Big Bend NP 500, 504
Big Hole NB 185
Big Sur Coast 466
Bighorn Canyon NRA 402
Blackfeet 54
Black Heritage Trail 344, 346
Black River 466
Blackstone River Valley 437
Blackwater River 466
Bodmer, Karl 55
Booker T. Washington NHS 341–342
Boone, Daniel 35
Booth, John Wilkes 302
Borglum, Gutzon 322
Borglum, Lincoln 323
Boston NHP 8
Boston African American 342–343
Bragg, Gen. Braxton 223–226, 279–281
Brice's Cross Rds. NB 221
Brown v. Board of Education 345–346
Brown, John 68, 69
Bryant, Harold C. 496
Bryce Canyon NP 502
Burgoyne, Gen. John 151, 169–171
Burnside, Gen. Ambrose E. 215–217, 238–242
Butcher, Devereux xiv, xv, 504, 505
Butterfield Overland Mail 130, 187
Buttrick, Maj. John 161

Cabrillo NM 11
Cabrillo, Juan Rodriguez 11
Caddo Culture Mounds Sites 466
Caddos 406
Cahokia Mounds 466
California NHT 445
Camp Fire Club of Amer. 504, 508
Canyonlands NP 497–498
Cape Cod NS 494
Cape Hatteras NS 504, 505
Cape Lookout NS 494
Carib–Tainos 119
Caribbean NF/Yunque 466
Carl Sandburg Home NHS 359–361
Carlsbad Caverns NP 502
Carpenters' Hall 72, 76
Carter, Jimmy 312
Carver, George Washington 338–350
Casas Grandes Culture Sites 466
Castillo de San Cristobal 127

Castillo de S. Felipe del Morro 127
Castillo de San Marcos 14
Castle Clinton NM 177
Caswell, Col. Richard 163
Catlin, George 55
Catoctin Mountain Park 403
Cayuse 145–147
Center for Nonviolent Soc. Change 353
Central Pacific Railroad 59–61
Chamizal N Mem. 16
Chancellorsville, Battle of 240, 244
Channel Islands NP 480, 497
Charbonneau, Toussaint 44
Charles Pinckney NHS 17
Charlie, Tagish 89
Chattahoochee River 405
Chattanooga, Battle of 226–226
Cherokees 197, 199, 442–444
Chesapeake & Ohio Canal xv, 17, 67
Cheyennes 192, 195, 202
Chicago Portage 438
Chickamauga & Chattanooga 221
Chickamauga, Battle of 224–226
Chickasaw NRA 406, 502
Chickasaws 3, 38, 199, 406
Chiricahua Apaches 187–188, 191
Chiricahua NM 490
Chitimachas 81, 82
Choctaws 199, 406
Christiansted NHS 21
Cicuye Pueblo 33, 100
City of Rocks N Res. 23
Civil War parks 209
Clara Barton NHS 335
Clark, Cap't. William 44–47, 91, 446–447
Clark, Col. George Rogers 152
Clatsops 45, 46
Coahuiltecans 121, 122
Cobscook Bay & Cutler Coast 466
Cochrane, Adm. Alexander 178
Cold Harbor, Battle of 272
Cole, Thomas, 466
Colonial NHP xv, 24, 480, 503
Columbus, Christopher 119
Comanches 102, 117, 122, 190, 195, 201, 202, 406
Congress Hall 75
Constitution Gardens 393
Constitution, U.S. xv, 74
Cornwallis, Gen. Charles Earl 29–30, 149, 155–157, 158, 160, 167
Coronado N Mem. 32
Coronado, Francisco V. de 32–33
Coulee Dam NRA 408
Cowpens NB 149
Craig, Bruce 494
Crater Lake NP 481
Crater, Battle of the 263
Creek Indian War 203–204
Creeks 199, 203–204
Crocker, Charles 59

Crows 55
Cumberland Gap NHP 34
Curecanti NRA 409
Custer, George A. 196, 205–207
Cuyahoga Valley NRA 410

Dams and Diversions 473
David Berger 438
Davis, Gary E. 497
Davis, Jefferson 225, 236, 254, 270, 273
Dayton Aviation Heritage 381
De Bell, Garrett 490–491
Death Valley NP 476, 497
Declaration House 72, 76
Declaration of Independence xv, 73–74
Declaration of Sentiments 338
Delaware & Lehigh Nav. Canal 438
Delaware Water Gap NRA 412
De Soto, Hernando 37–39
De Soto N Mem. 37
Dinosaur NM 473–474, 476, 477, 505
Dirty Devil River Canyons 467
Douglas, William O. 19
Douglass, Frederick 69, 350
Dugua de Mons, Pierre 112–113

Early, Gen. Jubal A. 227, 248, 259–262
Ebey's Landing NH Res. 40
Edgar Allan Poe NHS 362
Edison NHS 382
Edison, Thomas A. 382
Effigy Mounds NM 505
Eiffel, Gustave 136
Eisenhower, Dwight D. 301–302
Eisenhower NHS 301
El Morro NM xvi, 41
Eleanor Roosevelt NHS 336
Ellis Is. Immigration Museum 137–140
Ellis Island 134, 137–140
Emerson, Ralph Waldo 161
Emigrant Trail 467
Escalante River Canyons 467
Eugene O'Neill NHS 363
Evans, Rudulph 327
Everglades NP 477, 478, 505
Exploring Our Nat'l Parks & Mons., xvii, xix

Faneuil Hall 8–9
Faneuil, Peter 8
Father Marquette N Mem. 439
Federal Hall 42
Ferguson, Maj. Patrick 158
Filene Center 379–380
Fire Island NS 504
First Bank of the U.S. Bldg. 75
Fogelson, Mr.& Mrs. E.E. 103
Ford's Theatre NHS 302
Forrest, Gen. Nathan B. 221–222, 282
Fort Bowie NHS 187

Fort Caroline N Mem. 43
Fort Christiansvaern 21–22
Fort Circle Parks 227
Fort Clatsop N Mem. 44
Fort Davis NHS xvi, 190
Fort Donelson NB 229
Fort Dupont 228
Fort Foote 228
Fort Frederica NM 48
Fort Laramie NHS 192, 507
Fort Laramie Treaty 193, 206
Fort Larned NHS 194
Fort Marcy 227
Fort Mason 417, 419
Fort Matanzas NM 49
Fort McHenry NM 177
Fort Moultrie 235–236
Fort Necessity NB 50
Fort Point NHS xvi, 231–232
Fort Pulaski NM 233
Fort Raleigh NHS 51
Fort Scott NHS 197
Fort Smith NHS 198
Fort Stanwix NM 151
Fort Stevens 227, 262
Fort Sumter NM 235
Fort Union NM 201
Fort Union Trading Post 54
Fort Vancouver NHS 56
Fort Ward 228
Fort Washington Park 180
Fr. Damien 86
Franklin, Benjamin 76–77
Franklin Court 76
F. D. Roosevelt Mem. 303
Frederick Douglass NHS 346–347
Frederick Law Olmsted 364
Fredericksb'g & Spotsyl. xii, 233–244, 487
Free Quaker Meet. House 77
Freedom Trail 8, 11
Freer Gallery of Art 395
French Quarter 78–79, 82
French, Daniel Chester 318
Friendship Hill NHS 58
Frobisher, Ben. & Jos. 62
Frost, Robert 467

Gaget, Gauthier, & Compie 135
Gaines' Mill, Battle of 270–272, 275
Gansevoort, Col. Peter 151
Garfield, James A. NHS 311
Gates, Gen. Horatio 170–171
Gateway NRA 413, 494
Gateway Arch 83
General Grant N Mem. 304
George Rogers Clark NHP 152
George Washington Birthpl. 304, 503
George Washington Carver NM 348–349
George Washington Parkway 305
Geronimo 188, 191

Gettysburg Address 250–251
Gettysburg N Cemetery 247
Gettysburg NMP xv, 245, 250, 261, 286
Glacier NP 474, 479, 505
Glen Canyon Dam 475–476
Glen Canyon NRA 415
Glen Echo Park 365–366
Gloria Dei Church NHS 439
Glorieta, Battle of 100, 102–103
Golden Gate Bridge 231, 232
Golden Spike NHS 59
Gran Quivira 116–117
Grand Canyon NP 474–476, 483, 484, 488–489,
        490, 492, 497, 498, 499, 502
Grand Canyon Railway 488
Grand Council of Indians 200
Grand Portage NM 62
Grant, Ulysses S. 216–219, 225–230, 242, 243, 251,
        264–268, 272, 273, 276–278, 282–286.
        304, 329
Grant-Kohrs Ranch 64
Great Falls Park 420
Great Smoky Mtns. NP 482, 483, 485, 487, 502
Greene, Gen. Nathaniel 156, 160, 168
Green Springs H Dist. 439
Greenbelt Park 421
Guadalupe Mtns. NP 494
Guam, Battle of 296
Guilford Courthouse NMP 155

Haleakala NP 484
Hamilton Grange N Mem. 66
Hamilton, Alexander 66
Hampton NHS 367
Hansen's disease 85–86
Hansen, Armauer 85
Harpers Ferry 66
Harry S Truman NHS 306
Hawaii Volcanoes NP 484
Hawaiian Cultural Festival 110
Hawthorne, Nathaniel 162
Hayes, Alden C. 102, 103
Hells Canyon 467
Herbert Hoover NHS 308
Hetch Hetchy Dam 474
Hewett, Dr. Edgar L. 118
Hidatsas 91–93
Hill, Gen. A.P. 215, 239–241, 248
Hirshhorn Museum 395
Historic Camden 439
Home of F. D. Roosevelt 309
Homestead NM 69
Homestead Act 69
Hooker, Gen. Joseph 212, 225, 239–243, 245, 271
Hoover Dam 423–424
Hoover, Herbert 308–309
Hopewell Furnace NHS 383
Hopis 33, 71
Hopkins, Mark 59
Horseshoe Bend NMP 203

Howe, Gen. Sir William 151, 174
Hubbell Trading Post 71
Hubbell, John & Lina 71
Hudson's Bay Company 54, 56, 57
Hunt, Jane 338
Hunt, Richard Morris 136
Huntington, Collis P. 59

Ice Age N Scenic Trail 445
Ice Age N Scient. Res. 440, 445
Illinois & Michigan Canal 440
Independence NHP xv, 72
Independence Hall xv, 73–74
Inscription Rock 41
International Peace Garden 440

Jackson, Gen. Thomas J. "Stonewall" 213–214,
      238–242, 244, 258–260
James A. Garfield NHS 311
Jamestown 24
Jamestown Island xv, 24
Jamestown NHS xv, 28
Jarvis, T. Destry 498–499
Jean Lafitte NHP 78
Jefferson Expansion Mem. 83
Jefferson, Thomas xiii, 44, 83, 327–328
Jemez Mtns./Valles Caldera 467–468
Jemez State Monument 118
Jicarilla Apaches 201
Jim, Skookum 89
Jimmy Carter NHS 312
John F. Kennedy NHS 313
John Marshall House 468
John Muir NHS 368
Johnson, Andrew 299–301
Johnson, Lyndon B. 139, 313, 319, 320–321
Johnston, Gen. Joseph E. 216, 219, 225, 251, 252,
      256, 269, 270
Johnstown Flood N Mem. 85
Joliet, Louis 438
Jordan, Barbara 139–140
Juan Bautista de Anza NHT 446
Judah, Theodore 59, 61

Kalaupapa NHP 85
Kaloko–Honokohau NHP 86
Kamehameha I 88, 106, 109
Katmai NP 480
Kauai 468
Kearny, Stephen W. 197, 198
Kenai Fjords NP 490
Kenilworth Aquatic Gardens 394
Kennedy, John F. 313
Kennesaw Mountain NBP 251
Keweenaw NHP 384
Key, Francis Scott 178–179
Kidder, Alfred V. 102
King, Rev. Martin Luther, Jr. xiii, 352–353
Kings Canyon NP 474, 481, 483, 504
Kings Mountain NMP 158

Kino, Padre Eusebio F. 142–143
Kiowas 195, 202
Klondike Gold Rush NHP 89
Knife River Indian Villages 91
Kohrs, Conrad 64
Korean War Vets. Mem. 291
Kosciuszko, Col. Thaddeus 170, 173

Lafitte, Jean 78
Lafitte, Pierre 78
Lake Chelan NRA 422
Lake Erie, Battle of 182
Lake Mead NRA 423
Lake Meredith NRA 426
Lake of the Arbuckles 406
Lake Powell 415–417, 494
Lakotas 205–208
Lambert, Darwin 499
Las Humanas Pueblo 116–118
Lassen Volcanic NP 486
LBJ Boyhood Home 320
LBJ Ranch 320–321
Lee, Robert E. 68, 212, 213, 215–220, 238, 241–245,
      248–250, 254, 258–261, 265–266, 270–273
Lefebvre de Laboulaye, E.R. 135
Leopold, Aldo 468
Lewis & Clark NHT 446
Lewis, Cap't. Meriwether 44–47, 92, 446–447
Lexington Green 162
Liberty Bell Pavilion 77
Liberty Island 134, 136
Library Hall 76
Lillington, Col. Alexander 163
Lincoln Boyhood N Mem. 314
Lincoln Home NHS 316
Lincoln Memorial xiii, 317
Lincoln, Abraham xiii, 236, 238, 240, 245, 250–251, 254, 262,
      269, 270, 275, 284, 287, 302–303, 314–318, 319, 322, 323
Little Bighorn BNM 205
Longfellow NHS 370
Longfellow, Henry W. 370–371
Longstreet, Gen. James 224, 240, 246, 248, 249, 258, 259
Lowell NHP 386
Lyndon B. Johnson Grove 305, 319
Lyndon B. Johnson NHP 320

M'Clintock House 337, 339, 339
M'Clintock, Mary Ann 338
Mabilas 38
Maggie L. Walker NHS 350–351
Malibu Creek State Park 433, 434
Mammoth Cave 474, 479, 505
Manassas NBP xv, 229, 254, 255
Manassas, Battle of 1st 227, 254–258, 260, 276, 287
Manassas, Battle of 2nd 258–260, 268
Mandans 91–93
Manzanar NHS 292
Marquette, Jacques 439
Marshall, John 468
Martin Luther King, Jr., NHS 352

Martin Van Buren NHS 321
Martin, Terri 494
Mary McLeod Bethune NHS 354–355
Marye's Heights 238, 240, 244
Mather, Stephen T. 501
McClellan, Gen. George B. 212, 213, 226, 238, 243,
    257–259, 268–271, 274, 287
McDowell, Gen. Irvin 254–257, 268–269
McLoughlin House NHS 441
McLoughlin, John 56
McTavish, Simon 62
Meade, Gen. George G. 239, 240, 242, 245–249, 251
Merriam, John C. 503
Mesa Verde NP 483
Micronesia 468
Mikveh Israel Cemetery 77
Mimbres Culture Sites 468
Minute Man NHP 160
Misty Fiords 468
Mobile-Tensas R. Bottomlands 468
Mojave N Pres. 505
Monocacy, Battle of 227, 262–262
Monocacy NB 262–262
Monroe Elementary School 346
Moores Creek NB 163
Morgan, Gen. Daniel 149, 156
Mormon Pioneer NHT 447
Mormons 103, 129, 447
Morristown NHP 165
Mott, Lucretia 338
Mount Rushmore N Mem. xvi, 322
Mount Vernon Trail 305
Muir, John 368–369, 474
Museum of Westward Expansion 83

NAACP 345
Naiche 188
Natchez NHP 94
Natchez Trace 94
Natchez Trace NST 447
National Air & Space Museum 395
National Archives 395
National Audubon Society 474
National Catholic Conference 352
National Colonial Farm 105
National Council of Churches 352
National Council of Negro Women 354
National Gallery of Art 395
National Mall 395
National Museum of African Art 395
National Museum of Amer. History 395
National Museum of Natural History 395
National Park Standards 499, 502, 504–505, 508
National Park System Plan (1988) 506
National Park Trust 470, 507
National Parks Bulletin 501, 502, 503, 504
National Parks 494, 496, 497, 499, 504, 506
National Parks and Conservation Association. xvii, 465, 470,
    473, 474, 477, 478, 483–488, 490, 494, 495,
    498–500, 501, 502, 505–507, 508

National Parks Association 473, 501–506
National Parks in Crisis 506
National Prisoner of War Museum 211
National Recreation Areas 401
National Sculpture Garden 395
National Trails 445
National Zoological Park 396
Navajos 71, 103, 202
New Orleans Jazz NHP 372
New York Times, The 475, 479, 481, 483
Nez Perce 96–99, 145, 185–186
Nez Perce N Hist. Park 96
Nez Perce N Hist. Trail 99
Nez Perce, non-treaty 98, 186
Nez Perce War 98, 185
Ninety Six NHS 167
Nipomo Dunes 469
North Bridge 161
North Cascades NP 422, 431
North Country NST 448
North Fur Company 55
North West Company 62
NPCA: A Brief History 501

O'Neill, Eugene 363
O'odham (Pimas) 142–145
Ojibways 63
Old City Hall (Phila.) 76
Old Courthouse (St. Louis) 84, 84
Old Danish Customs House 22, 22
Old North Church 10
Old Point Loma Lighthouse 12, 13
Old South Meeting House 9
Old State House 9
Olmsted, Frederick Law 364
Olympic NP 505
Oregon Dunes 469
Oregon N Hist. Trail 448
Organ Pipe Cactus NM 476–477, 498
Osages 199
Other National Park System Areas 455
Our Endangered Parks 506
Overmountain Victory NHT 449
Owyhee Canyonlands 469
Oxon Hill Farm 427

Palo Alto Battlefild NHS 181
Palo Alto, Battle of 181–182
Parker, Isaac C. 200
Parker, Capít John 161
Park Waters In Peril 506
Paul Revere House 10
Peace of Paris (1763) 50
Peace of Paris (1783) 154
Pea Ridge NMP 263
Pea Ridge, Battle of 258, 263–264
Pecos NHP xiii, 99, 487–488
Pecos Pueblo 100–102, 487
Pemberton, Gen. John C. 284–286
Peninsular Campaign 258, 269, 270, 272, 275

Pennsylvania Ave. NHS 396
Perry's Victory Mem. 182
Perry, Oliver Hazard 182
Petersburg NB 216, 261, 264–268
Petroglyph NM 486
Philosophical Hall 77
Pickett's Charge 250
Pickett, George E. 249, 250, 266
Pig War 126
Pinelands 441
Pinkley, Jean M. 102
Pinnacles NM 497
Pipe Spring NM 103
Piscataway Park 104
Pitcairn, Maj. John 161
Platte NP 406, 502
Plessy v. Ferguson 345
Pocahontas 26, 28
Poe, Edgar Allan 362
Point Loma 11–13
Point Mugu SP 433
Point Reyes NS 418, 494, 505
Pollution, Air 481
Pollution, Noise 483
Pollution, Water 478
Pony Express 130, 450
Pony Express NHT 450
Pope, Gen. John 255, 257
Port Chicago Naval Magazine 441
Porter, Adm. David D. 285
Possible New Parks 465
Potomac Heritage NST 450
Powhatan, Chief 26
Powhatans 26–27
Presidio of San Francisco 417
Prince William Forest 428
Pritchard, Paul C. xiv, xv, 483, 495, 500, 506
Providence Plantations 111
Pu'uhonua o Honaunau xiii, 106
Pu'ukohola Heiau 109

Quapaws 3, 4, 5
Quarai Pueblo & church 116–118
Quinebaug & Shetucket Valley 443

Railroad History Museum 390
Rainbow Bridge NM 494
Raleigh, Sir Walter 52
Rankin, Jeanette 338
Red Hill Patrick Henry 443
Revere, Paul 161
Revolutionary War parks 149
Richmond NBP 216, 267, 268, 487
Richmond, Capture of 273
Robert Frost Farm 467
Rock Creek Park 396, 503
Rocky Mountain NP 487, 502
Roger Williams N Mem. 111
Rolfe, John 26
Roosevelt Campobello 444

Roosevelt, Eleanor 336
Roosevelt, Franklin D. 309–310, 334
Roosevelt, Theodore xiii, 323–327
Rosecrans, Gen. William 223–225, 279–280
Ross, Gen. Robert 178
Ross Lake NRA 431
Runte, Alfred 492
Russian American Company 133
Russian Bishop's House 133
Russian Orthodox Church 133

Saarinen, Eero 83
Sacagawea 44
Sagamore Hill NHS 323
Saguaro NP 486–487, 494, 497
Saint Croix Island IHS 112
Saint–Gaudens, Augustus 373–374
Saint–Gaudens NHS 373–374
Saint Paul's Church NHS 374
Salem Maritime NHS 114
Salinas Pueblo Missions NM xvi, 116
Salt River Bay NHP 118
San Antonio Missions NHP 121
San Francisco Maritime NHP 124
San Juan Island NHP 125
San Juan NHS 126
San Rafael Swell and Reef 469
Sandburg, Carl 359–361
Santa Fe Railway 202
Santa Fe Trail 102, 197, 201, 202, 450
Santa Monica Mtns NRA 433, 488
Saratoga NHP 169
Saugus Iron Works NHS 387
Sawtooth NRA 469
Science in the National Parks 496
Science Shortfall 496
Scott, Gen. Winfield 197, 198, 255
Scott, Hiram 128
Scotts Bluff NM 128
Second Bank of the U.S. 77
Selma-to-Montgomery NHT 451
Seminoles 199
Sequoia NP 481–483, 494, 496, 499
Seven Days' Battles 270–272
Sheldon Jackson Museum 134
Shenandoah NP 482, 494, 502
Shenandoah Valley battlefields 469
Sherman, Gen. William Tecumseh 221–225, 242, 251–253,
     278, 282, 283
Shiloh NMP 276, 277
Shiloh, Battle of 276–279, 284
Sierra Club 473, 474
Signers' Memorial 393
Sioux 92, 192–193
Siskiyou/Kalmiopsis 469
Sitka NHP 132
Smith, Capít. John 25
So. Christian Leadership Conf. 352, 452
Southern Pacific Railroad 61, 189
Spalding, Rev. Henry 96–97, 145

Spotsylvania Ct. Hse. Battle 237, 238, 239, 243, 244, 272
Springfield Armory NHS 172
St. Croix Riverway 479
St. George's Church 77
St. Leger, Col. Barry 151
Stanford, Leland 59
Stanton, Elizabeth Cady 338, 339
Stars–and–Stripes (U.S. flag) xv, 74
Star–Spangled Banner 178
Statue of Liberty NM xiv, 134, 509
Steamtown NHS 389
Steens Mountain 469–470
Stehekin Valley 422
Stones River, Battle of 223, 279–282
Stones River NB 223, 279–282
Stones R. N Cemetery 280
Storer College 68–69
Stuart, Gen. J.E.B. 242
Student Conservation Ass'n. 506
Student Non-Violent Coord. Cm. 352
Supreme Court, U.S. 84, 345

Taft, Wím Howard NHS 333, 334
Tagish 89
Tallgrass Prairie N Pres. 470, 507
Taylor, Gen. Zachary 181–182, 198
Tejas 122
Theodore Roosevelt Birthpl. NHS 325
Theodore Roosevelt Inaugural NHS 325
Thaddeus Kosciuszko 170, 173
Thaddeus Kosciuszko N Mem. 173
Theatre–in–the–Woods 379–380
Theodore Roosevelt Island 326, 503
Thomas Cole House 476
Thomas Jefferson Memorial 327
Thomas Stone NHS 140
Threats to parks 473
Tiguex 33
Timucuan E&H Pres. 141
Timucuans 141
Tlingits 132, 133
Tonti, Henri de 3
Too Many Cars 489
Topanga SP 434
Touro Synagogue 444
Trail of Tears NHT 199, 452
Trains of Discovery 492
Treaty of Fort Smith 199
Treaty of Guadalupe Hidalgo 182
Treaty of Medicine Lodge 196
Tumacacori NHP 142
Tupelo NB 265, 282
Tuskegee Institute NHS 356
Ulysses S.Grant NHS 329
Union Pacific Railroad 59–60, 130
Upper Missouri Outfit 54
Urban Impacts–External 486
Urban Impacts–Internal 488
Urban League 352
U.S. Presidents parks 297

USS Arizona Memorial 293
Utes 201

Valley Forge NHP xv, 174, 497
Valley of Fire SP 425
Van Buren, Martin 321
Vanderbilt Mansion NHS 376
Vanderbilt, Frederick W. 376
Vicksburg NMP 283
Vicksburg, Siege of 283–286
Victorio 191
Vietnam Veterans Mem. 294
Virginia Company 24, 26
Virgin Islands NP 505
Visitor Impact Management 506
Voyageurs NP 485

Walker, Maggie L. 350–351
Walt Whitman House 471
War for Independence parks 149
War in the Pacific NHP 296
Warren, Chief Justice Earl 345
Washington Monument 329, 513
Washington, Booker T. 341–342, 348, 356, 357
Washington, George xv, xvi, 28–30, 50–51, 73,
        165–167, 172, 174–176, 304, 305, 329
Wauer, Roland 119
Weir Farm NHS 377
Weir, J. Alden 377–378
Wharton, William P. 503
Whiskeytown NRA 435
White Bird Canyon, Battle of 98
White House, The 330, 503
Whitman Mission NHS 145
Whitman, Dr. Marcus 145–146
Whitman, Walt 471
William Howard Taft NHS 333
Williams, Roger 111–112
Williamsburg 31
Wilson's Creek NB 287–290
Wilson's Creek, Battle of 287–290
Winsor Castle 104
Wolf Trap Farm Park 379
Women in Military Hist. exhibit 232
Women in U.S. History parks 335
Women's Rights NHP 337
Wounded Knee 471
Wrangell–St. Elias NP 479, 507
Wright Bros. N Mem. 390
Wright, Martha 338
Wright, Orville & Wilbur 381, 390–392

Yard, Robert Sterling 501–502
Yellowstone NP 478–479, 480, 485, 487, 501, 502
Yorktown, Battle of 28–31
Yosemite NP 474, 483, 489, 490–492, 494

Zion NP 476, 479, 490, 494
Zuni Pueblo Indians 33, 71